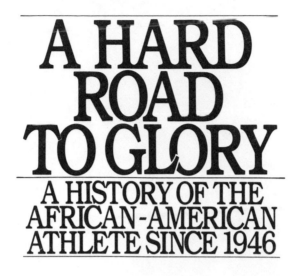

A HARD ROAD TO GLORY

A HISTORY OF THE AFRICAN-AMERICAN ATHLETE SINCE 1946

ARTHUR R. ASHE, JR.

A HARD ROAD TO GLORY

A HISTORY OF THE AFRICAN-AMERICAN ATHLETE SINCE 1946

WITH THE ASSISTANCE OF
KIP BRANCH, OCANIA CHALK, AND FRANCIS HARRIS

WARNER BOOKS

A Warner Communications Company

An Amistad Book

Warner Books, Inc., 666 Fifth Avenue, New York, NY 10103

A Warner Communications Company

Printed in the United States of America
First Printing: November 1988
10 9 8 7 6 5 4 3 2 1

Library of Congress Cataloging-in-Publication Data

Ashe, Arthur.
  A hard road to glory : a history of the African-American athlete
since 1946 / Arthur R. Ashe, Jr.
  p. cm.
  ISBN 0-446-71008-3
  1. Afro-Americans—Sports—History—20th century.   2. Afro
-American athletes.   I. Title.
GV583.A755 1988   88-20681
796′.08996073—dc19   CIP

Packaged by Rapid Transcript, a division of March Tenth, Inc.

To my wife, Jeanne, and my daughter, Camera

Contents

Foreword

This book began in a classroom at Florida Memorial College in Miami, Florida, in 1983. I was asked to teach a course, The Black Athlete in Contemporary Society, by Jefferson Rogers of the school's Center for Community Change. When I tried to find a book detailing what has surely been the African-American's most startling saga of successes, I found that the last attempt had been made exactly twenty years before.

I then felt compelled to write this story, for I literally grew up on a sports field. My father was the caretaker of the largest public park for blacks in Richmond, Virginia. Set out in a fanlike pattern at Brookfield Playground was an Olympic-size pool, a basketball court, four tennis courts, three baseball diamonds, and two football fields. Our five-room home was actually on these premises. Little wonder I later became a professional athlete.

My boyhood idol was Jackie Robinson, as was the case with every black kid in America in the late 1940s and early 1950s. But I had no appreciation of what he went through or, more importantly, what others like him had endured. I had never heard of Jack Johnson, Marshall Taylor, Isaac Murphy, or Howard P. Drew—icons in athletics

but seldom heralded in the post-World War II period.

These and others have been the most accomplished figures in the African-American subculture. They were vastly better known in their times than people such as Booker T. Washington, William E.B. Du Bois, or Marcus Garvey. They inspired idolatry bordering on deification, and thousands more wanted to follow. Indeed, in the pretelevision days of radio, Joe Louis's bouts occasioned impromptu celebration because, between 1934 and 1949, Louis lost only once.

But if contemporary black athletes' exploits are more well known, few fully appreciate their true Hard Road to Glory. Discrimination, vilification, incarceration, dissipation, ruination, and ultimate despair have dogged the steps of the mightiest of these heroes. And, only a handful in the last 179 years have been able to live out their post-athletic lives in peace and prosperity.

This book traces the development of African-American athletes from their ancestral African homelands in the seventeenth century through the present era. Their exploits are explored in a historical context, as all African-American successes were constrained by discriminatory laws, customs, and traditions.

As I began to complete my research, I realized that the subject was more extensive than I had thought. All of the material would not fit into one volume. Therefore, I have divided the work as follows:

Volume I covers the emergence of sports as adjuncts to daily life from the time of ancient civilizations like Egypt through World War I. Wars tend to compartmentalize eras and this story is no different. Major successes of African-Americans occurred in the ninteenth century, for example, which are simply glossed over in most examinations of the period.

Volume II examines black athletics during that vital twenty-year period between the World Wars. No greater contrast exists than that between the 1920s—the Golden Decade of Sports—and the Depression-plagued 1930s. The infrastructure of American athletics as we know it today was set during these crucial years, and the civil rights apparatus that would lead to integration in the post–World War II era was formalized. Popular African-American literature and its press augmented the already cosmic fame of athletes such as Jesse Owens and Joe Louis, who were the first black athletes to be admired by all Americans.

Volume III is set between World War II and the present. It begins with an unprecedented five-year period—1946 through 1950—in which football, baseball, basketball, tennis, golf, and bowling became integrated. These breakthroughs, coupled with the already heady showings in track and

boxing, provided enough incentive for African-Americans to embark on nothing less than an all-out effort for athletic fame and fortune.

The reference sections in each volume document the major successes of these gladiators. These records are proof positive of effort and dedication on the playing field. More importantly, they are proof of what the African-American can do when allowed to compete equally in a framework governed by a set of rules.

Each volume is divided into individual sport histories. Primary source materials were not to be found in the local public library and not even in New York City's Fifth Avenue Public Library. Chroniclers of America's early sports heroes simply left out most of their darker brothers and sisters except when they participated in white-controlled events. Much had to be gleaned, therefore, from the basements, attics, and closets of African-Americans themselves.

Interviews were invaluable in cross-referencing dubious written records. Where discrepancies occurred, I have stated so; but I have tried to reach the most logical conclusion. Some unintentional errors are inevitable. The author welcomes confirmed corrections and additions. If validated, they will be included in the next edition of this work.

Today, thousands of young African-Americans continue to seek their places in the sun through athletics. For some African-Americans the dream has bordered on a pathological obsession. But unless matters change, the majority may end up like their predecessors. Perhaps this history will ease the journey with sober reflections of how difficult and improbable the Hard Road really is. In no way, however, do I care to dissuade any young athlete from dreaming of athletic glory. Surely every American at some time has done so.

A word about nomenclature. Sociologists have referred to nearly all immigrant groups in hyphenated form: Irish-Americans, Italian-Americans, and Jewish-Americans. African-Americans are no different, and this term is correct. Throughout this book, I shall, however, use the modern designation *"black"* to refer to African-Americans. The appellations *Negro* and *colored* may also appear, but usually in quotes and only when I thought such usage may be more appropriate in a particular context.

Acknowledgments

A Hard Road to Glory would have been impossible without the help, assistance, contributions, and encouragement of many people. Initial moral support came from Reverend Jefferson Rogers, formerly of Florida Memorial College; Professor Louis "Skip" Gates of Cornell University; Howard Cosell; Marie Brown; my editor, Charles F. Harris; and my literary agent, Fifi Oscard. All made me believe it could be done. An inspiring letter urging me to press on also came from Professor John Hope Franklin of Duke University, who advised that this body of work was needed to fill a gap in African-American history.

My staff has been loyal and faithful to the end these past four years. I have been more than ably assisted by Kip Branch, who has stood by me from the first day; and by Ocania Chalk, whose two previous books on black collegiate athletes and other black athletic pioneers provided so much of the core material for *A Hard Road to Glory*. To my personal assistant, Derilene McCloud, go special thanks for coordinating, typing, filing, phoning, and organizing the information and interviews, as well as keeping my day-to-day affairs in order. Sandra Jamison's skills in library science were invaluable in the beginning. Her successor, Rod Howard, is now a virtual walking encyclopedia of information about black athletes, especially those in college. To Francis Harris, who almost single-handedly constructed the reference sections, I am truly grateful. And to Deborah McRae, who sat through hundreds of hours of typing—her assistance is not forgotten.

Institutions have been very helpful and forthcoming. The people at the New York Public Library Annex went out of their way to search for books. *The New York Times* provided access to back issues. The Norfolk, Virginia, Public Library was kind and considerate. This book could not have been done without the kind help of the Schomburg Library for Research in Black Culture in Harlem, New York. Its photography curator, Deborah Willis Thomas, found many photographs for me, and Ernest Kaiser followed my work with interest.

The Enoch Pratt Free Library in Baltimore, Maryland; the Moorland-Spingarn Library at Howard University in Washington, D.C.; and the Library of Congress not only assisted but were encouraging and courteous. The offices of the Central Intercollegiate Athletic Association, the Southern Intercollegiate Athletic Conference, the Mideastern Athletic Conference, and the Southwest Athletic Conference dug deep to find information on past black college sports. The National Collegiate Athletic Association and the National Association for Intercollegiate Athletics were quick with information about past and present athletes. The home offices of major league baseball, the National Basketball Association, the National Football League, and their archivists and Halls of Fame were eager to provide assistance. Joe Corrigan went out of his way to lend a hand.

The staffs at Tuskegee University and Tennessee State University were particularly kind. Wallace Jackson at Alabama A&M was helpful with information on the Southern Intercollegiate Athletic Conference. Alvin Hollins at Florida A&M University was eager to assist. Lynn Abraham of New York City found a rare set of boxing books for me. Lou Robinson of Claremont, California, came through in a pinch with information on black Olympians, and Margaret Gordon of the American Tennis Association offered her assistance.

Many people offered to be interviewed for this project. Two of them, Eyre Saitch, Nell Jackson, Dr. Reginald Weir and Ric Roberts, have since passed on, and I am truly grateful for their recollections. Others who agreed to sit and talk with Kip Branch, Ocania Chalk, or me include William "Pop" Gates, Elgin Baylor, Oscar Robertson, Anita DeFranz, Nikki Franke, Peter Westbrook, Paul Robeson, Jr., Afro-American sportswriter Sam Lacy, A.S. "Doc" young, Frederick "Fritz" Pollard, Jr., Mel Glover, Calvin Peete, Oscar Johnson, Althea Gibson, Mrs. Ted Paige, Charles Sifford, Howard Gentry, Milt Campbell, Otis Troupe, Beau Jack, Coach and Mrs. Jake Gaither, Lynn Swann, Franco Harris, Dr. Richard Long of Atlanta University, Dr. Leonard Jeffries of the City College of New York, Dr. Elliot Skinner of Columbia University, and Dr. Ben Jochannon.

Dr. Maulana Karenga of Los Angeles and Dr. William J. Baker of the Unversity of Maine offered material and guidance on African sports. Dr. Ofuatey Kodjo of Queens College in New York City helped edit this same information. Norris Horton of the United Golfers Association provided records, and Margaret Lee of the National Bowling Association answered every inquiry with interest. To Nick Seitz of *Golf Digest* and *Tennis*, I offer thanks for his efforts. Professors Barbara Cooke, Patsy B. Perry, Kenneth Chambers, Floyd Ferebee, and Tom Scheft of North Carolina Central University were kind enough to read parts of the manuscript, as did Mr. and Mrs. Donald Baker. Professor Eugene Beecher of Wilson College, an unabashed sports fan, shuttled many clippings our way.

To the dozens of people who heard about my book on Bob Law's *Night Talk* radio show and sent unsolicited but extremely valuable information, I cannot thank you enough. And to the hundreds of unsung African-American athletes who played under conditions of segregation and whose skills and talents were never known to the general public, I salute you and hope this body of work in some measure vindicates and redresses that gross miscarriage of our American ideals.

Finally, to my wife Jeanne Moutoussamy-Ashe, I owe gratitude and tremendous appreciation for her understanding, patience, tolerance, and sacrifice of time so I could complete this book.

Arthur R. Ashe, Jr.
1988

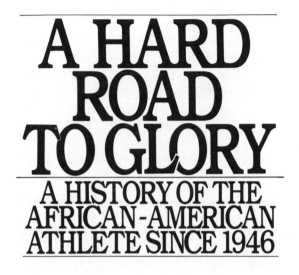

A HARD ROAD TO GLORY

A HISTORY OF THE AFRICAN-AMERICAN ATHLETE SINCE 1946

Introduction

For many including myself, the contemporary era of American sports begins in 1946, and for good reasons: the Second World War was over, many citizens had money in their pockets, and television was coming. In the first five years of this period, some extraordinary and historic changes and breakthroughs were effected. Baseball reasserted itself as the dominant spectator sport. Professional football merged two competing leagues and became stronger than ever, and professional basketball went through similar adjustments. Joe Louis retired undefeated in 1949 as the heavyweight boxing champion. With hurried preparations, the British staged the successful 1948 Olympic Games in London after a hiatus of a dozen years.

For black athletes, this five-year span was the most memorable sixty months in their sports history. Long-sought changes had finally come about because of the combined and persistent efforts of the entire black community. Jackie Robinson reintegrated the major leagues in 1947, a first time for a black, since 1884. Professional football became integrated for the second time since 1933, and the National Basketball Association (NBA) admitted blacks at last. Althea Gibson became the first black player in the National Tennis Championships at Forest Hills, New York. The American Bowling Congress (ABC) dropped the "Caucasians only" clause in its constitution. The Professional Golfers Association (PGA) settled out of court with Bill Spiller and Ted Rhodes in the two men's fight to play in the PGA. And President Harry S. Truman ordered the integration of the Armed Forces in 1948. Black athletes meant to take full advantage, but there were still more dues to pay.

The early civil rights movement had not paid much sustained attention to the past racial troubles of black sportsmen. Outside of black college varsity competition and Negro League baseball, there was no firmly entrenched athletic establishment to protect and defend black athletes. The black community could not completely support its own professional teams, and until the late 1930s, most assistance from civil rights groups went to individual athletes rather than to athletic teams seen as representing some clearly defined group. Sports were still regarded as fun and games, not worthy of the limited resources of black lawyers.

Even black scholars paid scant attention to sports. W.E.B. Du Bois had already called boxing "very, very immoral" and, with the exception of Edwin B. Henderson's book, *The Negro In Sports*, not a single notable book on black athletics had been

3

penned by a black writer. Sports was seen as ephemeral, short-lived experiences that offered momentary diversion. Sports was just not that important, some believed, when juxtaposed with other more pressing issues such as the vote in the South, lynchings, and the election of more blacks to political office. Yet the accomplishments of athletes and their influence on the black populace was evident. Jack Johnson and Joe Louis were, in their prime, the most famous black persons on earth, and their success stories should have been recorded by trained *black* historians other than by sports reporters.

The contemporary era has been little different. Nearly all the biographies and individual sports histories of black athletes are still written by whites, partly because publishing houses are not in contact with black writers. Still, the appreciation of the athletes' role in modern black history has been enhanced by their participation in the general struggle for equality. Henry Lee Moon presaged this connection between the athlete and the civil rights movement in his 1948 book, *Balance of Power: The Negro Vote.* He acknowledged that "The ballot, while no longer conceived of as a magic key, is recognized as the indispensable weapon in a persistent fight for full citizenship, equal economic opportunity ...and *recreational* [italics mine] facilities."[1] In the 1950s, white America began learning more about black America and one of the most influential messengers was the black athlete.

The 1950s was marked by the United States Supreme Court decision in *Brown* v. *Board of Education* (1954). While the Court ruled that separate-but-equal public school systems for blacks and whites were unconstitutional, the legal decision also meant that *all* Americans would finally have access to the best athletic facilities a local school district could afford. Better facilities meant better training, coaching, competition—and results. But the slow pace of integration of the three major professional team sports left the indelible impression that the equal rights battle was far from won in the athletic arena.

In the 1960s, black athletes were vital cogs in the machinery of the black social revolution. They manned picket lines, sat in at segregated lunch counters in the South, petitioned for redress of grievances at white colleges, demanded an end to discriminatory practices of white coaches, and even threatened to boycott that most cherished symbol of equal opportunity—the Olympic Games. Their power was strengthened by their new visibility generated through television, which, more than any other communications medium, has popularized sports. In addition, some black athletes became practically indispensable to the success of their teams.

Indispensable or not, studies showed black athletes were financially underpaid though their team and artistic value was higher. They were "stacked" into certain positions on teams because of the distorted and unrealistic racial perceptions of white coaches, and were summarily dealt with if they protested. They were still considered all brawn and no brains. Team owners had used black baseball players to keep the salaries of white players low, because it was believed black players attached more psychic value to careers as professional athletes than did white athletes; therefore better black players would work for less money, thus keeping their market value artificially lower than white players. This assumption proved true, and the professional teams took full advantage.

The 1970s brought free-agency, more opportunities for women, a rise in the power of player associations; a diminution in the number of American youngsters engaged in organized sports; the running craze; drug addiction; black professional team coaches, and the virtual abrogation of the hated contractual reserve clause in professional team sports. Suddenly, dozens of athletes were earning more money in one season than a college graduate made in a lifetime. Black athletes—most of whom came from our nation's underclass—found it difficult to adjust. Most had gone from sociologically lower-class amenities to upper-class bank accounts—skipping the middle class altogether.

By the mid-1980s, black athletes had almost completely rewritten the record books. They were the most dominant and charismatic players in the NBA, the NFL and the major leagues (which comprises the highest level of baseball played in the U.S.). Black tennis players and golfers had already won national and international titles. Track stars owned the sprint and jumping marks, and the higher weight divisions in boxing listed blacks as champions.

There were even two prominent black boxing promoters; a situation almost impossible in 1946.

No gains or successes came without a price, and athletes understood that more than nonathletes. Few experts right after World War II could have predicted that some black *athletes* would be making $2 million per year for playing games, and then losing most of it due to poor management. But ours is a free enterprise economic system where market forces of supply and demand, however imperfect, determine a person's economic value. Unfortunately, for every million-dollar-salaried black athlete, there were tens of thousands of young blacks who unrealistically thought they could earn it too. Professional sports became a means to an end to black degradation.

It was a glorious period—the years between 1946 and 1987. But the calendars were strewn with bankruptcies, broken homes, drug addictions, school dropouts, incarcerations, and hopeless dreams. The path to fame and wealth for all but a few black athletes has been "A Hard Road to Glory."

Notes

1. Henry Lee Moon, *Balance of Power: The Negro Vote,* (New York: Doubleday, 1948), 9.

Chapter 1

Baseball

The Noble Experiment Begins: Albert B. "Happy" Chandler was named the new major league commissioner on January 1, 1946, the year of Jackie Robinson's Montreal Royals debut as the first black player in organized ball since 1889. It was a fortunate choice for blacks. Chandler told black reporter Rick Roberts that "If they [blacks] can fight and die on Okinawa, Guadalcanal, in the South Pacific, they can play baseball in America. And when I give my word you can count on it."[1] Chandler's promise was needed, because some major league owners were scared stiff about the presence of blacks.

A secret report on the prospects for integrated baseball was supposedly written by a steering committee in 1946. The committee members included Ford Frick, the National League president; Sam Breadon of the St. Louis Cardinals; Phil Wrigley of the Chicago Cubs; William Harridge, the American League president; Larry McPhail of the New York Yankees; and Tom Yawkey of the Boston Red Sox, who urged the other committee members not to admit blacks. The vote was fifteen to one opposing blacks in the major leagues. Branch Rickey, the Brooklyn Dodgers' president and Jackie Robinson's mentor, was the lone dissenter.

This report was then destroyed by everyone but Chandler.

Rickey plotted ahead and made plans to ease Jackie's debut at Montreal. Meanwhile, the most perplexed group turned out to be the owners of Negro League teams. They suddenly realized that blacks would probably come into the major leagues one by one rather than through black teams that were a part of a recognized minor league. Some owners had dreamed of fielding a black team in the major leagues itself. An all-black team of first-rate players would be a big draw. It would never happen.

The Montreal Royals' spring training camp was at Daytona Beach, Florida. Jackie Robinson was newly-married to the former Rachel Isum, their trip from Pasadena to Daytona Beach was marred by being bumped from a plane flight, and having to move to the back of a bus on the last leg from Pensacola, Florida. The Robinsons were housed with a local black family rather than in the team hotel. Jackie had two other black players to talk with, since Rickey had also signed pitchers John Wright, and Roy Partlow to Montreal in February, 1946.

Finally, Opening Day arrived. April 18, 1946. Montreal's manager, Clay Hopper, a southerner himself, let Jackie play second base as the team played the Jersey City Giants at Roosevelt Stadium in Jersey City, New Jersey. In his first at bat, Jackie grounded weakly to short. But no matter, the "noble experiment" had begun. Jackie later collected four hits including a home run and two stolen bases; he made no errors.

While the people of Montreal accepted Jackie and Rachel with open arms, at other tour stops, he was taunted, jeered, and ridiculed. Baltimore, Louisville, and Syracuse were particularly bad. "I couldn't sleep," said Jackie, "and often I couldn't eat...we sought the advice of a doctor who was afraid I was going to have a nervous breakdown."[2] But he did endure, and eventually triumphed. In "the Little World Series" between Montreal and the Louisville Colonels of the American Association, Jackie batted .400 and scored the winning run in the final game. His performance capped a season sensational for any initiate. He led the International League with a .349 batting average, was second in stolen bases with 40, tied for first in runs scored with 113, was first in fielding average at .985, and was fourth in being hit by pitched balls that were thrown deliberately at him.

Perhaps the best accolade came from his southern manager, Clay Hopper, who told him: "You're a great ballplayer and a fine gentleman. It's been wonderful having you on the team."[3]

Jackie's performances were followed as closely as were Joe Louis' fights. The Negro Leagues' East-West Game drew 45,474 fans. The Cleveland Buckeyes of the NAL even signed a white pitcher, Eddie Klepp, for one season. Jackie gave black

baseball new meaning. Everyone took it more seriously. In March 1946, Rickey finally had signed Roy Campanella and assigned him to a Class AA team at Nashua, New Hampshire. (Rickey's team at Danville, Illinois, of the III League would not accept Campanella.) Campanella was joined there by a black pitcher named Don Newcombe, but Jackie's black teammate, John Wright, was released after two appearances.

Campanella had a good year, batting .290 in 113 games, and was acclaimed as Most Valuable Player. Newcombe pitched a 14–4 record for himself and posted a 2.21 earned run average. Both players were to make their own separate histories as future Dodgers. Yet life in the International League was not the same as life in the majors. It was still "let's wait and see."

There was even some talk that the racial climate in the major leagues was not fully ripe for Robinson despite his impressive statistics. On April 9, 1947, Brooklyn Dodger president, Branch Rickey made the following announcement: "Brooklyn announces the purchase of the contract of Jack Roosevelt Robinson from Montreal."

The white press was understandably cautious, and there were as many predictions about Robinson's success as there were white reporters. The influential New York *Daily News* even said he was a "thousand-to-one shot" against making the grade—and that, from a relatively liberal northern paper. *The Washington Post's* Shirley Povich editorialized by telling everyone to give Robinson the fair opportunity to prove himself irrespective of color. Southern papers simply wanted Robinson kept out of the league, and wrote at length about the logistical problems for black players such as housing, restaurants, and local ordinances against interracial sports.

Southern attitudes reflected the conclusions reinforced by most members of the steering committee, namely that

1. Integrationists are just trying to stir up trouble.
2. Negro fans will hurt attendance.
3. Negro players are not good enough yet.
4. Integration will hurt the Negro Leagues.
5. Segregation is good business.

At an address to faculty and students at Wilberforce University, a black college, on February 23, 1948, Rickey leaked a portion of this committee's conclusion, which said that "however well-intentioned, the use of Negro players would hazard all of the physical properties of baseball."[4]

The black press, however, viewed Robinson's breakthrough as the result of a long campaign to integrate the nation's most popular sport. While Rickey was given full credit in all quarters for having the guts to be the first to sign a black player, blacks felt he could not have done it without the constant pressure applied since the beginning of World War II. In 1944, Bill Veeck of the Philadelphia Phillies, a major league team, had suggested using blacks because of a shortage of white players due to the war. His suggestion was nixed by Commissioner Kennesaw M. Landis, who had always opposed black participation.

Joe Bostic, the fiery reporter for black Congressman Adam Clayton Powell's newspaper, *The People's Voice,* had sorely embarrassed Rickey on April 7, 1945, by showing up at a Dodger training camp in New York's Bear Mountain with two black players, pitcher Terris McDuffie and infielder Dave "Showboat" Thomas, for an impromptu tryout. Rickey was incensed. Bostic says Rickey "never spoke to me from that day until the day he died."[5]

The "End Jim Crow in Baseball Committee" was formed in New York City in 1945 with the support of the black press. With picket marches and meetings, that same year the National Association for the Advancement of Colored People (NAACP) started its "Double V" campaign that linked victory over the racist doctrines of Nazi Germany to victory over white racism at home. Tangible evidence of victory at home would be black participation in major league baseball.

After Robinson signed his historic contract, black papers fully recognized the milestone, but went to considerable lengths to put the entire issue in perspective. The New York *Amsterdam News* reminded readers that thousands of black GIs had died in Europe but "that Jackie Robinson, a young Negro who is intellectually, culturally and physically superior to most white baseball players, has signed a contract to play in a minor league [that] has caused a national sensation."[6]

Crisis, the NAACP's magazine, said a month later that Rickey was "...a deeply religious man with the fire of a crusader burning in his breast."[7] The *Pittsburgh Courier* wrote that Rickey's "...conscience would not permit him to wallow in the mire of racial discrimination."[8] The *Philadelphia Tribune* correctly prophesied that Robinson's signing was "but...the forerunner of the days when practically every team— even the Philadelphia Athletics in our city—will have one or more colored players on their teams, based solely on their ability to play..."[9]

The *Pittsburgh Courier*'s Wendell Smith and the *Baltimore Afro-American*'s Sam Lacy had followed Robinson's every move during the 1946 minor league season. They reported Robinson's generally favorable initial reception—though he was housed with black families during spring training—and suffered segregated seating during spring training games in the South. Rickey moved the entire Dodger pre-season camp from Sanford, Florida, to Daytona Beach due to the oppressive conditions of Sanford.

Black reporters warned black fans who planned to attend Robinson's games to behave themselves lest they make a bad impression. Wrote Smith: "The [black] guy who is so stimulated by the appearance of Robinson and [John] Wright in Montreal uniforms that he stands and rants and raves, yells and screams, before they have even so much as picked up a ball, is the guy who will be cheering them out of Organized Baseball rather than in."[10]

Lacy penned an Open Letter to Clay Hopper, Robinson's manager at Montreal, and wrote: "He [Robinson] is human regardless of the color of his skin. And, being human, he'll have "good" days and "bad" days and that you, like Jackie, are on the spot, if for no other reason than that you come from a section of the country that is generally regarded as hostile to Robinson's people."[11]

Having informed its readers of all developments since October 29, 1945, black reporters turned ominous when Rickey announced that Robinson would play for the Dodgers after all. Said the *Pittsburgh Cou-rier* on April 12, 1947: "If Robinson fails to make the grade, it will be years before a Negro makes the grade."[12] "This is IT!" was the Boston Chronicle's banner headlines reserved only for the most serious of stories: "TRIUMPH OF WHOLE RACE SEEN IN JACKIE'S DEBUT IN MAJOR-LEAGUE BALL."[13] In what today seems like a ridiculous suggestion, the *Chicago Defender* pleaded with black fans who wished to honor Robinson in his first circuit of major league cities not to "...hold up the game—in a ludicrous ceremony—to present him with a box of southern fried chicken..."[14]

Robinson persevered somehow in spite of name-calling, racial epithets, a black cat thrown at him in Philadelphia, and brushback pitches thrown at him by opposing pitchers. In all accounts of this first season, Robinson gave the highest praise to his wife, Rachel, who suffered along with him. On the field, he batted .297 with 12 homers, 48 runs batted in, and 16 errors at first base, plus leading the National League in stolen bases with 29—15 ahead of his nearest competitor. In the 1947 World Series, which the Yankees won four games to three, Robinson batted .259, had 7 hits, 3 runs batted in, and stole 2 bases. So much for his critics!

In retrospect, Robinson was a compromise selection as the first black player in organized ball since 1889. By the accounts and opinions of Negro Leaguers, he was not the best player—he only played forty-one games as a Kansas City Monarch. He was old for a rookie—twenty-eight in 1947. But he was intelligent, had four years of college behind him, was an Army lieutenant, had a stable marriage and an equally intelligent wife and, perhaps most important, he had demonstrated a combativeness that was surely necessary for survival in the major leagues. Still, quite a few veteran Negro Leaguers were upset that a relative newcomer should be given this first chance.

Could Branch Rickey have pulled off this "great experiment" twenty years earlier? Not a chance! World War II, the general liberal trend so evident in the United States since the Depression, the civil rights movement, the growing black voting strength in the northern cities, and the popularity of Joe Louis (the black heavyweight champion), all assisted Robinson and Rickey in their efforts. Robinson was ever-quick to pay homage to Louis as his forerunner. At Louis's funeral, Reverend Jesse Jackson eloquently reinforced this fact by saying: "Before there was a Jackie, there was a Joe!"

The geographical demographics of major league baseball also contributed to Rickey's plans. Though baseball was steeped in the biased traditions of the South, all the major league franchises were located in the northern or border states. In 1947, there were only sixteen teams—none south of Washington, D.C., or west of St. Louis. Population shifts and television would change all that in short order, and so would the infusion of black players, who brought speed, power, and daring to a staid old game.

Part I
BREAKING IN:
THE FIRST FOURTEEN YEARS

Branch Rickey's initiative was not matched by that of his fellow administrators on other teams. The period from Jackie Robinson's debut in April 1947 to 1953 can best be described as one of token integration. In this seven-year stretch, the National League added blacks at the rate of three every two years; the American League just one every two years. Some clubs would just not add any. The following is a list of the first black players on each team and their date of entry:

Jackie Robinson	April 1947	Brooklyn Dodgers
Larry Doby	April 1947	Cleveland Indians
Henry Thompson	July 1947	St. Louis Browns
Henry Thompson	July 1949	New York Giants
Sam Jethroe	April 1950	Boston Braves
Sam Hairston	July 1951	Chicago White Sox
Bob Trice	September 1953	Philadelphia Athletics
Gene Baker	September 1953	Chicago Cubs
Curt Roberts	April 1954	Pittsburgh Pirates
Tom Alston	April 1954	St. Louis Cardinals
Nino Escalera	April 1954	Cincinnati Reds
Carlos Paula	September 1954	Washington Senators
Elston Howard	April 1955	New York Yankees
John Kennedy	April 1957	Philadelphia Phillies
Ossie Virgil	June 1958	Detroit Tigers
Pumpsie Green	July 1959	Boston Red Sox

It took fourteen years for the major leagues to become integrated, and still in 1959, there was even an unwritten limit on the number of black players on a team roster, as well as on the field at any given time. If an owner thought his white fans might object to his fielding too many blacks, he would play it safe for he had much to lose. Singularly, the Dodgers in 1950 had four blacks—Jackie Robinson, Roy Campanella, Don Newcombe, and Dan Bankhead—and there were only a total of nine in the entire major leagues.

The Brooklyn Dodgers then became black America's team.

The Brooklyn Dodgers

While it is appropriate to say that black America turned its attention from Negro League baseball to major league ball in the late 1940s, and early 1950s, it is more appropriate to say blacks focused their attention on the Brooklyn Dodgers. The "Bums of Brooklyn," as they were affectionately dubbed, signed in sequence: Jackie Robinson, John Wright, Don Newcombe, Roy Campanella, Roy Partlow, Dan Bankhead, Joe Black, and Jim Gilliam as their first black players. Two of them, Robinson and Campanella, wound up in the Hall of Fame.

When he was about to be traded to the New York Giants on December 13, 1956, Robinson, who had played ten years, then retired. His best year was 1949 when he was first in the National League with a .342 batting average, first in stolen bases with 37, second in RBI's with 124, and second in hits with 203.

Robinson promised Rickey to keep his mouth shut, and suffered the racial abuse for his first two years in a Dodger uniform. But when the restrictions were removed in 1949–50, he became quite outspoken on and off the field—as was his natural bent. Most observers thought his actions were a means of venting his anger and frustration. The September 1951 issue of *Ebony* magazine even headlined a story entitled "Will Jackie Robinson Crack Up?"[15] The magazine's writer soberly remarked, "Jackie is a baseball player and not the executive secretary of the NAACP,"[16] an allusion to Robinson's remarks concerning the plight of blacks in America. That same year, he also set a new National League record for double plays by a second baseman with a total of 137.

Robinson's value to his team was unquestioned. During his ten years he played in six World Series; the team's lone win came in 1955. He played every position except pitcher and catcher, and is best remembered for his play at second base and his double-play partnership with shortstop Pee Wee Reese. His teammate, Roy Campanella, freely admitted, "Jackie could think so much faster than anybody I ever played with or saw."[17]

In 1962, his first year of eligibility, Robinson was inducted into the Hall of Fame, the first black player to be so honored. He then became a vice president of the Chock Full O' Nuts Corporation, and later one of the founders and the Chairman of the Freedom National Bank in New York City. He died on October 24, 1972, of complications brought on by diabetes. Without exception, Jack Roosevelt Robinson was the single most significant athlete—black or white—after World War II. He made possible the introduction and participation of other black athletes in all team sports. (See the Reference section for Robinson's record.)

Roy Campanella: He was Jackie Robinson's teammate for nine years. This 190-pound catcher from Philadelphia was a Negro Leagues veteran who began playing professionally at age fifteen. Born of an Italian father and an African-American mother, he was the youngest of four children. His baseball career started with local teams and then with an American Legion squad—as the only black player. His parents would not allow him to play on Sundays.

His primary Negro League affiliations were with the Bacharach Giants and Baltimore Elite Giants, beginning in 1935 at $60 per month. He credits Raleigh "Biz" Mackey, the great Negro Leagues catcher, with helping him. "I was his boy,"[18] Campanella said of Mackey. But Campanella claimed that "Josh Gibson was the greatest catcher—and ballplayer—he ever saw."[19]

Campanella once left the Negro Leagues, mistakenly thinking he had a possible spot with the Philadelphia Phillies. On October 17, 1945, he inadvertently declined an honest invitation from Branch Rickey to join the Dodgers. When Rickey did bring him aboard, he was asked to go to Nashua (New Hampshire), a Dodgers farm team, when Danville (Illinois) another team refused him because he was black. In 1948, after some time spent at the Dodger's St. Paul (Minnesota) farm club, managed by Walter Alston, he joined the Brooklyn Dodgers.

In 1950, Campanella fractured his thumb—a common occurrence among catchers who squat behind the plate some twenty thousand times a season—he recovered and played enough to win the National League Most Valuable Player Award three times—in 1951, 53, and 55. During the Dodgers' 1955 winning World Series, Campanella had 2 home runs, 4 RBIs, and 7 hits. Twenty-seven months later, tragedy struck at about 1:30 A.M. on January 28, 1958, on a winding, icy road near his home in Long Island, New York. Campanella's car skidded into a pole and he was left paralyzed from the chest down.

There were no seat belt regulations in 1958, and Campanella was not wearing one. His twenty-year playing career was over. After a difficult period of rehabilitation, he became an instructor with the Dodgers. On May 7, 1959, at the Los Angeles Coliseum (where the Dodgers played before Dodger Stadium was built), a crowd of 93,000 gathered to pay him homage. The crowd set a new attendance record for baseball, eclipsing the old record of 86,288 at the fifth game of the 1948 World Series in Cleveland between the Cleveland Indians and the Boston Braves. The Los Angeles Coliseum crowd was the largest paying audience ever assembled in honor of a black American. (See the Reference section for Campanella's record.)

The Dodgers had other outstanding black players during those early "difficult" times. Don Newcombe, Joe Black, and Dan Bankhead pitched, and Jim "Junior" Gilliam played second base. Newcombe joined the team in 1949 and promptly had a 17–8 season with a 3.17 earned run average, and was named National League Rookie of the Year. In 1951, he tied with Warren Spahn for the league lead in strikeouts with 164. After an Army hitch, he returned and posted a 20–5 season in 1955, but he had a dismal World Series. In 1957, the 6-foot 4-inch, 220-pound Madison, New Jersey native was 27–7. He finished his career at number thirty-two on the all-time list for winning percentage. After suffering bouts with alcoholism, he became a counselor.

Dan Bankhead posted a 9–4 record in 1950. Joe Black started with the Dodgers in 1952. After a 15–4 season, he became the first black pitcher to start the first game of a World Series in which the Dodgers won

4–2. But he lost two games, including the seventh against the New York Yankees. Gilliam joined in 1953 and played fourteen years, spending his entire working life with the team. He died on October 8, 1978, in Los Angeles.

Bill Veeck's Boys

Bill Veeck was a one-legged, shrewd baseball manager for the Cleveland Indians, who in 1947 bought the rights to Larry Doby, a brilliant outfielder, from Effa Manley's Newark Eagles for only $10,000. (Veeck had been turned down by his fellow white baseball magnates in 1944 when he wanted to hire blacks to play for the Philadelphia Phillies.) Doby, the team's brilliant, regular right fielder in 1948, was the first black player in the American League, hitting .301, the third highest on the team. A year later he was fifth in the league with 24 homers. In 1952, he led the league in slugging with an average of .541, including 32 homers, and 104 runs scored.

Doby, who like Jackie Robinson had a college background—at Virginia Union University—was on the short list of candidates for the job as the major league's first black manager in 1974. He was supposedly told by the Cleveland Indians' general manager, Ted Bonda, that "You're getting close."[20] The job went instead to Frank Robinson.

Luke Easter, a powerful outfielder, also got his break with the Indians. He led the league in home run percentage in 1952 with 7.1. The most phenomenal appearance, however, was that of Leroy "Satchel" Paige, the legendary black hurler from the Negro Leagues. In game five of the 1948 World Series between the Indians and the Boston Braves at Cleveland, Paige pitched in relief for two-thirds of an inning. Though Boston won the game 11 to 5, the Indians won the Series four games to two. Paige thus fulfilled a lifelong wish to play in the Series in the game from which he had been barred all his life.

Paige went on to play for the St. Louis Browns in 1951, 52, and 53. Then, in a noble gesture that qualified him for a major league pension, he was signed by the Kansas City Athletics in 1965 for one game in which he pitched three innings. He was fifty-nine years old. He finished perhaps one of the most fascinating careers ever experienced by a professional player, and was inducted into the Hall of Fame in 1971. (His major league record is listed in the Reference section.)

The New York Giants

Henry "Hank" Thompson broke in with the St. Louis Browns in 1947 but is associated more with the Giants. He threw right-handed but batted left-handed, an oddity. In 1951, he was part of the first all-black outfield in the major leagues—with Willie Mays and Monte Irvin of the Giants.

Monte Irvin: Monford "Monte" Irvin was one of the early leaders among the first generation of black players. He, too, had played in the Negro Leagues, and though he was in the majors for eight years, he was inducted into the Hall of Fame as a Negro League entrant in 1973. He batted over .300 three times, was in two World Series, in 1951 and 1954 (he stole home in the first game of the 1951 Series against the New York Yankees), and led the league in runs batted in with 121, in 1951. Irvin is particularly remembered for his helpfulness with younger players, including the great Willie Mays. He finished his career as an assistant to the commissioner.

Willie Mays: The third black player in the 1951 Giants outfield was Willie Howard Mays, a 5-foot 11-inch, 183-pound outfielder from Westfield, Alabama. The incomparable "Say Hey" kid—so called, because he forgot a teammate's name and blurted out: "Say Hey"—was born May 6, 1931, and spent his early years with an aunt after his parents divorced. He once played on a team with his father before joining the Birmingham Black Barons in the late 1940s.

Mays is thought by many baseball experts to be the best all-around player since World War II. He joined the Giants on May 25, 1951, earning a salary of $5,000 a year. He went to bat twelve times before getting his first hit, and had one hit for twenty-seven at-bats, before turning the corner and going nine for twenty-four—including six straight homers at one stretch. Mays thus began to fulfill the promise seen in him by Giants manager, Leo "The Lip" Durocher. Mays had been bought from the Birmingham Black Barons in 1950 for $10,000 and first assigned to Trenton Class B in the Interstate League where he hit .353 in 81 games. He then went to Minneapolis Class AAA, before going to the Giants.

While Jackie Robinson was serious and bore the brunt of being the first black player, Hank Thompson was the Giants' first black performer. However, it is Mays, whose youthful zest, enthusiasm, and gregariousness of spirit that forever remains as part of the game and captions his career. Mays was the first to admit that "I guess I talked too much."[21] No one doubted his abilities. When he joined the Giants in 1951, they were in fifth place. With him, they went on to win the pennant. He left the Giants in first place in 1952 when he went into the Army, that year, they finished second. The Giants in 1953, finished fifth, and when Mays returned in 1954, the Giants won the National League pennant again.

Mays became known for his basket-style technique of catching fly balls wherein he would hold his glove waist-high and palms up. (He claims he learned the technique in the Army at Fort Eustis, Virginia.) His most famous catch was an over-the-head basket-style nab of a long fly ball from the Cleveland Indians' Vic Wertz in the first game of the 1954 World Series at the Polo Grounds. The score was tied at 2–2 in the top of the eighth inning, and Larry Doby and Al Rosen were on base. Mays caught Wertz' drive, stopped, pivoted, and threw to Davey Williams to save a run. No runs were scored that inning, and the Giants won that game 5–2, plus the Series 4 games to none.

This 1954 Giants team was considered one of the best ever assembled, winning 97 games with a pitching staff that threw 19 shutouts. Mays won the major leagues batting title on the last day of the season with a three-for-four performance. New York gave the team a ticker-tape parade for their feat. Mays made the cover of *Time* magazine.

He could do everything well. He had power; he led the league three times in triples, four times in homers, and five times in slugging average. He could run; he led the league four times in stolen bases. He was durable; second only to Ty Cobb in total games by an outfielder with 2,843 (Cobb played in 2,943 games.) Mays was the first man to hit 30 homers and steal 30 bases in one season; he did it twice. He was also the first to hit 200 homers and steal 200 bases. Mays felt somewhat resigned to his talent: "Maybe I was born to play ball. Maybe I truly was."[22] Hank Aaron agreed: "Willie Mays was as natural in the way he plays baseball as he was about brushing his teeth..."[23]

Mays' career was not entirely rosy. He was the object of more than his share of "bean-balls," pitches thrown at players with the intent to injure or intimidate. Some black sportswriters often claimed that many of these incidents were intentional, and racially motivated. While not in complete agreement, Mays noted: "Every once in a while you read...it's the Negro players who get thrown at most of the time. That may be...some of the Negro players can hit pretty good."

In the 1960s, Mays was among the black athletes who were criticized for not being vocal enough about racial discrimination. Again, he was forthright in his opinion. "I don't picket in the streets of Birmingham [Alabama]" he stated, "I'm not mad at the people who do. Maybe they shouldn't be mad at the people who don't."[25]

When the Giants moved from New York City to San Francisco in 1958, Mays encountered the same types of problems faced by any black person moving to a new area. "I found I was disliked because I was from New York, and because I was a Negro, and because I was a threat to the legend of Joe DiMaggio..."[26]

Mays spent his last two seasons with the New York Mets in 1972–1973 and was a batting coach with the team during spring training. His lifetime statistics include 2,992 games—third on the all-time list; 3,283 hits—seventh on the list; and 660 homers—third among all major leaguers. To these numbers Mays replied, "I never played for records of any kind, only to win games. In fact, I don't think I have any records but whatever records there are, I'm in the top ten."[27]

Mays' work as a public relations consultant with a New Jersey casino after his retirement in 1973 caused the first black captain of the Giants (1964) and the highest paid major league player ($105,000 in 1963) to be disassociated, along with Mickey Mantle, from professional baseball by then commissioner Bowie Kuhn. Citing possible links with organized crime at the casino, Kuhn felt that Mays and former New York Yankee centerfielder Mickey Mantle should not be allowed formal relationships with the game because they were employed by gambling establishments. In March of 1985, Peter Ueberroth, the new commissioner, restored both Mays and Mantle to baseball's good graces.

Until 1953, the Dodgers, Indians, and Giants were the only teams that dared to employ more than a token number of black players. Between 1953 and 1959—the year the Boston Red Sox became the last franchise to integrate—the above three teams continued their leadership role. But there were other black players who began during these years, and one of them later broke one of the sport's most hallowed records.

Sam "The Jet" Jethroe, a Boston Braves switch-hitting speedster from East St. Louis, Illinois, led the National League in stolen bases in 1950 and 1951 with thirty-five each year. Bill Bruton, an Alabama-born outfielder for the Milwaukee Braves and the Detroit Tigers, led the National League in stolen bases in 1953, 1954, and 1955; in triples in 1956 and 1960; and in runs scored in 1960. Al Smith, who played for the Cleveland Indians, the Chicago White Sox, and the Baltimore Orioles, led the American League in runs scored in 1955. And Sam "Sad Sam" Jones, of Stewartsville, Ohio, pitched for the Indians, Cubs, Cardinals, Giants, Tigers, and Orioles over a twelve-year career beginning in 1951. Jones won twenty-one games with the Giants in 1959 and led the National League that year with an ERA of 2.83; he was first in strikeouts in 1955, 1956, and 1958.

Elston Howard deserves special mention. Howard was born in St. Louis, Missouri, and attended Vashon High School. After graduation, he played with the Kansas City Monarchs in the Negro Leagues before becoming the first black player for the New York Yankees in 1955. He began as an outfielder but was converted to catcher, and became the American League's first black Most Valuable Player in 1963. Howard was an anomaly among black players in the mid-1950s in that he was not a terror on the base paths. His manager, Casey Stengel, made reference to this point in saying in 1955: "Finally they give me a nigger, but they give me a nigger who can't run."[28] This durable catcher played for fourteen years in the major leagues and in ten World Series. He continued as a Yankee coach until his death in 1980.

In retrospect, the supremacy of black players in certain statistical categories at the time is not surprising. The major leagues were bereft of quality white players after World War II, and teams outdid themselves with bonus payments to attract the best they could find. As the relative cost of superior white players rose, talented low-cost black players became more desirable. Though records show that the mean batting average for black players—except pitchers—from 1953 to 1957 was 20.6 points higher than for white players, blacks were not paid accordingly.

In a December 1970 report by Anthony H. Pascal and Leonard A. Rapping for the Rand Corporation, it was reported that "no black player before 1959 received a signing bonus of $20,000 or more, while twenty-six white players received such sums in the same time period. In the four-year period from 1959 through 1961, forty-three white players received bonuses in excess of $20,000 while only three blacks received as much."[29] Black players were placed in an inferior bargaining position in the 1950s. They had no agents, and only Jackie Robinson and Larry Doby had, as a result of their college experience, enough knowledge of salary negotiation and its rigors. Blacks attached a higher psychic value to a career in professional sports than did their white counterparts. They were willing to suffer racial indignities like segregated lodging in order to play. Blacks had been in the major leagues for nine years before the last segregated player hotel, the Chase Hotel in St. Louis, gave in. Branch Rickey even advised blacks in a 1957 *Ebony* magazine article to "Cool it," and not press too hard, too fast, for their just rights and demands.

Blacks knew the game's reserve clause bound them for life to the first team that signed them, but that applied to whites as well. Jackie Robinson said soberly, "I knew

I was underpaid, but so were a lot of other Dodgers."[30] Hank Aaron freely admitted in his autobiography that "...I'd always been too easy to deal with. They'd offered me a contract and I'd nearly always signed without any argument."[31] Black sportswriter Sam Lacy was on target, when he said of black players of that period: "...The Negro is, generally, quicker to sign...there has never been a big Negro bonus player ...They're still signing for the opportunity."[32]

Black players in the 1950s thus served a dual role. In addition to performing at an above-average level, which it was assumed that they would do by the white owners, they were also used by owners to dampen the bonus payments to white players, while limiting the game's exposure to black players in general. As Gerald W. Scully noted in his historic book: "By checking bonus competition, baseball had altered the relative prices of black and white players and thus reduced the economic incentive of teams to hire blacks."[33] If one is to believe Scully's assertion, talent alone did not determine the number of black players signed between 1947 and 1961. These cold facts aside, blacks continued their outstanding play, and this first generation produced more future Hall of Fame inductees than did players who began in the 1960s, or 1970s.

Henry "Hank" Aaron: A titan alongside Willie Mays was Henry Louis "Hank" Aaron of Mobile, Alabama. Born February 5, 1936, during the Depression, Aaron was first discovered playing softball with the Mobile Black Bears. He wrote in his autobiography that he left home to join the Indianapolis

Clowns with two pairs of pants, two dollars, and two sandwiches. His meal money from the Clowns was $2 per day, and his salary was $200 per month. The Boston Braves signed him in 1952 and sent him to their Class C team in Eau Claire, Wisconsin, and then to their Jacksonville, Florida, franchise in 1953. He was the first black player in the South Atlantic ("Sally") League. He was Rookie of the Year at Eau Claire, and Most Valuable Player in the Sally League.

The 6-foot, 180-pound Aaron was a natural hitter, (though he used a cross-handed grip while playing for the Clowns, this deficiency was soon corrected.) He broke into the Braves' lineup on March 13, 1954, when Bobby Thompson broke his leg in a game against the Yankees. Aaron's salary was $8,000 a year. In only his third year in the majors, he led the National League with a batting average of .328, in hits with 200, in total bases with 340, and in doubles with 34; he was second in triples at 14; he was third in slugging average at .558, and in runs scored with 106. "Aaron was to my time what Joe DiMaggio was to the era when he played,"[34] said Mickey Mantle.

Aaron always seemed to play in the shadow of the more outgoing and gregarious Willie Mays, and like Mays, Aaron was named captain of his team—in 1969. Aaron passed Mays in the home run category in 1972 when he hit his 649th, a grand slam, and, until Mays caught up, Aaron was the only man to hit 500 home runs and the only man to have 3,000 hits. Between the two of them, Aaron and Mays were first in seven batting categories in 1957. Aaron helped the Braves win the 1957 World Series over the Yankees with a stupendous series batting average of .393, 3 home runs, and 11 hits.

Leroy "Satchel" Paige chats with Kansas City Monarchs teammate
Jackie Robinson in the summer of 1945. *(Courtesy of Ocania Chalk)*

Jackie Robinson signs his contract with the Brooklyn Dodgers in
October 1945. Branch Rickey, the Dodgers' president, looks on.
(Courtesy of the Los Angeles Dodgers)

The Brooklyn Dodgers' Jackie Robinson racing home to score against
Chicago Cubs catcher John Pramesa, in May 1952 at Ebbets field.
(Courtesy of the Los Angeles Dodgers)

Leroy "Satchel" Paige, in a pensive mood, finally makes it to the major leagues with the Cleveland Indians. *(Courtesy of George Brace)*

Brooklyn Dodgers players Roy Campanella, Jackie Robinson, and Gil Hodges greet General Douglas MacArthur and wife, Jean, July 1951. *(AP/Wide World Photos)*

The "Say Hey" Kid, Willie Mays, of the New York Giants, steals third against the Brooklyn Dodgers in 1955. *(Courtesy of Ocania Chalk)*

Willie Mays sharing a laugh with Monte Irvin (right). *(Courtesy of the Chicago Cubs)*

John "Buck" O'Neil, the first black coach in the major leagues. *(Courtesy of the Chicago Cubs)*

Hall of Famer Billy Williams, of the Chicago Cubs. For a time in 1964, Williams' batting average was .396. *(AP/Wide World Photos)*

Curt Flood, St. Louis Cardinals outfielder. Flood filed a suit contesting organized baseball's Reserve Clause, initiating the move to free agency. *(Courtesy of George Brace)*

Joe Morgan, the Cincinnati Reds' premier second baseman. *(Courtesy of the Cincinnati Reds, Inc.)*

Reggie Smith, the Los Angeles Dodgers' outfielder.
(Courtesy of the Los Angeles Dodgers)

Reggie "Mr. October" Jackson finishes a mighty
swing. *(Courtesy of the California Angels)*

Willie "Pops" Stargell, the Pittsburgh Pirates' slugging first baseman.
(Courtesy of the Pittsburgh Pirates)

Cincinnati Reds teammates Terry Francona and Kal Daniels welcome 1987 sensation Eric Davis after his home run against the Atlanta Braves in April. *(AP/Wide World Photos)*

The Baltimore Orioles' Eddie Murray connects for a home run against the Philadelphia Phillies' Charles Hudson in 1983 World Series game 5. *(AP/Wide World Photos)*

The St. Louis Cardinals' Willie McGee robs Gorman Thomas of a homer in a 1982 World Series game against the Milwaukee Brewers. *(AP/Wide World Photos)*

Dave Parker, the Cincinnati Reds' power-hitting outfielder. *(Courtesy of the Cincinnati Reds)*

Dwight Gooden, the New York Mets' Rookie-of-the-Year pitcher. *(Courtesy of the New York Mets)*

Rickey Henderson, the New York Yankees' fleet-footed outfielder.
(Courtesy of Yankees *magazine)*

Ozzie Smith, the St. Louis Cardinals' $2-million shortstop.
(Courtesy of the St. Louis Cardinals)

Jim Rice, Boston Red Sox all-star slugger.
(Courtesy of the Boston Red Sox)

The Montreal Expos' Andre Dawson snares a sure home run from the San Diego Padres' Terry Kennedy, in May 1984. *(AP/Wide World Photos)*

Dave Winfield, New York Yankees right fielder, heads for first base. *(Courtesy of* Yankees *magazine)*

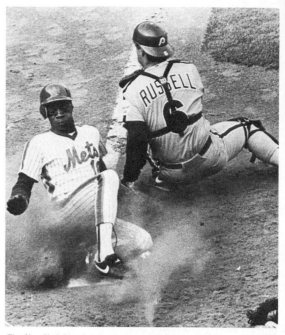

The master thief, Vince Coleman, of the St. Louis Cardinals, is tagged out by Houston Astros' catcher Mark Bailey, in May 1986. *(AP/Wide World Photos)*

The New York Mets' slugging right fielder Darryl Strawberry slides safely home under a late tag by Philadelphia Phillies' catcher John Russell, in April 1986. *(AP/Wide World Photos)*

Charles "Chuck" Cooper, the first black player in the NBA. *(Courtesy of the Basketball Hall of Fame)*

Nathaniel "Sweetwater" Clifton, one of the first three blacks in the NBA, in 1950. *(Courtesy of Ocania Chalk)*

Coach John McLendon (right) welcomes Dick Barnett, of Tennessee State University, to the Cleveland Pipers squad of the American Basketball League, on December 22, 1961. *(AP/Wide World Photos)*

UCLA All-America center Lew Alcindor (now Kareem Abdul-Jabbar) shows grace snaring a rebound during practice for NCAA semifinals against Drake University at Louisville, March 19, 1969. *(AP/Wide World Photos)*

Oscar "The Big O" Robertson, whom many believe to have been the best ever to play the game. *(Courtesy of the Milwaukee Bucks)*

Elvin "The Big E" Hayes, one of the NBA's most durable performers. *(Courtesy of Jay Goldberg)*

Wes Unseld, a man-mountain on defense for the Bullets. *(Courtesy of Wes Unseld)*

Number 19 of the New York Knicks, Willis Reed, exults with the game ball after helping the Knicks win the NBA title over the Los Angeles Lakers in the 1973 series. Jerry Lucas trails Reed. *(AP/Wide World Photos)*

The incomparable Julius "Dr. J" Erving (center) evades the block attempts by Kareem Abdul-Jabbar (left) and Don Ford, of the Los Angeles Lakers, December 1978. *(AP/Wide World Photos)*

Walt Frazier, of the NBA's New York Knicks, discussing the Hot-Shot Program for youngsters with former NBA Commissioner Larry O'Brien, 1975. *(AP/Wide World Photos)*

Lataunya Pollard Cal State-Long Beach '83	Holly Warlick Tennessee '81	Tara Heiss Maryland '78	Cindy Noble Tennessee '81
Jill Rankin Tennessee '80	Denise Curry UCLA '82	Lynette Woodard Kansas '81	Anne Donovan Old Dominion '84

Lataunya Pollard (top left) and Lynette Woodard (bottom, second from right), on team photo of the 1980 Olympic team. *(AP/Wide World Photos)*

Moses Malone, who went directly from Matoaca High School in Petersburg, Virginia, to the NBA. *(Courtesy of the Philadelphia 76'ers)*

Julius "Dr. J" Erving, one of the most acrobatic NBA performers since Elgin Baylor. *(Courtesy of the Philadelphia 76'ers)*

Jordon versus Bird. The Chicago Bulls' Michael Jordan finger rolls for 2 points over the Boston Celtics' premier forward, Larry Bird, in an April 26, 1987, game. *(AP/Wide World Photos)*

James Worthy, Magic Johnson's sidekick for the Los Angeles Lakers. *(Courtesy of ProServ, Inc.)*

The Los Angeles Lakers' Magic Johnson flips a "blind" pass over his shoulder past the Indiana Pacers' Dudley Bradley. *(AP/Wide World Photos)*

Clarence "Big House" Gaines, coach at Winston-Salem State University. *(Courtesy of Clarence Gaines)*

John Thompson, coach of the NCAA championship Georgetown University team. *(Courtesy of John Thompson)*

He was, quite naturally, named the National League's Most Valuable Player.

The normally somber Aaron admitted the Series was among his life's most exciting moments: "If you're playing in a World Series and your spine doesn't tingle some that first day you walk out of the clubhouse onto the field, you're dead and don't know it."[35]

Near the height of his career, Aaron admitted that he drew his original inspiration from a familiar source. "I got the idea I could play professional baseball when I heard that Jackie Robinson had broken the color barrier."[36] Aaron quietly suffered through his relative anonymity in the majors for twenty years, and then began to speak out: "For sixteen years no one knew I was playing baseball. Then suddenly last year [1972] everybody began to wonder where I came from."[37]

Seven years after signing a two-year contract with the Braves for $100,000 per year, Aaron broke baseball's most coveted record. On Monday, April 8, 1974, in a game against the Los Angeles Dodgers, Aaron hit his 715th home run to break Babe Ruth's major league record. This historic home run, was hit off of a black pitcher, Al Downing, and witnessed by a television audience of millions of Americans. Interest in Aaron's pursuit of Ruth's record did not help the Braves' attendance, and he had begun receiving hate mail as he neared home run number 715.

Having eclipsed the record, Aaron was quoted as saying: "When I hit it tonight, all I thought about was that I wanted to touch all the bases."[38] When Mrs. Babe Ruth was asked about Aaron's new record, she reportedly replied, "I don't care how many home runs Mr. Aaron hits. I just want to be left alone."[39]

Aaron retired after the 1976 season. His record is among the best of all time: 40 or more home runs eight times; 100 or more RBIs eleven times; and a batting average of .300 or more fourteen times. He is now vice president of player personnel for the Atlanta Braves, and a statue of him stands outside the front gates of County Stadium in Atlanta.

Ernie "Mr. Cub" Banks: Ernest "Ernie" Banks of Dallas, Texas, began playing for the Chicago Cubs on September 14, 1953. He was the second black Cubs player, following Gene Baker. The slightly built Banks—6-feet 1-inch, 180-pounds—had one of the most powerful pair of wrists the game had seen. His timing with a bat was uncanny. His 44 home runs in 1955 was the most ever by a shortstop, and his 5 grand slams that same season were also a record. Playing shortstop for nine of his nineteen years in the majors, he formed, along with second baseman Baker, the first black double-play combination in the majors.

Banks' best year was 1958 when he led the National League in at bats with 617, in home runs with 47, in home run percentage with 7.6 percent, in RBIs with 129, in slugging average with .614, and in total bases with 379. He was also second in runs scored with 119 and fourth in triples with 11. In 1962, at age thirty-one, Banks switched to first base. He is twelfth on the all-time list of consecutive games played at 717. The only black player ranked higher is Billy Williams with 1,117. Banks was the third black major league performer elected to the Hall of Fame—in 1977.

Frank Robinson: The fifth black Hall of Fame inductee to begin his career in the 1950s was Frank Robinson of Beaumont, Texas. And what a start he had, winning Rookie of the Year honors in the National League in 1956; that year, he also had 38 home runs and led the league in runs scored with 122.

Robinson was signed by the Cincinnati Reds out of Oakland, California's McClymonds High School. A high school basketball teammate of his was Bill Russell (who, at the time, had trouble making the team his first year). A high school baseball teammate was Vada Pinson, a black and future major league player. An outstanding schoolboy athlete, Robinson was All-City three years in a row in both baseball and basketball.

Robinson, who labored for three years in the minor leagues, was the youngest of ten children of divorced parents, who learned early on the value of dedication and hard work. Known by family, friends, and teammates to be very methodical about his craft during his early years, the results of Robinson's dedication were readily evident during his professional career, and he was usually found among the top five in home run production (including the 1962 season, when the National League leader's list was all black—Willie Mays, Hank Aaron, Frank Robinson, Ernie Banks, and Orlando Cepeda).

Robinson stands alone as the only major leaguer to be voted Most Valuable Player in both leagues—in the National League in 1961 as a Cincinnati Red, and in the American League in 1966 as a Baltimore Oriole outfielder. He is the only black player to win the game's "triple crown"—finishing first in batting average, home runs, and runs batted in, in 1966. That same year, Robinson became the first player to hit a ball completely out of Baltimore's Memorial Stadium—a 451-foot homer. His most historic contribution to the game, however, came in 1974 when he became the first black manager.

At 10:03 A.M. on October 3, 1974, Phil Seghi, the Cleveland Indians' general manager, announced that Frank Robinson would replace Ken Aspromonte as manager with a one-year, $180,000 contract. But unlike Aspromonte, who directed the team exclusively from the dugout, Robinson would be a player-manager. Lee McPhail, the American League president, said that Robinson's signing was "...second in importance only to Jackie Robinson's entry into baseball in 1947."[40]

Robinson made reference to his trailblazing namesake by saying at the press conference: "If I had one wish I was sure could be granted, it would be that Jackie Robinson could be here, seated alongside me, today."[41] Just before his actual debut as manager in 1975, he said: "My feelings are that this is the end of a long road, but the sacrifices were worthwhile to get here. I also have a feeling of gratefulness to all the people, black and white, who made it possible, the sacrifices of all the black players before me, and especially to Jackie Robinson, who's in my thoughts almost every time I put on a uniform. My only regret is that Jackie couldn't be alive to see this happen."[42] Robinson had prepared somewhat for this day by managing players for six years in Puerto Rico during the winter.

Robinson's selection as a manager was of tremendous importance to the black community. Activist and future presidential candidate Jesse Jackson noted, at an April 19, 1975, dinner honoring Robinson and Hank Aaron that "Frank Robinson is not a black manager! He is a manager who is black! Frank Robinson is not on trial, baseball is on trial!"[43] After hitting a home run in his first at bat as player-manager on April 8, 1975, he went on to be ejected three times during that season, and was suspended once by McPhail. In midseason, Robinson began to feel that the umpiring was biased against him, and a meeting was held among Robinson, Seghi, and McPhail to discuss this issue. He did not feel the fans were to blame, noting that, "As for fans, they don't come out to look at the manager. They look at the ballclub."[44]

Robinson's record as a rookie manager in 1975 was 79–80, good for a fourth place finish. He was later fired as the Indians' manager and hired as the San Francisco Giants' manager in 1981, a year in which two black men held managerial jobs—Robinson in San Francisco and Maury Wills in Seattle. Robinson was replaced as Giants manager in 1984, after compiling a 268–277 record. (See Reference section for Robinson's record as player and manager.)

The Boston Red Sox Give In

The total integration of black players in every major league franchise finally occurred in 1959 when Elijah "Pumpsie" Green of Oakland, California, was signed by the Boston Red Sox. It had been twelve years since Jackie Robinson's first day in the majors (coincidentally, blacks were approximately 14 percent of the leagues), and for the first time, dominated the record books. That year, blacks led in nine of twelve batting categories and two of twelve pitching categories. The top five stolen-base leaders were black—Willie Mays, Jim Gilliam, Orlando Cepeda, Tony Taylor, and Vada Pinson.

The first generation of black major league players had weathered many changes since Jackie Robinson's first appearance. Blacks even began playing for Japanese teams in 1952, when John Britton, Larry Raines, and Jonas Gaines were signed by the Hankyu Braves in Osaka. The Major League Players Association was formed in 1953, but remained largely ineffective until the mid-1960s. The United States Supreme Court ruled on November 19, 1953, in a 7-to-2 decision that baseball was indeed a sport and not a business subject to antitrust laws. In 1954, the Cotton States League began accepting black players while the Southern Association folded in 1957 without ever accepting a black player. The Chase Hotel in St. Louis finally integrated in 1955, the last holdout among player hotels.

President Dwight D. Eisenhower personally interceded in the integration brouhaha in 1956, when Roy Campanella, at Branch Rickey's request, went to Japan to play in some exhibition games. Initially, Campanella did not want to go, but the President pleaded, saying: "Campy, you just have to go to Japan. We have to impress upon these people that we do have democracy here, and we have to show them that we are not such bad people because of that atom bomb we dropped on Hiroshima."[45] Campanella was being used as a symbol of racial equality for a nation that still had far to go in this area.

In 1958, the Dodgers and Giants moved to Los Angeles and San Francisco, respectively, and that year marked the first time the percentage of black players in the major leagues approximated that of blacks in the general population. On the field, the carefully selected black players compiled awesome statistics and records in an incredibly short time. In the fourteen year period from 1946 to 1959, eight of the National League Rookie of the Year selections were black; nine of the MVPs were black; and an exceedingly high percentage of the game's leaders in stolen bases, runs scored, slugging average, and batting average were black. Unfortunately, these players were unwittingly being viewed as forerunners of future blacks who could only hit home runs and steal bases. While the primary concern of these pioneer performers was to establish a presence and a standard of play, the next generation would be concerned with issues like salary discrimination, segregation of black players by position, and the recission of the hated reserve clause.

PART II
1960 to 1969: TRIUMPHS, TRIALS, AND TREPIDATION

By 1960, black players were hardened veterans of major league ball. Enough of them had made their way to the top by every route possible to provide guidance for those who followed. The segregation of black players in the major league cities was "history," but off the field, they were still subjected to the racial indignities that any less famous black person encountered. This was especially true during spring training, which was held in the southern and southwestern states. The civil rights laws

that were passed in 1963, 1964, and 1965 only legally eradicated discriminatory treatment of blacks in public places.

The disproportionately high number of blacks killed in the Vietnam War; Muhammad Ali's refusal to be inducted into the armed forces; the overt demonstration by Tommie Smith and John Carlos at the 1968 Mexico City Olympics against racial treatment of black Americans in their home country, all had wide reaching repercussions—especially in professional baseball, where almost all of the black players felt compassion for the stands taken by all three men. Generally in sports, blacks felt freer to meet among themselves to discuss mutual, professional, societal, and international concerns.

Black members of team sports in particular became aware of their vulnerability, and of the risks of being too vocal in public about individual and collective grievances. Black athletes also grappled with the problems of being misunderstood, either because of their position and profession, or because they braved the waters to talk with members of the media during a time of antagonism between the black and white communities in the mid-1960s.

All major league managers were white until Frank Robinson appeared in 1974, although a few black coaches had been appointed. Team sports managers and coaches are, through historical precedence, autocratic and are used to having their orders obeyed with little or no discussion. They set standards for their players off the field as well as on. In the 1950s, black players, in the main, did as they were told, silently suffering and nursing their own private hurts, even when affected by decisions of a racist origin. Not so in the 1960s. The attitude of young Americans toward discrimination had turned defiant, and they demanded that their highly paid star athletes do the same.

Few black major leaguers were willing to play as public a role during the black social revolution in the mid-1960s as did Ali, Smith, or Carlos. Baseball players were the highest-paid of team-sport athletes, and the popularity of some, like Willie Mays, Hank Aaron, Frank Robinson, Willie Mc-Covey, and Bob Gibson was so widespread that only a hard core group of relatively young, college-educated protesters would criticize their words or actions. Like their counterparts in football and basketball, they were symbols of success to the average, wage-earning black American.

Hank Aaron probably spoke for many in his generation by saying in his autobiography: "I'm no crusader...never wanted to be."[46] He probably would not have been, even if he were not a ball player. After his retirement, Aaron became very vocal about his chances of being considered for a managerial slot. As previously mentioned, Mays also did not care for being attacked for not marching in the streets, and frankly stated that his critics "...shouldn't be mad at the people who don't."[47]

The black press had been careful in making parallels inside the defiant columns of their editorial pages because of the racial discrimination incurred by individual players. Having their own sets of racial problems, black players could be used by black papers' sportswriters and regular columnists as proof that discrimination was not confined to the man in the street, that it could and did happen to blacks who made more than $100,000 per year. It was difficult to criticize these heroes because nearly all of them came from humble backgrounds and their black fans supported and realized the difficulties they faced.

The Stacking Phenomenon in Baseball

In 1960, the American League began adding black players to its teams' rosters at a faster rate. Through to 1971, the rate of increase was 1.4 percent per year in the American League versus a rate of 0.6 percent for the National League. The percentage of black players on National League rosters, however, remained higher than that for the American League, and in no year during this period did the National League's average percentage dip below that of the American League. The twelve-year average for the National League was 25 percent, versus 18 percent of the American League.

The highest black representation in the National League up through 1971 was in 1967 and 1969, when it reached 29 percent. The Pittsburgh Pirates had the highest individual team average, in 1967, with 56 percent. The highest American League figure during those years came about in 1969, at 24 percent. The Cleveland Indians had the highest individual team average in 1968 at 40 percent. The ratio of black to white players would not get much higher in the future. On September 1, 1971, the Pittsburgh Pirates fielded an all-black team against the Philadelphia Phillies; the first time that had ever occurred.

These team figures for black players were two, and sometimes nearly three times that of the general population, but the players were not equally apportioned among the nine positions. Overwhelmingly, blacks were confined to the outfield, first base, and second base. In 1960, the ratio of black outfielders to black pitchers was 5.6 to 1, and in 1971, it had worsened to 6.7 to 1. Pascal and Rapping studied the racial composition of the leagues in 1968 and found that blacks made up 53 percent of the outfielders, 40 percent of the first basemen, 30 percent of second basemen, 26 percent of shortstops, 14 percent of third basemen, 12 percent of the catchers, and 9 percent of the pitchers. Thus black players were clearly "stacked" or limited on team rosters by position. (The "stacking" phenomenon was originally described by black Professor Harry Edwards of the University of California at Berkeley.)[48]

As to the relative dearth of black pitchers and catchers, there were several reasons put forth by observers. One was simply the purposeful exclusion because blacks were thought untrustworthy in these crucial positions. Another reason given was that pitchers and catchers required more pre–major league experience and interaction with coaches. Many blacks supposedly disliked spending time in the minor leagues, and some found it difficult to relate to white coaches, of mostly southern backgrounds. Outfielders, on the other hand, were expected to hit for power—a "natural" talent—steal bases, and make as few catching errors as possible. Not much coaching was needed. Still another theory brought forth was that aspiring, young black players emulated their heroes who were invariably black and, more than likely, were outfielders who earned large salaries.

Skin color gradations were even posited as a possible reason for the segregation of black players by position, and these observations are statistically relevant. Gerald W. Scully, who studied and wrote about discrimination in baseball, used the five skin color classifications found in G. Franklin Edwards' 1959 book, *The Negro Professional Class*—Very Light, Light Brown, Medium Brown, Dark Brown, and Very Dark—and related them to a player's position. Applying this code to a sample of 159 black players in the June 1969 issue of *Ebony* magazine, Scully found the following percentages of non-outfielders: Very Light, 80 percent; Light Brown, 67.9 percent; Medium Brown, 56.8 percent; Dark Brown, 53.5 percent; and Very Dark, 25 percent. Clearly, black players were also being segregated according to skin tone.

College experience was also a factor. While predominantly white colleges began recruiting black basketball, track, and football players in the 1960s, no such concerted effort was made for baseball players. Interest in black colleges dwindled after the 1930s and these schools never regained the interest for the Spring sport. (Southern University in Baton Rouge, Louisiana, was the only black college to win a national baseball title—the NAIA in 1959 under coach Bob Lee. Grambling, also in Louisiana, was NAIA runner-up in 1963 and 1964 under coach Ralph Jones.)

Pascal and Rapping reported a college graduation rate of 14 percent among white major leaguers in 1968, versus a 5 percent rate for American blacks, and 2 percent for Latin blacks. Though a smaller percentage of Latin blacks were college graduates, as a group they had more formal education than their American cousins. (Both white and black Latin players were forced to accept less than an intrinsic value in salary because their alternatives were not as profitable.) Of the 784 major leaguers studied, blacks had about twelve years of schooling, versus thirteen years for whites.

Therefore, black players coming into the major leagues before 1970 had to be superior players (as a group, black batting averages were 20 points higher). Blacks had no agents to bargain for them; less education than their white counterparts; fewer opportunities to play positions other than outfield, first base, and second base; less than a normal chance of playing an infield position if they were dark-skinned; a host of southern-oriented coaches to contend with; and a less than normal chance of becoming coaches and managers in the future, and still, they excelled.

The Batters

Hank Aaron, Willie Mays, Ernie Banks, and Frank Robinson were not the only stars at the plate between 1959 and 1969. There were others who earned spots in the record books in this difficult decade. Tommy Davis had a banner year in 1962, finishing first in hits with 230, in RBIs with 153, and in batting average with .346 (he also finished first in 1963 with a .326 batting average). Billy Williams of the Chicago Cubs had over 200 hits three times during this period and finished first in batting average and slugging average in 1972. Williams also holds the record for most consecutive games played by a black player, 1,117—fourth on the all-time list.

Willie McCovey was the first premier black first baseman. "Stretch," as he was called, was 6-feet 4-inches and 198 pounds. He played for twenty-two years—nineteen years for the Giants and three years for the San Diego Padres. He led the National League in home runs three times; with 44 in 1963, 36 in 1968, and 45 in 1969. He also led the league in RBIs twice, slugging average three times, and once in walks.

Willie Horton, of Arno, Virginia, starred for the Detroit Tigers in the American League for sixteen years. He batted over .300 three times, had over 20 home runs six times, and had a slugging average over .500 four times. He contributed to the Tigers' World Series victory in 1968 with a .304 average. (Some say his performance helped to avoid severe racial trouble in Detroit that year.)

Richie "Dick" Allen of Wampum, Pennsylvania, was a supreme hitter who had great difficulty adjusting to life in the major leagues. In his fifteen-year career with five teams—nine of them with the Phillies—he batted over .300 seven times, had 32 or more home runs six times, and a slugging average of .520 nine times. But he certainly had his problems.

Though he eventually became the game's highest-paid player in 1974 with a salary of $225,000, Allen's early career was marked by frustration. On July 3, 1965, he had a fistfight with white teammate Frank Thomas. Another fight occurred in a barroom on July 21, 1968. He frequently missed team planes, and finally he explained his feelings in an *Ebony* magazine article in July 1970: "I wouldn't say that I hate whitey, but deep down in my heart, I just can't stand whitey's ways, man... ...get right mad."[49] The late 1960s was a difficult time for all of black America.

The Runners

Black athletes have brought blazing foot speed to every sport they have attempted. This asset is considered by most experts to be God-given; in other words, fast runners are born, not made. Until 1960, the majority of black athletes who were participating in any organized sporting activity showed that they were specially endowed with, in addition to their other talents, the gift of speed afoot. Faced with a limited future in other occupations, these swift athletes often starred in several sports. In his very first year of major league play in 1947, for instance, Jackie Robinson led the National League in stolen bases with 29. In 1959, just twelve years later, the National League's entire top five stolen base leaders were black for the first time. Of all the major statistical categories, stolen bases have been most affected by the black athlete. The first of these record setters was Maurice "Maury" Wills of Washington, D.C.

Maury Wills: In 1915, the legendary Ty Cobb set what appeared to be one of the most durable records in the game: 96 stolen bases in a single season. His record lasted forty-seven years, until Maury Wills stole 104 bases in 1962. The 5-foot 10-inch, 165-pound Wills grew up in Washington, D.C., the son of a minister who had thirteen children. A star athlete at Cardozo High School, Wills was noticed and recruited after a talent hunt staged at Griffith Stadium, and after eight years in the minor leagues, he was called up to the Los Angeles Dodgers on June 1, 1959.

In the beginning, Wills suffered from a lack of confidence, but Dodger coach Pete Reiser buoyed his spirits, and he was on his way. In 1960, he stole 50 bases; in 1961, 35 bases. He was constantly improving his ability to "read" opposing pitchers. He noted, "Even before I get on base I have already decided whether or not I'm going to steal...I watch every move the pitcher makes...you always steal on the pitcher, not the catcher."[50] Toward the end of the 1962 season, it appeared that Wills might have a chance to break Cobb's record but few seriously considered this because the record seemed so unassailable. An *Ebony* magazine article on Sam Jethroe back in October 1950 had casually mentioned Cobb's record, saying, "Although there is little chance that Jethroe or any player will ever beat Ty Cobb's remarkable 1915 record of 96 stolen bases in a single season, Sam is given the best chance."[51]

With all of baseball now behind him, Wills set the new major league record of 97 stolen bases on September 23, 1962, in his 156th game of the season. Commissioner Ford Frick had ruled that Wills had to set a new mark within 154 games, though Cobb's 1915 record was set in 156 games. That year, Cobb played two extra games because of earlier ties, and two of his record total came during these additional games. The speedy Wills broke Cobb's record in a game against the St. Louis Cardinals with Larry Jackson pitching and Gene Oliver catching. Jackson threw to first base five times before throwing to home plate in a futile effort to forestall Wills' new mark. On September

7th, Wills had set the new National League mark of 82 steals, breaking Bob Bescher's record, set in 1911.

Wills finished the season with 104 steals having been thrown out only thirteen times. But Wills paid a high physical price. Sliding with an open "V" method with legs extended, his last 19 steals were painful. "My leg had turned an ugly purple, completely discolored from knee to hip..."[52] For his efforts, he was named the National League's Most Valuable Player for 1962. He also won the coveted Hickok Belt, which is awarded to the nation's top professional athlete.

He played for fourteen years in the major leagues and in four World Series. He also led the National League in stolen bases six times, and in at bats twice. In 1981 he was hired by the Seattle Mariners as the major's second black manager, but was released shortly thereafter. Later, he successfully weathered a drug-addiction problem. His son, Bump, also played in the major leagues for six years.

Wills had plenty of black company in the stolen base category during the 1960s. Every player listed in the National League top five in stolen bases from 1960 to 1970 is black. Other fleet base runners included Vada Pinson, who appeared in the top five six times; Tommy Harper appeared five times; Willie Davis six times; and Tony Taylor three times. The American League's Chuck Hinton appeared four times. But even Wills' record was not safe. The St. Louis Cardinals' Lou Brock broke Wills' record in 1974.

Lou Brock: Louis Clark Brock of El Dorado, Arkansas, is the only black Hall of Fame inductee who began his career in the 1960s. At 5-feet 11½ inches and 170 pounds, he was taller, stronger, and slightly faster than Wills. A left-hander, he was, of course, closer to first base than right-handers when at the plate. (Wills was a switch-hitter.) In 1967, Brock led the National League in at bats, runs scored, and bases stolen. He showed hitting power a year later when he led the league in doubles, triples, and stolen bases.

Brock had a fragile beginning. "Jim Crow was king," he says. "I was searching the dial of an old Philco radio and I heard a game in which Jackie Robinson was playing, and I felt pride in being alive. The baseball field was my fantasy of what life offered."[53]

In 1974, at age thirty-five, he erased Wills' record with 118 steals and a .306 batting average. He never stole even half that number again. Brock played for nineteen years, in three World Series, and was practical about his craft. "People equate stealing a base to winning a game. They don't equate a home run or a single to winning a game. A stolen base is designed to go from one base to another. It's part of the game."[54]

Brock is first on the all-time list of stolen base leaders with 938—he broke Cobb's record on August 29, 1977—and was first in total World Series stolen bases with 14. By the end of the 1984 season, the person representing the closest threat to Brock's record was Rickey Henderson, with

493. (See Reference section for Lou Brock's record.)

The Hurlers

Major changes took place in the 1960s that affected the success of pitchers. In 1961, the American League changed its structure and expanded to ten teams; the National League followed suit a year later. In 1964, a free-agent draft was started for all rookies. In 1965, it was decided that only 41 players from each team could be exempted when filling the rosters of expansion teams. Four years later in 1969, both leagues were expanded again—to twelve teams, each with two six-team divisions. One of the general effects of these changes was an increased demand for pitchers.

The quality of pitching was getting better by the early 1960s, but batting averages were going down, leading to duller games.[55] So the strike zone was enlarged in 1963. In 1969, the pitcher's mound was lowered in height from 15 inches to 10 inches—both measures helped the batter. (Black batters, meanwhile, continued their superiority at the plate. Their averages were 21.2 points higher than white batters from 1962 to 1965, and 20.8 points higher from 1966 to 1970.)

Though some of the most illustrious names in black baseball dating back to 1900 were pitchers, the major leagues gave them little note. In the 1950s there was Don Newcombe, Joe Black, Satchel Paige, and Sam Jones. In the 1960s there was Bob Gibson.

Robert "Hoot" Gibson: Bob Gibson was born on November 9, 1935, in Omaha, Nebraska, into very humble circumstances. He was one of seven children who lived in a four-room wooden shack without a father in the home. When he could sleep by himself, he did so on an army cot. He learned early on to deal with racial discrimination when he attended Omaha's Technical High School, which was fifty percent black yet refused him a spot on its baseball team in 1953. He did, however, star in track—broad jumping 22 feet—and in basketball.

As good an athlete as he was, Gibson received no college scholarship offers. He relied on his brother, Josh, to get him into Omaha's Creighton University, where he became the first black athlete there to play basketball and baseball. He played for a time with the Harlem Globetrotters basketball team. While playing for the Globetrotters, he accepted an offer from the St. Louis Cardinals to join their Class AAA team at Omaha, for a $1,000 bonus and a salary of $3,000 per year. Traded about in the minors, Gibson went from Omaha to Columbus, Georgia, then back to Omaha, then to Rochester, New York, back to Omaha, to the Cardinals and back to Rochester. Gibson finally made it to the Cardinals to stay, in 1960.

In a comparative analysis of two of the post World War II black pitchers, Don Newcombe's lifetime winning percentage of .623 was higher than Gibson's .591. Gibson's lifetime ERA of 2.91 was lower than Newcombe's 3.56; moreover, Gibson lasted longer—and against better-trained athletes. To be sure, he was wild at first, walking 119 batters in 1961. The following year, he led the league in shutouts with five. Three years later, in the 1964 World Series, he pitched a record 31 strikeouts to help the Cardinals defeat the New York Yankees four games to three.

Gibson gives much credit to Cardinal manager Johnny Keane. Keane believed in Gibson, and at a point preceding his own dismissal, told the young pitcher, "You're on your way, Hoot. Nothing can stop you now."[56] To the media Gibson was sometimes difficult, reticent, and withdrawn. The scars of his childhood were deeply felt. He frankly noted that, "In a world filled with hate, prejudice, and protest, I find that I too am filled with hate, prejudice, and protest."[57] He sounded much like Richie Allen.

Gibson astounded the baseball world in 1968—a year filled with inner-city rebellions, protest marches, the Mexico City Olympic demonstration by Tommie Smith and John Carlos, and Dr. Martin Luther King, Jr.'s assassination—when he won 22 games, 13 of which were shutouts. He struck out 268 batters and recorded an ERA of 1.12, the fourth-lowest in history and the best since Walter Johnson's 1.09 in 1913. In the World Series he struck out seventeen batters in the opening game, and thirty-five in his three appearances. His Series ERA that year was 1.67 and he holds the record for most strikeouts per 9 innings at 10.22. Satchel Paige notwithstanding, Bob Gibson was the best black pitcher the major leagues had seen. He is the only major league pitcher among black players in the Hall of Fame. (See Reference section for Bob Gibson's record.)

Most of the other successful black pitchers during this period were foreign-born. Ferguson Jenkins was Canadian, Luis Tiant was Cuban, and Juan Marichal was from the Dominican Republic. Only two others were American-born with outstanding records:

1. *Alphonso "Al" Downing* was from Trenton, New Jersey, and like Bob Gibson, played seventeen years in the major leagues. His lifetime ERA was 3.22, compiled with the New York Yankees, the Oakland Athletics, the Milwaukee Braves, and the Los Angeles Dodgers. He served up the ball that Hank Aaron hit to break Babe Ruth's home run record of 714. In 1964 he led the American League in strikeouts with 217; and in 1971, he led the National League in shutouts with 5.
2. *Earl Wilson* was born in Ponchatoula, Louisiana, and played eleven years in the majors. His lifetime ERA was 3.69 with the Boston Red Sox, the Detroit Tigers, and the San Diego Padres. His best year was 1966, when he won 18 and lost 11. He pitched in game three of the 1968 World Series for four and a third innings.

Unequal Opportunities: There would have been more black pitchers if they had had an equal chance to prove themselves. Like their nonpitching black brethren, they had little chance of remaining on team rosters as relievers or backups. In Gerald W. Scully's model that showed the relationship between length of time in the major leagues and starter status, black pitchers took 0.6 years longer than whites to achieve starter status. This condition would not improve much in the next fifteen years.[58]

The Curt Flood Supreme Court Case

In 1969, major league baseball decided to celebrate its centennial with a gala dinner held on July 21 in the nation's capital. Joe DiMaggio and Willie Mays were named as the first- and second-greatest living players, yet all was not well with the country's number-one sport. Earlier that Spring, the Major League Players Association had staged a boycott over disagreements concerning its pension fund, but that was mild compared to what was eventually set in motion on October 8 of the same year.

It was on that October day that Curt Flood, an outfielder with the St. Louis Cardinals, was told he was being traded to the Philadelphia Phillies. Flood felt that after fourteen years of solid service with the same team, he deserved better. Perhaps it was the memory of the unequal treatment of black players in 1959 when he began with the Cincinnati Reds. Perhaps it was the black social revolution in the mid-1960s and the assassinations of prominent black leaders. More than likely, it was all of that plus every white and black player's hatred of baseball's reserve clause, which bounded them for life to the first club that signed them.

Flood decided to fight the trade on the grounds that the reserve clause violated Federal antitrust laws. On December 13, 1969, the Players Association voted 25–0 to support his suit against major league baseball. Marvin Miller, an ex–steel workers union economist who was hired to be the

Players Association's director in 1966, secured former Supreme Court Justice Arthur Goldberg as legal counsel for Flood. Just after Christmas, Flood sent a letter to Commissioner Bowie Kuhn saying he would not play in 1970 for the Phillies.

Flood had wide popular support among the players, though many kept their support quiet lest they endanger their own careers. However, the feisty Richie Allen stated: "Curt Flood's doing a marvelous thing for baseball and many people don't know it. I don't have the intelligence to do what he's doing, but my hat's off to him."[59] Additionally, Jackie Robinson was fully and publicly supportive. He commented, "I think Curt is doing a service to all baseball players in the major leagues...all he is asking for is the right to negotiate...we need men like Curt Flood and Bill Russell...who are not willing to sit back and let Mr. Charlie dictate their needs and wants for them..."[60]

Flood himself felt the pressure early on. "Many people didn't understand. I got nasty letters. They thought I was trying to destroy baseball."[61] Flood was a proven talent, said his teammate Bob Gibson: "He has so much talent he frightens you."[62]

Kuhn's reply in late December stated that: "The reserve system was embodied in the basic agreements negotiated by the owners and the Association." Flood, however, contended that the Players Association had never agreed to the reserve system, that its legalities had always been questioned, and that the owners constantly refused to negotiate any changes to a system that kept players in bondage.

On January 17, 1970, Flood filed suit in

United States District Court for the Southern District of New York, and named the commissioner, the presidents of the National and American Leagues, and the twenty-four clubs as defendants. He asked for $4.1 million in damages. He had three goals: to invalidate his trade to Philadelphia, to become a free agent, and to end the reserve system.

On March 4, 1970, District Court Judge Ben Cooper denied Flood's request for an injunction and recommended a trial for hearing the case. This denial meant that Flood would indeed not play during the 1970 season. In that year, the average major leaguer's salary was $29,303 and seven of the ten players earning over $100,000 per year were black. On August 13, Judge Cooper ruled against Flood's suit. Flood promptly filed an appeal.

Gerald W. Scully had also studied the effects of the reserve clause on black players. Citing the low probability of a black player's being compensated on his true marginal value, Scully wrote, "The reserve clause may be an important factor in the racial pattern of compensation in baseball; its elimination could remove differences in salaries due to racial differences either in the reservation prices of the ball players or in bargaining strength."[63]

Eight months later, on April 8, 1971, a three-judge United States Appeals Court in the Second Circuit in New York City—Sterry Waterman, Wilfred Feinburg, and Leonard P. Moore—upheld Judge Cooper's denial. Flood appealed again, this time to the nation's highest court, which, on October 20, agreed to hear the case. Meanwhile, in 1971, Flood was playing his last major league season with the Washington Senators.

The following year on the vernal equinox (March 21) the Supreme Court began hearing Flood's case. In testimony before Justices Byron "Whizzer" White and Thurgood Marshall, major league baseball attorneys Paul Porter and Lou Haynes declared that Flood's case was more appropriately suited for labor-management negotiation and that the Players Association was the real plaintiff. Flood's attorney, Arthur Goldberg, argued in rebuttal that labor laws did not apply because the reserve system kept his client from playing in the minor leagues and in other countries.

Finally, on June 19, 1972, the Supreme Court ruled in a 5-to-3 decision that baseball could retain its unique status as the only professional sport exempted from federal antitrust legislation. But the Court urged Congress to resolve the issue. Voting in the majority were Justices Harry Blackmun, Warren Burger, Byron White, Potter Stewart, and William Rehnquist. In the minority were Justices William Douglas, Lewis Powell, and Thurgood Marshall.

This hearing before the nation's highest court was the second involving a black athlete. (The first had occurred in 1950 over the use of municipal golf courses in Miami Springs, Florida.) Curt Flood lost his court battle, but his fellow players would eventually win the war against the dreadful reserve clause. The first general strike in baseball history began during the Supreme Court's final deliberations on the Flood case.

Flood and the rest of the black major league players had come a long way since

Elijah "Pumpsie" Green completed the integration of all teams in 1959. Though vestiges of overt racial discrimination still existed here and there throughout the game, the fate of black players would now be inextricably intertwined with their white colleagues.

PART III
1970 to 1984: SUPER SALARIES, FREE AGENCY, AND DRUGS

The average black major leaguer who played during the adjudication of the Curt Flood Supreme Court case could not have imagined what lay ahead. There had been many changes in the last ten to twelve years but the rate of change would accelerate through 1984. In spite of the gains being made by black players, very little headway was being made in the appointment of black coaches, umpires, and managers.

The first black coach was John "Buck" O'Neill, who in 1962 was named by the Chicago Cubs.

(The first black umpire, Emmett Ashford, did not appear until 1966. Ashford was forty-eight years old and had umpired for more than a decade in the Pacific Coast League. Said Ashford just before officiating in the 1966 season Opening Day game, at which President Lyndon Johnson threw out the first ball, "I waited fifteen years for this, and now I'm finally here."[64])

The first black manager in organized ball was the former Chicago Cubs player, Gene Baker, who piloted the Pittsburgh Pirates' Class D farm team at Batavia, New York, in 1961. Nate Moreland had managed in the Arizona-Mexico League, but he did not have true manager status. Frank Robinson was the first black manager of a major league team—the Cleveland Indians in 1974.

Gerald W. Scully concluded from his study that, "The exclusion of blacks from managerial and coaching positions ...appears to be intimately linked to the underrepresentation of blacks in the infield...racial prejudice is responsible for this pattern."[65] This lack of black managers and coaches would change very little through 1984.

Scully had also constructed a model that showed, through empirical evidence, the statistical relationship in the late 1960s between compensation and three critical factors: performance, years in the leagues, and superstar versus nonsuperstar status. He found the following causalities:

1. Outfielders, the big hitters on a team, were paid more. For every 1 percent increase in lifetime slugging average, their salaries increased 2.3 percent.
2. For infielders, a 1 percent increase in lifetime batting average brought a 2.9 percent salary increase.
3. For outfielders, a 10 percent increase in time in the leagues brought a 4 percent increase in salary.
4. For infielders, a 10 percent increase in time in the leagues brought an 8 percent increase in salary.
5. For pitchers, a .1 percent increase in their strikeout-to-walk ratio brought a 3.4 percent increase in salary.

However, these statistical relationships did not apply to black players because:

1. It took black outfielders 0.2 years longer to achieve "regular" status, though they had batting averages nearly 20 points higher than whites.

2. It took black pitchers 0.6 years longer to achieve "regular" status.
3. Black infielders, though, achieved "regular" status 1.8 years faster than whites.
4. In positions where black representation was lowest—pitcher and catcher—the mean performance differentials were greatest.
5. Pay differentials between whites and blacks of equal ability persisted throughout for experienced players.
6. Blacks were forced to spend a longer time at peak performance to be paid equally.[66]

Scully's figures clearly showed that, even though there were a few black superstars earning top salaries as the 1970s began, their journeyman counterparts were severely undercompensated. The recission of the reserve clause and free agency for veterans would shortly change all that.

The ownership of major league teams had also changed during the 1960s. The traditional owner whose sole livelihood was his team gave way to corporate owners who brought more sophisticated business acumen to team management. These new corporate proprietors were less tradition-bound and less steeped in custom for custom's sake. The new breed of players—white and black—were almost forced to turn to professional negotiators or agents to bargain for them. This new state of affairs had never even dawned on players in Jackie Robinson's era.

Player Strikes and Free Agent Status

The Major League Players Association voted 663 to 10 in 1972 to stage the game's first general strike, a thirteen-day absence at the beginning of the season. (Black players voted overwhelmingly in favor of this action.) Curt Flood's Supreme Court case was being heard at the time. The following year, baseball was changed forever by an arbitrator's ruling in favor of two pitchers' grievances.

Pitchers Andy Messersmith of the Los Angeles Dodgers and Dave McNally of the Montreal Expos allowed the Players Association to file their grievances to a three-man arbitration panel. The panel, whose decision was binding, voted 2 to 1 on December 23, 1973, that both players were free agents. This ruling rocked the game at its very foundations. Appeals to the Federal District Court and United States Court of Appeals found in favor of the players. No doubt the courts were influenced by testimony from the Flood case. From then on, it was literally a whole new ballgame.

Peter M. Seitz, one of the arbitrators, even used a reference to the slavery of blacks to explain his reasoning. "I am not an Abraham Lincoln signing the Emancipation Proclamation. Involuntary servitude has nothing to do with this case. The decision does not destroy baseball. But if the club owners think it will ruin baseball, they have it in their power to prevent the damage."[67] The game's first free-agent draft was held on November 4, 1974, at the Plaza Hotel in New York City. Subsequently, the average major league salary jumped from $29,303 in 1970 to $46,000 in 1975, to $135,000 in 1980, and to $329,400 at the end of 1984. Nevertheless, labor disputes between management and players continued.

In 1976, the owners locked out the players for seventeen days during Spring training over unresolved differences. Five years later, on June 12, 1981, the players began the longest strike in American professional sport—fifty days, which involved the cancellation of 714 games. In each case, black players shared the same objectives as their white teammates, though evidence of "stacking" persisted through 1984.

Super Salaries and Super Problems

The general, steady increase in player salaries was jolted by the advent of free agency for veterans that began in late 1974. Players who became free agents could henceforth bargain independently with each team that drafted them. If a player and a team owner could not agree on salary, an arbitrator was brought in. The results over the next ten years were so favorable to players that those who "lost" in arbitration actually won anyway. The salaries of those who won in arbitration rose 94 percent over the ten-year period, and "losing" players' salaries rose 42.5 percent.

Rising player salaries caused a breakdown in some traditional baseball relationships. More frequently the inference was being drawn that a player's power and influence was proportional to his salary. Players began asserting themselves with coaches and managers more than before. Black athletes clearly understood their new bargaining position, and were vocal about it; before 1974 they had tended to mute their gripes. Willie Mays, for instance, wrote about his manager, Alvin Dark, in an article that appeared in *Newsday* (Long Island, New York) in late July 1964. Dark, speaking of the San Francisco Giants' problems, was quoted as saying: "We have trouble because we have so many Spanish-speaking and Negro players on the team. They are just not able to perform up to the white ball player when it comes to mental alertness...you can't make most Negro and Spanish players have the pride in their teams that you can get from white players."[68] At that time, there had been little if any public reaction to Dark's statement from black players.

However, by the mid-1970s, a white manager would not dare say such a thing publicly, and if he had, the resulting backlash could cost him his job. Another example of outspokenness involves Reggie Jackson, who began his career in 1967, and after stints at Kansas City, Oakland, and Baltimore, in 1977 became a New York Yankee. Jackson was, and still is, flamboyant, brash, cocky, and exciting. The late Elston Howard, a Yankee coach who was black, thought that his manager could not bear Jackson's media attention and large salary. Said Howard, "Billy [Martin, the Yankee manager] was jealous of him, hated the attention Reggie got, couldn't control him...the big part was that Reggie's black. Billy hated him for that. I believe Billy is prejudiced against blacks, Jews, American Indians, Spanish, anything...I think Billy wanted Reggie to fail more than he wanted the Yankees to win."[69]

Many black Americans supported Jackson's willingness to confront Martin in public. Not since Wilt Chamberlain had carried on his feuds with a series of coaches in the National Basketball Association had a black team-sport athlete demonstrated such rebelliousness. Jackson had panache. He owned five Rolls-Royces, had a candy bar—'Reggie"—named for him, a string of endorsements for shoes, cars, electronic equipment, gloves; part ownership in three auto dealerships, and was a commentator for ABC Sports.

Jackson proclaimed shortly after coming to New York: "The Yankee pinstripes are [Babe] Ruth and [Lou] Gehrig and [Joe] DiMaggio and [Mickey] Mantle. And I'm a nigger to them. I don't know how to be subservient."[70] But he had become a Yankee after ten years in which he had hit 23 or more home runs nine times. Three years into his stay in New York, he was still caustic: "I am a black man with an IQ of 160 making $700,000 a year, and they treat me like dirt...the problems were created by the money. The big salary made me more visible. I was scrutinized more."[71]

One of the most famous player-manager confrontations in American team-sport history took place less than a week after a *Sports Illustrated* article focused on Jackson and Martin. On July 17, Martin ordered Jackson to bunt in the tenth inning of a game against the Kansas City Royals with the score tied. Thurman Munson, the Yankee catcher, who gave Jackson the nickname "Mr. October," was on first base. With the Royals' infield moving in, Jackson attempted a bunt and backed off. He was then ordered to "hit away." Jackson disobeyed and tried another bunt—strike one. Ordered to hit again, he attempted another bunt—strike two. Martin was livid. Jackson attempted still another bunt and fouled it off—strike three.

Television cameras recorded, for the nation to see, the resulting verbal clash between Jackson and Martin in the Yankee dugout; a clash between a highly paid player and his manager who made less than a third his salary. The Yankees lost the game 9–7. That Jackson was black, and

Martin was white—and thought by most black players to be prejudiced—only added to the drama. Jackson was suspended without pay. Martin resigned a week later. Seven years later, Jackson acknowledged that, "I was not Billy Martin's favorite. I was the owner's favorite. And that caused a lot of problems."[72]

Drugs Take Center Stage

Personality differences between players and management were not the only problems exacerbated by high salaries. A more serious and permanent issue was the increasing drug use and addiction by some athletes. Traditionally, players had chewed tobacco and used their share of alcohol. Babe Ruth was famous for his drinking binges. Many players smoked cigarettes, and some even helped to advertise certain brands in the 1950s and early 1960s. The megasalaries players enjoyed after 1974 enabled many to indulge in more expensive addictions that, in some cases, caused irreparable physical and emotional damage.

The black American subculture was, and is, no stranger to illicit drugs. Nearly all of its communities, especially the urban ones, campaigned against drug use. Some drugs, however, like Cannibis (commonly known as "marijuana") and cocaine offered their users a temporary escape from a perceived reality that was often anxiety-ridden for a good number of blacks. Baseball players, with their high earnings, were just as vulnerable as the average wage-earner.

The use of amphetamines (or "uppers" as they are commonly called) began in the

1960s, but few recognized their use as constituting abuse. Usage did not seem to affect play nor did any managers believe that pennants were lost because of it. Not so with marijuana, alcohol, or cocaine. Beginning in the mid-1970s, local illicit-drug dealers began proselytizing players. "It [cocaine] was constantly available because of who I was,"[73] reported Dave Parker, who is black. Using cocaine was "sort of an in-thing to do." In addition, Dock Ellis, a black pitcher who began his career in 1968, said, "Every time I pitched in the big leagues, I was high. I tried to go naked [no drugs or alcohol] but couldn't do it...I didn't know how to wind up without the stuff [cocaine]."[74]

Legal authorities stepped in during 1980, when it became obvious that major league baseball could not police itself. The average salary that year was $143,756. Though blacks—American and Latin—and whites were affected, only eight black Americans were formally charged with possession, use, or abuse of controlled substances between 1980 and 1984.

Alan Wiggins of the San Diego Padres was arrested on July 21, 1982, for possession of cocaine. Wiggins completed a rehabilitation program and was suspended for thirty days; he later suffered a relapse and was suspended for a year.

Tim Raines, who led the National League for four years in stolen bases for the Montreal Expos, entered a rehabilitation center in October 1980 for cocaine abuse. The Expos' management believed cocaine addiction by some of their players caused the team to lose the pennant in 1982. Admitted Raines, "It [cocaine] certainly hurt my performance. I struck out a lot more; my vision was lessened...I'd go up

to the plate and the ball was right down the middle and I'd jump back, thinking it was at my head."[75]

Lonnie Smith said he spent $55,000 on cocaine between 1979 and 1983, while playing for Philadelphia and St. Louis. He voluntarily entered a drug treatment center on June 11, 1983, and eventually recovered.

Ken Landreaux of the Los Angeles Dodgers was treated in the winter of 1983 for cocaine addiction.

Willie Wilson and Willie Aikens of the Kansas City Royals, pleaded guilty on October 13, 1983, to federal misdemeanor drug charges following an investigation of their attempts to buy cocaine. Aikens and white teammate Jerry Martin served eighty-one days at the Fort Worth, Texas, correctional facility. Wilson recovered successfully, but Aikens' batting average dropped from .302 in 1983 to .205 in 1984, and his future is doubtful.

Vida Blue, who began his pitching career in 1969 and was the first black Cy Young Award winner in the American League, also spent time in jail on cocaine charges in 1983. He did not play at all for the Royals in 1984.

Pittsburgh Pirates pitcher Dock Ellis admitted on April 8, 1984, that he had taken LSD just before he pitched a no-hitter against the San Diego Padres on June 12, 1970.

These players were not alone in their addictions; they were merely the ones caught and legally charged. Foreign-born blacks like Ferguson Jenkins, Juan Bonilla, and Pasqual Perez, and white players like Len Barker, Ed Glynn, and Steve Howe, also suffered drug or alcohol problems during this period. Baseball's new commissioner, Pete Ueberroth, announced plans at the end of 1984 to launch a comprehensive testing program for all major league players.

Black major leaguers have proved to be generally much more susceptible to drug use than their white or Latin colleagues. In some settings, it is a sign of status to be seen as one who can afford high-priced drugs like cocaine. Experts have indeed admitted that short-term, intermittent use can heighten reflexes, dull pain, and effect moods of euphoria and well-being. Prolonged chronic use can induce addiction, loss of a sense of reality, and physical injury (such as a deviated septum in the nasal passage as a result of snorting cocaine). These addictions are a prohibitive price to pay for short-term professional sports glory, and they have created negative role model images for millions of young baseball followers.

EXCEPTIONAL ATHLETES

Despite the difficulties of adjusting to their new status as megabuck athletes, black American players rewrote the record books from 1970 through 1984. They hit, ran, fielded, threw, and fought their way to prominence, and into the hearts of many. The overall pressures they felt from their high salaries, in general, failed to dim their on-field performances.

The Hitters

Black rookies who began their careers in the late 1960s and beyond were much younger, on the average, than those who began in the Jackie Robinson or Bob Gibson eras. Major league scouts found talented players in high schools and began tracking their progress earlier. Predominantly white colleges began admitting more than a token number of black athletes in the mid-1960s, and the coaching staffs were better trained than ever. Black colleges continued to stress track over baseball as the Spring sport. Those blacks who chose to forgo or could not attend college headed for the minor leagues. As demonstrated in studies by George W. Scully, these selectees tended to be better players than their white counterparts.

Still no one—black or white—surfaced who had the all-around talents of a Willie Mays. Several black players enjoyed long careers because of their superior play at the plate, on the base paths, on the field, or on the mound. But blacks continued to be viewed by scouts, coaches, and managers as players who were simply naturally gifted as batters and fast on their feet.

Joe Morgan: Born in Bonham, Texas, he enjoyed a twenty-two-year career, and despite his diminutive 5-foot 7-inch and 150-pound build, he had no peer at second base. He enjoyed one of the highest onbase percentages in modern history, and with a lifetime batting average of .271, Morgan became the National League leader in triples in 1971 with 11, and in runs scored in 1972 with 122. Few have played with as much zest as Morgan, and his peers agree. Noted Willie Stargell, "He loved baseball as most men love a woman."[76] He is a sure bet as a future Hall of Famer.

Bob Watson: He played with the Houston Astros but seldom earned national recognition though his lifetime batting avearge is .295. Known as "The Bull," Watson stands 6-feet, 1½ inches and weighs

201 pounds. He has played outfield and first base for most of his career.

Lee May: Brother of Carlos May, also a major leaguer, he was another premier first baseman. He led the American League in RBIs in 1976 with 109. He played for eighteen years, and is now a coach for the Kansas City Royals.

Reginald Martinez "Mr. October" Jackson: Few players in professional baseball had the impact that Jackson enjoyed during his career. Born May 18, 1946, in Wyncote, Pennsylvania, this prodigious left-handed slugger attended Philadelphia's Cheltenham High School and Arizona State University on a football scholarship. He became a professional baseball player at the end of 1966 with the Kansas City Athletics and moved with the team to Oakland, California, in 1968. After playing in only 35 games in his rookie season in 1967, he was first-string thereafter, because of his bat. Leading the American League in strikeouts five times through 1984, he also led the league in home runs four times—hitting 47 in 1969.

Jackson dreamed of being a baseball megastar. He had cigar boxes of baseball cards as a youngster, imagined himself as a major leaguer, and when he finally made it, his self-assurance was frequently mistaken for arrogance. He publicly argued with his team owners. Having played his first year for $20,000, he held out for a raise to $60,000 in his second season, but settled for $40,000. He chafed under the orders that Athletics' owner Charles Finley gave manager John McNamara to bench him for not performing up to expectations. Jackson at one point saw a psychiatrist who finally helped him gain a truer measure of his problems.

In 1973 and 1974 the Athletics won the World Series with Jackson batting .310 and .286, respectively. He was finally a superstar. Traded to the Baltimore Orioles in 1976, he lasted one year there and then went to the New York Yankees. Yankees owner George Steinbrenner was not unlike Finley, and he did not mind paying top dollar for top talent. But Jackson had constant problems with manager Billy Martin.

Jackson's finest moment as a player came in the 1977 World Series in which the Yankees defeated the Los Angeles Dodgers 4 games to 2. In the sixth game, played at Yankee Stadium, he walked in his first at bat. In his second at bat, he homered off Burt Hooton on the first pitch with one man on base. In his third at bat, he homered again on the first pitch from Elias Sosa, again, with one man on base. In his fourth at bat, in the hushed eerie stillness before a home crowd, he homered still again on the first pitch—a knuckleball—from Charlie Hough.

In Jackson's own words, his feat was "...my most proud, individual, selfish, ego accomplishment. It was the greatest feeling I've ever had in baseball. I can't see it being duplicated."[77]

Jackson set or tied seven World Series records. They are: most homers in a World Series, 5; most runs scored, 10; highest slugging average in a six-game Series, 1,250; most total bases, 25 (tied with Willie Stargell); most extra-base hits in a six-game Series, 6; and most homers in consecutive at-bats, 4. With the legendary Babe Ruth he is tied in most total bases in one Series game at 12 and most homers in one game at

3. But *no one* had ever hit 3 consecutive homers in World Series competition on three consecutive pitches. On two occasions—in 1926 and in 1928, Ruth hit three home runs in one Series game, but not on first pitches three straight times.

The applause Jackson received after his third home run was deafening and lasted a full three minutes, as long as a boxing round. He was called out from the Yankee dugout three times for bows, though, few truly realized how historic his home runs had been. He had more than lived up to his nickname of "Mr. October."

Jackson signed with the California Angels in 1982 and was used primarily as a designated hitter. During his career, he has played in one divisional playoff series, ten league championship series, and on four of five winning World Series teams. Off-season, he works as a television commentator and has numerous business interests. (For a look at Jackson's record, see Reference section.)

Willie Stargell: "Pops" Stargell was, in the words of pitcher Bob Gibson, "...one of the strongest hitters I know."[78] At 6-feet, 2-inches, and 190 pounds, the left-handed Stargell was a terror at the plate. He was discovered in 1958 by Bob Zuck, the Pittsburgh Pirates' scout who also discovered Reggie Jackson, George Foster, and George Hendrick. The Pirates signed Stargell for $1,500 and none too soon, as his childhood was spent with an aunt in the Webster housing projects in Alameda, California, after his parents divorced. (Another Webster Project alumnus was Tommy Harper, a black major leaguer, who played with the Cincinnati Reds.) Life for Stargell in the minor leagues was a trying time. He was barred from the team hotel in Roswell, New Mexico. In Plainview, Texas, a white man once snuck up behind him and said, "Nigger, if you play in that game tonight, I'll blow your brains out."[79] He survived. Stargell joined the Pirates in 1962, and in his first at bat, hit a triple.

Stargell is one of the few players, black or white, who spent his entire career with one team, playing the outfield for twelve of his twenty-one seasons. His best years were 1971, 1973, and 1979. In 1971, he led the National League in home runs with 48 and batted .295. Two years later, he led the league in doubles with 43, in home runs with 44, in home run percentage with 8.4, in RBIs with 119, and with a slugging average of .646.

Like Reggie Jackson's performance in the 1977 World Series, Stargell had his own one-man show in the 1979 World Series. At one point in the Series, the Pirates had trailed 3 games to 1. In aiding the Pirates to an eventual 4 games to 3 victory over the Baltimore Orioles, Stargell had 12 hits, including 4 doubles. He scored 7 runs, drove in 7 others, and batted .400. His third home run, with one man on base in the sixth inning of the seventh game, put the Pirates ahead to stay. It was a stellar performance from one of the game's premier players. Stargell also orchestrated a now famous song, "We Are Family," made popular by the group Sister Sledge, that was the rallying cry for the Pirates in the Series. He is now a coach with the Atlanta Braves.

The Pirates had consistently used a high number of black players, and on September 1, 1971, they fielded an all-black team in a game against Philadephia. Dave

Parker, who then played for the Pirates, was quoted eight years later in *Ebony* magazine as saying, "You aren't going to see more than six blacks on the field at a time."[80] Dock Ellis, the former Pirates Pitcher who by 1979 had been traded five times, was also quoted in the same article as saying, "Maybe what we need is a black baseball player's association."[81] In baseball, the Pittsburgh Pirates had more black players than any other team.

Hal McRae: Born in Avon Park, Florida, McRae started as an outfielder, but spent more than half of his sixteen-year career as a designated hitter with the Kansas City Royals. He led the American League in doubles in 1977 with 54. However, his best year was 1982, when he led the league in doubles with 46 and in RBIs with 133. His slugging average in 1982 was an astounding .542. McRae played in three World Series— 1970, 1972, and 1980—with an aggregate batting average of .409.

Amos Otis: This 5-foot 11½-inch, 165-pound outfielder from Mobile, Alabama, has played seventeen years for only three teams—the New York Mets, Kansas City Royals, and the Pittsburgh Pirates. He twice led the American League in doubles—36 in 1970 and 40 in 1976—and also led the league in stolen bases in 1971 with 52. He batted .478 in the 1980 World Series while with Kansas City.

John Mayberry: A powerful 6-foot 3-inch, 215-pound first baseman from Detroit, Michigan, Mayberry played for fifteen years for four teams—Houston, Kansas City, Toronto, and the New York Yankees. He led the American League in walks in 1973 with

122 and in 1975 with 119; and a 6.1 home run percentage in 1975. He retired in 1982.

Ken Singleton: He came from New York City and enjoyed an outstanding fifteen-year career. A switch-hitter, this 6-foot 4-inch, 210-pound outfielder never led in any batting categories but remained among the leaders each year. His lifetime batting average is .282, and he averaged 71 RBIs per season during his career.

Reggie Smith: He spent seventeen years in the majors and twice led the American League in doubles—37 in 1968 and 33 in 1971—while with the Boston Red Sox. This switch-hitting outfielder also played in four World Series—1967, 1977, 1978, and 1979— and has the sixth-best all-time Series record for home run percentage—8.2. As a Los Angeles Dodger in the 1977 World Series, he hit three home runs and scored seven times, though the Dodgers lost to the New York Yankees. He retired in 1982.

Albert Oliver: "Mr. Scoop," as Oliver is called, is one of the game's best hitters with a seventeen-year batting average of .305. Playing outfield and first base, he has had eleven seasons with an average of .300 or better. Though he played for Pittsburgh and the Texas Rangers, he enjoyed his finest year in 1982 with the Montreal Expos, leading the National League in hits with 204, in doubles with 43, and in RBIs with 109.

George Foster: This 6-foot 1½-inch, 180-pound outfielder was born in Tuscaloosa, Alabama, and had spent sixteen years in the majors, as of 1984. The quiet, deeply religious Foster led the National League twice in home runs, with 52 in 1977 and 40 in 1978; in home run percentage in those same years, 8.5 in 1977 and 6.6 in 1978; in runs scored, 124 in 1977; three times in RBIs, 121 in 1976, 149 in 1977, and 120 in 1978; and in slugging average, .631, in 1977. His trade from the San Francisco Giants in 1971 to the Cincinnati Reds for an outfielder and a minor league pitcher was one of the biggest baseball faux pas of the decade. He has played in four League Championship Series and three World Series. In the Reds' four-game sweep of the New York Yankees, during the 1976 World Series, Foster batted .429, had 4 RBIs, and scored 3 runs.

Jimmy Wynn: He is from Cincinnati, Ohio, and is nicknamed "The Toy Cannon." He was not big for a major leaguer, 5-feet 10-inches, and 162 pounds, but he played fifteen years, principally because his on-base percentage was so high. He led the National League twice in walks, with 148 in 1969, and 127 in 1976. Unfortunately, he also led in strikeouts in 1967 with 137. Wynn played for Houston, the Los Angeles Dodgers, and the Atlanta Braves.

Don Baylor: At 6-foot 1-inch and 190 pounds, Baylor has carried a big bat for fifteen years, leading the American League in 1979 in runs scored with 120, and in RBIs with 139. The right-handed outfielder and designated hitter has played for the Baltimore Orioles, the Oakland Athletics, the California Angels, the New York Yankees, and the Boston Red Sox. He has participated in four League Championship Series.

George Scott: The "Boomer," as Scott was called, is from Greenville, Mississippi. He had a fourteen-year career, from 1966 to 1979, playing first base for Boston and Milwaukee. His best year was 1975, when he led the American League in home runs with 36 and in RBIs with 109. He recorded a slugging average of .500 in 1977. He retired in 1980.

Cecil Cooper: He is from Washington County, Texas, and is one of the few current players with a lifetime batting average over .300—.305 for fourteen years with the Boston Red Sox and the Milwaukee Brewers. He led the American League in doubles in 1979 with 44 and in 1981 with 35. Cooper twice led the league in RBIs— 122 in 1980 and 126 in 1983. He also played in two World Series.

Dave Parker: This giant of an outfielder—6-feet 5-inches, 230 pounds—has played for twelve years, eleven of them with the Pirates. In his third year in the majors, 1975, he led the National League in slugging average at .541. In 1977 he led the league in hits with 215, and doubles with 44, and in batting average with .338. A year later, he led in batting average at .334 and slugging average with .585. His lifetime batting average is .303, and he played in the 1979 World Series.

Dave Winfield: Winfield is one of the few black players from the frost belt, hailing from St. Paul, Minnesota, and he has played for a dozen years. He has been spectacular at the plate, his lowest season batting average being .265. Acknowledged as one of the best all-around athletes in the game, he was drafted by five professional teams in three sports. Though he led the National League in 1974 in errors by an outfielder, he recovered to win Golden Gloves titles in 1979 and 1980. After eight years with the San Diego Padres, he signed the then-largest baseball contract in history—with the New York Yankees for $13 million for ten years. He is also head of the Dave Winfield Foundation, a nonprofit organization that aids children in athletics and academics.

George Hendrick: He has been one of the most underrated and unheralded players during his fourteen-year career. Only twice has his slugging average dipped below .431. This 6-foot 3-inch, 195-pound outfielder was born in Los Angeles, California, and played for Oakland, Cleveland, San Diego, and St. Louis. He played in the 1972 and 1982 World Series.

Jim Rice: Some say Rice is the strongest hitter in baseball. A 6-foot 2-inch, 200-pound outfielder, he has played his entire career with the Boston Red Sox. Rice has led at least one league category for five seasons: In home runs with 39, and in slugging average with .593 in 1977; in at bats with 677, in hits with 213, in triples with 15, in home runs with 46, in RBIs with 139, and slugging average, an astounding .600, in 1978. In 1983, he led in home runs with 39 and in RBIs with 126. Rice's lifetime batting average is .303.

Andre Thornton: Thornton had plenty of childhood encouragement, since he was born in Tuskegee, Alabama, home of the famed black school, Tuskegee University (formerly Tuskegee Institute). He has played for eleven years, three and a half with the Chicago Cubs, half a year with the Montreal Expos, and seven and a half with the Cleveland Indians. This right-hander plays first base and is a designated hitter.

Eddie Murray: He was born in Los Angeles, California, and has been nothing short of exceptional during his eight-year career, all of it with the Baltimore Orioles. (His brother, Rich, also played for two years in the majors.) In 1981, Murray led the American League in home runs with 22 and in RBIs, with 78. He hit two home runs in the Orioles' four-games-to-one World Series victory over the Philadelphia Phillies in 1983.

The foregoing players had their own separate styles of batting, each of which produced outstanding results. The thrown baseball takes between 0.4 and 0.45 of a second to go from the pitcher's hand to home plate. The average swing of a batter takes about 0.28 of a second, leaving from 0.12 to 0.17 of a second for a hitter to decide whether he will make an attempt. Thus the ability to hit consistently takes uncanny coordination, natural ability, and nerve.

Some batters like Ernie Banks and Hank Aaron used their wrists to control their swing. Others like Reggie Jackson swung more from the shoulders. Moderate practice alone seems to keep natural hitters from altering an innate talent. Says Dave Winfield, "If I had to take an hour or two of batting practice every day, I'd be too tired to play baseball."[82]

Some batters stand away from the plate and some crowd the plate. Duke Snider said of Jackie Robinson, "...Jackie never got off the plate. I mean, Jackie would take one between the eyes before he'd get off the plate."[83]

Some batters hit for singles and doubles and some hit for home runs. In general, the smaller the player the more he is positioned near the top of the batting order, because his primary purpose is to get on base—by any means. Black players have long realized that the power hitters usually played in the outfield, at first base, and as catchers. But the high salaries went to the home run hitters. Reggie Jackson called his bat the "dues collector," and he leads the major league in striking out.

In just thirty-eight years, black players have rewritten hitting records in the major leagues, and they predominate in the long-ball categories—10 of the top 50 all-time slugging-average leaders; 11 of the top 50 in home runs; 10 of the top 35 in home run percentage; 11 of the top 48 in extra-base hits; and 10 of the all-time leaders in total bases. It seems ironic that blacks were kept out of organized ball for fifty-six years, when one considers the changes they have brought about in only thirty-eight years. With young players like Willie McGee, Willie Wilson, and Darryl Strawberry coming into their own, the future of black hitters looks unquestionably bright.

The Runners

In compiling the contributions that black players have made to baseball, none is more important than speed. For reasons that sociologists and coaches are still debating, blacks have also rewritten the record books for stolen bases. This is only the beginning of an issue. Managers have had to change their offensive and defensive strategies because of the availability of tremendously quick base runners.

Before 1946, when Jackie Robinson broke the color line, Ty Cobb held the single-season record for stolen bases—96 in 1915. If the assumption is true that major leaguers in Cobb's era were not as scientifically selected as they are today, then naturally gifted base runners had an advantage. Most experts thought confidently that Cobb's record would be safe forever. After all, pitchers and catchers are better trained and better athletes now than in the past. But we now know that, to be successful, most major league teams need players who can comfortably steal fifty to eighty bases per season. The overwhelming majority of these base stealers are black.

During the 1950s, the highest season stolen-base total was Luis Aparicio's 56 in 1959. Maury Wills broke Cobb's record in 1962 with 104 thefts, which seemed unbeatable even then. His nearest competitor that year was Los Angeles Dodger teammate Willie Davis with 32. The averages have continued to increase, and the fifth-place stolen-base leader recorded steals in the high 20s and low 30s by 1970.

By the early 1970s, managers had to change the job description for the first two batters in a lineup from a high batting average alone to a high batting average plus the ability to steal 30 bases. Not only did these speedsters help to win games, they were also exciting to watch. Television cameras focused on the duel between a runner at first base and the opposing pitcher and catcher. The success rate of premier base stealers began appearing in sports pages as regularly as those for batting averages and home runs.

Black players have had a near monopoly in this specialized art since the mid-1960s and have taken uncommon pride in pulling off spectacular steals. Each of the stolen base record breakers since Maury Wills has been black.

Eight years after Lou Brock broke Maury Wills' record with 118 steals, Rickey Henderson broke Brock's record with 130 steals in 1982. On his retirement after the 1979 season, Brock was the only man to hold the single season and career record in a major statistical category—118 steals in 1974 and 938 career steals. Stolen bases alone, however, do not tell the entire story about a player's true contribution. A table in the Reference section provides a more complete detail of the record holders and the years in which each set or broke a record.

Ty Cobb's batting average of .369 in 1915 was the highest of the four players. Though Wills came to bat more than the other three, he had fewer walks, 51, than Brock with 61, Henderson with 116, and Cobb with 118. In their respective record-breaking seasons, Brock scored 105 runs, Henderson scored 119 runs, Wills scored 130 runs, and Cobb scored 144 runs. Baseball fans argue interminably about who was the most productive or effective.

The all-time single-season leader in stolen bases in organized baseball, however, is none of the above players. He is Vince Coleman, an only child from Jacksonville, Florida, who in 1983 stole 145 bases while playing at Macon (Georgia) in the South Atlantic League. He now plays for the St. Louis Cardinals and is a switch-hitter like Maury Wills. He will certainly be a dominant factor in future Cardinal games.

Though none are holders of the single season record for stolen bases, there are black players who have excelled on the base paths. See the Reference section for a list of blacks who have averaged 30 or more stolen bases or more than 400 career stolen bases, since 1970.

In all likelihood, black players will continue to dominate this important category. These base stealers are heroes to thousands of young aspiring players—black and white. They earn large salaries and provide drama to a sport in which strategy is highly predictable. Baseball has changed materially since its standards of base stealing has risen. Black players can be justly proud of their achievements as the game's kings of the base paths.

The Pitchers

To date, Bob Gibson is one of only two black pitchers to be inducted into the Hall of Fame. By 1970, only Don Newcombe (1956) and Gibson (1968 and 1970) had won the Cy Young Award, given to the best pitcher in each league. Gerald W. Scully's research showed statistical evidence of racial discrimination against black pitchers and catchers through 1970, in spite of the exploits of Newcombe and Gibson.

The presence of black pitchers throughout the major leagues is so scant that, in the lists of all-time single-season leaders, there are only seven entries—all from four players—out of a total of 295. Of 1,052 pitchers listed in the lifetime pitching leaders categories, only 27 are black. Even today, it seems that major league baseball wants blacks to hit, run, and field, but not to pitch, or catch behind the plate. Some, however, have overcome substantial odds against their success and their records are worth noting. Since 1970, the following black pitchers have attained success in two of four statistical categories: 10 or more seasons in the major leagues; a total career winning percentage of .500 or better; a career ERA of 3.99 or lower; and 40 or more complete games.

Vida Blue: He is the only black Cy Young Award winner in American League history. He was born in Mansfield, Louisiana, one of six children. His father worked in the local mill. Blue was a high school athletic sensation, starring in football and baseball at DeSoto High. A Kansas City Athletics scout, Jack Sanford, discovered Blue when he struck out 21 batters in a game against Central High in Natchitoches, Louisiana. Blue was signed in 1967 for a $25,000 bonus, and he spent two years in the minors.

Blue pitched a no-hitter on September 21, 1970, during his first full season with the A's (who had moved to Oakland, California). In 1971, he was phenomenal, pitching eight shut-outs, with an ERA of 1.82, the best in the league. The following year, he had a highly publicized salary dispute with A's owner, Charles Finley. President Richard Nixon even took interest in this issue, and at one time declared, "He [Blue] has so much talent, maybe Finley ought to pay..."[84]

In 1971, Blue and Dock Ellis became the first two black pitchers to oppose one another in an All-Star game. Each pitched three innings, and the American League won 6–4. Five years later, Blue was involved in a landmark court ruling in which Commissioner Bowie Kuhn was upheld when he voided Finley's trade of Blue, Joe Rudi, and Rollie Fingers for $3.5 million to the New York Yankees. Kuhn said the prospective trade was bad for baseball.

On October 16, 1983, Blue pleaded guilty to charges connected with the possession and sale of cocaine. He spent time at a rehabilitation center in California and was restored to good standing in the majors at the end of 1984. He played for fifteen years with Oakland, San Francisco, and Kansas City. (For a look at Vida Blue's record, see Reference section.)

Rudy May: He is from Coffeyville, Kansas, and his career spanned sixteen years with four teams: The California Angels, New York Yankees, Baltimore Orioles, and the Montreal Expos. He had four years of sub-3.00 ERA performance, and pitched in three World Series games in 1981 for the Yankees.

Jim Grant: His nickname is "Mudcat," and he is from Lacoochee, Florida. He was largely unheralded in the 1960s until Charles Finley signed him in 1970 to the Oakland Athletics. His career lasted fourteen years, from 1958 to 1971, and he played for Cleveland, Minnesota, Los Angeles, Montreal, St. Louis, Oakland, and Pittsburgh. In the 1965 World Series, he won two games and lost one for Minnesota, who went on to lose the Series 4 games to 3.

Ray Burris: He played for twelve years and is from Idabel, Oklahoma. He has been on the rosters of the Chicago Cubs, the New York Yankees, the New York Mets, the Montreal Expos, and the Oakland A's. He pitched, and helped to win, one game for Montreal in the 1981 National League Championship Series.

John Odom: His nickname is "Blue Moon," and he played for thirteen years.

This right-hander played on three winning World Series teams at Oakland, in 1972, 1973, and 1974. His best year was 1968, when he won 16, lost 10, and posted an ERA of 2.45. He is one of only five black pitchers to toss a no-hit game, a 2 to 1 win over the Chicago White Sox, while playing for Oakland. He is from Macon, Georgia.

Jim Bibby: This 6-feet 5-inch, 235-pound right-hander, was born in Franklinton, North Carolina, and has played for twelve years. In 1980, he led the National League in winning percentage with .760. In his dozen years he has played for St. Louis, the Texas Rangers, the Cleveland Indians, and the Pittsburgh Pirates. In 1979, Bibby pitched ten and a third innings in two World Series games for a victorious Pittsburgh.

Dock Ellis: A 6-feet 3-inch, 205-pound switch-hitter from Los Angeles, California, Ellis has been one of the premier pitchers in major league history. His career lasted twelve years, during which he participated in five League Championship Series and two World Series. Ellis, who is right-handed, had only three years in which his winning percentage dipped below .500. On June 12, 1970, he pitched a no-hitter against the San Diego Padres, winning 2-0. (He later admitted he was under the influence of LSD at the time.) He pitched for Pittsburgh, the New York Yankees, the Oakland A's, the Texas Rangers, and the New York Mets.

Lynn McGlothen: He pitched for eleven years before his untimely death in 1984 at age thirty-four. He began with Boston in 1972 and also played for St. Louis, San Francisco, the Chicago Cubs, and the Chicago White Sox. His best year was 1974,

when he was 16–12. McGlothen was born in Monroe, Louisiana.

James R. Richard: This giant right-hander, who stood 6-feet 8-inches and weighed 222 pounds, had a strange ten years in the majors—all at Houston. He had a blazing fastball, but had trouble with control. He led the National League in strikeouts in 1978 with 303, and in 1979 with 313. He also led the League in walks on three occasions—138 in 1975, 151 in 1976, and 141 in 1978.

In 1980, Richard suffered a stroke that ended his career. He later successfully sued three of the four doctors who treated him, charging negligence. His case received nationwide publicity because just before his illness, many reporters and coaches thought Richard was not trying his best, an accusation some took to be racially motivated. Richard, who is from Vienna, Louisiana, tried a comeback but was unsuccessful.

Don Wilson: He, like Lynn McGlothen, is from Monroe, Louisiana, and he was James R. Richard's teammate at Houston from 1970 to 1974. This right-hander would have had even more good years had he not died prematurely in January 1975. His best year was 1971 with his record 16–10, and an ERA of 2.45.

Mike Norris: He was born in San Francisco, and spent his nine years in the majors with the Oakland Athletics. After five mediocre years, he won twenty-two games in 1980. The right-handed Norris had problems with drugs in 1983 and 1984, and in the latter year, he was arrested for possession of cocaine and marijuana. Though the charges were dropped for insufficient evidence, he did not play in 1984. It is hoped that rehabilitation will prepare him for future play.

Dwight Gooden: Gooden, 6-feet 2-inches and 190 pounds, is from Tampa, Florida. No pitcher—black or white—has been as impressive in his rookie year as has Gooden. He was 17–9 in 1984, his first year, with a 2.60 ERA, and a league-leading strikeout total of 276, for the New York Mets. Gooden's fastball, timed at 97 miles per hour, helped him record 300 strikeouts in 191 innings in his lone minor league season at Lynchburg, Virginia. Gooden broke Herb Score's rookie strikeout record of 245 with 276. He leaped into first place in the all-time single-season record books with an astounding 11.39 strikeouts-per-nine-innings performance in 1984. In 1984, he became the youngest player ever to appear in an All-Star game. In September 1984, Gooden set a National League record by striking out 32 batters in two consecutive games—16 each against Pittsburgh and Philadelphia. His strikeout/walk ratio was 3.78:1. He was deservedly named the National League's Rookie of the Year. Gooden is a product of the Belmont Heights Little League program in Tampa, which was started partially as a result of racial turmoil in his home city.

SUMMATION

The progress made by black players since Jackie Robinson first put on a Brooklyn Dodgers uniform has been outstanding. Were they alive today, players such as Bud Fowler, Moses Fleetwood Walker, Andrew "Rube" Foster, John Henry Lloyd, Josh Gibson, and Leroy "Satchel" Paige would hardly believe the good fortune of their modern counterparts. They would indeed be impressed by the achievements of a Dwight Gooden, a Dave Winfield, a Rickey Henderson, and an Ozzie Smith.

They would, however, be disappointed by the problems with drugs and the apparent stacking of black players in the outfield and at first base. Perhaps, as some expert observers have commented, the problems could easily have been worse. After all, the vast majority of black players have come from average black communities where anyone would have difficulty adjusting long-term to fame and riches beyond their fondest hopes.

All in all, baseball has been the fortunate recipient of the extraordinary efforts of blacks who excel at the game. In a short period of time, blacks have transformed a tradition-bound, patterned style of play into a more kinetic and energized festival of spectacular home runs, unsurpassed base running, and breath-taking catches in the outfield.

The Future? Black players seem certain to continue their superior play in any of their historically assigned positions. With more black infielders, there will be more coaches, and eventually more managers. This in turn will lead to a substantial presence in the front office of major league clubs. Only then can it be truly said that black Americans have achieved some semblance of amalgamation into the nation's pastime.

Notes

1. Don Rogosin, *Invisible Men: Life in Baseball's Negro Leagues,* (New York: Anthenum Press, 1983), 199.
2. Jackie Robinson, *I Never Had It Made,* (Greenwich, CT.: Fawcett Publications, 1972), 55.
3. Ibid., 58.
4. Bill L. Weaver, "The Black Press and the Assault on Professional baseball's 'Color Line,' October, 1945—April, 1947," *Phylon* (Winter 1979): 305.
5. *Sports Illustrated,* 20 April 1983.
6. *Amsterdam News,* 3 November 1945.
7. *Crisis,* magazine, (December 1945).
8. *Pittsburgh Courier,* 3 November 1945.
9. *Philadelphia Tribune,* 27 April 1946.
10. *Pittsburgh Courier,* 20 April 1946.
11. *Baltimore Afro-American,* 4 May 1946.
12. *Pittsburgh Courier,* 12 April 1947.
13. *Boston Chronicle,* 19 April 1947.
14. *Chicago Defender,* 26 April 1947.
15. *Ebony,* September 1951.
16. Ibid., 25.
17. Roy Campanella, *It's Good To Be Alive,* (Boston: Little Brown & Company, 1959), 285.
18. Ibid., 65.
19. *Negro History Bulletin* (February 1955): 71.
20. Russell Schneider, Jr., *Frank Robinson: The Making Of A Manager,* (New York: Coward, McCann and Geoghegan, 1976), 169.
21. Willie Mays and Charles Einstein, *Willie Mays: My Life In And Out Of Baseball,* (New York: E.P. Dutton & Company, 1966), 79.
22. *Ebony,* August 1955, 36.
23. Henry Aaron, *Aaron,* (New York: Thomas Y. and Crowell, 1974), 91.
24. Mays and Einstein, *Willie Mays: My Life In And Out Of Baseball,* 142.
25. Ibid., 26.
26. Ibid., 191.
27. *Sports Illustrated,* 25 March 1985, 84.
28. Art Rust, Jr., *"Get That Nigger Off The Field!",* (New York: Delacorte Press, 1976), 47.
29. Anthony Pascal and Leonard Rapping, *Racial Discrimination In Organized Baseball,* (Santa Monica: Rand Corporation, 1976), 28.
30. *Negro History Bulletin* (November 1960): 30.
31. Aaron, *Aaron,* 7.
32. *Negro History Bulletin* (November 1960): 30.
33. Gerald W. Scully, *Government And The Sports Business, Discrimination: The Case Of Baseball,* (Washington, D.C.: The Brookings Institution, 1974), 239.
34. Aaron, *Aaron,* 190.
35. Ibid., 98.
36. *Ebony,* August 1967, 130.
37. *Ebony,* September 1973, 149.
38. Rust, *"Get That Nigger Off The Field!",* 170.
39. Aaron, *Aaron,* 212.
40. Schneider, *Frank Robinson: The Making Of A Manager,* 14.
41. Ibid., 13.
42. Ibid., 51.
43. Ibid., 77.
44. *Ebony,* May 1975, 108.
45. Campanella, *It's Good To Be Alive,* 197.
46. Aaron, *Aaron,* 27.
47. Mays and Einstein, *Willie Mays: My Life In And Out Of Baseball,* 26.

48. Pascal and Rapping, *Racial Discrimination In Organized Baseball,* 47.
49. *Ebony,* July 1970, 93.
50. *Ebony,* May 1963, 40.
51. *Ebony,* October 1950.
52. Maury Wills and Steve Gardener, *It Pays To Steal,* (Englewood Cliffs, N.J.: Prentice-Hall, Inc., 1963), 67.
53. *International Herald Tribune,* 30 July 1985, 15.
54. Ibid., 15.
55. *Civil Rights Digest* (August 1972): 25.
56. Bob Gibson, *From Ghetto To Glory: The Story of Bob Gibson,* (Englewood Cliffs, N.J.: Prentice-Hall, Inc., 1968), 87.
57. Ibid., 30.
58. Scully, *Government And The Sports Business, Discrimination: The Case Of Baseball,* 257.
59. *Ebony,* July 1970, 94.
60. Doug Smith, Monograph, 1985, 5.
61. *Ebony,* March 1981, 56.
62. Gibson, *From Ghetto To Glory: The Story Of Bob Gibson,* 127.
63. Scully, *The Government And The Sports Business, Discrimination: The Case Of Baseball,* 268.
64. *Ebony,* June 1966, 65.
65. Scully, *The Government And The Sports Business, Discrimination: The Case Of Baseball,* 247.
66. Ibid., 257, 261.
67. The Baseball Encyclopedia, 6th ed., 21.
68. Mays and Einstein, *Willie Mays: My Life In And Out Of Baseball,* 267.
69. Maury Allen, *Mr. October: The Reggie Jackson Story,* (New York: New American).
70. Ibid., 174.
71. *Sports Illustrated,* 17 July 1978, 38.
72. *Inside Sports,* November 1985, 68.
73. *USA Today,* 12 September 1985, 1A.
74. *City Sun,* 2-8 October 1985, Al.
75. *New York Times,* 20 August 1985, Al.
76. Willie Stargell and Tom Bird, *Willie Stargell: An Autobiography,* (New York: Harper & Row, 1984), 75.
77. *Inside Sports,* November 1985, 69.
78. Gibson, *From Ghetto To Glory: The Story of Bob Gibson,* 159.
79. Stargell and Bird, *Willie Stargell: An Autobiography,* 65.
80. *Ebony,* October 1979, 90.
81. Ibid., 106.
82. *Forbes,* 26 September 1983, 180.
83. *Inside Sports,* November 1985, 74.
84. Vida Blue and Don Kowet, *Vida Blue: Coming Up Again,* (New York: G.P. Putnam's Sons, 1974), 123.

Basketball

After the Second World War, black basketball players were not as fortunate as their baseball brethren. In 1946, Jackie Robinson was playing for the Montreal Royals in the International League and followed that with an historic berth in the Brooklyn Dodgers' lineup in 1947. Nineteen forty-six for William "Pop" Gates and William "Dolly" King was quite different; both were playing in a white professional basketball league, but lasted only one season. Gates believes it was due to a racial incident involving Chick Meehan.

Gates was playing a game for the Tri-Cities Blackhawks against Meehan and the Syracuse Nationals; both teams were in the Basketball Association of America (BAA). As Gates relates the story: Meehan "...threw me down one time, and I said 'Chick, don't do that no more!' Well, he threw me down again, so I deliberately placed myself in the pivot. When he tried again, I threw *him* down and he got up whaling. So I got mine [punch] in first before he got his in. I made him bleed. That's the reason Dolly and I only played one season." [1]

Life in the BAA was difficult that season for Gates and King. They encountered the same housing problems the Negro League baseball players had, and solved them in the same manner: they coped. Most of the time they looked for a "Colored" YMCA, and sometimes they managed to stay with their white teammates. Gates mentions the Claypool Hotel in Indianapolis, Indiana, the Seneca Hotel in Rochester, New York, and a few others as being accommodating to black ballplayers.

This treatment of Gates and King should be, but is not surprising in comparison to the famous Harlem Globetrotters, whose housing was pre-arranged by Abe Saperstein, and who had a very successful season between 1947–48. That season included a 52-game winning streak, a victory in the Cuba Invitational, a victory over the Minneapolis Lakers and their star center George Mikan, and two movies, entitled The *Globetrotters Story* and *Go Man Go.* In the win over the Lakers at Chicago Stadium on February 20, 1948, Ermer Robinson drilled a 20-foot set shot after a pass from Marques Haynes at the buzzer.

The following year, the Globetrotters began the transformation from a serious team to one that entertained with fancy passes, trick shooting, and hilarious routines. They toured with an all-star squad of collegians and by 1951, the change was nearly complete, when they made their first round-the-world tour, playing 108 games in their twenty-fifth season. They still hold the attendance record of 75,000 in the Berlin Olympic Stadium and 50,041 in Rio de Janeiro, Brazil. As of the end of 1984, over 100 million people have watched the Globetrotters in action. They remain the world's best-known sports team.

In the late 1940s, the Globetrotters' success did not rub off on most other black teams. Except for the New York Renaissance squad, other all-black professional teams, like the Chicago Collegians, and the Chicago Studebakers struggled. Without a league, Collegians teammates Al Johnson, Ages Bray, Victor Kraft, Hank Blackburn, Anthony Payton, Bill Kelly, and Bob Farrell had nowhere else to go. The two competing white leagues had their own problems, and they finally decided that a merger was part of the answer but signing black players was another matter.

The *New York Age* announced the breakthrough in its October 9, 1948, edition: "Color Line Is Broken In Basketball Assn. of America: Six Join Chicago Stags." [2] Those six black pioneers were Henry Blackburn, Leon Wright, Irving Ward, George Raby, Arthur Wilson, and Leonard Jordan. Though none of them played in the National Basketball Association (NBA), they nevertheless widened the door opened by William "Pop" Gates and William "Dolly" King. The professional game has not been the same since then.

A GROWING BLACK TRADITION

The tradition inherited by black basketball players after World War II was perhaps the most fruitful of the major team sports. Unlike baseball and football, basketball tradition had included an all-black team generally recognized as the best in the world. This squad, the New York Renaissance, was unsurpassed in consistency and teamwork and, at its height in the late 1930s, thrilled many audiences. The Harlem Globetrotters also enjoyed a national reputation. However, both the Renaissance and Globetrotters teams owed a debt to the pioneer work of Dr. Edwin B. Henderson and Cumberland Posey. Henderson was instrumental in the early 1900s in developing the sport among blacks along the Washington, D.C.–New York City corridor from his base as Director of Physical Education for the Colored schools of the nation's capital and its local Colored YMCA.

After World War II, interest in the sport increased considerably. In particular, the northern urban areas became magnets for the best public school, college, and club players, most of whom played indoors in gyms and armories. More high schools fielded teams that improved the selection pools of college coaches, yet the sport that is today so identified with black America, developed most of its best talent on the public courts, which began to organize its play.

One of the prime innovators in the organization of public parks basketball competition was Holcombe Rucker, who began his summer leagues in 1946. From this New York City tournament came dozens of future professional players. Similar programs, like the Baker League of Philadelphia, sprang up in other urban areas from Baltimore to Los Angeles. These leagues have grown in sophistication to include academic counseling along with on-court play.

Uniqueness for Blacks: Basketball was an ideal athletic pursuit for the masses of black Americans in the immediate post--World War II period. Equipment requirements were minimal—just a basketball, some "gym shoes," and a court. Public courts were usually within walking distance of any black residential area in the northern cities. Most public courts used by blacks in the segregated South were found in school yards and Colored YMCAs and YWCAs.

Little coaching was needed to master basketball's basic offensive moves, and the small size of teams enabled most pickup squads to literally teach themselves. The sport was also less tradition-bound than baseball or football, so rule changes could be made more quickly to enhance its spectator appeal. Additionally, girls were encouraged to play since, in basketball's ideal form, there was supposedly little violent body contact. YWCAs, churches, clubs, and black newspaper-sponsored squads played in women's leagues.

The foregoing factors enabled black American communities to utilize their own resources to produce superior players. In the process, the players themselves built on the legacy of outstanding past performances from former Globetrotters and Renaissance players like Hilton Slocum, Eyre Saitch, William "Pop" Gates, "Fats" Jenkins, and William "Dolly" King. A distinctive "black" style of play developed that featured speed, uncommon jumping ability, and innovative passing skills. Though this style was frequently at odds with white coaches' philosophies of the late 1940s, it produced results and was extremely exciting to watch. Thus, it was only a matter of time

before the professional leagues admitted black players.

The Basketball Association of America Admits Blacks: In 1946, owners of some of the nation's largest northern indoor arenas sensed the increased popularity of basketball and formed the Basketball Association of America (BAA). Their main objective was to fill their empty arena dates with professional basketball games, though college and AAU basketball had a larger following. After much discussion and with an eye on the progress of Jackie Robinson in professional baseball, these proprietors decided to admit black players. In spite of the clash in 1946 involving "Pop" Gates and Chick Meehan, black participation was inevitable, due in large measure to Don Barksdale's play as the first black player on an Olympic team in 1948.

Within thirty years, black players, both men and women, would dominate what is now referred to as "the city game" at all levels of play.

THE AMATEURS

The Olympians: Since the YMCA gave birth to basketball and the organization was international in scope, it spread the hoop gospel quickly around the world. Inevitably basketball became an Olympic event. In the 1904 Games basketball was a demonstration sport, but at the 1936 Berlin Olympics its official debut was made on a dirt court turned muddy by rain. Twelve years later, at the 1948 London Olympics, Don Barksdale, an All-American from UCLA, earned a gold medal as part of the United States team. Barksdale, who was 6-

feet 5-inches, had played in the American Amateur Basketball League and had been named by California sportswriters to the all-time Pacific Coast Conference Team. Blacks would star, and in some cases dominate all succeeding Olympic competitions.

Though there was a strong black contingent of track athletes on the American Olympic squad in 1952, there were no basketball players. The United States defeated the previously undefeated Soviet Union squad 86–58. At the 1956 Games in Melbourne, Australia, Bill Russell and K.C. Jones starred, as the American team continued undefeated. To ensure that Russell, who was the most popular choice ever for All-American, would be present, President Dwight D. Eisenhower personally appealed to the University of San Francisco star: "We need you for our next Olympic team," Eisenhower told Russell. "I certainly hope we'll have you."[3] Russell replied, "I promise...I'll be on that Olympic team if I can make it." At the time, Russell characterized his participation on the Olympic team as his proudest moment. Later in his career, Russell would become very critical of his own country's racial policies.

The 1960 Olympic team featured the inimitable Oscar Robertson and Jerry West, a white player from West Virginia. The team averaged over a hundred points per game under coach Pete Newell (who figured prominently in future incidents involving black players).

The 1964 squad included five black players, all of whom continued to be selected from midwestern and western colleges. Walt Hazzard, of John Wooden's UCLA NCAA-winning team became the playmaker.

The 1968 competition was the first to feature important no-shows. At the proposed boycott of the Mexico City Games by black track and field athletes, some basketball players were supportive. Among those who were unavailable were: Bob Lanier, Elvin Hayes, Wes Unseld, Mike Warren, Lucius Allen, and Lew Alcindor (now Kareem Abdul-Jabbar). Coach Hank Iba called these missing black players "bad citizens."[4]

However, Spencer Haywood of the University of Detroit and Jo Jo White of the University of Kansas were not only eager to participate in the Olympics but were unafraid to speak about it. Said Haywood at the time, "I wake up in the morning thinking Olympics, I dream Olympics, I wrote to my mother about the Olympics."[5] Bill Russell had counselled Haywood about his views. White was also adamant in his feelings, saying "I make up my own mind and I've decided to play. I don't care if I'm the only one [black player]. They can go ahead and boycott. I'm playing."[6] Publicly at least, coach Iba made matters a little worse by saying "I don't think the Negroes playing for us will be bothered by the boycott."[7]

When the Olympics were over, Haywood's elation was undiminished. "When we won the final and took the victory stand and they draped those gold medals around our necks and played the national anthem, it sent shivers down my spine."[8] Nevertheless, the five black players on this 1968 team were criticized in some quarters of the black community.

In 1972, the American basketball squad lost its first game after sixty-three consecutive wins. The loss was to the Soviets on a controversial decision by the referee to set the clock back three seconds at the expiration of play. The Soviets were able to inbound the ball and get it downcourt for a quick layup before the three extra seconds had elapsed. The Americans refused to accept the 51–50 loss and did not show up to receive their silver medals.

The 1976 squad featured the second and third black twosomes from the same schools—Walter Davis and Phil Ford from the University of North Carolina at Chapel Hill, and Scott May and Quinn Buckner from Indiana University. There were still no representatives from predominantly white colleges in the deep South or from black colleges.

The 1980 overall Olympic black contingent was the largest ever, but they did not get a chance to play because of President Jimmy Carter's decision to boycott the Moscow Games.

In 1984 at Los Angeles, the University of North Carolina at Chapel Hill produced its fifth and sixth black Olympians in Michael Jordan and Sam Perkins. For the first time ever, one of the players, Patrick Ewing, was selected from a team with a black coach—John Thompson of the Georgetown Hoyas. Thompson had been an Olympic team assistant coach in 1976. George Raveling was appointed as an assistant coach for the 1984 squad.

The record of black achievement in Olympic competition is an enviable one. Were Edwin B. Henderson, Cumberland Posey, and Robert Douglas alive today, they would be justly proud of these accomplishments.

The Female Olympians: The United States fielded strong teams during the inaugural women's competition in 1976 and at the 1984 Games. The list of black female Olympians appears in the Reference section.

In the mid-1970s, women's basketball was just beginning to emerge as a possible professional sport. At the 1976 Games, the Soviet Union won the gold medal and the United States defeated Bulgaria 95–79 for the silver medal. The eight-year interim between the 1976 and 1984 Games was a period of unparalleled growth for women's basketball in America, and the squad at Los Angeles was the most highly touted assemblage ever seen on one team.

Though the 1984 team was well balanced, the stars were Cheryl Miller, Lynette Woodward, and Pam McGee; Miller was hailed as the best women's player in the history of the sport. Born and raised in Riverside, California, she came from a middle-class family that featured two other outstanding athletes. (Her brother, Reggie, played for UCLA, and another brother, Darrell, played professional baseball for the California Angels.)

Miller, who is 6-feet 3-inches, once scored 105 points in one game while at Polytechnic High in Riverside. She was also a member of two NCAA championship teams at the University of Southern California. Said former All-American Nancy Lieberman of Miller: "...Cheryl has revolutionized the game...she learned to do that the same way I did—we had to play like the guys...I think Cheryl is the best thing that could have happened to the game."[9]

McGee is one-half of a basketball playing set of twins. Her sister, Paula, did not make the cut for the Olympic team, yet she was present throughout to lend moral support. In a touching and heartwarming moment following her gold-medal performance against the Koreans, Pam presented her gold medal to Paula, who was already in tears over the medal ceremony. The scene was one of the most touching memories of the 1984 Olympic Games.

Lynette Woodward later made history herself in accepting an offer to become the first female member of the Harlem Globetrotters She had been the all-time leading scorer at the University of Kansas (topping even the totals set by Wilt Chamberlain). She was also the NCAA's top career scorer, for women's basketball, with 3,649 points—an average of 26.3 points per game.

The Black Colleges

The black colleges were primary beneficiaries of a continuing interest in basketball immediately following World War II. Athletically gifted black GIs returned home and headed for college, where tuition was paid for with G.I. Bill benefits. As was the case at predominantly white colleges, the sport became a coach-dominated game. Unlike his white counterpart, the black coach was most probably a teacher, as well.

The dominant powers in the early 1950s included North Carolina College (now known as North Carolina Central University) coached by Johnny B. McLendon; Virginia Union, coached by Tom Harris; Winston-Salem, coached by Clarence "Big House" Gaines; Morris Brown, coached by H.B. Thompson; and Florida A & M, coached by Ed Oglesby. The major schools were compressed into three conferences—the Central Intercollegiate Athletic Association (CIAA), the Southern Intercollegiate Athletic Conference (SIAC), and the Southwestern Athletic Conference (SWAC). A fourth conference, the Mid-east Athletic Conference (MEAC), would be added in the 1970s.

None of these schools had large gymnasiums, and their small budgets limited recruiting efforts to high school players within a day's drive. These efforts were augmented by word-of-mouth recruiting and the judicious use of former alumni. Though all but five black schools were located in southern or border states, it was not unusual for a southern team to have a starting five from Detroit, Chicago, or New York City. The mass migration of blacks from the South to northern factories during World War II had helped spread the word about black colleges.

The coaches who were able to consistently field conference winning teams were in many cases better known than some of their star players. None was better known than Johnny B. McLendon.

Johnny B. McLendon: He received his early training from the master himself—James Naismith, the Canadian YMCA instructor who invented the sport and later taught at the University of Kansas that McLendon attended. McLendon first earned fame at Tennessee State after joining the staff in 1954. Tennessee State president Walter Davis was an avid sports fan, and he truly believed that a winning team could only help to spread the word about his school.

Tennessee State became the first black college team invited to play in the National Association of Intercollegiate Athletics (NAIA) tourney in 1954. In March 1957, they won their first NAIA title at Kansas City. They defeated Southeast Oklahoma State 92–73 before eight-thousand fans, and became the first black college to win a national basketball title. The starting five on this historic team were Ron Hamilton, captain; John Barnhill; Henry Carlton; Jim Satterwhite; and Dick "Skull" Barnett. On the Eastern Airlines flight back to Nashville, a bomb threat was reported, but an investigation turned nothing up.

McLendon was hailed as the finest coach in black intercollegiate athletics. No black school before 1957 had ever won a national title against a white school in any sport. Tennessee State repeated as NAIA champions in 1958 and 1959. The 1958 victory was gained over Western Illinois 85–73, and Dick Barnett was named Most Valuable Player. The 1959 win came over Pacific Lutheran 97–87 and contributed to Barnett being a three-time NAIA All-American, who finished his collegiate career with 3,209 points.

In 1961, McLendon shocked Tennessee State's administrators by resigning to become the first black professional basketball coach of the Cleveland Pipers of the new American Basketball League (ABL). The prime force behind the ABL was Abe Saperstein, the owner of the Harlem Globetrotters. In January 1962, McLendon submitted his resignation to Pipers president George Steinbrenner. Steinbrenner had withheld salary checks to players because he was supposedly irritated over their play. McLendon stood up for his players, saying, "I cannot stand by and see a good group of young athletes intimidated."[10] Later, when Ralph Wilson bought the Pipers from Steinbrenner, McLendon was brought back.

Years later, Steinbrenner was again involved in a feud with another black, Reggie Jackson, when Steinbrenner became the principal owner of the New York Yankees baseball team in the 1970s.

Clarence "Big House" Gaines: He made his mark at Winston-Salem State University in Winston-Salem, North Carolina. In 1967, he became the first black college coach to win an NCAA title—in NCAA Division II. He finished his career with eight CIAA Conference victories, more than any other coach. Just as Johnny B. McLendon was closely associated with Dick Barnett, Gaines was instrumental in the development of Earl Monroe, who achieved fame during his National Basketball Association (NBA) career.

Dave Whitney: He enjoyed tremendous success as the coach at Mississippi's Alcorn State Univeristy. He won eight SWAC titles between 1969 and 1984, the period when predominantly white southern colleges began recruiting black athletes.

The mid-1970s was a particularly difficult transition period for black colleges. Bobby Vaughn, the CIAA's president, noted in 1976 that: "The competition for the good players is much greater. We're so far behind in finances, just like everything else."[11]

"Big House" Gaines, remarking on the paradoxical situation of black colleges, said,"The only thing that keeps us on an even keel is so many kids are playing basketball that the supply is greater than the demand...I'm not playing the University of Indiana with all those seven footers."[12] First Gaines and then Whitney realized that they could no longer rely on recruiting exclusively the best black talent.

Through the 1984-85 season, Whitney's teams earned 416 victories in twenty-one years. Later, he was appointed as a member of the Olympic Trials coaching staff, and guided Alcorn State to four NCAA Playoff Tournaments, and two National Invitation Tournament (NIT) berths.

Conference Champions: Though most black NBA players played at white schools, the black colleges maintained their interest in basketball and a fourth major conference, the MEAC, was formed in the early 1970s in response to increased demand. The list appears in the Reference section.

National Champions: A surprising number of black schools have won NAIA, NCAA II, and NCAA III national titles. The list appears in the Reference section.

Black Women Score Victories: Black females had traditionally concentrated on track and field as their major athletic outlet. When men's basketball became a revenue-producing sport, few black college athletic directors were willing to give "equal time" to women's games which were events usually open to the public free of charge. Title IX of the Education Amendments Act of 1972 changed that, and all universities receiving federal funds had to provide varsity sports for women who wanted them. Cheryl Miller, the University of Southern California star, told *Sports Illustrated*: "Without Title IX I wouldn't be here." [13]

Two black schools have won national women's titles: South Carolina State, coached by Willie Simon, won the Association for Intercollegiate Women's Athletics II (AIAW II) title in 1979; and Virginia Union, coached by Louis Hearn, won the NCAA II

title in 1983. In NAIA Final Four competition, Texas Southern finished second in 1981 and Dillard finished third in 1984. In NCAA II Final Four competition, Tuskegee finished second in 1982 and Virginia Union finished second in 1984.

Vivian Stringer: The best-known of female coaches, she began at Cheney State in Pennsylvania in 1971. Her eleven-year record there was 251–51. Her 1981–82 squad reached the final of the first NCAA Women's Championships, losing to Louisiana Tech, 76–62. She left Cheney State for the University of Iowa in the spring of 1983, and on February 3, 1985, she coached Iowa against Ohio State in front of the largest crowd ever to see a women's basketball game—22,157.

By the late 1970s, women's basketball was a serious endeavor among its participants and bore little resemblance to the genteel game played right after World War II. As Lusia Harris of Delta State soberly noted, "You have to get rough with the sport. You have to be tough." [14]

The White-College Experience

Some white-college conferences including the Ivy League and schools in the Mid-west, the Middle Atlantic, and on the Pacific coast continued allowing blacks on their basketball teams, but southern and southwestern schools, and the Big Ten Conference, did not. This situation existed when the college game was more popular than the professional version. Ed "Ned" Irish had begun his college basketball doubleheaders at Madison Square Garden in 1936, and they were extremely popular.

However, by 1950, the idea began to take hold that "if blacks were good enough to fight in World War II, they were good enough to play anywhere in America." Unfortunately, some black basketballers were named in some of the most damaging scandals to beset the college game.

Blacks eventually dominated all college basketball, but they have suffered through periods of blatant exploitation and are frequent victims of illegal schemes involving gambling, point shaving, receiving unaccounted sums of money, recruiting violations, and broken promises. Contributing factors include the low socioeconomic class of the players, their relative lack of sophistication, their lack of knowledge of the rules, their naiveté, and temptation.

The first recorded incident occurred in 1951. Arthur Daley, the *New York Times'* esteemed sports columnist, described the atmosphere. "...the gambling craze has swept the country," he wrote, "with the avariciousness of a prairie fire...the satanic gimmick is the point spread."[15] Bettors on athletic contests used to wager using "odds," but by this time, they began using the "point spreads" that are common today.

Manhattan College (New York City) players Hank Poppe and Jack Byrnes, both white, confessed to District Attorney Frank Hogan that they "shaved" points in five games in return for money. Junius Kellog, a black player from Portsmouth, Virginia, reported his bribe offer to Manhattan coach Kenny Norton. His actions were lauded in the biggest sports scandal since the "fixed" World Series games of 1919. The *Pittsburgh Courier*'s Wendell Smith said, "Junie Kellog rates a special salute from the entire sporting world."[16]

Further investigation showed that between 1947 and 1950, eighty-six games in New York City and twenty-two other cities were fixed by thirty-two players at seven schools. Even the University of Kentucky, referred to in the black community as the "Blue Grass Bigots," lost their National Invitation Tournament title of 1949 due to point shaving.

In 1961, there was another fixing scandal involving a total of forty-seven players. This time Connie Hawkins, an eighteen-year-old black freshman at Iowa, was falsely implicated. Hawkins was a much-lauded player from Brooklyn's Bedford-Stuyvesant neighborhood and Kareem Abdul-Jabbar (formerly Lew Alcindor) once said of him: "I've seen the best in the NBA, but I've never seen anybody better than Hawkins."[17]

Hawkins was wrongfully accused by Dave Budin, a former Brooklyn College player and public-school teacher, of acting as an intermediary in fixing games. Budin's partner in the illegal scheme was Jack Molinas, who masterminded the fixed games and was prosecuted by District Attorney Frank Hogan. Though he was never charged or prosecuted, Hawkins was blackballed by the NBA and sued the organization for $6 million. This 6-foot 8-inch star finally began to play professionally in the American Basketball League with the Pittsburgh Pipers in 1967. Hawkins and the NBA finally settled out of court for $1 million. His lawyers had been so sure of Hawkins's innocence that they spent $35,000 of their own money to defend him.

Pressure intensified on black athletes as they helped to win games and to fill arenas. In response to the increasing competitiveness of the college game, the rules were amended in 1972 to make freshman student-athletes eligible for varsity competition. This meant that eighteen-year-old black players, most of whom came from low socioeconomic backgrounds, without proper social or legal counseling, would be even more vulnerable on and off the court. In 1975, Moses Malone of Petersburg, Virginia, became the first player—white or black—to go directly from high school to the professional basketball ranks.

By 1976, roughly 1,250 colleges had varsity teams, and recruiting was the key to a winning program. Naive black families were now promised unheard of, and illegal amounts of money, and favors in return for their sons' (and later their daughters') promise to attend certain schools. Hundreds of promises were broken when the players' eligibility was used up. Less than ten percent graduated (most would not have been admitted to college in the first place without the benefit of "special exemption" rules). But the presence of two competing leagues, the NBA and the ABA, increased the number of available jobs.

In some cases, illusions began in high school. Billy Harris, a black high school star in Chicago in 1969, tells of his treatment before his demise. "An athlete is not part of the [high school] student population...Hey man, I got paid. In high school, I got free lunches, clothes. I went to the prom in a limo. I had money."[18] Harris eventually went to Northern Illinois, was drafted by the Chicago Bulls in the seventh round, and was eventually cut.

Current NBA star Isiah Thomas' brother Gregory at one time accused Indiana's coach Bobby Knight of wanting to exploit his brother during a recruiting interview. The exploitation of blacks by whites is a common belief held by the black community at large. The fiery Bobby Knight, who prided himself on his professional integrity, lashed back and plainly told Gregory, "You're an asshole and you're a failure, and the worst thing about you is that you want Isiah to fail the way you did...I'm getting out of here. I'm sorry we lost you."[19] In the end, Thomas did go to Indiana, and is now one of the NBA's premier performers. The altercation between Knight and Gregory Thomas displayed the overall tension of the recruiting process in the mid-1970s.

There were also many incidents of college coaches and assistant coaches having altered the academic records of high school and junior-college athletes to make them eligible. One coach who was caught was Manny Goldstein, an assistant at the University of New Mexico, who admitted doctoring the records of Craig Gilbert, an Oxnard Junior College transfer student. Goldstein later resigned, and the head coach, Norm Ellenberger, was fired. Arizona State University also admitted doing a similar thing. Many black athletes spent a year or two at a junior college before transferring to a major NCAA Division I school because their grades or SAT/ACT test scores were low.

Some black student-athletes were passed right through the college system as though they were in public schools, lacking even the ability to read or write. The most widely noted example is Kevin Ross, who attended Creighton University by way of Wyandotte High School in Kansas City, Kansas. Ross shocked the sports world by enrolling in Westside Prep in Chicago *after* his senior year at Creighton. "I went to school for sixteen years, and then four years at college. When I got out, I couldn't even read a menu or a street sign,"[20] Ross said. Billy Ray Bates, who played for the Portland Trailblazers, said he had a similar problem. John "Hot Rod" Williams, the Tulane University player who was charged in 1984 with accepting illegal payments while in school, and who was later tried and found innocent, said of his college-entrance SAT exam: "I couldn't even read the English part."[21]

Illegal Payments: As the Billy Harris case shows, money and other favors are used freely to corrupt and coerce white and black athletes. The more important the athlete, the bigger the payoff. Wilt Chamberlain, for instance, wrote in his controversial book, *Wilt*, that in the mid-1950s "I guess I got about $15,000 or $20,000 while I was there [University of Kansas]...I never kept any records."[22] The NCAA later put Kansas on probation, but this was after Chamberlain's departure, and before his disclosure.

Basketball players were more likely to receive these payments, since one good player could easily make a difference. Booster clubs, that were loosely associated with the school, but nevertheless zealous in their support supplied cars, money, girls, and jobs to some players. If a player did not perform up to expectations, these fringe benefits sometimes disappeared. Black players were expected to be grateful and not make waves—like demanding that white fraternities admit them or dating white coeds.

A highly publicized scandal in 1984 involved the academically troubled John "Hot Rod" Williams. Williams, of Sorrento,

Louisiana, came from a broken home—he never knew his mother and saw his father once a year—but he was the Metro Conference's Player of the Year in 1984. In 1985, he and David Dominique, also black, were tried for sports bribery (point shaving) in New Orleans. Both were freed when after trials in both state and federal courts, the prosecutors failed to prove their cases.

At Memphis State, some players were allegedly getting as much as $1,500 per month in illegal payments. Keith Lee, their star black player, was supposedly promised money for his mother by coach Dana Kirk, according to *Sports Illustrated* sources. A check of the records showed that only 4 of 38 Memphis State players graduated between 1973 and 1984, none of them black. To make matters worse, a Tennessee government audit showed that, between 1980 and 1984, 109 Memphis State basketball and football players received federal grants that were legally reserved for needy, academically eligible students. Blacks, therefore, lost out in two ways: they were illegally used to field winning teams and never graduated; plus their fees were paid for from funds earmarked for scholastically eligible, but destitute students—many of whom were also black.

The Spencer Haywood Case: One of the most controversial cases in all of college sports involved a poor black youngster from Silver City, Mississippi. Spencer Haywood, a 6-foot 9-inch, 215-pounder who moved to Chicago and eventually attended the University of Detroit, was the hero of the 1968 Olympic basketball team, who did not want to wait to turn professional. In 1969, the NBA had a rule against signing college players before they had used up four years of eligibility; the ABA, however, was not so strict.

At age nineteen, Haywood signed three separate contracts with the ABA's Denver Rockets without benefit of legal counsel. The first, in August 1969, called for $450,000 for three years, and was also signed by his friend and adviser, Will Robinson, who is also black. Two months later, Haywood signed another contract with the Rockets for $500,000 for three years plus $3,000 per year for ten years to be invested. Finally, in April 1970, he signed a third contract with the Rockets for $1.9 million for six years, and the rival NBA showed interest.

Haywood realized that he would be more valuable in the NBA, and with the assistance of a lawyer, Al Ross, tried to invalidate his Rockets agreement, even though he had been designated ABA MVP and Rookie of the Year. Sam Schulman, owner of the NBA's Seattle Supersonics, asked permission to sign Haywood. By a vote of fifteen to two, Schulman's request was denied by the NBA. Schulman signed Haywood anyway to a $1.5 million contract for six years, plus payments of $100,000 per year for fifteen years. The Rockets then petitioned for and received a temporary injunction against Schulman.

On March 30, 1971, in Los Angeles, Judge Warren Ferguson in a summary judgment ruled the four-year college stay illegal and that Haywood could play for Seattle pending a final resolution. College administrators and most white sportswriters were brutal in their denunciation of Haywood. College officials feared for their programs, and Roger Stanton, a Detroit reporter, may have spoken for many when he said, "He [Haywood] is ungrateful, misguided, uneducated and irresponsible...In his greed for wealth, he has stopped at nothing."[23] But Haywood was a better athlete than student at the time.

Now the NBA and ABA tried to limit the pregraduation signings to "hardship" cases, but that was eventually scuttled. Henceforth, college players could turn professional any time they chose.

Considerations and Temptations: Not all college coaches were devious and deceitful. Some were just indifferent. NBA Hall of Fame inductee Elgin Baylor recalled that in the early 1950s, "White colleges did not explore black high schools...[they] didn't know anything about us. I went to the College of Idaho for the first year on a football scholarship."[24]

At the NCAA Western Regionals in Dallas in 1957, a cross was burned on a vacant lot across from where Wilt Chamberlain and his Kansas teammates stayed. Oscar Robertson, another NBA Hall of Fame inductee, was the lone black on the University of Cincinnati squad, and he had to stay at a black college, Texas Southern University, when his team played in Houston in 1959. Life for a black on a white college campus was (and still is) a lonely existence since there were (and still are) only a few other blacks. Nearly a decade later when blacks were protesting, they were accused of not being thankful for their "coveted" positions.

Texas Western University (now University of Texas at El Paso) won the 1966 NCAA title with an all-black starting five. They beat Kentucky 72–65 in the finals. The school had only 250 black students among a population of 10,000, and it was supported, in part, by black tax dollars. Yet, school athletic officials referred to blacks as "niggers" and expressed amazement when black students sought improved conditions.

Texas Western's Assistant Athletic Director, Jim Bowden, was quoted as saying, angrily, "This was the first institution in Texas—right here!—that had a colored athlete and George McCarty, our athletic director, was the coach who recruited him...McCarty's done more for 'em than this damn guy Harry Edwards that's coming in here to speak. George McCarty's done more for the nigger than Harry Edwards'll ever do if he lives to be 100."[25]

The black social revolution of the mid-1960s *forced* black athletes on white campuses to be more assertive. When University of California coach Rene Herrerias dismissed Bob Presley for not cutting his Afro hairstyle, a faculty committee discussed the matter and Herrerias was replaced. John Wooden, UCLA's coach of ten NCAA titles, was tolerant of the new black assertiveness, though, he did tell a reporter that "I feel it's outside influences trying to use the Negro athletes."[26]

In 1968, Notre Dame fielded its first all-black starting five with Austin Carr, Sid Catlett, Colis Jones, Bob Whitmore, and Dwight Murphy. When they were greeted with boos from their own fans, they demanded an apology before they would play again. However, it is important to remember that in 1956, Notre Dame had joined with the University of Dayton and St. Louis University in withdrawing from the Sugar Bowl tournament in New Orleans, because a Louisiana law forbade interracial sports.

For some whites, racial progress had been too fast, especially in the period from 1966 to 1970. The on-court results were obvious. According to a report on 246 integrated college teams in 1970, approximately two-thirds of all blacks were starters, "regardless of region, size, and type of school."[27] Furthermore, between 1958 and 1970, blacks were only 29 percent of the total of players, but accounted for nearly half the points scored.

General Gripes: During the late 1960s there were enough black athletes on white-college campuses to press for reforms. Along with the football and track athletes, black basketball players complained about off-campus housing, low academic expectations from coaches, sarcastic and racial slurs from coaches, a belief that coaches assumed blacks could play in more pain than whites, a lack of black cheerleaders, the scarcity of black faculty and advisers, and a quota system that favored whites at the expense of more talented blacks. Stu Inman, who later became an assistant coach with the Portland Trailblazers, was told in 1960 at the University of Idaho, "Stu, out here we only play three of them [blacks] at a time."[28] Inman left the school.

To be sure, black athletes must shoulder *some* of the blame for their predicament. The overwhelming majority of black basketball players had visions of a professional career when they entered college. Most were academically unprepared and would never have been admitted under ordinary circumstances. By the mid-1970s, there had been enough stories in the press about black exploitation to warn even the most cynical among them. During the recruiting period of Moses Malone, one quote from Lefty Driesell, the University of Maryland's coach, was obviously in part jest, but much publicized. Driesell said of Malone, "I don't care if you never go to class. Hell, don't go to class. They'll kick you out after seven months, but in the meantime we'll have had a pretty good basketball team."[29]

Proposition 48: "By 1980, the NBA had only a 20 percent graduation rate among its players, black and white. The average salary was $185,000. There were roughly 15,000 players in NCAA-affiliated schools and another 700,000 on high school squads."[30] Blacks, however, had the lowest high school test grades and SAT/ACT scores. Those who went to college seldom graduated. At the University of Georgia, for example, only 4 percent of blacks graduated between 1974 and 1984, as opposed to 63 percent of whites. The American Council on Education, made up of college presidents, felt they had to do something about this exploitation of black athletes.

What emerged, in 1983, was NCAA Proposition 48, that sought to impose mandatory academic minimums for all scholarship athletes. To be eligible for college varsity competition, a player had to have a C average in high school courses that normally led to graduation, plus either a combined score of 700 on the SAT exam, or 15 on the ACT exam. Once in college, the student-athlete had to maintain a "C" or 2.0 grade average to remain athletically eligible.

While white-college officials and coaches realized that the proposal was probably a good idea, reaction among black-college administrators was surprisingly mixed. Some, like Southern University's Jesse Stoner, thought it was a plan to rid collegiate athletics of superior black athletes. Reverend Jesse Jackson, one of the most prominent black leaders, thought the plan was motivated by some who felt black athletes were just "too good." Others, led by Hampton University president William Harvey and black sociologist Harry Edwards, thought the proposal was long overdue. Scheduled for implementation in August 1986, the proposal was amended, and is now in use.

An Outstanding Record: Despite the problems, no one could say the black athlete did not measure up on the court. From the 1954–55 season when Bill Russell and K.C. Jones led the University of San Francisco to the NCAA Championship, to the 1983–84 championship season at Georgetown, blacks have continued to play a major part in college basketball. Along the way, some coaches have proven their respect for black athletes: Dean Smith at North Carolina; Bobby Knight at Indiana; John Wooden at UCLA; Al Maguire, formerly of Marquette, and Denny Crum at Louisville; among others. And John Thompson, the black head coach of the Georgetown "Hoyas," deserves special mention.

The son of a hardworking tile factory worker and a domestic, Thompson attended John Carroll High School in Washington, D.C., and later Providence College. After two years with the Boston Celtics, Thompson earned his master's degree in guidance counseling at the University of the District of Columbia. His coaching career began at St. Anthony's High in Washington, D.C., and he went to Georgetown in 1972.

Thompson has been known as an overprotective coach, to his critics, he replied "I think I probably am overprotective, but I don't think that's bad...I'm nervous about the responsibility of 15 people who belong to somebody else."[31]

He guided his 1982–83 team to the NCAA finals, but lost when Freddy Brown made a bad pass in the last thirty seconds of the game against North Carolina. In one of the most dramatic moments in college television sports history, Thompson shocked millions of viewers by putting his arm around Brown in a consoling gesture. Most people expected outrage from him. Thompson, however, was nonplussed about his totally unexpected act. People, he said "...made me a saint because I put my arm around Freddy Brown...Shucks, man. What was I suppose to do? Chop off his head?"

On April 3, 1984, Thompson's squad, led by Patrick Ewing, won the NCAA title over Houston, 84–75. Ewing led a team that held its opponents to a 39.5 field-goal percentage—an NCAA record. Like Michael Jordan one year before him, Ewing was the 1984–85 college Player of the Year.

There is every indication that black players will continue to excel in college basketball. Lists of the African-American male John Wooden awardees and the African-American All-Americas since 1950 appear in the Reference section.

Black Female Collegians: Black colleges were generally unable to afford the expense, or find the space to field top-ranked women's teams. Most aspiring players through the mid-1960s were found on AAU-affiliated club teams. The women's liberation movement and the passage of Title IX of the Education Amendments Act of 1972 forced most major colleges to form women's squads. First, the Association of Intercollegiate Athletics for Women (AIAW) led the way for most varsity sports, but it was superseded by the NCAA in the mid-1970s.

Notable among the black women stars were Lusia Harris of Delta State, Lynette Woodard of Kansas, Pam and Paula McGee of the University of Southern California, and Cheryl Miller, also of the University of Southern California. Through the 1960s, most women's teams played with six on a team and a regulation-sized basketball. Now the teams use five players and a slightly smaller ball. The exciting play at the 1984 Olympic Games and at schools such as Iowa, Texas, Louisiana Tech, Old Dominion, Delta State, and St. Joseph's shows that women's basketball can indeed by very inspiring.

THE PROFESSIONALS

After World War II, professional basketball took a distinct backseat to the college game. There had been a rich black professional history, with the New York Renaissance and the Harlem Globetrotters to draw upon. By the late 1940s, the Renaissance's best days were behind them, and Abe Saperstein did not want his Globetrotters to join the new professional leagues. The Globbies, as the Globetrotters were sometimes called, had a near monopoly on the best black talent, and Saperstein wanted to keep it that way.

In 1948, for instance, the Globbies played the powerful all-white Minneapolis Lakers, led by the great George Mikan, and split a pair of games at Chicago Stadium. They won the first game 61–59 before 18,000 fans, but lost the second 75–60. There was no doubt in the mind of any professional team owner that blacks were among the best players around. When the Basketball Association of America was formed in 1946, it agreed to sign black players, so it became only a matter of time before blacks were signed by the National Basketball Association.

The thirty-four-year period between the admittance of the first three black players in the NBA in 1950 through to 1984 can be divided into three eras: 1950 to 1959–60, Breaking In; 1960 to 1973, Wilt Chamberlain and Bill Russell reigns; and 1974 to 1985, the Kareem Abdul-Jabbar Era.

1950 to 1960: Breaking In

The Basketball Association of America team owners were primarily interested in filling empty arenas. Doing so with blacks, initially presented two problems: 1. many BAA owners booked Globetrotter games— that outdrew BAA games—in their arenas; and 2. Saperstein wanted to continue his monopoly of the best black talent. Saperstein, however, could not hold the tide forever.

The first three blacks signed to play in the NBA for the 1950–51 season were: Chuck Cooper, of Duquesne University, who signed with the Boston Celtics; Earl Lloyd, of West Virginia State, who went to

the Washington Capitols, and Nathaniel "Sweetwater" Clifton, of Xavier University, who went to the New York Knickerbockers. The first black player to be drafted by the NBA was Harold Hunter of North Carolina College. Hunter was signed by the Baltimore Bullets, traded to the Capitols, and then cut.

In that first historic season, Cooper played in 66 games and had 562 rebounds, 174 assists, and 615 points for a 9.3 average. Clifton played in 65 games and had 491 rebounds, 162 assists, and 562 points for a 8.6 average. Lloyd played in only seven games because the team disbanded on January 9, 1951. As auspicious a start as these three players had, Globetrotter owner Saperstein was not pleased.

As Wilt Chamberlain noted in his book, "Abe [Saperstein] wasn't very happy when the NBA first started to integrate. Walter Brown, one of the founders of the NBA, was the owner of the Boston Celtics, and he was going to sign Chuck Cooper as the first black man in the league. Abe went crazy. He threatened to boycott Boston Garden."[32]

Since the Globetrotters were no longer assured of the best black players, and the team was not going to join the NBA, they decided to change their format to one that entertained spectators with comical routines and fancy ball handling, rather than playing serious basketball. They even made a movie, *The Globetrotters Story*, that debuted in 1951, and was the introduction for the black actress Dorothy Dandridge.

The Globbies continued as one of the most famous sports teams on earth, traveling the globe and performing before popes and kings. Stars like Marques Haynes,

centage, and fourth in rebounds. Not until the 1956–57 season did a black player, Maurice Stokes, lead the league in a category. That year, Stokes averaged 17.4 rebounds per game, almost three more per game than Bob Petitt.

Stokes began with the Rochester Royals in the 1955–56 season and finished the year second in rebounding. Unfortunately, on March 15, 1958, Stokes suffered a paralyzing stroke that ended his career. Stokes's white teammate, Dick Ricketts, remembered the stroke, which occurred on an airplane. Said Stokes to Ricketts, "Dick, every bone in my body pains me. I feel like I'm going to die."[40] After a period of recovery, a benefit game was organized by Jack Twyman, another of Stokes's white teammates.

Twyman treated his care of Stokes like a privilege, "I had to take care of Mo'. The rest of the team was leaving town. I was a hometown guy. It was my responsibility...taking care of Mo' has made me a better man."[41]

Hal Greer: The first of the speedy black guards in the NBA was Hal Greer of Marshall University. Players like Bob Cousy were excellent ballhandlers and passers, but they did not have Greer's blazing speed and ability to literally break open defenses. Guy Rodgers and Greer both began their NBA careers in the 1958–59 season, just one year after the St. Louis Hawks became the last all-white team to win the NBA championship.

Within two years, Rodgers was second in the assists category and Greer was second in field-goal percentage, a spectacular feat for a guard who had to shoot primarily from long range. Wilt Chamberlain was forthright in his appraisal of Rodgers: "Guy Rodgers...was the best ball handler I ever saw—better than Cousy or Jerry West or Oscar Robertson or Walt Frazier or Pete Maravich or anyone."[42] Both Rodgers and Greer were prototypes of the new and faster NBA guard whose jobs were to direct a team's offense, execute steals, and play a solid defensive game.

Greer played fifteen years in the NBA, for the Syracuse Nationals and the Philadelphia 76'ers. He led his teams in average points scored three times and is one of the few players to perform in three separate decades.

Sam Jones: Jones is the second black Celtics player to be inducted into the Hall of Fame. He played at North Carolina College (now North Carolina Central University)—where he was also a member of the tennis team—in Durham. Jones later found his niche with the Celtics. His career spanned thirteen seasons, during which time he was on ten championship teams. He is best remembered for his banked shots off the backboard, and for his willingness to take the last shot in the closing minutes of a tight game.

He was never flashy, but publicly contented himself with being a part of the Celtics dynasty, and one-half of "the Jones boys"—with K.C. Jones. Celtic Coach Red Auerbach stated that Jones was one of the most selfless players in the game and that he understood the value of each player being assigned a special role (a lesson Jones no doubt learned at NCCU). Jones later coached at NCCU and at Federal City College in Washington, D.C.

An Era Closes: It is surprising to many that ten years elapsed before the last all-white NBA team, the St. Louis Hawks, signed a black player in 1959. The Hawks were also the last all-white squad to win the NBA title, in 1958. There were only eight teams in the league in 1959 and, like the Washington Redskins in football, the Hawks were the southern-most team, geographically, and in manner of operation. The Hawks were the South's team.

Still, basketball in this decade became an obsession for thousands of black youngsters who had dreams of a professional career. The fact that two of the first three black players in the NBA in 1950 were from black colleges was highly significant. That was not the case in either baseball or football. Even the percentages seemed favorable. From three players on eleven teams in 1950, the black presence grew to twenty-three players on eight teams ten years later.

The rule changes, especially the twenty-four-second clock adopted in 1954 were advantageous to traditional black playground styles of play. That same year, three blacks, Earl Lloyd, George King, and Jim Tucker, were the first to play for an NBA Championship team, the Syracuse Nationals. Blacks realized they were pioneers and that they were being judged by higher standards than those for whites. Like their baseball counterparts, black players endured instances of overt discrimination but, in the main, they felt privileged to be professional players earning salaries high above those of most wage-earning blacks and whites.

Finally, the period also marked the debut of the two most dominant players in the history of the game—Bill Russell and Wilt Chamberlain. Their personal battles and those of their respective teams provide the boundaries for the next era in the professional game.

1960 to 1973: Russell and Chamberlain Reign

Superstars in every sport need other superstars by which to measure their performances. When Bill Russell came into the league in 1956 he led the Celtics to their first NBA title. During that same year, Wilt Chamberlain began his collegiate career at the University of Kansas scoring 52 points and grabbing 31 rebounds in his first varsity game. However, the Kansas squad lost to North Carolina in the NCAA finals, 54–53. Chamberlain left Kansas after one more season and played for the Globetrotters during the 1958–59 season.

Chamberlain later signed with the Philadelphia Warriors, chiefly because Warriors owner Eddie Gottlieb had territorial rights to him. In his first NBA game on October 24, 1959, against the New York Knickerbockers, Chamberlain scored 43 points and grabbed twenty-eight rebounds. Fourteen days later, he faced Russell for the first time and saw his first fall-away jumper blocked by his new adversary. Their rivalry had begun, and Russell had the upper hand.

Wilt Chamberlain: The NBA had decidedly better players when Chamberlain made his debut, than when Chuck Cooper began with the Celtics in 1950. Cooper's salary was under $10,000, whereas the top salary in 1959 was $25,000. Players were

Reece "Goose" Tatum, Meadowlark Lemon, and Curly Neal thrilled thousands. Haynes had graduated from Langston University and was a dribbler nonpareil. In 1953, he formed a rival group, the Harlem Magicians, and also played with Lemon's Bucketeers and with the Harlem Wizards. Lemon was a superb showman, but according to Haynes, Tatum's public image belied his dislike for whites.

While Haynes readily acknowledges that "no one will ever match him [Tatum]" for having been one of the sports world's most famous personages, Tatum's funeral was a nonevent. Haynes and his wife drove to Fort Bliss, Texas, for the services, but they were ten minutes late arriving at the cemetery. Seeing no one around, Haynes asked the grave diggers what they missed. Sadly, they were told that nothing happened. "They [the funeral directors] drove up, backed the hearse up to the grave, lowered the casket and took off."[33] Haynes bought a Bible for $2.98 and read the Lord's Prayer and the twenty-third Psalm for his friend Goose Tatum.

Slow Pace: The first black players in the NBA were forwards. The first black "big man" was Ray Felix, 6-feet 10-inches, who went to the Baltimore Bullets in 1953. Felix found the pace of the game slower than necessary in the early 1950s. Coaches wanted disciplined ball handling and passing. Spectators wanted to stop the slowdowns caused when a team with a substantial lead began to stall. In the 1954–55 season, the NBA adopted a twenty-four-second rule that required teams to attempt a shot within twenty-four seconds of inbounding the ball, and limited teams

to 6 fouls per period. These rules speeded up play, and the change came none too soon for William Fenton "Bill" Russell, who would combine with Bob Cousy and K.C. Jones to form the most winning professional team since World War II.

Bill Russell: Russell changed the classic theories about the way the game should be played. At the University of San Francisco he led his team to two NCAA titles, over LaSalle, 77–63 in 1955 and over Iowa, 83–71 in 1956. He suffered only one loss in his college career, a 47–40 decision to UCLA in 1954. At the end of 1955, the NCAA doubled the width of the foul lane from six to twelve feet—"the Russell rule"—because Russell had been so dominating a rebounder.

No one had ever played defense so well before. More specifically, as Celtic coach Arnold "Red" Auerbach said, "Nobody had ever blocked shots in the pros before Russell came along. He upset everybody."[34] Players were afraid to drive toward the basket, and the Celtics won their first NBA title; the first of eleven NBA titles with Russell. The 6-foot 10-inch Russell, who was born in Monroe, Louisiana, also recognized his impact. "No one had ever played basketball the way I played it," noted Russell, "or as well. They had never seen anyone block shots before...I like to think I originated a whole new style of play."[35]

Russell's inimitable playmaker teammate, Bob Cousy, succinctly summed up his friend's worth: "He meant everything. We didn't win a championship until we got him in 1957, we lost it when he was injured in 1959, and we won it back when he was sound again in 1959."[36] Such was the relative value of one player in a sport like basketball. In addition, Auerbach stressed teamwork wherein every player had a specifically defined role to play. Auerbach also decided to utilize the faster speed of black players to his advantage by installing a "full court press" and allowing blacks to play the playground game they learned as youngsters—within limits.

Russell did have his detractors. In 1958 when he was the NBA's Most Valuable Player, the sportswriters did not name him to the all-NBA team; the insult still rankles Russell today. The overall pressure on Russell almost caused him to have a nervous breakdown in the 1963–64 season. Nevertheless, for the 1966–67 season he was named player/coach of the Celtics, the first black coach in a major sport since World War II. He later coached the Seattle Supersonics, and is currently the head coach of the Sacramento Kings.

Russell, a born leader, played through the transition period from the racial slurs that characterized the mid-1950s to the empowerment of the NBA Players Association and the era of six-figure salaries. He still remembers the game's quota system when he began. "In America," he noted then, "The practice is to put two black athletes in the basketball game at home, put three on the road, and put five in when you get behind..."[37] No American athlete has won as many championship titles in major sports as has Bill Russell.

Elgin Baylor: This Hall of Fame forward for the Los Angeles Lakers (previously the Minneapolis Lakers) was the first to impress crowds with an ability to seemingly defy gravity. The 6-foot 8-inch Baylor came from Washington, D.C., and its Spingarn High School. He attended the College of Idaho on a football scholarship and then transferred to Seattle University. Baylor was a 1958 first round draft choice of the Lakers.

Baylor stated that his amazing body control was "a gift from God"[38] although as a youth he had spent thousands of hours practicing on the public playgrounds of the nation's capital. As good as his on-court record was, his very presence was instrumental in the strengthening of the Players Association. In 1964, just before the All-Star Game that year, the players were poised to strike over the lack of an adequate pension plan. Lakers owner Bob Short sent word to Jerry West, a white player, and Baylor that they had better play—or else. Short's ultimatum to two of the game's best united the players, and the owners gave in under pressure from ABC Television to begin the game.

Baylor was named captain of the Lakers and was one of the game's most popular players. He played on one championship team, 1971–72, in his fourteen-year career. The Lakers lost to the Celtics six times in the NBA playoffs during the same period. After his retirement he became coach of the New Orleans Jazz. However, racial slurs and the lack of local support made life difficult for him and his black players. Phrases like "We're not going to make this an all-nigger team" were common, said Baylor. "Black players couldn't wait to be traded."[39]

The first black players having been big forwards, it is therefore not surprising that Ray Felix was the first black player to show up in more than one statistical category. He was fifth in scoring, fifth in field-goal per-

more accurate and better trained. The average field-goal percentage of the top ten scorers in 1950 was .432—versus .449 for the top ten in 1959. Chamberlain, however, was in an altogether different class.

Wilt, who was one of eleven children (two died), was born on August 21, 1936, in Philadelphia, Pennsylvania. He graduated from the city's famed Overbrook High School and attended the University of Kansas for two years. He was such a dominating force that *Look* magazine featured a story about him entitled "Why I Am Quitting College," an unprecedented occurrence for a black college player. Since NBA rules prohibited the signing of players before their college class graduated, Chamberlain spent the extra year with the Globetrotters.

Chamberlain was an immediate sensation in the NBA. No one, not even the great George Mikan, ever matched his offensive prowess; he was able to score almost at will. He was named the league's MVP after his first season. Though he led the NBA in offensive statistics and never fouled out of a game during his professional career, Chamberlain was tagged with a "loser" label early on, because his teams failed to win titles. His first NBA title came in 1967, seven years after his rookie season.

As a youngster, Chamberlain led his Christian Street YMCA to a national championship and helped Overbrook to two All-City titles and three All-Public school titles. He also won shot-put titles in track and field at Overbrook and at Kansas. Part of this success was his uncommon coordination on a long frame. He was 6-feet 3-inches at twelve years of age, and was extremely dedicated to succeeding in athletics. "I'd

practice afternoons and evenings and weekends, and during the summer I'd practice all day long, working on my moves and my shots and my passing and my rebounding."[43] Chamberlain eventually grew to 7-feet 1¹⁄₁₆-inches and weighed 265 pounds. He was possibly the strongest professional athlete in a major sport.

While Chamberlain continued to pile up individual NBA honors, his teams failed to match the success of Bill Russell's Celtics. Though both men were superb athletes, they were different in many ways. Russell stayed with one team for his entire career; Chamberlain changed teams twice, from the Philadelphia/San Francisco Warriors to the Philadelphia 76'ers and then to the Los Angeles Lakers. Russell got along with his coach Red Auerbach and was eventually made player/coach himself; Chamberlain constantly feuded with his coaches. Russell was a leader in the NBA Players Association; Chamberlain was not. Yet Chamberlain was never afraid to speak his mind or follow his own dictates. "I never have been known for my humility."[44] Nor was he afraid to face black militants in the mid-1960s. In the early 1970s he admitted that "...I do not support the militant black power 'hate whitey' types like Stokeley Carmichael and H. Rap Brown, and some of the early Black Panthers."[45] Chamberlain even publicly supported Richard Nixon for President in 1968 and attended the Republican Convention, much to the chagrin of most blacks. (He did so on the basis of a private and prolonged conversation with Nixon on a plane ride from New York City to Los Angeles.)

Chamberlain also freely admitted dating white women at a time when it was frowned upon by many in the black community, and by reporters who covered his games. He said, "Back when I was getting started in the NBA, most sportswriters—like most whites—didn't like that interracial sex one bit."[46] He inadvertently incensed many black women with a passage from his book, *Wilt*, published in 1973, which sought to explain his dating philosophy: "I live in America, where there are more white women than black women available to date...I meet more white women than black women...I don't give a s— what color a girl's skin is."[47] Though the statement itself was more of an observation than a defense of his right to date whomever he pleased, it nevertheless was cause for much discussion among blacks at a time when black militancy was high and the women's liberation movement was just getting started.

Throughout their careers, however, Russell and Chamberlain remained good friends. They even picked one another up at the airport when their respective teams arrived to play each other. These two giants left the professional game much better off than it was when they began. Russell set defensive standards and a winning percentage that remain the standard today. While Chamberlain's offensive output may perhaps never be equalled in so many different categories; both men's contributions have forever marked the sport.

Back-Court Generals: As teams moved from the era of tokenism in the 1950s to fielding the best five players on their rosters regardless of race, they were forced to acknowledge the superior speed and leadership of black guards. While theories abounded to explain the growing black point guard presence in the NBA, few argued with the results. Though some wanted to believe in the superior genetic endowment of blacks for physical expression, the more objective reasoning was that black players were simply more highly-motivated, practiced longer and harder, and made a stronger commitment to the game at an earlier age than whites.

However characterized, these exceptional players led the NBA's statistical record books for free-throw percentage, assists, field goals, and points. Hal Greer, Guy Rodgers, Sihugo Green, Lenny Wilkens, Dick Barnett, K.C. Jones, Walt Hazzard, Wally Jones, Dave Bing, Al Attles, Norm Van Lier, Clem Haskins, Art Williams, Nate Archibald, Archie Clark, Flynn Robinson, Eddie Miles, Randy Smith, Herm Gilliam, Charlie Scott, Jimmy Walker, Calvin Murphy, Jo Jo White, Walt Frazier, Earl Monroe, and Oscar Robertson, to name just some of them.

Lenny Wilkens, K.C. Jones, and Al Attles went on to coaching careers in the NBA. Walt Frazier led the New York Knicks to an NBA title in 1970 with a seventh-game performance against the Lakers that included 36 points, 7 rebounds, 19 assists, and 5 steals. Calvin Murphy, at 5-feet 9-inches, was one of the few black players under six feet. Earl Monroe performed in the quintessential black playground style. Nicknamed "the Pearl" as a professional, he was known as "the Black Jesus" on the public courts of his native Philadelphia and at Winston-Salem State College under coach Clarence "Big House" Gaines. This 6-foot 3-inch wizard was a favorite with the Baltimore Bullets and the New York Knicks fans. No guard, though, could match the all-around skills of Oscar Robertson.

Oscar Robertson: Robertson was the modern game's first big guard at 6-feet 5-inches and 210 pounds. He could—and did—do everything well. He was born on November 24, 1938, in Charlotte, Tennessee, the son of a divorced sanitation worker. Like his black counterparts in the 1950s, he suffered his share of turmoil on and off the court. Under coach Ray Crowe, Robertson guided Indianapolis' Crispus Attucks High School team to two state titles in three years, the first black school to achieve that goal. Traditionally, Indiana's winning high school team was feted with a parade through their hometown but, Crispus Attucks' principal, Russell Lane, was warned to temper their celebrations since they had defeated a white school, Shortridge, in the finals. Instead of being led through the center of town as usual, Robertson's team was taken to Northwestern Park, a remote part of town, by police to avoid racial incidents. Robertson never forgot this slight.

Robertson's motivation was no different than any other black youngster. "I practiced all the time...we didn't have any money and sports was the only outlet we had."[48] His views did not change much when he attended the University of Cincinnati, though he was the first college player to lead the NCAA in scoring three consecutive years. Yet he had become so disillusioned with his life that he said, "All I want is to get out of school. When I'm through, I don't want to have anything to do with this place."[49]

Robertson signed with the Cincinnati Royals in 1960 for $100,000 for three years and helped to draw more people into the arena than in the Royal's three previous seasons combined. His steady but brilliant play impressed NBA veterans immediately, but he rankled under the NBA's disguised quota system for blacks. "We [blacks] all know it. A lot of good Negro ball players should be in the league but generally only four or five spots are open on a team. Boston has five, I think. St. Louis has five...I don't know. It makes you wonder."[50]

Robertson's best year was the 1963–64 season when he averaged 31.4 points per game, led the league in assists with 868, and led the league in free-throw percentage with .853. The Royals had their best season ever, with 55 wins and 25 losses. Amazingly, it took four years before he was finally offered a product endorsement—for a basketball!

At the suggestion of Jack Twyman, Robertson ran for and was elected president of the NBA Players Association in 1966. He later helped hire Larry Fleischer as the Association's counsel. Under his leadership, the NBAPA established collective bargaining with the owners.

In 1971, Robertson finally won an NBA title, with the Milwaukee Bucks, where he played with Lew Alcindor (Kareem Abdul-Jabbar). He retired in 1974.

Front-Court Stars: The average fan can readily understand someone who is under 6-feet 4-inches tall being exceptionally coordinated. But the intricate moves shown by men averaging 6 feet 8 inches or taller seem somehow extraordinary. Players like

George Mikan, Clyde Lovellette, and Bob Petitt—all white—were outstanding in their time. However, by the mid-1960s, the black big men brought their own distinctive style of play to the hardwood. While most of them had come from solid college experiences, they had learned to play in black environments where they impressed one another with the latest moves.

In the period between 1960 and 1973, the following black forwards and centers appeared among the lists of statistical leaders: Willie Naulls, Walter Dukes, Wayne Embry, Walt Bellamy, Johnny Green, Bob Boozer, Ray Scott, Gus Johnson, Nate Thurmond, Lucius Jackson, Zelmo Beaty, Jim Barnes, Bob Love, Bill Bridges, Leroy Ellis, Chet Walker, Wes Unseld, Paul Silas, Bob Lanier, Elmore Smith, Elvin Hayes, Willis Reed, Spencer Haywood, Curtis Rowe, Bob Dandridge, Cazzie Russell, Lou Hudson, Connie Hawkins, Joe Caldwell, and Sidney Wicks. During the fourteen-year period, 101 of the top 140 NBA rebounding leaders were black.

Through the 1984–85 season, Elvin Hayes had played in more NBA games, 1,303, than anyone else. He was also first in minutes played at 50,000, third in field goals, and fourth in blocked shots. Paul Silas was second in games played and eighth in rebounds. Among NBA career scorers, Walt Bellamy was ninth, Bob Lanier was thirteenth, and Chet Walker was fifteenth.

Willis Reed: Reed was the extremely popular captain of the New York Knicks and is best remembered for his heroic play in the 1970 seven-game championship series win over the Lakers. Reed had a painful hip injury and was a doubtful starter for game seven. However, he hobbled onto the court at Madison Square Garden and promptly sunk his first two field goals to provide an emotional lift for his team. The Knicks won 113–99 for their first championship.

Reed attended college at Grambling State in Louisiana and later coached the New York Knicks and the Creighton University team. He was elected to the Hall of Fame in 1981.

Off-Court Problems: In addition to the unwritten but evident quota system for blacks through the 1960s, there were other problems that surfaced. The point shaving scandal kept Connie Hawkins from signing with an NBA team. Black players were not united enough and the NBAPA was not strong enough at the time to challenge this snub, which was based solely on unproven testimony from an indicted gambler. When Hawkins finally joined the Phoenix Suns in 1969, he led the team in scoring with a 24.6 average.

The Spencer Haywood case had also caused enmity among black players. Some black superstars even turned their backs on Haywood, an unprecedented occurrence in basketball, baseball, or football. Most did not understand at the time that Haywood had signed his ABA contract without benefit of counsel, and they erroneously connected the final resolution of his lawsuit to a merger of the ABA and NBA, which was fought by black players, because it would have reduced the competition for their talents.

The Russell-Chamberlain era was one

of tremendous growth in the sport. Salaries rose, television coverage increased, and the caliber of play improved substantially; due in large measure to the excitement created by this new generation of blacks.

1973 to 1985: The Kareem Abdul-Jabbar Era

At the end of the 1960s, Wilt Chamberlain was recovering from knee surgery and the New York Knicks were about to win their first NBA title. Professional sports were providing a welcome diversion from the evening television news programs that showed the numbers of American and Vietnamese soldiers being killed in Southeast Asia. ABC Television renewed its NBA contract for another four years in spite of the league's 58 percent black roster. The rival ABA was 54 percent black in 1969.

The minimum salary for players was $15,500 with the average salary being $43,000. Statistically, blacks began the 1970s with fourteen of the top twenty scorers, five of the top ten field-goal shooters, seven of the top ten free-throw shooters, seven of the top ten assists leaders, and seven of the top ten rebounders. For all players, the average of the top ten in field-goal percentage was an impressive .527, compared with .432 in 1951 and .449 in 1959. Unquestionably, players were not only faster, they were also better. However, for a time there was another league to contend with.

The NBA/ABA Merger: In the Fall of 1966, the American Basketball Association (ABA) began operating with eleven teams. It was clear that more large cities wanted teams than the NBA was willing to include. As a marketing ploy, the ABA introduced the 3-point field goal for shots made 25 feet or more, and they played with a red, white, and blue ball. Inevitably, a bidding war erupted between the two leagues and salaries began to rise—60 percent between 1967 and 1971—and some NBA players jumped to the ABA. The interleague competition was a boon to black players, and several, including Elgin Baylor, Wilt Chamberlain, and Nate Thurmond, began earning more than $100,000 per year by 1968.

The ABA had its best opportunity for long-term stability if, in 1969, it could sign Lew Alcindor (now Kareem Abdul-Jabbar). The ABA's commissioner was George Mikan who plainly stated, "If Lew joined our league, it would be the equivalent of the [New York] Jets beating the [Baltimore] Colts in the Super Bowl."[51] But the ABA did not get Alcindor, because he asked for a bonus atop the ABA's offer and Mikan turned him down. Mikan mistakenly thought Alcindor was just negotiating. Mikan's error turned out to be one of the most costly in American team-sport history. Alcindor later declared, "The ABA had the inside track but they had blown it."[52]

Though the NBAPA filed a class action suit in 1970 to block a proposed merger of the two leagues, the leagues eventually did merge in 1975 and the NBA was flooded with a wealth of talent.

Before the merger, however, there were some racial difficulties that plagued some ABA teams. For instance, the Dallas franchise removed four of their ten blacks from its eleven-man roster, as a Dallas official was quoted as saying, "Whites in Dallas are simply not interested in paying to see an all-black team and the black population alone cannot support us."[53]

These problems notwithstanding, the ABA in its ten-year existence had provided professional jobs for dozens of black players and had helped increase salaries for players in both leagues.

High Salaries Change Relationships:

Along with the merger proceedings of the ABA and NBA came a dissolution of the reserve system, which, as in baseball, bound a player to a team for the duration of his career. As salaries soared, so did the problems that black players had in keeping their new fortunes. In addition, alongside the box scores were stories of the profligacy of many players, most of whom were black. Said the July 17, 1978, issue of *Sports Illustrated* of Marvin "Bad News" Barnes, "After...Barnes signed his $2.1 million contract with St. Louis of the ABA in 1974, he spent $125,000 in six weeks. A silver Rolls-Royce, a diamond ring for each hand, a ruby necklace spelling NEWS and 13 telephones..."[54]

In 1975, Moses Malone became the first high school player to skip college altogether and go directly to the NBA. He had averaged 36 points per game, 26 rebounds, and 12 blocked shots in his high school senior year. He was so heavily recruited that his mother developed an ulcer. But she did remember the moment her son decided to become a professional. She said, "I didn't even think about him going pro until he came into the Safeway and told me to quit work..."[55]

"Jumping" Joe Caldwell, a ten-year veteran of the ABA and NBA who once earned $210,000 per year, was broke and divorced by 1977.

Opinions about their relative economic worth varied among black players, but nearly all of them came from humble and religious beginnings. The following are sample comments from four players at the time:

Elvin Hayes: "No athlete is worth the money he is getting, including me."

Julius Erving, who remembered his poor childhood: "I have this habit. I was always so poor that if I had a dime I made sure when I went to bed that dime would be there when I got up...in the beginning I was taken advantage of. Players have to be careful that they don't get used and cast aside."[56]

George Gervin: "We put a lot of wear and tear on our bodies. We're sacrificing ourselves to give fans something to see. If that's not work, what is?"

Wayne Embry: "Many players are now more concerned about protecting their earning power than performing. So the quality of basketball is not what it used to be. The fans pay an inflated price for a tarnished product—all because of greed."

Embry's comment was echoed by many white sportswriters. The general feeling among white fans was that "...the declining intensity in play confirmed their suspicions of innate black laziness...[the] perception that black players were not 'putting out.'"[57] Ted Stepien, the Cleveland Cavaliers owner, said he thought attendance would rise if there were more white players. In New York City, the Knicks were sometimes referred to by some whites as the New York Niggerbockers. Some owners, though, were still prepared to pay top dollar for the best talent. In 1981, Los Angeles Lakers owner, Jerry Buss, gave Earvin "Magic" Johnson a twenty-five-year, $25-million contract, the largest total sum in team-sports history.

Due to the intense pressure to play and with players receiving such large sums, their relationships with coaches changed dramatically. Coaches simply lost much of their authority. Few of their high-priced players were hesitant in speaking up about their concerns, even as the pressure mounted to perform up to expectations. Subsequently, many players succumbed to using illegal drugs, especially cocaine. In the seventies, they had begun using marijuana. Elgin Baylor noted that: "There were guys that smoked marijuana and drank [alcohol] through the late sixties, but no one was doing cocaine."[58] That had all changed by the mid-1970s. Even Kareem Abdul-Jabbar, who came from a solid middle-class family, admitted to an early problem: "I found myself coming out of college and all of a sudden I had some money in my pocket and I was curious enough to try it [cocaine]...I ended up altering my personality so much that I was some type of race car driver and I ended up spinning my car out..."[59]

John Lucas, another product of a middle-class environment, admitted his addiction: "I became bored by what I was doing [playing basketball]. I wanted to seek some adventure. I let my teammates down, I let myself down. I lost some money. Lost my job."[60]

Michael Ray Richardson was one of the most publicized drug users. He came from a broken home, one of seven children of a twice-divorced mother in Lubbock, Texas. At one time, he was a severe stutterer. When he first joined the New York Knicks he bought a Rolls-Royce, but coach Willis Reed counselled him and persuaded him to sell it. Richardson stated that "the lifestyle that basketball has created for me, I can't handle that...maybe I'd be better off driving a truck."[61] He was waived from the NBA's New Jersey Nets for the 1982–83 season because of his problem. "When they put me out of the league, I started spending all my cash...about 60 or 70 grand easy. I've heard of guys that spent two or three million, so $60,000 is not really that much."[62]

There were many other drug abuse problems, as drugs had been an ever-present problem in many black communities for years. But the aforementioned case histories failed to dampen the enthusiasm of tens of thousands of black youngsters who still aspired to professional basketball careers at the expense of other, and more viable options.

The Vicious Cycle Continues: As the rewards of a professional basketball career increased, so did the temptation to push through the nation's public-school systems those athletically gifted but academically unprepared players. The sport became an obsession in many black communities in the late sixties and early seventies. And why not? Basketball players were the highest-paid team-sport athletes, and basketball courts were within walking distance of nearly every black American.

Many blacks graduated from high school with an elementary reading-skill level. The overwhelming majority of black professional players were from families in lower socioeconomic groups. As such, they were more inclined to spend the thousands of hours of practice necessary to make their high school and college teams. The lack of modern facilities was not a deterrent. Elvin Hayes remembered practicing with a "raggedy old wooden backboard nailed to an old light pole"[63] and playing three or four games a day.

Black colleges, the centerpieces of black culture in the South, continued to see basketball in the 1970s as a more inexpensive varsity sport than football. They derived free nationwide publicity from winning teams. Alcorn A & M, for example, would have been virtually unknown outside the black community and the South if it were not for their basketball and football squads. Thus, these institutions continued trying to field the best teams possible. Their record has been impressive.

A list of professional basketball players from both white and black colleges can be found in the Reference section.

Back-Court Stars in the Abdul-Jabbar Era: On the average, players during the last dozen years have been bigger, faster, and better trained than ever. All were born after World War II and have little recollection of the problems experienced by players of the 1950s such as Oscar Robertson and Elgin Baylor. Public-school facilities, especially in the South, improved tremendously in the 1960s, and black athletes took maximum advantage. Whereas players in the mid-1960s began playing in a distinctive black style, their counterparts in the 1970s and 1980s further widened the differences between black and white players. White players with exceptional ball-handling skills, like Pete Maravich, were prized commodities. Joe Jares of *Sports Illustrated* referred to Jerry West and John Havlicek, both whites, as "collector's items."

By the early 1980s, white guards were rare indeed. The list of black guards who appear among the leaders in NBA statistics from 1972 to 1985 includes Frank Johnson, Allen Leavell, Lafayette Lever, Kelvin Ransey, Kenny Higgs, Rickey Green, Kevin Porter, Phil Chenier, Slick Watts, John Lucas, Henry Bibby, Phil Ford, Norm Nixon, Ray Williams, Earvin "Magic" Johnson, Maurice Cheeks, Randy Smith, Lucius Allen, Tom Henderson, Mike Gale, Lionel Hollins, Jo Jo White, Ricky Sobers, Quinn Buckner, Butch Lee, Clarence "Foots" Walker, Walter Davis, Armond Hill, Dudley Bradley, Terry Furlow, Sonny Parker, Robert Reid, Geoff Huston, Andrew Toney, World B. Free, John Moore, Darwin Cook, Isiah Thomas, Mark Aguirre, and Michael Jordan. These players had spent more hours practicing, had been more highly trained, had been more highly motivated, had been more highly paid, and were simply better than their white counterparts in any previous generation.

Some were among the most well-known faces and names in America. Earvin "Magic" Johnson, at 6-feet 9-inches, was much taller than most guards and was an instant success. He guided Everett High School in Lansing, Michigan, to a state title and then in 1979, while only a sophomore steered Michigan State to the NCAA title. He brought a wondrous smile and boundless enthusiasm to the Los Angeles Lakers and within five years he had helped to win two NBA titles as well.

There were definite advantages to being in a franchise in important media cities like New York, Los Angeles, Chicago, Washington, D.C.–Baltimore, Philadelphia, Boston, and San Francisco. Walt Frazier, for instance, whose nickname was "Clyde" (so named because the stylish clothes he wore reminded some of bank robber Clyde Barrow), would not have been as well known had he played for Cleveland. Likewise, "Magic" Johnson graced the nation's papers and sports magazines largely because he was based in Los Angeles. The size of the city was secondary to its media importance, and for this reason the best players wanted to play where they received the most publicity.

Some players created their own persona. Lloyd Free legally changed his name to World B. Free. George Gervin, known as "The Ice Man," was a 6-foot 7-inch guard, who was eleventh on the list of all-time NBA scorers at the end of the 1984–85 season. Only two other guards on the list, Oscar Robertson and Hal Greer, were ahead of him.

At the end of the 1979–80 season, the leaders in assists and steals—the two categories most associated with guards—were all black for the first time. But by the early 1980s, roughly 80 percent of the league was black, so it was no longer meaningful to speak of their statistical dominance.

Front-Court Status: The list of the game's premier big men who play the forward and center positions is not as long as that for the guards. There are simply fewer highly talented players over 6-feet 8-inches. Therefore, a good big man is much more valuable than a good little man. Con-

sequently, the same names surface over and over again in those categories—points, field goals, rebounds, and blocked shots (a category first documented in 1972–73)—associated with front-court players. Players exclusive of those already named from the previous period, but who played during the Abdul-Jabbar era include: Bob McAdoo, Happy Hairston, Sam Lacey, Clifford Ray, Garfield Heard, Don Smith, Curtis Perry, Jim Chones, Sidney Wicks, Harvey Catchings, Lloyd Neal, George McGinnis, Artis Gilmore, Larry Kenon, Otto Moore, Bob Dandridge, John Drew, Billy Knight, Tree Rollins, Joe C. Meriweather, Marvin Webster, Leonard "Truck" Robinson, Robert Parish, Terry Tyler, Dan Roundfield, Caldwell Jones, Adrian Dantley, Cedric Maxwell, Kermit Washington, Jamaal Wilkes, Bill Cartwright, Buck Williams, Larry Smith, Moses Malone, Cliff Robinson, Julius Erving, David Thompson, Albert King, Bernard King, Terry Cummings, Larry Nance, Alton Lister, Herb Williams, and Darryl Dawkins.

A very good argument can be made that the foregoing players are among the world's best athletes. There is a consensus among sportswriters and fans that the incredible coordination shown on a basketball court by players such as Julius Erving, Larry Bird, Bill Walton, Kareem Abdul-Jabbar, and Bernard King is nothing short of astounding. In the sport of basketball, it is simply not enough to be tall; stamina, strength, timing, and intelligence are also needed. It is no surprise then that the all-time leaders in the majority of offensive, rebounding, and blocked-shot categories are centers and forwards. In one category, blocked-shots, the entire top ten are all black. Several of these players alone are worth the price of admission. Julius Erving is perhaps the most physically gifted and acrobatic performer yet seen. The only comparable player in past years was Elgin Baylor. Erving specializes in intricate plays such as dunks that frequently begin with just one step from the foul line and end with different maneuvers each time. He is one of the few players who can literally have fans shaking their heads in disbelief.

Black players took pride in mastering assorted ways of dunking the ball. White players seldom attempted anything approaching the razzle-dazzle shown by blacks. And fewer still give labels to their favorite dunk, as did Darryl Dawkins. Dawkins, who like Moses Malone and Bill Willoughby went straight to the NBA from high school, broke several fiberglass backboards with his powerful slam dunks. He called this shattering move his Chocolate Thunder Flyin' Robinzin Cry'in Teeth Shakin' Glass Breakin' Rump Roastin' Bun Toasting' Wham Bam Glass Breaker Am Jam.

A Need to Regroup: In the early 1980s the black domination of the NBA was cause for serious concern among the owners and league officials. In spite of the natural talent displayed by black players, many continued to feel black player presence and dominance of the sport was the root cause of declining audience attendance. One team official was blunt in his sentiments: "It's race, pure and simple. No major sport comes up against it the way we do. It's just difficult to get a lot of people to watch huge, intelligent, millionaire black people on television."[64]

Correspondingly, fans had read and became tired of salary squabbles, illegal drug use, too many games, and lethargic play. As such, fan support began to decline. In 1982, ten of twenty-three NBA teams were for sale or facing liquidation. So it was that Larry Bird, the best white player in the NBA, was viewed as "the great white hope," but he was the only one. To save money, and possibly franchises, the NBAPA and the league agreed in 1983 to a shorter television schedule, revenue-sharing, and a team cap on salaries.

The league also enacted a tough new drug law that called for the expulsion of any player caught using illegal substances. Expelled players could petition for reinstatement in two years. If a player volunteered for treatment, he could receive it at league expense the first time, but had to pay for treatment a second time. There was no third chance.

The 1984–85 season, though, was a promising year. A revised television schedule and the presence of Michael Jordan, the sensational rookie from the University of North Carolina, gave the league a big lift. Jordan's college coach, Dean Smith, was effusive in his praise: "I've seen other great athletes but Michael also has the intelligence, the court savvy…he was a hero so many times at the end of games—it was uncanny. It really was."[65] Aside from some jealousy shown toward him at the 1985 All-Star Game, his rookie debut was cause for celebration. In the endorsement field, his basketball shoe, Air Jordan, was the largest selling ever, $70 million. This is a tremendous increase from the paltry offers to Oscar Robertson twenty years earlier.

Indeed, total NBA revenues at the end of the 1984–85 season were $192 million, in third place behind baseball at $625 million, and football at $700 million. Like it or not, much of it was due to the exciting play of blacks.

A Look Back: The game has come a long way since 1891 when James Naismith nailed two peach baskets to a wall. Black players have weathered many difficulties since 1908, when Edwin B. Henderson began the first serious inner-city competitions between New York City and Washington, D.C. Much credit is due to those pioneering teams—Monticello, the Loendi Big Five, the Savoy Big Five, the New York Renaissance, the Philadelphia Tribune Girl's Team, the Harlem Globetrotters, Tennessee State, Winston-Salem State College, and Alcorn A & M.

Henderson himself cannot be thanked enough for his contributions, In addition, coaches and officials like Cumberland Posey, Robert Douglas, Abe Saperstein, Holcombe Rucker, Clarence "Big House" Gaines, Johnny B. McLendon, Vivian Stringer, Dave Whitney, Bill Russell, John Thompson, Lenny Wilkins, and K.C. Jones have been outstanding.

Neither can we forget such players as Hilton Slocum, Ora Washington, "Fats" Jenkins, William "Pop" Gates, William "Dolly" King, Isadore Channels, Don Barksdale, Chuck Cooper, Wilt Chamberlain, Bill Russell, Hal Greer, Oscar Robertson, Lusia Harris, Kareem Abdul-Jabbar, Earl Monroe, Michael Jordan, Lynette Woodard, and Cheryl Miller.

When one thinks of the black athlete, thoughts inevitably settle on three sports— boxing, track and field, and basketball. Through thousands of hours of practice and dedication, black American athletes have mastered the nuances of the world's second most popular team-sport. Though alternative avenues of self-expression are now open that were closed as recently as fifteen years ago, ethnic pride in basketball excellence is now at stake. We can therefore expect more of the same in the future.

Notes

1. William "Pop" Gates, telephone interview with author, 24 April 1985.
2. *New York Age,* 9 October 1948.
3. *Ebony,* April 1956, 52.
4. Bill Libby and Spencer Haywood, *Stand Up For Something: The Spencer Haywood Story,* (New York: Grosset and Dunlap, 1972), 41.
5. Joe Jares, *Basketball: The American Game,* (Chicago: Follet Publishing Company, 1971), 194.
6. Ibid.
7. Ibid.
8. Libby and Haywood, *Stand Up For Something: The Spencer Haywood Story,* 41.
9. *Sports Illustrated,* 20 November 1985, 129.
10. *Ebony,* March 1962, 109.
11. *Ebony,* May 1976, 153.
12. Ibid.
13. *Sports Illustrated,* 4 March 1985, 9.
14. *Ebony,* February 1977, 92.
15. *New York Times,* 1 January 1951.
16. *Pittsburgh Courier,* 27 January 1951.
17. *Ebony,* February 1970, 42.
18. *Sports Illustrated,* 19 May 1980, 54.
19. David Halberstam, *The Breaks of the Game,* (New York: Alfred A. Knopf, 1981), 227.

20. *Miami Herald,* 16 February 1985.
21. *Sports Illustrated,* 22 April 1985, 37.
22. Wilt Chamberlain and David Shaw, *Wilt: Just Like Any Other 7-Foot Black Millionaire Who Lives Next Door,* (New York: MacMillan Publishing Company, 1973), 48.
23. Libby and Haywood, *Stand Up For Something: The Spencer Haywood Story,* 120.
24. Elgin Baylor, telephone interview with author, 19 August 1985.
25. "The Black Athlete, Part 3," Jack Olsen, *Sports Illustrated,* 15 July 1968, 30.
26. *Newsweek,* 15 July 1968, 56.
27. *Civil Rights Digest* (August 1972): 26.
28. Halberstam, *The Breaks of the Game,* 352.
29. *Commonwealth Magazine,* February 1983, 37.
30. *Sports Illustrated,* 19 May 1980, 60.
31. *Ebony,* February 1985, 96.
32. Chamberlain and Shaw, *Wilt: Just Like Any Other 7-Foot Black Millionaire Who Lives Next Door,* 94.
33. *Sports Illustrated,* 22 April 1985, 85.
34. Jares, *Basketball: The American Game,* 106.
35. Ibid., 67.
36. Ibid., 99.
37. Harry Edwards, *The Sociology of Sports,* (Homewood, IL: The Dorsey Press, 1973), 213.
38. Elgin Baylor, telephone interview with author, 19 August 1985.
39. Ibid.
40. *Ebony,* April 1959, 59.
41. Ira Berkow, *Oscar Robertson: The Golden Year,* (Englewood Cliffs, N.J.: Prentice-Hall, Inc., 1971), 48.
42. Chamberlain and Shaw, *Wilt: Just Like Any Other 7-Foot Black Millionaire Who Lives Next Door,* 113.
43. Ibid., 14.
44. Ibid., 3.
45. Ibid., 55.
46. Ibid., 111.
47. Ibid., 259.
48. Berkow, *Oscar Robertson: The Golden Year,* 122.
49. *Ebony,* March 1960, 118.
50. Berkow, *Oscar Robertson: The Golden Year,* 136.
51. Jares, *Basketball: The American Game,* 141.
52. Ibid.
53. Edwards, *The Sociology of Sport,* 214.
54. *Sports Illustrated,* 17 July 1978, 48.
55. *Commonwealth,* February 1983, 68.
56. *Sports Illustrated,* 17 July 1978, 36-41.
57. Benjamin G. Rader, *American Sports* (Englewood Cliffs, N.J.: Prentice-Hall, Inc., 1985), 299.
58. Elgin Baylor, telephone interview with author, 19 August 1985.
59. *New York Times,* 2 October 1985.
60. Ibid.
61. Ibid.
62. Ibid.
63. Elvin Hayes, *They Call Me The Big E,* (Englewood Cliffs, N.J.: Prentice-Hall, Inc., 1978), 25.
64. *Esquire,* February 1985, 114.
65. "Show Time," Barry Jacobs, *Inside Sports,* November 1985, 24.

Chapter

3

Boxing

≈≈

Joe Louis' Legacy: The Brown Bomber retired (for the first time) in 1949 after a dozen years as the world heavyweight champion. Although he had tax difficulties with the Federal Government most everyone, especially black Americans, loved him. To black Americans he was larger than life. To boxing impresarios, he was money in the bank, someone who could be counted on to "fill the house." Memories of the controversial first black heavyweight champion, Jack Johnson, haunted Louis and, with the help of his managers, John Roxborough and Mike Jacobs, he strove to make amends.

There were other black champions during the Louis era, such as Henry Armstrong and Sugar Ray Robinson, but they did not have Louis' following. Louis dutifully served in the Army, and was an inspiration to fighters the world over. Partly because of his reputation, boxing made some key organizational changes in the 1940s. In 1944, the Gillette Company began sponsoring weekly bouts at Madison Square Garden, and in 1949, James Norris founded the International Boxing Club (IBC), in order to stage live televised fights.

The general mood of optimism surrounding the sport after World War II had resulted in part from Louis' image. For

blacks, the combination of Louis and Jackie Robinson between 1946 and 1949 formed a major part of their postwar euphoria. These two athletes even contributed to the confidence of those in the Civil Rights Movement.

Though Louis carried boxing through some difficult times, he left it in less than ideal sets of hands. Manager Mike Jacobs' contemporaries were more concerned with profitability than with boxing's traditions, especially the small clubs, which were the life-blood of the sport. A new *modus operandi* was forthcoming.

Among the growing number of black ex-professional fighters, only one, Harry Wills, had managed to retire financially sound. The September 1946 issue of *Ebony* magazine reported that "Out of the million dollars he earned in more than twenty years in the ring, Wills today still has a big piece invested in two big Harlem apartment houses and two country estates...and an annual income of more than $25,000."[1] Matters would get worse before they got better.

New Boxing Environment: In 1949, the International Boxing Club (IBC) was founded by James Norris. The IBC virtually controlled the sport for ten years via shrewd agreements among boxers, arenas, and television. It was extremely difficult for any fighter to secure a championship bout without Norris' involvement.

There were 85 million television viewers in the United States in 1950, but Norris was not sure whether white America would watch mixed-race bouts without protest if blacks won most of them. Though the number of sets amounted to less than ten percent of American homes, boxing matches were full of racial symbolism and metaphor. Would southern whites, for instance, boycott Gillette shaving products because of its sponsorship?

Mike Jacobs wrote a thought-provoking article in the May 1950 issue of *Ebony* magazine entitled "Are Negroes Killing Boxing?" His answer was essentially no, and he added that "Negroes are entitled to whatever dominance of boxing or any other sport they achieve."[2] Hence, Jacobs achieved a reputation in the black community somewhat akin to that of Branch Rickey, the Brooklyn Dodgers president who signed Jackie Robinson to a contract as the first black major league baseball player of the modern era.

James Norris also sought to include blacks in the IBC administration. He hired Truman K. Gibson, Jr., to become a matchmaker at Chicago Stadium. Gibson, a lawyer, had helped arrange the Army boxing tours for Joe Louis, and had promoted the Sugar Ray Robinson–Jake LaMotta bout in 1951.

The IBC concentrated on staging bouts on closed-circuit television, the first being between Joe Louis and Lee Savold. This pulled fans away from the small clubs, and total boxing receipts slumped to only $4 million dollars for 1950. By 1954, there were roughly five televised boxing shows per week. A year later, the IBC was under investigation for violation of antitrust laws.

For the next four years, the IBC fought to retain its stranglehold on the sport. However, on January 12, 1959, the United States Supreme Court upheld a lower court ruling that the IBC had indeed violated federal antitrust laws. Two years later, Frank "Blinky" Carbo, an alleged organized-crime figure and Norris associate, was sentenced to twenty-five years in prison for conspiracy and extortion.

Between 1949 and 1953, the IBC promoted thirty-six of forty-four world title bouts. Consequently, black boxers and their managers were forced to operate within IBC confines. The demise of the IBC in 1959 paved the way for more competitor-oriented promotion in the 1960s. From the time of Joe Louis' retirement in 1949 through 1984, black boxers made more money than all other black professional athletes combined. What initially promised to be a vertical monopoly of all weight classes ended up with a concentration of black champions in the middle and upper weight divisions. Theirs is an enviable record in the ring, matched only by the predominance of black professional basketball players in the 1980s.

The 1950s
Featherweights: 119–126 lbs.

Sandy Saddler: He was, pound for pound, one of the hardest punchers in the history of the sport. In 162 official bouts, he scored 103 knockouts (KOs). (Twenty-eight of his first thirty-eight professional bouts were KOs.) He fought the champions of seven countries before securing a title bout. Saddler began his professional career in 1944, and averaged 14 bouts per year through 1951. He was best known for his four bouts with Willie Pep between October 29, 1948, and September 26, 1951. Saddler won the vacant junior lightweight title in 1949, but after one defense, relinquished it. He served in the United States Army in 1952–53, and he retired following an automobile accident in 1956. There would be no more black junior lightweight champions for almost thirty years.

Davey Moore: This Lexington, Kentucky, native was also the 1952 AAU bantamweight champion. His professional career began in 1953. He won the featherweight title from Hogan "Kid" Bassey on August 19, 1959, and defended it four times. He lost his title to Sugar Ramos on March 21, 1963, and died two days later of head injuries suffered in the bout. There have been no black featherweight champions since.

Lightweights: 127–135 lbs.

Ike Williams: This feisty battler won the National Boxing Association (NBA) title from Juan Zurita in 1945, in a second-round KO. He then won the world title two years later from Bob Montgomery. Williams, who admitted to heavy gambling losses in golf games, turned professional in 1940 and, retired four years after losing to James Carter in 1951.

James Carter: A South Carolina native, Carter was the first man to hold the same World title three times. After winning the title from Ike Williams, he lost it to Lauro

Salas. He regained it from Salas, lost it to Paddy deMarco, then regained it again from deMarco. Wallace "Bud" Smith finally ended Carter's career hopes in 1955.

Wallace "Bud" Smith: He turned professional after winning the 1948 National AAU title. Seven years later he won the world title from James Carter in fifteen tough rounds and successfully defended against him four months later. He lost the title to Joe Brown in 1956, after holding it for fourteen months. He retired in 1959, and died in 1973.

Joe "Old Bones" Brown: Born and raised in New Orleans during the Depression, Brown began his career in the military as the all-service lightweight champion. He turned professional after World War II and proved to be a durable fighter. After winning the world title from "Bud" Smith in 1956, he kept it five years and two months—longer than any lightweight title-holder since Benny Leonard in 1917–23.

Brown acquired the nickname "Old Bones" because he won the title at age thirty-one. A very hard puncher, he was feared by many fighters in the welterweight class. His eventual conqueror, Carlos Ortiz, referred to him as "a murderous puncher...a good left hooker, terrible body puncher."[3] Perhaps his most interesting bout was against Ralph Dupas in Houston, Texas, in 1958. Dupas, also from New Orleans, sued in his home state to prove he was not white. If Dupas had been listed as black, he would have circumvented Louisiana's rule, at the time, barring interracial sports. Louisiana refused to change his racial classification, so subsequently the fight was held in Houston. Brown won before 11,000 fans.

Eighteen years passed before another black lightweight champion was crowned.

Welterweights: 136–147 lbs.

Sugar Ray Robinson: Sugar Ray (formerly Walker Smith, Jr.) turned professional in 1940 and spent the 1940s as a welterweight. He won the world title from Tommie Bell in fifteen rounds on December 20, 1946. However, Robinson had a problem keeping his weight below the 147-pound limit. After winning the Pennsylvania middleweight title on June 5, 1950, from Robert Villemain, Robinson decided to become a permanent middleweight, and he subsequently relinquished his welterweight title after defeating Charley Fusari on August 9, 1950.

Johnny Bratton: He moved to Chicago from his native Little Rock, Arkansas. He turned professional in 1944 at age seventeen and won the vacant NBA title seven years later over Charley Fusari. He held his crown just two months and four days, losing it to Kid Gavilan.

Johnny Saxton: Saxton had an enviable amateur career, winning thirty-one of thirty-three bouts, the AAU crown, and the Golden Gloves in his hometown of Newark, New Jersey. After winning the world title from Gavilan in fifteen grueling rounds in 1954, he lost it six months later to Tony deMarco by a fourteenth-round KO. Saxton regained the title from Carmen Basilio in 1956 and lost it again six months later.

Virgil Akins: After a short amateur career of fourteen wins in fifteen bouts, this St. Louis, Missouri, fighter won the vacant world title by defeating Vince Martinez in 1958 on a fourth-round KO. He had defeated Isaac Logart in an elimination bout just three months earlier. Akins kept the title exactly six months, losing it to Don Jordon on December 5, 1958. A serious eye injury in 1962 forced him into retirement.

Middleweights: 148–160 lbs.

The story of the middleweight division in the 1950s is the story of Sugar Ray Robinson. He was unquestionably the most colorful boxer of the decade, and many experts have rated him pound for pound as the best ever. Before he had even reached his prime as a middleweight, he was named among such greats as John L. Sullivan, Joe Gans, Henry Armstrong, and Joe Louis. Dan Parker, of the *New York Mirror,* said in his column on February 14, 1951, that Robinson is "the greatest combination of brains, brawn, and boxing skill the modern prize ring has seen."[4]

One of Robinson's antagonists, Carl "Bobo" Olson, said Sugar Ray was "the greatest fighter that ever lived."[5] Another opponent, Paul Pender, added, "He was the greatest puncher that ever lived, with a repertoire of punches that nobody could throw…a great left hook, a great right-hand uppercut, a great right-cross."[6]

As early as 1950, Robinson had acquired a reputation as being difficult. He was labeled "boxing's bad boy." A few times he failed to appear for scheduled bouts, claiming misunderstandings with promoters. In 1947, the New York State Athletic Commission suspended him for thirty days for failing to report a bribery attempt. Yet by the black public in particular, he was idolized.

Robinson made constant reference to the sorry state of many ex-fighters. "A broke fighter is a pitiful sight...most fighters end up broke...I certainly don't intend to finish my career battered and broke."[7] However, he sometimes failed to heed his own advice. Perhaps no fighter believed more in his own invincibility. After all, he had survived life as a ghetto street kid in Detroit's Black Bottom district.

Born Walker Smith, Jr., on May 3, 1921, to Walker and Leila Smith, he learned to box at the Brewster Center two blocks from his home. When he was eleven he moved with his mother and sister to New York City's Hell's Kitchen neighborhood. They later moved to Harlem, where he began boxing in the Police Athletic League program.

His natural skills attracted the attention of George Gainford of the old Salem-Crescent Athletic Club. Gainford encouraged young Smith and showed him how to evade the rules against amateur fighters collecting prize money. When a youngster won a bout, Robinson recalled, "they give you a watch and then buy it back for ten dollars."[8]

He acquired his new name in Kingston, New York, when he was forced by local officials to produce his AAU card. Since he did not have one, he was persuaded by Gainford to use Ray Robinson's card as a substitute. Unknown outside Harlem, he was able to make the switch undetected. (The real Ray Robinson was born in Richmond, Virginia, on August 25, 1919.) As such, Robinson decided to keep his new name.

Robinson received his nickname from Jack Case, a writer for a Watertown, New York, newspaper, who noted to Gainford after watching him, "That's a real sweet fighter you've got there. As sweet as sugar."[9]

Robinson, who was 5 feet 11½ inches tall, began as a featherweight, winning the Golden Gloves title. He also won all of his eighty-five amateur bouts, sixty-nine by KO, forty of them in the first round. His professional debut came on Nobember 4, 1940, at Madison Square Garden, where Henry Armstrong was the headliner. Robinson moved about the ring effortlessly, partly because of dancing lessons and in part because of natural ability. Harry Wills stressed to him that "Balance son, balance is the fighter's most important asset."[10] Robinson himself freely acknowledged that "Rhythm is everything in boxing."[11]

He spent many hours with Joe Louis at Louis' training camp in Greenwood Lake, New York, and agreed to allow Louis's manager, Mike Jacobs, to arrange some of his bouts. All the time, though, he kept Gainford by his side. Robinson was intensely loyal to his friends. After sixteen months in the Army, from February 1943 to June 1944, he married former Cotton Club (New York City) dancer Edna Mae Holly and resumed his ring career. He was proud of the fact that during the war, he helped to integrate the entertainment shows at Keesler Field in Mississippi.

Robinson won his first world middleweight crown on Valentine's Day 1951 from Jake LaMottta on a thirteenth-round TKO. He was thirty years old, and euphoric about his feat. The IBC had been forced to give him a title shot when he won the Neil Award. IBC president Jim Norris wanted

Robinson to get rid of Gainford but he refused. To punish Robinson, Norris withheld his title bout as long as possible.

Before a scheduled defense with Randy Turpin in England, Robinson traveled to Paris to train and to entertain with a nightclub act. (During an audience with the French President and his wife, the impulsive Robinson suddenly reached out and kissed Madame Vincent Aurial on the cheek.) As a result of being undertrained, he lost his crown to Turpin on July 10, 1951, in fifteen rounds.

The rematch at the Polo Grounds in front of 61, 370 fans on September 12 of that year set a record for gate receipts in a non-heavyweight fight: $767,626.17. Sugar Ray won the title for a second time by a 10-round TKO. (Turpin, who was also black, eventually lost his money and committed suicide.) Following victories over Carl "Bobo" Olson and Rocky Graziano, he tried to win the light-heavyweight title from Joey Maxim.

On an oppressively hot and humid June 25, 1952, Robinson came within six minutes of winning. With the night-time temperature at 104 degrees, he collapsed on his stool at the end of the thirteenth-round. All three judges had him ahead at the time: 10–3; 9–3–1; 7–4–2. Robinson said after the fight, "The heat didn't get me. God willed it that way."[12] He then decided to retire to show business.

After two and a half years of less than spectacular success on the stage, Robinson returned to the ring at age thirty-four. Incredibly, he won the middleweight crown for a third time from Carl "Bobo" Olson on a second-round KO in Chicago. He lost it to Gene Fullmer on January 2, 1957, in fifteen

rounds and then astounded the sports world once more with his fourth title victory—a fifth round KO over Fullmer on May 1, 1957. Robinson became the first man to win a world title four times. Following a fifteen-round title defense loss to Carmen Basilio on a split decision, he won a fifth middleight title on March 25, 1958, over Basilio at Chicago, also in fifteen rounds.

As much as fans marvelled at his prowess at age thirty-seven, they knew he had money troubles. He owed hundreds of thousands of dollars in back taxes by the time of his third title win. Robinson was unabashedly loose with his hard earned purses. "There were nights when I'd go through $500 in handouts when I had it on me."[13]

Joe Glaser, who was brought in to help rearrange his financial matters, eventually foreclosed. The Internal Revenue Service then put liens on his purses. For a time, Robinson earned $500,000 and never saw a dime of it. His wife, Edna Mae, divorced him, his café was closed, and his Cadillac was sold. "Only me was left."[14] "I went through four million dollars, but I have no regrets."[15]

At age forty Robinson was still fighting. He lost twice to Paul Pender in 1960. He retired for good in 1965 and devoted his time to the Sugar Ray Robinson Youth Foundation in Los Angeles. He is most remembered by the public for his bouts against Jake LaMotta, Carl "Bobo" Olson, and Carmen Basilio, but boxing experts remember his unexcelled boxing skills over a quarter of a century.

Robinson's career was summed up this way by Jimmy Jacobs, owner of the world's largest collection of fight films:

"Sugar Ray Robinson...was probably the greatest fighter of all time—lightweight, welterweight, or heavyweight."[16]

Light-heavyweights: 161–175 lbs.

This weight division was also a one-man show during the fifties. Joey Maxim was the champion. Sugar Ray Robinson tried to win the title as a middleweight, but failed because he collapsed at the end of the thirteenth-round. But Archie Moore (formerly Archibald Lee Wright), at age thirty-seven, took Maxim's crown on December 17, 1952.

Moore was one of the cagiest boxers ever to lace on a pair of gloves, but his road to the World title was difficult. He says he was born on December 13, 1913 in Benoit, Mississippi and later moved to St. Louis, Missouri. He learned to box in reform school and turned professional at age twenty-three. After seventeen years of boxing, that included 170 bouts, he finally received a shot at the title.

Moore had been the number-one contender for five years, and five former champions passed up opportunities to fight him. As champion, Moore was the second oldest light heavyweight title holder (Bob Fitzsimmons was forty-one). To prepare for Maxim he was forced to lose sixteen pounds.

Since there was little demand for light heavyweight bouts during the early 1950s, Moore fought most of the time as a heavyweight.

Maxim demanded the most one-sided prize money split in memory. He was to be guaranteed $100,000 while Moore was to receive $800 plus expenses. After his fifteen-round win, Moore refused to let his manager lift him in the air in a victory hug.

"Turn me loose!" he demanded. "Don't do that. Just slip my robe on my shoulders. Be cool. Don't get excited. There's nothing to be excited about. I could have won this thing twelve years ago. This is nothing new to me. Be cool."[17] He dedicated his victory to Argentine President Juan Peron, a long-time friend and supporter.

During his career his fighting weight varied from 152 to 192 pounds. At one time he was ranked number three among heavyweights. Because of limited competition in the heavyweight ranks, Moore was given a chance to win the world heavyweight title from Rocky Marciano on September 21, 1955, but he was knocked out in the ninth round in a bout shown in 133 theaters and drive-ins in ninety-two cities. The NBA finally lifted Moore's light heavyweight title on October 25, 1960, because of inactivity, though the New York State Athletic Commission and the European Boxing Union waited another two years to do the same.

The NBA action was not without justification. Fourteen months after his loss to Marciano, Moore fought a second time for the world heavyweight title—this time against the young Floyd Patterson for Marciano's vacated crown on November 30, 1956. The forty-three-year-old Moore lost in a fifth-round knockout at Chicago in front of 14,000 fans. In the three-man elimination contest, Moore received a bye, while Patterson defeated Tommy "Hurricane" Jackson in a split twelve-round decision.

Moore's last light heavyweight title defense was a win in fifteen rounds over Giulio Rinaldi at Madison Square Garden, on June 10, 1961. Now forty-eight years old, he was known as the "Old Mongoose." Less than a year later he fought a ten-round draw with Willie Pastrano in Los Angeles.

Moore's next to last career bout was against a brash, fast-talking, lightning quick young heavyweight named Cassius Clay. Twenty-eight days short of his forty-ninth birthday, November 15, 1962, Moore lost on a knockout in the fourth round in Los Angeles. No fighter in his weight class had lasted as long with his skills intact. One of the best defensive boxers ever, he retired without a loss in his division after winning the title. His three losses were to men who either had won or would eventually win the heavyweight title.

Heavyweights: 191 lbs. and Above

Ezzard Charles: He had a most bizarre history on his way to the world heavyweight title. Born in Lawrenceville, Georgia, in 1921, he later moved to Cincinnati, Ohio. His parents divorced and his father, a janitor, allowed him to be raised by his grandmother. Charles began his boxing career at age fourteen as a featherweight, he eventually won the Golden Gloves middleweight title twice and was the 1939 AAU National middleweight champion. He turned professional shortly thereafter, but had a lackluster career until 1947 when an opponent, Sam Baroudi, died after their bout.

Though greatly affected by Baroudi's death, Charles now had a reputation as a hard puncher despite his tall, angular frame. Trained by the famed Ray Arcel, Charles fought Jersey Joe Walcott for the vacant NBA title on June 22, 1949, and won in fifteen rounds at Chicago. Charles was twenty-eight and Walcott was thirty-five. Even though Joe Louis had retired, he was still considered by many fight fans to be heavyweight champion. As Louis needed money badly, it was no mere coincidence that he and Charles fought for the title on September 27, 1950, in New York City. Charles won in fifteen rounds and was the second of only three men to defeat Louis during the Brown Bomber's professional career.

With the heavyweight division so muddled at the time, Walcott earned another chance at Charles' title. Charles could not sustain the onslaught from the shorter and more aggressive Walcott, and he lost his title in 1951. Three months after Charles' loss to Walcott, Joe Louis lost to Marciano. The lack of any clear-cut contenders allowed Charles to fight three more times for the world title, but he failed each time. One of the most underrated champions, Charles died of lateral sclerosis in 1965.

"Jersey" Joe Walcott: He was born January 31, 1914, at Merchantville, New Jersey—(hence the nickname "Jersey" Joe.) he began his professional career during the Depression, preferring to scrounge out a living in the ring rather than selling apples on street corners. As Walcott fought most of his bouts within fifty miles of New York City, he had a local following.

Joe Louis gave Walcott a title shot on December 5, 1947, at Madison Square Garden. Almost everyone who saw this battle—writers and fans alike—agree that Walcott should have been given the decision. He knocked Louis down twice, but back-pedaled in the fourteenth and fifteenth rounds and lost a split decision.

The first knockdown was in round one, and Louis was up at the count of two. The next knockdown was in round four, and Louis was up at the count of seven. It was evident to the 18,194 fans that Louis' best days were behind him. The referee, Ruby Goldstein, gave the fight to Walcott. But judges Marty Monroe and Frank Forbes scored it 9–6 and 8–6–1, respectively, for Louis. In a rematch at Yankee Stadium six months later, on June 25, 1948, Louis knocked out Walcott in the eleventh round in front of 42,657 fans.

Walcott's title victory over Ezzard Charles on July 18, 1951, at the age of thirty-seven was his fifth championship opportunity. He lost his title on a thirteenth-round knockout to Rocky Marciano in Philadelphia on September 23, 1952. Though he eventually won over $1 million dollars in purses, he lost most of it in bad investments. He later became the New Jersey State Athletic Commissioner and was inducted into boxing's Hall of Fame, in 1969.

Floyd Patterson: His life as a boxer was nothing short of a rags-to-riches story with a fairy-tale ending. Patterson was born on January 4, 1935, to an extremely poor family in Waco, North Carolina. His family later moved to New York City in search of a better life. But the sensitive and emotionally troubled young Patterson was unable to adjust.

Patterson became a delinquent and a truant, who hid out in subway tunnels in order to avoid going to school. He picked fights with anyone who made fun of his dirty and ill-fitting clothes. His mother even once sent him to a detention center to keep him out of trouble. Finally, arrangements were made to send him to the Wiltwyck School for troubled youngsters. The move proved a fortunate one. There, he learned to box, starting as a middleweight. His brother, Frank, who won the New York Golden Gloves 160-pound title in 1949, became his hero.

Patterson had incredibly fast hands, and as an amateur he developed his famous peek-a-boo defense, saying he could appreciate "the importance of avoiding being hit."[18] Patterson won the Golden Gloves title, and he also earned a berth on the 1952 Olympic Boxing Team as a middleweight. He won the Gold Medal. He also gained the National AAU middleweight title that year.

After Patterson turned professional his manager, Cus D'Amato, became obsessed with the IBC's intentions toward him. D'Amato, some thought, believed the IBC wanted to take Patterson away from him and to force Patterson to fight for the heavyweight crown. Patterson claims D'Amato wanted him to win Archie Moore's light heavyweight crown before tackling the heavyweight division. In any event, after Rocky Marciano retired in 1955, Patterson (who sustained a broken right hand) defeated Tommy "Hurricane" Jackson in a split twelve-round decision for the right to meet Archie Moore for Marciano's vacated crown. The twenty-one-year-old Patterson needed just five rounds to dispose of Moore, who was twenty-two years his senior. It was a strange contest, pitting the world light heavyweight champion against an opponent who was a natural light heavyweight himself. The $114,257 purse was for Patterson "riches beyond my wildest dreams, but insignificant compared to what was to come."[19]

Patterson's first title defense was significant because it was not promoted by the IBC. He was constantly nagged by critics, who claimed he was not worthy of the title, that he was just a blown-up light heavyweight with quick fists and a big heart. Consequently, these same critics were not surprised when the Swede, Ingemar Johansson took Patterson's crown on June 26, 1959, at Yankee Stadium.

Johansson, a four to one underdog, knocked Patterson down seven times to win by a technical knockout in the third round. The fight had been delayed one day because of rain and only 21,961 fans showed up. A sensitive and giving man, Patterson had attended graduation ceremonies at his old school, P.S. 614, just before the fight. The loss devastated him. "I felt I had let so many people down, all of America."[20]

Six days short of a year later, Patterson became the first heavyweight champion to regain his title, scoring a fifth-round knockout over Johansson at the Polo Grounds. It was the highlight of his career, and it was done without D'Amato's assistance (D'Amato's license had been revoked on November 24, 1959.) Almost 32,000 fans and a closed-circuit audience of half a million paid over $2 million dollars to witness Patterson's comeback. And on March 13, 1961, Patterson defeated Johansson for the second time, at Miami Beach on a sixth-round knockout. It was to be his last shining moment in the ring.

Against the strong objections of D'Amato, who was again advising him, Patterson fought Charles "Sonny" Liston on September 25, 1962. He lost by a knockout two minutes, six seconds into the first round. Liston, an ex-felon, who was generally dis-

liked and, feared, outweighed Patterson by twenty-five pounds, 212 to 187, as well as having a thirteen-inch reach advantage. Their encounter was, in retrospect, the most publicized fight since Jack Dempsey–Gene Tunney.

Nearly 19,000 fans at Chicago's Comiskey Park paid $665,420 and another 600,000 people in closed-circuit theaters paid over $4 million to view the fight. It was the first time the champion had been knocked out in the first round, and it was the third-fastest knockout in the history of the heavyweight title. Amazingly, Liston had boxed only five official rounds in the past two years.

Patterson felt that his ego, and the nation's prestige were on the line, so he tried to slug it out with the much stronger Liston. "When the bell rang, I was like a robot...The President of the United States (John F. Kennedy), Ralph Bunche...the millions of letters...made Liston a bad guy...pressure...the President...said to me 'make sure you keep that championship.'"[21]

In the eyes of white America, this was a fight between a "good nigger" and a "bad nigger." Dr. Charles Larson, president of the United States National Boxing Association, vehemently opposed the bout and said he spoke for millions of Americans: "I will use my personal influence to prevent Liston being matched against Patterson. In my opinion, Patterson is a fine representative of his race, and I believe the Heavyweight champion of the World should be the kind of man our children could look up to,,,"[22]

Less than a year later, on July 22, 1963, Patterson lost for the second time to Liston

at Las Vegas, in two minutes and ten seconds of the first round. The bout had originally been scheduled for April 4, but was
postponed because Liston had hurt his
knee playing golf.

After his bouts with Liston, Patterson
faced the "greatest"—Muhammad Ali. On
November 22, 1965, Patterson, outweighed
by 16 pounds, lost in 12 rounds to Ali at Las
Vegas, Nevada. Ali, a recent convert to the
religion of Islam, taunted and teased Patterson before and during their bout. "You're
nothing but an Uncle Tom Negro, a white
man's Negro, a yellow Negro. You quit twice
to Liston. Get into the ring and I'll lick
you."[23]

No black athlete had ever publicly
spoken so disparagingly to another black
athlete. Moreover, their bout came amidst
an emotional period in black American
history, when demonstrations and marches
were front page-news and Congress was
inundated with civil rights bills. Ali, who
was racially defiant in public, had a tremendous following among young blacks. Consequently, Patterson had likened his bout
with Ali to a "moral crusade."

Almost all viewers of the fight agreed
that Ali could have won the match much
sooner than round 12. But he purposefully
dragged it out, preferring to "punish" Patterson. All through the fight Ali kept up a
verbal barrage, saying to Patterson, "Come
on, America, come on white America!"[24]

Just before the fight Ali tendered one
of his soon to be much noted poems, one
specifically derogatory in tone:

"I'm going to put him flat on his back,
so that he will start acting Black,
because when he was champ he didn't do
    as he should,

he tried to force himself into an all-white
neighborhood."[25]

Floyd Patterson ended his career with
his brains intact and money in the bank. He
was the first black world champion since
Harry Wills to retire financially secure. He
was also the first Olympic Gold Medalist to
go on to win a world title. More importantly
to him, he was highly respected among his
peers.

As the decade of the 1950s came to a
close for black athletics, the United States
Supreme Court effectively ended the IBC's
monopoly; the Internal Revenue Service
agreed to forgive all of Joe Louis' debts in
1960. The next ten years were much more
contentious. They were to be dominated by
the black social revolution, the death of a
United States President, and the quickest
and most talkative heavyweight champion
the world had ever seen.

THE MUHAMMAD ALI ERA

The new occupational and career opportunities that arose for blacks after World
War II did not deter a significant number of
youngsters from a boxing career. As the
1960s began, there were many political
victories yet to be won, and boxers were
still the highest-paid athletes in the world.
The availability of internationally televised
bouts and the three Olympic Games since
the war had helped to spread the popularity
of the sport. Also, Third World countries
began training top-flight fighters in the
lower weight classes.

With the IBC now a thing of the past,
organized crime tried to control the major
contenders. Consequently, Senator Estes
Kefauver of Tennessee began a probe of the

sport in 1960, and concluded that organized crime did indeed have substantial influence. The NBA, in a move to reflect its more international scope, changed its name to the World Boxing Association (WBA) in 1962, and it was soon joined by a rival sanctioning body, the World Boxing Council (WBC), which seemed much more representative of Third World countries. African-American fighters made their marks in the heavier weight classes of both groups.

Welterweights: 141–147 lbs.

Curtis Cokes: Cokes won the Texas State title in 1965, and the Southern title in December of that year. After winning an elimination tournament to determine the successor to Emile Griffith, he won the world title from Jean Josselin on November 28, 1966. Cokes had previously defeated Manuel Gonzales on August 24, 1966, for the vacant WBA title. But the 5-foot 9-inch, 145-pound fighter from Dallas lost his title to Jose Napoles in thirteen rounds at Los Angeles on April 18, 1969. He failed in another attempt against Napoles two months later. There would be no more black American welterweight champions until Ray Leonard in 1979.

Light Heavyweights: 161–175 lbs.

Harold Johnson: He won the WBA title from Jesse Bowdrey at Miami Beach, Florida, in a ninth-round technical knockout on February 7, 1961, to capture Archie Moore's old title. Moore, however, would still be recognized as champion by the rest of the world for one more year. Johnson then

captured the World title from Doug Jones on May 12, 1962, and lost it thirteen months later to Willie Pastrano in a fifteen-round split decision at Las Vegas.

Initially, Pastrano was hesitant about meeting Johnson. "I didn't want to fight Harold Johnson...that animal...a fighter's fighter...greatest defensive boxer I've ever seen...a perfectionist."[26] Johnson and his father, Phil, shared the interesting historical note of having both lost to "Jersey" Joe Walcott—Phil in 1936 and Harold in 1950.

Bob Foster: He was perhaps the most powerful punching light heavyweight champion since John Henry Lewis. Born in Albuquerque, New Mexico, on December 15, 1938, he won the title from Dick Tiger in 1968 at Madison Square Garden. The result was never in doubt, as Foster scored a fourth-round knockout. Like Archie Moore, Foster kept the title a long time—nearly six years. He retired undefeated as a light heavyweight.

Though Foster successfully defended his title fourteen times—a record for a light heavyweight champion—his purses were not nearly as lucrative as those for the heavyweights or some welterweights. Foster made an unsuccessful challenge for the world heavyweight title, losing to Joe Frazier in 1970. He lost an NABF title fight to Muhammad Ali in 1972. He later became a sheriff in his native Albuquerque.

Heavyweights: 191 lbs. and Above

Charles "Sonny" Liston: No contender for the heavyweight title was so generally disliked as Liston, not even the Jack Johnson of 1908. Liston's troubled childhood mirrored that of Archie Moore and

Floyd Patterson. Born on May 8, 1932, in Pine Bluff, Arkansas, he was one of twenty-five children his father had by two wives. His father later abandoned his families, and Liston moved to St. Louis, Missouri.

When he was eighteen years old, Liston was incarcerated in the Missouri State Penitentiary for robbing a service station. He learned to box there and was released to the custody of Frank Mitchell, the black owner of the St. Louis *Argus* newspaper. Despite winning the 1952 Golden Gloves title and then turning professional, he would never completely erase his image as a street hoodlum.

Liston was arrested again in 1956 for assaulting a policeman and was sentenced to nine months in a workhouse, in addition to having his boxing license revoked. His troubles with the law and his suspected links with organized crime made it nearly impossible for him to secure fights. He was eventually relicensed, after falsifying his prison record.

One year before Liston fought Floyd Patterson for the title, his manager was Joseph "Peppy" Barone, a known friend of Frank "Blinky" Palermo, Frankie Carbo, and Johnny Vitale—all alleged organized crime figures. Liston's police record at the time showed nineteen arrests. In February of 1962, Liston obtained a new manager, Jack Nilon, and secured a shot at the title.

Liston knocked out Patterson in their title bout within two minutes and six seconds of the first round, on September 25, 1962. Joe Louis stated: "Liston is stronger than any man I've seen."[27] Two months later, after defeating Archie Moore, Cassius Clay said to Liston at ringside, "You're next. You must fall in eight [rounds]."[28] To which

Liston replied, "You couldn't lick a Popsicle."

Seven months after defeating Patterson for the second time, Liston faced Cassius Clay at Miami Beach. It was the most discussed heavyweight fight in years, and was replete with racial and social demagoguery. Clay referred to Liston as "a big ugly bear," (a comment only a black man could have gotten away with at the time). Liston had made matters worse with a heartfelt statement he made after returning home from a European tour soon after the bombing of the Birmingham, Alabama, black church and the killing of four little girls: "I'm ashamed to say I'm in America."[29] The white press had a field day.

But Clay's reputation in white America was also in transformation. He had met the black Islamic leader Malcolm X in Detroit in 1962, and Malcolm was now his spiritual advisor. Malcolm stated that "...it was Allah's intent for me to help Cassius prove Islam's superiority before the world...people everywhere scoffed at Cassius Clay's chances of beating Liston."[30]

As for Clay, he mixed the practical with the spiritual. Against Liston, he planned to copy Sugar Ray Robinson's strategy against Jake LaMotta: hit and run. At the weigh-in Clay seemed out of control. His plan was to psych out Liston, to "mess with his mind." He entered the ring against Liston truly believing he was divinely destined to win. "It is prophesied for me to be successful!"[31] he roared. "I cannot be beaten." Clay even gave up staying in a plush white Miami Beach hotel, preferring to stay at the black-owned Hampton House motel.

A huge thunder storm drenched Miami

just two and a half hours before fight time. Consequently, only 8,297 patrons attended the bout. Liston, a seven to one favorite, was guaranteed 40 percent of the live gate, television, radio, and movie rights; Clay got 22.5 percent. The promotion was a financial flop. But in the ring a new era in boxing had begun.

Clay was in constant motion while Liston kept looking for an opening for his lethal right hand. At the start of the seventh round, Liston refused to leave his stool, claiming later that he could not move his left arm.

Alleged ties to organized-crime continued to follow Liston, and many people thought that the fight was fixed, since $50,000 of Clay's purse was paid by Intercontinental Promotions (ICP), in which Liston was a stockholder. Half of Liston's shares in ICP were held in Sam Margolis' name, a known friend of "Blinky" Palermo's. As a result, the sports press made the assumption that Liston owed money to Palermo.

The second fight on May 25, 1965, in Lewiston, Maine, between Liston and Muhammad Ali (Clay changed his name a day after their first fight), was even more controversial than the first one. Coming just three months after Malcolm X's assassination and two months after Ali's failure to pass an Army preinduction mental examination, the fight was over in one minute, fifty-two seconds of the first round. There was even a mixup over the exact time the fight ended.

Ali nailed Liston with what ringsiders say was a phantom right hand and Liston hit the canvas at 1:42. But referee Jersey Joe Walcott somehow miscounted. At one point, *Ring* magazine publisher Nat Fleischer shouted to Walcott, "Joe, the fight is over!" Walcott finally stopped the bout two minutes and twelve seconds into the round.

Liston was never the same again. In 1969, he was knocked out by Leotis Martin in the ninth round of a NABF title fight. A year later he was dead of a drug overdose in Las Vegas.

Muhammad Ali (formerly Cassius Marcellus Clay, Jr.): When young Cassius Clay, Jr., decided to become a boxer he could not have picked a more difficult period to begin. Born during World War II on January 17, 1942, in Louisville, Kentucky, he had his first boxing lessons in the mid-fifties. At first, the 4-foot, 87-pound novice only wanted to learn to fight in order to keep older and bigger boys from taking his bicycle. His teacher was an Irish-American cop named Joe Martin.

In 1953, nineteen fighters died as the result of injuries suffered in the ring. Consequently, the January 1955 issue of *Ebony* magazine headlined an article titled "Should Boxing Be Abolished?" In addition, boxers continued to find themselves in dire financial straits. (Sam Langford, named one of the ten greatest athletes of the first half-century, died penniless in a Boston nursing home on January 12, 1956.) Why, then, did a young man like Cassius Clay, who was from a comfortable home with a solid nuclear family, choose professional boxing as a career? *Because he was good; in fact, he was very good.*

In 1958, when he was only sixteen, Clay won his hometown's Golden Gloves light heavyweight title and reached the quarter finals of the Golden Gloves Tournament of Champions in Chicago. He stood 6 feet tall and weighed 170 pounds. While in Chicago he heard for the first time about Elijah Muhammad, leader of the Black Nation of Islam.

The year 1960 was an incredible one for Clay. He was graduated from Louisville's Central High School number 376 in a class of 391. In the ring that year he won his sixth Kentucky Golden Gloves title; the Tournament of Champions in Chicago; the National Golden Gloves; the AAU title; and an Olympic Gold Medal—all as a light heavyweight. The year before, he had won the National Golden Gloves and the AAU titles. But he lost in a bid for the United States Pan-American Games Boxing Team.

By the time of the 1960 Olympics in Rome, Clay had already earned a deserved reputation as a loudmouthed, brash, and cocky fighter. He was, in actuality, the most publicly vocal black athlete since Jack Johnson. Neither white nor black Americans knew what to make of him. After defeating Zbiegniew Pietrzykowski in the Olympic finals for his fortieth consecutive win, he was asked what he wanted next. "I want money, plenty of it!"[32]

Clay, during his stay in Rome, refused to back down from giving his opinion on weighty issues. In answer to a Soviet reporter's question about the condition of blacks in America, he shot back: "To me, the USA is still the best country in the world, counting yours."[33] But when he returned to Louisville as an Olympic champion he realized that life for him had not changed because of his new fame. "With my gold medal actually hanging around my neck, I couldn't get a cheeseburger served

to me in a downtown Louisville restaurant."[34] Clay later threw his Olympic Gold Medal into the Ohio River, in a gesture of racial defiance of American hypocrisy.

As colorful and controversial as he was, a respected group of white Louisville businessmen with an intent to capitalize on Clay's notoriety, agreed to form a syndicate to sponsor their newly acknowledged hometown hero. The syndicate members were Archibald M. Foster, Patrick Calhoun, Jr., Gordon Davidson, William S. Cutchins, J.D. Stetson Coleman, William Faversham, Jr., James R. Todd, Vertner D. Smith, Sr., George W. Norton IV, William Lee Lyons Brown, E. Gary Sutcliffe, and Robert W. Bingham. The syndicate agreement was arranged by a black lawyer, Alberta Jones, who received $2,500 for her services and was later fired. (Clay had also received management offers from Archie Moore, Rocky Marciano, and Cus D'Amato.)

In return for 50 percent of Clay's earnings in and out of the ring, the syndicate gave him a $10,000 bonus to sign, an $80,000 guarantee over the first two years, $6,000 for the next four years, and all training expenses. The agreement was to last six years, from 1960 to 1966.

Leaving behind an amateur record of 161–6, Clay fought his first professional fight at Freedom Hall in Louisville on October 29, 1960. He collected $2,000 for a six-round decision over Tunney Hunsaker. Immediately after his win, he signed Angelo Dundee as his trainer for $125 per week.

Clay began calling the round in which his opponents would fall, beginning with Alex Miteff on October 7, 1961. He claimed he patterned his showmanship after the wrestler "Gorgeous" George Wagner. By now known by an assortment of nick-names—the Louisville Lip, Cash the Brash, Gaseous Cassius, Mighty Mouth, Clap Trap Clay, and Kentucky Rooster—he correctly named the knockout round in thirteen of seventeen fights. "Humble people I've found don't get very far. If you're a nice guy people trample on you."[35]

After defeating forty-nine-year-old Archie Moore on November 15, 1962, Clay set his sights on the recently crowned heavyweight champion, Charles "Sonny" Liston. Between the Moore and Liston bouts, his boxing skills were questioned and his verbal pronouncements debated. On June 18, 1963, the Englishman Henry Cooper knocked him down in their bout, leading experts to believe he could not take a punch. A month later, he made a phonograph record, "I Am The Greatest." *Ebony* magazine ran an editorial that focused on his value and worth to the black community.

During this period Clay became more and more attracted to Islam. He made frequent trips to Chicago and Detroit to meet with Malcolm X and Elijah Muhammad. A day after winning the world heavyweight title for the first time, he changed his name to Muhammad Ali, which means "worthy of all praise." While the black sports press tolerated this conversion, only a few white sports figures—Howard Cosell, Bud Collins, and Robert Lipsyte, among others—continued to support him.

Ali disdained his appellation as a "Black Muslim." "That is a word made up by the white press. I am a black man who has adopted Islam...I love to be black, and I love to be with my people..."[36]

Ali's spiritual mentor, Malcolm X, had been forthright about his young disciple. "Clay....is the finest Negro athlete I have ever known, the man who will mean more to his people than Jackie Robinson was, because Robinson is the white man's hero. But Cassius is the black man's hero. Do you know why? Because the white press wanted him to lose...because he is a Muslim. You noticed nobody cares about the religion of other athletes. But their prejudice against Clay blinded them to his ability."[37]

On February 26, 1964, Ali made a simple announcement. "I believe in the religion of Islam. I believe in Allah and peace...I'm not a Christian anymore."[38] His troubles were just beginning.

Ali rolled over his opponents, taunting them in the ring. He railed at Liston in Maine during their second bout, "Get up and fight, you bum!" The state of Massachusetts and the WBA refused to sanction this fight. He married Sonji Roi on August 14, 1964, and divorced her in January 1966, claiming she would not agree to Muslim customs.

In February 1966, Ali was reclassified 1-A by the Selective Service. He immediately issued his negative response in the form of a poem:

"Keep asking me, no matter how long
On the war in Viet Nam, I sing this song
I ain't got no quarrel with the Viet Cong."

Nearly three hundred theaters cancelled contracts for Ali's bout with Ernie Terrell. Getting no response from American promoters, Ali fought in Europe, where he was served with a notice for failing to pay alimony. His syndicate contract with the Louisville businessmen expired prematurely in October of 1963.

Ali finally secured Houston, Texas, as the site for his fifteen-round bout with Terrell on February 6, 1967. Before the fight, Terrell had referred to Ali as Cassius Clay. In the ring Ali called Terrell "a dog" and kept asking him, "What's my name?" The bout set an indoor attendance record of 37,321. Ali stated afterwards: "I am an astronaut of boxing. Joe Louis and Dempsey were just jet pilots. I'm in a world of my own."[39]

Ali was ordered to report to the Army induction center in Houston on April 28. "For months I've drilled myself for this moment,"[40] he said later, "but I still feel nervous. I hope no one notices my shoulders tremble." Three times Ali refused the call for "Cassius Clay" to step forward and be inducted into the United States Army. The voice of the induction officer noticeably wavered.

After signing an official document stating his refusal on religious grounds Ali walked out of the building to a chorus of cheers from supporters and students from Texas Southern University. Eight days before his induction procedure, he had declared: "I am not going ten thousand miles from here to help murder and kill and burn poor people simply to help continue the domination of white slave masters over the darker people."[41] Without waiting for an indictment, the WBA and the NYSAC stripped Ali of his title.

Ten days later, on May 8, a federal grand jury indicted Ali for failing to submit to the draft. He confided to Sugar Ray Robinson, "I'm afraid, Ray. I'm real afraid."[42] Robinson recalled that "That night...His eyes were glistening with tears—tears of torment, tears of indecision."[43] On the phone with his mother the day before, Ali

was tearfully told, "G.G. [his mother's nickname for him], do the right thing...take the step."[44]

On June 19 and 20, Judge Joe Ingram of the United States District Court for the Southern District of Texas tried the Ali case and sentenced him to five years in jail and a $10,000 fine. Ali posted bail and was released.

Some prominent black athletes publicly came to Ali's support; Lew Alcindor, the UCLA basketball player; Bill Russell, player/coach of the Boston Celtics; Sid Williams and Walter Beach of the Cleveland Browns; Curtis McClinton of the Kansas City Chiefs; Bobby Mitchell and Jim Shorter of the Washington Redskins; Willie Davis of the Green Bay Packers; and Gale Sayers of the Chicago Bears. The traditional black civil rights leaders, however, were very wary about publicly supporting Ali.

With the assistance of lawyer Hayden Covington, Ali appealed his case first to the Fifth Circuit Court of Appeals and then to the United States Supreme Court. (The Fifth Circuit Court upheld the District Court verdict). Ironically, Covington's sister was married to General Lewis Hershey, the Director of the Selective Service System.

For two years thereafter, boxing was in a state of limbo. Ali, twenty-five years old at the time of his induction refusal, spent twenty-nine months in exile. With the war in Vietnam at its peak, he was sought as an antiwar speaker. "My main livelihood is coming from my appearances at colleges, black and white...support for me is high."[45]

On June 28, 1970, the United States Supreme Court, in an 8–0 decision, declared Ali free because of a technical error by the Justice Department. At first, Justice William Brennan was the only one of the Supreme Court's Justices willing to hear the Ali appeal—known as *Clay v. United States.* His case had come before the Court two terms before, but the Court had refused to hear it. But when the Court heard that the FBI had illegally tapped Ali's phone, they changed their minds.

The original vote (with the black Justice Thurgood Marshall abstaining because he had been the federal government's Solicitor General when the case began), was 5–3 against Ali. But Justice John Harlan's clerk convinced him that Ali was genuine in his beliefs and "For all practical purposes, Ali was opposed to all wars."[46]

Subsequently, an additional vote was taken and the Court deadlocked 4 to 4. Justice Potter Stewart proposed that the Court simply set Ali free because of the wiretap. Though Ali thanked Allah and the Court for "recognizing the sincerity of the religious teaching that I've accepted"[47] in the words of Woodward and Armstrong, "He did not know how close he had come to going to jail."[48]

While most black Americans and anti-war protesters were jubilant over Ali's release, veterans groups and President Richard M. Nixon were incensed. "...you know Cassius Clay is Nixon's pet peeve"[49] Jackie Robinson told Nelson Rockefeller. "Nixon hates his guts."

Now relicensed, Ali trained in Miami before leaving for an exhibition at Morehouse College and a bout with Jerry Quarry in Atlanta. Before leaving Miami he received two packages in the mail: one contained a decapitated black chihuahua dog and the other a hanged doll with a note

saying: "To Cassius Clay, From Georgia." Ali meant to use this fight and a win over Oscar Bonavena as tune-ups for Joe Frazier, the new WBA titleholder.

The Ali-Frazier bout on March 8, 1971, at the new Madison Square Garden became known as "The Fight." Frazier had come up the hard way, winning both the NYSAC and WBA titles. (In January 1970, three men laid claim to a heavyweight title: Jimmy Ellis, WBA; Frazier, NYSAC; and Ali, recently deposed as WBC champion.) Over 20,000 fans in Madison Square Garden and 1.3 million on closed-circuit television saw Frazier defeat Ali in fifteen of the toughest rounds in memory. The fight truly lived up to its billing.

Ali was his old self again. In answer to Frazier's warning that he would come out "smokin'," Ali said, "Well, smokin's bad for the lungs, gives you cancer... Maybe this will shock and amaze ya, but I'm gonna retire that Joe Frazier."[50] When the fight ended, both combatants had to go to the hospital. Frazier would not fight for the next ten months.

After winning the NABF title in 1971, Ali lost to Ken Norton on March 31, 1973. Norton used hypnosis as part of his training for this bout, and he fractured Ali's jaw in the first round. Ali regained the NBAF title from Norton on September 10, 1973, and prepared to defend it against Frazier on January 28, 1974. (George Foreman held the world title as a result of a win against Frazier on January 22, 1973.) Ali defeated Frazier in twelve rounds at Madison Square Garden in a fight witnessed by a 20,746 live gate and a closed-circuit audience of 1.1 million. The total gross receipts were roughly $25 million.

Ali then signed to meet George Foreman for the world title on October 30, 1974, in Kinshasa, Zaire—a bout billed as "The Rumble in the Jungle." Foreman, viewed as the strongest heavyweight since Liston, fell in the eighth round before 62,000 screaming Zaireans. Ali, then age thirty-two, became the second man to regain the heavyweight title. It was also the first heavyweight title fight on the African continent. Don King, a black promoter and an ex-felon, had arranged this $10 million fight with Zaire's President Mobutu.

Ali used what he called his "rope-a-dope" technique to tire out Foreman. He simply leaned back against the ropes and protected his head, allowing the much stronger Foreman to punch and, thereby, burn himself out. Foreman, however, said he followed the instructions of his trainer, Dick Saddler, who advised him to "get it over with quickly."

Ali had his third and final meeting with Frazier on September 30, 1975, in Manila, the Philippines. Dubbed "The Thrilla in Manila" and "Super Fight III," it was hailed by many who saw it as the greatest fight in the history of the sport. The two fighters went at it non-stop for fourteen rounds. With his boxer's body bruised and battered, trainer Eddie Futch refused to let Frazier come out for round 15. He cut Frazier's gloves off to end the fight. "Sit down, son. It's all over," Futch said. "No one will ever forget what you did here today."[51] Ali stated it was "...The hardest fight I've ever had in my life—the deadliest and the most vicious...me and Joe Frazier had rumbled together this night for the last time. And it's over. The dinosaurs met for the last time..."[52] In the postbout press conference it was Frazier who said, "I hit

him with punches that would bring down walls." Ali spoke of a feeling like being close to death.[53] Frazier was magnanimous in defeat. Brotherly, he said to Ali, "You one bad nigger. We both bad niggers. We don't do no crawlin'."[54]

At age thirty-six, Ali lost his world title to Leon Spinks on February 15, 1978, in a fifteen-round split decision in Las Vegas. Though undertrained and overweight, Ali roared, quoting General Douglas MacArthur, "I shall return." And return he did. On September 15, 1978, before the largest-ever indoor boxing audience, 63,350 at the New Orleans Superdome, he regained the WBA version of his title—becoming the first man to win the heavyweight title three times. Spinks, who held the title only seven months, lost a unanimous fifteen-round decision.

Ali retired for the second time (the first time was in early 1970) and then came back to lose to WBC champion Larry Holmes, on October 2, 1980. Holmes "carried" Ali through eleven rounds at Caesar's Palace in Las Vegas. Ali was almost thirty-nine years old.

This extraordinary athlete retired and is now a Muslim minister. No one had a greater influence over the sport since Joe Louis. Ironically, Ali's rise to prominence came amid the black social revolution of the 1960s and America's distress over the Vietnam war. He was a hero to thousands of young people the world over but a pariah and an embarrassment to the American government. In retrospect, one must agree with Ali's self-assessment: he was The Greatest.

Ernie Terrell: He was one of the tallest heavyweights since Primo Carnera, standing 6-feet 6-inches and 200 pounds. He was born on April 4, 1939, in Chicago, and after turning professional in 1957, fought there almost exclusively until 1962. He won the vacant WBA title over Eddie Machen on March 5, 1965, in Chicago. He then lost in a bid for the world title to Muhammad Ali on February 6, 1967, in fifteen rounds. In the WBA Elimination Tournament in 1967, he lost in twelve rounds to Thad Spencer. He retired four months later.

Terrell's bout with Ali was marked by much name calling. Terrell referred to Ali in the prefight buildup as Cassius Clay, and experts believed Ali deliberately prolonged this fight to punish Terrell. (*See* MUHAMMAD ALI.) After a two-year retirement, Terrell returned to the ring and eventually lost a twelve-rounder to Chuck Wepner on June 23, 1973, for the United States heavyweight title. He retired for good with a 46–9 professional record.

Jimmy Ellis: This Louisville, Kentucky, native's primary claim to fame at the beginning of his professional career was as Muhammad Ali's sparring partner. However, Ellis, who was born on February 24, 1940, soon earned the right through the WBA Elimination Tournament to fight Jerry Quarry for that group's vacant title. He won in fifteen rounds in Oakland, California.

The Elimination Tournament had been held to name a successor to Ali's vacated title. The boxers in the tournament included Floyd Patterson, Oscar Bonavena, Jerry Quarry, Karl Mildenberger, Ernie Terrell, Thad Spencer, Jimmy Ellis, and Joe Frazier. (Frazier later refused to join the group.)

After defeating Floyd Patterson in fifteen rounds in his first title defense, Ellis

lost to Joe Frazier in a bid for the vacant world title on February 16, 1970. Ellis, who stood 6-feet 1-inch andd weighed 205 pounds, was managed by Angelo Dundee. This clever fighter with a solid left jab retired in 1975 after losses to Muhammad Ali, Ernie Shavers, and Joe Frazier (for the second time).

Joe Frazier: "Smokin' Joe" was born in Gullah country, in Beaufort, South Carolina, on January 12, 1944. He was unquestionably one of the hardest-working fighters in the history of the ring. If Ali's style was "hit and run," Frazier's could be classified as "hit, and hit again." He first fought professionally in Philadelphia after the winning an Olympic heavyweight Gold Medal in 1964.

Copying the syndicate formula used for Muhammad Ali, Frazier was also sponsored by a group of white businessmen. Known as Cloverlay, Inc., these investors capitalized their group at $250 per share. Their return was eventually a whopping 1,350 percent, or $3,350 per share. Frazier got to keep 50 percent of his purses while the other 50 percent was split between Cloverlay and his manager/trainer, Yancey Durham, 35 percent and 15 percent, respectively. They were encouraged to invest because Frazier had won thirty-eight of forty amateur bouts as well as the Golden Gloves title in 1962, 1963 and 1964.

Known as "Billy Boy" as a teenager, Frazier began boxing in a Police Athletic League gymnasium to lose weight. He developed his tremendous upper-body strength while working in a meat packing plant in Philadelphia. His first eleven fights were won by KOs, none of which lasted more than six rounds. After defeating

George Chuvalo on July 19, 1967, he refused to join the WBA Elimination Tournament that began less than a month later, on August 5. Instead, Frazier opted to pursue the vacant NYSAC title and won it by defeating Buster Mathis on March 4, 1968, in an eleventh-round knockout.

With Ali in exile, Frazier's path to the world title was easier. He won it against Jimmy Ellis, then the current WBA champion, on February 16, 1970, in a fifth-round KO. His first world-title defense was against the light heavyweight champion, Bob Foster, whom he overwhelmed in a second round knockout. That set the stage for his three meetings with Ali.

In one of the sport's epic battles, Frazier defeated Ali in the first of their three fights. (See Muhammad Ali.) Though he won this encounter over fifteen of the most outstanding rounds ever seen, he was so battered in his face, chest, and arms that he could not fight again for ten months. After two successful defenses, he lost his world title via a second-round KO to George Foreman. It was the most embarrassing loss of his career.

Frazier was a three to one favorite over Foreman, but the challenger knocked him down six times in less than six minutes. Using the same "go for broke" style as he employed against Ali, Frazier was never given a chance to even loosen up. Foreman waited for openings to deliver his lethal right hand and simply overpowered Frazier, whom he outweighed by sixteen pounds.

Frazier lost his next two battles with Ali, a twelve-rounder in New York for the NABF title on January 28, 1974, and a fourteenth-round TKO in Manila, The Philippines, on October 1, 1975. (See Muhammed Ali.) His second fight with Foreman was a nontitle affair on June 15, 1976, and he lost in a fifth-round KO. By then Foreman had lost his world title to Ali in Zaire.

Frazier finally retired in 1981 and devoted himself to the career of his son, Marvis, a promising young heavyweight. He was elected to Boxing's Hall of Fame in 1980. His short but brilliant career of 37 professional fights included 27 knockouts, 5 victories by decision, 1 draw, 1 loss by decision, and 3 losses by knockouts. He was one of the most popular fighters since World War II.

THE SEVENTIES

When the decade of the seventies began, it reminded boxing observers of the early fifties. The glamour division—the heavyweight class—was muddled, and three separate fighters claimed the title for three separate sanctioning bodies: Jimmy Ellis for the WBA; Joe Frazier for the NYSAC; and Muhammad Ali, as the deposed and exiled WBC champion.

Additional weight classes had been introduced to boxing during the previous fifteen years. The International Olympic Committee had inserted more weight classes in its program, and American television had encouraged more classes, as there would be more champions to promote. But even though boxing was now more accessible, black American champions continued to be concentrated in the higher-weight classes. In the seventies, there were no black American champions in the following divisions: flyweight, junior featherweight, featherweight, bantamweight, junior lightweight, lightweight, and junior welterweight.

There were other changes, as well. Joe Louis' image had become altered as a result of the black social revolution of the sixties. In his prime, he was the most well-known black man on earth. Unfortunately, for the first ten years following his retirement, he was seen as the victim of bad financial management and of his own spending habits. However, during the sixties, it became standard practice among a new, young, and iconoclastic generation of black historians to lump him among the "Uncle Toms" of the post-war period. Nevertheless, sentiment toward Louis had changed again by the mid-seventies. While he had continued to be a hero to black Americans thirty-five and over, those who had castigated him ten years before were now more realistic. Louis worked as a greeter at the Caesars' Palace Hotel and Casino in Las Vegas and his mental faculties were failing. In essence, he had white America tending to his needs in the end.

In the ring, black boxers finally began assuring their financial futures. Two in particular, Larry Holmes and Ray Leonard, would end their careers as the wealthiest of all black athletes. Black promoters like Don King and Butch Lewis competed against their white counterparts, (e.g., Bob Arum and Jerry Perenchio) to stage the most attractive bouts. Subsequently, for the first time in twenty years, stars in the lower-weight divisions outdrew the heavyweights.

Welterweights: 141–147 lbs.

Wilfredo Benitez: He was born in the Bronx, New York, on September 12, 1958, and was managed and taught by his father. This 5-feet 10-inches, 154-pound elusive and talented fighter is more closely identified with the Hispanic community than the black community. He fought nearly six years as a professional before his first loss—to Ray Leonard at Las Vegas on November 30, 1979, via a fifteenth-round TKO.

Benitez first attracted international notice when he won the World Junior Welterweight title in San Juan, Puerto Rico, on March 6, 1976, from Antonio Cervantes. Three years later, he won the WBC welterweight title from Carlos Palomino in San Juan on January 14, 1979, in fifteen rounds. Benitez was very difficult to hit and a master of defense and counterpunching. After losing his welterweight title to Ray Leonard, he won the WBC Junior Middleweight title from Maurice Hope at Las Vegas on May 23, 1981, via a twelfth-round knockout. He lost this crown to Thomas Hearns on December 3, 1982, at New Orleans in fifteen rounds. Benitez was one of only a handful of fighters to win titles in three separate weight divisions.

"Sugar" Ray Charles Leonard: No black fighter was as carefully managed—financially and athletically—as Ray Leonard. Born on May 17, 1956, in Wilmington, North Carolina, this showstopper was named after the blind black singer. His father, Cicero, also a boxer, moved his family to Washington, D.C., in 1960. Young Ray sang in his church's choir and learned to box at the Palmer Park Recreation Center. His lightning quick hands and blazing foot speed helped him to earn a National Golden Gloves 132-pound title in 1972. After winning an Olympic Gold Medal in the 1976 Montreal Games, Leonard became an instant hero and was acclaimed as a "can't miss" future titleholder. Sarge Johnson, the assistant United States Olympic boxing coach, said, "Pound for pound, Leonard is the finest fighter I've seen in thirty years of working with the amateurs."[55] Head Boxing Coach Pat Nappi added, "Sugar Ray is the best amateur I've ever seen, and that includes Muhammad Ali."[56]

Leonard had originally planned to give up boxing after the Olympics to attend college. Less than a week after his win in Montreal, he was sued by his local county officials because the mother of his son, Ray Junior, had filed for welfare payments. He then changed his mind about pursuing a professional boxing career. Like Ali and Frazier before him, he used a syndicate of businessmen to initially back him. Twenty-four sponsors put up $21,000, as Leonard promised repayment within four years at 8 percent interest. He paid them back after his first professional fight. His earnings from this inaugural bout were a record $38,000, which stood until Ed "Too Tall" Jones left the Dallas Cowboys football team to try his hand in the ring. (Jones collected $70,000 for his first professional fight.) With the help of his lawyer, Mike Trainer, he formed Sugar Ray Leonard Enterprises and in 1977 he negotiated a six-fight, $320,000 package deal with ABC Television. In 1979, ABC upped the ante to $1 million for five fights.

Trained by Angelo Dundee and his good friend Janks Morton, Leonard won the NABF title from Pete Ranzany at Las Vegas on August 12, 1979. Three months later he acquired the WBC title via a fifteenth-round knockout of Wilfredo Benitez at Las Vegas on November 30. A showman and a crowd pleaser, Leonard's popularity was nearly unbounded.

Leonard's idolatry from white boxing fans caused slight resentment in the black community. While not oblivious to his standing in Black America, he was forthright with an explanation: "Blacks criticize me because I'm so popular with whites."[57] Part of black America's problem with Leonard was that he avoided getting vocally involved in any racial issues. Leonard had earned more than $3 million in his first three years as a professional and many believed the money had simply gone to his head.

In the ring, he was remembered for his championship fights against Benitez, Roberto Duran, and Thomas "Hit Man" Hearns. After winning the WBC title from Benitez on national television, he lost it in fifteen rounds to Duran in Montreal on June 20, 1980. He had incensed his Panamanian opponent by saying "I'll kill you"[58] before their fight. Their combined ring records listed 98 wins and 1 loss. The fight was so close that the judges' score cards read 148–147, 146–144, and 145–144.

Before their return bout on November 25 of that year, Leonard sought to rile his Latin adversary by incessantly talking about what strategy he would pursue during the fight, just as Ali had tried to do against Sonny Liston. Leonard regained the World title when Duran refused to continue fighting during the eighth round. Duran, baffled by Leonard's ability to hit and run, literally gave up, saying, *"No mas, no mas"* (Spanish for "no more, no more"). From his two bouts with Duran, Leonard had grossed more than $16 million, more than the combined career winnings of Joe Louis, Sugar Ray Robinson, Floyd Patterson, and Archie Moore.

Leonard then stepped up one weight class and captured the world junior middleweight crown from Ayub Kalule in Houston on June 25, 1981, in a ninth-round KO. He followed this with a spectacular fourteenth-round TKO of Thomas Hearns on September 16, 1981, unifying both the WBA and WBC welterweight titles.

Following his bout with Hearns, Leonard underwent surgery for a detached retina and retired after one last bout in 1984 to pursue a career as a television boxing commentator for HBO. Along with Muhammad Ali, he was the most charismatic boxer of the seventies and eighties.

Light Heavyweights: 161–175 lbs.

Marvin Johnson: Like so many before him, Johnson had a sensational amateur career. In 1972, he won the National Golden Gloves light heavyweight title and an Olympic Bronze Medal as a middleweight. Born on April 12, 1954, in Indianapolis, Indiana, the left-handed Johnson turned professional in 1973 and won eleven of his first twelve bouts by knockouts.

In 1977, after winning the vacant NABF title by defeating Matthew Saad Muhammad (formerly Matthew Franklin), Johnson won the WBC version of the title from Mate Parlov of Yugoslavia on December 2, 1978, via a tenth-round knockout. After losing his WBC title to Muhammad on April 22, 1979, via an eighth-round knockout, he won the WBA version from Victor Galindez in New Orleans on November 30, 1979, in an elev-

enth-round KO. Four months later he lost his WBA title to Eddie Mustfa Muhammad (formerly Eddie Dee Gregory) in Knoxville, Tennessee, via an eleventh-round knockout. Though he held both versions of the title, he kept neither for more than four months.

Matthew Saad Muhammad (formerly Matthew Franklin): Muhammad did not start out as well as his contemporaries. He was born Matthew Franklin on August 5, 1954, in Philadelphia, Pennsylvania. He was also known as Maxwell Antonio Loach. His coversion to Islam produced his current name. He suffered losses in his first and third years as a professional and a draw in his second year, but managed to win the vacant NABF title over Marvin Johnson on July 26, 1977, in a twelfth-round KO.

Almost two years later, he defeated Johnson again for the WBC version of the title. He then blossomed as a light heavyweight, successfully defending the title eight times before losing it to Dwight Muhammad Qawi (Dwight Braxton). Qawi defeated him again in a rematch for the WBC title on August 7, 1982, in Philadelphia, via a sixth-round KO.

Heavyweights: 191 lbs. and Above

George Foreman: He came from humble beginnings, and was one of the most physically imposing boxers ever seen in the ring. He was born on January 22, 1948, in Marshall, Texas, and grew to a height of 6-feet 3-inches and weighed 220 pounds. Foreman had a rough childhood in the streets of Houston, where he snatched purses and engaged in petty larcenies. He publicly claims that he was saved by the Job Corps and football player Jim Brown.

Those who knew Foreman in Houston understood when he later declared, "I got out of that (purse snatchings) right quick because I never wanted to hurt anybody...sometimes, I would like to find those people I did that to and give them some money."[59] "We'd end up dropping the purse when a woman would cry: 'Lord Jesus, don't take my money.' It hurt us so we would leave the purse."[60] But he still angered many black Americans by waving a small American flag at the 1968 Summer Olympics, after winning the Heavyweight Gold Medal.

Foreman compiled an impressive knockout record—42 in 47 professional fights—a feat that even Joe Louis could not match. On January 22, 1973, he became only the second former Olympic Heavyweight Gold Medalist to win the World title, by defeating Joe Frazier in Kingston, Jamaica, in a second-round knockout. Before this fight, Foreman had been extended to ten rounds only three times.

Foreman defended his title against José Roman and Ken Norton in a combined total of three rounds for both bouts. The Norton victory enabled him to meet Muhammad Ali, who had defeated Joe Frazier two months earlier. Foreman entered the Ali fight in financial trouble and hired President John F. Kennedy's brother-in-law, Sargent Shriver, to assist him.

Foreman was a three to one favorite over Ali, the NABF titleholder, in their bout in Kinshasa, Zaire, on October 30, 1974. In this first-ever heavyweight title fight in Africa, Foreman tired badly after seven rounds and was floored by Ali in the eighth. (*See*

Muhammad Ali.) Foreman's feared right hand, which he called his "anywhere punch," never landed on ali's head. The "Rumble In The Jungle," as this bout was known, attracted 62,000 fans.

Though he never again fought for a title, Foreman will be remembered for his knockout record. He is now a minister.

Leon Spinks: Spinks was the lightest heavyweight champion since Jimmy Ellis. Standing 6-feet 1-inch and weighing 205 pounds. Born on July 11, 1953 in St. Louis, Missouri, this ex-Marine won the light heavyweight gold medal at the 1976 Montreal Olympic Games. His brother, Michael, won the Olympic middleweight gold medal.

In Spinks' second year as a professional and in only his eighth fight, he surprised Muhammad Ali in Las Vegas on February 15, 1978, winning the world title in fifteen rounds. Exactly seven months later, he lost it to Ali in New Orleans in fifteen rounds. After losing to Larry Holmes in Detroit for the WBC title on June 12, 1981, he won the vacant NABF Cruiserweight (190 lbs.) title over Jesse Burnett in McAfee, New Jersey, on October 31, 1982, in twelve rounds.

Kenneth Howard Norton: Like Leon Spinks, Norton was an ex-Marine who started his professional career later than most—at age twenty-four. He was born on August 9, 1943, in Jacksonville, Illinois, and grew to 6-feet 3-inches and weighed 220 pounds. So well proportioned was his physique that he could have had a career as a model, which he sometimes tried.

For the first six years of his career, he never fought outside of Southern California.

He then arranged a bout with Muhammad Ali for the NABF title in San Diego, and won in twelve rounds. He underwent hypnosis before this bout in an attempt to correct some bad boxing habits, and broke Ali's jaw in the first round. After losing the NABF title to Ali, six months later, he lost to George Foreman for the World title in a second-round knockout in Caracas, Venezuela, on March 26, 1974. Following another loss to Ali for the World title on September 28, 1976, in New York City in fifteen rounds, he was proclaimed the WBC champion two years later.

Norton became the WBC champion because Leon Spinks, the world champpion, refused to defend the WBC portion of the title against an assigned challenger. Norton then lost his WBC crown to Larry Holmes in Las Vegas on June 9, 1978, in fifteen rounds. He retired to a career in movies and sports management, following a first-round KO by Gerry Cooney on May 11, 1981, in New York City.

Larry Holmes: Without a doubt, Holmes has been the most underrated and under-publicized heavyweight champion in history. It was Holmes' (or any heavy-weight's) misfortune to have come to prominence when Muhammad Ali and welterweight Sugar Ray Leonard were garnering most of the headlines. Born on November 3, 1949, in Cuthberth, Georgia, this 6-foot 3-inch, 220-pound heavyweight turned professional at age twenty-four.

Following a twelve-round win over Earnie Shavers in 1978, Holmes won the WBC title from Ken Norton on June 9 of that year. After seven successful WBC defenses he unified the vacant World title by defeat-ing Muhammad Ali on October 2, 1980, in an eleventh-round knockout at Las Vegas. Ali was thirty-eight years old and only a shadow of his former self, clearly no match for Holmes.

Although Holmes ducked no fighters, his knockout record was generally unappreciated. As of the end of 1984, he had 33 KOs in 46 bouts. He has a powerful left jab that keeps his opponents at bay. In late 1983, he helped in the organization of the International Boxing Federation (IBF), which is run by Bob Lee, a black former Commissioner for the New Jersey State Boxing Commission. His last official defense as WBC champion was against Marvis Frazier, son of former world champion Joe Frazier.

John Tate: Tate was big for a modern heavyweight, 6-foot 4-inches and 240 pounds He was born in Marion City, Arkansas, on January 29, 1955, and turned professional at age twenty-two. After only three years of professional fighting, he defeated the South African Gerrie Coetzee on October 20, 1979, in Pretoria, South Africa, for the vacant WBA title. Five months later, he lost it to Mike Weaver in a fifteen-round KO on March 31, 1980, in Knoxville, Tennessee.

THE EIGHTIES

The end of the seventies saw Larry Holmes defeat Muhammad Ali on October 2, 1980. Though Ali fought and lost to Trevor Berbick over a year later, the world knew he was finished. Professional boxing in the eighties was characterized by the creation of more weight classes and a material increase in the size of purses. Gone was much of the racial turmoil that had distinguished the beginning of the previous decade, and there were no relevant Supreme Court cases looming or waiting to be heard. There were no marches in the streets by black students and the Vietnam war had been over for half a decade. The U.S.-led boycott of the 1980 Moscow Summer Olympics hardly made a difference in boxing. There were so many international amateur competitions for aspiring American fighters that, despite the forfeiture of a possible medal, their talent could still be showcased.

The influence of organized crime was hinted at only to the extent that the gambling palaces in Las Vegas went out of their way to stage the most attractive bouts. Two of the most successful and well-known promoters were black—Don King and Butch Lewis. Surprisingly, the biggest gate attraction was a welterweight, not a heavyweight. That had not been the case since Joe Louis retired and Sugar Ray Robinson, a middleweight, claimed the fight world's adulation.

Though 1980 began with black World champions in the heavyweight, light heavyweight, and welterweight divisions, within four years other black champions in six additional weight classes would join them.

Bantamweights: 113–118 lbs.

Jeff Chandler: He was the first black American bantamweight champion since Harold Dade won the title in 1947. Born on September 3, 1956, in Philadelphia, Pennsylvania, this 5-foot 7-inch, 120-pounder was undefeated as a professional for seven years. He won the WBA World title from Julian Solis on November 14, 1980, and, after nine successful defenses, he lost it to

Richard Sandoval via a fifteenth-round knockout on April 7, 1984.

Junior Featherweights: 119–122 lbs.

Leo Randolph: Born on February 27, 1958, in Tacoma, Washington, Randolph went on to win an Olympic Gold Medal as a flyweight in 1976. Randolph, 5-feet 5-inches and 122 pounds, had a very short career—19 bouts in three years. He won the WBA title from Ricardo Cardona in a fifteenth-round KO on May 4, 1980. He lost it three months later to Sergio Palma by a KO in the fifth round.

Junior Lightweights: 127–130 lbs.

Roger Lee Mayweather: He won the WBC title on January 19, 1983, in an eighth-round KO over Samuel Serrano in San Juan, Puerto Rico. It was only his fifteenth professional fight. After two defenses, he lost his title to Rocky Lockridge in a stunning first round KO. Mayweather was born on April 24, 1961, in Grand Rapids, Michigan.

Ricky "Rocky" Lockridge: He took longer to become a contender than Mayweather. After winning the New Jersey and USBA titles, he met Eusebio Pedroza for the WBA title and lost in fifteen rounds on October 4, 1980. Ten months after losing a second WBA title bout to Pedroza in fifteen rounds, he defeated Mayweather for the WBC title on February 26, 1984, in a first-round knockout.

Lightweights: 131–135 lbs.

James Hilmer Kenty: Within three years of his professional debut, Kenty won the WBC title from Ernesto Espana in Detroit,

Michigan, on March 2, 1980, by a ninth-round knockout. Born July 30, 1955, and managed by the shrewd Emanuel Steward, Kenty defended his title three times before falling to Sean O'Grady, in fifteen rounds on April 12, 1981. He has had only two losses in eight years.

Junior Welterweights: 136–140 lbs.

This weight class has been one of the best for black Americans in the eighties. Few experts expected this much success.

Saoul Mamby: Mamby was born on June 4, 1947, in the Bronx, New York, and bar mitzvahed into the Jewish faith at age thirteen. He had been fighting professionally for nine years before he lost his first chance at the WBC title in 1977. He finally won it two and a half years later against Sang-Hyun Kim of Korea on February 23, 1980, by a fourteenth-round KO. He lost it to Leroy Haley in 1982. He was unsuccessful at regaining it from Haley in 1983. He also lost a second try at regaining the title from Bill Costello in 1984, in a twelve-round decision.

Aaron Pryor: It is astonishing that Pryor managed the self-discipline to fight at all. Born on October 20, 1955, in Cincinnati, Ohio, he stated, "I was a kid nobody paid any attention to. Some nights I just said to hell with it and slept in a doorway."[61]

Though Pryor won the WBA title from Antonio Cervantes in Cincinnati, by a fourth-round KO in 1980, he is best known for his two bouts with the Nicaraguan, Alexis Arguello. Both wins were knockouts, the first in the round fourteen and the second in round ten. Pryor's style was nonstop hitting, and reminded observers of a smaller Joe Frazier. He abdicated his WBA title after the second Arguello fight, but has been recognized as IBF champion since. He has earned over $4 million in his undefeated career.

Leroy Haley: He was one of the least-known champions. Fighting almost exclusively out of Las Vegas, this 5-foot 6-3/4-inch, 140-pound native of Garland County, Arkansas, won the WBC title from Saoul Mamby on June 26, 1982, in fifteen rounds. He lost it to Bruce Curry less than a year later.

Bruce Curry: The brother of welterweight Donald Curry, Bruce was born March 29, 1956, in Marlin, Texas. After winning the NABF title, he won the WBC title from Leroy Haley on May 20, 1983, in twelve rounds. He lost it to Bill Costello by a tenth-round knockout in 1984.

John T. "Bump City" Bumphus: This stringbean of a fighter had an enviable amateur career—winning the 1977 AAU featherweight title, the 1979 Golden Gloves lightweight title, and the 1980 National AAU light welterweight title. In his fifth year as a professional, he won the vacant WBA title from Lorenzo Garcia in fifteen rounds, on January 22, 1984. He lost it to Gene Hatcher five months later by an eleventh-round knockout.

William Donald "Bill" Costello: After five years as a professional, Costello defeated Bruce Curry for the WBC title on January 29, 1984, at Beaumont, Texas, by a tenth-round KO. He was undefeated as of the end of 1984. He was born in Kingston, New York, on April 10, 1956.

Welterweights: 141–147 lbs.

Ray Charles "Sugar Ray" Leonard:
(*See* 1970s, Welterweights.)

Thomas "Hit Man" Hearns: Few fighters in the late seventies or eighties have been as exciting as Hearns. Standing 6-foot 1-inch and weighing 145 pounds, Hearns has one of the most feared right hands in the history of the division. His first seventeen bouts were won by KOs, as were thirty of his first thirty-two. Managed by Emanuel Steward, Hearns had trouble booking fights, such was his reputation.

Born on October 18, 1958, in Memphis, Tennessee, Hearns moved to Detroit where he won the WBA title from Pipino Cuevas on August 2, 1980, in a second round knockout. In one of the most exciting title bouts of the eighties, he lost in a bid to unify the world title to Ray Leonard at Las Vegas on September 16, 1981, in a fourteenth-round TKO. Earlier in the fight Hearns had rocked Leonard with right hands, but Leonard recovered enough to stop the taller Hearns in the fourteenth.

Hearns also captured the WBC version of the junior middleweight title from Wilfredo Benitez at New Orleans on December 3, 1982, in fifteen rounds. He later stepped up one weight class because of a lack of competition. On June 15, 1984, he unified the world junior middleweight title by defeating WBA champion Roberto Duran, in a second-round knockout. He thus became one of the few fighters to lose in a chance for a world title in one division and later win a world title in a heavier weight class. Currently he is the WBC light heavyweight champion.

Donald "Cobra" Curry: Born September 7, 1961, at Fort Worth, Texas, this 5-foot 10-inch, 147 pounder won the 1979 National AAU title before turning professional. After winning the NABF and USBA titles, he won the vacant WBA version on February 13, 1983, by defeating Jun-Sok Hwang in fifteen rounds. The brother of Bruce Curry, Donald was, at the end of 1984, still the WBA champion and undefeated.

Milton "Iceman" McCrory: Along with Thomas Hearns, McCrory gave Detroit a powerful boxing twosome in the eighties. Managed by Emanuel Steward, McCrory won the vacant WBC title when he defeated Colin Jones on August 13, 1983, in twelve rounds. At the end of 1984, McCrory was still champion and undefeated in twenty-two fights.

Junior Middleweights: 148–154 lbs.

Ray Charles "Sugar Ray" Leonard:
(*See* 1970s, Welterweights.)

Davey Moore: Though another Davey Moore died as a result of ring injuries in 1963, this Davey Moore was born in the Bronx, New York, on June 9, 1959. He had two losses in sixteen fights by the end of 1984. In only his ninth professional fight, Moore won the WBA title from Tadashi Mihara in Tokyo, Japan on February 2, 1982, via a sixth-round knockout. He lost the title after three defenses to Roberto Duran on June 16, 1983, by an eighth-round KO.

Thomas "Hit Man" Hearns: (*See* 1980s, Welterweights.)

Mark Medal: Medal won the IBF title by defeating Earl Hargrove on March 11, 1984, in a fifth-round knockout.

Middleweights: 155–160 lbs.

"Marvelous" Marvin Hagler: Hagler is arguably the most well-known boxer in the world today. This left-hander, who was born on May 23, 1954, in Newark, New Jersey, was the 1973 National AAU middleweight champion. Now fighting out of Brockton, Massachusetts, he paid his ring dues before defeating Alan Minter for the World title on September 27, 1980, in London, England. It was his fifty-fourth professional fight. He had drawn with Vito Antuofermo for the world title ten months earlier in Las Vegas in fifteen rounds.

There were racial overtones to the Minter bout. During the preflight buildup, Minter was quoted as saying, "I don't intend losing my title to a black guy."[62] After Hagler's third-round knockout of Minter, fans threw bottles at the ring and the new champion needed a police escort to leave the stadium.

Hagler has a nonstop, aggressive style that reminds fans of Joe Frazier. His bald pate is now his trademark. He has never been knocked out in sixty-four fights, as of the end of the 1984, and he has had ten successful defenses of his title. Carlos Monzon holds the record of fourteen defenses for the middleweight division.

Light Heavyweights: 161–175 lbs.

Eddie Mustafa Muhammad (nee Eddie Dee Gregory):   He was born April 30, 1952, in Brooklyn, New York, and won the WBA title from Marvin Johnson on March 31, 1980, by an eleventh-round knockout. After two defenses he lost his title to Michael Spinks in fifteen rounds. His first chance to fight for the title came in a losing fifteen-round effort against Victor Galindez in 1977. He has never been knocked out in fifty bouts.

Michael Spinks: He is the brother of the former heavyweight champion Leon Spinks. Born July 13, 1956, in St. Louis, Missouri, he won an Olympic Gold Medal as a middleweight in 1976. In his fifth year as a professional, he won the WBA title from Eddie Mustafa Muhammad on July 18, 1981. On March 18, 1983, he unified the vacant world title by defeating Dwight Muhammad Qawi in fifteen rounds at Atlantic City. He is currently undefeated in twenty-five bouts, seventeen were won by knockouts.

Dwight Muhammad Qawi (formerly Dwight Braxton):   He did not impress his managers until his third year as a professional. Standing only 5-feet 6¾-inches and weighing 174 pounds, most experts thought he was too short for the likes of Michael Spinks and Eddie Muhammed. He won the WBC title from Matthew Saad Muhammad in Atlantic City, New Jersey, on December 19, 1981, via a tenth-round knockout. He lost his opportunity for the vacant world title against Michael Spinks, losing a fifteen round decision on March 18, 1983.

Heavyweights: 191 lbs. and Above

Micheal Dwayne Weaver: He was born on June 14, 1952, in Gatesville, Texas, and has had a very erratic career as a professional. But with the lack of a dominating talent in division during the early seventies, and with three separate sanctioning bodies, he was able to work his way through the ranks. After winning the California, the vacant NABF and USBA titles, he was knocked out by Larry Holmes as he challenged for the WBC title. Weaver managed to win the WBA title from John Tate at Knoxville, Tennessee, on March 31, 1980, in a fifteenth-round knockout.

Afterwards, he traveled to racially troubled Bophuthatswana, South Africa, to defeat Gerrie Coetzee and retain his WBA title. He later lost his crown to Michael Dokes in 1982, on a first-round knockout. His main vulnerability seemed to be a susceptability to a knockout punch. In thirty-eight total professional fights, Weaver has lost six by knockouts.

Micheal "Dynamite" Dokes: Born on August 10, 1958 in Akron, Ohio, Dokes stands 6-feet 3-inches and weighs 227 pounds. He turned professional at age eighteen and is managed by Carl King, the son of Don King. He did not lose a bout in his first seven years, and he won the WBA title from Mike Weaver on December 10, 1982, in a first-round knockout. He lost the title via a tenth-round knockout to Gerrie Coetzee, on September 23, 1983. It was his only loss in thirty bouts.

Tim "Terrible Tim" Witherspoon: Born December 27, 1957, in Philadelphia, Pennsylvania, Witherspoon was given a WBC title bout with Larry Holmes on May 20, 1983. He lost in twelve rounds, but when Holmes vacated his title Witherspoon won it with a twelve-round victory over Greg Page on March 9, 1984. Five months later, he lost the WBC title to Pinklon Thomas in twelve rounds.

Pinklon "Pinky" Thomas, Jr: He was born in Pontiac, Michigan, on February 10, 1958, and was a drug addict at age thirteen. Though he dropped out of school in the tenth grade, this 6-foot 3-inch, 216-pound heavyweight returned to get his G.E.D. Diploma. Training in Joe Frazier's gymnasium in Philadelphia, he had only three amateur fights before turning professional. In his last bout of 1984, on August 31, he won the WBC title from Tim Witherspoon in twelve rounds. Thomas, a very powerful puncher, has compiled a stellar knockout record—twenty in twenty-six fights. He is undefeated as of 1984.

Gregory Edward Page: Page is one of the biggest active professional boxers. Born on October 25, 1958, in Louisville, Kentucky, he is 6-feet 3-inches and weighs 240 pounds. He simply overpowered his amateur competition in winning the 1977 and 1978 National AAU titles, and the 1978 National Golden Gloves title. Fifteen of his first sixteen professional bouts were won by knockouts. After winning the USBA title, he lost to Tim Witherspoon in twelve rounds for the vacant WBC title in 1984. However, he won the WBA title from Gerrie Coetzee on December 1, 1984, in an eighth-round knockout. The title fight with Coetzee took place in South Africa.

Page was under tremendous pressure not to fight in that racially torn country. However, he was managed by Don King, who owned the promotional rights to this title bout, and King reportedly sold his promotional rights for $1 million to a South African promoter who staged the fight.

EPILOGUE

The boxer was black America's—and indeed all America's—first athletic hero. The sport itself has ancient beginnings and is considered the ultimate contest in individual competition. Black fighters have been a part of boxing history in its entirety and black Americans were part of that first generation of scientific pugilists.

Bill Richmond and Tom Molineaux were the first recorded black American athletes in recognized international sports. Exactly one hundred years after Molineaux's illegal defeat in 1810, Jack Johnson won a racial psychological victory in defeating Jim Jeffries, a "white hope" sent to put him in his place. Though he lost his title in exile in 1915, his mastery of "the sweet science" was unquestioned.

Johnson's successor as the next black heavyweight champion was Joe Louis, who became a near deity to many blacks while other black champions in the lower weight classes continued to succeed. No group of black athletes in any sport had as much influence on the morale of black America and the psyche of white America as did the boxers. Always the wealthiest of athletes, only a few managed to survive their ring careers financially secure.

At the end of 1984, black Americans held world titles in seventeen weight divisions, from bantamweight to heavyweight. It is an outstanding record, matched only by the predominance of the black athlete in professional basketball. Perhaps the day will soon come when young black men will view the sport as just another alternative among occupational opportunities. But until that day the ranks of the black American prizefighters will continue to be from that sector which feels there is no other way to survive in a society where boxers (and other professional athletes) have a greater earning potential than most college graduates.

Notes

1. *Ebony,* September 1946, 25.
2. Mike Jacobs, "Are Negroes Killing Boxing?", *Ebony,* May 1950, 29.
3. Peter Heller, *In This Corner: Forty World Champions Tell Their Stories,* (New York: Simon & Schuster, 1973), 369.
4. Bert Randolph Sugar and *Ring* magazine, *The Great Fights,* (New York: Rutledge Press, 1981), 119.
5. Heller, *In This Corner: Forty World Champions Tell Their Stories,* 322.
6. Ibid., 378
7. *Ebony,* November 1950, 77, 79.
8. Dave Anderson, *Sugar Ray Robinson,* (New York: New American Library, 1970), 33.
9. Ibid., 47.
10. Ibid., 43.
11. Ibid., 62.
12. Sugar and *Ring* magazine, *The Great Fights,* 130.
13. Anderson, *Sugar Ray Robinson,* 182.
14. Ibid., 253.
15. Ibid., 278.
16. Ibid., 177.
17. Heller, *In This Corner: Forty World Champions Tell Their Stories,* 314.
18. Floyd Patterson and Milton Gross, *Victory Over Myself,* (New York: Bernard Geis Associates and Random House, 1962), 45.
19. Ibid., 141.

20. Heller, *In This Corner: Forty World Champions Tell Their Stories,* 344.
21. Ibid., 345.
22. John Cottrell, *Man Of Destiny: The Story of Muhammad Ali,* (London: Frederick Muller Press, 1967), 73.
23. Ibid., 210.
24. Ibid., 243.
25. Ibid., 239.
26. Heller, *In This Corner: Forty World Champions Tell Their Stories,* 394.
27. Cottrell, *Man Of Destiny: The Story of Muhammad Ali,* 115.
28. Ibid., 89.
29. Ibid., 120.
30. Ibid., 173.
31. Ibid.
32. Ibid., 30.
33. Benjamin G. Rader, *American Sports,* (Englewood Cliffs, N.J.: Prentice Hall, Inc., 1983), 330.
34. *Newsweek,* 15 July 1968, 57.
35. Cottrell, *Man Of Destiny: The Story of Muhammad Ali,* 39.
36. Ibid., 158.
37. Ibid.
38. Ibid., 157.
39. Ibid., 319.
40. Muhammad Ali, *The Greatest: My Own Story,* (New York: Random House, 1975), 171.
41. Cottrell, *Man Of Destiny: The Story of Muhammad Ali,* 335.
42. Anderson, *Sugar Ray Robinson,* 265.
43. Ibid., 266.
44. Ali, *The Greatest: My Own Story,* 159.
45. Ibid., 177.
46. Bob Woodard and Scott Armstrong, *The Brethren,* (New York: Simon & Schuster, 1979), 137.
47. Ibid., 138.
48. Ibid., 139.
49. Ali, *The Greatest: My Own Story,* 286.
50. Harry Carpenter, *Boxing: An Illustrated History,* 146.
51. Sugar and *Ring* magazine, *The Great Fights,* 182.
52. Ali, *The Greatest: My Own Story,* 414.
53. Carpenter, *Boxing: An Illustrated History,* 158.
54. Ibid., 415.
55. Alan Goldstein, *A Fistful of Sugar,* (New York: Coward, McCann and Geoghegan, 1981), 67.
56. Ibid.
57. *Ebony,* July 1982, 34.
58. Ibid., 35.
59. *Ebony,* April 1973, 39.
60. Ibid., 40.
61. *Sports Illustrated,* 9 September 1985, 28.
62. Carpenter, *Boxing: An Illustrated History,* 164.

Sandy Saddler (left) hovers above Willie Pep (right) during his win on October 29, 1948. *(Source unknown)*

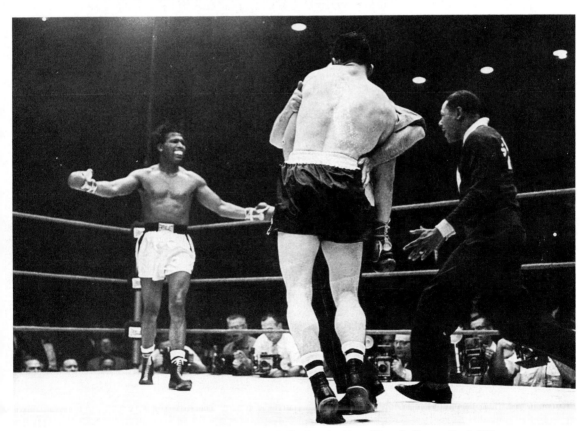

Sugar Ray Robinson exults after knocking out Gene Fullmer to regain his championship at Chicago Stadium, on May 1, 1957. *(AP/Wide World Photos)*

Ezzard Charles (left) connects with a left to the body of Wayne Bethea at New York City's St. Nick's Arena on May 21, 1956. Bethea won. *(AP/Wide World Photos)*

Joe "Old Bones" Brown (right) lands a right to the jaw of George Araujo in a bout on October 10, 1952. Araujo won the bout in the next round. *(AP/Wide World Photos)*

Archie Moore showers after winning the World Light Heavyweight title over Joey Maxim on December 18, 1952. *(AP/Wide World Photos)*

Jersey Joe Walcott (right) unloads a left hook on Ezzard Charles in a bout on June 5, 1952. *(Source unknown)*

Sugar Ray Robinson (right) lands a one-two combination on Jake LaMotta in a bout on February 15, 1951. *(AP/Wide World Photos)*

Cassius Clay, shown as he won the decision over the Russian Guennadiy Chatkov in the quarter-finals on September 3, 1960, in Rome, Italy. Clay, who later changed his name to Muhammad Ali, subsequently beat Anthony Madigan, of Australia, and Zbigniew Pietrzykowski, of Poland, to win the gold medal in the light heavyweight class. *(AP/Wide World)*

Floyd Patterson is directed to a neutral corner by referee Billy Regan as Sweden's Ingemar Johansson kneels head down after a knockout, at Miami Beach on March 13, 1961. *(AP/Wide World Photos)*

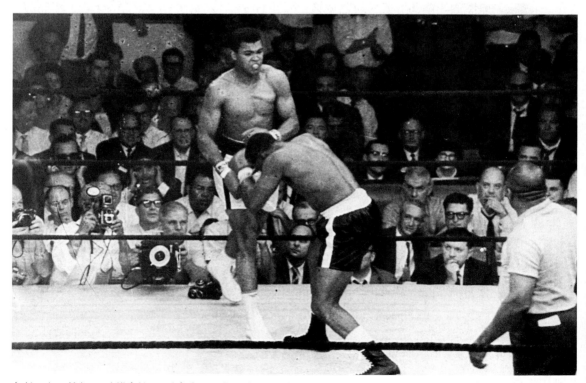

In his prime, Muhammad Ali (white trunks) flattens Sonny Liston in their second meeting, in Lewiston, Maine, in 1965. *(AP/Wide World Photos)*

Muhammad Ali, standing, shouts defiantly at a prone Sonny Liston in Lewiston, Maine. *(Courtesy of Neil Leifer/*Sports Illustrated*)*

Bob Foster, of Albuquerque, New Mexico, watches as Argentina's Andres Selpa is counted out, in Washington, D.C., on February 28, 1967. *(AP/Wide World Photos)*

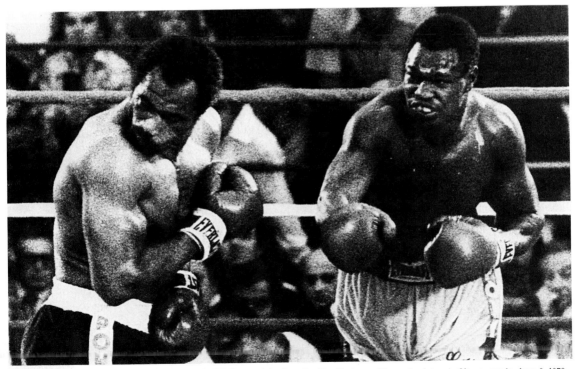

Larry Holmes (right) delivers a right to the jaw of WBC Heavyweight champion Ken Norton on his way to victory in fifteen rounds, June 9, 1978, at Las Vegas. *(AP/Wide World Photos)*

Howard Davis (right), 1976 Olympic Lightweight champion, wins a ten-round split decision over Larry Stanton at Orlando, Florida, on May 13, 1978. *(AP/Wide World Photos)*

Muhammad Ali is helped by trainers and handlers after winning a fourteenth-round TKO victory over Joe Frazier at Manila on October 1, 1975. Some say this fight helped cause the Parkinson's Syndrome Ali later suffered. *(AP/Wide World Photos)*

Challenger George Foreman sends Joe Frazier to the ropes in the second round, at Kingston, Jamaica, on January 22, 1973. Foreman won after 1 minute 35 seconds in the second round. *(AP/Wide World Photos)*

Joe Frazier (left) and George Foreman (right). Foreman lands a right to Frazier's jaw in a bout in Kingston, Jamaica. *(Courtesy of Neil Leifer/Sports Illustrated)*

Muhammad Ali nails Floyd Patterson on the head in the sixth round, at New York City's Madison Square Garden. Ali won with a seventh-round TKO, on September 20, 1972. *(AP/Wide World Photos)*

Joe Frazier (left) and Jimmy Ellis size up one another before meeting at Madison Square Garden. Frazier won on February 16, 1970, to take the WBA title. *(AP/Wide World Photos)*

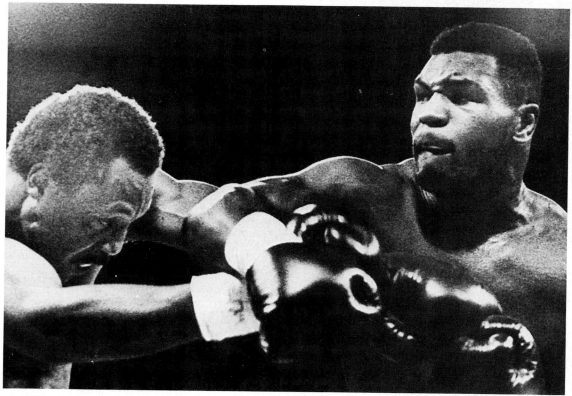

"Iron" Mike Tyson completes a right to the head of challenger Pinklon Thomas, at Las Vegas on May 30, 1987. Tyson retained the WBC and WBA Heavyweight titles with a sixth-round TKO. *(AP/Wide World Photos)*

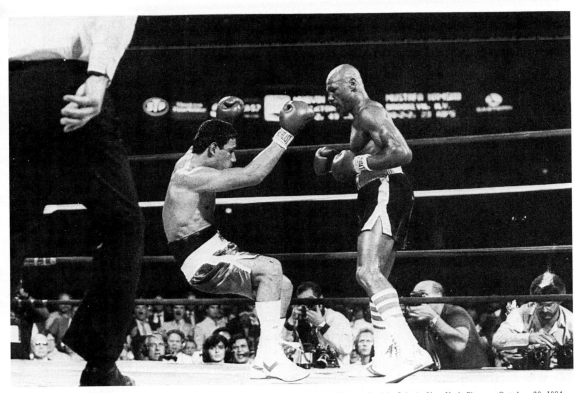

"Marvelous" Marvin Hagler watches Mustafa Hamsho hit the canvas in the WBA Middleweight title fight in New York City, on October 20, 1984. Hagler retained the title. *(AP/Wide World Photos)*

The "Hit Man," Thomas Hearns (right), throws a right at Pablo Baez at Houston on June 25, 1981. Hearns won on a fourth-round TKO. *(AP/Wide World Photos)*

Michael Spinks holds WBA and WBC championship belts aloft after unifying the titles with a win over Dwight Braxton at Atlantic City, on March 19, 1983. ABC's Al Michaels is at left, and promoter Butch Lewis is in the white suit. *(AP/Wide World Photos)*

Sugar Ray Leonard lands a right to the jaw of Roberto Duran. Duran lost the WBC Welterweight title after saying *"No mas, no mas"* ("No more, no more"), at New Orleans on November 25, 1980. *(AP/Wide World Photos)*

Claude "Buddy" Young (with the ball and wearing a leather helmet), in action with the New York Yankees against the New York Giants on December 3, 1950. The Yankees lost, 51–7. *(AP/Wide World Photos)*

Marion Motley, Jim Brown's predecessor as a power running back for the Cleveland Browns. *(Courtesy of the Cleveland Browns)*

Hall of Famer Len Ford of the Cleveland Browns. *(Courtesy of the Cleveland Browns)*

Bill Willis, of the Cleveland Browns, a pioneer in the early years of NFL integration. *(Courtesy of the Cleveland Browns)*

The diminutive Joe Perry, of the San Francisco 49'ers, the NFL's first player with back-to-back 1,000-yard seasons. *(Courtesy of the San Francisco 49'ers)*

Dick "Night Train" Lane, a bone-crushing tackler as a defensive back. *(Courtesy of the Detroit Lions)*

Jim Brown *(Courtesy of the Cleveland Browns)*

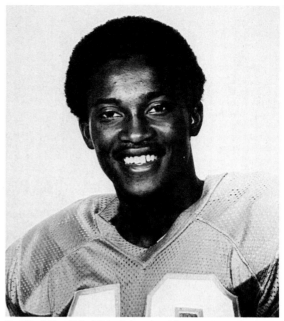

Paul Warfield, a Hall of Fame inductee and feared wide receiver. *(Courtesy of the Miami Dolphins)*

The incomparable Jim Brown, of the Cleveland Browns, who held the NFL all-time total rushing record until Walter Payton arrived. *(Courtesy of the Cleveland Browns)*

Hall of Fame guard Jim Parker, who played for Ohio State and the Baltimore Colts. *(AP/Wide World Photos)*

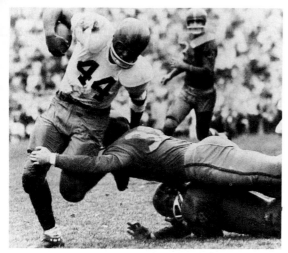

Syracuse University's Ernie Davis (number 44), the first black Heisman Trophy winner, in 1961. *(AP/Wide World Photos)*

Orenthal James "O.J." Simpson (number 32), of the Buffalo Bills, was the most exciting NFL runner in the 1970s. *(AP/Wide World Photos)*

Gayle Sayers, of the Chicago Bears. Some say he was the nimblest runner ever. *(Courtesy of the Chicago Bears)*

Coach Alonzo "Jake" Gaither, the Papa Rattler of Florida A&M's championship teams. *(Courtesy of Florida A&M University)*

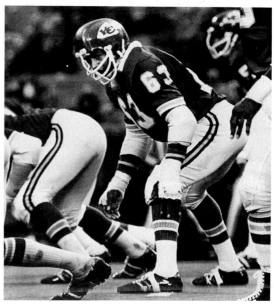

Hall of Famer Willie Lanier (from Maggie Walker High in Richmond, Virginia) assumes his linebacker position for the NFL's Kansas City Chiefs. *(Courtesy of the Kansas City Chiefs)*

Franco Harris, of the Pittsburgh Steelers, among the top four in NFL all-time rushing yardage. *(Courtesy of Mr. Franco Harris)*

Left to right: South Carolina Governor Richard Riley, George Rogers, Mrs. Grady Rogers. Rogers was celebrating his 1980 Heisman Trophy Award. *(AP/Wide World Photos)*

Lynn Swann (University of Southern California), the Pittsburgh Steelers' high-flying wide receiver. *(Courtesy of Mr. Lynn Swann)*

Charlie Joiner, of the San Diego Chargers, hauls in a touchdown pass over the Philadelphia Eagles' Evan Cooper in 1986. *(AP/Wide World Photos)*

The Chicago Bears' Walter Payton (from Jackson State University in Jackson, Mississippi), the NFL's leading rusher. *(Courtesy of the Chicago Bears)*

Bobby Mitchell (left), Paul Warfield (center), and Bobby Bell (second from right) receive their Hall of Fame busts on July 30, 1983, with Sonny Jurgensen and Sid Gillman (right). *(Courtesy of the Football Hall of Fame)*

Eddie Robinson, coach of the nationally famous Grambling State University team. *(Courtesy of Mr. Eddie Robinson)*

Willie Totten, of Mississippi Valley State University, fires away against Grambling University in 1984. Totten broke all black college passing records for total yardage. *(AP/Wide World Photos)*

Richard Dent, of the Super Bowl–winning Chicago Bears, stops the Minnesota Vikings' Alfred Anderson with a shirttail pull. *(AP/Wide World Photos)*

The sensation of the 1985 NFL season, William "The Refrigerator" Perry, lands at the London airport with wife, Sherry, for a game against the Dallas Cowboys in 1986. *(AP/Wide World Photos)*

Herschel Walker (University of Georgia), the most heralded runner in collegiate play in the early 1980s. *(AP/Wide World Photos)*

Marcus Allen (number 32), of the Los Angeles Raiders, in action against the Pittsburgh Steelers. *(AP/Wide World Photos)*

Lawrence "LT" Taylor, of the NFL's Giants, accepts the Schick Trophy as Most Valuable Player for 1986. *(AP/Wide World Photos)*

Chapter 4

Football

Football was the perfect post–World War II sport for a victorious America. The war had just been won over a German foe led by a maniacal and immoral figure—Adolf Hitler. As the country turned to the business of repairing itself, football seemed to offer a means of relieving, temporarily at least, the bloody image of battle. Hundreds of thousands of Americans died in World War II. A couple of dozen public-school and college players died of injuries during the football season, and hundreds were injured. But casualty was considered a price worth paying because the game exemplified the toughness and moral resolve that enabled the Allies to win the war over the Germans, Italians, and Japanese. Though professional football was just coming into its own, college football was the second most popular sport in 1950.

Black Americans were no less optimistic than whites about their country during this period. A contingent of civil rights leaders were laying the groundwork for the Supreme Court and congressional challenges for the next twenty years, and new black-owned periodicals like *Ebony* magazine, which published its first issue in 1946, would henceforth help black America define itself. Jackie Robinson was successfully integrating major league baseball.

The Basketball Association of America, which began in 1946, admitted blacks, and even the West Side Tennis Club in Queens, New York, the site of the National Tennis Championships, admitted Althea Gibson for the first time in 1950.

Optimism was solidly grounded due to the popularity of college football, and a general improvement in race relations. The first game between a white and a black college was held in New York City in 1947. Wilberforce University, the oldest black college in the country, defeated Bergen College of New Jersey 40–12. In November of that same year, the Willowtree Athletic Club of Washington, D.C., played the white Philadelphia Vulpine Athletic Club to a 6–6 tie in Durham, North Carolina. Here was an example that made national news.

A black 6-foot 4-inch, 225-pound tackle from Harvard University, Chester "Chet" Pierce, played in a precedent-setting game against the University of Virginia in October 1947. Though Harvard was defeated 47–0, the loss was of secondary importance. Pierce was warmly received by the school that Thomas Jefferson founded and was given a standing ovation in the fourth quarter when he was removed for a substitute. The incident, he noted, "...thrilled me beyond description."[1] Virginia officials had asked their students to vote on whether their team should play against a Harvard team that included a black player. The vote result was a resounding "yes."

Quick to realize the importance of the moment, the *Richmond* (Virginia) *Afro-American* newspaper added this editorial: "It is our fervent hope that our white leaders who control the affairs of this state will take the cue from these youth and open the doors to all of our state colleges to all our youth on the basis of educational qualifications—before the courts force them to do it!"[2] The University of Virginia, a major school, had never admitted black students before. World War II was over, but for black southern athletes, another war was about to begin anew. Though the future looked bright, progress would be slow at first.

At least in part, football mirrored the changes that the nation was undergoing. Returning black soldiers who wanted to resume educational opportunities they had postponed, were forced to attend historically black colleges, or forego post-secondary education altogether. Acceptance at white colleges remained difficult, as these schools had unwritten quotas for blacks in their student bodies and on their athletic teams. Professional football, much more vulnerable than the college game, was also cautious about signing black players. As a result, three separate histories developed and became important: black college football, white college football, and professional football.

Football in 1946 was the backbone of the black colleges' varsity sports programs. It had a history dating to the 1890s and it

was, as it is today, a primary revenue producer. Baseball at black colleges lost its luster during the Depression, and gymnasiums for basketball and indoor track were not modern enough to ensure a large following during the winter. Many college presidents relied on the success of their football teams to help create a favorable image for their schools. The most important dates on black America's social calendar were the dates of athletic events, especially in the South. For many black college graduates the most important of these was the homecoming football game of their alma mater.

College teams after World War II owed much to the perseverance of pioneers like Cleveland Abbott of Tuskegee University (formerly Tuskegee Institute) and Eddie Hurt of Morgan State. Players like Alfred "Jazz" Bird of Lincoln University (Pennsylvania) and the incomparable Ben Stevenson of Tuskegee were still talked about in the late 1940s, as being the best ever. Those opinions were hearsay, of course, as no more than a few thousand people at a time ever saw the aforementioned players perform. There was no television before the war, and black college games were seldom broadcast on radio. The black print media and word of mouth were almost exclusively responsible for these player's stardom.

Meager Facilities: In the late 1940s, no black college stadium held more than ten thousand seats. However, a few schools tried renting fields in major league parks, as did the Negro League baseball teams. Equipment was not "state of the art" even for the period and, with the exception of ex-

G.I.s, just a few of the players were from school systems with sophisticated football programs. Some schools like Tuskegee continued to make their own uniforms. Still, the brand of football these teams played was entertaining, and highly competitive.

Coaches Are Teachers First: Winning black coaches remained, as they had been before the war, almost mythical figures. They were expected to be benevolent dictators. They turned players from second-rate segregated high school systems that used simple plays into student athletes who frequently won berths on professional teams. Unlike his counterpart at a major white school, the black college coach usually taught classes and coached other sports. While his skills were questionable in the minds of most white professional team owners, black coaches did, between 1946 and 1970, have one substantial advantage: a near monopoly in recruiting the best black talent from among their southern brethren. Until the late 1950s, there were no professional teams in any major sport based in the South. Thus football served as a magnet for many blacks who did not migrate northward. (Many famous black athletes like Joe Louis, Jesse Owens, and Willie Mays were southern-born but earned their fame in the North.) Consequently, it was just a matter of time before football in the Southeastern Intercollegiate Athletic Conference (SIAC) and the Southwestern Athletic Conference (SWAC) equalled that in the Central Intercollegiate Athletic Association (CIAA.)

An indication of the rapid dispersal of talented athletes throughout the black college system is the following list of players, their schools, and the NFL professional teams that signed them from 1946 to 1959:

Hal Turner	Tennessee State	Detroit Lions
Maurice Bassett	Langston University	Cleveland Browns
Henry Mosley	Morris Brown	Chicago Bears
J.D. Smith	North Carolina A & T	Chicago Bears
Robert Jackson	North Carolina A & T	New York Giants
Sherman Plunkett	U. of Maryland, E. Shore	Baltimore Colts
Johnny Sample	U. of Maryland, E. Shore	Baltimore Colts
John Parker	North Carolina Central	Los Angeles Rams
Jack Springs	Alcorn State	Pittsburgh Steelers
Frank Purnell	Alcorn State	Green Bay Packers
Roosevelt Brown	Morgan State	New York Giants
Charles Robinson	Morgan State	Baltimore Colts
Charles Brackins	Prairie View A & M	Green Bay Packers
Herman Lee	Florida A & M	Chicago Bears
Willie McClung	Florida A & M	Pittsburgh Steelers
Paul Younger	Grambling	Los Angeles Rams
Willie Davis	Grambling	Cleveland Browns

These seventeen players were the first from black schools to sign with National Football League teams. They show that the CIAA—of which only North Carolina A & T, University of Maryland Eastern Shore, Morgan State, and North Carolina Central were a part—was no longer totally dominant. By the 1970s and 1980s, there was an almost complete reversal in conference strength, and a realignment of conference membership left the CIAA the weakest of the five major black college groupings.

In the interim, many schools with solid football histories were forced to drop the sport because of its cost. In particular, schools with student-body enrollments of less than 1,500 found it extremely difficult to field teams. The traditional black Land Grant schools, which were partially supported by state tax funds, and Howard

University, which got much of its support from the federal government, were luckier than the smaller private schools. However, some private institutions, like Hampton Institute and Morehouse College, were able to provide a quality education and a quality football team.

By the early 1970s, the options were clear for those schools wishing to retain the sport: (1) conference rearrangements were made to strengthen the schedules in order to weed out the grossly weaker teams; (2) state-supported schools made full use of their allocations and specialized in only those sports that had a solid following; (3) every effort was made to regionally televise as many games as possible, in order to increase local support; (4) the all-important recruiting function was modernized to include a wider group of athletes from which to choose; (5) coaching staffs were increased and more use was made of former NFL players; (6) larger stadiums were built to comfortably accommodate larger crowds; (7) the schools maximized the public relations use of their own success in sending players on to the NFL. But the survivors still could not match the NCAA Division I–A white schools when it came to providing resources and inducements.

A list of all black college conference winners from 1950 through 1984 can be found in the Reference section.

Few black student-athletes wanted to attend a black school without a football team if they could attend a predominantly white school with a team. College administrators were well aware of this desire, and they made conscious efforts to keep the sport if at all possible. Scholar athletes who have been recruited during the 1980s have

been reared on a steady diet of televised football and many, if not most of them, have looked forward to the fall schedules of games pitting nationally known and ranked white college teams against one another. The halftime shows by these schools' bands have also shown to be added attractions which have influenced decisions by these athletes to attend white colleges over black ones.

These schools also recruited outstanding players though white schools began siphoning prime black prospects in the mid-1970s and 1980s. Two players from black colleges, Roosevelt Brown and Willie Davis, were inducted into the Football Hall of Fame. No doubt more will follow. A complete list of past NFL players from historically black colleges and universities appears in the reference section.

Black College Coaches and Their Records: The enviable record of black college players signed by professional teams is primarily due to the intense dedication of their coaches. These men were, and continue to be, supreme authority figures for hundreds of young black men. Many have been like second fathers to their players, who often come from single-parent families. To other players these coaches represented their first sustained exposure to systematic discipline.

The majority of these players were seldom involved in the types of recruiting scandals of the past, simply because there were no illegal slush funds available for dispensing loose cash. Additionally, their academic transcripts did not need doctoring because black schools have, as a matter of course, accepted, educated, and graduated student athletes who had been refused admittance for one reason or another by white schools. Also, there was no stacking of players by position, as frequently happened at white schools. Just as black college quarterbacks, for example, were switched to other positions in the NFL, so were black high school quarterbacks switched at white colleges.

By the mid-1960s, black coaches began receiving their just due from the white critics. In 1966, Eddie Robinson of Grambling was voted by the Football Writers Association as having done more for the College Division (smaller schools) game than anyone else in the last twenty-five years. In 1978, Robinson was invited to interview for the head coaching position with the Los Angeles Rams, the first black to be seriously considered. (In 1980 the NFL began inviting black college coaches to training camps with professional coaches and their assistants.) Though he was not truly interested in leaving Grambling for a chance at the professional ranks, Robinson told his players before he left for Los Angeles that "...I need to go to open the doors for you. The way things are looking, I don't think I'd take it, but I'm obliged to go."[3]

While Eddie Robinson is certainly the best-known black football coach since World War II, he is not alone in possessing expertise. Though he has sent more players, sixty-nine, to the NFL than any other, he is second to Florida A & M's Jake Gaither in conference titles won, twelve, to eight for Robinson. Gaither, known as "the Papa Rattler" of his stellar teams, is in that legendary class with Eddie Hurt and Cleveland Abbott. However, Robinson may surpass

them all. See the Reference section for a list of the names, college teams coached, conferences, and the total number of titles won by the top black college coaches.

These coaches are among the most successful in any sport. They have been an invaluable asset not only to their institutions but to black America and our nation as well.

Player Records: No player from a black college has ever won a Heisman Trophy or an Outland Trophy, awarded to the nation's premier college player and lineman, respectively, each year. But the complete list of 528 professional players from black schools attests to their abilities. One player, Walter Payton of Jackson State, holds SWAC and NFL rushing records. The black college career leaders in rushing, passing, pass receiving, and punting from 1950 through 1984 are shown in the Reference section.

These superior athletes knew before they signed their college letters of intent that they were not going to appear on ABC Sports' nationally televised Game of the Week on Saturdays during football season. They knew no one would hand a packet of ten-dollar bills to them each week. Nor did they expect to get to travel too far from the school's campus. But they did know that every effort would be made to ensure their graduation and that, since the 1970s at least, professsional scouts would be aware of who they were and what they could do. The rest was up to them.

The Future: There are now four major black-college conferences and some independents. The list of black schools offering serious varsity programs is smaller than it was in 1950. Faced with the hard choice between academic integrity and a mediocre football team, many college presidents wisely chose the former. Those programs that have survived have done so despite their relatively small resource base. Some games are now regionally telecast and Black Entertainment Television (BET) has brought games and showcased players to black communities (in California and Washington, for example) that had never seen them before.

Black college football has a bright future. While some schools will understandably place more emphasis on academic programs, others will work out a compromise that retains football's competitiveness, while eschewing other varsity sports. Football is as much a part of college life as any other extracurricular activity. A winning team is generally good for morale and even the most astute scholars recognize its value. Importantly, and more than ever, black schools are now able to draw upon a large reservoir of potential coaches. These schools have shown an unusual degree of ingenuity and creativity through some difficult times. Continued future success is a certainty.

BLACKS AT WHITE COLLEGES

Following World War II, football at white colleges was the nation's second most popular sport after major league baseball. The huge sellout crowds for some school games enabled many schools to field well-equipped teams that had as many as four or five coaches. Many of these schools, like Ohio State, Michigan State, and the University of Illinois, were Land Grant institutions that were established under the Morrill Act of 1890. All of them were partially supported by black tax dollars, but they limited black enrollment and varsity sports competition to a handful. Southern white schools, by custom, simply ignored the very idea of blacks as students or athletes. To southerners college football was their major league sport.

However, nationally known black student athletes have come from these schools since the 1890s. William H. Lewis, of Amherst, was the first black All-America named by Walter Camp. Frederick Douglass "Fritz" Pollard, of Brown University, was the first black All-America running back. Camp said Paul Robeson of Rutgers was "the greatest end that ever trod a gridiron." Other outstanding players included Duke Slater, Joe Lillard, Jerome "Brud" Holland, William "Dolly" King, Jackie Robinson, Kenny Washington, Brice Taylor, Robert Marshall, and Doc Keller. Most of these superb athletes were running backs or ends and, like everybody else before two-platoon football was introduced, played both offense and defense.

Few, if any of them, ever lived on campus. Though they were applauded on the field, they were unwelcome in the dormitories. (Even Paul Robeson, who had a superior singing voice, was not allowed to join the Princeton Glee Club.) The housing issue was especially nettlesome. William "Bill" Willis, of the University of Illinois in the mid-1940s, remembered that "We lived so far from campus that it is really difficult to walk back and forth so far three or four times a day."[4]

Still, black athletes on white college

teams were nationally known. *Ebony* magazine's first cover story on an athlete, for instance, was on UCLA's Kenny Washington. When Washington entered UCLA, the school's athletic budget was $121,529 in debt. When he left, they had $47,033 in the bank. Such was the drawing power of a few of these stars.

Conditions for blacks had been gradually improving outside of the southern colleges. Jackie Robinson's breakthrough in professional baseball rippled across all major team sports. A symbolic victory of sorts was won on New Year's Day in 1948, when Wally Triplett and Denny Hoggard, both Penn State players, became the first blacks to perform in a Cotton Bowl Game. Penn State tied Southern Methodist University, 13–13. That same year Levi Jackson, a 5-foot 10-inch, 185-pound running back, was named captain of the Yale team. (Francis Gregory, a black player, was captain of the Yale Divinity School team in 1899, after being named captain at Amherst the year before). Ironically, the Yale fight song, "Boola Boola," was penned by the famous black writer, James Weldon Johnson, and his brother.

Also in 1948, tiny Lafayette College in Pennsylvania rejected a Sun Bowl bid at El Paso, Texas, because their black player, Dave Showell, would not be allowed to play. Such moral stands were lauded by black Americans.

Sanity Code: Nearly all of these black players had attended school on scholarships that were legally offered to those in need. This policy was known as the Sanity Code, and it was intended to keep the richer schools from signing all of the best players.

However, in 1952, the NCAA repealed the Sanity Code to permit a limited number of scholarships for each member school regardless of need. This repeal marked the beginning of the collegiate scholarship system that we know today, from which thousands of black athletes have benefited.

1950 to 1958: The Breakthrough

The decade of the 1950s began on a sour note. The United States Military Academy at West Point, New York, expelled all but two of its varsity team members for cheating on exams. This was a bitter blow, as there were also scandals in college basketball. These incidents were the first graphic examples of how misplaced varsity sports were becoming in college life. The Ivy League reacted by putting spring practice on hold and tightening scholarship standards. There were other reported cases of doctored academic transcripts, and the American Council on Education (ACE) proposed a ban on postseason bowl games.

Some incidents were blatantly racist in nature and received national publicity. On October 20, 1951, during a game between Drake and Oklahoma A & M, Johnny Bright, a black Drake running back, was punched by Wilbanks Smith, an Oklahoma lineman, and suffered a broken jaw. In 1950, Bright had set an NCAA rushing record of 2,400 total yards. When Missouri Valley Conference officials refused to investigate the matter, Drake withdrew from the conference.

According to one report, "Bright was knocked unconscious three times in the first seven minutes of the game,"[5] and Smith "...hit him on every single play in the first seven minutes, whether or not Johnny had the ball." This example was used by white southern colleges as justification for not allowing blacks to play. The Missouri Valley Conference was vilified in the black press for its refusal to formally investigate this incident.

The second major occurrence took place in 1955. Georgia's governor, Marvin Griffin, decided to ban Georgia Tech from playing in the Sugar Bowl in New Orleans because their opponent, the University of Pittsburgh, had a black player, Bobby Grier. In tones similar to those used by Alabama governor George Wallace at the University of Alabama years later, Griffin said the South "...stands at Armageddon—we can not make the slightest concession [integration] to the enemy."[6]

Two thousand Georgia Tech students stormed the state capital in Atlanta to protest Griffin's decision. Griffin had made Georgia Tech look silly and the South abnormally petty. His decision was exacerbated because just a year before the United States Supreme Court outlawed "separate but equal" public school systems, which the South supported. As ludicrous as Griffin's stand was, it took another decade before the Sugar Bowl and the Blue-Gray games allowed blacks to play.

Outstanding Players: The black press closely watched the progress of black players at white colleges. Yards gained and passes caught were weekly headlines in their sports sections. In the late 1940s, Mel Groomes and George Taliaferro were at Indiana. Wally Triplett and Denny Hoggard played at Penn State. "Deacon" Dan Towler was at Washington & Jefferson. Bernie

Custis played quarterback at Syracuse. Playing the end position, Bob Mann and Len Ford, along with running back Gene Derricotte, were part of the University of Michigan's "point a minute" team and they helped Michigan defeat the University of Southern California (USC) 49–0 in the Rose Bowl in 1948. Four years later, Addison Hawthorne became the first black on USC's team in twenty-five years. In the mid-1950s, Bobby Watkins and Jim Parker starred at Ohio State. In 1956 Parker was the first black winner of the Outland Trophy, awarded to the nation's top collegiate lineman.

In 1957, Bobby Mitchell starred at Illinois. A year later, two quarterbacks, Mel Myers at Illinois and Sidney Williams at Wisconsin, made history. Williams had attended the racially troubled Central High in Little Rock, Arkansas. But the two most significant student-athletes of this period were Jim Brown and Prentiss Gault.

Jim Brown attended Syracuse University, and would go on to become the best running back the game had ever seen. But his years at Syracuse were not without problems. This 6-feet 2-inches, 220-pound power back was brought up on St. Simons Island, Georgia. He moved to Manhasset, Long Island, in New York, and attended Manhasset High School, where he was All-State in football, basketball, and track. In all, he won thirteen varsity letters in high school and averaged 38 points per game in basketball.

Brown was not on scholarship at Syracuse. A forty-five man syndicate organized by a white friend paid his expenses. Though he had been a gang warlord in high school, in college Brown displayed awesome athletic abilities. He lettered in four sports—football, track, basketball, and lacrosse. At Syracuse, where he majored in recreation, he was the only black player on the football team. In a basketball game against Colgate on November 17, 1956, he scored 43 points. He also set a single-season football rushing record of 986 yards in eight games and was named Most Valuable Player in the 1957 Cotton Bowl game. He was the school's first All-America running back. He also was named All-America in lacrosse. The Cleveland Browns made him their first-round draft choice.

Brown got into trouble because he dared to date white coeds. He was given such a difficult time about it that he later declared, "...I felt that I had promptly been viewed as a potential troublemaker and threat to Caucasian women."[7] No one, however, doubted his ability to run the football.

Prentiss Gault made history when the University of Oklahoma's coach, Charles "Bud" Wilkinson, signed him in 1958. Gault was the first black player at a major southern white school. Wilkinson had near deity status as a coach. He began in 1948 and, during one stretch, won thirty-one games in a row before losing to Kentucky in 1951. His teams had another winning streak of forty-seven from 1953 to 1957. Southern white college football was enjoying a resurgence in strength in the 1950s and Wilkinson, with his polite, gentlemanly manner, was the perfect coach to use the first black player.

Irrespective of Wilkinson's bold move, it was just a matter of time before all colleges began using black players. Blacks were seen constantly in starring roles in televised games and, in spite of local at-tempts to hold back the tide of integration, blacks were soon seen on teams once considered bastions of white supremacy.

1959 to 1970: Lonely Superstars

In the dozen years following Prentiss Gault's breakthrough at Oklahoma, the increasing numbers of black players faced new sets of difficulties. And for those at schools with a history of black participation, the same problems remained. There were still only a few dozen black students at the largest of these universities. Housing was always, and continued to be the number-one gripe. Off-campus, apartment landlords frequently refused to rent to black students, and university administrators did little to assist. In the early 1960s, few white schools dared to use black cheerleaders, who would certainly be seen on television, and thus possibly alienate potential donors. But it would be the mid-1960s before groups of black students and athletes pressed demands for reform.

On the field, certain positions were still reserved for white players, and unwritten quotas for blacks remained. Black players who were clearly superior to some whites were sometimes benched. Coaches were extremely sensitive to the feelings of alumni groups, who were overwhelmingly white and wanted to see white players in positions of prominence. Continuing to show their mettle, some black players even earned national honors as substitutes.

William Burrell, who played at the University of Illinois in the late 1950s, said, "After earning a position on the first team, blacks were seldom allowed to start in the game...the alumni association had much influence on the make-up of the starting line-up. I actually made All-America from the second team. The coaches were prejudiced as were most of the players. There were lots of conflicts."[8]

Heisman Trophy Winners: Problems or not, black players were generally acknowledged for their performances. In 1961, Ernie Davis, a Syracuse running back, was the first black awarded the Heisman Trophy. During this same period two other black running backs, Mike Garrett in 1965 and O.J. Simpson in 1968, won this coveted honor, given to the nation's outstanding collegiate player. These honors embarrassed southern schools, some of which by 1968, had yet to sign even one black player.

Rules and Strategy Changes: Along with their national recognition, black players seemed to readily fit the new offensive strategies adopted by college coaches. Before the mid-1950s, the single-wing and single-platoon teams were the norm. But new rules allowed free substitutions as in the NFL, and the split-T backfield formation, which called for exceptional speed from ball carriers, was popularized. Black players began assuming larger roles as running backs.

Player Militancy: As the number of black football players increased, they felt more inclined to voice their grievances. Their larger presence also coincided with the black social revolution that took place in the mid-1960s. They were not alone as their counterparts on basketball and track teams joined to protest the lack of attention to off-campus housing, black cheerleaders, the stacking of players by position, the

dearth of black faculty members, and the insensitivity of some coaches and their assistants.

Players in this period were sophisticated enough to know whether or not a particular school was suited for them. As recently as fifteen years before, a black player would not have had much selectivity. The years between 1964 and 1970 were particularly appealing to an outstanding player because the southern schools had yet to begin recruiting blacks in large numbers. Consequently, a player like, say, Gale Sayers, was offered several dozen scholarships to top northern schools.

Sayers, for example, wound up at the University of Kansas, after declining an offer from the University of Nebraska. (He found out that Nebraska had forty-four black athletes and two black girls enrolled.) No black player could have been so picky in 1950. But even at Kansas, in his senior year, he felt obliged to participate in a sit-in to protest housing conditions.

In 1967, black players on the University of California at Berkeley football team boycotted spring practice to support suspended black basketball player, Bob Presley. John Erby was soon named as the first black assistant coach at UCB. A year later, players at Michigan State delivered a list of demands, drafted by black professor Robert Green, to coach Biggie Munn.

In October 1969, fourteen black players at the University of Wyoming publicly criticized the Mormon church and appealed to their coach, Lloyd Eaton, to support their right not to play against Brigham Young University, a Mormon school. The Mormon religion at the time, taught that blacks could not attain to the priesthood, and that they were tainted by the curse of Ham, a biblical figure. Eaton, however, summarily dropped all fourteen players from the squad.

That same month, the University of Washington played a game against UCLA without its thirteen black players. Four of the players had been suspended by coach Jim Owens for refusing to make a pledge of loyalty to the university. Such was the attitude of football coaches in the 1960s who had difficulty adjusting to a more assertive black athlete.

Black Quarterbacks: The most important position on any football team is that of quarterback, and blacks were thought by coaches, alumni, and fans to be lacking the necessities for playing this position. Indeed, very few were given a chance and a coach risked his job if a black quarterback did not succeed. Critics could point to any number of "failures." But there were some successes. Willie Thrower played the position for a short time with the Chicago Bears in 1953. Sandy Stephens at Minnesota, Wilbur Hollis (an Iowa quarterback who led his team to Big Ten co-championship honors in 1960), Jim Raye at Michigan State, and Ron Burton at Colgate were all successful quarterbacks at white schools. John McClusky became Harvard's first black quarterback in 1964.

Marlin Briscoe, who stood only 5-feet 11-inches and weighed 180 pounds, set quarterback records at the University of Omaha. During his career he rushed for 1,318 yards, passed for 4,935 yards, and completed 333 of 609 passes for 52 touchdowns. Briscoe did get a chance to play his position in the NFL. Gene Washington of

Stanford was more pragmatic. Washington switched from quarterback to wide receiver for the San Francisco 49'ers. For him, "It was strickly a matter of economics. I knew a black quarterback would have little chance in pro ball unless he was absolutely superb."[9]

James Harris had his own set of problems. Harris played at Grambling in Louisiana under Eddie Robinson. He wanted desperately to play quarterback in the NFL, but was ready to accept another position. "I prepared myself to play other positions. A cat named Marlin Briscoe played QB for Denver [Broncos] the year before me, so that did open a few doors. It turned out to be just like coach Robinson said…As a black QB they are constantly trying to switch you to another position."[10] Later, Harris became even more bitter, saying, "You [blacks] get two types of opportunities to play QB in the NFL. A chance and a 'nigger' chance."[11]

Harris' black contemporaries at white schools also faced an historically entrenched, dictatorial attitude from coaches who viewed any dissent as an erosion of their leadership. Some of these players simply could not adjust. As one observer noted: "Many coaches thought that beards, Afro hair styles, and interracial dating symbolized personal license and a rebellion against authority."[12]

The South Caves In: Though Bud Wilkinson pioneered the playing of black quarterbacks with Prentiss Gault at Oklahoma, his southern colleagues moved more slowly. Schools in the border states—Texas, Virginia, Kentucky, and West Virginia—were quicker to sign blacks than were schools in Alabama, Mississippi, Georgia, and Louisiana. But in a December 1967 *Ebony* magazine article, Alabama coach Bear Bryant was quoted as saying: "The time is coming when in this entire area (the Deep South), you won't see too many of these boys [blacks] going away."[13]

Simultaneously, the black college coach watched as his racial advantage in recruiting the best black talent withered to a fraction of what it once was. In that same *Ebony* article, Florida A&M coach Jake Gaither sadly said, "It's [integration] hurting us."[14] In retrospect, blacks who chose to attend white schools traded the increased publicity for a lesser chance at graduation. It is arguable that their chances at a professional career were jeopardized, since records show a large number of NFL players coming from black schools. But the public impression was certainly present in the 1960s that a good black player desiring a professional career was better off at a white school.

White Conference Firsts: The first black players in the three major southern white college conferences had many offers from black schools but chose to break new ground. In the Southwest Conference, Jerry LeVias entered Southern Methodist University and Warren McVea entered the University of Houston. In the Atlantic Coast Conference, Freddie Summers attended Wake Forest; and in the Southeast Conference, Nat Northington and Greg Page chose Kentucky.

For their part, these schools were not shy in explaining why blacks were welcomed on the field, if not in their fraternity houses. Said a Kentucky Sports Information Director: "...the blacks have given us something we haven't had—speed. And speed is the name of the game."[15] In the next fifteen years, black players looked for more than just a chance to play football. They realized they were not graduating and something had to be done.

1970 to 1984: Consolidation

In the early 1970s, white coaches were zealous in their recruitment of the most talented black players. While players at black colleges completed their eligibility under NCAA rules, some of their cousins at white schools were sorely tempted by illegal offers of complimentary tickets for resale, cars, clothes, money, jobs, women, tampered transcripts, and inflated grades.

Jerry LeVias, recalled that while at SMU, he paid someone "a couple grand"[16] to help him get good grades in his senior year. Gerald Taylor, a linebacker at Texas Christian University, admitted receiving about $200 every two weeks, "...not a lump sum or anything."[17] To be sure, some of these transgressions occurred at black schools, but they were never the norm.

Lest anyone doubt the rationale for such efforts, Oklahoma coach Barry Switzer did not condone the practices but had an answer: "Recruiting, not coaching, is the name of the game."[18]

Georgia Tech, which in 1955 was barred from attending a bowl game because its opponent had a black player, played its first black quarterback, Eddie McAshan, in 1970. Some Georgia Tech alumni stopped contributing monies, but times had changed for good. A source of many of these violations were from booster groups that frequently acted without the knowledge of coaches or college presidents. Most schools began appointing faculty advisors whose sole function was to liaise with the athletic departments and their support organizations.

By the mid-1970s, most white schools had more experienced and younger coaches. Many of the older, traditional, and racist coaches were replaced by men who had had more contact with blacks as players and as people. Even the ratios had changed. In ten years, according to one report, "the player/coach ratio had gone from thirty to one in 1966 to eight to one in 1976."[19] In addition, few scholarship athletes played more than one sport, with the exception of some football players who were on track teams. It was not unusual for a major college to spend $5 million on their football program. Too much was at stake and football receipts paid for the other non–revenue producing sports like tennis, swimming, volleyball, etc. The white colleges *had* to have the best athletes they could find.

Thus, it is no surprise that an increasing number of Heisman Trophy winners were black. In the fifteen-year period between 1971 and 1984, ten awardees, 67 percent, were black. And all of them were running backs. The complete list of black Heisman trophy winners can be found in the Reference section.

These players had passed the most thorough scrutiny of any group of team athletes in history. They had once been one of a little more than a million high school players and were some of the 42,000 that played at NCAA-affiliated schools in several divisions. In 1981, a former college player, Dennis Green, became the first black football coach at a predominantly white school, Northwestern.

But even in the 1980s the motivation for the black athlete remained basically the same as twenty years before. Marcus Allen, the 1981 Heisman Trophy winner from USC, said matter-of-factly, "Sports is a way out of the ghetto."[20] This enthusiasm, however, continued to make naive black high school athletes vulnerable to illegal recruiting schemes and payoffs.

Adjustment Problems: The pressure on the high school athlete had intensified by 1971, when the NCAA voted to allow varsity participation by freshmen. Knowing that black athletes ran a higher-than-average chance of becoming academically ineligible before their class graduated, coaches were forced to sign only the bluest of blue-chip players. Most of these players were woefully ill-prepared for college-level studies and graduation rates were shockingly low.

Marino Casem, coach at predominantly black Alcorn State in Mississippi, said in the mid-1970s, "We've been integrated for six years now and there's been only one graduate in the whole state."[21] Casem's reference was to black football players in white colleges since 1970. Robert Hill, coach at Mississippi's Jackson State, a black school, added, "We try to sign 30 boys we think are blue chippers. White schools don't necessarily think they're blue chippers. We look for size. White schools want glamour boys who gained all the yards."[22]

Yet the white coach, like the black coach, knows that the job is to win. If he does not win, he knows, he will be replaced. With an NCAA limit of ninety-five scholarships per school, the pressure is intense. Former Georgia Tech coach Pepper Rogers put it best: "If I were coaching at a school where you could give a guy five hours of correspondence courses during the summer to keep him eligible, hell, yes, I'd give'em to him. So would every other football coach, to my knowledge. Why? Because that would be the rule at that school, and the alumni are going to fire me and my wife and my kids and my assistant coaches and their families if a 6-foot 2-inch, 220-pound halfback who can run the 40 [yards] in 4.5 [seconds] isn't eligible and we don't win football games."[23]

Nearly all of the 6-foot 2-inch, 220-pound half-backs who run 40 yards in 4.5 seconds are black.

Proposition 48: In a move meant to alleviate the growing public outcry over the exploitation of black athletes at white colleges, the NCAA adopted Proposition 48 in early 1983. This proposal, recommended by the American Council on Education, took effect in August 1986. It simply stated that for a freshman college athlete to be eligible for varsity competition at an NCAA Division I school, he or she must have scored at least 700 on the SAT College Entrance Exam or 15 on the ACT Exam and have attained a C average in eleven core subjects that normally lead to high school graduation. Furthermore, to remain eligible, an athlete must maintain a C average in courses that lead to college graduation.

Though the success of white college basketball teams would be more adversely affected, college football teams in general had a greater number of black players, who were affected by the proposal. In early 1985, Proposition 48 was amended to include an indexing formula to allow low SAT or ACT scores to be compensated for by higher grade-point averages.

The Future: Black players are no longer novelties on college teams, even though quarterbacks are still anomalies. Blacks have played every position with distinction, and they dominate the Heisman Trophy selections. However, their low grade-point averages, low graduation rates, and off-campus problems persist. Television viewers normally see former players as assistants on major college teams; only a few have become head coaches. None, though, has been picked as coach of a school with a serious varsity program.

As long as the black community is economically exploited and oppressed, it will continue to place high value on athletic careers, and the concentration will continue to focus on bringing forth superior players. By the year 2000, one can expect that a black school like Grambling will be invited to a major bowl game against a white school with a black head coach. And maybe, just maybe, no one will care who is playing which position on the field.

THE PROFESSIONAL GAME

Following World War II, professional football was third in the pecking order of major sports, after baseball and college football. Part of the reason was the lingering idea in the minds of some that all professional players were just mercenaries in disguise.

Baseball players could be excused, since few of them had attended college, but most professional football players were different. Even the college administrators had adopted a Sanity Code to limit athletic scholarships to those in need. They were clearly afraid of unbridled competition for talent. But the demand for more professional teams was there nonetheless.

The All American Football Conference (AAFC) was organized in 1946 and, after much discussion, promptly allowed its teams to sign blacks. The Cleveland Browns were the first to follow through and took Marion Motley, a running back from the University of Nevada at Reno, who in 1968, became the first black player in the Hall of Fame. An upstart league, the AAFC took a chance on blacks before Jackie Robinson had fully proven himself on the baseball diamond. Though the league had eight teams, only six signed blacks in its four-year existence.

The following blacks were the first on their respective teams in the AAFC:

1946	Marion Motley, RB	Cleveland Browns
1947	Buddy Young, RB	New York Yankees
	Elmore Harris, RB	Brooklyn Dodgers
	Bert Piggott, RB, DB	Los Angeles Dons
	Ezzrett Anderson, E	Los Angeles Dons
	Bill Bass RB, DB	Chicago Rockets
1948	Joe Perry, RB	San Francisco 49'ers

In the same time period, the National Football League (NFL) signed fewer blacks and only three teams—the Los Angeles Rams, the New York Giants, and the Detroit Lions—did so. The AAFC was also first to sign players from black schools though, most did not make the cut. Robert Drummond of Tennessee State was signed by the

Dodgers, and in 1948 the Yankees signed Fred "Cannonball" Cooper of Virginia Union and Tom Casey, a World War II veteran from Hampton Institute.

Other forces that enhanced the reception of blacks in 1948 were Jackie Robinson's outstanding showing in baseball, the gold medals won by blacks at the London Olympic Games, the signing of blacks in the Basketball Association of America, and Ralph Bunche's diplomatic success in the Middle East.

No one could have imagined the success that lay ahead for black football players. As in baseball and basketball, an era of tokenism (lasting seventeen years) transpired before every team in the merged NFL had at least one black player. Forty years later, the tokenism was gone, but conditioned ideas about the suitability of blacks for certain positions remained. Along the way, blacks would supplant old records and set new ones.

Tokenism: 1946 to 1962

It took seventeen years to integrate the NFL. The Washington Redskins were the last to do so in 1962, when they signed Bobby Mitchell. George Preston Marshall, the Redskins' owner, had a near monopoly on the allegiance of southerners and did not want to lose it. He had secured a network of radio stations to carry Redskins games. But losing seasons forced him to give in to the inevitable. From Kenny Washington and Woody Strode in 1946 to Mitchell in 1962, the list of the first blacks on individual NFL squads grew longer and longer.

These players were always stars. But for the first four of these seventeen years, they competed with another league for the nation's attention.

AAFC: The All-American Football Conference was organized in 1946 by Arch Ward, the sports editor of the *Chicago Tribune* newspaper. Their teams were the first to use air travel as standard practice and the first with a fourteen-game schedule. The first blacks were the Cleveland Browns' Marion Motley and Bill Willis, both of whom made the All-AAFC team that first year. But though the AAFC had wealthy owners, they were short on staff and front office personnel.

Buddy Young of the Yankees' franchise recalled that "The weakness of the AAFC was in overall coaching and player depth. Some of the coaches had never been associated with pro football and didn't realize the necessity of having more than eleven or fifteen good players. In college, you could get by that way but in the pros you must have depth."[24]

Awesome talent enabled Marion Motley to dominate AAFC offensive statistics. In 1948, he led in rushing with 964 yards to become the first black player to lead professional football in that category. That same year, William "Dolly" King of the Chicago Rockets was fourth in receptions with 647 yards. (King also played professional basketball.) In 1949, the AAFC's last year of operation, Joe Perry was on the All-League team. Black players on AAFC teams from 1946 to 1949 are listed in the Reference section.

National Football League: For the first fourteen years of the NFL's existence, from 1920 through 1933, blacks participated. Stars like Frederick Douglass "Fritz" Pollard,

Paul Robeson, Duke Slater, and Joe Lillard thrilled thousands. But in 1934, at the height of the Depression, the owners began enforcing a gentleman's agreement to keep blacks out because of complaints from white players over the lack of jobs. In 1946, blacks were back in the lineups when Kenny Washington and Woody Strode, both from UCLA, donned uniforms for the Los Angeles Rams. (It seems no accident that this breakthrough occurred on the West Coast, where football was the first major professional sport introduced and where its tradition was not as strongly entrenched.) Strode played end, and Washington was a running and defensive back. In an era of limited substitutions, both played offense and defense. Washington was outstanding, gaining 444 yards in 1947 in twelve games (including a 92-yard run against the Chicago Cardinals), for fourth place among rushers.

Emlen Tunnel: A year later, the New York Giants signed a future Hall of Fame inductee in Emlen Tunnel, a World War II veteran from Garrett Hill, Pennsylvania, who had attended Toledo University and the University of Iowa. Tunnel had survived a torpedoed ship in World War II and was a "walk on" (meaning he made the team unrecruited) for the Giants. He played the safety position and was brilliant, setting an NFL record of 79 interceptions for 1,282 yards. Tunnel played for fourteen years, was in nine Pro Bowls, and was an All-Pro four times.

Giants coach Jim Howell said Tunnel "...ranked head and shoulders above the other defensive players..."[25] During his last three years, 1959 through 1961, he played under the legendary Green Bay Packers coach, Vince Lombardi. That same year, the Detroit Lions added Mel Groomes of Indiana University and Bob Mann from the University of Michigan.

In 1949, the last year of the AAFC's existence, the Los Angeles Rams made history by signing the NFL's first player from a black college, Paul "Tank" Younger of Grambling University. Younger had been the best player in the black college system since Ben Stevenson. He had scored sixty touchdowns in four years and was a two-time All-America. He developed a fearsome reputation—he was jailed for five days once for hitting his mother-in-law. The Detroit Lions also added Wally Triplett, the running back from Penn State.

Though only four seasons elapsed before the demise of the AAFC, black players had proven themselves on the field and with the crowds. Some, like Marion Motley, Kenny Washington, and Emlen Tunnel had made themselves indispensable. But financial losses in the AAFC forced their owners to seek a merger with the NFL. The new and stronger NFL, which began in 1950, became the most attractive league in the history of American sports.

A New NFL: Three AAFC franchises—the Cleveland Browns, the San Francisco 49'ers, and the Baltimore Colts—were merged into the NFL in 1950, and a new rule allowing free substitutions was effected. More and larger teams meant more jobs for an increasingly popular sport. NFL games drew over 2.7 million fans in 1956 and the owners petitioned Congress for exemption from antitrust laws that major league baseball enjoyed. But the Supreme Court ruled

otherwise in 1957 in *Radovich* v. *NFL*. The owners could, however, package their televised games. That same year, the NFL Players Association was organized.

On August 22, 1959, the American Football League was formed by Lamar Hunt and K.S. "Bud" Adams and listed franchises in New York City, Oakland, Buffalo, Houston, Denver, Los Angeles, Dallas, and Boston. It means more jobs for black players and more incentive for black youngsters to devote themselves to careers in professional sports, while avoiding other perverse avenues. These developments came before the passage of the civil rights laws of the mid-1960s.

The average NFL salary in 1959 was $9,200, but pay had not kept up with inflation since 1949. There were forty-eight black players in 1959, or 12 percent of the total; they were attracted more by the fame, than by the fortune. Nearly all of them were locked into certain positions; they were expected to run the ball, catch it, and keep their mouths shut.

Marion Motley: He continued his outstanding play for the Browns, leading the NFL in rushing, the first black to do so, in 1950 with 810 yards. In one game against the Pittsburgh Steelers, on October 29, he averaged 17.09 yards per carry for a total of 188 yards. His black teammate, Bill Willis, was a stalwart at the guard position and was later inducted into the Hall of Fame.

Ollie Matson: He came out of Trinity, Texas, the University of San Francisco, the Army, and the Olympic track team (he won a Bronze Medal in the 400-meter run) to lead the Chicago Cardinals in 1952. The former All-America outgained the NFL leader in his rookie year. Tank Younger was All-NFL at outside linebacker, part of the Rams' "Bull Elephant" backfield in the early 1950s, and was third in rushing in 1954.

Joe Perry: Perry was fifth in rushing in 1951, but two years later made history as the first black player to rush for more than 1,000 yards—1,018 yards. In 1954 he did it again, running for 1,049 yards to become the first player—white or black—to surpass 1,000 yards two straight seasons. He led the NFL both times and earned a bonus of $5 for every yard gained. In another first, the top three rushers in 1954 were all black— Perry, John Henry Johnson, and Younger. Perry was elected to the Hall of Fame in 1969.

Jim Brown: Brown was in a class by himself. He became, simply, the best the game had yet seen at running a football. He was also coveted by the New York Yankees in baseball and the Syracuse Nationals in basketball. His rookie salary was $12,000, plus a signing bonus of $3,000. In his first year in 1957, he gained 942 yards to lead the NFL. Against the Rams alone, he gained 237 yards.

Odd as it may seem since he had such a tumultuous career, Brown was quiet as a rookie. "I kept my mouth shut,"[26] he said. Brown had trouble renting an apartment where he wanted to in Cleveland, and he was among the first black athletes to freely admit that players frequently had their priorities in the wrong order. "I tooled into [college] All-Star camp in my spanking new covertible...from my bonus money and thirty-six months of time payments..."[27] Of course, his salary did go up, from $12,000

in 1957 to $32,000 in 1960, to $45,000 in 1962.

Brown's black teammate, Milton Campbell, did not fare as well. Campbell, like Ollie Matson, was an Olympian but he was castigated because he had a white wife. Campbell recalls a conversation with Browns coach Paul Brown in which Brown asked him, "Why'd you get married?"[28] Campbell replied, "For the same reason you got married." Yet the Browns quarterback Otto Graham was quoted as saying, "We've never cared whether a player was colored, white, green, or red—just so he did his job."[29]

Later, the Giants offered to take Campbell if he were "free and clear." They never called, so Campbell played in Canada with the Hamilton Tigercats, where he found the same kind of discrimination; he scored a touchdown on each of the first five times he carried the ball.

Campbell could not call on the Players Association then. The NFLPA was woefully weak at the time, and individual black players had their own sets of problems. No team had more than three blacks at a time from 1946 through 1962. There were no black assistant or head coaches, and no black player representatives. Few civil rights organizations seemed interested in the plight of a relative handful of players, so moral support was lacking; yet they played under enormous pressure.

Jim Brown set standards that remain today. He led the league in rushing in eight of his nine years, and held the total career rushing yardage record for nineteen years. Esteemed *New York Times* sportswriter Red Smith said, "For mercurial speed, airy nimbleness, and explosive violence in one package of undistilled evil, there is no other like Mr. Brown."[30] Added Grambling University coach Eddie Robinson, "The amazing thing about Jim is that he did what he did in only nine seasons."[31]

Brown formed the Black Economic Union after his playing days were over to assist black-owned businesses. Later, he followed the lead of Paul Robeson and Woody Strode, and became an actor. His most famous role was that of a troublemaker-turned-good-guy in *The Dirty Dozen.*

Len Ford: He was a 6-foot 5-inch end at the University of Michigan, the Los Angeles Dons in the AAFC in 1949, and the Cleveland Browns in 1950. He set records during his career and was inducted into the Hall of Fame in 1976. Bob Mann also appeared in the record books in 1951, while finishing fourth in receptions with 696 yards at Green Bay.

Lenny Moore: The premier receivers of the period were Lenny Moore from Penn State and Bobby Mitchell from Illinois. Moore was the second black receiver among the NFL top five, amassing 687 yards and scoring seven touchdowns in 1957 for the Baltimore Colts. Quarterback Johnny Unitas and Moore were the most feared passing duo of their time. In one stretch, Moore caught touchdown passes in eighteen straight games. In the 1959 NFL championship game, Moore caught a touchdown pass and black teammate Johnny Sample intercepted two, one for a 42-yard score.

Dick "Night Train" Lane: The running backs and receivers were not the only stars of the period. Lane led the NFL in interceptions twice, with fourteen in 1952—a record—and ten in 1954. He entered the Hall of Fame in 1974. Willie Wood of the Green Bay Packers led the league in punt returns in 1961 and in interceptions in 1962.

Roosevelt Brown: Brown, a tackle, left Morgan State in 1953 to join the New York Giants, where he played for thirteen years. An All-Pro eight years, he was inducted into the Hall of Fame in 1975, the first from a black college. Gene "Big Daddy" Lipscomb was another fearsome lineman who terrorized offenses with the Rams and then the Colts. Lipscomb unfortunately died prematurely of a drug overdose, a problem that was to plague black players beginning in the late 1970s and continuing into the 1980s.

Uncommon Progress

From Marion Motley and Kenny Washington to Jim Brown and Lenny Moore, black players made uncommon progress in their first seventeen years in professional football. Many suffered racial abuse from team members, opposing players, coaches, and fans. But they were aware they were the first wave of black performers and had to make good.

They were also buoyed by the success of blacks in other sports. From 1957 through 1962, Blacks had reached the top in baseball with Willie Mays, in track and field with Rafer Johnson and Wilma Rudolph, in basketball with Bill Russell and Wilt Chamberlain, in tennis with Althea Gibson, and in boxing with Cassius Clay and Sonny Liston. Their fortunes could only improve. From just two players in 1946 to over 12 percent of the NFL in 1960, they showed what could be done given the opportunity. In the next dozen years blacks had to contend with problems of another competing league and the continuing belief among coaches that they were unfit for certain positions.

Acceptance: 1963 to 1971

If it took seventeen years for blacks to be listed among all NFL teams, it took another nine years to play at every position. The first blacks hired were running backs and ends, players who influenced future trends. The following factors kept blacks primarily relegated to the positions of running back, end, safety, and cornerback: (1) some black and white high school coaches intentionally steered talented players into the safe "black" positions; (2) few white colleges had outstanding black quarterbacks who knew sophisticated offenses; (3)there were no black NFL coaches or assistants to help correct the erroneous assumptions; (4) white professional coaches worried about morale among white players if blacks were put in some positions; (5) there was little outside pressure from influential whites to change; (6) the NFLPA did not press the issue in the early 1960s; and (7) neither the NFL nor the AFL took a public stand until 1965.

By 1960, it was clear that television had a love affair with the sport. The AFL had begun operating and, between both leagues, there were franchises in every section of the nation. The current commissioner of the NFL, Alvin "Pete" Rozelle, assumed his stewardship on January 26, 1960. Professional football was on a roll

and none of the proprietors wanted to change the formula.

"In 1960, however, blacks made up only 5.5 percent of the linebackers and guards. There were no regular centers, kickers, punters, or quarterbacks at all."[32]

The conclusions drawn were: (1) blacks cannot be trusted at certain positions because they are not smart enough; (2) they will have shorter careers and thus lower pensions because their jobs are fraught with a high risk of injury; (3) they do not make good leaders; (4) they wind up competing with one another for the same positions; and (5) a quota is implied.

The theory most advanced by sociologists to explain this dilemma was that of "centrality," meaning positions calling for more responsibility and interaction among two or more players were "central" slots and were reserved for whites. Quarterbacks, centers, offensive guards, and linebackers had to "talk" to their teammates. Safeties, wide receivers, cornerbacks, tackles, and running backs operated more on their own. That blacks had led the NFL in rushing in six of the ten years before 1960 was not lost on their followers. Blacks also led the AFL in rushing and receiving in its first year.

University of California at Berkeley sociologist Harry Edwards, who led the proposed Olympic boycott by black athletes in 1968, qualified the centrality theory by saying the "relative outcome control" or "leadership responsibility" was more important than centrality alone. Whatever the reasons, coaches, scouts, fans, and many players themselves tended to believe the stereotyped roles. But blacks seemed willing enough to trade being forced into just four or five positions for the glory of setting rushing and receiving records.

Jim Brown firmly agreed that blacks were being confined. "There are black positions. A lot of coaches are kind of stupid. They don't know anything about black people or black players. We obviously know they don't want blacks at quarterback because that takes brains. Every time you hear them talk about a black leader, they say he leads by example. If he's smart, 'Well, he's a troublemaker.'"[33]

For fifteen years, black players knew they were being discriminated against, but said little about it publicly for fear of losing their jobs or being labeled a troublemaker. After all, it was explained, before 1946 they did not play at all.

More Problems: Salary disputes and evaluations were also issues. Already being made to feel inferior as individuals, blacks suffered in compensation as well. Until the early 1970s, few football players used agents to negotiate their contracts, and average salaries were lower than for either basketball or baseball. Players were encouraged to keep their salaries a secret. According to Jim Brown, a player in the 1960s was "...unaware of his teammates' salaries, has no reliable measuring stick for deciding how much money to ask...players have only a vague idea of their worth."[34] But with full or nearly full stadiums, owners had little incentive to raise salaries.

Another contributing factor affecting the professional game in this decade was the southern white colleges' continued refusal to recruit blacks. In essence, a part of the feeder system still discriminated, thus lessening the criticism at the top. The Sugar Bowl did not allow blacks to participate until 1965, when Louisiana State beat Syracuse 13–10. That same year the AFL moved their East–West game out of New Orleans when some black players complained they were barred from some public social clubs that were open to their white teammates. To his credit, AFL Commissioner Joe Foss acted swiftly in this regard and moved the game to Houston's Jeppesen Stadium. This incident helped to slightly sour Jim Brown's final year.

Blacks were afforded little outside endorsement income as well. Corporations wishing to capitalize on an athlete's appeal to the general public shied away from black players. Jim Brown, the most prolific runner the game had witnessed, had practically no offers. Economist Roger Knoll even coined the phrase "the Jim Brown phenomenon" to describe the notion that a star's outside earning potential was determined more by his or her fame than skill. Brown's reputation off the field was always suspect in the press and, if Brown could not get endorsements, it was reasoned, other blacks were also of dubious value.

As proof of these perceptions, the August 1972 issue of *Civil Rights Digest* reported that "for seventeen of twenty-six professional teams replying to queries, 75 percent of endorsement slots offered went to players at "central" (white) positions."[35]

Outstanding Field Performances: In spite of the problems, blacks scored on the field with their own particular style of play. Exceptional pride was taken by the runners and receivers. These were *black* positions and they wanted to keep it that way. Jim Brown not only set the yardage standards, he helped entrench the very image of the quintessential black runner—powerful, fast, and blessed with tremendous balance.

Gale Sayers: He took up where Jim Brown left off and was one of only two black runners who began their careers in the 1960s to make the Hall of Fame. Sayers came from a very poor family in Wichita, Kansas, where he was born on May 30, 1943. Sayers starred in track and football in high school and then naively signed seventeen college letters of intent. Finally settling on the University of Kansas, he was sensational on the field, though he was once ejected for shoving an Oklahoma State player who had called him a "nigger." He was also arrested in his senior year for taking part in a sit-in to protest off-campus housing discrimination. He signed with the Chicago Bears before graduation, but later returned to Kansas to not only finish but to earn his master's degree.

Sayers was not a power runner in the mold of Jim Brown. Brown was 6-feet 2-inches and 218 pounds; Sayers was 6-feet 2-inches and 205 pounds. Veterans agreed he was the shiftiest runner yet seen. No one could change directions like this Kansas cyclone. On November 5, 1965, he scored a record six touchdowns in a game played on a muddy field against the San Francisco 49'ers. Bears coach George Halas said Sayers' performance "...was the greatest football exhibition I've ever seen in my life." Sayers' sixth touchdown was on a kickoff return after he had been taken out of the game at running back.

In another game against the 49ers, in November 1968, Sayers was block-tackled by Kermit Alexander and his knee was injured. But the following year he led the league in rushing with 1,032 yards and was the highest-paid player. He developed a warm friendship with white teammate Brian Piccolo who died of cancer (their relationship was developed into a film entitled *Brian's Song*). Sayers retired in 1970 when his injured knee took away his mobility completely.

Other Stars: Other players who led the NFL in rushing were Leroy Kelly of Cleveland, in 1967–68, and Larry Brown of the Washington Redskins in 1970. The great wide receiver Bob Hayes starred during his collegiate years at Florida A&M under coach Jake "Papa Rattler" Gaither. He went on to win a gold medal in the 100-meter race in the 1960 Olympics and then a Super Bowl ring with the Dallas Cowboys. His case, however, is a special one.

In 1965, Hayes caught 46 passes for the Cowboys for 1,003 yards, an astounding 21.8 yards-per reception average. Unfortunately, in April 1978, Hayes was arrested for selling cocaine and sentenced to five years in prison. He served eleven months and was released. Filled with remorse for his deed he admitted that, "I'm guilty and I'm wrong. I've paid the price in my image and my respect. People see me as Bob Hayes, the dope dealer, not Bob Hayes the citizen. It hurts."[36]

Among the receivers, Bobby Mitchell led the league in 1962, Charley Taylor in 1966–67, Clifton McNeil in 1968, and Dick Gordon in 1970. Cleveland Browns standout Paul Warfield, who came from Ohio State and who led the league with 52 receptions during his 1964 rookie season, was touted as the most acrobatic receiver until

Lynn Swann joined the Pittsburgh Steelers in 1974.

In the 1973 Super Bowl, the 6-foot, 188-pound Warfield caught a 47-yard touchdown pass from Bob Griese to help the Dolphins defeat the Redskins 14–7. Along with Larry Csonka and Jim Kiick, Warfield left the Dolphins and joined the fledgling World Football League in 1974. The WFL folded after one season. Warfield was inducted into the Hall of Fame in 1983.

Charley Taylor: Taylor, of the Redskins, was the first black receiver to lead the league twice in receptions. His career lasted thirteen years and he was inducted into the Hall of Fame in 1984. He broke Don Maynard's NFL reception record in 1975 with 635 catches.

Line Players: The linemen of the period included some legendary names. Carl Eller, Alan Paige, and Jim Marshall made up three-fourths of the Minnesota Vikings' "Purple People Eaters" defensive line. Lamar Lundy, Rosey Grier, and David "Deacon" Jones made up three-fourths of the Los Angeles Rams' "Fearsome Foursome." Deacon Jones made the Hall of Fame in 1980.

Another Hall of Famer, Willie Davis, helped the Green Bay Packers win Championships in 1961, 1962, 1965, 1966 and 1967. Davis, from Texarkana, Arkansas, played ten years, then earned a master's degree in business administration, which he used as a launching pad for a highly successful business career. In 1967, his teammate, Dave Robinson became the first black All-Pro outside linebacker since Tank Younger in 1951. In the 1966 NFL championship game against the Dallas Cowboys, Robinson tackled quarterback Don Meredith to stop a Cowboy drive and help the Packers win 34–27. Robinson was also instrumental in convincing coaches that blacks made outstanding players at this "thinking" position. Willie Lanier from Morgan State also starred at linebacker for the Kansas City Chiefs, who won the Super Bowl in 1970.

Another teammate of Robinson and Davis was Herb Adderly, heralded as the best cornerback the game had seen. He was All-Pro five times and, in the second Super Bowl, in 1968, intercepted a pass from the Oakland Raiders' Daryl Lamonica to ensure a Packers victory, 33–14. Adderly joined the Hall of Fame in 1980.

In 1962, Willie Wood was the first black player to lead the league in interceptions. He doubled as a premier punt returner, returning 14 for an average of 16.1 yards in 1961, the highest average until Bob Hayes ran back 15 punts for an average of 20.8 yards in 1968.

American Football League: In the same year that Pete Rozelle became the NFL commissioner, the AFL began operating. Black players led the new league in rushing and receiving in that first season—Abner Haynes in rushing with 875 yards and Lionel Taylor in receiving with 92 passes for 1,235 yards. The AFL was much less hesitant in using any player in any position than the tradition-bound NFL. AFL play emphasized the passing game.

Abner Haynes scored 19 touchdowns for the Dallas Texans in 1962. Cookie Gilchrist left the Canadian Football League to play with the Buffalo Bills that same year and promptly led the AFL in rushing with

1,096 yards. In 1962 four of the top five AFL rushers—Gilchrist, Haynes, Clem Daniels, and Curtis McClinton—were black. Even though in 1963 there were 46 blacks in the AFL and 100 in the NFL, 56 were linemen—41 were halfbacks, 33 were defensive backs, 16 were fullbacks, and there were no quarterbacks—stacking of blacks was still evident.

Despite continued patterns of racism and attitudes of superiority on the part of the AFL and NFL, both leagues and players benefited from the rivalry. The bidding war of 1966 for draft choices cost the two leagues a combined total of $6 million. A "peace" agreement was signed that year and resulted in the first Super Bowl between the two leagues; the portended merger of the AFL and the NFL occurred in 1970. It is difficult to say whether or not the quality of play in the AFL was equal to that of the NFL, but black players dominated in many statistical categories. Outstanding black players in the AFL achieved notable records of play.

New Role Models: By the late 1960s, black players brought a new style of play to the football field, one born of pride in their accomplishments, an increased assertiveness effected because they were no longer tokens, and the rise in levels of self-esteem brought about by the black social revolution. And blacks accentuated their success. Nicknames were given to some, with the full cooperation of the white owners. Football was entertainment and the flashy, brash antics of some black players was enjoyed by the home crowd. These athletes—black and white—were removed from their pedestals and made to look

human. The civil rights laws had been passed in the mid-1960s and blacks felt freer to be expressive and to show off in front of tens of thousands of people.

A white quarterback, Joe Namath of the New York Jets, who flouted the customary rules of decorum for athletes, was emulated by blacks. Said Johnny Sample, the black cornerback, "Our heroes were a new breed of players. Men like Joe Namath who wore their hair long and bragged about how good they were replaced the men like Johnny Unitas, the clean-cut All-American-kid type."[37] Like their counterparts in baseball and basketball, black football players no longer automatically kept their mouths shut as did Jim Brown in his rookie year. But with this new image came a new set of problems.

By the beginning of the 1971 season, black players had increased their numbers at center, quarterback, offensive guard, linebacker, punter, and kicker from 5.5 percent in 1960 to 8.4 percent. Whites in these positions increased their numbers 10 percent from the 1960 level to 42.3 percent. "In the three "whitest" positions—quarterback, center, and offensive guard—10.4 percent had been playing for ten years. Only 5.8 percent of blacks in the "blackest" positions had been around that long."[38] Full acceptance was still not complete, and seemed a long way off.

1972 to 1984:
Super Players, Super Salaries, Super Bowls

In the early 1970's, tickets for NFL games became more sought after than those for any other type of athletic contest. Corporations bought up sections of season tickets, and sellout crowds were the norm rather than the exception. There was a constant demand to make the game more exciting, and fans, especially those watching on television, wanted more scoring; rules were changed to accommodate them, and in nearly every instance black players benefitted because, aside from the white quarterbacks, they were the most gifted performers on the field.

The Super Runners: The hashmarks on the field that determined where the ball is placed for each "down" and the uprights on the goalposts were both narrowed in 1972. The former rule change enabled shifty runners to gain more yards because there was now more room on either side of where the ball was centered. Ten players gained more than 1,000 yards that year. Six years later, the NFL schedule was increased to sixteen games, two more than before. These changes ushered in an era of super runners. Black players who gained more than 1,000 yards per season are listed in the Reference section.

Orenthal James "O.J." Simpson: As of 1970, blacks had led the league in rushing fifteen times since 1950 and nine times since 1960. But no runner since Jim Brown captured the imagination of fans as did Simpson. He attended the famed McClymonds High in Oakland, California, then a junior college, and then transferred to the University of Southern California, where he won the Heisman Trophy. In 1969, he signed a $250,000 contract for three years with the Buffalo Bills. Simpson was the best broken field runner since Gale Sayers, and won the respect of his peers. Said Franco Harris, the

brilliant fullback for the Pittsburgh Steelers, "I...consider O.J. Simpson *the* running back...He, to me, had so much natural ability. I know there's no way I can touch him."[39]

Simpson reset the yardstick by which premier runners were measured, and he gained on average 200, rather than 100 yards per game. On December 16, 1973, Simpson replaced the challenge of gaining 1,000 yards per season with his record-shattering mark of 2,003 yards, which he set in a game played against the New York Jets. Three years later on November 25, 1976, he set a new single-game rushing record of 273 yards against the Detroit Lions. Though he never played in a Super Bowl, he was acknowledged as the premier runner of the 1970s. On August 3, 1985, he was inducted into the Hall of Fame, along with Joe Namath. Simpson made one of the smoothest retirement transitions of any player, becoming an actor, movie producer, television commentator, and a man much sought after for commerical endorsements.

John Brockington of the Green Bay Packers became the first player to gain over 1,000 yards in each of his first three seasons. Don Woods set an NFL rushing record for a rookie, of 1,162 yards in 1974; a record that would be broken four more times in nine years—all by black runners.

Franco Harris: Harris was a mainstay for the Pittsburgh Steelers for over a decade. This son of an African-American father and an Italian mother had a chance to surpass Jim Brown's NFL rushing record, but a 1984 contract dispute with the Steelers forced him to sign with the Seattle Seahawks, and forestalled that possibility. Upon retirement, the thirty-four-year-old Harris remained 363 yards short of the record.

Harris may be most remembered for "The Immaculate Reception," a pass he caught in the Steelers' 1972 playoff game against the Oakland Raiders. The pass, intended for John Fuqua, bounced off of Raider defender Jack Tatum and into the arms of Harris, who raced 60 yards for a touchdown. The score at the time was 7–6, in favor of Oakland, with fourth down and 10 yards to go and 22 seconds remaining in the game. The Steelers won 13–7.

In 1975, Harris set a Super Bowl record of 158 yards rushing, against the Minnesota Vikings. He broke Matt Snell's record of 121 yards, set in 1969. Harris is sure to make the Hall of Fame.

Walter Payton: The runner who did eventually break Brown's NFL record was Walter Payton. He attended Jackson State in Mississippi, and is the only runner to set a all-time rushing record for his college conference and the NFL. Nicknamed "Sweetness", Payton has played for the Chicago Bears his entire career. On November 20, 1977, he broke O.J. Simpson's single game rushing record, gaining 275 yards against the Vikings on forty carries. On October 7, 1984, he broke Jim Brown's career rushing record of 12,312 yards in a game against the New Orleans Saints.

Payton was modest about his success and paid homage to Brown. "Jim Brown's still the greatest,"[40] he said. "The thing I want is not to be known as the best, but to be known as giving the best of myself." Like Franco Harris, Payton is destined for the Hall of Fame in his first year of eligibility.

Tony Dorsett: Dorsett, from the University of Pittsburgh, is number seven on the NFL's career rushing list. A Heisman Trophy winner before joining the Dallas Cowboys in 1977, he was the first NFL player to gain more than 1,000 yards in his first five seasons—an outstanding performance.

Earl Campbell: He was one of twelve children born to a poor family from Tyler, Texas. At the University of Texas he gained 4,444 yards, captured the Heisman Trophy, and was named the Southwest Conference's Player of the Decade, a stellar honor in football-mad Texas. Campbell always had a serious demeanor concerning his athletic accomplishments. He said, "Most kids have a chance to be a kid. I never was a kid too long. I was raised without a father, so I grew up fast."[41]

Campbell set a rookie rushing record of 1,450 yards in 1978 for the Houston Oilers and, in 1980, had ten 100-yard games and four 200-yard games for a total of 1,934 yards. His relationship with Oiler coach Bum Phillips was exceptionally close and led Phillips to say on more than one occasion that Campbell was like a son to him. Few white coaches would have been so public with a comment like that a decade ago.

At the end of the 1984 season, sixteen of the top twenty career rushing leaders were black and three of them—O.J. Simpson, John Henry Johnson, Floyd Little—had spent some time in the AFL. Others deserve mention. Duane Thomas, a troubled but talented runner for the Cowboys, was the hero of the 1972 Super Bowl. (Five years later he filed for bankruptcy, claiming $4.66

in assets and $26,979 in debts.) Otis Anderson broke Earl Campbell's rookie rushing record in 1979 with 1,605 yards.

In the thirty years between 1950 and 1980, blacks won the rushing title twenty-six times, and ten times between 1970 and 1980. Two runners who seem destined for the Hall of Fame are Eric Dickerson and Marcus Allen. Dickerson attended Southern Methodist University and set another rookie rushing record of 1,808 yards in 1983, for the Los Angeles Rams. A year later he smashed O.J. Simpson's single season rushing record with a 2,007-yard performance. And he surpassed Simpson's record in only the fifteenth game of the season, against the Oilers at Anaheim Stadium.

Allen was a Heisman Trophy winner for the University of Southern California and was the Los Angeles Raiders Most Valuable Player in the 1984 Super Bowl.

Many theories have been advanced to explain the predominance of blacks as the premier runners in professional football, but most conclusions point to an early cultural emphasis on the sport itself, early screening of the most talented players, positive reinforcement from peers and schools, good coaching, a high personal achievement index, and a feeling grounded in racial pride that the potential rewards are worth the effort. Young black boys could point to few other endeavors that offered as high a psychic and monetary return as did sports and its glamor positions. Running backs are among the most publicized athletes in all of sports.

The Receivers: Of all the offensive maneuvers, none is as exciting as the long pass caught by the acrobatic wide receivers and tight ends. Both positions call for superior athletic skills, but the wide receiver is generally the speedier of the two. A handful of them appear over and over in the record books: Harold Jackson, Cliff Branch, John Jefferson, Harold Carmichael, Charlie Joiner, Lynn Swann, Ahmad Rashad (formerly Bobby Moore), James Lofton, Kellen Winslow, Art Monk, Drew Pearson, Gene Washington, Roy Green, John Stallworth, Mark Clayton, Mark Duper, Wesley Walker, and Charlie Brown.

Lynn Swann of the Steelers is best remembered for his Super Bowl performances. In 1976, Swann's 64-yard touchdown reception against the Cowboys helped the Steelers win 21–17. His 42-yard reception in 1980 aided in a 31–19 win over the Rams. Swann's teammate, John Stallworth, caught two touchdown passes in that same game.

In 1980, Kellen Winslow, John Jefferson, and Charlie Joiner of the San Diego Chargers became the first threesome from the same team to each amass more than 1,000 yards receiving. Joiner was the NFL all-time leader in receptions with 657, at the end of 1984. Winslow, a tight end, set a record for receptions for that position with 89 in 1980. The next year, he set another record of 5 touchdown receptions in one game against the Raiders. But he is best remembered for his one-man show against the Miami Dolphins in the 1981 AFC playoff game, a 41–38 win for the Chargers. In that game, Winslow had 13 pass receptions for 166 yards—including a touchdown—and blocked Uwe von Schammann's field goal attempt in the last minute of regulation time. His performance was one of the premier efforts in the history of the sport. The average size of tight ends by then had increased from 6-feet 3-inches and 228 pounds in 1974 to 6-feet 4-inches and 236 in 1984, such were the physical demands on this important position.

All receivers were aided in 1978, when the rules were changed to disallow corner-backs and outside linebackers from block-ing past five yards from their side of the line of scrimmage. This change freed the most elusive receivers, and yardage totals soared. It is doubtful that as many players would have gained as many yards without this change. As of the end of the 1984 season, half of the top twenty all-time receiving leaders were black.

The Secondary Leaders: The second-ary is that part of the defensive team that plays behind the line of scrimmage. The players incude the linebackers, corner-backs, and safeties. An overwhelming ma-jority of cornerbacks and safeties are black, and almost all of these men have patterned their styles of play after Emlen Tunnell, Dick "Night Train" Lane, and Sam Huff (the white linebacker who during the 1950s was a standout with the New York Giants).

Ken Houston of the Houston Oilers set an NFL record with 4 touchdowns on inter-ceptions in 1971. In 1980, Houston ex-tended the NFL record by scoring 9 touchdowns on interceptions. Houston's teammate, Vernon Perry, had four intercep-tions in the Oilers 17–14, 1979 AFC playoff win against the Chargers.

The secondary elite consists of those players with ten or more interceptions in a single season. They are shown in the Refer-ence section.

Punt and Kickoff Return Specialists: The last group of players with a substantial amount of black participation is the unit known today as the special teams. These men make up a group of athletes who, with recklessness and abandon, perform a vari-ety of tasks. Many rookies obtain their "rights of passage" into the NFL with these special teams. Those who return kickoffs and punts are ranked according to the number of yards gained per attempt. Ranked number one among black players and number four overall among punt retur-ners is Billy "White Shoes" Johnson, with a career return average of 12.3 yards. Among kick-off returners, Gale Sayers tops the NFL list with an astounding 30.6 yard average. No other player has a career average of 30 or more yards per return on kick-offs. The complete list of punt and kick-off return leaders is found in the Reference section.

Outstanding Linemen: The most un-sung of all players are the linemen who, with the exception of William "The Re-frigerator" Perry of the Chicago Bears, sel-dom, if ever touch the ball to advance with it. Yet their jobs are vitally important if their teams are to score. Even the best among them are usually unknown to those outside their cities or conferences. Perhaps the best way to recognize their worth is to list those named to the All-Pro squads, an elite group selected to represent the most talented. The complete list of black All-Pro players is found in the Reference section.

The Black Quarterbacks: The first black professional quarterback to play reg-ularly was Marlin Briscoe, who in 1968 played for the Denver Broncos of the then American Football League.

Back in 1953, Willie Thrower played a few downs as quarterback for the Chicago Bears, but never as a regular. Blacks were still not trusted at all positions then, especially at quarterback. Briscoe came in to replace Steve Tensi, who broke his collar bone. The 5-foot 11-inch Briscoe had completed 333 of 609 passes and thrown for 52 touchdowns, while attending the University of Omaha.

Some college quarterbacks, like Gene Washington of Stanford, assumed they would not be given a fair chance at playing the position and prepared themselves to adjust in the professional ranks. Briscoe wound up playing wide receiver. Others like James Harris and Joe Gilliam chose not to switch. Harris, it was learned, was not particularly fast and he had bad knees. O.J. Simpson added that Harris also "...tended to drill some of his passes too hard..."[42] It was obvious to all that the first regularly playing black quarterback would have to be exceptional in every way.

In the early 1970s the controversy over the lack of a black NFL quarterback reached new levels. Harris decried the discrimination, and certain white coaches were singled out for attention. Briscoe, who was no longer playing the position, pointed at Lou Saban: "He's cut every black quarterback, except Gilliam, who has been in the league. He cut me, he cut Jimmy Harris, he's cut Karl Douglas and he cut Matt Reed. This man's track record has to indicate he's a racist."[43] Yet, Saban is credited with introducing a new offense, while coaching the Buffalo Bills, which was built around O.J. Simpson.

There is little doubt that many coaches did not trust blacks at quarterback and other "thinking" positions because of their own conditioned prejudices. D. Stanley Eitzen and David C. Sanford reported that a survey of NFL coaches indicated that 47 percent were either born in the South or played their college football there. Consequently, it is not surprising to find instances where black quarterbacks were discriminated against by white coaches.

Two black quarterbacks who regularly play the position are Doug Williams from Grambling University, who played with the Tampa Bay Buccaneers, and Warren Moon, who left the Canadian Football League to play for the Houston Oilers for $1.1 million per year in 1984. Willie Totten of Mississippi Valley State should have an excellent chance in the NFL at this position.

Super Salaries

Football has historically paid lower salaries than either baseball or basketball. In the 1950s, to some players, football was considered just an exciting part-time job. Most made under $10,000 a year, and bonuses like the $5 per yard gained awarded Joe Perry many years ago, was considered ample. Jim Brown signed for $12,000 as a rookie in 1957, the same year the NFLPA was organized. By 1970, the average salary was only $23,000, and in 1975 it was only $39,600.

NFL team owners had little incentive to raise salaries. Stadiums were full or nearly so, and there was evidently a large psychic reward felt by players for being a part of the game. A reserve system similar to the one in baseball was in force until 1977, which allowed a team to select, retain, control, trade, and sell players, as well as resolve disputes. After the NFL and the AFL signed their "peace agreement" in 1966, Congress gave the new NFL an exemption from antitrust laws. Correspondingly, the NFLPA organized strikes in 1968, 1970, and 1974. Additionally, the players association won a court case—*John Mackey* v. *NFL*—in 1975. Mackey, then a black player with the Baltimore Colts, was the president of the NFLPA. A year later, in the court case *Yazoo Smith* v. *NFL,* the NFL draft was declared illegal.

In 1977 the NFL and the NFLPA signed an agreement whereby $15 million in past compensation was awarded to the NFLPA—salaries began soaring. But with the agreement and escalating salaries, came problems with illegal drugs, particularly cocaine. Bob Hayes, formerly of the Dallas Cowboys, spent eleven months in jail for selling cocaine. Former Miami Dolphin Eugene "Mercury" Morris was sentenced to twenty years for the same offense. Thomas "Hollywood" Henderson received a four-year sentence for sexual assault that was induced by cocaine and alcohol. Other players like Charles White, Rickey Young, and Chuck Muncie were also mentioned in the press as having problems with cocaine.

Under the new Executive Director of the NFL Players Association, Gene Upshaw, who is black, the organization had spent considerable resources on education and rehabilitation, but the drug problem still remains critical today. Not only have many players ruined their family lives, they have depleted their own resources as well—a heavy price for an average career of four and a half years in a sport that usually leaves its participants with permanent injuries.

Problems with Agents: Ill-advised players also fell victim to sales pitches by unscrupulous agents who wanted to negotiate their contracts. Black players were relatively unsophisticated in handling large sums of money, and nearly all had family and friends who asked for financial favors. Agents used false promises and dubious incentives to sign players as clients. Willie Gault noted, "One agent knew of my religious background and he said God had sent him to represent me."[44] Gault was not alone.

Other black players were victims of bad investment advice (this happened to basketball and baseball players as well). The most highly-publicized case was that of running back Tony Dorsett who, in 1985, saw the Internal Revenue Service attach two of his homes for $400,000 in back taxes. Though his predicament was widely known because he is a superstar, he was not the only player to be a victim of unsound investment advice.

Super Bowls

The Super Bowl games of the NFL have been the ten highest rated individual television shows on the air—that includes all shows. The first game was not a sellout and was played in 1967, before the formal merger of the NFL and the AFL. These contests represent the ultimate test under pressure, and the tension involved is unsurpassed in any sport. More than a third of the entire American population watch some portion of these games. Blacks have starred in each game, and their Super Bowl highlights, and outstanding performance in NFL championship games before 1967 follow.

1950 Marion Motley of the Cleveland Browns is the first black player in an NFL Championship Game

1956 Roosevelt Brown of the New York Giants is second starter.

1957 Jim Brown is first to score, on a 29-yard run. His counterpart as fullback was John Henry Johnson of the Detroit Lions.

1959 Lenny Moore caught one touchdown pass and Johnny Sample intercepted two passes—one for a touchdown—for the Baltimore Colts.

1961 Willie Davis and Willie Wood help the Green Bay Packers shut out the Giants, 37–0.

1965 Willie Davis, Dave Robinson, Herb Adderly, and Willie Wood assist Green Bay in a 23–12 win over the Browns.

1967 Super Bowl I. Willie Wood intercepts a pass thrown by Len Dawson of the Kansas City Chiefs, to help preserve Green Bay's 35–10 victory.

1968 Super Bowl II. Herb Adderly intercepts a pass and scores on a 60-yard touchdown in the fourth quarter against the Oakland Raiders. The Packers win 33–14.

1969 Super Bowl III. The New York Jets win over the Baltimore Colts 16–7. Matt Snell sets rushing record of 121 yards.

1970 Super Bowl IV. Otis Taylor catches a 46-yard pass for Chiefs in a 23–7 win over the Minnesota Vikings. Mike Garrett also starred.

1971 Super Bowl V. John Mackey catches a 45-yard touchdown pass to help the Colts to a 16–13 win over the Cowboys.

1972 Super Bowl VI. Jethro Pugh, Herb Adderly, Mel Renfro, Duane Thomas, and Cornell Green help hold off the Miami Dolphins in 24–3 win for the Cowboys.

1973 Super Bowl VII. Paul Warfield catches a 47-yard touchdown pass for Dolphins in their 14–7 win over the Washington Redskins.

1974 Super Bowl VIII. Curtis Johnson intercepts a pass at the Dolphins goal line in a 24–7 Dolphins win.

1975 Super Bowl IX. Franco Harris breaks Matt Snell's record with 158 yards rushing, for the first Pittsburgh Steelers title win in 42 years.

1976 Super Bowl X. Lynn Swann catches a 64-yard touchdown pass with 4:25 remaining in the Steelers 21–17 win over the Cowboys.

1977 Super Bowl XI. Willie Brown scores on a 75-yard intercepted pass in the Oakland Raiders 32–14 win over the Minnesota Vikings.

1978 Super Bowl XII. Rick Upchurch had a 67-yard kick-off return, but his Denver Broncos lost to the Cowboys, 27–10.

1979 Super Bowl XIII. John Stallworth catches touchdown passes of twenty-eight and seventy-five yards in the Steelers 35–31 win over the Cowboys.

1980 Super Bowl XIV. Lynn Swann and John Stallworth catch touchdown passes in the Steelers 31–19 win over the Los Angeles Rams.

1981 Super Bowl XV. Cliff Branch catches two touchdown passes for the Raiders, who defeat the Eagles 27–10.

1982 Super Bowl XVI. Eric Wright of the San Francisco 49'ers intercepts a fourth period pass to set up a field goal. The 49'ers win 26–21.

1983 Super Bowl XVII. Alvin Garrett of the Washington Redskins catches a four-yard TD pass. The Redskins beat Miami 27–17.

1984 Super Bowl XVIII. Marcus Allen rushes for a Super Bowl record 191 yards in the Los Angeles Raiders 38–9 victory over the Redskins.

SUMMARY

Black participation in football has come a long way since the first intercollegiate contest in 1892, between Livingstone College and Biddle College (now known as Johnson C. Smith University). Perhaps more comfort should have been taken when William H. Lewis was named as an All-America at Harvard University before the turn of the century.

Some of the men of black America's sports legends are football players. Besides Lewis, there is Fritz Pollard, Alfred "Jazz" Bird, Paul Robeson, Robert Marshall, Duke Slater, Jerome Holland, Ben Stevenson,

Kenny Washington, Emlen Tunnell, Jim Brown, Gale Sayers, Herb Adderly, O. J. Simpson, Walter Payton, Franco Harris, Lawrence Taylor, Lynn Swann, and Charlie Joiner.

In the African-American culture, football is an integral part of the social fabric. Black college reunions are set around football contests. Public school popularity for boys is, in part, a function of one's stardom on athletic teams, especially football. Yet many expert observers decry the many hours spent by young black boys in pursuit of an athletic scholarship or a professional career, to the neglect of their studies. Some have termed it a cultural shame. Others allude to Langston Hughes' dictum that "everyone has a right to dream."

What Lies Ahead?   There is still no black head coach of a top-twenty ranked college team, nor of an NFL squad. No blacks serve as general managers of NFL teams. Though there have been blacks at every position, the numerical predominance at running back, wide receiver, cornerback, and safety leaves the undeniable impression that they are still not fully trusted at quarterback, center, linebacker, and as kickers and punters.

There is no indication that blacks will find football any less appealing in the future. They will continue to appear at their "historical" positions and they will still find subtle, and sometimes overt racial barriers in other occupations. Until the black poverty rate decreases by 100 percent, sports will continue to be viewed by most of the black community as the quickest legitimate way out of their condition. As the second most "macho"—next to boxing—of the major sports, football has a special appeal to young boys bent on proving their manhood through a physically violent game.

Hopefully, one day, when black youngsters make the decision to play football, they will do so not because there are no other apparent occupational choices, but because of a true love for the sport.

Notes

1. Sam Lacy, "Harvard Ace Makes History, Team Bonus," *Baltimore Afro-American,* 18 October 1947.
2. Editorial, *Richmond* (Virginia) *Afro-American.*
3. *New York Times,* 3 November 1985, 53.
4. *Social Science Quarterly,* (March 1975): 944.
5. *New York Times,* (October 1985).
6. *New York Telegram and Sun,* 3 December 1955.
7. Jim Brown, *Off My Chest,* (New York: Doubleday and Company, Inc., 1964), 117.
8. Donald Spivey and Thomas E. Jones, "Intercollegiate Athletic Servitude," *Social Science Quarterly,* (March 1975): 945.
9. *Civil Rights Digest,* (August 1972): 23.
10. *Black Sports,* January 1974, 42.
11. *Ebony,* November 1974, 167.
12. Benjamin G. Rader, *American Sports,* (Englewood Cliffs, N.J.: Prentice-Hall, Inc., 1983), 333.
13. *Ebony,* December 1967, 32.
14. Ibid.
15. *Ebony,* December 1970, 134.
16. Douglas S. Looney, "Deception In The Heart Of Texas," *Sports Illustrated,* 30 September 1985, 30.

17. Ibid.
18. Rader, *American Sports,* 24.
19. Ibid., 267.
20. *Ebony,* November 1983, 148.
21. *Ebony,* September 1976, 110.
22. Ibid.
23. *Sports Illustrated,* 19 May 1980, 42.
24. *Official Encyclopedia Of Professional Football,* (New York: New American Library, 1977), 121.
25. *Ebony,* November 1957, 99.
26. Brown, *Off My Chest,* 7.
27. Ibid., 20.
28. Milton Campbell, telephone interview with author, 23 September 1985.
29. *Ebony,* December 1955, 105.
30. Brown, *Off My Chest,* vii.
31. *Ebony,* December 1984, 88.
32. *Social Science Quarterly,* (March 1975): 950.
33. *Black Sports,* November 1973, 56.
34. Brown, *Off My Chest,* 76.
35. *Civil Rights Digest,* (August 1972): 22.
36. *Los Angeles Times,* 25 July 1984, Part VIII, 23.
37. Rader, *American Sports,* 260.
38. *Social Science Quarterly* (March 1975), 950.
39. *Inside Sports,* August 1984, 20.
40. *Ebony,* December 1984, 88.
41. *USA Today,* 27 September 1985.
42. O.J. Simpson, *O.J.: The Education Of A Rich Rookie,* (New York: The Macmillan Company, 1970), 66.
43. *Ebony,* November 1974, 167.
44. *Ebony,* September 1984, 154.

5

Golf

XXXXXXXXXXXXXXXXXXXXXXXXXXXXXXXXXXXXXXXXXXXXXXXXXXXX

After the Second World War, the major battles in golf for blacks came in courts of law rather than on the courses. The Michigan delegation to the Professional Golfers Association (PGA) annual meeting in 1943, had forced a clause in the PGA Constitution that limited membership to whites only. Three of the best black golfers—Bill Spiller, Ted Rhodes, and Madison Gunter—decided to challenge that rule in a $10,000 PGA event in Richmond, California, in January of 1948. Spiller was a four-time United Golfers Association (UGA) champion, and heavyweight champion Joe Louis' personal instructor. These three players sued the PGA and the Richmond Golf Club for $315,000 for refusing their entries. Spiller and Rhodes had qualified by finishing 25th and 11th, respectively, at the Los Angeles Open the previous week. Spiller had even tied the great Ben Hogan in the first round with a 68.

Each player sued on two counts for $5,000 against the club and $100,000 against the PGA, for a total of $315,000. The PGA then agreed to rescind its "caucasians only" policy in return for the suit being dropped. In claiming victory, Spiller noted: "This is bigger than just trying to get into that Richmond Open. We've got to break golf Jim Crow down. I want my kids playing with your kids."[1] Rhodes added, "Those guys don't hit the ball any better than we do. All we need is a chance to get in there and shoot with them."

But the PGA was not like major league baseball. Herb Griffis noted that after paying $2,100 in legal fees, "...if it proved anything, it demonstrated that the PGA could maintain the status quo by insisting that its regulations be followed to ensure orderly development of the tournament business."[2] Graffis never mentioned how the case was finally resolved, only that "after the customary fussing around and publicity, the case was settled out of court." A very strange and misleading account. Yet, more lawsuits were on the way as the number of UGA events increased and more women like Thelma Cowan took the game seriously.

Black Golfers Take Legal Action: The number of black golfers after World War II rose so quickly that segregated public courses could not accommodate the demand. These athletes decided to follow Spiller, Rhodes, and Gunter, and seek legal recourse, which was significant in two respects: first, it marked the first time the black upperclass legally involved itself in sports, and second, the resulting verdicts had ramifications in other sports that also involved the use of public facilities.

A black dentist, Dr. P. O. Sweeny, of Louisville, Kentucky, sued the Parks Department in December of 1947 for the right to use all municipal courses and the Iroquois Amphitheatre. He was turned down by Judge Lawrence Speckman, who ruled, "Social equality between persons of the white and colored races or, in fact, between persons of the same race cannot be enforced by legislation or the courts."[3]

Undaunted, more suits were filed, most of them by black business professionals. Federal Judge W. Calvin Chesnut ruled that Baltimore, Maryland's, Carroll Park course was not of equal standard with the three public courses exclusively reserved for whites. In June 1948, he ordered all the city's public courses open to all.

By 1950, civil rights organizations had become an integral part of these legal actions. The National Association for the Advancement of Colored People (NAACP) viewed these suits as being worthy of their efforts because the outcome involved the use of public facilities paid for, in part, with black tax dollars. Charles P. Lucas, the NAACP's Cleveland, Ohio, local secretary, successfully petitioned the Ohio Court of Appeals to order the Lakeshore Club to open its facilities to blacks. The club used public facilities for its clubhouse and course.

A restricted public course also occasioned the first case in black sports to reach the United States Supreme Court. In March 1950, the Florida Supreme Court upheld the right of Miami Springs to confine black players to one day per week on its lone public course. Joseph Rice, represented by NAACP attorney Franklin Williams, appealed to the United States Supreme Court. In October, the U.S. Supreme Court ordered the Florida Supreme Court to reconsider its decision.

This decision in turn encouraged more black golfers across the country to press for equal access to public facilities. Within the next five years, major suits were filed in Atlanta, Georgia; Nashville, Tennessee; Baton Rouge, Louisiana; Winston-Salem, North Carolina; Fort Worth, Texas; Houston, Texas; Charlotte, North Carolina; Pensacola, Florida; and Jackson, Mississippi.

The resulting court decisions reflected regional traditions. Some cities in the South built new eighteen-hole courses for blacks while others simply opened their public courses to all. The 1954 *Brown* v. *Board of Education* Supreme Court decision offered an added incentive to blacks who sought to use facilities subsidized with public tax funds. The United States Golf Association, a white body, reported nearly 3.8 million golfers on five thousand courses in 1955.

While the UGA itself never filed any lawsuits, their members continued to be legally barred from the Professional Golfers Association's (PGA) events. Prominent black professionals like Howard Wheeler and Ted Rhodes were forbidden to play PGA tournaments by the 1943 PGA decision that barred blacks.

At the annual PGA meeting that year, the Michigan delegation proposed a constitutional amendment. It read, "Professional golfers of the Caucasian race, over the age of eighteen years, residing in North or South America, and who have served at least five years in the profession (either in the employ of a golf club in the capacity of a professional or in the employ of a professional as his assistant) shall be eligible for membership."[4]

When the wisdom of this amendment was challenged, a Michigan delegate replied, "Show us some good golf clubs Negroes have established, and we can talk this over again."[5] The amendment passed.

The Ladies Professional Golfers Association (LPGA), formed in 1948, also barred blacks, though no specific racial clause was included in their constitution.

The UGA in the Fifties: The UGA devoted most of its organizational efforts and resources to increasing its membership, the number of clubs, and is sponsoring events. Unlike the major team sports, there was no group of well-coached black professionals waiting to "tear up" the circuit. It was rare for any black professional to play on a well-manicured golf course, nearly all of which were to be found in private clubs.

The majority of UGA clubs were concentrated in the Northeast and Midwest. It was 1954 before the UGA held its first national event in the South, in Dallas, Texas. Unlike its black counterpart in tennis, the American Tennis Association, the UGA seldom had much influence on its white counterpart, the United States Golf Association. The USGA did not reserve any places in its United States Open for UGA qualifiers as did the United States Lawn Tennis Association for the ATA.

While the best black players were not as recognizable as, say, Satchel Paige or Buddy Young, their records were notable.

Howard Wheeler was a five-time UGA National Professional winner between 1933 and 1958. He was famous for his unorthodox "cross-handed" grip. (He had his right hand near the butt of the club.) Ted Rhodes won the UGA Professional title three consecutive years, from 1949 to 1951, and again in 1957.

Among the women, Thelma Cowan and Anne Gregory headed the field. Cowan won the UGA National title in 1947, 1949, 1954, and 1955. But many observers hailed Anne Gregory, from Gary, Indiana, as the best black woman golfer ever. She won the UGA title in 1950, 1953, 1957, 1965, and 1966. She won her first UGA title at the Joe Louis Invitational in 1946. In 1950, at age thirty-three, Gregory won six of the seven events she entered. She was also an accomplished tennis player.

In spite of her successes, Gregory was not aiming for a professional career. She said, "My main thought...is my little girl...I will not let golf get between me and my family, although I love the game."[6]

Charlie Sifford: The most famous black golfer between World War II and 1970 was cigar-chomping Charlie Sifford from Charlotte, North Carolina. Sifford hustled bets like the other pros from anyone foolish enough to play with him, and he was a fixture at UGA events. "We didn't have no other way to play,"[7] he observed. Black newspapers, which had begun sponsoring golf tournaments, lowered their contributions if Sifford were not entered.

Sifford was a six-time winner of the UGA National Professional title, including a streak of five in a row between 1952 and 1956. In the opening round of the 1955 Canadian Open at Montreal, Sifford shot a 63 to lead the pack. Arnold Palmer had a 64. In 1957, Sifford became the first black player to win a significant title in a predominantly white event, the Long Beach (California) Open. His winner's check was $1,500.

Sifford's personal history typified the difficulties of his fellow black professionals. He started caddying at age nine in Charlotte. At thirteen, he won a caddy tournament by shooting a 70. The first prize was ten dollars and a case of Pepsi-Cola. He then moved to Philadelphia and worked as a teaching professional (for black entertainer Billy Eckstine, among others) and chauffeur. But golf was his love.

Said Sifford, "All I had was a stupid head, a raggedy golf game and determination to be a golfer; one of the best in the world, not a *black* golfer."[8]

In 1959, the PGA rescinded its "Caucasian only" clause and on September 1, Sifford became the first black person to receive a PGA card as an "approved player," a classification usually reserved for foreigners. (Sifford received his Class A card in 1964. PGA records show that Dewey Brown was its first black member, in the 1920s. Brown was a caddy and shop assistant in New York City and Philadelphia. His best-known teaching position was at the Buckwood Inn at Shawnee-on-Delaware.) It is perhaps important to note that President Dwight D. Eisenhower, an avid golfer, made no public attempt to try to change PGA policy.

But a PGA card did not guarantee equal treatment. Developing a reputation as a surly character, Sifford simply would not grin and bear unequal treatment. He recounted a key incident in the 1960 Greater Greensborough Open: "I had a good chance to get in the Masters if I finished good... suddenly, I was intercepted by five white men who started following me around the course. They threw beer cans, jumped up and down when I attempted to concentrate on a shot, called me 'nigger' and many other vile names."[9]

Part of Sifford's "surly" attitude may also have been passed on to him by Bill Spiller, a top black golfer of the 1940s, who would stand outside the gates to private clubs that held PGA events with a protest sign in hand.

Separating the attitudes of the white professional from that of the club official, Spiller noted that the "...white players are sympathetic to the black players trying to get on. But no one wants to rock the boat."[10] Spiller sued the PGA in 1948.

Black baseball legend Jackie Robinson encountered a similar problem when he received an invitation to join a private club: "I was invited to join one club, and the admission board approved me. But eight ladies objected and I didn't make it."[11]

In spite of his travail, Sifford became the first black player to win a major PGA event, the Los Angeles Open in 1969. Anna Robinson, founder of the UGA Hall of Fame, holds Sifford in the highest regard. "Mr. Sifford was our dream child in that Mr. Robert Hawkins had the dream—forty-seven years ago—that black golfers could

participate on the trail, and Mr. Sifford was the realization of that dream."[12] Sifford now plays on the PGA Seniors circuit.

The Charlie Sifford Record

1952–56, 1960	UGA Professional Champion
1957	Long Beach Open
1964	Puerto Rican Open
1967	Hartford Open
1969	Los Angeles Open (first major black PGA victory)
1975	PGA Seniors Open
1980	Suntree Seniors Open

Career Earnings: $339,000 on PGA Tour and $251,000 on PGA Seniors Tour.

The Fifties End on a Positive Note: In spite of the tribulations of black professionals and troubles on some public courses, real gains were made and the future looked brighter by the end of the decade. The UGA named its first woman officer, Mrs. Parrish Brown, as UGA Tournament Director. In the twenties, her late husband, Edgar Brown, was one of America's first black tennis stars.

Ethel Funches won the first of her seven UGA National titles in 1959, a feat that lasted for fourteen years. That same year, Bill Wright of Kansas City, Missouri won the National Public Links title over Frank Campbell, 3 and 2, at the Wellshire Links in Denver, Colorado. The twenty-three-year-old Wright was a student at Western Washington College.

With the PGA's racial qualifications gone and more blacks willing to spend the time sharpening their games, a dramatic rise in the presence of black golfers was forthcoming.

Breakthrough—The Sixties: Three factors helped golf rid itself of its image as a sport for the privileged classes. First, President Dwight D. "Ike" Eisenhower, a former Army general and hero of World War II, loved the game. Television screens showed Ike on the links as often as in the Oval Office. The resulting publicity was a godsend to the USGA and the PGA. Second, television coverage of tournaments increased in the late fifties. (In 1956, there were only 5½ hours of golf on television all year and the number of courses had actually declined since the end of World War II.) Third, Arnold Palmer's "go for broke" style helped attract the casual sports fan. Palmer was not born to wealth, and his swing resembled something learned from an Army manual. He won the 1960 U.S. Open in Denver, Colorado, and was seven shots behind the leader going into the final round. "Arnie's Army," as the press called his faithful followers, included many blacks who also lacked the polished strokes of someone who had taken dozens of lessons. Nearly all the black professionals were self-taught.

Pete Brown was no exception. Born in Jackson, Mississippi, Brown overcame chronic back problems to win the UGA Professional title in 1961–62 and was the first black player to win a PGA satellite event, the 1963 Waco Open in Burneyville, Oklahoma. A former caddy, he began playing when he was fifteen.

Brown was quick to credit Sifford with opening the doors for other blacks. Said Brown, "The PGA tour is really together, and the man mainly responsible is Charlie Sifford. People don't really know what that man went through during his early years on the tour...Charlie helped wipe out bias in sport."[13]

Brown's victory came just as the civil rights movement effected the passage of a flurry of bills in Congress. Passed during President Lyndon Johnson's administration, they were aimed more at public than private facilities. But these new laws did not materially affect professional golf at first. Nearly all PGA events were held at private clubs. The U.S. Open, however, was a USGA-sponsored tournament that came under criticism for patronizing clubs that had discriminatory membership policies.

In 1967, Renee Powell became the first black woman on the LPGA tour. She had won the UGA Women's title in 1964. Raised in East Canton, Ohio, Powell was the daughter of a teaching golf professional who owned his own course. She was joined for a time on the LPGA tour by former tennis great Althea Gibson, who tried with modest success to make a switch from tennis to golf.

Powell's father, William, who played on the Wilberforce University team, taught his daughter to play when she was only three. As an accomplished junior player, Powell had difficulty entering tournaments. Later, she remembered her first weeks on the LPGA tour, "At first it was rather difficult being on the tour as the only black female. There were racial slurs, hate mail, threatening letters, but it really didn't disturb me."[14] She now teaches golf and devotes time to golf clinics for public links juniors.

Lee Elder: Robert Lee Elder was the second black golfer to make significant inroads on the PGA tour and, like Charlie Sifford, he paid his dues along the way in UGA events. Born July 14, 1934, in Dallas, Texas, Elder played on the local Tennison Public Links when he was not caddying. He spent time in Los Angeles and then moved to Washington, D.C. He was a four-time winner of the UGA National Professional title and a protégé of Ted Rhodes.

Elder turned professional in 1959 and received his PGA card in 1967, as a thirty-three-year-old rookie. It is not unusual for beginning black professionals to be much older than their white counterparts. Elder cites the monetary outlay and the lack of sustained interest as the primary reasons that make college golf scholarships difficult. He noted, "Ninety percent of the black players started as caddies, and now the golf cart has just about killed the caddie."[15]

Elder finished "in the money" in his first nine PGA events in 1968, an auspicious beginning since he was sponsoring himself on the tour. In August, at the Firestone course in Ohio, he found himself going head-to-head with the incomparable Jack Nicklaus in a five-hole "sudden death" playoff on national television. Though he lost, Elder was hailed and praised as a comer. His showing, and Sifford's 1969 PGA win at Los Angeles, raised high expectations for black golfers. Total PGA prize money in 1969 was $5.5 million.

In 1971, Elder became the first black American to play in the South African PGA Open. He later played an exhibition against Gary Player in neighboring Swaziland. At the time, South Africa was trying to improve its international image and decided to allow select foreign nonwhite athletes into its major sporting events. The world light heavyweight boxing champion, Bob Foster, and the former U.S. Open tennis champion, Arthur Ashe, were also allowed into South Africa within two years of Elder's visit. Elder also won the Nigerian Open that same year.

During Elder's seventh year on the PGA tour, he earned a bid to that most symbolically important of all tournaments—the Masters at Augusta, Georgia. Two years earlier, he had expressed irritation at not being invited after having compiled such a good record. He won his berth by virtue of his first PGA victory, the Monsanto Open. So on April 10, 1975, he teed off as the Masters' first black entry.

He complained, "Why should I, who have served in the military and fought for my country, be invited to play in apartheid South Africa, and yet be denied the opportunity to play in the Masters."[16]

About the same time, Charlie Sifford had similar sentiments about the site of the Masters. "The Masters is the last stronghold of bias. It is a lily-white club, and the white people seem to want to keep it that

Lee Elder's Record

1963, 1964, 1966, 1967	UGA National Professional
1971	Nigerian Open
1974	PGA Monsanto Open
1976	PGA Houston Open
1978	PGA Greater Milwaukee Open
1978	PGA Westchester Classic
1984	PGA Seniors Suntree Classic
	PGA Seniors Hilton Head

Career Earnings (PGA and PGA Seniors): $1,118,974

Other Honors: 1977 Charles Bartlett Award by Golf Writers of America
1978 *Ebony* magazine, One of Five Outstanding Athletes
1979 Afro-American Golfer Hall of Fame, Golfer of the Decade
1979 Ryder Cup Team

way…one thing about that Augusta deal, they discriminate on all sides. They don't allow any white caddies to work there, even for Jack Nicklaus and Arnold Palmer. Everybody must use the resident caddies, and they are all black."[17]

Elder won three more PGA events before retiring to the Senior's Tour. In 1979, he was black America's first Ryder Cup Team member.

The last player in the sixties to win a UGA National Professional title and earn a PGA card was Jim Dent. The 6-foot 1-inch, 230-pound Dent won the UGA in 1969 and is still a tour regular. Ethel Funches, the best black female golfer since Anne Gregory, opted not to try the LPGA tour. Funches won the UGA Women's National title in 1959, 1960, 1963, 1967, 1968, 1969, and 1973.

Calvin Peete: When the decade of the 1970s began, those blacks in a now growing middle class, who were most interested in golf, could now provide their children with the lessons necessary for creating a solid foundation in the sport. But few young blacks seemed interested in putting in the practice time required. Of those who did, the primary purpose seemed to be more for social advantages rather than for a crack at the professional ranks. The first generation of middle-class black parents who had been given new opportunities as a result of the civil rights gains of the 1960s, they were not about to risk their children's futures on careers in professional sports.

It appeared, then, that future black players would continue to come from the ranks of caddies, who often neglected school for the sake of carrying bags and replacing divots for up to $20 for eighteen holes. Black caddies were divided into two different groups: those who remained at one club all year or at one club during the summer "up north", and at another club in the winter; and those that followed the PGA tour. Though many of them were married, most of them spent as much as nine months a year away from their families.

As the use of golf carts increased in the early seventies, the younger caddie began looking elsewhere for work. The older caddie, who often had been working for thirty years, knew no other line of work. And while his knowledge of a particular course was unquestioned (as was the case with "Stovepipe"), the golf cart was faster. In a time of rising maintenance costs, a club manager needed not only to charge more in fees but to try to get members to complete their rounds in a shorter amount of time. The days of the "club caddie" were numbered.

Nearly all the blacks who earned their PGA cards in the seventies had caddied at some time. Examples are: Curtis Sifford (Charlie Sifford's nephew), Willie Brown, Cliff Brown, Nate Starks, Rae Botts, Lee Carter, Ron Terry, Jim Thorpe, and George Johnson. Many were enticed to play because golf was, by 1970, on television almost five hours per week. Arnold Palmer had been named by the Associated Press as Athlete of the Decade, ahead of such performers as Rod Laver, Johnny Unitas, and Wilt Chamberlain. By 1973, the PGA Tour offered $8 million in prize money in seventy-six events.

Calvin Peete was different. He was never a caddie, never played in the UGA, and did not hit a golf ball until he was twenty-three. But he became the best black golfer in history. Born on July 18, 1943, in Detroit, he was one of nineteen children of his twice-married father. Reversing a trend common during World War II, Peete moved south and grew up in Pahokee, Florida.

Peete had a job selling wares to the migrant farm workers who travelled up and down the East Coast picking fruit on a seasonal basis. With a small diamond inset in a front tooth, he was a veritable gypsy most of the year. His northernmost landing point was usually Rochester, New York, where friends always tried to get him to try golf. And he always refused, commenting, "Who wants to chase a little ball around under the hot sun?"[18]

Telling him that they were taking him to a clambake, Peete's friends took him to a golf course one day and literally forced him to either play with them or just tag along and watch. He played—and has been hooked on the sport ever since. He recalls that "Just about that same time I saw a tournament on television and learned that Jack Nicklaus was making around $200,000 a year chasing that ball. I figured I could be happy with one-third that amount, so I decided to give it a try."[19]

Peete practiced as much, as long, and as often as he could. He was told by all the experts that he would never amount to much, because he could not straighten his left arm completely. He had broken it as a child and most experts believed a straight left arm—for a right-handed player—was necessary to hit the ball consistently straight. He proved them all wrong.

With the approval of his wife, Christine, he persevered. He turned professional in 1971, and after his third try at winning his

PGA card, he finally succeeded in 1975. The 5-foot 10-inch, 165-pound former itinerant salesman found that his card guaranteed only equal opportunity, a far cry from the $200,000 that Jack Nicklaus earned. In 1976, Peete finished ninety-fourth on the PGA tour with $22,966 in winnings. A year later, he did worse: 105th on the tour with $20,525 in winnings. In his third year, he was worse still: 108th on the tour with $20,459 in winnings. But he did finish fifth at the New Orleans Open.

In 1978, at thirty-five years of age, Peete found his form and vaulted to twenty-seventh on the money list and earned his first victory in the Greater Milwaukee Open. (A year earlier, Lee Elder had won this same event.) Peete's 19 under par set a new course and tournament record. That same year, he finished second in the Quad Cities Open and third in the Southern Open. He became the second black golfer to earn over $100,000 a year, with an income of $122,481.

After finishing forty-third on the 1980 money list, Peete came back in 1981 to finish number one on the tour in driving accuracy and in greens in regulation (the latter category refers to a player's ability to land his ball on the putting green on the first shot for par 3's, the second shot for par 4's, and the third shot for par 5's). His stroke average in 1981 was 71.35.

In 1982, Peete became the second black multiple winner, capturing the Greater Milwaukee Open for the second time, the Anheuser-Busch Classic, the BC Open, and the Pensacola Open. Peete also had his best finish in a Grand Slam event (U.S. Open, PGA, British Open, and Masters), third place in the PGA Championship.

Again he was number one in driving accuracy and greens in regulation.

But Peete was still not a fully accredited PGA member. The PGA required its players to be high school graduates if they wished to compete as members of the Ryder Cup Team. Peete had never finished high school. In August 1982, after having studied with the assistance of his wife, who was a part-time teacher, he passed the Michigan General Equivalency Test— twenty-four years after leaving high school. *Ebony* magazine presented their Black Achievement Award to him that same year.

He won two more PGA titles in 1983, as well as a place on the prestigious Ryder Cup Team. He also won the Ben Hogan Award. He missed winning the Vardon Trophy by one one-hundredth of a point: 70.62 for Peete to 70.61 for Raymond Floyd. He finally won the Vardon Trophy in 1984, with

Calvin Peete's Record

1967	Turns professional
1975	Earns PGA card on third attempt
1979	PGA Greater Milwaukee Open
1982	PGA Greater Milwaukee Open
	PGA Anheuser-Busch Classic
	PGA BC Open (Endicott, New York)
	PGA Pensacola Open
1983	PGA Georgia-Pacific Atlanta Classic
	PGA Anheuser-Busch Classic
1984	PGA Texas Open

Career Earnings through 1984: $1,249,829

Other Awards: 1982 Leads PGA in driving accuracy and greens in regulation

1983 Leads PGA in driving accuracy and greens in regulation

Golf magazine All-America Team

Golf Digest magazine "Most Improved Player" Award

Golf Writers Association's Ben Hogan Award.

a 70.56 scoring average. Jack Nicklaus was second. Said Peete of this award, "It's almost like winning a major tournament to me."[20]

At the end of 1984, Peete was the winningest player on the PGA tour for the preceding four years. He had come a long way—from selling pots and pans to farm workers to the pinnacle of the professional golf world. His story is, without question, one of the most amazing in sports.

The Future: Charlie Sifford had no illusions about his breakthrough on the PGA Tour. As good as he was, he knew few other black golfers stood much of a chance against the highly disciplined and well-coached tour regulars. "I never thought that my victories would create a lot of Black golfers,"[21] noted Sifford. "I got a lot of attention, and I think it helped some, but there are too many other things that keep a lot of blacks from the courses."

The traditional route to professional status for black athletes (except boxers) has been through public school programs and college competitions. Precious few blacks have been able to make the golf teams of NCAA Division I or II schools. Michael Cooper played at Arizona State in 1975 and was the Cook County (Illinois) titleholder in 1974, but he was an outstanding exception.

Black college teams seldom attain high rankings in national competition. Tuskegee University (formerly Tuskegee Institute), Wilberforce, and Howard University have achieved some fame for their golf programs. No black school has its own eighteen-hole course, and at this time there simply is no imperative to create one.

John Organ, Howard University coach, agrees with Sifford: "Most young Blacks can't see golf; it's like tennis where (Arthur) Ashe is the only one out there. There's no money for years. The kids can't see the money, because golf is a long range thing that requires lots of hard work."[22] Calvin Peete adds that blacks "...have to play harder than the whites. They've had the breaks. We haven't."[23]

By 1980, the role of the UGA as a stepping-stone to the PGA for blacks was beginning to change. USGA junior events had more black participation than ever before, and promising players saw a less influential UGA in the future. Jim Thorpe foresaw the UGA limitations early in his career. "Sure I played in the UGA,"[24] he insists. "...In 1970, I won twenty-seven of thirty-three tournaments. But I didn't learn anything in the black tournaments. You had to put up entrance money on the first tee."[24]

While that is a candid personal assessment of the UGA, no one can deny the association's overall worth to the black golfer since its formation in 1926. There is one bright hope, however, and she may one day accomplish on the LPGA Tour what Sifford, Elder, and Peete did on the PGA Tour. Her name is LaRee Sugg.

LaRee Pearl Sugg: Not far from the campus of Virginia State University in Petersburg, Virginia, is the Lee Park Golf Course. There, in 1975, a six-year-old pig-tailed youngster took her first golf lessons. She was a natural. Her grandfather, Dr. James Nelson, a former teacher at Virginia State University, insisted that his grand-daughter begin properly.

Sugg took lessons from a PGA professional, Russ Pike, at the Fort Lee Golf Course, and was winning tournaments at age eleven. Her success is proof that players need not grow up on plush private courses. (Lee Trevino is also a product of public courses.) At Matoaca High School in her native city, she compiled the best junior record of any black aspirant in history. Though only time will manifest her displayed promise, her record to date deserves recognition.

LaRee Sugg's Record

1981	1st Place	Ohio State Juniors
	1st Place	Ping Junior Classic
	1st Place	Southern Junior Classic
	1st Place	Eastern Airlines Junior Classic
	1st Place	Johnny Miller Junior Classic
	1st Place	North-South Junior Classic
1982	1st Place	Tar Heel Junior Open
	2nd Place	Keystone Junior Invitational
	4th Place	North-South Junior Classic
1983		LPGA Pro-Am (with Beth Daniel)
	1st Place	Ohio Junior Classic
	1st Place	Tar Heel Junior Open (Girls 12–15)
	1st Place	North-South Juniors (Girls 12–13)

Other Awards:

1981	*Golf* magazine All-America (11 and under)
	World of Junior Golf All-America
1983	*Golf* magazine All-America (Girls 12–13)

Lee Elder, the first black man to play in the Masters, must have had LaRee Sugg in mind when he reflected on the importance of early preparation. "Oh, I think there will always be some black player coming around,"[25] he mused. "I'd like to see blacks represented in the PGA. I know the young ones can play as well as anyone if they get the same kind of start as the whites." Perhaps Sugg and others like her will prove him right.

Notes

1. *Daily Worker,* August 1948.
2. Herb Graffis, *PGA: Official History Of The PGA Of America,* (New York: Thomas Y. Crowell Company, 1975), 276.
3. A.S. "Doc" Young, *Negro Firsts In Sports,* (Chicago: Johnson Publishing Company, 1963), 166.
4. Graffis, *PGA: Official History Of The PGA Of America,* 236.
5. Ibid.
6. *Chicago Defender,* 14 October 1950.
7. Charlie Sifford, phone interview with author, 3 May 1985.
8. *Ebony,* September 1969, 49.
9. *Black Sports,* July 1973, 32.
10. Skip Hollandsworth, "Blacks on Tour," *Sportsweek,* 9 May 1980.
11. Negro History Bulletin, (November 1960): 28.
12. Guil Jones, "Past Greats," *Black Sports,* July 1973, 67.
13. C.L. Lamarr, "Black Pros," *Black Sports,* July 1973, 37.
14. Lena Williams, "Renee Powell On Tour," *Black Sports,* May 1974, 41.
15. Hollandsworth, *Sportsweek,* (May 1980), 5.
16. *Ebony,* May 1973, 134.
17. Dick Edwards, "19 Years Is A Long Time To Be In The Rough," *Black Sports,* July 1973, 35.
18. *1983 PGA Tour Guide,* 126.

19. Ibid.

20. Calvin Peete, Publicity Monograph.

21. Hollandsworth, *Sportsweek,* (May 1980), 5.

22. *Black Sports,* July 1973, 74.

23. Hollandsworth, *Sportsweek,* (May 1980), 5.

24. Lamarr, *Black Sports,* 54.

25. Skip Hollandsworth, "Blacks On Tour," *Sportsweek,* 9 May 1980, 6.

Chapter 6

Tennis

America's best black tennis players waited with the same sense of urgency after World War II as did the Negro League baseball players. But there were material differences with a sport like tennis, as opposed to baseball. Baseball was the nation's pastime—however racist at the professional level—while tennis was clearly associated with the upper socioeconomic classes. Baseball games were played at stadiums open to the public; tennis tournaments were typically held at private clubs and sponsored by the United States Lawn Tennis Association (USLTA). But the mood set by Jackie Robinson in baseball encouraged black athletes in all sports to challenge *any* "whites only" policies. The first to try in tennis was a slim Californian named Oscar Johnson, who had plenty of credentials.

Johnson, with a national reputation of sorts, had come east to play. In August 1948, he was the first black player to win a USLTA-affiliated national event—the National Junior Public Parks at Los Angeles' Griffith Park. He was also the Pacific Coast Junior winner in 1946–48 in singles and doubles. (Johnson led his high school, Thomas Jefferson, to the Southern League title. His coach there was the black former USC football star, Brice Taylor, who had

assembled a tennis team made up of athletes who had never before played.)

Four months later, Johnson entered the USLTA National Junior Indoors at St. Louis and was accepted, only to be rebuffed by tournament officials. Johnson was aided in St. Louis by Richard Hudlin, a former tennis team captain at the University of Chicago, and Frank Summers, a black attorney from East St. Louis, Illinois. Hudlin accompanied Johnson to the armory where the event was held. Upon reaching the desk, the director, seeing Johnson carrying several rackets, testily inquired, "What are you doing here, boy?" Johnson replied, "I'm here to play in the tournament, my application was accepted. My name is Oscar Johnson."[1]

The director looked down the list and found Johnson's name. "Well, I'll be damned. But you won't play here, boy."[2] Hudlin and Johnson turned around and walked out. Hudlin and Johnson expected the reply; they had already written a telegram to send to the USLTA in New York. The USLTA soon answered and forced the local officials to admit the eighteen-year-old California youngster. Johnson reached the quarterfinals before losing to a future top-ranked American, Tony Trabert.

Johnson and other blacks like him were largely self-taught. Most of them started learning the game in their mid teens, and unless their parents played and instructed them, few developed orthodox strokes. Johnson learned by watching. "With some of these schools we'd play against, I figured that some of these guys were taking lessons, so I would watch the number-one player...and I'd copy what I saw...sometimes I'd jot it down and then I'd go home and practice in front of the mirror. I did that for three years, cause we didn't have any coaching."[3]

Johnson later met Pancho Gonzales—a Mexican-American soon to be the world's number-one player—at the Exposition Park courts, which were situated where the present parking lot for the Los Angeles Sports Arena is located. Both Johnson and Gonzales experienced a quasiracist arrangement peculiar to quite a few cities, where the races were not rigidly segregated. They were allowed to use the public courts, but they could not join the Olympic Tennis Club, which used the courts as its home base.

Johnson, however, was lucky enough to reach his peak in the post–World War II era, when the entire sports community was opening its doors to blacks for the first time. In 1953, he became the third black male to play in the USLTA Nationals at Forest Hills. The first black player, however, was Althea Gibson, in 1950.

Althea Gibson: It is ironic that the first black female athlete to gain and hold world dominance did so in a sport that featured relatively little black participation. The im-

age of tennis in black communities also suffered. Tennis was associated with the upper classes and it was not considered masculine, as it was not a contact sport. Yet, apart from those reservations, it was a demanding discipline that required extraordinary athletic ability and stamina. Althea Gibson had them both.

Gibson was a typical tomboy. Born on August 25, 1927, in Silver, South Carolina, she spent her early years in pool halls, at bowling alleys, and on basketball courts. She would often play hooky from Harlem's Public School 136, in order to play these sports. At age three, she had been sent to New York City by her parents, Daniel and Annie Gibson, to live with her Aunt Sally. Her father even taught her how to box. "I did my athletic thing."[4]

Gibson wielded her first racket of sorts on a Police Athletic League "play street" on 143rd Street in Harlem. What she saw that first day was the game of paddleball, designed in part for the narrow streets of New York City. She recalled, "Even then, I had a little skill in hitting the ball."[5] She was hooked. For the next two summers, Gibson and her friends played paddleball at every opportunity. Soon, she was the best player in her neighborhood, male or female.

At the beginning of her third summer of paddleball—1940—the play street director, Buddy Walker, gave Gibson her first tennis racket and told her to take some lessons from Fred Johnson at the Harlem River courts on 152nd Street and Seventh Avenue. Impressed with her ability, the Cosmopolitan Tennis Club invited her to become an honorary member. At the time, she was living in a home for troubled girls.

She kept quiet about her housing situation because "The Cosmopolitan members were the highest class of Harlem people and they had rigid ideas about what was socially acceptable behavior."[6]

As her tennis prowess increased, she dropped all other athletic pursuits except bowling—at one time she had a 195 average. "I could have been a professional bowler."[7] she thought. She began tennis lessons with the one-armed Fred Johnson in 1941. A year later she promptly won her first tournament, the American Tennis Association (ATA)–sanctioned New York State Junior Girls, by defeating Nina Irwin, a white player, in the finals. (The ATA is the Black counterpart to the USLTA.) In the 1942 ATA Nationals, she lost to Nana Davis in the finals of the junior girls. The raw side of her persona surfaced.

"Althea was a very crude creature," recalled Nana Davis (now Davis-Vaughn). "She had the idea she was better than anybody...After I beat her, she headed straight for the grandstand without bothering to shake hands. Some kid had been laughing at her and she was going to throw him out."[8] Because of the war, there was no ATA Nationals event for Gibson to participate in in 1943, but in 1944–45 she was national junior champion.

At the 1946 ATA Nationals, Gibson lost in the finals of the Women's Singles 6–4, 7–9, and 6–3, to Roumania Peters. But during the tournament she had attracted the attention of two physicians, Hubert A. Eaton and R. Walter Johnson. (Johnson had been in a varsity running back at Lincoln University Pennsylvania in the mid-1920s.) They were to change her life.

As was the case with the best black athletes in other sports during the mid-forties, Gibson was seen as one who could make a breakthrough in white tennis circles when the right time arrived—which appeared to be soon. There was, however, one hitch: she had never graduated from high school, though she was, in 1946, nineteen years old. With prompting from Sugar Ray Robinson, who would win the world welterweight title four months later, Gibson decided to accept the offer from the two doctors to live with them while she completed her education.

Gibson lived with Dr. Eaton during the school terms in Wilmington, North Carolina, and with Dr. Johnson in Lynchburg, Virginia, in the summers, all the while coming to terms with racism—southern style. In the summer of 1947, after her sophomore year, she played in nine ATA women's tournaments and won them all, including the Nationals over her old nemesis, Nana Davis. She graduated high school in June 1949 (Sugar Ray Robinson paid for her class ring). Eventually, she won ten consecutive ATA National titles, breaking Ora Washington's record.

At the ATA Nationals in 1949, the notion was brought to Gibson by Dr. Eaton that she might play at Forest Hills in the USLTA Nationals. The ATA had been informed that if her entry was sent in for the USLTA Eastern Indoors later that year, it would be accepted. The white tennis body did not want to be accused of lagging behind the gains made by Jackie Robinson three years before. Gibson reached the quarterfinals of both the Eastern Indoors and the National Indoors in successive

Charles Sifford wipes away tears after winning his first PGA title, the
Greater Hartford Open, in August 1967. His score was 12 under par
272. *(AP/Wide World Photos)*

Lee Elder, the first black golfer to play in the Masters at Augusta,
Georgia. *(Courtesy of Rose Elder)*

Anne Gregory, seven-time United Golfers Association women's
champion. *(Courtesy of the United Golfers Association)*

Calvin Peete, of Ft. Myers, Florida, clutches, his heart in mock
surprise as he watches his putt fall for a birdie at the 1985 Phoenix
Open. Peete won the tournament and $81,000. *(AP/Wide World Photos)*

Jim Thorpe hits a chip onto the green. *(Courtesy of ProServ, Inc.)*

Laree Sugg, a UCLA student-athlete from Petersburg, Virginia. *(Courtesy of Joseph Jones)*

U.S. Davis Cup team captain Arthur Ashe (left) signs an autograph while John McEnroe prepares for practice in a Davis Cup match against Australia at Portland, Oregon, October 1981. *(AP/Wide World Photos)*

Althea Gibson in action, winning the 1957 Wimbledon title.
(Courtesy of LeRoye Productions)

Rodney Harmon at the Grand Prix event in Stowe, Utah, August 1982.
(Courtesy of Michael Baz)

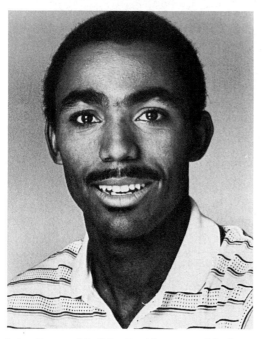

Rodney Harmon, of the University of Tennessee and Southern
Methodist University, was the NCAA Doubles victor.
(Courtesy of Advantage International)

Chip Hooper moving with total concentration. *(Courtesy of ProServ, Inc.)*

Dr. Screen poses with Hampton University's NCAA Division II championship tennis team of 1976. Left to right:
Bruce Foxworth, Roger Guedes, Dr. Robert Screen, Airton Silva, Rodney Young. *(Courtesy of Dr. Robert Screen)*

Left to right: the Duke of Kent, Zina Garrison, and the Duchess of Kent. Garrison accepts her Wimbledon Junior Girls' championship trophy. *(Courtesy of Advantage International)*

Zina Garrison, shown at the U.S. Open at Queens, New York.
(Courtesy of Russ Adams Productions)

Leslie Allen in action at the Murjani WTA championships, February 1983, Amelia Island, Florida. She is playing Amy Holton.
(Courtesy of Carol L. Newsom Associates)

Lori McNeil at the U.S. Open, also in September 1987.
(Courtesy of Russ Adams Productions).

In 1948 Alice Coachman became the first black woman to win an Olympic gold medal. She set the record with a 5-foot 6-inch high jump in London, England. Coachman is shown here during school days at Tuskegee. *(Courtesy of Tuskegee University)*

Eighteen-year-old Jean Lane, of Wilberforce University, defeats Stella Walsh in the National AAU 200-meter dash at Ocean City, New Jersey. Lane's time was 25.2 seconds, a new meet record. *(AP/Wide World Photos)*

Alice Coachman, of Tuskegee Institute (now Tuskegee University), wins the 100-meter dash at the National AAU Championships on August 5, 1946. Stella Walsh (with glasses) was second. *(AP/Wide World Photos)*

Alice Coachman clears the bar at 5 feet 6⅛ inches to win the 1948 Olympic gold medal in high jump. D. J. Tyler of Great Britain cleared the same height, but Coachman had fewer misses. *(AP/Wide World Photos)*

Alice Coachman atop the victory stand after winning a gold medal for a high jump at the 1948 Olympic Games in London on August 7. Coachman was the first black female to win an Olympic gold medal. Second was D. J. Tyler, and M. O. Ostermeyer was third. *(AP/Wide World Photos)*

Lillie Purifoy (second from left) comes in second in *Philadelphia Inquirer*'s women's 50-yard low hurdles on January 23, 1948. The winner was Nancy Cowperthwaite, of the German-American Athletic Club. Purifoy won the event in 1947. *(AP/Wide World Photos)*

Members of the U.S. Olympic 400-meter relay team relax at their Uxbridge quarters in England, August 8, 1948, reading British press reports of their disqualification after finishing first in the event. The Olympic jury of appeal viewed movies and other pictures before ruling on the U.S. appeal against the verdict. Left to right are: Mel Patton, Harrison Dillard, Lorenzo Wright, and Barney Ewell. *(AP/Wide World Photos)*

Wilma Rudolph is shown breaking the tape to win the gold medal in the 200-meter dash at the 1960 Olympics in Rome, Italy. Her time was 24.0 seconds. *(AP/Wide World Photos)*

Edward S. Temple, women's track coach, Tennessee State University, and U.S.A. head women's track coach for the 1960 and 1964 Olympics. *(Courtesy of Edward S. Temple)*

Wilma Rudolph anchors the U.S. women's 400-meter relay team to a gold medal at the Rome Olympics in 1960. Rudolph's teammates were Lucinda Williams, Barbara Jones, and Martha Hudson. The winning time was 44.5 seconds. *(AP/Wide World Photos)*

Rafer Johnson, Olympic Decathlon gold medalist in 1960, boards plane with the American Maccabian Squad from Israel in August 1961. *(AP/Wide World Photos)*

Wyomia Tyus hits the tape first, ahead of Edith McGuire (second from left), to finish 1-2 in the Tokyo Olympic Games 100-meter dash in 1964. At left is Marilyn White. *(AP/Wide World Photos)*

Jesse Owens (left) congratulates Ralph Boston, enjoying a hot dog, after Boston bettered the American indoor long jump mark to 26 feet ¼ inch in March 1961. *(AP/Wide World Photos)*

Bob Hayes of Florida A&M clocks a 9.9-second 100-meter dash (the first 100-meter dash run under 10 seconds) in the semifinal heat at the Tokyo Olympic Games in 1964. *(AP/Wide World Photos)*

Jim Hines, of the Houston Striders, edges out Ronnie Smith at 1968 U.S. Championships in 100-meter dash. Both clocked 9.95 seconds. *(AP/Wide World Photos)*

John Carlos and Tommy Smith at the 1968 Olympic Games.
(AP/Wide World Photos)

Bob Beamon soaring to a wind-aided long jump of 27 feet 6½ inches at the Olympic Trials at Lake Tahoe in 1968. *(AP/Wide World Photos)*

Dr. Leroy Walker, of North Carolina Central University, shows Olympic sprinter Willye White a photo of herself, at 1972 Munich, Germany, Olympic Games. *(AP/Wide World Photos)*

The 1976 U.S. 4 × 400 winning relay team. Left to right: Fred Newhouse, Benny Brown, Herm Frazier, and Maxie Parks. Time: 2 minutes 58.65 seconds. *(Courtesy of Heinz Kluetmeier/*Sports Illustrated)

Diane Dixon won the first heat of the 1,600-meter relay race in 1984, setting the pace for the team to win the gold.
(Courtesy of Focus on Sports*)*

Martin Epps, head track coach at Jackson State University.
(Courtesy of Handy's Photo Service)

Evelyn Ashford set a world record in the 100-meter race at the 1984 Olympics, with a time of 10.97 seconds. She is a two-time gold medal winner. *(Courtesy of John McDonough/*Sports Illustrated)

Renaldo Nehemiah cracked the 13-second barrier in the 110-meter hurdles with a time of 12.93 seconds. *(Courtesy of* Focus on Sports*)*

Mike Conley won a silver medal in the 1984 Olympics for the triple jump with a record of 56 feet 4½ inches.
(Courtesy of the University of Arkansas)

Valerie Brisco-Hooks, a triple gold medalist in the 1984 Olympics at Los Angeles, shown here at the IIAF/Mobil GP at Oslo, Norway. *(Courtesy of All Sport)*

Willie Banks in action during his school days at the University of California at Los Angeles. *(Courtesy of UCLA)*

Carl Lewis is the first Olympic performer to win four track and field gold medals in one Olympiad since Jesse Owens in 1936. *(Courtesy of the University of Houston)*

Edwin Moses, a master of the 400-meter hurdles. Here he is going for the gold at the 1984 Olympiad. *(Courtesy of Rich Clarkson/Sports Illustrated)*

Jackie Joyner-Kersee is shown here at the Olympic Sports Festival in 1986. She is a silver medalist in the heptathalon. *(Courtesy of All Sport)*

Greg Foster steps down from the last hurdle to win the 110-meter hurdles at the U.S. Olympic Trials in 1984. At left is Dennis Brantley, of Texas Southern University. *(AP/Wide World Photos)*

weeks. "I was made to feel right at home by the other girls."[9] Her treatment was in sharp contrast to that received by Jackie Robinson from his fellow ballplayers.

The USLTA said nothing, though, about Gibson entering their upcoming 1950 summer grass-court tournament season. Then suddenly, it occurred to them that unless she was allowed to play in the tune-up events leading to the USLTA Nationals at Forest Hills, she could not possibly give her best performance. Enter Alice Marble, a white former USLTA singles champion. In a stirring letter in *American Lawn Tennis* magazine, Marble challenged the USLTA to quit their wavering and allow Gibson to participate.

In the July 1950 issue, Marble wrote:

"On my current lecture tours, the question I am most frequently expected to answer is no longer: 'What do you think of Gussie's panties?' For every individual who still cares whether Gussie Moran has lace on her drawers, there are three who want to know if Althea Gibson will be permitted to play in the Nationals this year. Not being privy to the sentiments of the USLTA committe, I couldn't answer their questions, but I came back to New York determined to find out. When I directed the question at a committee member of long standing, his answer, tacitly given, was in the negative. Unless something within the realm of the supernatural occurs, Miss Gibson will not be permitted to play in the Nationals.

"He said nothing of the sort, of course. The attitude of the committee will be that Miss Gibson has not sufficiently proven herself. True enough,

she was a finalist in the National Indoors, the gentlemen admitted—but didn't I think the field was awfully poor? I did not. It is my opinion that Miss Gibson performed beautifully under the circumstances. Considering how little play she has had in top competition, her win over a seasoned veteran like Midge Buck seems to me a real triumph.

"Nevertheless the committee, according to this member, insists that in order to qualify for the Nationals, Miss Gibson must also make a strong showing in the major eastern tournaments to be played between now and the date set for the big do at Forest Hills. Most of these major tournaments—Orange, East Hampton, Essex, etc.—are invitational, of course. If she is not invited to participate in them, as my committee member freely predicted, then she obviously will not be able to prove anything at all, and it will be the reluctant duty of the committee to reject her entry at Forest Hills. Miss Gibson is over a very cunningly-wrought barrel, and I can only hope to loosen a few of its staves with one lone opinion.

"I think it's time we faced a few facts. If tennis is a game for ladies and gentlemen, it's also time we acted a little more like gentle people and less like sanctimonious hypocrites. If there is anything left in the name of sportsmanship, it's more than time to display what it means to us. If Althea Gibson represents a challenge to the present crop of women players, it's only fair that they should meet that challenge on the courts, where tennis is played. I know those girls, and I can't think of one who would refuse to meet Miss Gibson in competition. She might be soundly beaten for a while—but she has a much better chance on the courts than in the inner sanctum of the committee, where a different kind of game is played.

"I can't honestly say that I believe Miss Gibson to be a potential champion; I don't know. In the Indoors she played under tremendous pressure, but there were moments when she exhibited a bold, exciting game that will doubtlessly improve against first-class competition. Whether she can achieve championship status here or abroad depends no more on her lovely strokes than what Althea Gibson finds within herself when the chips are down. If she can do it, a proud new chapter will have been added to the history of tennis. If she cannot, we will have seen nothing more and nothing less than one more youngster who failed to live up to her initial promise. But if she is refused a chance to succeed or to fail, then there is an uneradical mark against a game to which I have devoted most of my life, and I would be bitterly ashamed.

"We can accept the evasions, ignore the fact that no one will be honest enough to shoulder the responsibility for Althea Gibson's probable exclusion from the Nationals. We can just "not think about it." Or we can face the issue squarely and honestly. It so happens that I tan very heavily in the summer—but I doubt that anyone ever questioned my right to play in the Nationals because of it. Margaret DuPont collects a few freckles—but who ever thought to omit her name for such a reason? The committee would have felt pretty foolish saying, 'Alice Marble can't play because of that tan', or 'We can't accept Margaret DuPont; she gets freckles on her nose.' It's just as ridiculous to reject Althea

Gibson on the same basis—and that's the truth of it. She is not being judged by the yardstick of ability but by the fact that her pigmentation is somewhat different.

"If the field of sports has got to pave the way for all of civilization, let's do it. At this moment tennis is privileged to take its place among the pioneers for a true democracy, if it will accept that privilege. If it declines to do so, the honor will fall to the next generation, perhaps—but someone will break the ground. The entrance of Negroes into national tennis is as inevitable as it has proven to be in baseball, in football, or in boxing; there is no denying so much talent. The committee at Forest Hills has the power to stifle the efforts of one Althea Gibson, who may or may not be the stuff of which champions are made, but eventually she will be succeeded by others of her race who have equal or superior ability. They will knock at the door as she has done. Eventually the tennis world will rise up en masse to protest the injustices perpetrated by our policymakers. Eventually—why not now?

"I am beating no drums for Miss Gibson as a player of outstanding quality. As I said, I have seen her only in the National Indoors, where she obviously did play her best and was still able to display some lovely shots. To me, she is a fellow tennis player and, as such, deserving of the chance I had to prove myself. I've never met Miss Gibson but, to me, she is a fellow human being to whom equal privileges ought to be extended.

"Speaking for myself, I will be glad to help Althea Gibson in any way I can. If I can improve her game or merely give her the benefit of my own experiences, as I have many other young players, I'll do that. If I can give her an iota more of confidence by rooting my heart out from the gallery, she can take my word for it: I'll be there."[10]

Marble's eloquent riposte to the USLTA's prejudiced attitude had an immediate, though measured, response.

After a rebuff at New Jersey's Maplewood Country Club, Gibson was accepted at the Orange Lawn Tennis Club in South Orange, New Jersey, and at the USLTA National Clay Courts in Chicago. Harold LeBair of the USLTA then passed word to Bertram Baker of the ATA that Gibson would be accepted at the Forest Hills for the USLTA Nationals. Behind the scenes, the ATA hierarchy had worked feverishly to get Gibson accepted at Orange and Chicago. To the New Jersey State tennis officials who kept her out of the event at Maplewood, Arthur Francis, Baker's assistant, sent a blistering note deploring the association's "snobbishness, prejudice, and bad judgment."[11]

Gibson stayed in Harlem with her longtime friend, Rhoda Smith, and was delighted when Sarah Palfrey Danzig, a nationally ranked player, agreed to take her to the West Side Tennis Club at Forest Hills for practice. When the Nationals began, she won her first-round match easily and then had to face the three-time Wimbledon and 1947 United States champion, Louise Brough. This encounter erased all doubt as to Gibson's potential.

Playing on the Number One Court adjoining the Stadium Court, Gibson began tensely, losing the first set, 6–1. Her nervousness gone, she won the second set, 6–3, as the stands became packed with spectators expecting an upset. The deciding set was a seesaw affair and Gibson took a 7–6 lead; then a thunderstorm struck. Before the stands were cleared, lightning had knocked one of the stone eagles that stood atop the Stadium off its pedestal. Play was called off until the next day. Gibson remembered feeling "...that the delay was the worst thing that could have happened to me."[12]

Althea could not sleep that night. The next morning the match was resumed before a full house and Brough won her serve to 40–30. In the next game, tied at 7–7, a jittery Gibson double-faulted and made a loose volley error to go down, 7–8. She saved one match point at 40–15, but lost the match on the next point. A glorious beginning for a young black athlete in the citadel of American tennis. She had opened the door; others would follow. When she returned to Florida A&M University for the fall semester, she was given a hero's welcome.

Official notification of Gibson's acceptance at Forest Hills came during the ATA Championships at Central State College at Wilberforce, Ohio. Everyone present was jubilant, knowing a major event was about to take place. With undisguised pride, Baker read the following passage to America's best black players: "The year 1950 will...go down in the history of the American Tennis Association as the beginning of a new era...many of us have worked untiringly for years to witness the day when our players would be accepted for competition in the National Championships of the USLTA. That day has come. It was not brought about by senseless agitation or unwarranted demands, but by cultivation of good will thereby acquiring the genuine friendship of individuals without whose aid the door would not yet be open to us...Althea Gibson will play at Forest Hills...on Monday, August 28."[13]

A sizable faction of the ATA, however, had disagreed with the means by which Gibson's entry was obtained. Their principal objection was the implied quota of black players to be allowed entry in the Nationals. In an article in the November 1960 *Negro History Bulletin*, Bill Davis, the ATA Men's Champion, said he believed "the number is five. They won't take more than five Negroes."[14]

Dissidents thought more attention should have been paid to breaking down the barriers that made qualification for the Nationals next to impossible. As matters stood then, the only way blacks could play at Forest Hills was through a recommendation by the ATA. While all were still pleased with Gibson's acceptance because of her abilities, many black players wanted the ATA to take a stronger stand regarding USLTA sanctioned events that barred players because of race and/or religion.

Dr. Johnson Begins Junior Development Programs: Althea Gibson's acceptance at Forest Hills immediately heightened interest in the sport among blacks. But black tennis officials were aware of the difficulties and racial barriers that lay ahead. Though the ATA had been in existence since 1916, it had no paid staff, and any attempts to launch a long-range junior development program among black youth would have to result from the efforts of intensely dedicated individuals. Dr. Johnson felt up to the task and, though frequently involved in major disagreements with the ATA, he envisioned a permanent summer program for the best young black talent.

Johnson, who gave priority to recommendations from trusted friends across the country, began bringing talented youngsters to his three-story home in Lynchburg, Virginia.

Financial support came from wherever he could find it, but principally from his own pocket. His son, Robert Johnson, Jr., recalls his father's initial interest in the best black college players. "He had started originally getting collegians primarily to help them with their game. Then he finally realized that he had to reach way back to get some of the younger players."[15]

Dr. Johnson became the tournament director of the Central Intercollegiate Athletic Association (CIAA) Championships. But having seen the best in the world at Forest Hills, he knew the best black college players stood little chance of progressing very far because their early training had been haphazard and primarily self-imposed. An incident that occurred in Charlottesville, Virginia, in the spring of 1951 presented a challenge that could be addressed within one day's drive of his Lynchburg home.

Going home from Washington, D.C., through Charlottesville on Route 29, Dr. Johnson noticed a large white-and-red sign on the outside wall of the gymnasium of the University of Virginia. It read "USLTA National Interscholastic Championships." Assumming that this event featured the nation's best high school players, he stopped his car to investigate. Finding no black participation, he located the tournament director and established his credentials as Althea Gibson's mentor. After an hour's discussion, he convinced officials to do for black high school players what the USLTA had done for the ATA at Forest Hills. He would bring the two finalists from an all-black qualifying event to Charlottesville the following year.

The initial results were disastrous. Both players lost, 6–0, 6–0, in the first round. But Dr. Johnson vowed to himself that he would produce a player who would one day win this event.

In 1953, the CIAA held its annual event at segregated Brookfield Playground in Richmond, Virginia. One of the participants was Ronald Charity, a student at Virginia Union University just two blocks away. Charity had been giving lessons to the son of Arthur Ashe, Sr., the park's caretaker. Arthur Ashe, Jr., was only ten, but showed an unusual aptitude and eagerness for the sport. Charity recommended Ashe's inclusion in Dr. Johnson's summer program. The elder Ashe agreed. Though Ashe became, in the summer of 1953, the youngest of Dr. Johnson's pupils, he soon became the centerpiece of the program.

While Althea Gibson continued her studies at Florida A&M and improved her tennis abilities, Ashe joined a constantly changing group of young players at Dr. Johnson's home. Over the years, this entourage included Hubert Eaton, Jr., Thomas Hawes, Bonnie Logan, Billy Wynn, and Linwood Simpson from North Carolina; Ralph Long from Atlanta; Gwen McEvans and Drew Williams from Detroit; Ethel Reid, Horace Cunningham, Juan Farrow, and Elmer Reid from Lynchburg; Bob Davis, Sydney and Luis Glass from New York City;

Beverly Coleman and Willis Fennell from Los Angeles; William Nielson, Doug Smith, Sid Moore, Jr., and Henry Livas from Hampton, Virginia; Charles Brown and Joe Williams from Durham, North Carolina; and Willis Thomas, Jr., from Washington, D.C.—among others.

But Dr. Johnson's task was not only to fashion a training scheme for his charges. Much aware of the discrimination and the highly social nature of the sport, he was forced to list a special code of behavior as well. His players were to be unfailingly polite at all times; their tennis attire was to be clean and white; and above all, they were never to cheat, because Johnson assumed that white tournament directors would use any excuse to deny entry to black players.

The Johnson-trained players, with the assistance of their local coaches, began winning most of the ATA local and national titles. Tennis became an obsession for some of his students. Travel to and from tournaments was by car and, as Dr. Johnson's son explained, "We'd talk about the game all the way."[16] Though not every player blossomed under his strict regiment, enough of them enjoyed the experience and established sectional and national reputations.

The number-one fantasy among these young players was to play and win the Nationals at Forest Hills. Althea Gibson's entry in 1950 was followed by the first black male performers, Dr. Reginald Weir and George Stewart, in 1952. Though both Weir and Stewart lost in the first round, all black observers felt it was just a matter of time before one of their own won the event. They did not have long to wait.

Althea Gibson Breaks Through: Althea Gibson continued making inroads in American tennis. Her debut at Forest Hills came just two years after Alice Coachman became the first black woman to win an Olympic Games Gold Medal. Gibson was becoming black America's most talked about female athlete. Her photograph appeared regularly in the black press, and she was good friends with Sugar Ray Robinson and his wife, Edna. In March 1951, she was the first black accepted in a major event in the South—the Good Neighbor Championships in Miami. Three months later, Joe Louis paid the airfare for her first trip to Wimbledon.

In 1952, Gibson came under the tutelage of Sydney Llewelyn, a Jamaican-born teaching professional living in New York City. Llewelyn had met Gibson at the Cosmopolitan Tennis Club in Harlem, the best-known black tennis facility on the East Coast. Said Llewelyn, "I changed her forehand grip from a continental to an eastern, and I gave her what I call the Theory of Correct Returns."[17] Till now Gibson had advanced primarily because of her exceptional athletic ability and her overall aggressiveness. The change from a continental to an eastern grip added more power to her forehand, and Gibson agreed that she improved her ability to make tactical changes during matches.

Althea had a USLTA ranking of 9 in 1952, 7 in 1953, and 13 in 1954. But she departed on an extended tour for the United States State Department in 1955 with Ham Richardson, Karol Fageros, and Bob Perry that enabled her to work on her game without the pressures of tournament play.

She won eighteen of nineteen events, and her confidence soared. By 1956, she was ready.

In the spring of 1956, she became the first black player to win one of the sport's Grand Slam events (they are Wimbledon, and the U.S., French, and Australian Opens), capturing the French title in singles and doubles. A month later she was a two-to-one favorite to win at Wimbledon, but she had to settle for a doubles victory with Angela Buxton. That winter she toured Australia and won the Asian Championships in Ceylon (now Sri Lanka). She was now nearly as well known in black America as Jackie Robinson and Sugar Ray Robinson.

In 1957 and 1958, she was the world's undisputed number one female player. Her first Wimbledon title in 1957 was over Darlene Hard, 6–3, 6–2. She was personally received by Queen Elizabeth II, who said, "My congratulations, it must have been hot out there." Telegrams arrived at her Wimbledon hotel by the dozens, including messages from Sugar Ray Robinson, President Dwight D. Eisenhower, Averill Harriman, and Williston High School in Wilmington, North Carolina. Back in New York, she was accorded that rarest of honors, a ticker-tape parade down Broadway, and presented the key to the city by Mayor Robert Wagner.

Three months later, Gibson added that most sought-after crown for all tennis players in America, the Nationals at Forest Hills. She defeated her old nemesis, Louise Brough, in the finals, 6–3, 6–2. She also won the Mixed Doubles title with Kurt Nielsen of Denmark. She was a member of the U.S. Wightman Cup Squad and was given the Babe Didrickson Zaharias Trophy as Female Athlete of the Year. She could do no wrong. Or could she?

Gibson complained of "being Public Enemy No. 1 to some sections of the Negro press...they say I'm bigheaded, uppity, ungrateful..."[18] She was criticized severely by some black writers for not being more aggressive on the issue of racial equality. Said Gibson in her 1958 book, "I am not a racially conscious person. I don't want to be. I see myself as just an individual."[19] Other black athletes like Hank Aaron, Willie Mays, and Emlen Tunnel would occasionally suffer such criticism.

She repeated her Wimbledon and U.S. Open victories in 1958. Though she had lived like a queen on the world tennis circuit, she had no permanent job. Unlike other young women competitors, she could not afford to just play the tournaments from year to year. She was thirty-one years old and needed to begin thinking of her life after tennis. She took the unprecedented step of turning professional at a time when there were few women professionals.

Her short career as a playing professional came one decade too soon. After a year as the opening match for a men's Professional Tour, she devoted herself to golf and a singing career (Ed Sullivan had invited her to sing on his Sunday-night variety show). She was later named to the New Jersey State Athletic Commission, and is now a highly respected teaching professional in Montclair, New Jersey. She was black America's first internationally famous female athlete.

Gibson's victories provided ongoing encouragement for Dr. Johnson's junior

Althea Gibson's Record

1944–45	ATA Junior Girl's Singles
1947–56	ATA Women's Singles
1948–50, 1952–55	ATA Mixed Doubles (with R. Walter Johnson)
1956	French Women's Singles
	French Women's Doubles (with Angela Buxton)
1957	Wimbledon Women's Singles
	U.S. Women's Singles
	U.S. Mixed Doubles (with Kurt Nielsen)
	Australian Women's Doubles (with S. Fry)
1958	Wimbledon Women's Singles
	U.S. Women's Singles

Member, U.S. Wightman Cup Team, 1957–58

players. Along with the increasing acceptance of black athletes in the major team sports and with a psychological boost from the United States Supreme Court decision in 1954 banning segregated schools, Dr. Johnson's teenagers found more doors opened to them. One of them, Arthur Ashe, Jr., took full advantage of these new opportunities and became black America's next tennis star.

Ashe Breaks Through: Under Dr. Johnson's guidance, Ashe made more progress than his fellow black juniors. After winning three ATA Boy's titles, he became the first black junior to receive a USLTA National ranking. In 1958, he was ranked number five among all U.S. juniors. A year later, he became one of the youngest-ever entrants at Forest Hills, losing to Rod Laver at only sixteen years of age. He had qualified as one of the ATA's nominated players.

In 1960, Ashe won his first of three consecutive ATA Men's Singles titles and moved from his native Richmond, Virginia, to St. Louis, Missouri, for his senior year of high school. Feeling that Ashe needed year-round practice not available in Richmond, Dr. Johnson arranged for him to stay with former University of Chicago tennis team captain Richard Hudlin, who taught history at famed Sumner High School. That fall, Ashe won his first USLTA National title, the Junior Indoors. He also became the first black member of the U.S. Junior Davis Cup Team.

In June 1961, Ashe captured an event surrounded in symbolism for his coach Dr. Johnson. On the very same courts where, nine years ago, Dr. Johnson's first two black high school representatives lost, 6–0, 6–0, in the first round, Ashe won the USLTA National Interscholastics. Though the title itself was not nearly as important as some others, it was the first USLTA National title to be won by a black player in the South.

On the basis of his win in the 1960 Junior Indoors and a semifinal showing at the Orange Bowl Junior Championships, Ashe was awarded a full scholarship to UCLA by coach J.D. Morgan. Ashe had never visited UCLA and had never met Morgan before arriving as a freshman. Morgan stated quite forthrightly to Ashe that "UCLA has a long history of black athletic participation beginning with Dr. Ralph Bunche back in the twenties. Even though I never met you before you arrived here on campus, I had you thoroughly checked out and I was satisfied that you would have no academic problems. And your tennis record speaks for itself."

Ashe blossomed at UCLA, where he often played against another black varsity player, Doug Sykes, from the University of

California at Berkeley. Unfortunately, Ashe's freshman year was marred by an incident involving the Balboa Club in Orange County. The club held an annual event, and routinely invited the best players from the top regional college teams to attend. Ashe was pointedly not invited, though his freshman teammates at UCLA were asked to participate.

In spite of the intentional oversight, for the first time in his life Ashe was surrounded by the best the sport had to offer. Richard "Pancho" Gonzales, the world's number-one player, not only offered encouragement but spent many hours with him on court. Francisco "Pancho" Segura, also one of the world's best in the forties and fifties offered assistance. Ashe played on a freshman team many considered to be among the best ever. Charles Pasarell, a close friend and the nation's number-one junior; Dave Reed, the number-one junior in Southern California; and Dave Sanderlin, who defeated Ashe in the National Junior Championships, were teammates for four years.

In 1963, Ashe became the first black player to win USLTA National Men's event, the Hardcourt title in La Jolla, California. Ten years before, Oscar Johnson had been the first black player accepted into this event, then held in Salt Lake City.

Three weeks after winning the Hardcourts, a very fortunate event occurred. After playing in an exhibition at the California Club in West Los Angeles, Ashe was approached by a female club member who asked him his future plans. Ashe replied, "Well, we've got the Intercollegiates coming up, and if I can find enough money I'll try to go to Wimbledon."

The lady then asked, "How much does it cost?"

"About eight hundred dollars," Ashe said as he prepared to leave with Pasarell.

"Wait right here a second and I'll be right back," she politely ordered and disappeared down the hall.

Three minutes later, she reappeared and handed Ashe eight crisp one-hundred dollar bills and said, "I'll be looking for your results in the (Los Angeles) *Times*." The lady was Julianna Ogner, whose husband owned a car dealership in Beverly Hills; she had simply gone into the club's card room and cajoled eight club members into giving her one hundred dollars each for Ashe's first trip to Wimbledon.

Later that summer, Ashe was named to the U.S. Davis Cup Team by Captain Robert Kelleher. He played his first match against Venezuela as a substitute after the outcome had been decided. Kelleher then opted to let Ashe remain in school rather than play in the remaining matches that year. Two years later, Ashe won the NCAA title and helped UCLA capture the team honors. In the fall of 1965, he spent three months in Australia, winning four tournaments and learning to play on grass. He returned to UCLA in the spring of 1966 to finish his degree requirements and then, with a six-week stint at ROTC summer camp at Fort Lewis, Washington, in between, headed for Australia before beginning a two-year stretch as an Army officer.

In 1965 through 1967, the United States lost in Davis Cup competition to Spain, Brazil, and Ecuador, respectively. The Ecuador loss was particularly painful for Ashe, who lost his two singles matches. Though he later regrouped and captured the USLTA National Clay Court title, the summer of 1967 was a low point in his career.

The Army allowed Ashe time off for Davis Cup duty in 1968. The team, under the captaincy of Donald Dell, recaptured the Cup from Australia in December. Along the way, two events occurred that changed the very direction of his life: the proposed boycott of the Mexico City Olympic Games by black American athletes and the first U.S. Open Tennis Championships.

One of the motivating factors behind the proposed boycott of the Olympic Games was the system of racial segregation in the Republic of South Africa, known as "apartheid." South Africa was entered in the Davis Cup competition in 1968 and was slated to meet the United States in the third round. Ashe was in a quandary. Should he play for the United States if the two countries met? Though he never had to decide, because South Africa lost to West Germany, a conversation he had with Cliff Drysdale, a white South African player, in June 1968 convinced him the issue would not disappear anytime soon.

Drysdale told Ashe that even if he did apply for a visa to play in the South African Open, he would not be allowed to participate. The South African government's system of apartheid did not allow sports contests between blacks and whites. Ashe immediately recognized a parallel with his predicament as a junior player in his native Virginia. He had been systematically kept out of USLTA-sanctioned events there because of race.

As a junior player, Ashe's chances of making the United States Junior Davis Cup Team had rested on the results of five major events, two of which denied him entry: the Kentucky State Juniors and the National Jaycees (he was denied entry in the Virginia State Jaycee qualifying event). He was not about to let this discrimination happen again. Though he did not have to play against South Africa in 1968, the plight of the black South African became a major issue with him throughout his adult life.

Two years later, after a second formal denial of his visa application to play in South Africa, Ashe read the official response to his request. Ashe, reported Frank Waring, South Africa's Minister of Sport, on January 28, 1970, "would not be allowed to enter South Africa as a member of the United States team to compete in the South African Open tennis championships or for any other reason due to Ashe's general antagonism toward South Africa's racial policies."[20]

Added Gary Player, South Africa's premier white golfer, "The Arthur Ashe case is probably the last straw to make our isolation in the field of sports complete."[21]

The second major event for Ashe in 1968 was his victory in the first United States Open Tennis Championships at Forest Hills. The sport was opened to professionals as well as amateurs in April of that year and the Nationals was a prize-money event for the first time. On a hot streak that lasted two months, Ashe was undefeated, from the middle of July until a semifinal loss in the Pacific Southwest in the third week in September. Included in that streak were wins in the United States Amateur at Brookline, Massachusetts, followed by his five-set U.S. Open win over Tom Okker in the final, 14–12, 5–7, 6–3, 3–6, 6–3.

Still an Army officer, Ashe was given the rare accolade of a cheer by the entire Corp of Cadets at the U.S. Military Academy where he was assigned, as well as a meeting with President Lyndon B. Johnson. He was also given another award, this one tinged with irony: The U.S. Jaycees Ten Outstanding Young Men (TOYM) Award, from the same group whose Virginia representatives had denied his entry in their State Junior Tennis event.

Ashe appeared on the cover of *Life* magazine and on the nationally syndicated political talk show *Face the Nation,* the first athlete so honored.

Black America now had a woman and a man on the list of Grand Slam tournament winners. The door was open. While Althea Gibson and Arthur Ashe proved to young black players that it could be done, the civil rights movement in the sixties achieved the changes necessary to guarantee access to all public tennis facilities to all Americans. Dr. Johnson was joined by an increasing number of black coaches who rushed to fill the void. The twenty years between 1960 and 1980 were to be a watershed period in the development of black professional players.

On July 31, 1979, Ashe suffered a mild heart attack and retired from professional tennis. But he assumed the captaincy of the Davis Cup Team in September 1980. As one of three founders of the National Junior Tennis League in 1968, he was instrumental in bringing tennis instruction to public parks and playgrounds. (The NJTL was merged into the United States Tennis Association in 1984 and continues to be one of the prime sources of quality instruction for minority youngsters.)

Ashe also served as a former president of the Association of Tennis Professionals (ATP), the players union, and was instru-

Arthur Ashe's Major Tournament Record

1955	ATA 12-and-under Singles
	ATA 12-and-under Doubles (with Willis Thomas)
1956	ATA 15-and-under Doubles (with Willis Thomas)
1957–58	ATA 15-and-under Singles
1958	ATA 15-and-under Doubles (with Willis Thomas)
1960	ATA 18-and-under Singles
1960–62	ATA Men's Singles
1961	ATA Men's Doubles (with Ron Charity)
1960–61	USLTA Junior Indoors
1961	USLTA Interscholastics
1963	USLTA Hardcourts
1965	NCAA Singles and Doubles (with Ian Crookenden)
1967	USLTA Clay Courts
1968	USLTA National Open
1970	USLTA Indoor Doubles (with Stan Smith)
1970	Australian Open
1971	French Open Doubles (with Marty Riessen)
1975	Wimbledon
1977	Australian Open Doubles (with Tony Roche)

Davis Cup Team member 1963–70, 75, 77–78

Davis Cup Captain 1981–84

mental in planning the Wimbledon withdrawal of players in 1973 that resulted in the players' right to play their own schedules. In addition, he is Chairman of the Board of the Black Tennis and Sports Foundation, a nonprofit body devoted to assisting black athletes and sports organizations.

Both Althea Gibson and Arthur Ashe have continued to assist the ATA and other groups that foster the development of black players.

The Open Era Begins: Permanent changes occurred in the sixties in black tennis. Even before "open" (amateur and professional in the same event) tennis be-

gan in 1968, black players nationwide were offered more quality instruction, and opportunities to play increased. Players not overtly associated with black clubs or the ATA held their own. Doug Sykes, University of California at Berkeley varsity member, won the 1961 National Public Parks Men's Singles title. Bonnie Logan, who in 1964 began a seven-year streak of ATA Women's Singles titles, was clearly the best since Althea Gibson.

But ATA events began losing some importance to black players as traditionally white-only events admitted all qualified players. No longer did the best black talent seek to advance their careers by winning ATA titles. Part of the problem was the historic concentration of ATA member clubs east of the Mississippi River. Only twice since the 1917 inaugural event, had the ATA Nationals been played west of St. Louis—in San Diego in 1975 and 1982. Consequently, more and more talented black players declined to travel to the East Coast each summer to play in the ATA events.

Some blacks, however, began in ATA competition and quickly graduated to the more difficult USLTA junior circuits. One such player was Juan Farrow, who literally lived next door to Dr. Johnson's tennis court. He showed early promise in winning the 1968 ATA 12-and-under Singles title. He became the first black player to win a USLTA National Junior title, capturing the Boy's 12-and-under, Boy's 14-and-under, and Boy's 16-and-under Indoor Singles titles in 1970, 1972, and 1973, respectively. He was coached by Dr. Johnson. He later attended Southern Illinois University on scholarship and captured the small-college title.

Horace Reid of Atlanta won the USLTA

Boy's 16-and-under Clay Court Doubles title with Billy Martin in 1971. Lawrence "Chip" Hooper won the USLTA Boy's 12-and-under Doubles with Juan Farrow in 1970. Diane Morrison of Los Angeles captured the National Public Parks Girl's 16-and-under Singles title in 1972, and added the ATA Women's Singles Crown three years later. Black youngsters showed they could hold their own when given the chance.

In 1972, the entire nation had a chance to see how good black tennis players could be when the ATA Men's Singles final was televised from Boston. Ashe recalls the players in the men's locker room at the West Side Tennis Club during the U.S. Open being fascinated by this clay-court match between Arthur Carrington and Horace Reid. For the first time ever, the white tennis community at large caught a glimpse of an ATA event and was truly surprised at the high level of competition.

The civil rights era of the sixties and the beginning of Open tennis in 1968 proved to be powerful incentives for young aspiring black players. As the seventies began blacks were no longer novelties in the major events. They were prepared to take their chances at the earliest opportunity. Only the high expense associated with the lengthy learning period deterred some players. The solution proved to be a refinement of the approach used by Dr. Johnson when he began his program in 1951. With one or two exceptions, the best black players from 1970 to 1984 were products of the nation's public parks.

No Longer a Novelty: Beginning in the early seventies, the ATA Men's Singles titles were increasingly won by hardened veterans of years of keen competition. Though the ATA Nationals retained its social amenities, the best senior players more than likely had college experience. In particular, black schools like Hampton University and Texas Southern University fielded teams that began competing with predominantly white schools. The most talented young blacks also began appearing regularly on the rosters of some of the best NCAA Division I schools. Horace Reid and Luis Glass played at UCLA. Rodney Harmon played at the University of Tennessee and graduated from Southern Methodist University. Diane Morrison and Lloyd Bourne played varsity tennis and graduated from Stanford University. The black tennis player had arrived.

Black foreign tennis players also appeared for the first time on the international circuit. William N'Godrella of New Caledonia played for France. Evonne Goolagong, an Australian who is part Aborigine, became a Wimbledon Singles winner. Richard Russell and Lance Lumsden of Jamaica had scored an upset Davis Cup doubles victory over the American team of Arthur Ashe and Charles Pasarell in 1966. But as fate would have it, Ashe made a discovery in the winter of 1971 similar to his own discovery in 1953.

On a private tour of East and West Africa six months after the death of Dr. Johnson on June 28, 1971, Ashe made a scheduled stop in Yaounde, Cameroun, in West Africa. He was accompanied by Tom Okker, the newlywed Charles Pasarell, and Marty Riessen. As the foursome approached the center court at the little club in Yaounde, they noticed a lanky but talented young player volleying at the net.

Ashe recalls: "I was immediately struck by two things: he was exceptionally good for eleven years old, and he didn't look to be pure African. Right away I figured he was of mixed blood, and I was right. We played for about ten minutes, and during one game he served a clean ace against me. I had never seen such a talented eleven-year-old player before—white or black."

The player's name was Yannick Simon Noah. Following conversations through a translator—neither Noah nor his French mother spoke English—Ashe agreed to try to arrange for the French Tennis Federation to sponsor the youngster. Philippe Chatrier, the French Federation President, took Ashe at his word and brought the young Noah to Nice, France, to be included in the French National Junior training program.

Noah had experienced discrimination in the Cameroun because of his white French mother, Marie Claire. His African father, Zachariah, had been a professional soccer player. Said Noah, "I have never had a problem being black, but the Cameroun Federation never supported me. The reason, my mother was white."[22] Noah went on to become the champion of France and one of the world's top five players.

In addition to the rise in the fortunes of black players, black coaches also made their marks. Robert Johnson, Jr., Dr. Johnson's son, continued teaching in the Washington, D.C., area. Two black college coaches, Dr. Robert Screen of Hampton University and Herbert Provost of Texas Southern University, fielded outstanding varsity squads. Robert Binns, John Wilkerson, Horace Reid, Arthur Carrington, and Benny Sims—all former ATA Men's Singles

winners—began careers as coaches. Willis Thomas, Van Hooks, Bob Davis, Eddie Davis, Amelia Myers, Zack Davis, and Emily Moore also established reputations as coaches.

Dr. Screen's record at Hampton deserves special recognition. In 1976, Hampton became the first black school to capture an NCAA team title, the Division II crown. Screen's squads had dominated the Central Intercollegiate Athletic Association (CIAA) since 1970. His fifteen year record was 296–69, for a winning percentage of 81.1.

Herbert Provost coached Stan Franker to the NAIA Singles title in 1974, and the doubles team of Benny Sims-Glenn Moolchan to the NAIA Doubles crown in 1975. Both Screen and Provost witnessed an expanding schedule during the seventies.

One year before Hampton University's NCAA Division II title, Arthur Ashe won the coveted Wimbledon Singles title in a popular win over Jimmy Connors. At the time of the event in June 1975, Ashe was being sued by Connors for libel. Ashe had remarked in an article that Connors was "seemingly unpatriotic" for not playing in the Davis Cup competition for America. Two weeks following Ashe's four-set Wimbledon victory, by the scores of 6–1, 6–1, 5–7, and 6–4, Connors dropped his suit.

Ashe's win was a popular victory, though two years earlier he had led the mass withdrawal of players from that event. But he acknowledged that while his third Grand Slam title was certainly noteworthy, black America should not raise its hopes too high just yet. "If you live in a black community and you want to be a tennis player, you have to leave it, because the black community is currently lacking in expertise, facilities, competition and instruction."[23]

Ashe was essentially correct in his assessment. Whereas the nation's public schools and parks turned out black basketball, football, baseball, track, and boxing participants by the hundreds, black tennis champions amounted to only a small percentage of what it should be.

As Ashe neared retirement in 1979, the black presence on the men's and women's professional circuit was established. In the junior division, Rodney Harmon, of Richmond, Virginia, and Zina Garrison, of Houston, Texas, won national USTA (the USLTA had removed "Lawn" from its name) titles. While Harmon captured the 1979 USTA Boy's 18-and-under Doubles crown, Garrison amassed more USTA National Junior titles than any other black player— seven in all, including the U.S. Open and Junior Wimbledon titles. Garrison's coach, John Wilkerson, had won the ATA Men's Singles crown in 1971, thus becoming the first black coach to develop a Wimbledon winner on his own.

In the early eighties, there were more black women professionals than men on the world circuit. Black women who had tried their hand included Leslie Allen of New York City, Andrea Buchannan of Los Angeles (she was accidentally killed in a shoot-out in Los Angeles), Kim Sands of Miami, Camille Benjamin of Bakersfield, California, Michaela Washington of Michigan, Diane Morrison of Los Angeles, Lori McNeil of Houston, Texas, and Renee Blount of St. Louis, Missouri.

Black men on the professional tour had included Ashe, of Richmond, Virginia, Horace Reid of Atlanta, Georgia, Arthur Carrington of Elizabeth, New Jersey, Benny Sims of Boston, Massachusetts, Todd Shelton of San Diego, California, Chip Hooper of Sunnyvale, California, Marcel Freeman of Long Island, New York, Lloyd Bourne of Glendale, California, and Rodney Harmon of Richmond, Virginia.

In the thirty-five years between 1950 and 1984, black tennis players made unprecedented strides. Beginning with a quota system by which the ATA nominated no more than five blacks for the Nationals at Forest Hills, black players won more than sixty USTA National and international titles. They became members of the Wightman Cup and Davis Cup teams. Black schools won NCAA and NAIA National titles. Black umpires like Titus Sparrow, Jason Smith, Augustus Jenkins, and Claranella Morris officiated in Grand Prix events. Black coaches won National titles. It was an incredible performance in a short time.

Notes

1. Oscar Johnson, Interview Los Angeles, California, 10 August 1984.
2. Ibid.
3. Ibid.
4. Althea Gibson, Interview with author, New York City, N.Y., 8 May 1984.
5. Ibid.
6. Althea Gibson, *I Always Wanted To Be Somebody*, (New York: Harper and Brothers, 1958), 29.
7. Althea Gibson, Interview with author, New York City, N.Y., 8 May 1984.

8. Gibson, *I Always Wanted To Be Somebody,* 33.

9. Ibid., 55.

10. Alice Marble, Letter, *American Law Tennis,* July 1950.

11. Gibson, *I Always Wanted To Be Somebody,* 68.

12. Ibid., 72.

13. Hubert A. Eaton, *Every Man Should Try,* (Wilmington, NC: Bonaparte Press, 1984), 34.

14. *Negro History Bulletin* (November 1960).

15. Robert Johnson, Jr., phone interview with author, 5 May 1985.

16. Ibid.

17. Sydney Llewelyn, telephone interview with author, 22 April 1985.

18. Gibson, *I Always Wanted To Be Somebody,* 159.

19. Ibid., 158.

20. Harry Edwards, *Revolt Of The Black Athlete,* (New York: The Free Press, 1970), xviii.

21. Ibid., xix.

22. *Ebony,* June 1981, 84.

23. *Ebony,* November 1975, 150.

Chapter

7

Track and Field

In the immediate post–World War II era, black track stars were known for their sprinting and jumping. Jesse Owens and his black Olympic teammates had helped America to a team victory in Berlin in 1936. However, by 1948, no black runners held world records for distances greater than 880 yards (some critics charged that blacks were genetically built for shorter races). But in the hurdles, it was imagined that they *should* excel, since this event involved jumping over ten rather short obstacles as fast as possible. Not so. Though, on paper, blacks seemed suited for it, only a handful had mastered the techniques to set world-class marks, and it was also viewed as an event for those who could not make the "first team" in the 100-yard and 220-yard dashes. But for William Harrison Dillard Baldwin-Wallace College, such talk made no difference.

Coming on strong in the late 1940s, Dillard tied the American record in 1946 in the 220-yard hurdles at 22.5 seconds. That same year, he won the AAU 200-meter hurdles title at 23.3 seconds, a new AAU record. He repeated the feat with an identical time in 1947. Elmore Harris, formerly of Morgan State and later with the Shore Athletic Club of New Jersey, had been AAU 200-meter hurdles winner in 1944, the same

year he was AAU 400-meter champion. Indoors, he claimed three AAU titles before the 1948 London Olympics.

In the weight events, blacks had never made much headway. To this day, no black man has won an Olympic medal in the discus, shot put, or javelin. Theodore Cable had a chance in 1912, but was injured; and Thomas Anderson in 1920 failed to place. In the shot put, Lilburn Williams of Xavier University had tossed the 16-pound shot 53 feet 7 inches in 1939 to win the AAU Outdoor title, a first for a black-college athlete. This distance would have won the event in the 1936 Berlin Olympics. But help was on the way.

Woodrow "Woody" Strode of UCLA recorded heaves of 51-feet 6-inches; Archie Harris had noteworthy tosses while attending Indiana University; and Bill Watson of the University of Michigan placed in the shot put in the NCAA's.The best ever, however, was Charles Fonville of the University of Michigan, who was a coholder of the world record set on April 17, 1948, at 58-feet ¼-inch. Fonville set his record at the Kansas Relays in Lawrence, after being forced to stay in private housing in the black section of the city. Earlier, he and Harrison Dillard had been assured that they could stay with their teammates. Incensed, Dillard also pro-

178

ceeded to set a world record of 13.6 seconds in the 110-meter high hurdles in the same arena. New records; same old racism. Fonville, who like Jesse Owens paid his own way through college, injured his back just two weeks after his record toss and could not try out for the 1948 Olympic squad. Those black athletes who *did* make the Olympic team represented the widest range of talent ever seen.

1948: The XIVth Olympiad at London, England

A record 4,062 athletes from fifty-eight nations participated in the 1948 Olympics in London, England, amidst a continuing buildup from the rubble of World War II bombings. One hundred and thirty-eight events were held between July 29 and August 14. Fifty-eight black American athletes sailed for London with their teammates aboard the *S.S. America.*

Pre-Olympic hopes in the black community were very high. Most people expected many medals from the fifty-eight-member black contingent, but these self-same supporters failed to take into account the general improvement of training methods and athletes around the world. In the end, blacks returned with eight gold, two silver, and three bronze medals in track and field.

The twenty-five-year-old Dillard, nicknamed "Bones" by his friends, provided the major surprise among the men. He had come into the 1948 AAU Nationals with eighty-two consecutive hurdles victories, but failed to qualify for the U.S. team. He got to London by finishing third in the 100-meters and then won the gold medal.

Noted Dillard: "I was twenty-five years old when I made the team. It was the realization of a childhood dream and it is about as far as the amateur athlete can go...I remember standing on the victory stand facing the huge scoreboards at the end of the stadium. I remember standing at attention seeing the flag being raised before some 75,000–80,000 people, including the King and Queen of England. I could feel the hair stand up on the back of my neck. It was a tremendous feeling. It was almost as if I could feel my whole athletic life flickering in front of me."[1]

Malvin Whitfield of Ohio State was simply the best combination 400–800 meter runner of his day. In June of 1948, he began a six-year period in which he would lose only three of sixty-nine races at either 800 meters or 880 yards. Like Dillard, he went on to win more medals in the 1952 Olympics.

Harold Norwood "Barney" Ewell, of Penn State, was thirty years old when he won his medals. (In the 4 × 100-meter relay, Ewell was part of a squad that was three-quarters black. The white member was Mel Patton.) He was also an accomplished broad jumper. Unfortunately, he lost his amateur status just after the Olympic Games for accepting an excessive number of prizes from grateful townsfolk in his native Harrisburg, Pennsylvania.

William S. "Willie" Steele followed the path left by a former West Coast jumper Cornelius Johnson. Six years before, Steele was the AAU Junior broad jump winner. He was the 1947 AAU and NCAA titleholder, and in 1948 after winning the NCAA title again, he became only the second jumper in history—apart from Jesse Owens—to break the 26-foot barrier twice. He attended San Jose State.

Lorenzo Christopher Wright competed for Wayne State College and, like Dillard, backed into the team. He was primarily a broad jumper, but finished fourth at the Olympics. On the relay team, he was a last-minute substitute for Ed Conwell, who had an asthma attack.

Herbert Paul Douglas, Jr., hailed from the University of Pittsburgh. At the Olympic Trials he gave his career-best leap of 25 feet 3 inches, but could not repeat the distance in London. He came within one inch of finishing second.

Edward Conwell and Dave Bolen were also members of the track and field squad, but did not place.

A monumental milestone was reached when Alice Coachman (Davis) became the first black woman to win a gold medal in Olympic competition. She had the added distinction of being the only American woman to win a gold medal in track and field at that Olympiad. She still holds the record for most victories in the national AAU Outdoor High Jump without a loss— ten in a row between 1939 and 1948. She attended both Tuskegee and Albany State. Coachman is a member of the National Track and Field Hall of Fame, the Helms Hall of fame, the Black Athletes Hall of Fame, the Tuskegee Hall of Fame, the Georgia State Hall of Fame, and the Bob Douglas Hall of Fame.

Audrey Mickey Patterson of Tennessee State College began that school's streak of female Olympic medalists. At the Trials, she finished second in the 100-meters and won the 200-meters. She failed to make the finals in the 100-meters in London.

There were seven blacks on the women's squad, all from either Tuskegee or Tennessee State. Besides Coachman, others from Tuskegee included Theresa Manuel, Nell Jackson (who in 1956 became the first black head track coach of an American Olympic team), and Mabel Walker. Heriwentha Mae Faggs and Emma Reed were Patterson's teammates from Tennessee State. Faggs, who was only sixteen years old, was eliminated in the semifinals of the 200-meters.

The 1948 Olympics marked the end of an extraordinary period in black track exploits. In the sixteen years between the Olympic Games in 1932 and 1948, blacks established their supremacy in the sprints and jumping events, and served notice that the distance and weight events were not out of reach. While the next twenty years witnessed more victories, higher black expectations would be met with stiffening resistance from collegiate and Olympic authorities. More importantly, sports like track and field became valuable adjuncts to the maturing civil rights movement which swept the nation.

At the end of the war, the leadership roles of the YMCA's and church teams had been superseded by well-organized clubs, Police Athletic League competitions, and college teams. Blacks who did not or could not attend college were forced to find clubs that would accept them. The black college itself was beginning to lose its elitist image in the black community, but its track and field facilities paralleled the degree of sophistication of its football program. Football and track athletes used the same field, so if the football field was modern, the track facilities would be the same.

Still, as late as 1948, even the best-equipped black schools had serious shortcomings. There was, except in rare cases, little expertise in distance coaching; records made on black tracks were not recognized internationally; training equipment was seldom state of the art.

Two years later, black track stars were given a taste of a future problem in which they were to play a major role. In June 1950, following the AAU Championships held at the University of Maryland and at Morgan State College (the first National AAU meet held at a black school), selections were made for international teams to travel to Europe and South Africa. One black athlete listed South Africa as his fifth choice but was turned down, and AAU authorities were criticized for deliberately keeping blacks off the team because this country practiced overt racial segregation.

The AAU had last sent a team to South Africa in 1931, but the public announcement of that country's official racial policy of "apartheid" in 1948 had provided critics with new weapons of protest. The official 1950 AAU squad was all-white.

Politics aside, black and white track athletes could not have imagined what lay ahead: The sheer number of events would increase fifty percent, especially for women; new competitions like the Pan-Am Games would surface; new sanctioning bodies like the Association for Intercollegiate Athletics for Women (AIAW) and the National Association of Intercollegiate Athletics (NAIA) would be organized; the National Collegiate Athletic Association (NCAA) would subdivide according to enrollment size and degree of participation; and the growth of the junior and community college system would provide more opportunities to compete.

But the grandest competition of them all, the Olympic Games, would continue to bring together the world's best athletes every four years and provide a common denominator around which the entire planet could peacefully focus, at least, for two weeks.

1952: The XVth Olympiad at Helsinki, Finland

This second Olympiad since World War II was significant because it marked the first appearance of a team from the Soviet Union. The United States was caught up in the "red scare," brought about in part by Senator Joseph McCarthy, who held accusatory hearings and suspected Communist infiltration in every government department. Even *Ebony* magazine, the most widely read periodical in the black community, joined the bandwagon in headlining an article entitled "Can Negro Athletes Stop The Russians?"

The white American Olympian Bob Mathias noted, "There were many more pressures on the American athletes because of the Russians than in 1948. They were in a sense the real enemies. You just loved to beat 'em. You just had to beat 'em.[2]

However, Milton Campbell, the black silver medalist in the 1952 Olympic Decathlon, said, "We [black athletes] didn't make that big a deal of it."[3]

Strangely, the United States at the time had no well-coordinated program to train Olympic athletes. Training was left entirely to schools, clubs, and the AAU. The Pan-Am Games were organized in 1951 for the first time as a prelude to the Olympics themselves. (The Pan-Am Games would be held every four years in the year preceding the Olympic Games.) The American contingent was part of a total of 5,294 men and 573 women to compete at Helsinki.

Black Americans won fourteen medals at Helsinki. Their results are shown in the Reference section.

For Harrison Dillard, known as "Bones," his were the third and fourth gold medals in successive Olympaids. Called by General George Patton "the best goddamn athlete I've ever seen,"[4] Dillard was 5-feet 10-inches and weighed only 150 pounds. He had attended East Technical High School in Cleveland, Ohio, the same school that had produced Jesse Owens, and Baldwin-Wallace College. Though acknowledged as the greatest hurdler of his time, Dillard missed qualifying in his specialty event for the 1948 Olympic team; he made the team as a sprinter and won the 100-meter dash.

After that 1948 Olympic win, Dillard's black teammate Norwood "Barney" Ewell cried out, "I won, I did it!" But the Panamanian Lloyd LaBeach told him "No, Bones win."[5] Dillard's victories in 1952, however, were never in doubt. He finished his career with fourteen AAU and six NCAA National titles.

The 1952 Olympiad was also the second for Mal Whitfield, an Ohio State University product. Undoubtedly the finest 400/800-meter runner of his time, between June 1948 and October 1954 Whitfield lost only three of sixty-nine races of 800 meters or 880 yards. He repeated as gold medalist in the 1952 Olympic Games 800-meter run. He eventually captured five AAU titles and

five indoor and outdoor world records. In the late fifties and early sixties, he spent time in Africa training various Olympic teams. In 1955, he was the first black recipient of the James E. Sullivan Award, given to the nation's premier amateur athlete.

Andrew Stanfield, a graduate of Seton Hall University, represented the New York Pioneer Athletic Club. In addition to capturing six IC4A titles in the 100-yard and 60-yard dashes, he set a world record of 20.6 seconds in the 220-yard dash in 1951.

Jerome Biffle won the NCAA long jump title in 1950 while at the University of Denver. When he won his Olympic gold medal, he was an Army private.

Mae Faggs started out in a New York PAL program and later attended Tennessee State, where she was coached by Ed Temple. She won five AAU titles in the 100/200-meters and a gold and a silver medal in the 1955 Pan-Am Games. She was given credit by Wilma Rudolph for providing invaluable assistance during Rudolph's career.

Catherine Hardy attended Fort Valley State in Georgia. She won three AAU indoor and outdoor titles.

Barbara Jones was, at fifteen years and one hundred twenty-three days, the youngest American female to win an Olympic gold medal in track and field. She started in the Chicago Catholic Youth Organization (CYO) and attended Tennessee State. Jones won three AAU titles between 1953 and 1957.

Meredith Gourdine went to Cornell, where he won the IC4A long jump title and the 220-yard hurdles in 1951. He finished ahead of Biffle in the trials and at the AAU, but had to settle for second in Helsinki. The initial favorite in the long jump was George

Brown of UCLA. But Brown, who is Black, fouled three straight times during the finals at Helsinki.

Milton Campbell was a seventeen-year-old high school student from Plainfield, New Jersey, when he won his 1952 Olympic silver medal. He also won the 1953 AAU Decathlon title, with 7,235 points. Harold Bruguiere, his high school coach, said, "He is beyond a doubt the greatest athlete in all around ability I have ever seen."[6] Inexplicably, he noted, "No black college ever contacted me—none. I had sixty-three offers but no offers from a black school."[7] This has to be one of the most serious oversights by black colleges in track history.

Ollie Matson who attended the University of San Francisco, tried to make the 1948 United States Olympic team in the 400-meters, but failed. He did win two medals at the 1952 Games. Better known for his football prowess, he played professionally for the Chicago Cardinals, the Los Angeles Rams, the Detroit Lions, and the Philadelphia Eagles.

1956: The XVIth Olympiad at Melbourne, Australia

The success of black athletes at Helsinki was shown on television and on movie newsreels. Only Joe Louis and Sugar Ray Robinson enjoyed much international adulation at the time. For Mae Faggs, Catherine Hardy, and Barbara Jones, their gold medals represented the height of acclaim for black female athletes. The 1952 United States Women's Olympic squad consisted of only ten athletes (and a manager) competing in only nine events. Nineteen fifty-six would be different.

Among black colleges, Morgan State continued in its premier role, especially in relay events. In 1955, the State team won the AAU Indoor relay crown. On May 6, 1954, Roger Bannister of England finally broke the four-minute barrier in the mile—3:59.4, only to see it broken six weeks later on June 21 by John Landy in 3:58.

Ted Corbitt, the black marathoner, enjoyed success in winning the 1954 AAU Philadelphia and Detroit marathons. Another notable showing was a sixth-place finish in the 1952 Boston marathon. In 1955, at age thirty-five, he finished tenth in a field of 160 at Boston.

Noteworthy for blacks were three political events that took place between the 1952 and 1956 Games. First, President Harry S. Truman desegregated the Armed Forces, thereby desegregating its sports programs and guaranteeing the best training and coaching possible for black GIs. Second, in a monumental 1954 United States Supreme Court decision, the justices declared that "separate but equal" public schooling for blacks and whites was unconstitutional. It was immediately assumed by many that black students would soon enjoy the same athletic opportunities as white students.

The third event affected the 1956 Games more directly. Before the Games began in November, the Soviet Union invaded Hungary, and Great Britain, France, and Israel seized the Suez Canal from Egypt. Holland, Spain, and Switzerland withdrew from the Games over the Soviet invasion, and Lebanon, Iraq, and Egypt withdrew over the Suez seizure. The International Olympic Committee tried to remain aloof from it all.

America's black athletes took notice of these incidents, trained hard, and returned with eighteen medals. These medalists are listed in the Reference section.

Milton Campbell, who attended Indiana University, won the gold medal in the decathlon. Surprisingly, he attempted only five decathlons during his career—the Olympic Trials in 1952 and 1956, the Olympics in 1952 and 1956, and the 1953 AAU which he won. He considered himself a hurdler first and a decathlete second.

Lee Calhoun became the first black male athlete from a black college to win an Olympic gold medal. Trained by the famed black coach at North Carolina Central, Dr. Leory Walker, Calhoun set an Olympic record and is the only man to win two Olympic high hurdles titles. He also won AAU, NAIA, and NCAA titles in 1956 and 1957. After a brief suspension of his amateur status, he won his third AAU and a Pan-Am title in 1959.

At the 1956 Olympic Trials, Charles Dumas was the first human to break the seven-foot barrier in the high jump. He had tied for first place in the high jump at the 1955 AAUs, but won it outright in 1957–59. Representing the University of Southern California, he finished sixth in the 1960 Games.

Greg Bell won the 1955 AAU Long Jump title and added the NCAA title in the 1956–57 and the AAU Indoor title in 1958.

Charles Jenkins was a surprise Olympic winner in the 400-meter run. His teammate, Lou Jones, had set a world record during the Trials at 45.2 seconds, but could

do no better than fifth place in Melbourne. Jones led for most of the race, but was passed by four runners near the end. A Villanova University student, Jenkins won the AAU title in 1955, the IC4A title in 1955 and 1957 and set a world record for the 500-yard run in 1956. He eventually succeeded his college coach, Jumbo Elliot, at Villanova.

Lou Jones partly atoned for his lapse in the 400-meter run by sharing victory in the 1600-meter relay along with Jenkins and white teammates Jesse Mashburn and Thomas Courtney. A graduate of Manhattan College, he set his first world record in the 400-meter run at the 1955 Pan-Am Games.

Ira Murchison and Leamon King shared gold medals in the 400-meter relay with Thane Baker and Bobby Morrow. Murchison, who stood only 5-feet 5-inches, ran for both Iowa and Western Michigan and in 1956 set a world record of 10.1 seconds in the 100-meters at a military meet in Berlin, Germany. This graduate of Wendell Phillips High in Chicago also won the AAU 60-yard title in 1957 and the NCAA 100-yard title in 1958. King set a world record of 9.3 seconds for the 100-yard dash in 1956 and won the AAU title in 1957.

Rafer Johnson won the AAU decathlon in 1956 and, after winning a silver medal in Melbourne, he never lost again. He also qualified for the 1956 Games in the long jump, but did not participate because of injury.

Andrew Stanfield returned to capture a silver medal in his second Olympics and Josh Culbreath of Morgan State captured a bronze in the 400-meter hurdles. Culbreath was AAU champion in 1953-55. In 1957 at

Oslo, Norway, he set a world record of 50.5 seconds in the 440-yard hurdles. He was black America's first premier intermediate hurdler.

The women's squad, coached by Nell Jackson of Tuskegee Institute (now Tuskegee University), produced its first Olympic and world record by a black American female in the person of Mildred McDaniel. Not only did Mildred set a world and Olympic record, she also defeated the former record holder, Iolanda Balas of Roumania. Three years later, McDaniel won the high jump at the Pan-Am Games.

Willye White, nicknamed "Red", participated in a record five Olympiads and won medals in two—1956 and 1964 (a silver medal in the 400-meter relay). She won the AAU Outdoor long jump title ten times and in 1962, the Indoor title. A graduate of Tennessee State University, White also won the Pan-Am long jump title in 1963. She was truly one of America's greatest female athletes.

Mae Faggs, Isabelle Daniels, and Wilma Rudolph all hailed from Tennessee State and were coached by Ed Temple. Along with Margret Matthews, who held the American record of 19-feet 9¼-inches in the long jump, the three Tigerbelles from Tennessee State finished third in the 400-meter relay behind Australia and Great Britain. Daniels won twelve AAU Indoor and Outdoor sprint titles.

But better days lay ahead for Wilma Rudolph. One of twenty-two children from Clarksville, Tennessee, she had a deformed left foot as a child and wore a brace on her right leg for five years between the ages of seven and twelve. She was only sixteen when she participated at Melbourne. She shared in the bronze medal in the 400-meter relay after being eliminated in a preliminary heat in the 200-meter run.

1960: The XVIIth Olympiad at Rome, Italy

America wrestled with internal racial contradictions during the four years between the XVIth and the XVIIth Olympiads. What observers thought would be a peaceful transition from segregation to integration in public schools, as ordered by the Supreme Court, was not the case. In school systems where the change did take place, black coaches were usually assigned secondary positions.

Black colleges, however, made historic advances. For the first time, NAIA titles were won in basketball, baseball, football, and track in this four-year period. The familiarity of the black college coach, such as Ed Temple of Tennessee State (who succeeded Nell Jackson as Head Women's Track Coach for the 1960 United States Olympic squad), with international competition had paid off.

No group made greater strides during these forty-eight months than black female track stars. They seemed to be more team-oriented than their male counterparts and relied more on the advice of their coaches. Even travel to meets was now more bearable, because these athletes went as a group rather than as individuals. No black female—no matter how good she was—wanted to go to a strange place alone.

Nell Jackson recalls that "the distance we traveled on our way to a meet was determined by how far the next black college was from our location. Because we had no public places to stay in the fifties, we relied on the South's black colleges to house us."[8]

These considerations were of paramount importance, and it is not difficult to understand why the black colleges rather than the predominantly white colleges nurtured the first generations of black female track stars. Subsequently, Fred Thompson, who began his Atoms Track Club in 1959 as a coed venture in Brooklyn, New York, soon dropped his young male runners and concentrated solely on training the girls. Says Thompson, "...I had to phase out the boys because by the time they got into high school they had other things to interest them. But at that time, there wasn't one intramural program for girls' athletics."[9] Because of the increased interest in track among girls in the public schools, the USOC created a Women's Advisory Board in 1958.

With renewed vigor, black athletes came to Rome and won more gold medals than ever.

Rafer Johnson had the honor of carrying the American flag during the opening ceremonies in Rome. He must have drawn even more competitive inspiration from this experience because he set a new Olympic record in the decathlon. After his retirement from track, he became very involved in community programs in California. He was with Democratic presidential candidate Robert F. Kennedy the night he was assassinated in Los Angeles in 1968. It was Johnson who grabbed the pistol from the hands of Kennedy's assassin, Sirhan Sirhan. At the 1984 Los Angeles Games, Johnson

was accorded the honor of lighting the Olympic torch above the Coliseum.

Ralph Boston won medals in three Olympiads—a gold in 1960, a silver in 1964, and a bronze in 1968. Just before the Rome Olympics in August, Boston broke Jesse Owens' long jump record with a leap of 26 feet 11¼ inches. In 1961, he broke his own world record two more times and, in 1964 and 1965, he broke the record three additional times. With the exception of Edwin Moses, Boston is the only track athlete ever to break a world record on six occasions.

Boston also won the AAU Outdoor long-jump title six straight years (1961 to 66) and the Indoor title in 1961. As a Tennessee State student, he won the NCAA Outdoor title in 1960. Throughout his career, he was one of the most highly respected athletes in the sport, and was known for encouraging other athletes during difficult times.

Otis Davis, from Tuscaloosa, Alabama, was a Sergeant in the Air Force in 1960. Though he never ran in an organized race until he was twenty-five, he later became the fourth black Olympian to set a world record. Davis attended the University of Oregon as a basketball player and then discovered his sprinting talents.

Willie May came into his own in his senior year at Indiana University. He finished second to Lee Calhoun in the 1960 Olympic Trials and the Games.

Lester Carney enjoyed football more than track. Playing for Ohio University, he was later drafted by the Baltimore Colts but never played professional ball.

Irvin Roberson, who attended Cornell, won the 1959 Pan-Am Games long-jump title and came very close to winning the title at Rome. He later played professional football for six years at San Diego, Oakland, Buffalo, and Miami.

Hayes Jones won six AAU hurdles titles and, from March 1959 through 1964, fifty-five consecutive indoor races. He was also Pan-Am and NCAA champion in 1959. This hurdler had such speed that he was part of the 1961 world-record 400-meter relay team. In 1964 he finally won a gold medal in the 110-meter hurdles.

John Thomas, along with Ray Norton, was a hard luck story at Rome. He was the first man to exceed 7 feet indoors, when he leaped 7 feet 1¼ inches in 1959. He was only seventeen. Coming into Rome, the 6-foot 4¾-inch Thomas had jumped over 7 feet thirty-seven times, but had to settle for a bronze medal. He explained, "When I passed [his turn] at 6 feet 11½ inches, it wasn't a psychological maneuver. I always liked to go up in two-inch increments...I'd never heard of any of the Russian jumpers...Brumel...we were 5–5 over the years...it was always the U.S. versus Russia. Freedom versus Communism. Us versus them. It was the only barometer."[10]

Thomas' reference to Valeri Brumel was an explanation of his 1964 Tokyo Olympic loss. Though both jumpers reached 7-feet 1¾-inch at Tokyo, Brumel won because of fewer misses. Thomas won seven AAU Indoor and Outdoor titles, two NCAA titles and six IC4A Indoor and Outdoor titles while at Boston University.

Other 1960 Rome disappointments were Ray Norton's last-place finishes in the 100-meter and 200-meter dashes. Norton, who attended San Jose State, had run 10.1 seconds for the 100-meter and 20.1 seconds for the 200-meter runs. To worsen matters, he caused his 400-meter relay team to be disqualified because of a bad baton pass that caused Stone Johnson to miss out on a gold medal.

Norton had an explanation for his miserable showing. At an Olympic tune-up meet before Rome, he recalls, "...John Thomas found out I was afraid of snakes. He came up behind me with a garter snake and held it up to my face. I jumped so high, I wrenched my lower back...I got to Rome with a bad case of dysentery from a train ride...in ten days, I went from 187 pounds to 167..."[11]

No such bad luck befell Wilma Rudolph or her 400-meter relay teammates. Rudolph captivated the world with three gold medal performances, and she became the first black female to win a gold medal in a sprint event. Though she sprained her ankle the day before her first race, she won the 100-meter final by six yards. She won the 200-meter final in the rain.

Rudolph received much encouragement along the way. At the Penn Relays one year, Jackie Robinson told the then unheralded young runner, "...don't let anything, or anybody, keep you from running. Keep running."[12] She won the AAU 100-meter title four straight years, from 1959 to 1962, the 200-meter title in 1960, and three AAU Indoor titles.

More than any other athlete, Rudolph is credited with stirring interest among females in track events. Noted Nell Jackson, "Wilma's accomplishments opened up the real door for women in track because of her grace and beauty. People saw her as beauty in motion."[13] To help underprivileged children she later formed the Wilma Rudolph Foundation in Indianapolis, Indiana.

Rudolph's teammates, Martha Hudson, Lucinda Williams, and Barbara Jones, all attended Tennessee State. Hudson won the AAU Indoor 100-yard title in 1959; Williams won AAU 220-yard titles in 1957-59; and Jones won AAU 100-meter titles in 1953 and 1954 and the 100-yard title in 1957.

Earlene Brown is still the only American woman to win a medal in the shot put. She won eight AAU National titles and Pan-Am Games gold medals in 1959 in the shot put and discus. Brown set American records in 1960 with a 54-foot 9¼-inch shot put and a discus throw of 176 feet 10 inches.

1964: The XVIIIth Olympiad at Tokyo, Japan

Black colleges made concerted efforts to upgrade their track programs in the early sixties. Three different schools won NAIA titles between 1960 and 1964. Public-school integration of athletic teams proceeded according to local custom, but black tracksters continued to concentrate on the sprinting and jumping events. The sit-ins, protest marches, and economic boycotts so typical of this period in American history had more influence on college sports than public-school sports.

Internationally, South Africa had participated in the 1960 Olympics for the last time, but there were last-minute attempts to include them in 1964. Soviet delegates to the IOC first made protests over South Africa's presence in 1960. Black activist/comedian, Dick Gregory, called for an international boycott of the 1960 Games. He was joined in this view in 1964 by Mal Whitfield who said in an *Ebony* magazine article in

1963, "...It is time for American Negro athletes to join the civil rights fight—a fight that is far from won."[14] Both Gregory and Whitfield recognized a connection between the treatment of blacks in America and in South Africa.

Black American athletes left Tokyo in 1964 with nineteen American and world records to their credit. The medalists are listed in the Reference section.

Bob Hayes was awesome in winning the 100-meters by a 7-foot margin. In the 400-meter relay final, he ran the anchor leg and made up a 9-yard deficit to win ahead of the Frenchman, Jocelyn DeLecour. Hayes, who attended Florida A&M University, and ran in an awkward style, said of his Olympic performance, "It's the 'most satisfying feeling I've ever had in athletics." San Jose State coach Bud Winter added, "...he ran like he was pounding grapes into win."[15]

Hayes, 5-foot 11-inches, and 186 pounds at the time, performed the impossible on the last leg of the 400-meter relay final. Richard Stebbins, who ran the third leg in the relay, remembered that "The Japanese are reserved people. But they came to their feet, even those in the Emperor's box."[16] Some people say Hayes actually clocked 8.6 seconds for his last leg to make up the 9-yard deficit.

Hayes' standard reply to those who considered him the fastest of "The World's Fastest Humans" was, "I'm just a country boy goin' to the city with taps on my tennis shoes."[17]

Henry Carr was a superb sprinter. Besides winning the NCAA 220-yard title in 1963 for Arizona State and the AAU title in 1964, he twice set world records in the 200-

meter—20.3 seconds in 1963 and 20.2 a year later. He was the best 200/400-meter runner of his time.

As a student at Villanova, Paul Drayton was part of the 1961 400-meter relay team that set a world record of 39.1 seconds. He was the AAU 200-meter champion in 1961 and 1962.

John Rambo, who attended Long Beach State in California, was the 1964 NCAA high jump title holder and won the AAU Indoor title in 1967 and 1969.

Ulis Williams was Henry Carr's teammate at Arizona State. He was part of the 1600-meter relay teams that won the AAU title in 1962 and 1963, the NCAA title in 1963, and tied for the 1964 NCAA title.

Wyomia Tyus of Tennessee State is the only Olympian to successfully defend the 100-meter title. She is tied with Wilma Rudolph and Valerie Brisco-Hooks for most gold medals by a female runner—three. She is tied with Rudolph for most medals—four. She also won five AAU titles at 100-meters, 100-yards, 200-meters, and 200-yards; three AAU Indoor 60-yard titles; and was Pan-Am champion in 1967 at 200-meters. She could lay fair claim to the title of "Greatest American Female Olympian."

Edith McGuire was only the second black female to win three medals at the same Olympiad. She was also an accomplished long jumper, winning this event at the AAU Indoor and Outdoor meets in 1963. She was also AAU 200-meter champion in 1964 and Indoor champion in 1965 and 1966.

Marilyn White won the AAU 220-yard Indoor title in 1963 as a student at UCLA. She ran the third leg on the 400-meter relay team at Tokyo.

Changing Conditions: In the mid-sixties, black track stars faced a world different from that of their predecessors fifteen years before. The rivalry with the Soviet Union was in high gear; the USOC was much more organized, although the despised Avery Brundage was still firmly in charge; television coverage made national heroes of some athletes overnight; the national political atmosphere was charged with the black social revolution; black colleges were starting to feel the negative effects of inflation on their athletic budgets; black female track stars were, in the words of the black writer Maya Angelou, "sheroes"; the track calendar was crowded with more events, meets, and more records; and the sport itself continued to lure most of its black performers from the black underclass.

By now, black athletes had an emotional attachment to the sprinting and jumping events. Among themselves they considered it culturally treasonous to lose in these specialty contests. Whether or not they believed the theories about the genetic physical superiority of black sprinters, they behaved as if the theories were true.

When interviewed by *Newsweek* magazine, Tommy Smith replied, "Everything is hustle and bustle for a young black. Run to the bus, run with other kids, run from the cops. Maybe that's how we get so good at sprinting."[18] In the same issue of *Newsweek,* a white polevaulter countered by saying blacks did not go in for other events "...because distance running and vaulting are too much work for them."[19]

Said Lee Evans, the Olympic gold medalist: "We were bred for it. Certainly the black people who survived in the slave ships must have contained a high proportion of the strongest."[20] Though Evans and others like him *believed* this line of reasoning was incorrect, this did not deter negative thinking.

Though track, like boxing, is among the black "big five"—track, boxing, baseball, football, and basketball—it has little in common with its more brutal "cousin" sport, boxing. And unlike boxing, there is no money to be made on the track; the athletes are in it for the glory and the fame and little else.

Only a handful of black track athletes wrote their autobiographies, but from those that did, a sobering portrait can be drawn. Most of them came from broken homes, were chronic truants, cared little about school initially, were exploited at the predominantly white colleges, and had little if any attention paid to them after their usefulness was exhausted.

Bob Beamon, for instance, "...lived in a crowded ghetto apartment with his stepfather and his stepfather's wife, his grandmother and his great-grandfather and, eventually, two stepbrothers and a stepsister."[21]

Vince Matthews, a gold medalist in the 1968 Games, spoke for many other blacks when he said of his more fortunate black colleague, Wayne Collett, "...some people had said that Wayne didn't have the will to go all the way, that his black middle-class background and taste for good wines, classical and Oriental music and smart clothes didn't jive with the demands of a race like the 400 [meters]."[22] Matthews' comment was more a generalization than a stab at Collett.

Many were painted as hedonists. Bob Beamon began drinking alcohol at age seven and graduated to marijuana and wine before straightening out. John Carlos did the same. They were, as Beamon wrote, "desperate for attention."[23] Of course, not all black track athletes were like this, thanks in large measure to black college coaches and some caring white coaches as well.

It is thus easier to understand why most of the supreme public sacrifices made by black athletes were by those who felt they had little to lose. Against this backdrop, the buildup to the 1968 Olympic Games began.

The Olympic Project for Human Rights: There were more angry black athletes in more sports in the mid-sixties than at any other time. Challenges to authority and protests over discriminatory practices were everyday occurrences. The Olympic Project for Human Rights (OPHR), organized by black San Jose State sociology professor Harry Edwards, was a logical extension of the overall racial climate. Pointedly, Dr. Edwards said to his early critics, "The roots of the revolt of the black athlete spring from the same seed that produced the sit-ins, the freedom rides, and the rebellions in Watts, Detroit, and Newark..."[24]

On the opening day of classes at San Jose State in September 1967, a rally of seven hundred people resolved to disrupt the first game of the football season against the University of Texas at El Paso (UTEP) to protest racial discrimination. On October 7, Dr. Edwards formed the Olympic Committee for Human Rights (OCHR) in his home. It was decided that formal and organized protests were needed to redress the increasingly difficult conditions for black athletes. The OCHR formed the OPHR.

Six weeks later, at a strategy session in Los Angeles (on November 22 and 23), the particpants—including activist James Foreman, Lew Alcindor (now Kareem Abdul-Jabbar), Lee Evans, Tommie Smith, and Otis Burrell—issued the following closing statement: "Black men and women athletes at a Black Youth Conference held in Los Angeles on the 23rd of November, 1967, have unanimously voted to fully endorse and participate in a boycott of the Olympic Games in 1968."[25]

Alcindor had been passionately eloquent in his remarks. He told the Conference, "Everybody knows me...last summer I was almost killed by a racist cop shooting at a black cat [man] in Harlem...Somewhere each of us has got to make a stand...I take my stand here."[26]

The statements were a direct challenge to the USOC and a clarion call to black athletes in all sports. After deciding to deliberately avoid the traditional civil rights groups like the National Urban League and the NAACP, a conference was held in the American Hotel in New York City on December 15, attended by Louis Lomax, Floyd McKissick, and Dr. Martin Luther King, Jr.

A list of demands were drawn up and directed to the USOC, the World Boxing Association, the World Boxing Council, the New York State Athletic Commission, and the New York Athletic Club. The demands were:

1. The restoration of Muhammad Ali's titles.
2. The removal of Avery Brundage as head of the USOC.
3. The continued exclusion of South African and Rhodesian teams from the United States and the Olympic Games.
4. The hiring of two additional black coaches to the Olympic track team—but not Stanley Wright.
5. The appointment of two blacks to the policymaking committee of the USOC.
6. The desegregation of the New York Athletic Club.

Muhammad Ali had been summarily stripped of his heavyweight title, and his fellow black athletes wanted justice done. Brundage was intensely disliked for his crass insensitivity to black problems and his hard-line aversion to mixing politics and sport. Both South Africa and Rhodesia practiced official racial segregation at the time, and the committee deemed their continued athletic exclusion mandatory.

Stan Wright, who is black, had been appointed as an assistant coach for the 1968 United States squad but, he was, like Jesse Owens, considered at the time to be an "Uncle Tom." In answer to the demand concerning blacks on the USOC Executive Committee, Avery Brundage was quoted as replying, "I think there should be a qualified Negro on the USOC Board. I think Jesse Owens is a fine boy and might make a good representative." *[sic]*[27]

The reaction to the OPHR's proposed boycott was loud and diverse. Black athletes themselves were by no means totally supportive. Sample opinions provide clues to the mood of the times. Among those in favor of the boycott: Bill Gaines, a sprinter, said, "I'm fully prepared to do anything necessary to dramatize the plight of black people in this country." Lee Evans noted that "There is need for anything that brings about unity among black people and points up the fact that successful blacks maintain their ties with the black community." Ralph Boston declared that "If we decide on some kind of protest, I'd be less than a man not to participate. I'd be letting myself down, my family, my race."[28]

In a dissenting opinion John Thomas said, "How much pride can you lose by emerging an Olympic champion?" Larry Livers, an AAU hurdles champion, replied, "I would rather see boycotts against domestic indoor and outdoor meets. That's where the black is really exploited...I would support that kind of boycotting." Willye White said, "I can't see passing up the Olympics...I am an athlete."[29]

The New York Times' heralded white sports columnist Red Smith declared that athletics have been "the Negro's best friend." The great Jesse Owens was quoted as saying, "I am not in accord with those who advocate a boycott of the Olympic Games...athletics help youngsters who do not have the money to go on to colleges of their choice..."[30]

But Professor Charles Hamilton of Columbia University, the coauthor of *Black Power* with Stokely Carmichael, declared, "The boycott is very necessary. It gives us another way to confront the system."[31] An *Ebony* magazine poll found only 1 percent of black athletes agreeing with the boycott, 71 percent against it, and 28 percent undecided. The OPHR clearly lacked support among the rank and file in early 1968.

An interim boycott against the New York Athletic Club (which had no black members and few if any Jewish ones) meet on February 15, 1968, was moderately successful. Led by Catholic groups, the invited high school teams withdrew; the service academies withdrew; and the Soviets canceled. That very morning, newspapers had headlined the readmittance of South Africa to the Olympic Games by a secret ballot of seventy-one members at an IOC meeting in Grenoble, France. South Africa had agreed to integrate its Olympic team, though it still planned to hold segregated Olympic trials. A three-man IOC delegation to South Africa, that included an African, had reported the reforms. However, only nine black athletes crossed the picket line at Madison Square Garden, where black activist H. Rap Brown suggested the arena be blown up. Intense emotion surrounded the OPHR.

Said O.J. Simpson of the NYAC meet: "I wouldn't run that weekend if my mother was holding the meet." Harry Edwards angrily declared after hearing of South Africa's readmittance: "Let whitey run his own Olympics."[32] Within two weeks of South Africa's readmittance, nearly all African nations and some Third World nations withdrew from the 1968 Games.

The OPHR and the South African issue effected the first major partnership between the black athletes of Africa and America. It also dramatized the gap between the first generation of post–World War II black athletes and their mid-sixties successors. During the 1967-68 academic year, black athletes at thirty-seven predominantly white colleges had raised demands for more black coaches, faculty, trainers, and cheerleaders, and expressed sympathy with the OPHR.

Two months after the NYAC meet,

UTEP Track Coach Wayne Vandenburg summarily dropped six blacks from his team (including Bob Beamon) for refusing to run against Brigham Young University (BYU). BYU was a Mormon institution which adhered to that religion's belief that blacks were damned by the Biblical curse of Ham. (The football coach at the University of Wyoming had done the same thing for the same reasons.) UTEP President Joseph Ray refused to rescind Vandenburg's dismissals. Racial tensions across the country were already near the boiling point because of Dr. Martin Luther King's assassination by a white man on April 4.

The next major national meet was the AAU championships. It was decided among the participating black athletes that if two-thirds of them agreed to boycott before the Olympic Trials were held, then the boycott was on. Just before the Trials in July, a meeting of approximately forty athletes was convened by Dr. Edwards at Pomona, California. During the previous week, the IOC had changed their position on South Africa and barred it from the Games. The growing attention paid to the proposed boycott and the euphoria over South Africa's expulsion, encouraged the black athletes to use the Trials for symbolic racial gestures of solidarity.

The USOC became aware of the proposed actions at the Trials at Pomona, and reacted by cancelling the victory ceremonies. Subsequently, the USOC stated that the Trials were not the real Trials and transferred these Olympic qualification events to Lake Tahoe, California—ostensibly for high altitude training for Mexico City's atmosphere at 7,349 feet. This sudden move appeared to be aimed more at the OPHR than for its practical benefits. Surely,

blacks reasoned, the USOC could plan better than that.

Avery Brundage made matters worse when he was quoted as saying, "It seems a little ungrateful to attempt to boycott something which has given them [blacks] such great opportunities."[33]

At Tahoe, where the victory ceremonies were also cancelled, twelve blacks went on record as supporting the boycott and thirteen were against. Support for the OPHR had grown. Those who agreed to boycott were released from the group's pledge to "Do Your Own Thing." There would be no demonstrations at the Trials. The following month, on August 15, a National Conference on Black Power was held in Philadelphia, and there the OPHR became an integral part of the nation's black social revolution.

Within a year, a small but determined group of black athletes had succeeded in focusing the world's attention on their plight and that of black America. They arrived in Mexico City buoyed by the past year's experience, and left with a record total of twenty-seven Olympic medals in track and field—nineteen of them gold, and seventeen world records.

1968: The XIXth Olympiad at Mexico City, Mexico

This Olympiad is remembered principally for two events: Bob Beamon's new world record in the long jump and the victory stand demonstration by Tommie Smith and John Carlos. After all the meetings, caucasing, and reconsiderations, most black athletes were not sure what they were going to do as a form of protest. But they did know they were ready to perform.

On October 14, Jim Hines and Charles Greene (nursing a sore leg), finished first and third in the 100-meter dash. At the AAU Nationals that year, Hines from Texas Southern University, became the first man to clock a legal sub-ten-second reading for that event—9.9 in a semi-final heat. Greene attended the University of Nebraska and was a six-time NCAA Indoor and Outdoor 100-meter champion, and a four-time AAU Indoor and Outdoor winner in the century distance. According to Matthews, Hines refused to shake hands with Brundage during the medal ceremonies. Lee Evans and Tommie Smith watched from the stands.

Some black athletes were dissuaded from protesting by offers from sports companies. Vincent Matthews wrote that "...payments contributed to the reluctance of many to become totally committed in The Olympic Project for Human Rights."[34] Also, during a pre-Olympic stopover at Denver, Colorado, for outfitting and processing, the athletes agreed that a boycott was out of the question—though several proposals, such as the wearing of black arm bands and uniforms, were discussed.

On October 16, Smith and Carlos finished first and third in the 200-meter dash finals. While waiting under the stands for the awards ceremonies, Smith pulled two black gloves, purchased by his and Evans' wives, from his bag and gave the left glove to Carlos. On the spur of the moment they agreed on their gesture, which would be witnessed around the world and forever change the image of the black American athlete.

On the victory stand during the playing of America's National Anthem, Smith raised his right black-gloved fist high and straight above his head, and Carlos raised his left black-gloved fist as well. Smith wore a knotted black scarf around his neck and both wore long black socks and no shoes. Both stood with heads bowed, eyes closed, not saying a word. The deed was done.

What had prompted such courage in such a public forum? Smith was born in Acworth, Texas, on June 5, 1944; one of eight children of a migrant farm worker. He set four world records in 1966, in the 200-meters and 220-yard dash; a year later he set more world marks in the 400-meters and 440-yard dash. His world record at Mexico City was his seventh. In addition, he was AAU and NCAA 200/220 champion in 1967, and AAU 200-meter champion in 1968.

His statement to WABC-TV's Howard Cosell, after the race, succinctly explained his feelings: "I wore a black right-hand glove and Carlos wore the left-hand glove of the same pair. My raised right hand stood for the power in black America. Carlos' raised left hand stood for the unity of black America. Together they formed an arch of unity and power. The black scarf around my neck stood for black pride. The black sock with no shoes stood for black poverty in racist America. The totality of our effort was the regaining of black dignity."[35]

John Carlos was born in New York City on June 5, 1945, and, after withdrawing from East Texas State because of racial discrimination, he enrolled at San Jose State. "In Harlem, you're not brought up to take what they do in Texas."[36] In his mind, nothing the USOC could do to him would be worse than what he had already experienced. His best ever performance was a nonratified clocking of 19.7 seconds in illegal spiked shoes for 200-meters, at the

1968 Olympic Trials. In 1969, he was AAU and NCAA champion at 200-meters and 220-yards, and equaled the world records in the 60-yard dash and the 100-yard dash.

Smith and Carlos were ejected from the Olympic Village by the IOC and subjected to vilification at home. Carlos said his "parents caught hell. They didn't really understand at the time. They seemed to be ashamed to be my parents."[37] (Carlos later played professional football and, at the 1984 Games, was named as a special assistant for the USOC.)

Lee Evans felt duty bound to do something since he and Smith were good friends. Their wives had bought the black gloves. Just before the 400-meter final, Evans, Larry James, and Ron Freeman were approached by a visibly nervous and shaking Douglas F. Roby, the USOC president, Stan Wright, and several other USOC officials. In a stammering voice, Roby warned against any demonstrations.

James screamed at Wright, "Listen, you better get this sonofabitch out of here, or I'll punch him in the mouth."[38]

On the victory stand in the rain afterwards, Evans, James, and Freeman, who finished first, second, and third, respectively, wore black berets and saluted. Evans set a world record in this event which still stands.

While at San Jose State in 1968, Evans won the NCAA 440-yard title, five AAU titles, and was a member of the 1972 Olympic 1600-meter relay team. James attended Villanova and won the NCAA Indoor 440-yard title three straight years, and the Outdoor title in 1970. Though Freeman, of Arizona State, finished with a Bronze Medal he ran the fastest 440-meters on record—43.2 seconds—on the second leg of the 1600-meter relay.

After Matthews, Freeman, James, and Evans set a world record in the 1600-meter relay, they mounted the victory stand with their left hands under their jackets. After receiving their medals, they gave a salute and stood in a military at-ease position during the National Anthem. Matthews would perform in the 1972 Games, winning a second gold medal in the 400-meter run.

Rod Smith, Pender, Greene, and Hines set a world record in the 400-meter relay. At the 1968 AAU Nationals, both Smith, of San Jose State, and Hines shared a new world record of 9.9 seconds for 100-meters. Pender had made the Olympic finals of the 100-meters in 1964 and 1968, but placed sixth each time. A graduate of Adelphi University and later a career Army officer, he tied world Indoor marks in 1972 for 50-yards and 60-yards.

Davenport and Hall finished first and second in the 110-meter hurdles. Hall, from Villanova University, had set an Olympic record of 13.3 seconds in his first semifinal heat, but came in second in the final. Davenport, nicknamed "Cool Breeze", had made the 1964 team but never made the finals. He later competed on Olympic Teams in 1972, 1976, and was one of the first of two blacks in the Winter Olympics in 1980. As a student at Southern University he won the AAU Outdoor hurdles in 1965-67, and tied for first place in 1969. He was one of the greatest hurdlers ever.

The athletic event of the 1968 Olympiad and perhaps in all of recorded sports history was Bob Beamon's unparalleled performance in the long jump. Beamon had remained aloof from the OPHR events up until Mexico City, being one of the nine blacks to run in the NYAC meet in February because he wanted a free plane ticket home to New York. But in 1968, before coming to the Games, he had a string of twenty long jump wins in twenty-one meets. A few weeks before the NYAC meet, at the NAIA Indoors, Beamon set a world indoor record of 27 feet 1 inch. In March at the NCAA Indoors, he completed an historic double— winning both the long jump in a world record leap of 27 feet 2¾ inches, and two hours later the triple jump at 52 feet 3 inches.

On the day of his unprecedented feat, he was driven to the Estadio Olympico in a chauffeured limousine provided by a friend. While warming up he said to Ralph Boston, "I feel I can jump twenty-eight feet today." Charley Mays, the third American jumper, noticed Beamon's wife, Bertha, sitting in the stands. Totally relaxed, free of tension, and, as the fourth scheduled jumper, Beamon was content to watch his lesser talented Olympic colleagues. But it was beginning to cloud up and it looked like it would rain. At 3:36 P.M. his number, 254, was called, and all he wanted to do was get in a good leap before it rained. After removing his warm-ups he stood at the end of the long jump runway, 130 feet from the take-off board; nineteen strides from where he stood.

Beamon went through his own pre-jump check list, rehearsing the jump in his mind like an Army general planning an invasion. Indeed, he meant to attack the take-off board. Of the track events, perhaps only the pole vault, the high jump, and the long jump lend themselves to large percentage increases in world marks, if all the right elements converge in perfect order. That

day, Bob Beamon was in sync with the universe.

After Beamon's right foot perfectly pushed off the take-off board, "...he soared, his mind went blank, and his power of hearing, curiously, deserted him. The whole stadium went silent. His fists were clenched, his arms flung out for balance. He spread his knees and lifted them waist-high, his feet leading the way, his upper torso surprisingly erect."[39] Ralph Boston said, "I thought he would never come down."[40]

Beamon's first thought was that the jump felt good, perhaps more than 27 feet 6 inches. He then had to wait longer than normal for an official measurement; the marshalls quickly discovered that his jump was so long that their optical equipment was not designed to measure that great a distance. The outer limit was 28 feet, even in Mexico City's rarified air. After getting a new tape, the officials measured Beamon's distance—8.9 meters or 29 feet 2½ inches. But no, that was not humanly possible. A different set of officials measured it again. The result was the same. Twenty-nine feet, two and one-half inches. The most superlative accomplishment in the history of recorded sports.

In a daze, Beamon's mind was like a jammed switchboard, overloaded and temporarily unable to fully comprehend reality. Anxiously, he said to Boston, "What do I do now? I know you're gonna kick my ass." But Boston, called "the Master" by Beamon, knew it was all over for everybody else; he had just witnessed a once-in-a-millennium event from front and center. Beamon had exceeded the World Record by *almost two feet!* "No, no" said the Master, "I can't jump that far." The Russian jumper, Igor Ter-

Ovanesyan dryly intoned, "After that jump, the rest of us are children."[41]

Within minutes, Beamon's brain sorted out reality from illusion, the present from that somnambulant state induced by his effort. It had all seemed so easy, so effortless; there was no strain. Without knowing it and with no sense of embarrassment or chagrin, he sank to his knees and covered his face with his hands, his heart pounding. "Tell me I'm not dreaming. It's not possible. I can't believe it. Tell me I'm not dreaming." And then it started to rain. Later, Beamon with black socks on in a show of support for Smith and Carlos, tried a second jump and went 26 feet 4½ inches. Boston won the bronze medal.

Edward Caruthers, a 1967 Pan-Am Games high jump gold medalist from Arizona State, posted a personal best of 7 feet 3½ inches, but had to settle for a silver medal behind Dick Fosbury, whose jumping style was later termed "the Fosbury flop."

The black women Olympians were no less brilliant at Mexico City. Wyomia Tyus became the second black female to win more than one gold medal in a single Olympiad, and the first to set world records in two events. She repeated as gold medalist in the 100-meters. She finished her Olympic career with three golds and one silver medal.

Barbara Ferrell, Margaret Bailes, and Mildrette Netter were Tyus' relay mates in the 400-meter relay. Ferrell, of Los Angeles State and the L.A. Mercurettes, won the Pan-Am Games 100-meters in 1967, and qualified for the U.S. Olympic Team in 1972, but did not win a medal. Bailes, of the Oregon Track Club, was only seventeen at the time. She was the 1968 AAU 100-meter champion and twice equaled the world record of 11.1 seconds. Netter attended Alcorn A & M and was on the 1972 Olympic 400-meter relay team.

Madeline Manning's career was among the longest—nearly fifteen years. From Tennessee State, she was a six-time AAU winner at 800-meters, a Pan-Am Games winner, a World University Games winner in 1966, and an Olympic Silver Medalist in 1972. She would have been a contender in 1980, if President Jimmy Carter had not forced a U.S.-led boycott at Moscow. Manning was easily the best female 800-meter runner the United States had ever produced. She is now an ordained minister.

Although the OPHR did not effect a boycott of the 1968 Games, it furnished startling evidence that the American athletic community could no longer take black athletes for granted. Changes were made as a result of the OPHR effort and other protest movements with similar aims. Conferences were held from coast to coast to consider the hiring of more black staff members. The Pan-African Games, organized by Dr. Leroy Walker in 1971 at Duke University, saw black athletes from Africa and America participating; the black American team won, 117–78.

But as Abraham Ordia, president of the Supreme Council For Support In Africa, jokingly said of the Pan-African Games, "There is no way Africa can lose this meet. Why? Because the best athletes on America's teams also come from Africa."[42]

Two other results from the Mexico City Games are noteworthy. Jesse Owens wrote another book entitled, *I Have Changed,* in which he sought to let people know that his beliefs on some issues had altered and that he saw a need for more direct action on racial matters. Though some earlier critics scoffed at this change of heart as being too late, others welcomed his metamorphosis.

As Vince Matthews pointed out, most team members at Mexico City considered Owens to be "…a messenger sent by the USOC to determine the mood of black athletes."[43] Owens had been publicly rebuffed at a meeting of black and white athletes on the night following Tommie Smith's and John Carlos' demonstration. Some were even more hostile. Said Willye White: "I live in the same town as Jesse Owens, Chicago. We're both black athletes, but the only time I ever see Jesse Owens is at the Olympics every four years."[44]

Another item of interest was an announcement by Kenneth Pitzer, the president of Stanford University. In November 1969, Pitzer announced that Stanford would henceforth honor what he called an athlete's "Right of Conscience." This Right would allow the athlete to boycott an event which he or she had deemed personally repugnant. Though it was not heartily endorsed by other schools, it was nevertheless a breakthrough.

1972: The XXth Olympiad at Munich, West Germany

While the Mexico City Olympics were remembered in part for the victory stand demonstrations by Tommie Smith and John Carlos, the Munich Olympics are remembered for the massacre of eleven Israeli Olympians by their Palestinian kidnappers and a record seven gold medals in swimming won by Mark Spitz. It was not an especially memorable Olympics for black Americans.

Seven gold medals were earned and two world records were set. The medalists are listed in the Reference section.

Vincent Matthews came back from the 1968 Games to win his second gold medal. Milburn was simply brilliant at Munich where automatic timing to hundredths of a second was used for the first time. He was a three-time AAU champion, a two-time NCAA winner, and Pan-Am winner in 1971. Like his predecessor, Willie Davenport, he matriculated at Southern University.

Randy Williams became the youngest Olympic long jump winner at nineteen. He won the silver medal in Montreal in 1976 and qualified for the team in 1980. From the University of Southern California, he was NCAA titleholder in 1972 and AAU winner in 1972–73.

Black, Taylor, Tinker, and Hart sound like the name of a law firm, but these four runners set a new world record in the 400-m relay. Black, from North Carolina Central, won two medals. He was NCAA, NCAA-College Division, and NAIA champion in 1971. Taylor just missed edging out Valeri Borzov in the 100-meter final where he was the only American finalist. (Eddie Hart and Rey Robinson failed to make it to the starting line in time for their heats.) A Texas Southern student, Taylor was AAU 100-meters champion in 1972. Tinker went to Kent State and ran the third leg on the 400-meter team.

Eddie Hart, running for the University of California at Berkeley, and Rey Robinson had qualified in their first heat, but failed to show up in time for the second heat and were disqualified. Like Howard Porter Drew in 1912, Harrison Dillard in 1948, and Ray Norton in 1960, Hart was considered almost a sure winner. At the Finals Trials he had equaled the world record of 9.9 seconds for 100-meters. In addition, he was NCAA 100-yard dash winner in 1970.

Hart and Robinson thought their heats were scheduled after the 10,000-meter heat, but they were really scheduled earlier. The USOC had posted one set of schedules but the coaches had another set of times. The Games officials allowed no exceptions.

Arnie Rey Robinson, whose real first names were Clarence Earl, attended San Diego State and was a NCAA winner in 1970. He was the Pan-Am titleholder in 1971, and his six AAU titles is matched only by William DeHart Hubbard and Ralph Boston. Winning a bronze medal in 1972 in the long jump, he roared back at Montreal four years later to take the gold.

Wayne Collett of UCLA finished second behind Matthews in the 400-m run, though he had won the Trials event. During the anthem ceremony, Matthews stood casually with his warm-ups undone, and was pointedly uninterested in respecting the American flag. Collett stood next to Matthews on top and appeared even more deliberately disrespectful throughout the playing of the anthem. For this behavior they were banned for life by the IOC. The massacre of the Israeli athletes was thus not the only tense moment at Munich, although it certainly seemed the darkest day in Olympic history.

By the 1972 Olympiad, black male athletes were much more assertive and less willing to obey orders. They were world class athletes and each had his own way of training, which frequently clashed with opinions of Head Coach, Bill Bowerman. Luckily, the black Assistant Coach, Hoover Wright of Prairie View College, was helpful.

There was even a possibility that another boycott attempt would be made, because the IOC had allowed the Rhodesian team to participate under the flag of Great Britain. With his experience at Mexico City in his mind, Matthews persuaded John Smith, Lee Evans, Wayne Collett, and Chuck Smith to issue the following statement in solidarity with Ethiopia and Kenya, which were threatening to pull out:

> "In the light of the Rhodesian acceptance into the Games, the United States Black athletes now in Olympic Park believe it imperative to take a stand concerning the issue. We denounce Rhodesia's participation and if they are allowed to compete, we will take a united stand with our African brothers."

Later, the IOC changed its policy and banned the Rhodesian squad which, it was then found out, had black athletes. Thus the statement, written by Chuck Smith, referred to a moot issue but the point was nonetheless made.

When Matthews and Collett came off the victory stand, they knew that life would never be the same. Matthews' mother was crying and his fiancée was angry. Collett, from a solidly middle class family, was engaged to be married in two weeks and his family back in California was stunned.

Matthews' motives stemmed in part from America's institutionalized racism, and in part from his lack of satisfaction from his weaker Mexico City protest. Correspondingly, Collett was loud and clear, saying to ABC's Howard Cosell, "I didn't stand at attention on the victory stand because I couldn't do it with a clear conscience...I feel that, looking back on it now, my actions on the victory stand probably will mirror the attitude of white America toward blacks—total, casual as long as we're not embarrassing them."[45]

For their actions, Avery Brundage sent the following letter to Stan Buck, the USOC president:

Dear Mr. Buck,

The whole world saw the disgusting display of your two athletes, when they received their gold and silver medals for the 400 m. event yesterday.

This is the second time the USOC has permitted such occurrences on the athletic field. It is the Executive Board's opinion that these two athletes have broken rule 26, paragraph 1 in respect of the traditional Olympic spirit and ethic and are, therefore, eliminated from taking part in any future Olympic competition.

Yours sincerely,
Avery Brundage

Matthews eventually secured a job as a payroll coordinator for a youth project and Collett became a lawyer. While the bannings at Munich did not get the same international exposure as the demonstrations at Mexico City, they were still grave evidence of the black distrust felt toward USOC authorities, and the residual resentment toward white America by black youth.

Mable Ferguson, Cheryl Toussaint, and Madeline Manning shared their silver medal victory with Kathy Hammond, a white runner. Ferguson was only seventeen at the time, but she had already won the AAU 400-meter title in 1971, and in 1973 she added National titles in the 400-yard and the 220-yard dashes.

Toussaint was outstanding at the 400/440 and 800/880 distances. A New York University graduate and a product of Fred Thompson's Atoms Track Club in Brooklyn, New York, she won the Nationals title at 880 yards in 1970–73 but was eliminated in the heats at Munich. She also held the world record in the Indoor 600-yard dash. Another of Thompson's athletes, Gail Fitzgerald, competed in the Pentathlon in 1972 and 1976 but did not win a medal.

1976: The XXIth Olympiad at Montreal, Canada

The Olympics at Montreal coincided with the 40th anniversary of the 1936 Games at Berlin. The United States had fought in three major wars—World War II, Korea, and Vietnam—since then. The Supreme Court had integrated the nation's public schools, more facilities had been built, and the coaching and competition was vastly improved. How much progress had been made on the track?

Black athletes continued to dominate the sprinting and jumping events but the results were uneven. Since 1936, thirty-nine men had either set or equaled the world record in the 100-meter dash—twenty-five of them black Americans. The record in

1936 was set by Jesse Owens at 10.2 seconds with hand-held timing; by 1976, it was 9.9 seconds. Owens had once said of a sub-ten-second time, "They'll never do it...Mathematics will bear me out."[46] Jim Hines ran a 9.9 second, 100-meter dash on July 10, 1968.

In the 200-meters, Owens also had the 1936 world record at 20.7 seconds but in 1976 the record was 19.8 seconds, set by Don Quarrie (of Jamaica) who was also black. During that forty-year period, twenty men equaled or set new world records at this distance—twelve of them black Americans. But significantly, all the world record holders in the 100-meters, the 200-meters, and the 400-meters from 1968 through 1984 were black.

The figures seem to add weight to theories that sprinters are "born" but the longer sprints require more than natural ability. The fact that so many blacks are sprint record holders does not mean that blacks are better natural sprinters; but that more athletically inclined blacks took an active interest in sprinting than did the general white population.

(In 1972, Dr. Delano Merriwether, a physician who was the first black medical student at Duke University Medical School, ran the 100-yard dash in 9 seconds. He had never run before 1970, and he never trained.)

In 1936, Archie Williams, a black quarter-miler, had the 400-meters world record at 46.1 seconds; and by 1976 the record was down to 43.8 seconds—set by Lee Evans. In 1967, Tommie Smith became the only man ever to hold the world record at both 200-meters and 400-meters, an astounding accomplishment.

The first black female world record holder in the 100-meters or 200-meters was Wilma Rudolph in 1960, at 11.3 seconds and 22.9 seconds, respectively. Only two other black runners, Wyomia Tyus and Barbara Ferrell, either set new records or tied existing records in the 100-meters. Rudolph stands alone as the only black world record setter in the 200-meters.

Ten of the record setters in the long jump are black Americans, and the record was raised from 26-feet 8-inches in 1936 to Bob Beamon's phenomenal 29 feet 2½-inch leap in Mexico City in 1968. In the High Jump, six of the first sixteen record holders were black—John Thomas was the last one in 1960.

While the men's track teams at black colleges had, by 1976, won NAIA and NCAA Division II titles, the women finally broke through two years after the Munich Olympics, when Prairie View A & M College in Texas won the AIAW title. Coached by Barbara Jacket, this team won the Outdoor title and repeated in 1976. The country was just beginning to catch up in women's athletics, due in large measure to the passage of Title IX of the Education Amendments Act passed by Congress in 1972.

But as much progress as was made in the United States, the rest of the world—Eastern Europe in particular—made even more with their ultra-scientific approach to all track and field events. In the 1976 Olympic Games in Montreal, no black Americans won gold medals in any individual sprinting events. The medalists are listed in the Reference section.

The star of this Olympiad was Edwin Moses, a physics major from Morehouse College. He was born in Dayton, Ohio, on

August 31, 1955. Few track experts realized that he would dominate his event (the 400-meter hurdles) as no other athlete had ever done before. Moses constantly spoke of the lessons in life learned at Morehouse, a black all-male college in Atlanta. He noted, "At Morehouse, we learned to do without, and we had to make adjustments and sacrifices. But we were highly motivated."[47]

After setting a world record at Montreal of 47.6 seconds, he lowered it on several occasions and currently holds it at 47.02. In the 1984 Games at Los Angeles, Moses was accorded the honor of giving the Athlete's Oath. He is one of the most highly respected athletes in the world today.

Millard Hampton, from UCLA, had won the 200-meter Olympic Trials in 20.10 seconds, but settled for second place at Montreal. Hampton's 400-meter relay mates, Steve Riddick, John Jones, and Harvey Glance were among the world's best sprinters in the mid '70s. Riddick, of Norfolk State, reached the semifinals of the 100-meter competition at Montreal; Jones attended the University of Texas and went on to a professional football career with the New York Jets; and Glance won the 1976 NCAA 100-yard and 220-yard dashes. Glance, of Auburn, won the NCAA 100-yard title again in 1977.

Herman Frazier, Maxie Parks, Benny Brown, and Fred Newhouse won the 1600-meter gold medal but did not set any records. Frazier attended Arizona State and won the NCAA 440-yard dash in 1977, and tried to make the United States Winter Olympic team in 1980 as a bobsledder. Parks, of UCLA, was a AAU champion in 1976. Brown, also of UCLA, earned his relay spot by finishing fourth in the Trials. New-

house, from Prairie View A&M, should have made the 1972 team, but made up for it with two medals in 1976. His third-leg time was 43.8 seconds.

James Butts, from UCLA, was NCAA triple jump champion in 1972. Like Newhouse, Butts just missed making the team in 1972. Dwayne Evans attended the University of Arizona and also won the 1979 AAU 200-meter title.

Dr. Leroy Walker of North Carolina Central University was named Head Coach for the Men's team at Montreal, and former Olympian Lee Calhoun was one of his assistants.

Debra Sapenter, Sheila Ingram, Pam Jiles, and Rosalyn Bryant all won silver medals in the 1600-meter relay. The United States did not win a gold medal in this event until 1984. Sapenter, from Prairie View A&M, won AAU titles in 1974–75; Ingram set a new American record 51.31 seconds for 400-meters at Montreal in the quarterfinals but lost it hours later to Sapenter (she set a new record of 50.90 seconds in the semifinals but lost that one minute later to Bryant who ran a 50.62 clocking.) Jiles, of Dillard University and LSU, was a better 200-meter runner and was the 1975 Pan-Am Games 100-meter champion.

Rosalyn Bryant was from Chicago, and attended Long Beach State. She was easily one of the best sprinters in the late '70s. Her anchor leg time in the 1600-meter final of 49.7 seconds assured the silver medal. She was also AAU Indoor title holder in 1975 and 1977.

Dr. Evie Dennis scored a victory of sorts in 1976, by becoming the first black woman officer of the USOC.

Amidst the 1976 Games was an African boycott by thirty countries over New Zealand's presence. New Zealand had entertained a rugby team from racist South Africa earlier in the year and, to protest New Zealand's action, the Supreme Council for Sport in Africa called for a mass withdrawal. Black American athletes were not pressured by African Olympic officials to participate, though many sympathized with this protest. The world was thus deprived of a potential world record 1500-meter race between Filbert Bayi of Tanzania and John Walker of New Zealand.

Walker had set a new mile record of 3:49.4 minutes the year before. In 1973, Reggie McAffee had become the first black American to run a mile under four minutes. The distance races, in particular the mile and the marathon, had become more popular than the sprints, since the running craze matured in the United States.

In other developments, the IOC began allowing athletes to receive regular salaries from sports firms in 1974, as long as the monies were paid to national associations or bona fide clubs in good standing with the International Amateur Athletic Federation (IAAF). This certainly rid the sport of some of the on-going under-the-table payments to athletes. In a profound, though unrelated matter, the Canadian Olympic officials left their government with a debt of roughly one billion dollars.

The United States was forced to withdraw from the 1980 Moscow Olympics by President Jimmy Carter, because of the Soviet Union's invasion of Afghanistan in 1979. Japan, West Germany, and Canada also withdrew as a measure of protest. Though many decried the intrusion of politics into the Games, in reality, the Games had been used as political footballs since 1900. Black American athletes expressed only lukewarm or no support for President Carter's actions.

Two years before, Congress passed the Amateur Sports Act which empowered the USOC to coordinate America's efforts in the Games and appropriated $16 million to fund the effort. The fielding of superior Olympic teams had by then become an everyday preoccupation of the USOC, and the increased attention paid off at the 1984 Games at Los Angeles, even though the Soviet Union and its allies boycotted in retaliation for President Carter's action in 1980.

1984: The XXIIIrd Olympiad at Los Angeles, California

World record performances had slowed down in the eight years since America's last Olympic appearance in 1976. No new men's records were set in the 100-meters, 200-meters, 400-meters, long jump, or triple jump. Renaldo Nehemiah, a black American hurdler, finally cracked the thirteen-second barrier in the 110-meter hurdles in August 1981, with a time of 12.93 seconds. The women, however, lowered the 100-meter mark from 10.88 seconds to 10.79 seconds and the 200-meter mark from 22.06 seconds to 21.71 seconds. American companies like Colgate-Palmolive began sponsoring women's track meets and participation jumped considerably. But women did not cash in heavily with endorsements, or in fees paid by meet promoters.

The United States team for the Los Angeles Games was one of the most talented ever seen, and of the fifty-seven American medals won in track and field forty-one were won by blacks. The black medalists are listed in the Reference section.

Carl Lewis was unquestionably the star of this Olympiad. He received more pre-Olympic publicity than any athlete had ever experienced before, and he lived up to expectations. Lewis, born in New Jersey and a student at the University of Houston, did not set any individual world records, but he did set a new Olympic record in the 200-meter dash finals. He won the 100-meter dash by 8 feet, the largest margin ever. His winning long jump distance of 28 feet and ¼ inch, was achieved on his first leap. Only four men have ever jumped over 28 feet and only Bob Beamon and Lewis have jumped over 28 feet 6 inches.

Lewis is a flashy performer who seems somewhat misunderstood by his fellow competitors and his fans. He is very much an individual thinker who does not hesitate to do things his way. He was criticized by some for not trying for a longer distance in the long jump, but no one came within a foot of his initial jump. Brooks Johnson, the black Head Coach of the men's team, did not press Lewis or try to change his mind.

Lewis was the first Olympic performer since Jesse Owens in 1936, to win four track and field gold medals in one Olympiad. He is certainly the most versatile track star since Owens, and stands the best chance of breaking Bob Beamon's long jump record of 29 feet 2½ inches set in 1968.

Sam Graddy, from the University of Tennessee, was part of the 400-meter relay team with Emmit King, Willie Gault, and Carl Lewis, who set the world record in Helsinki in August 1983 in 37.86 seconds. Along with Ron Brown, Calvin Smith, and Carl Lewis, Graddy helped set another world record in the Olympic 400-meter relay in 37.83 seconds. The second place Jamaican team was 79/100ths of a second behind. The Lewis-Baptiste-Jefferson sweep in the 100-meters was the first such all-United States victory since 1912.

Babers spent his early life in West Germany where his father was stationed in the Air Force. McKay was a Georgia Tech freshman who had won the NCAA Indoor and Outdoor 440-yard titles. In the 110-meter hurdles, Foster, from UCLA, was favored but was edged out by Kingdom in the finals.

Edwin Moses, almost twenty-nine, picked up where he left off at the 1976 Games. He held the world record for the 400-meter hurdles and won the Olympic event by a margin of 38/100ths of a second over Danny Harris. Before the final in Los Angeles Moses had an unbeaten streak of 102 races, eighty-nine of them in the finals. By the end of the year, Moses had extended his unbeaten streak in his specialty to over 105 races, the longest by any track athlete in any event. Of the ten best times in his event, nine of them belonged to him.

Al Joyner won the triple jump over Mike Conley by a margin of only 8/100ths of a meter. When his sister, Jackie, won her silver medal on August 4, she and Al became the first brother-sister track and field medal winners on the same day. Al, nicknamed "Sweetwater," attended Arkansas State and is 6-foot 1-inch and is considered a stringbean at 168 pounds. Conley, of the

University of Arkansas, was 1984 NCAA triple jump champion.

Earl Jones' Bronze Medal in the 800-meter run was the first medal by a black American at that distance since 1952.

The black female Olympians were brilliant. Of twenty-four total medals won by American women, eighteen were by blacks. Valerie Brisco-Hooks joined the select company of Wilma Rudolph and Wyomia Tyus as a triple gold medal winner. She set new Olympic records in the finals of both the 200-meter and 400-meter dash.

As a triple winner, Brisco-Hooks had reason to expect endorsements of the type previous multiple winners had enjoyed from the corporate world. The response to her, however, was initially lukewarm but heightened considerably ten months after the Games. Mary Lou Retton, who is white and who won a single gold medal in the Gymnastics competition, was the prime recipient of corporate attention. The black press duly noted this discrepancy which only served to reinforce the black community's basic distrust of corporate America.

Evelyn Ashford, a UCLA graduate, might have been a triple winner but she settled for first place in the 100-meters and as anchor on the 400-meter relay team. Historically, Ashford had been very reclusive and rarely gave interviews or talked with opponents. But in Los Angeles she was more engaging and, against her lost chances at the 1980 Games, was determined to come in a winner. Alice Brown's second place finish came just 3/100ths of a second ahead of Merlene Ottey-Page of Jamaica.

Benita Fitzgerald-Brown won the 100-meter hurdles over Shirley Strong of Great Britain—by 4/100ths of a second. Kim Turner was 18/100ths of a second behind Strong. In the 400-meter hurdles final, Judi Brown desperately tried to sprint to the finish but missed winning by 59/100ths of a second.

Alice Brown partly atoned for her silver medal in the 100-meter dash by helping Jeanette Bolden, Chandra Cheeseborough, and Evelyn Ashford win the gold in the 400-meter relay. Cheeseborough later added a third medal to her second place one in the 400-meter dash with a gold medal finish in the 400-meter relay. Along with Brisco-Hooks, Sherri Howard, and Lillie Leatherwood, Cheeseborough helped set a new Olympic record in the 1600-meter relay final. Leatherwood and Howard were joined by Diane Dixon and Denean Howard in winning the first heat to put them into the finals. Dixon and Denean Howard were then replaced by Brisco-Hooks and Cheeseborough in the final, and this latter foursome set the new Olympic record. (Dixon once failed gym class at Brooklyn's Tech High, but was encouraged by Fred Thompson of the Atoms Track Club who told her she had Olympic potential.) It was the first Olympic record set by American women in this event.

Jackie Joyner (now Jackie Joyner-Kersee) was unable to match her performance in the Trials where she scored an American record of 6,520 points in the heptathlon. That would have been good enough for a gold medal at Los Angeles. Her Olympic score of 6,385 points was 5 points shy of Glynis Nunn's effort of 6,390. Bob Kersee, the black Head Coach at UCLA (now Joyner's husband), says Joyner is the best female athlete he has ever seen. Joyner is a solid 5-foot 10-inch, 145-pound athlete, who says basketball is her favorite sport.

There were many other black Olympic hopefuls who did not win medals but nevertheless are outstanding performers. Sydney Maree, a naturalized American born in South Africa, was injured and missed the 1500-meter run competition. David Patrick and Andre Phillips missed in the 400-meter hurdles; Larry Myricks and Tyke Peacock in the high jump; Jason Grimes in the long jump; Tony Banks in the 400-meter dash; David Mack in the 800-meter run and the 1500-meters; David Robinson and Johnny Gray in the 800-meters; and the veteran Rod Milburn in the 110-meter hurdles.

Among the women, Carl Lewis' sister, Carol, and Jodi Anderson missed in the long jump. Lewis has, at 22 feet 10-3/4 inches, the second best jump ever for an American. Anderson holds the American record in this event at 23 feet and was a heptathlon competitor as well. Delisa Floyd, wife of former sprinter, Stanley Floyd, had become a mother and was unable to perform.

Other world class female athletes who either failed to make the team or missed capturing a medal included Dianne Williams in the 100-meter dash; LaShon Nedd and Rosalyn Bryant in the 400-meters; Robin Campbell in the 800-meters, and Missy Gerald in the 100-meter hurdles.

Female athletes had come a long way since before World War II. Nell Jackson tells of feeling two separate attitudes toward women. Outside the Tuskegee community, "…there was a stigma against women participating in sports; that it was unfeminine, unladylike."[48] But there was no such stigma at Tuskegee in the late '30s and early '40s.

Furthermore, Jackson believes that "Sports helped to break the [racial] ice in the South. We went to meets in Oklahoma and Texas where all the athletes were housed in community gyms and Army bases."[49] By 1984, racial restrictions seemed gone and the social stigma had disappeared, but the best black female performers were still concentrated in black colleges; selected clubs in New York City, Philadelphia, Chicago, and Los Angeles; and at predominantly white colleges on the West Coast. Ahead of tennis and basketball, track was the primary outlet for aspiring black American female athletes.

The Black Colleges

At the end of World War II, the major black college conferences were the Central Intercollegiate Athletic Association (CIAA), the Southeastern Athletic Conference (SEAC), and the Southwest Athletic Conference (SWAC). By the end of 1984, there were six black major conferences including one for unaffiliated schools. While it was difficult to qualify for participation in the NCAA events, the NAIA, which began including track and field in 1952, gave black schools an entry into world competition. It was a godsend for hundreds of black athletes who did not attend the large NCAA-affiliated institutions.

Seven years after the NAIA began track competition, Winston-Salem State Teacher's College, coached by Wilbur Ross, won the Outdoor title—the first national title won by a black school outside the traditional group of historically black colleges. In 1974, Prairie View A&M, coached by Barbara Jacket, won the AIAW title—the first national title by a black college women's team. (The complete list of national titles won by black colleges is listed in the Reference section.)

Jackson State, coached by Martin Epps, won the 1978 AIAW Women's Cross Country title.

The list of championships represents an astounding record amassed in such a short time. Few black schools have large student body populations, which makes their productivity even more amazing. Since track is the only major school sport with an international following, school administrators feel that outstanding teams are worth the expense in favorable publicity alone.

The Black College Coach

The profile of the successful black coach was outlined by the approach taken by Cleveland Abbott, Tuskegee's innovative leader in the mid-1920s. At that time, nearly all black coaches were teachers as well. Ed Hurt, who coached at Morgan State for forty years, was the head coach for football, basketball, baseball, and track. He was not alone in this regard. Other pioneers in track included William Bennett at Virginia State University, Nell Jackson at Tuskegee, George Wright and Al Priestly at Xavier, Wilbur Ross at Winston-Salem and Maryland Eastern Shore, Ed Temple at Tennessee State, Dr. Leroy Walker at North Carolina Central, and Stan Wright at Texas Southern.

SUMMARY

The foot race is probably mankind's oldest nonviolent form of athletic competition. Recorded history is replete with mention of these contests. Ancient Olympic athletes and spectators were male and the competitors performed naked. The black African ancestors of today's black Americans came by their running prowess out of a necessity to capture wild game for food. It was considered a great tribal honor to be chosen in these hunting parties in which only the swiftest and strongest could belong.

Travel journals and Frederick Douglass' autobiography mention foot races as forms of leisure activities among slaves before the Civil War. After this conflict, running competitions became highly organized and black participation was evident from the beginning. The Walking races, the "Go As You Please" six-day races, and the Bunion Derbies all had black participation.

William Tecumseh Sherman Jackson was the first collegiate star as a middle distance runner. George Poage followed as the first black Olympian in 1904. He was followed by Dr. John B. Taylor and, in 1911, Howard Porter Drew who was the first black world record holder of a sprint title.

Following World War I, black runners developed a reputation as sprinters and jumpers only, when in fact, the major shortcoming was a lack of quality instruction in the middle and long distance races at black colleges. In the 1920s, the so-called Golden Decade of Sports, the numbers of blacks on track teams at predominantly white schools could be counted on two hands.

All sorts of racist and supposedly objective and scientific theories were advanced to explain the "natural" superiority of black sprinters and jumpers when no such racially-based talent existed. As late as 1975, *Track and Field News* (T & FN), the bible of the sport, headlined an article entitled "IS BLACK FASTEST?" *Track and Field News* polled a cross-section of college coaches and found that 35 percent believed that blacks were physically superior to whites.

James "Doc" Counsilman, Indiana University's world famous swimming coach, felt that, "The Black athlete excels because he has more white muscle fibers, which are adapted for speed and power, than red fibers, which are adapted for endurance."[50] To this claim Wilbur Ross, the black coach at Winston-Salem State, answers, "This whole supremacy myth is a white athlete's cop-out. He has been so brainwashed by the racist white society that he has a preference role to fulfill."[51]

Brooks Johnson, the black Head Coach for the 1984 Olympic Men's team, says, "I call it the 'sprinter's syndrome'...the overpowering drive and compulsion to do what you have to do right now, to get the rewards right now."[52] Stan Wright believes part of the blame rests with black coaches themselves, noting, "We Black coaches believed we were superior in the sprints and this was the only place we could run—or coach. This was a learned concept."[53]

Theories aside, no one can question the results. Deprived of equal opportunities for competition before 1960, black athletes have made up for lost time since then. In any historic rendition of this and most other sports, the black American athlete is sure to be listed among the best of all time.

Notes

1. Delores T. Broots, "Black Olympians: 1948–1980" *Dollars and Sense,* (June–July, 1983), 29.
2. Benjamin G. Rader, *American Sports,* (Englewood Cliffs, N.J., 1983), 304.
3. Milton Campbell, telephone interview with author, 23 September 1985.
4. *Los Angeles Times,* Part VIII, 25 July 1984, 8.
5. Ibid., 9.
6. *Ebony,* November 1953.
7. Harold Braguieve, Interview with Kip Branch, 23 September 1985.
8. Nell Jackson, telephone interview with author, 4 December 1984.
9. *New York Times,* 18 March 1985, C-1.
10. *Los Angeles Times,* 24 July 1984.
11. *Los Angeles Times,* 24 July 1984.
12. Wilma Rudolph, *Wilma,* (New York: New American Library, 1977), 79.
13. Nell Jackson, telephone interview with author, 4 December 1984.
14. *Ebony,* 1963.
15. *Los Angeles Times,* Part VIII, 25 July 1984, 16.
16. *Los Angeles Times,* Part VIII, (Mal Florence), 25 July 1984, 23.
17. Vince Matthews, *My Race Be Won,* (New York: Charterhouse, 1974), 89.
18. *Newsweek,* 15 July 1968, 56.
19. Ibid.
20. James Michener, *Sports In America,* (New York: Fawcett Crest, 1976), 208.
21. Dick Schaap, *The Perfect Jump,* (New York: New American Library, 1976), 30.
22. Matthews, *My Race Be Won,* 9.
23. Schaap, *The Perfect Jump,* 30.
24. Harry Edwards, *The Sociology of Sport,* (Homewood, IL.: The Dorsey Press, 1973), 72.
25. Harry Edwards, *Revolt of the Black Athlete,* (New York: The Free Press, 1970), 55.
26. Ibid., 53.
27. *Ebony,* March 1968, 112.

28. *Ebony,* March 1968, 188.
29. Ibid., 116.
30. Edwards, *Revolt Of The Black Athlete,* 131.
31. Ibid., 116.
32. *Sports Illustrated,* 28 February 1968, 25.
33. *Newsweek,* 15 July 1968, 57D.
34. Matthews, *My Race Be Won,* 173.
35. Edwards, *Revolt Of The Black Athlete,* 104.
36. *Newsweek,* 15 July 1984, 59.
37. Delores T. Broots, *Dollars and Sense,* 44.
38. Matthews, *My Race Be Won,* 198.
39. Schaap, *The Perfect Jump,* 94.
40. Ibid.
41. Ibid., 96.
42. *Ebony,* October 1971, 146.
43. Matthews, *My Race Be Won,* 191.
44. Ibid., 194.
45. Matthews, *My Race Be Won,* 355.
46. *Ebony,* September 1959, 110.
47. *Ebony,* May 1984, 100.
48. Nell Jackson, telephone interview with author, 4 December 1984.
49. Ibid.
50. *Track and Field News,* February 1975.
51. Ibid.
52. Ibid.
53. Ibid.

Chapter 8

Additional Olympic and Other Sports

BOWLING

Blacks have had great difficulties in bowling. Bowling began in the midwest and is the most popular indoor athletic activity for the average citizen. In cities where there were few alleys but a sizeable black population, racial friction was inevitable. Consequently, by the late thirties, blacks decided to form their own association of clubs. Thus, was born the National Negro Bowling Association (NNBA).

The NNBA was organized on August 20, 1939, in Detroit. The primary factor in its formation was the "Caucasians only" clause in the constitutions of the white American Bowling Congress (ABC) and the Women's International Bowling Congress (WIBC). Clubs from the following cities were represented at the inaugural NNBA meeting: Detroit, Cleveland, Cincinnati, Columbus, Toledo, Indianapolis, Chicago, and Racine, Wisconsin.

The first officers were president Wynston T. Brown; vice president L. Huntley; secretary Richard Benton; treasurer Brownie Cain; and organizer, Henry Harden. They resolved to encourage

"...Negroes to develop their skills in the game of Ten Pins" and later to participate "...actively in the fight for equality in bowling..."[1]

In 1939, the NNBA held its first tournament in Cleveland. Although only men competed in this first event, women began one year later. Chicago, Detroit, and Cleveland produced the best black bowlers during the Second World War. Teams from these three cities won every NNBA National men's team and doubles event in all but three years. In the men's singles (up to 1950), only players from Indianapolis and Newark broke the three-city monopoly in nine years of play. The NNBA suspended play from 1943 to 1945, and changed its name in 1944 to the National Bowling Association (NBA).

Competition among the best black bowlers was keen in the early years. In the men's singles, no player won the NBA title more than once, but in the all-events category, two Chicago bowlers, Merrit Thomas and G. Walker, each won twice. In 1950, Ben Harding became the first participant to win the singles and the all-events titles in the same year.

210

Among the women, Hazel Lyman and Virginia Dolphin each won the singles and the all-events in the same year. Doris Largent won the all-events title two times, in 1949–50.

As more blacks found time to practice, and more lanes were constructed, their scores rose. Wherein a men's singles score of 589 won the NBA title in 1939, by 1950 a score of 650 was needed. The men's all-events winner bowled 1662 in 1939, but a score of 1843 was the winning tally in 1950. The women's singles winner in 1939 bowled 483, whereas a 609 was needed in 1950. This trend continued into the fifties.

While the winning scores were rising, advances were made in the fight against discrimination. In June 1948, a National Committee for Fair Play in Bowling was formed, with Mayor Hubert Humphrey of Minneapolis as chairman. This committee met in New York City to consider steps to be taken to persuade the ABC to open its tournaments to all qualified bowlers. Eighteen months later, the ABC and WIBC repealed their "Caucasians only" clause and, in 1951, any qualified bowler was eligible for ABC and WIBC events.

The ABC and the WIBC were forced to act because of lengthy out-of-court maneuverings in 1950, and the threat of a law suit. The two groups dropped their constitutional racial clauses, which kept membership for whites only. Assistance was given to the NBA by the white union leader Walter Reuther, and Father Carow, a Catholic priest based in Brooklyn, New York, who were of immense influence behind the scenes. A year before, black, oriental, and white bowlers held a protest tournament in New York City, that presaged the 1950 court action. J. Elmer Reed, a founder and NBA historian, and Eric de Freitas, a black Trinidadian, worked tirelessly to organize the protest event and the court action.

In an August 1974 *Black Sports* magazine article on De Freitas, writer Joe Marcos stated, "It was Eric who joined up with other prominent blacks as well as whites to force the issue, which finally was resolved when, under heavy threat of lawsuits, the ABC relented its ban."[2] De Freitas had been active in black bowling organizations for over thirty years. He was a teaching professional at the Madison Square Garden Lanes, in New York City.

Black American's Most Popular Sport: In 1947, *Ebony* magazine listed bowling as the number one sport among blacks. Fifteen thousand keglers (as bowlers are called) participated every night across the country, and in Bermuda. Like its tennis counterpart, the American Tennis Association, the NBA had a Bermuda chapter, or senate.

William "Jack" Marshall of Montgomery, Alabama, who had played in the Negro Baseball Leagues for the Kansas City Monarchs, was the acclaimed number one bowler, though he never won the NBA title. The Brunswick-Balkes Callender Company sponsored a sixteen-week tour of black bowling centers, that featured Marshall.

As popular as bowling had become, it was, nevertheless, initially concentrated among blacks in the midwest and eastern sections of the country. It was not until 1971, that a women's NBA winner came from a non-midwest or non-eastern area. (Wanda Bruce hails from Los Angeles, California. Joe Calloway, the 1984 men's NBA victor, is from Denver, Colorado.)

Bowling's lack of seasonality was also an attraction. Though most major tournaments were held during the fall and winter months, lane owners devised marketing strategies to make their lanes profitable all year long, hence the appeal to women. After World War II, thousands of returning black GIs took over the jobs their wives, girlfriends, mothers, sisters, and aunts had assumed during the war years. With spare time on their hands for recreation, black women learned to bowl. It was, without a doubt, the most popular sporting activity for black women by the middle 1950s.

The great heavyweight champion Joe Louis and Ted Page, one of the outstanding performers in the Negro Baseball Leagues, also were instrumental during the formative years of organized black bowling. In addition to his golf interests, Louis established a large, twenty-four-lane alley in Detroit in 1942, and was often seen participating in the competition. (The first black-owned lanes were built in 1940 by William Pierson in Cleveland, Ohio.) By way of his involvements in bowling and golf, Louis endeared himself even more to the working as well as upper class blacks, who were more likely to be found on the golf course. Ted Page was also a lanes owner in Pittsburgh.

Blacks Join the ABC: The NBA never envisioned itself as a permanent substitute for the ABC. William DeHart Hubbard, the NBA president in the 1950s and first black gold medalist in the long jump in the 1924 Olympic Games, said the NBA provided a point of entry into the ABC for blacks. This capability was needed because of the sport's "social" nature.

In the 1950s, before the civil rights movement effected a public accommodations congressional bill, bowling was included in a group of what were termed the "social sports"—swimming, golf, and tennis. Each entailed, in the natural course of its activity, constant social interaction among the participants. Entire families often joined in. Teenagers' dating plans frequently revolved around bowling, and social clubs had bowling teams. It became obligatory, therefore, for blacks and whites to habitually segregate themselves in certain parts of bowling establishments, out of choice and to avoid any embarrassment.

Some blacks flourished under these difficult circumstances. On May 24, 1951, at St. Paul, Minnesota, blacks participated for the first time in ABC National competition. A team from Detroit, that trained at Joe Louis' alleys, finished in 72nd place and won $600 in prize money. This team, representing Allen & Sons Supermarkets (Lafayette Allen tied for first place in the 1960 NBA Nationals), had the following members: Maurice Kilgore, George Williams, William Rhodman, Clarence Williams, and Lavert Griffin. As a team, they began shakily with a game of 886, but finished with tallies of 989 and 1,035. As a twosome, Rhodman and Clarence Williams rolled a 1,278-point game for 22nd place. Individually, Kilgore had a 619 series average, George Williams a 582, Rhodman a 596, Clarence Williams a 588, and Griffin a 525. Though all were admittedly nervous at the outset, they were favorably received and this historic breakthrough did not go unnoticed.

Seven years later, Kilgore was the first black kegler to bowl on television. The 5-foot 9-inch, 205-pound bowler compiled a total score of 678, to earn $225 at the Faetz-Nielsen Lanes in Chicago. "It was the biggest step in the history of the game except for the Negro's acceptance to the American Bowling Congress," said Matt Nielsen, the show's producer.

NBA Champions: In spite of the ABC breakthrough, the NBA continued to grow. Though bowling kept its image as a social sport, it acquired the further reputation as being "blue collar" by the mid-sixties. Lane fees were low, thus keeping the sport within the financial means of nearly everyone.

As bowling became more and more the primary means of active athletic participations by the white working man and woman, bowling assumed a social significance not accorded tennis, golf, or swimming.

Blacks had just begun to feel more comfortable in NBA events when interracial teams formed under business auspices in the late fifties and early sixties. Bowling, black sociologists noted, was for a time the only non-workplace social activity between and among blacks and whites in the lower middle class income strata.

Bowling among blacks kept its midwest and eastern geographical focus through 1984. Because there were so many excellent players, the list of NBA Nationals winners changed constantly. Subsequently, there has emerged a select roster of double-winners of NBA Nationals titles (winning both the singles and all-events title the same year); bowlers who, through dedication, practice, and natural talent, set themselves apart from their competitors.

The highest and lowest winning singles scores in NBA history were Alphonso T. Harris' 845 in 1983 and Jimmy Jones' 589 in

Men and Women Doubles Winners

1941	Hazel Lyman
1949	Bob Robinson
1950	Ben Harding
1952	Ruth Coburn
1953	William Rhodman
1956	Beverly Adams
1962	Al Rotunno
1965	J. Wilbert Sims
1969	Clyde Wilson
1971	Wanda Bruce
1974	Joseph Woodlock
1980	Laura Jones
1983	Alphonso T. Harris

1939. For the women the highest and lowest scores were Mattie Worthy's 744 in 1979 and Edna Conner's 483 in 1939.

Individual women stars of black bowling included Ruth Coburn and Doris Miller of Cleveland; Sadie Dixon of Chester, Pennsylvania; Mac Gordon of Chicago; Wanda Bruce of Los Angeles, and Laura Jones of Indianapolis, Indiana. Professional bowling for women is, at present, regional in scope.

The Black Professionals: In 1960, Fuller Gordy of Detroit, Michigan, became the first black professional bowler. His family, who started Motown Records, was also in the construction business. As such, he was one of a handful of young blacks who could afford to consider a career on the Professional Bowlers Association (PBA) tour.

Bobby Williams was the first black presence on the PBA's nationally televised program, debuting at the PBA United States Open in January 1972, at Madison Square Garden. He was quick to point out his primary obstacle at the beginning, "...the money problem. To do well on the tour, you have to stay out and bowl every week. To do that you must have a sponsor to pay the bills. Finding one isn't all that easy if you're black."[3]

Charlie Venable of Brooklyn, New York, was just as candid. As a rookie professional on the PBA tour in 1973, he lamented, "...it's tough getting sponsors, and you must work hard and sacrifice to be a pro bowler. If a black bowler can break through and win, it will be easier for him, and all black bowlers."[4]

Other Distinctions: Black bowling figures have made inroads outside the lanes as well. Don Scott was a member of the American Machine & Foundry (AMF), Advisory Staff. Joe Ferguson heads the New York branch of the ABC. In 1978, J. Elmer Reed was inducted into the ABC Hall of Fame for Meritorious Service. Reed's and others' stories about black bowlers can be seen at the National Bowling Hall of Fame and Museum in St. Louis, Missouri.

CREW

The sport of crew evolved out of a love of boat racing, which was America's first leisure activity to draw large crowds. It dates back to biblical times and beyond. The first recorded race was around 1500 in Venice, and there is even a reference to women racing in 1529.

African antecedents abound for this endeavor. European goods and slave traders wrote and spoke of the proficiency of the boats and oarsmen in West Africa. At the Bight of Benin, near the mouth of the Bonny River, the Portuguese observer,

Pacao Pererie, found canoes that held eighty men and were the largest he had yet seen. Jean Barbot, an agent of the French Royal Africa Company in the 1600s, was impressed with the boatmen of Wida (now Ouida) in the Republic of Benin (formerly Dahomey).

The skilled boatmen in Western Africa were an absolute necessity for the river systems, as their tributaries were the primary routes for trade into the interior. The famed rivers of Africa—Nile, Gambia, Niger, Volta, Congo, Zambezi, and Limpopo, etc.—were mysterious and perilous at best. (No European knew the direction of the Niger River until the 1790s; nor its mouth until 1830. The source of the Nile remained a puzzle to Europeans until the mid-1800s.) Boat racing thus became a means of selecting the most able and trustworthy teams of oarsmen, and honor and status were bestowed upon these African nationals.

In traditional African society many citizens believed—some still do—that there was a "river god." Consequently, a religious dimension also prevailed. It did not take much to believe that this god at times may have favored one set of oarsmen over another. Possibly, the winners of races were thought to be under the protection of this deity.

Racing in America: Boat races were the first mass spectator sports simply because there were some natural rivalries and room to accompany everyone. No stadium or waterway had to be built and the nearest river or canal was sufficient. Races were typically held on Saturday afternoons, and they became fixtures on the social calendars of bourgeois society. Lavish dinners were planned after the races, and white matrons competed to see who could throw the best affairs.

The sports press covered the races and reported the winners and their times. Unfortunately, the coverage was sometimes disdainful to blacks. The *Spirit of the Times* newspaper reported on a race in Louisville in 1839; the account read: "The beauty and the fashion of the city were there, ladies and gentlemen, loafers and laborers, white folks and 'niggers' all along the levee."[5]

An account from a southern lady whose father owned quite a few slaves stated: "My father owned large twelve-oared boats, in which we made frequent trips...the most delightful music I listened to was the wild songs of those athletic boatmen on the water...our men would ply their oars with renewed energy and challenge their neighbors to a race."[6]

In 1851, before the Civil War, the first America's Cup race was held around the Isle of Wight, off the coast of *England*. The United States' entry, *America*, won and renewed interest in racing, though the America's Cup races were for yachts.

A year later, the sport of crew distinguished itself from mere boat racing when it served as the nation's first ever intercollegiate contest. Harvard and Yale raced at Lake Winnepesaukee for the amusement of hotel guests, but passions ran so high that both schools planned to compete in other sports. Crew boats were sleek, handcrafted boats called "sculls," that were specially designed for maximum speed. Up to seven or eight oarsmen rode the sculls and each numbered place called

for different abilities. For instance, in reply to a question as to which position a rower was seated, he or she might say "I rowed number four oar" for his school or club.

Black Participation: Black colleges have seldom tried crew as a varsity sport, though Howard University attempted it for a time. Hampton University began a boat club (the school is twenty minutes from the Norfolk, Virginia, Naval Base) in 1912, but had no other black school with which to compete.

In 1915, Joseph E. Trigg manned the number seven oar at Syracuse University. And he was the first known black athlete on a varsity team. Harriet Pickens and Hilda Anderson later rowed at Smith College. But it was left to a Connecticut College coed to put her stamp on the sport.

At the 1976 Olympic Games at Montreal, Canada, Anita De Franz won a bronze medal in this sport. She attended the University of Pennsylvania Law School at night, while training for the Olympics. She grew up in Philadelphia, Pennsylvania, into a family of athletes. Her father, grandfather, and uncle played at the Colored YMCA and she wanted to follow. She had her dreams and "...always wanted to be an athlete."[7]

De Franz had some difficulty at Connecticut College because "...it is a very, very social sport...the social pressures are immense."[8] Her solution was to completely separate her rowing and non-rowing life. Some of her friends were completely unaware of her rowing experiences. When she objected to President Jimmy Carter's decision to withdraw the Olympic team from the Moscow Games in 1980, she was "...harrassed, received phone calls, hate mail, etc., while trying to make the team."[9] Yet that same year she was still awarded the Olympic Order Medal for lifetime contributions to the sport, an honor bestowed by the International Olympic Committee. At present, she practices law in Los Angeles and is a member of the Executive Committee of the U.S. Olympic Committee.

Pat Spratlan followed in the footsteps of De Franz and was a member of the 1984 Olympic Team. She attended the University of California at Berkeley, and is from Seattle, Washington. There are sure to be more black collegiate and Olympic medalists soon.

CYCLING

The first noted black cyclist since Marshall "Major" Taylor was Oliver "Butch" Martin, Jr., who rode for the Unione Sportiva Italiana Club of New York City. Martin has a black father and an Italian mother, which explains his membership in an Italian-American club. He was on the 1964 United States Olympic Team and placed twelfth in the American Bicycle League's National Roadrace in 1967.

Nelson Vails: Twenty years after Martin's debut as a member of the U.S. Olympic Team, another black racer, Nelson Vails, made history by capturing a silver medal in the 1984 Olympic sprint competition. Nicknamed "the Cheetah," Vails began serious riding as a messenger in the streets of his native New York City. He was born in Harlem and won his first race in 1981, at age twenty-one.

Vails made no secret of his disappointment in not winning the gold medal to his teammate, Mark Gorski. "I came out to complete a mission today," he noted after the race, "and I went back to home base without accomplishing it."[10] That sort of competitive spirit helped Vails to a Pan American Games gold medal in his event in 1983. He now trains under the auspices of the U.S. Olympic program in Colorado Springs, Colorado. Both Vails and the Olympic team coaches feel future black participation would be a welcome development.

FENCING

Fencing grew out of the ancient arts of war with the sword. The three events in international competition are the foil, a lightweight blade that tapers to a blunt point, the epee has a bowl-shaped guard and a rigid 35-inch blade tapering to a sharp point blunted with a metal stop for fencing, and the saber, a light dueling sword with an arc-shaped guard and tapering flexible blade of fluted H section that is not more than 41⅜ inches long, and has one full cutting edge and an 8-inch cutting edge on the back at the tip. Each requires different skills but the basic moves are the same. These contests are held on a running board or strip, and a score is made when a participant touches an opponent with either the tip or blade. Most contestants are now wired electronically with a protective chest protector to help record a "hit."

Black participation began in earnest after World War II, and most participants started through the urgings of a friend (nearly all began after finishing high school). Nikki Franke, the 1975 American Fencers League of America (AFLA) foil champion, said, "There were not very many black fencers even when I began [1960s]."[11] The typical black fencers club would be virtually unknown to most of the community, and no black college has ever had a varsity team. The first prominent black fencer was Richard Henry, who was captain of the Springfield College team in 1926.

Black Fencers

Sophronia Pierce Stent: The YMCA/YWCA organization was the first source of inspiration for black fencers. Stent was captain of the New York University team and became the first black woman accepted into the Amateur Fencer's League of America, in 1951. She learned to fence at the Harlem YWCA. Other Y's in northern cities offered fencing instruction but no blacks ever reached national prominence from that base.

College Champions: The first national title earned by a black fencer went to Bruce Davis who won the NCAA foil competition for Wayne State (Detroit) in 1957–58. In 1971, Edward Ballinger of NYU, was the Intercollegiate Fencing Association (IFA) champion in the foil. That same year Tyrone Simmons of the University of Detroit won the same title in NCAA competition; he won again in 1972. Simmons was also part of the University of Detroit's NCAA winning three-man team that same year, along with Ken Blake and Fred Hooker.

In 1981, Peter Lewison was an NCAA All-American in the saber for the City University of New York. The first black saber winner was NCAA champion Peter West-brook of NYU, who won the title in 1974. The second black saber NCAA winner was Michael Lofton of New York University in 1984. There have been no black winners in any major competitions in the epee division.

Among black women fencers, Ruth White of NYU learned at the Baltimore YWCA, and was the 1971-72 National Intercollegiate Women's Fencing Association (NIWFA) winner in the foil. White was National (under 19) champion in 1969. She learned under some of the best Hungarian coaches in the sport, including Bela de Csajaghy. White, now a physician, was the first black to appear on the cover of *American Fencing* magazine.

Sharon Montplaisir of Hunter College (New York City), was NIWFA champion in 1984. Nikki Franke was never a collegiate standout, but she became the women's team coach at Temple University, and steered her squad to four consecutive NCAA Final Four appearances—1981 through 1984.

It is no accident that most of the superior black fencers have come from the Ivy League and East Coast colleges, where the traditions are the strongest. That trend is not likely to change. Nearly all black fencers have belonged to private fencing clubs in their area, and have competed in amateur events sponsored by the AFLA which, in 1983, changed its name to the United States Fencing Association (USFA).

Black Club Fencers: Most black fencing clubs started at local YMCA/YWCA's or armories used by the National Guard. Membership in the USFA guarantees access to competition and a chance to make the

Olympic team. It is also where the best coaches are to be found. As Peter Westbrook, a black member of the New York Fencers Club remarked, "It is so important to have a good coach in fencing."[12]

Westbrook believes that black participation has suffered because there is no money to be made in the sport. Westbrook began when his mother allowed him to take lessons to keep him out of trouble. Though he later received a fencing scholarship to NYU, after attending Essex Catholic High (New Jersey), his base was provided by a club affiliation.

Melodie Jones is quick to echo Westbrook's admonition about making money from the sport. "When the kids start out, the first thing they ask is 'Do you make any money from fencing?'"[13] Westbrook has done well, however, in ten years of teaching for the New York City Recreation Department.

Discrimination has been a consideration. Nikki Franke notes that there were "...no obvious barriers put up other than those in society in general."[14] Westbrook, on the other hand, felt more resistance. Of mixed oriental and black parentage, he felt "...there was some difficulty (racial) at first but once you get high up, you can erase those warped notions."[15] Both fencers are firm in their belief that a good club membership is essential to advancement.

Two of the most promising black clubs are the Alcazar Fencing Club in Cleveland, Ohio, and the Horizons Club in Brooklyn, New York. Bill Reith is the coach at Alcazar where Melodie Jones, a teenager, and Wilbur Wheeler, who was ranked in the top twenty in the under-twenty-one age group,

train for major competitions. The Horizons coach is Cottrell Jenkins Jones who trained Nikki Franke and others. Horizons is located in Bedford-Stuyvesant, a predominantly black section of Brooklyn, New York.

Black coaches like Reith, Franke, and Jones believe blacks could become excellent fencers if properly exposed to sound instruction. Even Csaba Elthes, Westbrook's Hungarian-born coach, told his star pupil, "If blacks were involved in fencing today, no question the sport would be predominantly black soon."[16]

The Black Olympians: The first black member of an American Olympic squad was Uriah Jones, a former AFLA winner, who was on the team in 1968. Four years later, Ruth White, Bart Freeman, and Tyrone Simmons made the squad.

In 1976, Peter Westbrook made his first appearance and finished 13th in the saber. Two of his black teammates that year were Edward Ballinger and Edward Wright. Before President Jimmy Carter called off American participation in 1980, Franke, Westbrook, and Mark Smith earned spots on the Olympic team.

At the 1984 Olympiad, Westbrook made history by capturing a bronze medal in the saber. It was the first fencing medal of any kind for an American since 1960. Westbrook's other black teammates were Michael Lofton, Smith, Lewison, and Sharon Montplaisir. Semyon Pinkhasov, Montplaisir's coach, thinks his pupil has a chance for a medal in the foil in the 1988 Olympic Games.

The presence of black fencers is sure to increase in years to come.

FIELD HOCKEY

The first prominent name to surface in field hockey was Ketura "Kitty" Waterman Cox, who played for New York University in the early 1940s. She was named to the Northeast field hockey team in 1947. Cox later became the field hockey coach at Queens College in New York, from 1952 to 1976.

Stars in this sport seldom received much fame outside the confines of women's athletics. But since it is an Olympic sport, interest has remained high. Black colleges have typically not shown much interest in field hockey, and all the prominent black players have earned their prominence at white schools.

C. Vivian Stringer, the current women's basketball coach at Iowa State, was on the Mid-East field hockey team. Lacrosse star, Tina Sloan Green, was on the United States National field hockey team in 1969. Green was women's coach at Temple University from 1974 through 1979, and founded the Philadelphia Inner City field hockey program in 1980.

Though she was not a college player herself, Dr. Alpha Vernell Alexander was a consultant to the United States Field Hockey Association in 1980.

Gloria Jean Byard: She is perhaps one of the best black field hockey players ever. She was the first black to earn a position on the United States National Team, in 1974. Byard remained a member for the next two seasons, and toured Trinidad with the team in 1978. This Glassboro State College alumna was also a first team All-College selection in 1974-76.

Black females have recently made impressive strides in the sport and, since 1981, include three first-team All-Americans among their numbers. Undoubtedly more will succeed as the numbers of black female students at predominantly white colleges increase.

GYMNASTICS

The sport of gymnastics is derived from the ancient skills of tumbling, those acrobatic maneuvers performed by traveling circuses and court jesters. References to tumbling in African oral history abound, and the physical abilities required by practitioners— agility, strength, stamina, suppleness, coordination—were and still are prized in African life. Some of these tumbling games took place at night under a full moon, when the participants tried to execute the most difficult jumps possible. In front of the assembled villagers to the accompaniment of drums, flutes, and stamping feet, athletes attempted to outdo one another. These exercises and the childhood games associated with them survived the "middle passage" of enslaved Africans brought to these shores during the fourteenth through the nineteenth centuries.

The children of these slaves continued to play the games which were passed down to them by their parents and grandparents. But as other forms of play came into prominence, they were put aside in lieu of more formalized activities that stressed competition. In the mid-1800s, the German-American Turner Societies, which preceded the YMCA movement, started exercise classes in large groups that featured movements similar to the gymnastics routines seen today. In fact, the word "gymnastics" is taken from the word "gymnasium," the German term for high school. When the United States public school systems began after the Civil War, these exercises or calisthenics started to become a standard part of play periods.

All-black military units were also adept gymnastics practitioners. This sport was very popular in the 1890s, just before basketball became a favorite Winter activity. Black soldiers in makeshift gyms passed their free time jumping the wooden horse and climbing a greasy pole. An observer from the *Army and Navy Journal* was so impressed that he wrote of their abilities in the edition of March 12, 1904: "They danced, walked, lay down, sat and kneeled on a slack wire, turned handsprings over three or four men, sometimes using only one hand; others by grasping one another by the knees became a human wheel, and rolled around the room; others played on the horizontal and parallel bars with such rapidity that it was hard to tell when one feat was finished and another commenced."[17] None of these men had any coaching; it was just a learned skill that must have been resurrected from their cultural history.

Black Gymnasts

Gymnastics was slow to be accepted as an Olympic sport and was in a constant state of flux after World War I. (Some Olympiads offered gold medals for prowess in the use of Indian clubs, which looked like elongated and oversized bowling pins.) Gradually the sport evolved into routines set around the pommel horse, parallel bars, uneven parallel bars, rings, and mat exercises.

Since public-schools used gymnastic activities more for training rather than for competition, they seldom had a mass following. But televised events in Olympiads in the 1970s, featuring appealing and diminutive female Soviet and Roumanian gymnasts, changed the sport's image. The sport has seen phenomenal growth since the early 1970s, and black performers have taken part.

Mike Carter: The first black gymnast with a national reputation was Mike Carter, a three-time All-America at Louisiana State University (1973-75.) The LSU teams were undefeated in two of the three years of his attendance—1973 and 1975.

Carter's specialties were the floor exercises, the all-around, and the parallel bars. He finished fourth in the all-around and eleventh in the parallel bars in 1973; third in the floor exercises and sixth in the all-around in 1974; and third in the all-around in 1975, all in national collegiate competition. Said Carter's coach, Armando Vega, "Every gymnast has some weaknesses. Mike has no weaknesses. By that I mean no weak event."[18]

Ron Galimore: The son of Chicago Bears football great Willie Galimore began his gymnastics training with nary a black role model in sight. "When I got interested in gymnastics in 1969, I didn't have anybody black to look up to."[19] He was not alone.

This Tallahassee, Florida native also attended Louisiana State for his first two years of college—1977–79. He then transferred to Iowa State for the 1979–81 seasons. Galimore was phenomenal in college, becoming the *only* gymnast to win NCAA individual titles in four different years. He recorded the only perfect score ("10") during the NCAA Championships.

Galimore was Midwest All-around winner in 1978–79; holder of seven Iowa State records; scored a "10" in the 1980 Big Eight Championships; was NCAA vaulting champion in 1978, 1980, and 1981; was All-America in 1980 and 1981; was awarded the Nissen Certificate as the country's outstanding senior gymnast; was AAU champion in vaulting and floor exercises; and was a member of the abortive 1980 U.S. Olympic Team. His international experience includes the 1978 Coca-Cola International Invitational in Canada; the 1977 World University Games; and the 1977 United States tour of Bulgaria.

Diane Durham: Durham is black America's first internationally ranked female gymnast. Considered a sure medalist for the 1984 Olympics, she unfortunately injured herself just before the competition. This Houston, Texas–based star was also the first black gymnast to achieve prominence at an early age.

Durham is one of the most versatile athletes around. As proof, she was United States Junior Champion in 1981 and 1982 in the floor exercises, vault, parallel bars, and balance beam. She repeated the following year as National Senior winner in the same events. By the time the 1984 Olympics neared, she was the winner in the above-mentioned events in the Pre-Olympic Games and was on the national team for a major meet against the People's Republic of China.

Her strongest ally is her mother, who travels and counsels her young prodigy. Durham is sure to be a contender for Olympic honors in 1988.

Nearly all world class gymnasts began young and have trained under private coaching. Blacks have not taken to this activity, in part, because it is not a major public-school sport and because private lessons are expensive. However, black girls in particular are thought to be prime candidates for future gymnasts because of their fluidity of movement and dance prowess. Black males, of course, now have Galimore and Carter to emulate. If and when black colleges develop varsity programs, they will further stimulate much interest in the black community.

ICE HOCKEY

There has been precious little black American participation in ice hockey. Blacks have preferred team sports like football, basketball, and baseball. Of the four major team sports, ice hockey has the fewest black American followers. There was only one black American player on a college team—Henry Beckett at Springfield College (Massachusetts)—in 1903–1906. In 1938, Charles Brooks played for the city of Medford, Massachusetts, and later practiced with the Boston Bruins of the National Hockey League (NHL). But hockey is international and the Soviet Union alone has over one million players, who love this sometimes brutal sport played on an ice skating rink.

The game began with British soldiers in eastern Canada in the mid-1800s. They were looking for a Winter sport to play on the frozen lakes near their camps and simply adapted traditional ball games— played on a field with goals at either end— on ice. The Canadians have been the best players ever since. Former Governor-General Lord Stanley donated a cup in his name, which is still today the highest prize in the sport.

Though this work chronicles the achievements of black American sports figures, in this particular sport, the black Canadians cannot be left out.

Black Canadian Stars

Willie O'Rhee: The name Willie O'Rhee may possibly conjure up some distant Irish playwright but it is in fact the name of the first black hockey star. O'Rhee was born in Frederickton, New Brunswick. Like all Canadian youth, he spent much time on the ice rink. O'Rhee got so good that he became the first black player in the National Hockey League (NHL) in 1957–58, playing for the Boston Bruins.

After a couple of years in the minor leagues, O'Rhee played in forty-three games for the Bruins in the 1960–61 season; he scored four goals and had ten assists. He then began nineteen years in the minor leagues, including seven years with the Los Angeles Blades. O'Rhee noted that he had few racial problems. "I was received really good, but there was some name calling in Chicago and Detroit. But it went in one ear and out the other. I made it a point to myself that I would have to take a certain amount."[20] After his career was over, he looked back fondly and was proud "Not to be the first black in the NHL, just to play in the NHL".[21]

Alton White and William Riley: Alton White was the second black professional player. He was born in Nova Scotia, which was also home to George Dixon, the first black world boxing champion. White played for the Los Angeles Sharks in 1973. Riley was also from Nova Scotia and played professionally in the 1970s.

Grant Fuhr, Tony McKegney, Ray Neufeld: Fuhr is perhaps the best-known black player ever. This adopted son of a Canadian couple is the goalie for the world champion Edmonton Oilers. McKegney is a forward for the Minnesota North Stars and Neufeld plays forward for the Hartford Whalers. As of the end of the 1984–85 season, they were the only black players in the NHL.

Black American Stars

While there have been many black American players in the northern tier of states that border Canada, none has played in the NHL. There was simply never enough peer pressure among blacks to sustain interest, and no role models could be found to emulate. In addition, the northern tier of the nation contains the smallest percentage of blacks, and they are attracted to sports which feature their own in starring roles on television. Hockey's central focus is the club experience rather than a school game, which means an outlay of money above that for basketball or baseball. But there have been some college players who have done well.

Lloyd Robinson: He returned from World War II service with the all-black 92nd Division to play at Boston University. This Wellesley, Massachusetts, native majored in physical education and played left wing on the varsity squad. He was in the NCAA playoffs in 1948, at twenty-two, the first American-born black to do so.

Robinson believed his home city's small size was an asset. "I was lucky that I was brought up in Wellesley and not in a more crowded area, like the South End of Boston."[22] What Robinson meant was that in Boston a black child would be more likely drawn to football, basketball, or baseball.

Donald Seale and Ed Wright: Seale played varsity hockey at Clarkson University from 1954–57. Wright played college hockey at Boston University and coached at the State University of New York. Wright's career as a player lasted from 1967–70, but he did not appear to relish the experience. "I think to a certain extent I was relieved when I took off the B.U. jersey for the last time," he said, "to know that the frustrations that had occurred in the game, the battles I had, the difficulties throughout my playing career were over…it was a total relief to take that jersey off for the last time."[23]

In 1974, Wright was appointed coach at SUNY and expressed his views differently about the sport. "I like to think that my experiences have been varied enough…that I'm capable of handling any situation."[24] He was the first black appointed as coach of a college hockey program.

Val James: James was born in one of the most unlikely places for a hockey player— Ocala, Florida. He became good enough to play in the Eastern Hockey League (EHL) for the Erie (Pennsylvania) Blades, and the Rochester Americans in the American Hockey League (AHL) in the mid-1970s. He had a tryout with the NHL's Detroit Red Wings in 1980, but was cut.

According to James, the racial epithets have not stopped since O'Rhee's days. The 6-foot 2-inch wingman said: "I've come to expect the name-calling now. Some nights I can take it, but others, I feel like going up into the stands, grabbing somebody and beating the hell out of them."[25] James' sentiments are not surprising since professional hockey fans are among the most raucous.

The outlook for future black hockey stars is a continuance of the status quo, as there is only a minimal amount of interest in the sport in the black American community.

ICE SKATING

Like ice hockey, ice skating has very few black American participants and its appeal is more toward females than males. There are no high school or college ice skating teams, so training and competition is a private affair. In addition, scoring is done by a panel of judges whose collective judgments decide a performer's rating. Television has brought this beautiful sport into our living rooms, and it is among the most watched of Winter Olympic events. Though many have tried, there have been only four black Americans who have earned widespread acclaim.

Mable Fairbanks: She was the first prominent black skater; she won enough amateur competitions to turn professional in 1951. The diminutive, 5-foot 3-inch, 130-pound native of Seminole Indian Territory, Florida, was featured in numerous black newspapers and magazines as a member of several ice shows.

Linda Allen: She matured as an amateur skater only to be denied a chance at an Olympic medal because President Jimmy Carter withdrew the American team from the 1980 Moscow Olympics. She grew up in Los Angeles and attended Culver City High School. As was the case with so many young athletes who take up individual sports, Allen used skating to help her overcome an introverted personality:

"The sport is a means of self-expression. I used to be shy."[26]

Bobby Beauchamp: This slim 6-foot, 160-pound native of Los Angeles was the first black male to earn high honors. In 1979, he was second in the junior world event and in the United States junior men's competition. His rigorous, thirty hours per week training under coach John Nicks, brought more honors as a senior performer. In 1981, he was seventh among American senior men and placed sixth in the NHK Trophy event in Japan.

In 1982, he maintained his number seven national ranking and was sixth in the Skate Canada event. After placing fourth nationally in 1983, he dropped to eighth in 1984 and ninth in 1985.

Debi Thomas: Thomas realized the dream of every budding skater, to win an Olympic medal, becoming a medalist in the 1988 Winter Olympics. She is, by far, the best black American performer in history. Born on March 25, 1967, in Poughkeepsie, New York, the 5-foot 6-inch, 115-pounder finished second in the 1980 United States Novice Ladies event, thirteenth in the Senior Ladies in 1983, sixth in the National Seniors in 1984, and second in 1985.

Thomas credits her 1983 victory in the Criterium International du Sucre in France for boosting her confidence. "It was the best thing that's ever happened to me."[27] Her British-born coach, Alex McGowan thinks Thomas has the ability to be the best. She would like to perfect her "figures" routine and to add a "triple flip" to her maneuvers.

Like other athletes in special sports, she needed a sponsor to help with the enormous expenses involved in training and competing. Her goal, said Libby Slate, was "to become the first U.S. black woman to win an international Senior singles meet."[28] She did so in capturing the United States and World Figure Skating titles in 1986. So far Thomas' race has been a minor factor. "Being black hasn't really affected me as a skater that much. I think it's affected other people more. After I won [in France] for instance, I got a fan letter from a young skater in Ohio who said that she was black and proud of my achievement."[29] She is now a Stanford University student.

JUDO

Judo, which means "the gentle way" in Japanese, evolved from the oriental martial arts. It became a sport when brought into focus by Jigoro Kano, its most famous performer, in the mid-1880s. It was to be a demonstration sport in the 1940 Olympic Games, but World War II intervened. Judo had enough of an international following that it blossomed at the 1964 Games in Tokyo.

George Harris: Harris, the first black American to reach the international level, was part of a multi-ethnic Olympic team at the 1964 Games. The other judo members were Ben Campbell, an Indian; Jim Bregman, a Jew; and Paul Maruyama, an Oriental. Harris is a former Air Force boxer who had competed in the Golden Gloves and once fought Archie Moore. When first introduced to judo, he asked, "What the hell is that?"[30] Harris, who competed as a heavyweight, lost to Anzor Kiknadze of the Soviet Union in the quarterfinals.

Allen Coage: Judo was removed from the Olympic Games in 1968, but reinstated for good in 1972. Four years later at the Montreal Games, Coage won a bronze medal as a heavyweight and then became a professional wrestler.

Edward Liddie: Before the 1984 Olympic Games, Liddie was one of five black American possibilities for the United States team. Although Fred Hand of Philadelphia and James B. Thompson did not make the team, Army Lieutenant Leo White, Doug Nelson, and Liddie did win berths. Neither the twenty-six-year-old White nor the twenty-four-year-old Nelson won a medal, but Liddie captured a bronze medal in the 132-pound extra lightweight class.

Paul Maruyama, the American coach, said Liddie needed only to believe in himself. Liddie finished fourth in the 1983 World Championships in Moscow and came into the Olympic Games feeling confident. He has a chance at another medal in the 1988 Olympic Games in Seoul, Korea.

Since judo is primarily a club sport with no varsity programs in either high schools or colleges, the prospect for more black participation will probably remain spotty at best.

LACROSSE

History: According to many sports historians, lacrosse is the oldest organized athletic activity in North America. It originated with Native Americans and there is evidence that the Iroquois Indians may have played a variation of the game in pre-Columbian times. White Canadians learned it from them and brought it to the United States. Originally mainly concentrated in Ivy League schools and the service academies, it now enjoys widespread appeal in the college system. Blacks have not been prominent in the sport simply because it has limited geographical appeal, and no nationally known role models for hopefuls to emulate.

Modern lacrosse is played on a grass field that is one hundred and ten by sixty yards. Ten players are on each team. At each end of the field is a net into which a small ball is slung from a stick with a mesh pocket attached at its top. A goal is scored when the ball lands in the area inside the nets. The term "lacrosse" is the French phrase for "the cross", which is what early French Canadian observers were reminded of when they saw the sticks used by the Indians.

Pre–World War II Players: Albert F. Lewis, a black Canadian goalie, is the first player mentioned in a starring role. He was a member of the Cornwall Club in Ontario in the late 1880s and played on the Canadian National Team from 1888–91. Said J. Allen Lowe, a Canadian expert, Lewis was "...the only colored man who has ever played on a championship team in Canada...a first class player, at his best he was a star of the first magnitude."[31]

When Joe Lally picked his All-Time Canadian team and penned his book, *Fifty Years of the Best,* he said, "...Albert Lewis...was looked upon in the lacrosse world as the cleanest, most finished, and best player from that day to this [1944]."[32]

Black participation in lacrosse languished until 1939, when Simeon F. Moss of Princeton, New Jersey, played for Rutgers University. He was the first known black player on a college team. According to Roberts, Moss' picture was the first taken of a black player in a lacrosse uniform since Lewis.

Two years later Lucien Victor Alexis, Jr., of New Orleans played for Harvard University in the 1941 and 1942 seasons. In 1941 he was benched in a game against the United States Naval Academy at Annapolis, Maryland, because they objected to playing against a black man. Academy officials gave Harvard's coach three choices: one, in return for benching Alexis, the Academy would bench a player of comparable worth; two, Navy would forfeit the game; or three, the Academy superintendent would phone Harvard authorities and discuss the matter.

Initially, Harvard's athletic director, William J. Bingham, withstood the challenge, but he finally succumbed and instructed his coach, Richard Snibbe, to bench Alexis. Alexis immediately returned home, twenty-four hours ahead of his teammates. But the howl of protest from students and outside groups was heartening. A student petition to Bingham declared in part: "By yielding to the Naval Academy's demands, Harvard has taken an indefensible

position in the eyes of a democratic nation." The American Federation of Labor wrote: "...there is no justification for the discrimination practiced by the United States Naval Academy..." Roy Wilkins, then Assistant Secretary of the National Association For The Advancement Of Colored People (NAACP), wired: "...Navy policy... illustrates perfectly the hypocrisy of the war-cry against totalitarian cruelties, while practicing the same doctrines here in America."[33] The senior Alexis, of New Orleans, was a Harvard graduate—class of 1918.

Nevertheless, the swap was made and Navy won 12–0. Thirty-five years later, in 1976, black midshipman George Moore became the Naval Academy's first lacrosse varsity member.

College Players After World War II:
The popularity of lacrosse increased dramatically after the war and more talented athletes were persuaded to play. The NCAA did not sanction the sport until 1970. Its appeal was still too regional to warrant a true national following. However, All-Americas were named, and black players made up a sizeable portion of the lists. Milton Roberts' article cites some of the star players.

Jim Brown: Lacrosse traditionalists were quite unprepared for Jim Brown, the football player, who played the midfield position for Syracuse University in 1955–56. Brown had never played the sport until he came to Syracuse; out of curiosity, he decided to try it. He immediately overwhelmed the opposition and set new standards of play. Said Gardner Mallonnee, a former All-America himself and coach at Johns Hopkins University, after seeing

Nikki Franke, Temple University's fencing coach and one of America's best female fencers. *(Courtesy of Nikki Franke)*

Peter Westbrook, a bronze medalist in the 1984 Olympic Games. *(Courtesy of Peter Westbrook)*

Ron Galimore, former Iowa State gymnastics All-America.
(Courtesy of Iowa State)

Diane Durham, 1984 Olympic hopeful, on the balance beam.
(Courtesy of Diane Durham)

Mike Carter, of Louisiana State University, performing an "Iron Cross" on the rings, 1975. *(Courtesy of Louisiana State University)*

John Mackey, the NFL star, was also an All-America lacrosse performer. *(Courtesy of Syracuse University)*

Jim Brown, of Syracuse University, was acclaimed the best lacrosse
midfielder ever seen. *(Courtesy of Syracuse University)*

Debi Thomas, the 1986 American and world figure skating champion. *(Courtesy of David Leonardi)*

Charles Sampson, professional rodeo star, riding a bull. *(Courtesy of the Professional Rodeo Cowboys Association)*

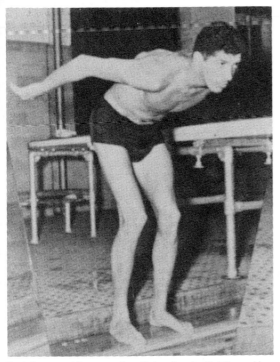

Frank Stewart, of Tennessee State University, who tied the world
mark for 50-meters, 1949. *(Courtesy of Tennessee State University)*

Trent Lyght, Arizona State University star. *(Courtesy of Conely Photography)*

Nathan Clark, Ohio State All-America, 1961.
(Courtesy of Ohio State University Archives)

Chris Silva, UCLA All-America in the freestyle, takes off. *(Courtesy of UCLA)*

Beverly Robinson, a 1982 winning player for Tennessee State University. *(Courtesy of Rick Stewart)*

United States Women's Volleyball Team

Laurie Flachmeier **Julie Vollertsen** **Jeanne Beauprey** **Carolyn Becker**

Debbie Green **Rita Crockett** **Kim Ruddins** **Flo Hyman**

The 1985 Women's National Volleyball Squad. Rita Crockett and the incomparable Flo Hyman were team members. *(Source unknown)*

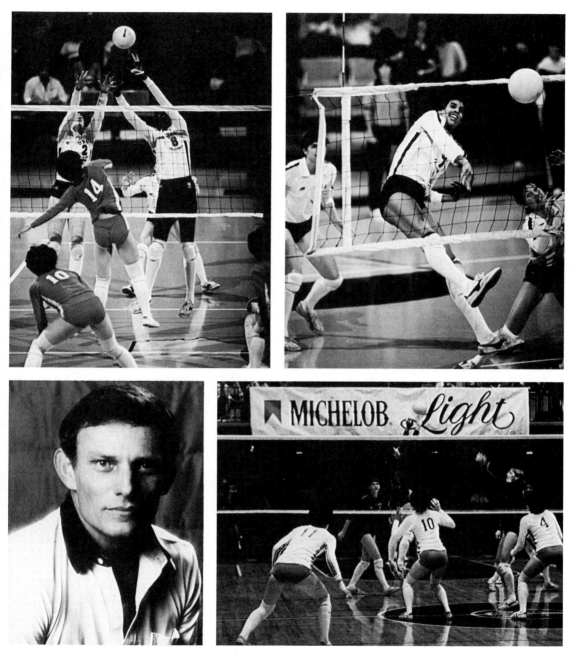

The USA Women's National Volleyball Team. Team coach Dr. Arie Selinger is shown at lower left. *(Source unknown)*

Kim Oden of Stanford University, the next black superstar. *(Courtesy of Tim Davis Photography)*

John H. Davis of Brooklyn, New York, hoists 396 pounds in the "Clean and Jerk" to win the Pan American Games gold medal in 1951.
(AP/Wide World Photos)

Bobby Douglas, head wrestling coach at Arizona State University.
(Courtesy of Arizona State University)

Chris Campbell, NCAA All-America wrestler from the University of Iowa. *(Courtesy of the University of Iowa)*

Brown play in the 1957 North-South Game, "Brown is the greatest lacrosse player I've ever seen, and that includes all the great (Johns) Hopkins and Mount Washington players I've watched over the past thirty years."[34]

More specifically, critics were impressed with Brown's speed. Charley Clark, former president of the Intercollegiate Lacrosse Association, was awed. "It's amazing that a man with his size can be not only fast but so graceful. Why, the way he whirls and dodges is unbelievable."[35] In truth, college lacrosse had been played with mediocre athletes, players who possibly did not or could not make the football team. There were superior athletes around but no one bothered to recruit them.

Another telling anecdote is recounted by Kevin Conwick, a former Colgate University All-American. Colgate had just put in new nets for a game against Syracuse, and the first time Brown came down the field he fired the ball so hard that it put a hole in the net. Said Conwick, "Our goalie spent the rest of the day keeping out of his way."[36]

In 1957 Brown was the first black player in the North-South Game. Though he played only half the game, he scored five goals and had two assists to lead the North to a 14–10 upset win. Brown helped to popularize lacrosse among general sports fans and to serve as a role model for future black players.

Other College All-Americas: Jim Brown was not the only black star to emerge from our nation's colleges. Don Peppers was the first black player selected for the South's All-Star team, in 1958. Though he was not an All-America, John Mackey, the football player, was selected as a midfielder for the North-South Game in 1963, but declined due to a prior commitment.

Wendell Thomas played for Towson State in Baltimore from 1971 through 1974, where he also participated in wrestling and football. He was the 1974 NCAA Division II Player of the Year and a first team All-America.

John Sheffield, from the University of Pennsylvania, was the first black All-America from an Ivy League school. This 6-foot 2-inch athlete played the center position from 1972 through 1974. Said his coach, Jim Adams, "Johnny didn't realize how strong he was. He probably could have maimed some people."

Ed Howard made All-America as a defenseman for Hobart College in 1979 and played in the North-South Game. He started out on the "B Team" after quitting the freshman basketball team. Hobart was NCAA Division II champions in 1976–77, finalists in 1978, and quarterfinalists in 1979, when Howard made the All-America list.

James Ford set Rutgers University scoring and assist records of 201 and 131 points, respectively, while playing the attack position from 1977 through 1980. He had played in high school and was highly recruited. In 1979, Ford was named an Honorable Mention All-America after scoring 43 points for the season. Rutgers was 33–13 while Ford played there.

Albert Ray was a two-time high school All-America before coming to Rutgers where he made All-America in 1982. His specialty was the "face-off" that begins the game. According to his coach, Tom Hayes,

Ray was successful eighty-eight percent of the time, a phenomenal percentage. He played in the North-South Game.

Rick Sowell, of Washington College (Maryland), was named NCAA Division III, Third Team All-America in 1984. He had played the attack position at Cobbleskill Community College (New York) for two years before transferring to Washington, where he played midfield. Sowell scored twenty-three goals and had eight assists in his first year as a Division III performer.

Though lacrosse is not a major sport by conventional standards, it continues to lure more black athletes because of the basic physical skills required. It is still concentrated primarily in the northeast quadrant of the nation, and few black high schools have programs. Nearly all black players at predominantly white colleges had never played the game before they went to college.

Morgan State University, the First Black College Power: "This is a black man's game!"[37] screamed Earl Banks, Morgan State's football coach, after watching a lacrosse practice on campus one day. This black school rose to national prominence after only six years of intercollegiate play, and in 1975 achieved a number ten ranking in the College Division. One of their players, Miles Harrison, was the first player from a black school to be selected to play in the North-South Game.

Banks' telling comment, particularly in light of the fact that he was a highly successful football coach at Morgan, was in essence saying that black athletes could, and would do well on a lacrosse field. Speedy football players in particular make

good mid-field candidates because of their bulk and because swiftness is highly prized. Lack of formal introduction to the sport before college is not a hindrance to most athletes since the game can be learned quickly.

Other Morgan State stars have included Wayne Jackson, who in 1973 was a College Division Third Team All-America and North-South Game designate, and Dave Raymond, an attack man, who was College Division Honorable Mention All-America in 1974. Raymond was, for a time, the school's all-time scoring leader with 218 career points.

James "Poopie" Williams returned from the Vietnam War to become captain of Morgan's team in 1974. He died tragically while trying to mediate a quarrel. A white member of the Morgan squad was Courtney Servary, who was a Third Team College Division All-America in 1975. In 1978, the school produced an All-America, in NCAA Division I competition, Joe Faulks. He became the most celebrated lacrosse player ever from a black institution.

Few black schools have lacrosse teams. As it is not a revenue-producing sport, the expense required for an activity so little known in the black community is seldom worth the effort. But undoubtedly more will give it a try in the future.

Black Women Performers: The first women players started in British private schools in the early 1900s, when Victorian standards of behavior were still the norm. As was the case for men, women began here in America in the small, elite, private New England colleges like Vassar, Smith, and Wellesley. Black participation began here as well and spread when the Association of Intercollegiate Athletics for Women (AIAW) was founded. Later, the NCAA sanctioned some events.

Black women have gained honors in AIAW and NCAA competition in this uniquely American sport.

Black Club Players: According to Milton Roberts, the first black club player was Harold Rumsey, who played for the Manhasset Lacrosse Club in Long Island, New York, in the 1940s. Most clubs are concentrated along the eastern seaboard and games are sponsored by the United States Club Lacrosse Association. The USCLA also sponsors a club version of the North-South Game.

Other black club players mentioned by Roberts include Larry Palmer of the Philadelphia Lacrosse Club in 1971–72; Val Emery, Jr., for the Mount Washington Club in 1971; Dean Rollins of the New York Lacrosse Club; Morgan Holley of the Chesapeake Lacrosse Club; and former college player, Wendell Thomas of the Maryland Lacrosse Club.

Serious observers of the sport believe that black participation can only increase. The physical skills involved are similar to those in other sports, especially football. A more serious impediment may be the upper class image that the sport enjoys and the fact that there is no professional tour. The lack of black coaches is mentioned as a problem, but the lack of public-school involvement supercedes this consideration. The best hope for more black participation will have to come from competitions sponsored mainly by black colleges.

MOTOR RACING

The sport of motor racing was bound to occur sooner or later, after the German Gottlieb Daimler improved the internal combustion engine, in 1885. He attached his crude engine to a bicycle and duplicated the effort with a boat on the Seine River. Then a Frenchman, Emile Levassor, created the machine in 1894 that most closely approximates today's automobile. Three years later, the first major race was held in Paris, on a route that stretched from the center of the city to Versailles and back.

In the United States the first major run was on November 28, 1895, and was sponsored by the *Chicago Times Herald* newspaper. The winning speed averaged 7½ miles per hour, and the prize of $2,000 was won by Frank Duryea. The first Indianapolis 500 race was staged on Memorial Day, May 30, 1911, and was won by Ray Harroun, who drove a Marmon Wasp at an average speed of 74.59 miles per hour. This first Indy 500 was open to whites only. The year before, the newly-formed American Automobile Association suspended America's most famous driver, Berna Eli "Barney" Oldfield, for an unauthorized race against Jack Johnson, the black heavyweight boxing champion.

Black drivers had impromptu races just before and during the First World War. Their prime motivating factors were the sheer fun of this sport and an avid interest in automobile mechanics. In the 1920s, some groups of black drivers formed and tried to arrange circuits of races, but sponsorship was next to impossible. In Los Angeles, for instance, the Western Race

Drivers Association had a rally at Ascot Park in 1925. One of the drivers, "Ace" Foreman, was described by the *California Eagle* (Los Angeles) newspaper as being ...a demon behind the wheel."[38] In Georgia, the Negro Men's Automobile Racing Association was organized.

The most famous black driver of the period, though, was Rojo Jack, who was assisted by none other than Barney Oldfield. Jack started racing in his teens in the early 1920s and was a recognizable face at many events. Part of his problem may have been his size. He reportedly weighed about 250 pounds, which may have slowed him down a bit. He continued to drive until the late 1930s, when he lost the use of an eye in an accident.

One of the largest races on record for blacks occurred on August 2, 1924, at Indianapolis in a 100-mile Derby organized by William Rucker (twenty-two drivers lined up for a prize offered by Harry Earl). With the exception of Lincoln Bailey, Henry Lewis, and Edward Givens, the best drivers in the country were on hand. The winner was Malcolm Hannon in his Frontenac. His winning time was one hour, forty-three minutes, and forty-two seconds. Only three cars finished.

Black drivers never could amass the resources to maintain a career on the racing circuit. They were seldom allowed on the white-run tracks and the prize money was not enough to be considered a living. Drivers had to be experienced in every facet of automobile knowledge—mechanics, body-building, engineering, and so on. It is little wonder that most black drivers raced only for the thrill. It was not until after World War II, that any significant breakthroughs were effected in what is today termed "stock car" racing. Stock car racing is specifically oriented toward the blue-collar fan, since the car used is an adapted version of that found in any auto dealers show rooms. Stock car racing has a large following in the South, Midwest, and Southwest. The geography, locale and racial customs of these U.S. areas have been factors in discouraging blacks from entering this sport. As for Formula One and Formula 5000 races, the enormous expense alone is enough to deter anyone, unless a sponsor is available. Still, blacks have been part of the stock car racing scene since its beginnings and most recently have made significant impressions in the higher-speed Formula races. (Formula designations refer to engine size. Formula One is the most powerful of all—and the fastest.)

Mel Leighton: Leighton, who was from Iowa, was the first black driver featured in *Ebony* magazine, in August 1948. He finished "in the money" in 1947, in twenty-seven of forty races, using a Riley Special on a Model B (Ford) chassis. He also found racism to be a potent obstacle. Concerning his then future chances Leighton said, "The only thing that might stop me is the unwritten lily-white clause of the American Automobile Association (AMA)."[39] Though the AMA never had a "Caucasians Only" clause written into its by-laws, they nevertheless enforced a ban on black drivers in some places.

Wilbur Gaines: He had been around as a stock car racer longer than Leighton, and had certainly paid a heavy price for his involvement. Featured in the September 1951 issue of *Ebony* magazine, he listed two broken collar bones, a fractured right leg, a fractured left arm, burns on his hands and chest, and many bruises and lacerations.

Gaines was a member of the Hurricane Racing Association in Chicago, a group of fellow drivers who banded together out of mutual self-interest. But this 5-foot 11-inch driver started rather humbly in Kalamazoo, Michigan, with a horse-drawn delivery wagon. Later, he became a chauffeur for a limousine service and began racing on Sundays in local meets. At his peak, he never made over $3,000–6,000 per year on the track and was not above trying a few stunts for bonuses.

Said Gaines, "In the old days [1920s] drivers got extra money for turning their cars over. A complete turn would net around $200."[40] So many drivers received bad necks from this experience that Gaines invented the roll bar to protect drivers during flips. Gaines was still racing cars into his sixties.

Wendell Oliver Scott: Wilbur Gaines notwithstanding, Scott, who was from Danville, Virginia, was the first black driver since Rojo Jack to earn a national following. He has had the most prominent career of any black performer. Scott came from the "Crooktown" section of Danville and received his first driving job with the local taxi company. After an Army hitch with the 101st Airborne unit, he started hauling illegal whiskey from hideaway stills to the Danville Fairgrounds.

"There were just a few blacks attending the races then," said Scott. "Most of the time me and a friend were the only two blacks in the stands. He'd often ask me if I'd have the nerve to get out there and run. I'd tell him, 'shucks, yes' I could do it."[41]

In 1971, Scott was duped by the white promoter of the Charlotte (North Carolina) Motor Speedway (CMS), when told that he, Scott, would be supplied with a "first-class car" to race at the CMS. Though the promoter had honorable intentions, Scott felt the promoter bowed to pressure from white drivers to deliver a less than first-class car and he never had a chance. The embarrassment haunts Scott to this day. But one white Grand National (GN) driver, Earl Brooks, did assist Scott and this gesture was not forgotten.

Scott had always wanted to race on the prestigious Grand National (GN) circuit but could not muster the resources until 1961. He had won eighty Sportsman and forty Modified races, and the 1959 Virginia State Championships. Outright prejudice kept him from qualifying for the GN tour. "I'll never forget my first race in Georgia, a Sportsman event at Lakewood Speedway. When I got there...the promoter told me he'd gone all the way to the Chamber of Commerce for permission for me to run, that he was glad I was light-skinned, for me to stay in my place and everything would be all right. I wasn't permitted on the track that day until an ambulance for blacks arrived. If I wrecked, the ambulance for whites couldn't take me to the hospital."[42]

Scott finally made his GN debut in 1961 at the Spartenburg (South Carolina) Fairgrounds. He finished in the top ten five times and earned $3,240 in 1961. He also earned $7,000 for eleven top ten finishes in

1962. His biggest win came in the National Association of Stock Car Auto Racing (NASCAR) GN 100-mile race at Jacksonville, Florida in 1964. It was his first and only GN victory. But even that was marred in controversy.

"Everybody in the place knew I had won the race...but the promoters and NASCAR officials didn't want me out there kissing any beauty queens or accepting any awards. They wanted Buck Baker (who was second) to take care of that. That was all right. All I wanted was credit and my money. Later on, I received a trophy, but it wasn't the right one. It was a block of wood worth no more than three bucks. But I still have it as a reminder of what I suffered through to get it."[43]

Scott's best year was 1969, when he won $27,542. Serious white critics had begun to applaud his perseverance. Said his local *Danville Commercial Appeal:* "In his own way, a Danville Negro had done as much for race relations in the Deep South as Dr. Martin Luther King and all the marchers in Selma, Alabama."[44] Though he meant well, the reporter's comment showed a clear misunderstanding of the gravity of race relations in the Deep South in the mid-1960s.

Scott's career earnings were nearly $180,000, and nearly all of it went to maintaining his cars. He turned sixty on August 29, 1981.

Benny Scott: No relation to Wendell Scott, he won the 1969 Southern California Stock Car Title at age twenty-seven. Three years later he was part of the first integrated corporate effort to win a starting position in the Indianapolis 500. The company, Van-

guard Racing, had several black stockholders, including Leonard Miller, Paul Jackson, and the football player, Brigg Owens. The other black driver was Coyle Peek. Unfortunately, Vanguard was unable to attain its goal.

Before Scott's involvement with Vanguard, he made his reputation in Formula B cars and then upgraded to Formula 5000, with a more powerful engine. Most thought his lack of success in the latter category was due to being promoted too quickly without first gaining enough experience to handle the faster cars. Both Scott and George Wiltshire, another black NASCAR driver, were shy about sponsorship arrangements because of the Wendell Scott incident in 1972.

Willie T. Ribbs: He came from a racing family. His father, William T. "Bunny" Ribbs raced nearly everything on wheels. The younger Ribbs was born in 1957, and began racing early in and around San Jose, California. He had his leg broken when he was nine, while watching a race in which two people died.

Ribbs attended the Jim Russell Driving School and headed for Europe where he won the 1978 Dunlop Championships. He landed a Budweiser sponsorship in 1983 for the Trans-Am circuit, and earned Rookie of the Year honors. This brash—some say cocky— 5-foot 11-inch, 160-pounder also trains seriously, spending time with Muhammad Ali's former aide, Drew "Bundini" Brown, at the Joe Louis Memorial Gym in Santa Monica, California. As of the end of 1984, he was managed by Don King.

Ribbs is also quick to give credit to Wendell Scott. "My heart bleeds for Wendell

Scott. He was racing in southern stock car races...in Alabama and in the 1950s and '60s. I take my hat off to Wendell Scott. Just for him to have the stick-to-it-iveness."[45]

Ribbs knows what sticking to it means. He was involved in a shoving incident in 1984, with fellow (white) driver Bob Lobenburg, in Atlanta. He was fined $1,000 and disqualified from the race. Was it worth it? somebody asked. "Yeah, if you let somebody get away with it once, it could go again and the next time it could be your life. I don't take any nonsense. I don't care if it's Lobenburg or Mario Andretti."[46] This led to his withdrawal from the Neil DeAlley Racing Team just before the start of the Atlanta meet. Nevertheless, he had recorded Trans-Am victories at Daytona Beach and Brainerd in 1984, and wound up driving for Team Roush Protofab. In the future more will certainly be heard from Ribbs.

Overall future progress for black drivers will be slow. The costs are enormous, the rewards meager, and the risks are the highest of any major sport. Few are willing to risk money and life in this precarious pursuit. Perhaps the sport will attract more figures like Hardy Allen, who was Grand Prix driver Dan Guerney's pit crew chief in 1970, or even Cheryl Glass, who hopes one day to drive in the Indianapolis 500.

POWER BOAT RACING

Power boat racing is to water what wheeled and foot racing are to land. Its adherents are just as daunting and always looking to eke out one more iota of speed. As for black participation, the story is entirely told with

the saga of the Arthur Kennedy family of St. Louis, Missouri.

By the mid-1950s, Arthur Kennedy, Sr., and his son, Arthur "Butch" Kennedy, Jr., were the only black members of the National Outboard Association (NOA). The elder Kennedy had attended Tuskegee Institute (now Tuskegee University), and began racing in 1947, when he was thirty-one. The younger Kennedy began racing at age eight.

Arthur Sr. raced professionally and won nearly $500 in 1954, while winning twelve of thirteen events, including a speed record on the Ohio River. His racial background, he noted, was not a problem. "Once the guys get to know you, they forget all about color and think about competition."[47]

Arthur Jr. is still racing and his record is impressive. Here are a few of his accomplishments:

1955	Set two NOA records for the one-mile straightaway
1966–68	Was undefeated in 100 horsepower class
1968	Won NOA High-Point Championships
1974	Finished in 1st place in the Bermuda Four-Hour TART marathon
1978–79	Won the Schaeffer Cup for the Mod U Class
1983	Finished in first place in the Division Parker Enduro and then joined the Bob Hauser Racing Team. Won Lake Havasu Classic.
1984	Named as team driver for Mercury.

Though Kennedy was injured in 1983, he refused to let that setback keep him from the water. At the end of 1984, the forty-one-year-old racer was still at the wheel. It is unlikely that many blacks will surface as champions in the near future, and Arthur

Kennedy, Jr.'s records will stand as a testament to perseverance and dedication.

RODEO

Rodeo events grew out of those activities performed by cowboys in the Old West in the late 1800s. A black performer, Bill Pickett, is credited with being the first outstanding bulldogger, a feat whereby a rider on a horse must chase a young calf, jump from his horse to bring the calf to an up-ended position, then tie his legs in the shortest amount of time. Pickett's contemporary was Nat "Deadwood Dick" Love, who was born a slave in June 1854, and was a champion roper in cowboy contests in the late 1800s. Most of the major events took place in what was called "Stampede Week," where cowhands from hundreds of miles around would gather to see who was best at shooting and handling calves, horses, and bulls. Other black cowboys whose names appeared in the literature of the time were George Hooker, "Pinto Jim", "Bronco" Jim Davis, and Sam Johnson.

Though there is now a national rodeo circuit, the performers are no longer cowboys. Few of them "punch cows" for a living, most have regular jobs and they try their hands at the sport to make some extra money.

The first *modern* black rodeo performer was Myrtis Dightman of Crockett, Texas, who, in his best year, 1968, made $16,000. As a bullrider, he was ranked third by the Professional Rodeo Cowboy Association in 1967 and 1968. For most blacks, though, the bruises are not worth the effort, and more than one rider has suffered permanent injury from bulls and bucking horses.

However, there were four other rodeo performers with national reputations. Clarence LeBlanc of Okmulgee, Oklahoma, finished first in average points in the 1978 International Finals Rodeo in steer wrestling; five years later in 1983, he was runner-up in the national steer wrestling competition. He won the Southern Region title as well as the World title.

Charlie Sampson is the best-known current rodeo performer. Sampson, from Los Angeles, California, made his fellow riders take notice when, as a bullrider, he won $13,000 at the National Finals Rodeo in 1981. In 1982, he not only won the Winston Rodeo Series, but was awarded the World title as well, the first black rider to earn this top ranking.

Sampson added the Sierra Circuit title in 1984, and won $68,366 as a fourth place finisher in 1985. He also qualified for the National Finals Rodeo for five consecutive years—1981–85. This personable rider became so popular that he began appearing in advertisements in magazines.

Irvin Williams, of Tulsa, Oklahoma, was black America's first high school rodeo champion. He won the Oklahoma state bullriding title for high school students in 1983, and qualified in 1983–85 for the International Finals rodeo in the fourteen–sixteen age group. Barring unforeseen injuries, young Williams should add more titles as he gets older.

The last important figure in the sport is not a rider. He is a "producer" whose name is Thyrl Latting of Robbins, Illinois. He breeds horses and bulls for the rodeo circuits and has done rather well. His bareback horse, "Phoenix," earned the highest honors from the International Professional Rodeo Association (IPRA) in 1979 and 1980. "Baldysocks" was named Saddle Bronc Horse of the Year in 1980. Two other Latting horses, "Feedlot" in 1981, and "Limber Lambert" in 1982, were also named bareback Horse of the Year. His champion bull, "Evil Knievel," was named the Central Region's Bull of the Year in 1982.

These little-known but accomplished black athletes represent further proof that the black athlete, in any sport where there is legitimate interest and support, will emerge an outstanding performer alongside or above his or her white counterpart.

SKIING

Skiing programs have been formed at many colleges, and the National Collegiate Athletic Association does sanction official events.

David Lucy: The first instance of black participation on a college team was that of David Lucy, from North Conway, New Hampshire, who skied for Denver University in 1960.

Bonnie Saint John: The 1980s have seen blacks beginning to get heavily involved in the sport. Recently, the National Brotherhood of Skiers was formed by a group of avid blacks. They are encouraging other blacks to take up the sport and to think seriously about training for national and international competitions. Their most highly-publicized effort has centered around the assistance given Bonnie Saint John, a black Harvard student whose right

leg was amputated above the knee when she was five years old.

Saint John began skiing in 1980 to overcome her feelings that she was "...a fragile, handicapped girl sitting by a window."[48] In the 1984 Handicapped Olympics in Innsbruck, Austria, she finished in first place and became the second fastest female handicapped skier. In recognition of her dedication as a scholar and an athlete, she was awarded a Rhodes Scholarship to study at Oxford University in England.

SOCCER

Soccer, or football as it is termed outside the United States, is the world's most popular team sport. There was a time in the late nineteenth century, when soccer and rugby may have earned the popularity that American-style football enjoys today. Americans went through a period of rejecting distinctly British sports after the Civil War. Rather than take up cricket, Americans chose baseball, and football over rugby.

The first black athletes to take soccer seriously here were West Indians who immigrated to America and studied at black schools. The first black star was William E. Kindle, who played soccer and rugby at Springfield College in Massachusetts, in 1911. Ten years later, John H. Burr also played at Springfield and then became an instructor in physical education at Howard University. Burr was followed by Robert Gilham at Springfield in 1924–26. Perhaps the best of these college players was Garth B.M. Crooks, who starred at Howard in 1924–26.

Soccer's popularity today is unquestioned and many of its most talented players have been black. Edison Nascimento of Brazil, better known as Pele, is generally recognized as being the all-around best ever. Likewise, most of the talented black players in America still have West Indian and African backgrounds. In the 1980s, soccer began attracting more interest among middle-class black americans, but it remains a relatively minor sport among the underclass, from which most professional black athletes come.

Howard University: This federally-funded school in Washington, D.C., has long had a sizable percentage of black foreign students. Since nearly all of them grew up with a familiarity with soccer, they have accounted for the bulk of Howard's teams. Under the guidance of Lincoln Phillips, a Trinidadian, they won national titles in 1961, 1971, and 1974.

After a third place finish in the National Association of Intercollegiate Athletics (NAIA) playoffs in 1959, Howard won the NAIA title in 1961 at Lock Haven, Pennsylvania, by defeating Newark College of Engineering (New Jersey), 3–2. The members of that squad included Cecil Durham, Alex Romeo, Noel Carr, Carlton Hinds, Charles Aloysius, and Vic Henry. They all were also accorded All-NAIA honors. The other key players included Winston Alexis, Ernie Ipke, Winston Cooke, and Martin Pardarath.

Ten years later, Howard won the NCAA Division I crown over St. Louis University, 3–2, at Miami, Florida. They later forfeited the crown because some players were ineligible for varsity competition. However, the team was undefeated in its fifteen-game schedule. The team members were Keith Acqui, Ian Bian, Mari Diane, Alvin Hender-

son, Edward Holder, Tony Martin, Don Simmons, Stan Smith, Sam Tetteh, Steve Waldron, W. Yaller-Arthur, Michael Selassie, Alfred Desmond, Ron Daily, Tony Donkwu, Mike Billy Jones, Z. Haptemariam, Trevor Mitchell, Olusegun Onadeko, Charles Pyne, Andy Terrell, and Mike Tomlinson. Keith Acqui was an All-America that year and remains the school's all-time leading scorer.

The 1974 win was also against St. Louis University, 2–1, in overtime. The members of this squad were Samuel Acquah, Richard Davy, Ian Bain, Andrew Terrell, Tunde Balogun, Keith Tulloch, Yomi Bamiro, Lincoln Peddie, Bertram Beckett, Kenneth Ilodigwe, Michael Selassie, Keith Lookloy, Trevor Leiba, Paul Pingle, Dominic Ezeani, Miywa Sanya, Sunday Izevbigie, and Neil Williams. Acquah, Davy, and Bain were All-Americas. Lincoln Phillips was the coach for each team.

Alabama A&M: In the late 1970s, this Alabama school became the second soccer power among black institutions. It, too, had a foreign coach, Salah Yousif. Yousif guided his squad to the NCAA Division II title in 1977 and 1979; and a runner-up finish in 1978. In 1981, the school was runner-up in the NCAA Division I playoffs.

Currently, the most sought after black American player is Alfonso Smith, Jr., of Ellenwood, Georgia. Richard Rottkov, the public relations director for the United States Soccer Federation (USSF), said just before the 1984 Olympics that the twenty-year-old Smith "...is one black player who is an excellent candidate"[49] for the American team. Smith played for the University of Tampa.

All expert observers believe black

American athletes would make excellent soccer players if there were more community support and interest. But very few public high schools with large black student enrollments stress soccer, and there are still few quality black American coaches. However, the sport is growing in the suburban areas of the major cities and in the South. Its main advantage is its low cost. A ball, some shoes, and a playing area are enough. For this reason alone, more black colleges are considering soccer as a major sport. The future looks very promising.

SOFTBALL

Softball is a somewhat slower and less dangerous version of baseball. It is played on a regular baseball diamond, but the distance between the bases is sixty feet instead of ninety feet. The softball itself is so named because it is larger and softer than a standard size baseball. Ball sizes vary but the two most common are the twelve-inch and sixteen-inch, the latter being used in Chicago for barehanded play.

According to the Amateur Softball Association (ASA), nearly twenty-three million people play on organized teams. These players compete to reach any one of thirty-three national championships and four world championships. Black players have played an integral role in the ASA and, along with bowling and volleyball, have considered softball a primary vehicle for competitive team play.

Black Players in the Hall of Fame

Frankie Williams:　He is from Seymour, Connecticut, and made his mark with the Raybestos Cardinals in Stratford, Connecticut. In his first season, 1957, he batted .404 and his feat was mentioned in *Ripley's Believe It or Not*. He led his team in hitting in seven of ten years, and batted over .400 on three occasions, becoming the first player in the Atlantic Seaboard League to do so in more than one season.

This second baseman was named to the ASA All-American team in 1957, 1958, and 1962. At one time, he held four all-time individual marks. Williams retired at the end of the 1966 season. He holds a masters degree from Springfield College in Massachusetts.

Charles Justice:　Justice was known as the Satchel Paige of softball and also played basketball with the Harlem Globetrotters in 1935, 1936, 1938, 1939, and 1940. His pitching career lasted more than thirty years, and he recorded 873 wins and only 92 losses. On eight occasions he struck out the maximum twenty-one batters in a seven-inning game, and on six occasions he pitched perfect games.

His primary team affiliations were with the Pontiac Big Six from 1936–1942, Flint M&S Orange in 1945, and the Toronto Tip Top Tailors in 1949–50. With the Tailors in 1949, he won the national fast pitch title and placed second in 1950. In the 1950 World Tournament, Justice won five games, lost two, and struck out forty batters.

In 1974, he was the forty-seventh player to be inducted into the Hall of Fame. He died on November 7, 1974, at age sixty-one.

Billie Harris:　Harris, of Arizona, gained fame as a pitcher and utility player. Her career lasted from 1948–75. Harris was a three-time ASA All-American, as a pitcher and utility player in 1958, and mostly as a pitcher in 1969. At the 1958 nationals, she won five games, lost two, and had an incredible ERA of 1.40. In the 1969 nationals she won four games, batted .400, and was the event's Most Valuable Player.

From 1953–75 she played in the Pacific Coast Women's League and compiled an aggregate batting average of .260. In 1963, she pitched two perfect games (four during her career). She also pitched seventy no-hitters. Harris was considered among the best at the "drag bunt" and was exceptionally fast. Now living in Glendale, Arizona, she was inducted into the Hall of Fame in 1982.

Softball has been extremely important in the athletic development of black America since World War II. Nearly every boy, and most girls, at one time has played or at least watched baseball. The gentler softball is familiar and easy to understand. A good case can be made that softball, with its thousands of teams, is more American than baseball. Certainly, more people play it than have played baseball. Except for bowling, more black men and women belong to softball teams than to teams in any other sport.

SPEED SKATING

Speed skating is a minor sport which enjoys its greatest visibility during the Winter Olympic Games. Skaters race around an oval ice-covered track, and events are classified into sprints and distance races. Training facilities are very scarce and the competition has been dominated in the past by foreign athletes, though Eric Heiden, a white American, is considered one of the best ever.

Black Skaters

Gayle Ann Fannin: She was born in Brooklyn and attended St. John's University in Queens, New York, while training for the 1964 Winter Olympic Games. Though she was unsuccessful, her effort did not go unnoticed. She did, however, win the New York State title.

Erroll Fraser: He is also from Brooklyn and, like Eric Heiden, was a cyclist. He managed to gain a berth as a cyclist in the 1971 Pan-American Games Trials, and then tried speed skating. Though his efforts were chronicled in the black press, he was never as successful as Gayle Fannin.

Fraser was a sprinter and competed in the 500-meter, 1000-meter, and 1500-meter events. His motivation for trying such an improbable sport came, he said, when he saw American Ted McDermott win a gold medal in the 1964 Winter Games. "...McDermott beat him [Evgeny Grishin, the Soviet's best] by one-tenth of a second...that kind of inspired me; I liked the sport mentally."[50]

Fraser trained by watching films of champion skaters and paid his own way to meets just to watch and learn. "People looked at me like I had just come out of a spaceship from Mars. They had never seen a black skater before,"[51] he said. When the world mark for 500-meters was 38 seconds, Fraser's best time was 42.2 seconds. In the 1000-meters at the time, the world mark was 117.6 seconds and Fraser's best was 128.2.

Fraser's noble attempt deserves acknowledgment and congratulations.

It is likely that black Americans will figure prominently in this sport in the foreseeable future.

SWIMMING

Swimming for sport came as naturally to mankind as foot races. However the various events that make up a swimming meet today—freestyle, breast stroke, butterfly, back stroke—were unheard of centuries ago. Until the 1800s, races were freestyle and conducted on smooth lakes or ponds. In Africa, nations located near the oceans and the great river systems had excellent swimmers. For them, swimming was a matter of survival and contests were used to select the strongest and swiftest. In America, slaves swam for sport *and* for profit. Slaves along the southeast coast—the Sea Islands of the Carolinas, and Georgia— were widely known for their prowess in diving for shell fish and other sea life.

The first formal swimming meets among blacks began on Independence Day in 1911, in Washington, D.C. In connection with national celebrations, the Interscholastic Athletic Association (ISAA) and the local Colored YMCA invited area schools to participate. Dr. Edwin B. Henderson was the meet coordinator and plans were made to teach more black children to swim. The lack of facilities hampered this effort, and caused considerable friction between whites and blacks in many northern cities. The second major migration of blacks from the South to the North was underway and recreational amenities for them were grossly inadequate. The 1919 race riot in Chicago was caused in part by problems in that city's sports accommodations.

But by the 1920s some northern public schools had pools, and blacks were beginning to excel. Clarence Gatliffe was named to the varsity at Detroit's Cass Tech High School in 1925, and Anita Gant, a Washington, D.C., school teacher, starred in local meets in the 1920s. But the most outstanding performer was Inez Patterson of Philadelphia. She began winning medals in junior high school and at McCoach playground. Dr. Henderson called Patterson "One of the greatest athletes of all time."[52] Patterson was also a track star for the *Philadelphia Inquirer* Girls Track Team. She lettered in five sports at Temple University.

While Inez Patterson's exploits were commendable, she was an exception. Swimming became an "in" sport after the 1928 Olympics, because American Johnny Weismuller had by then won a total of five gold medals in two Olympiads. But blacks were little interested; so much so that this comment appeared in the black-owned *California Eagle* newspaper on August 30, 1934: "No colored swimmers in the last Olympic Games, none in the ones before that or before those. Well isn't it high time we showed the world that we can swim as well as sprint, jump and box."[53]

Few blacks seemed willing to spend the time necessary for competition other than in local meets because there were almost no black role models, no scholarships available at black colleges, and no professional competition. Morris Jackson and Emily Jeter caused a brief stir by qualifying for the 1935 National AAU swim meet. In addition, John Strothers of Pittsburgh finished second in his city's outdoor junior 50-meter freestyle event in 1938. A year later, Charles Pinderhughes swam at Dartmouth College and John Pinderhughes made the varsity swim team at Springfield College (Massachusetts).

Other Restrictions: Blacks were also held back because of strongly held taboos concerning disease and social custom. It was erroneously thought by many whites that blacks had communicable diseases that would spread if the races swam together. Thus, most city councils, with their all-white memberships, preferred to have separate pools for blacks and whites. If that were not possible or practical then certain days were reserved for the exclusive use of each racial group. The silliest objection was to black male swimmers appearing near nude in front of white women. There were even some instances of pools sitting empty in the middle of the summer because there was not enough money to build a separate pool for blacks; whites refused to swim in mixed facilities. In Ferndale, Michigan, in 1941, for example, a pool at Lincoln High sat empty for years because blacks and whites were forbidden to swim together.

As a result, blacks were seldom able to reach their potential unless they happened to live in an area with no restrictions or were stationed at military bases in northern states. Yet the "colored" YMCA/YWCA's continued to turn out talented performers.

World War II and the U.S. Navy: Although the Navy was by far the most racist of the U.S. armed forces through the 1950s, it did provide the first substantial oppor-

tunities for black swimmers and divers. The Navy built a pool at Hampton Institute (now Hampton University) in 1942, to assist black sailors in their training. Hampton was a mere twenty-minute drive from the Navy's largest base in Norfolk, Virginia. Another Naval center with a strong black swimming program was the Great Lakes Naval Training Center in Wisconsin. Most of the Navy's black instructors were trained at one of these two facilities.

A second motivating factor to Navy pool building was the emphasis on physical fitness during the war. Groups such as the American Red Cross actively campaigned to persuade every citizen to learn to swim not only for safety's sake but for the physical conditioning involved. The sport enjoyed more publicity during this period than at any previous time.

Post–World War II Surge: After the war, public and private pool construction soared. In 1948, the Central Intercollegiate Athletic Association (CIAA), the oldest black college conference, began its swimming and diving championships. That same year, Richard McGriff of Eastman, Georgia, enjoyed press attention as a promising nineteen-year-old diver at George Washington High School in New York City. The future looked bright.

There were also a number of lawsuits filed by blacks who were denied access to public facilities and/or limited to swimming on certain days of the week. According to noted sports writer A. S. "Doc" Young, disgruntled blacks began to organize a "...series of 'wade-ins' at municipal southern pools."[54] Golf, tennis, and swimming were the sports most resistant to the integration of nonwhites into the mainstream of their activities.

This pressure forced the appointment of Sylvius Moore, Hampton's swimming coach, to the staff of the National Aquatic School in 1954. But the times registered by black swimmers remained below national and international standards. However, within thirty years, black Americans would be listed among collegiate winners, and one would be a serious contender for the Olympic team.

Black College Winners: Only three black college conferences—the CIAA, SIAC, MEAC—have held swimming championships, and none has done so continuously since it started. In fact, there have been no championships held for any of the conferences since 1980. There are three reasons for this decline in interest. One, the best black swimmers began attending predominantly white schools; two, the conferences were severely imbalanced; and three, some black schools stopped their swimming programs to save money. As a result, the same schools won most of the time.

As the record shows, only eight different schools have ever won conference titles, but without a well-balanced conference schedule, repeated victories became shallow. Some schools did retain their teams, but they now compete against white schools in their local area. No black school has ever won a national title in NAIA, AIAW, or NCAA competition.

Tennessee State University: Morgan State, Tennessee State, and Howard University had the best black swim teams in the 1950s. Tom "Friend" Hughes was Tennessee State's coach from 1945–69, and was the acknowledged dean of black college coaches. His teams were perennial winners and he produced some outstanding swimmers, including two national champions.

Hughes' first star performer was Frank Stewart, from Chicago, who specialized in the freestyle. In 1947, Stewart's time of 20:02 minutes was the ninth fastest in the world for the 1500-meters. The best time was 19:15.4. Stewart was also an instructor at the Great Lakes Naval Training Center during World War II. After watching Airman Second Class Stewart swim during a war meet, one white Chicago sports reporter exclaimed, "I found there are some Negroes swimming within a sneeze of world's records, who race down a pool faster than one can walk or run. The greatest of these Negro stars is Frank Stewart."[55]

A panel of sportswriters named Stewart and Tom Hughes as the two greatest black swimmers of the first half of the twentieth century. In 1945, Stewart won the Far Western AAU 100-meter freestyle in a time of 1:02.5 minutes, and was Pacific Coast champion in the 50-meter and 100-meter free style. In 1946, he equalled the world's record for the 50-meter freestyle with a time of 25.4 seconds. Five years later, in 1951, he equalled the 220-yard freestyle record of 2:20.1 minutes and set a new 440-yard freestyle world record with a time of 5:20.3 minutes. Stewart had begun his career at Chicago's International YMCA in 1936, when he was only eleven years old. He later attended Wendell Phillips High School before joining the Navy and graduating from Tennessee State with degrees in Physical Education and Chemistry.

Donald E. Jackson followed Stewart as Tennessee State's next freestyle standout. He starred in the 100-meters, 200-meters, and 400-meters from 1949–52. Stanley Gainor was a middle-distance freestyle artist from 1950–53. Leroy Jones was an excellent short-distance sprinter there from 1953 through 1956. However, in John Swann and Clyde James, Tennessee State produced two more national winners.

In 1958, Swann won the NAIA 100-meter butterfly and broke many CIAA records. In 1960–61, Clyde James won the NAIA 100-yard backstroke and was named an NAIA All-America both years. Swann and James were black America's first national collegiate champions from black schools.

Hampton's coach, Sylvius Moore, understood why black collegiate swimmers began falling behind in the early 1960s. "The lack of coaching was a big problem. There were also not too many black high schools with swimming teams and the YMCA's for black kids did not all have pools. So most of them never had the year round encouragement. Also, very few black swimming clubs were formed. Nearly all the good white swimmers had belonged to clubs before they even got to college...Most of our boys came from upper-class families because the black kids from ordinary circumstances played football, basketball, baseball, and track. The upper-class boys played tennis and a few could swim. These kids also had very high graduation rates."[56]

As proof of Moore's assertions, Morehouse College, which maintains the highest of entrance qualifications, has won more conference titles, sixteen, than any other black school.

Quality swimmers from other schools include Roy Fagan of Morgan State and Sandra Ann Arrington, who became the first female diver on Howard University's men's team.

As for women's teams, Alabama A&M in Huntsville has dominated since 1980. They have competed against white schools such as Vanderbilt, Georgia Tech, and the University of Kentucky. Lori Reid, a high school All-America from Chicago, has swum the 100-yard breast stroke in 1:13.93 minutes. Cathy Merriweather of Detroit specializes in the 100-meter and 200-meter butterfly, and is black America's first All-America female swimmer. Coach Freddie Wyckoff has done an outstanding job with his team.

Black college coaches have had a difficult time in amassing quality teams. While recruiting has been the primary hinderance, most continue to persevere. The following list shows the top black college coaches, their school, their conference, and the number of titles to their credit.

JAMES "PINKY" HAINES	Morehouse	SIAC	16
TOM JOHNSON	Howard	CIAA	8
W.A. CAMPBELL	Albany State	SIAC	6
SYLVIUS MOORE	Hampton	CIAA	6
STU BROOKS	Morgan State	CIAA	4
JAMES MACK	Morgan State	MEAC	3

Other outstanding coaches include Dr. James Hawkins and John Ewbanks of West Virginia State; Clarence Pendleton and John Burr of Howard; and Lawrence Thornton, French Jackson, and Robert Bethel at

Hampton. Nearly all of these men believe that black college swimming programs have a promising future. The missing link is the lack of enough competitive varsity programs in high schools with large black enrollments.

Black Swimmers at White Colleges:

The three primary advantages of white college programs over those at black colleges are: (1) better facilities; (2) more uniformly good coaching; and (3) more intense competition. However, until the 1960s, blacks were discouraged from varsity participation in most white schools. The first to make a national impression was Nathan Clark, who swam for Ohio State in 1962–63. In 1963, he was ranked fourth nationally in the 200-meter butterfly and sixth in the 100-meter butterfly. He was named an All-America that same year.

Rick White of Brooklyn, was a three-time world champion high diver and captain of the American team at the 1973 International Team Championships. He spent two years at Long Island University, but left because he was not satisfied. "I left LIU after two years. No one was ready for a black diver. I could see no future in college diving…many old time judges never got used to me and gave me a hard time scoring. But I always had the respect of the other divers."[57]

Other than Rick White's diving reputation, a decade passed before another collegiate winner, Fred Evans, surfaced. As one black reporter mentioned, "What many younger black swimmers—and white coaches—need is proof and inspiration. Proof that all good swimmers don't have to be raised in $60,000 houses. Inspiration that all those hours in the pool swimming boring repetitions and fighting swelling pain can lead to glory."[58]

Evans swam for the University of Illinois at Chicago, and was a star in his native Washington, D.C., before college. Many in the nation's capital recognized his potential. Said Jane Stafford, who codirected swimming clinics for the Phillips' 66 company, "He's the same to swimming around here for blacks as Arthur Ashe was to tennis for a nation of blacks. And if he could become a national champion it would open the door for black swimmers everywhere."[59] Evans did just that.

At UIC, Evans was the NAIA champion in the 100-meter breast stroke, and repeated as NCAA Division II winner in this event in 1976 and 1977. He finished in third place in the NCAA's in 1975. Evans was later inducted into the United States Swimming Hall of Fame.

Bob Murray attended the University of Michigan from 1978 to 1981, and was the first black champion of a conference of predominantly white schools in Division I of the NCAA. In 1978, he was Big Ten champion in the 50-meter freestyle and set a school record at 20.91 seconds. Murray was also a member of the winning 400-meter and 800-meter relay teams. A year later, he repeated as a member of the winning 400-meter relay team. In 1980, he was Big Ten champion in the 50-meter and 400-meter freestyle.

Trent Lyght set an Arizona State University record in the 100-meter breast stroke of 56.53 seconds in 1981, and was ranked thirteenth by the NCAA in this event in 1979.

The best black American swimmer

ever, however, is Chris Silva. He attended UCLA from 1981–84. His best year was 1982, when he was a member of the winning PAC 10 400-meter relay team, that also won the NCAA title. He was a silver medalist in the 1983 World University Games at 400-meters. Silva was named an All-America in 1982 and 1983 for the 50-meter freestyle, the 400-meter freestyle, and the 400-meter medley relay. In 1984, he had a world ranking of fourteenth in the 50-meter freestyle.

Coaches at white colleges no longer consider black swimmers rarities, Silva is proof of that. But there is an understanding of why they do not see more: "There's no money in swimming, so you can't blame them..."[60] said Jack Hanes, UCLA's coach in the 1970s. That economic consideration still applies today.

A word must be added for Walter Hutcherson, the swimming coach at the Los Angeles Twenty-eighth Street YMCA in the 1950s, and Charles A. "Tuna" Chapman, a marathoner. In 1959, Hutcherson's junior team of black swimmers finished second in the AAU Junior Olympic 200-meter freestyle. The star performer was ten year old Charles Edward Spann, III, who was the AAU 50-meter breast stroke winner in his age category in a time of 44.5 seconds. In the late 1970s, Tracy Parker also won some junior titles as a fifteen year old competitor.

Charles Chapman is from Buffalo, New York, and is the only noted black marathon swimmer. On August 24, 1981, he became the first black to swim the English Channel, a 37½-mile trip from Dover, England, to Sangatte Bay, France. His time was 13 hours and 10 minutes and compares very favorably with the 21 hours 45 minutes it took Matthew Webb to do it first in 1875.

Chapman began swimming at the Humboldt YMCA in Buffalo when he was six, and began swimming long distances in 1978. His future plans include attempts at swimming the Nile River and the Sea of Galilee.

Experts do not expect any major breakthroughs for black swimmers in the forseeable future. There are no professional events, high school programs are spotty at best, there are few black swimming clubs, and black college varsity teams are being cut because of costs and a lack of interest. Still, the potential is there and no one should be surprised if in the future a black swimmer qualifies for the United States Olympic Team.

TABLE TENNIS

Table tennis, or Ping Pong as it is more popularly called, originated in England in the early 1900s, as a result of new technologies emanating from the Industrial Revolution. Ping Pong balls are made of celluloid and their light weight makes them ideal for this miniature version of lawn tennis.

The best players before and during World War II were the Czechoslovakians and Hungarians. The Chinese, Scandinavians, and Americans have done well since 1950. The sport demands lightning quick reflexes, excellent hand-eye coordination, and stamina.

Black Players

According to *Ebony* magazine, a 4-foot 8-inch twelve-year-old from Newport News, Virginia, Ronnie Hobson, was the first black

American champion. He won the U.S. Open for Under-sixteens, Under-thirteens, and the Junior Men's Doubles with Bill Keim, in 1960. Joy Foster, a young black girl from Kingston, Jamaica won the Girl's title. Sol Hairston, Hobson's teammate, was a runner-up. They were among eight black players from Newport News to participate in the U.S. Open, the first blacks to do so.

Many churches, YMCA/YWCAs, Boy's Clubs, Police Athletic Leagues, and neighborhood recreation centers across the country promote Ping Pong. But few black players view it as more than recreation. In 1971, however, the sport figured prominently in international diplomacy.

In that year, George Braithwaite, the nation's fifth-ranked player, was the only black among a group that toured the People's Republic of China on a goodwill trip. These Ping Pong players were specifically selected to act as cultural ambassadors preceding President Richard M. Nixon's visit there. The United States and China had not had diplomatic relations since 1949.

Braithwaite was born in Guyana, South America, but now lives in New York City and works at the United Nations. He won the U.S. National Class "B" Championships in 1966, and the Class "A" title in 1968. In 1970, he was appointed to the American team that toured Nicaragua, Guatemala, and El Salvador. Braithwaite was on the Pan-American Team in 1983, and won the Canadian International Open singles, Senior singles, and doubles in 1984. The U.S. Table Tennis Association named him their Amateur Athlete of the Year in 1984.

Ping Pong remains a very popular indoor recreational sport, but is unlikely to enjoy much greater support among blacks, since there is no professional circuit.

VOLLEYBALL

Volleyball is thought by many to be the world's most popular non-professional player team sport. Nearly every high school and college has an intramural program and it is a favorite with beach goers. Basketball star Wilt Chamberlain used beach volleyball as a reconditioning regimen in 1969, when he severely wrenched his knee. Since there is no professional circuit, the sport has not been pursued seriously by black players past the intramural level.

However, in 1977, Tuskegee Institute's (now Tuskegee University) women's team became the first from a black school to win an AIAW-sanctioned state title. Under coach Tiny Laster, they defeated the University of Montevallo 15–4, 15–7, 11–15, 15–8. The team members included Angela Cox, Sophia James, Linda Jones, Gwen Harvey, Evelyn McWay, Peggy Murray, Brendolyn McCarty, Elizabeth Lockett, Johnnie Tolberg, Shirley Underwood, and Fran Vincent.

In addition to Tuskegee, Howard University and St. Augustine have fielded the best black women's teams in the 1980s. Men's competition at black schools is not as well developed as that of the women.

The biggest impression made by black volleyball players came from three women who were part of the 1984 Olympic squad. Flo Hyman, a 6-foot 5-inch spiker, Rita Crockett, and Rose Magers helped steer the American team to a silver medal finish against China. Hyman, who was thirty years old in 1984, was the star of the team.

She was the top hitter at the 1981 World Cup Tournament. Rita Crockett was named All-World in 1982. Both were members of the 1980 Olympic team that could not compete because of President Jimmy Carter's decision to boycott the Moscow Olympics. Hyman and Crockett had played together since 1978.

This entire women's team made supreme sacrifices to train for the 1984 Games. "Almost all of the players had to leave school and give up college scholarships to train with the team full-time in [coach Ariel] Selinger's regimented atmosphere...none went to school...and none had jobs."[61] But they were all proud of their silver medals.

Future black stars are more than likely to come out of our nation's colleges, and more of them will be women. The game requires a high level of athletic ability but most black male athletes will not choose a sport with no professional outlet. With Hyman, Crockett, and Magers having led the way, more black female Olympians will earn berths on future American teams.

WEIGHTLIFTING

Weightlifting seems to have stemmed from some primal urge in males to demonstrate their physical superiority. While people in African ancestry did not display any particular emphasis on contests of this sort, certain European tribes made an art of it. The Highland Games of the Scots included competitions to see which man could toss heavy objects the greatest distance. The hammer-throw, the discus, and the javelin are mere variations on the general idea of defying the laws of gravity.

In the United States, the sport has only recently moved out of the back rooms of YMCA's and made use of modern techniques and computer analysis. Weightlifting, though, is not to be confused with "bodybuilding," in which participants try to mold perfectly proportioned physiques. Weightlifters try to do what the name implies—lift heavy weights over their heads with their arms straight and their bodies in control.

The history of black Americans in the sport dwells on three men: John Davis, John Terry, and James Bradford. Davis is one of the legends of the sport.

John Davis: He was born in Brooklyn, New York, and won his first world's title, the light-heavyweight championship in 1938, when he was only seventeen. After becoming a heavyweight lifter, he held the world "clean and jerk" record of 402 pounds for a time.

Davis had an impressive physique: a 47-inch chest, 31-inch waist, 24½-inch thighs, 16½-inch calfs, 16-inch biceps, and stood 5-foot 8-inches and weighed 180-pounds at age eighteen. Few doubt that if there had been no World War II, Davis would have won gold medals in the cancelled 1940 and 1944 Olympics. By the time his career was over, he had won twelve National titles, six World titles, two Olympic gold medals, and a Pan-American Games title.

When officials of the 1984 Olympic Games heard that Davis was dying of cancer, they named him a special representative, though he could not attend. He died in 1984.

John Davis' Record

United States National Champion in
1939-1940 as a lightheavyweight (82.5
kilograms) and in 1941-43, 1946-48, and
1950-53 as a heavyweight.
World Champion in 1938 as a lightweight
and in 1946-47, and 1949-51 as a
heavyweight.
Pan-American Games Champion in 1951
and 1955 as a heavyweight.
Olympic Games Champion in 1948 and
1952 as a heavyweight.
Notable Achievements:

1. First of only three men to win eight
consecutive World and Olympic
championships.
2. First amateur to clean and jerk more
than 400-pounds—402¼-pounds in 1951.
3. Member of the Helms Hall of Fame.
4. Member of Black Athletes Hall of Fame.

John Terry: He was a featherweight lifter
who was born in Pittsburgh, Pennsylvania.
The featherweight limit is 60 kilograms or
132¼ pounds. Terry held the world record
in 1938, for a snatch of 215 pounds (or 97.52
kilograms), and a year later he became the
first featherweight to deadlift 600 pounds.
He was a member of the 1936 Olympic
team and was the National Champion in
1938–41. He is now deceased.

James Bradford: He is from Washington, D.C., and was second to John Davis
in the 1952 Olympic Games as a heavyweight. The 245-pound lifter startled everyone by returning eight years later to earn
another silver medal in the 1960 Games in
Rome. He was National Champion in
1960–61.

Albert Hood gained some recognition
as a lifter in the 123-pound class as a junior,
but has not figured prominently in senior
competition. Black participation has been
limited by the lack of role models. There are
many aspirants but, outside of preparations
for international competition, little assistance or coaching is available. The sport
today is dominated by the eastern Europeans. Most Americans use weightlifting to
strengthen themselves for other sports like
wrestling, football, and bodybuilding. The
sport is not likely to witness a great surge of
black interest in the near future.

WRESTLING

Wrestling is best described in the Encyclopedia Britannica as a "weaponless
combative sport...among the oldest vari-
eties of sporting endeavor known to mankind."[62] It is an apt description since
ancient drawings, engravings, and literature refer to this commonplace activity.
Among African peoples, wrestling has always been mentioned as the subject of lore
and oral history. Grand prizes and the
highest national honors accrued to its
winners.

"Belt wrestling" was popular in ancient Egypt and Mesopotamia and most old
cultures viewed the sport as a substitute for
war or the symbolic death of an adversary.
African warriors used wrestling techniques
as conditioning exercises. In North America, Native Americans were wrestling long
before the Europeans reached these shores.
The sport was also very popular among
slaves in America during their free time.

There are three wrestling styles in use
today: loose, catch-hold, and belt-and-

jacket. Points are scored by forcing one's opponent out of a position, toppling an opponent, forcing an opponent into certain supine positions, holding an opponent immobile for a certain length of time, or forcing an opponent to submit.

Black Professional Wrestlers: Most Americans have acquired their image of the sport through professional events on television. These contests are usually held between wrestlers who are part athlete and part entertainer. Much of what is seen is staged and the blows to the face and chest are "pulled" to avoid serious injury. Yet these contestants are trained in crowd-pleasing techniques, and professional wrestling shows are among the most popular in America. As these contestants are athletes, they deserve mention.

Before 1960, most black professional grapplers were forced to wrestle among themselves. But Edward "Bearcat" Wright announced in Gary, Indiana, that year that he would no longer wrestle in places that barred integrated bouts. The National Association for the Advancement of Colored People (NAACP) supported his move and soon blacks were able to book matches against white opponents. In most black-versus-white bouts, the black wrestler is postured as the symbol of moral rectitude and his white opponent is the villain.

"No match is dearer to the hearts of wrestling promoters than one that has overtones of ethnic warfare, and there is a fairly brisk demand for Negro wrestlers, virtually all of whom are good guys. Although promoters prefer their crowds intense, to employ Negroes as villains before white audiences would be to invite a lynching."[63]

Some of the more famous black pro-

fessional wrestlers included Edward "Bearcat" Wright, Reggie "Sweet Daddy" Siki, Buster "The Harlem Hangman" Lloyd, Bobo Brazil, "Seaman" Art Thomas, Don Blackman, Rufus Jones, Frank James, Woody Strode (the former UCLA athlete), Dory Dixon, Jim "The Black Panther" Mitchell, and Jack Claybourne. Even Joe Louis, the former heavyweight boxing champion, turned to the sport after his ring days were finished. Two black female stars were Dinah Beamon and Sweet Georgia Brown.

Black College Wrestling: Black college interest has been intermittent, and Morgan State has perhaps the oldest history. No black school has ever won an NAIA or NCAA national title. Only two conferences, the CIAA and the MEAC, have solid and unbroken wrestling championship events. The pattern in both conferences shows winning streaks by certain schools that last up to five years, only to be replaced by another school that enjoyed another multi-year streak.

Only eleven schools have earned conference honors since 1950: Howard with eight; Lincoln with seven; Morgan State and Virginia State with six each; Elizabeth City, Winston-Salem State, and South Carolina State with five each; Norfolk State and North Carolina A&T with two each; and Delaware State and Livingstone with one each. The complete list of conference winners by year is listed in the Reference section.

Howard University changed its conference affiliation in 1972 from the CIAA to the MEAC. The names of the leading coaches, their schools, conference affiliation, and the number of titles won are:

JOHN ORGAN	Howard University, CIAA (6), MEAC (2), total 8
ROBERT GARDNER	Lincoln University, CIAA 7
HULON WILLIS	Virginia State, CIAA 6
THURLIS LITTLE	Elizabeth City, CIAA 5
JAMES RAGLUND	S. Carolina State, MEAC 5
JAMES PHILLIPS	Morgan State, MEAC 3

In the 1970s, some of these schools began competing against predominantly white schools when intra-conference competition became limited. As a result, a few of their wrestlers earned national honors. In 1980, William Smith of Morgan State became the first wrestler from a black college to win the NCAA Division II 158-pound title. His teammate, Greg Veale, won the 167-pound crown in 1983. Davis was named as the Outstanding Wrestler by the NCAA Division II for his weight class in 1984. Coaches are very encouraged by recent results and more progress is expected in the near future.

Black Wrestlers at White Colleges

Robert Douglas: Any discussion of black wrestling figures in predominantly white college competition must begin with Robert Douglas. Born in Belaire, Ohio, he was an outstanding athlete at Bridgeport (Ohio) high school, where he won three letters in football, four in baseball, and four in wrestling, including two state wrestling titles.

He then attended West Liberty State College (West Virginia) where he won the 1962, NAIA 130-pound title, before switching to Oklahoma State University where he was Big Eight champion in the 147-pound division, in 1965. His major collegiate, na-

tional, world, and Olympic records are listed in the Reference section.

Douglas continued as a coach after his playing days were over, becoming the first black in such a position at a major institution (Don Benning was the first black coach at a predominantly white college, Omaha University, in 1964). Before assuming the coaching position at Arizona State, Douglas spent time at the University of California at Santa Barbara, Oklahoma State, Cornell (New York), and Iowa State. In his eleven years at Arizona State, he has compiled a record of 139 wins and 56 losses for a winning percentage of 71.3. He has authored four books on wrestling and was an assistant coach of the 1984 United States Olympic Team.

NCAA Champions: Black America's national collegiate winners are among the least known of its premier athletes. Wrestling is not considered a major sport by black Americans, and college matches are seldom on television except during the NCAA playoffs or in certain sections of the country. In addition, the sport's main focus of support is in the Midwest rather than the populous East or South. Of the thirty-seven black NCAA winners since 1957, only one is from a southern school. The emphasis on football in the South is so strong that, except for those in the lighter weight divisions, athletes who might try wrestling are often encouraged to play football instead.

The list of black NCAA winners is surprisingly lengthy and covers the weight classes from 118 pounds to the heavyweight division.

Lee Kemp of Madison, Wisconsin, won his division three times and was a five-time National Open freestyle winner, a three-time World Cup winner, and a Pan American games gold medalist.

Darryl Burley was one of only four wrestlers to reach the NCAA Finals four times. He was also voted as Wrestler of the Year by *Wrestling News* in 1983.

NAIA Winners: Among the champions at the smaller schools, Roy Washington of the University of Nebraska at Omaha (UNO) sets an excellent example. He was the first black NAIA victor in 1968, and followed with repeat victories in 1969–70. Mel Washington and Herb Stanley are two other multiple winners. Washington won in 1969–71, and Stanley in 1978–79. Don Benning, a 1958 graduate of Omaha University and coach at UNO, was named Coach of the Year in 1970—positive proof that blacks can be attracted to and star in wrestling. Individual NAIA champions are listed in the Reference section.

National and World Titleholders

By the late 1960s, black Americans had acquired the skills through college training and club bouts to compete on a national and international level. The armed forces, local wrestling clubs, and company-sponsored teams recruited and sent talented grapplers to tournaments. This was not possible nor probable in the early 1950s, as a match between black and white competitors was considered racially provocative. Until that time, even professional wrestlers avoided interracial bouts.

As the statistics show, clubs in the Midwest dominate the winners column. In fact, only two black winners of national events came from clubs east of Michigan— Greg Gibson and Ron Carlisle were Marines

stationed at Quantico, Virginia. The National Open and World champions in freestyle and Greco-Roman (no grabbing below the waist or using the legs to trip) are listed in the Reference section.

Pan-American and Olympic Games Winners

Black Americans have fared well in Olympic competition but better in the Pan-American Games. The names are familiar. Lloyd Keaser, Greg Gibson, Carl Adams, Robert Douglas, Jimmy Jackson, and Lee Kemp are standouts who made their marks in other competitions as well.

Few sports require a training regimen as rigorous as wrestling. Exercise physiologists believe it to be one of the most strenuous activities. Sustained physical exertion is the norm and concentration is a must. While the list of black collegiate, national, and international winners may be surprising, the trend begun by Robert Douglas in the early 1960s promises even better results and more winners in the future.

Notes

1. *NBA Brochure.*
2. *Black Sports,* August 1974, 46.
3. John Pozenal, "Black Bowling Pros," *Black Sports,* April 1974, 39.
4. Chuck Pezzano, "Charlie Venable," *Black Sports,* February 1974, 60.
5. Benjamin G. Rader, *American Sports,* (Englewood Cliffs, N.J.: Prentice-Hall, 1983), 41.
6. Mary Howard Schoolcraft, *Letters On The Condition of The African Race In The U.S. By A Southern Lady* (Philadelphia, Pa.: T.K. and P.G. Collins Printers, 1852), 12.

7. Anita De Franz, telephone interview with author, 14 August, 1985.

8. Ibid., De Franz Interview.

9. Ibid.

10. *Los Angeles Times,* Part VIII, 4 August 1984, 4.

11. Nikki Franke, telephone interview with author, 12 August 1985.

12. Peter Westbrook, telephone interview with author, 13 August 1985.

13. *The City Sun,* 5-11 June 1985, 28.

14. Nikki Franke, telephone interview with author, 12 August 1985.

15. Ibid.

16. Ibid.

17. *Army and Navy Journal,* 12 March 1904.

18. *Ebony,* December 1974, 108.

19. *Ebony,* January 1983, 44.

20. Ira Winderman, *Ft. Lauderdale News,* 13 February 1985, 3C.

21. Ibid.

22. *Boston Globe,* 25 February 1948.

23. *Black Sports,* February 1974, 43.

24. Ibid.

25. *Jet* magazine, 30 April 1981.

26. *Ebony,* June 1977, 48.

27. *Focus,* December/January 1985, 38.

28. Ibid.

29. Ibid.

30. *Los Angeles Times,* Part VIII, 28 July 1984, 29.

31. Milton Roberts, "Lacrosse," *Black Sports,* May 1976, 19.

32. Ibid.

33. *Daily Worker,* 14 April 1941.

34. Val Pinchbeck, Athletic Publicity Director, Syracuse University, 1962.

35. Ibid.

36. *(Great Running Backs in Pro Football, Jim Brown: The Greatest,* p. 49.

37. Milton Roberts, "Lacrosse," *Black Sports,* May 1976, 18.

38. *California Eagle,* 18 September 1925.

39. *Ebony,* August 1948, 36.

40. *Ebony,* September 1951, 49.

41. Bob Myers, "Turn Back In Anger," *Stock Car Racing,* July 1973, 20.

42. Ibid., 22.

43. Ibid., 23.

44. *Ebony,* May 1966, 62.

45. Hal Lamarr, "Have Car, Will Travel," *Black Southerner,* September 1984, 64.

46. *The City Sun,* 3-9 April 1985, 24.

47. *Ebony,* October 1955.

48. *New York Times,* 18 December 1985, A-19.

49. Richard Rottkov, public relations director (USSF), 1984.

50. *Black Sports,* November 1974, 34.

51. Ibid.

52. Edwin B. Henderson, *The Negro in Sports,* (Washington, D.C., Associated Negro Press, 1949), 237.

53. *California Eagle,* 30 August 1934.

54. A.S. Young, *Negro Firsts In Sports,* (Chicago, IL.: Johnson Publishing Company, 1963), 181.

55. White Chicago sportswriter.

56. Sylvius Moore, telephone interview with author, 20 July 1985.

57. *Ebony,* October 1974, 52 & 54.

58. *Black Sports,* September 1974, 21.

59. Ibid.

60. *Ebony,* December 1974, 144.

61. *Los Angeles Times,* Part VIII, 27 July 1984.

62. *The New Encyclopedia Britannica,* 15th Edition, Volume 19, 1024.

63. *Saturday Evening Post,* 12 February 1966.

ADDENDUM

When work began on *A Hard Road To Glory* a decision was made to terminate the third volume at the end of 1984. But so much has happened since then that a brief review of 1985, 1986, and of a part of 1987 is in order. It seems fitting to end with the fortieth anniversary celebration of Jackie Robinson's debut as a Brooklyn Dodger on April 15, 1947. On that day, Robinson went hitless in a game against the Boston Braves at Ebbets Field in Brooklyn. The Braves' starting pitcher Johnny Sain also happened to be the last man to pitch to Babe Ruth.

The celebration was, however, marred by some rather racist remarks made by the Los Angeles Dodgers' vice-president for player personnel, Al Campanis. Though Campanis had been with the Dodgers organization for forty-four years, and played shortstop when Robinson was at second base, he let on to ABC Television's Nightline host Ted Koppel that blacks "...may not have some of the necessities to be, let's say, a field manager, or perhaps a general manager." He further added that blacks "...may not have the desire to be in the front office."[1] These words became a *cause celebre* throughout the country and Campanis was dismissed by the Dodgers' president, Peter O'Malley. Campanis is probably of good character, but he displayed the fact that many professional baseball executives still harbor the belief that blacks do not have the "right stuff" to manage teams or organizations.

In a column by the *New York Times'* sports columnist Dave Anderson it then surfaced that Peter O'Malley's late father, Walter, did not want to see Robinson as a manager. Anderson quoted the elder O'Malley as saying back then: "Robinson can't manage himself; how do you expect him to manage 25 ballplayers."[2] Rachel Robinson, Jackie's widow, was reported to be "...shocked and appalled and horrified and angry because I hadn't expected it."[3]

The Campanis affair was not the only off-the-field incident to make the headlines in the national pastime of baseball. In December 1985, Tommy Harper, a black ex-Boston Red Sox player and coach, was fired by that organization because his work was "inferior." In actuality, he was dismissed because he complained about Red Sox Spring training activities at the Elks Club in Winter Haven, Florida. The club does not permit black membership. The United States Equal Opportunity Commission investigated the incident and agreed with Harper. An out-of-court settlement ensued.

On a more pleasant note, three more African-Americans were inducted into the

Hall of Fame. Willie McCovey was enshrined at Cooperstown, New York, in 1986. Billy Williams and former Negro Leaguer, Ray Dandridge, made it in 1987. McCovey made it rather easily, but Williams was ushered in on January 13, 1987, in his sixth year of eligibility. A Chicago Cubs player, Williams was named on 86 percent of the ballots. He had a .290 career batting average, 426 home runs, 1,476 runs batted in, and his streak of 1,117 consecutive games played is the second longest in National League history.

Ray Dandridge's election by the Veterans Committee was especially pleasing since he was one vote short in 1986. He began with the Detroit Stars in 1933, in the Negro Leagues and later played with the Minneapolis Millers. The 5-foot 7-inch, 175-pound third baseman whose nickname was "Squat," might have been called up to the majors in the early 1950s, but a black fellow player named Willie Mays was given the nod instead. Dandridge, from Richmond, Virginia, said his induction was one of the happiest days of his life. Also happy was Bo Jackson, the former Auburn University football Heisman Trophy winner who switched to professional baseball. Jackson was batting about .500 for the Kansas City Royals after his first twenty-eight at-bats in the 1987 season. One of his hits was a broken bat, grand slam home run against the Detroit Tigers.

Basketball continued to lead the major sports in recognizing black managerial talent. On the professional level, Don Chaney was appointed coach of the Los Angeles Clippers and Hall of Famer Elgin Baylor was appointed general manager. K.C. Jones of the Boston Celtics, Lenny Wilkins of the Cleveland Cavaliers, and Bernie Bickerstaff of the Seattle Supersonics continue in their positions as head coaches. In NCAA schools, Bob Wade left Baltimore's Dunbar High School to fill the vacancy created at the University of Maryland when Lefty Driesell was dismissed, after the death of former Maryland player Len Bias. Wade, forty-one, was given a five-year contract. He compiled a 341–25 record at Dunbar High School. He is a Morgan State University alumnus and played professional football with the Baltimore Colts, Washington Redskins, Pittsburgh Steelers, and the Denver Broncos.

At Memphis State University Larry Finch replaced the former white coach Dana Kirk; John Chaney is at Temple University; Clem Haskins is at the University of Minnesota; George Raveling is at the University of Southern California; Walt Hazzard is at UCLA; John Thompson, who was named Coach of the Year for 1986–1987 by United Press International, is at Georgetown University; and Vivian Stringer is at the University of Iowa.

The Harlem Globetrotters basketball team added two women—Lynette Woodard and later Jackie White. Michael Jordan, from the University of North Carolina and now the Chicago Bulls, has dazzled crowds with his uncommon abilities. He is recognized as the most exciting player in the game today and, for 1986–1987, became only the second NBA player in history to score more than 3,000 points in a single season. On November 22, 1986, he set another NBA record of eighteen straight points against the New York Knicks; reminiscent of the sixteen straight points scored against the Knicks by Isiah Thomas in a

1984 playoff game. In balloting for the All-Star Game for the 1986–1987 season, Jordan broke all records with a vote tally of 1,141,733.

Jordan's theatrics have come none too soon, as Julius "Doctor J" Erving retired at the end of the 1986–87 season. Erving's last "lap around the NBA track" was a sentimental journey unlike any seen in modern sports. He was literally showered with gifts and affection from adoring fans. His transition to civilian life was eased by his already close involvement and partial ownership of a large bottling franchise by a major soft drink firm. Erving is going to be sorely missed and fondly remembered by millions for his inimitable feats of body control. He has been an outstanding example and role model for the nation's youth.

At the collegiate level, the 6-foot 3-inch Cheryl Miller of the University of Southern California (USC), has been acclaimed the best female player in the history of the sport. After being named All-America for four years and NCAA Player of the Year three times, she graduated in 1986, with a degree in communications. She led the United States team to gold medal victories in the 1986 World Championships and the Goodwill Games in Moscow that same year. With her in the news was 6-foot 1-inch Clarissa Davis of the University of Texas, who scored 24 points and grabbed fourteen rebounds in her alma mater's win over USC in the 1986 NCAA Finals. Katrina McClain, a 6-foot 2-inch forward at the University of Georgia, may follow Davis with national honors.

At the United States Naval Academy, 7-foot 1-inch David Robinson was the 1986–1987 College Player of the Year, and became the first Navy player to score over 2,000 career points. He did it against East Carolina on January 3, 1987, in a 31-point effort. Ralph Tally of Norfolk State University was the NCAA Division II Player of the Year in 1986. Elvin Hayes, formerly of the University of Houston and the NBA, finally earned his college degree in December 1986. On March 30, 1987, Keith Smart of the Indiana University, made a sixteen-foot jump shot from the corner with five seconds remaining on the clock to seal a 74–73 NCAA Finals victory over Syracuse University.

Two other players in college basketball are worth noting. Wake Forest had Muggsy Bogues, a 5-foot 3-inch—yes, 5-foot 3-inch—senior guard, who while the shortest player in NCAA competition was among the quickest and most elusive. The other is Thomasina Robinson, who at forty-six played on the junior varsity at New York City's Hunter College. According to her, she played just for the sheer fun of it.

In boxing, black America has its first heavyweight champion who is a college graduate. James "Bonecrusher" Smith of Lillington, North Carolina, knocked out Tim Witherspoon on December 12, 1986, to win the WBA title. Smith, who received his degree from Shaw University, subsequently lost to Mike Tyson. Tyson had become the latest in a long line of black heavyweight champions stretching back to Jack Johnson in 1908. Tyson is the youngest ever heavyweight (WBC) winner by virtue of his stunning victory over Trevor Berbick in November 1986. At the time of his win, Tyson was twenty years, four months, and twenty-two days old. Floyd Patterson, who previously held the distinction as the youngest champion, is now the second-youngest, though he remains the first heavyweight champion to win, lose, and regain the title.

Three other epic battles took place since the end of 1984. "Marvelous" Marvin Hagler defeated Thomas "Hitman" Hearns in three of the most exciting rounds of boxing ever seen. The first round of this encounter was three minutes of nonstop, windmill slugging, jabbing, bobbing, and hooking. The consensus was that this initial round was the most thrilling three minutes, since the last round of the "Thrilla in Manila" between Muhammad Ali and Joe Frazier. Hagler retained the undisputed middleweight championship.

Thomas Hearns took his loss to Hagler in stride, gained another ten pounds, and won the WBC Light-heavyweight title by knocking out Dennis Andries. Finally, on April 6, 1987, "The Super Fight" was staged between Hagler and Sugar Ray Leonard. Leonard, who had retired twice in the past, returned and amazed a live Caesar's Palace crowd in Las Vegas, Nevada, and a closed-circuit television audience, with a split-decision win in twelve rounds. Entering this bout, Hagler had career earnings of $25 million, versus $42 million for Leonard. Bob Arum, the promoter, guaranteed Hagler $12 million, and Leonard received a minimum of $11 million.

In some astute maneuvering, Leonard's manager, Mike Trainer, gave up the money edge to Hagler in exchange for a twelve-round limit and thumbless, ten-ounce gloves. Leonard is now the most financially successful boxer in history. In spite of the woeful imbalance of ruined lives and bodies, boxing continues to have a mesmerizing hold on black America. It is the third most-watched sport on television by blacks following professional wrestling and professional basketball.

Professional football kept us glued to our television screens on Sunday afternoons and Monday evenings. The Chicago Bears' 1986 Super Bowl win, spotlighted its hero of the season—William "The Refrigerator" Perry—an ex-Clemson University star who, at 320 pounds, played both offense and defense. Sadly, the incomparable Walter Payton, the game's most prolific runner, did not score in his team's victory. Between seasons the Professional Football Hall of Fame, in 1987, added three blacks to its hallowed pantheon: John Henry Johnson, who played for the San Francisco 49'ers, the Pittsburgh Steelers, and the Houston Oilers; Gene Upshaw, the current president of the NFL Players Association and a former Oakland Raider; and "Mean" Joe Greene, a stalwart on the defensive front line of the Pittsburgh Steelers.

Charlie Joiner, the 5-foot 11-inch, 183-pound wide receiver for the San Diego Chargers, finally retired in 1987 after playing in 239 games. He caught 750 passes for a total of 12,146 yards and 65 touchdowns. This former Grambling University star, whose professional career began in 1969, has become a receivers' coach for the Chargers.

Controversy continued over the lack of a single black head coach in the NFL, at a time when 57 percent of the team rosters are black. As of the beginning of the 1987 season, thirty-eight assistant coaches are black versus fourteen in 1980. Leading candidates for head coaching positions appear to be Jimmy Raye of the Atlanta Falcons and Tony Dungy of the Pittsburgh Steelers. The San Francisco 49'ers have four black assistants. In January 1987, the Atlanta Falcons conducted a wide and rather public search for a head coach, and finally settled on Marion Campbell (white), who had guided a previous Falcons team as head coach, to a 6–19 record in the mid-1970s. Campbell's lifetime professional coaching record was twenty-three wins, forty-eight losses, and one tie.

In the black collegiate ranks, the SWAC and SIAC continued to outpace the CIAA and MEAC in publicity and on-field performance. NCAA Rule 5 (1) (j), better known as Proposition 48, has had a damaging effect on recruitment for these conferences, but public sentiment for action over the possible exploitation of student-athletes is strong. (Rule 5 (1) (j) mandated SAT scores of 700 or better, or ACT scores of 15 or better with a combination of upwardly scaled grade-point-averages of high school athletes who want to become eligible for NCAA varsity competition.)

In predominantly white schools in NCAA Division I, the combined annual spending on varsity football alone is now roughly $1 billion, yet graduation rates for black players remain around 20 percent, within two years of the expiration of their athletic eligibility. For a change, the inattention to the special needs of blacks on white college campuses knows no geographical boundaries. Observers still recall that September 12 evening in 1970, when the University of Alabama was humiliated by the University of Southern California with its black fullback, Sam "Bam" Cunningham. Cunningham scored three times against Alabama Coach Bear Bryant's all-white defensive unit to help his team to a 42–21 victory. Though southern major college football decided for good that night to integrate their athletic teams, black student-athlete graduation rates remain unconscionably low. As for black head coaches at NCAA Division I-A schools, three institutions qualify: Northwestern University with Francis Peay; Ohio University with Cleve Bryant; and the University of Nevada at Las Vegas with Wayne Nunnelly.

Most of the recent interest in track and field has been created by black women. Jackie Joyner-Kersee won the fifty-seventh Sullivan Award in March 1987, presented annually to the nation's top amateur athlete. In the summer of 1986, she set a world record in the heptathlon at the Goodwill Games in Moscow, with 7,148 points, only to better that mark at the United States Olympic Festival in Houston three weeks later with 7,158 points. Wilma Rudolph, forty-six, who in the 1960 Olympic Games won three gold medals, was named head women's track coach at DePauw University. And Dianne Dixon set a new American record in the 400-meter run with fifty-two seconds.

Renaldo Nehemiah, the world record holder in the 110-meter hurdles, returned from a brief career as a wide receiver for the San Francisco 49'ers, to reinstatement as an amateur for track events. The International Amateur Athletic Federation (IAAF) will allow him to run in its sanctioned meets, but the ex-UCLA star Greg Foster shows no sign of letting Nehemiah back in the winners circle. Foster has dominated the 110-meter hurdles since Nehemiah left.

On February 27, 1987, Mike Conley, the

former University of Arkansas jumper, set a new world record in the triple jump at 58-feet 3¼ inches. The twenty-four-year-old Conley's record occurred at the National Indoor Championships at New York City's Madison Square Garden. The track world is astir over a teenager named William Reed who at 6-feet and 175 pounds is the best quarter-miler prospect since Lee Evans. A student at Philadelphia's Central High School, the sixteen-year-old Reed has run the 400-meters in 44.52 seconds. Perhaps he may break Evans' record set at the 1968 Mexico City Olympics.

Outside the Big Five sports, substantial progress was made. In tennis, black players won three more national titles. In July 1986, Martin Blackman became the first black male to win the boys' crown, the United States Tennis Association (USTA) National sixteen-and under singles event at Kalamazoo, Michigan. Blackman defeated Michael Chang 6–4, 6–3 in the finals; the first time in the history of the USTA that two minority athletes met in the championship round of this prestigious event. The 6-foot 2-inch Blackman was born in the Bronx, New York, but grew up in Barbados, where his father is the governor of that nation's central bank. In college play, Otis Smith, III, played in the number one singles slot for UCLA, as did Don Freeman at Rice University in Houston, Texas. Smith—with Dan Nihirney—also won the 1986 USTA National Amateur Doubles title.

In female activities, on November 29, 1986, Jeri Ingram of Silver Spring, Maryland, won the USTA sixteen-and-under indoor doubles (with Carrie Cunningham) title over Amy Novotny and Karen Gallego 4–6, 6–2, 6–2. Less than a month later, she won the National Amateur indoor singles crown in Mt. Vernon, Virginia. Katrina Adams, a student at Northwestern University and a member of the USTA Junior Federation Cup Team, won the doubles title in Bradenton, Florida, on segment two of the USTA Womens' Circuit in July 1986. Iwalani McCalla of California was named the Most Improved Junior for 1986, by the USTA.

In professional play, more history was made on September 21, 1986, when two black women, Zina Garrison and Lori McNeil, met in the finals of the Eckard Open in Tampa, Florida. McNeil prevailed 2–6, 7–5, 6–2. This encounter put two black women into the world's top fifteen ranked players.

On the golf course, Calvin Peete continued to lead the PGA tour in greens in regulation. Jim Thorpe finally made the million-dollar club. The thirty-seven-year old Thorpe won the top prize of $150,000 in the PGA Seiko event in November, 1986, that put him over the million-dollar mark. Thorpe also won the Seiko event in 1985.

In figure skating, the whole world applauded Debi Thomas, who in 1986 won the United States and World titles. This nineteen-year old pre-medical student at Stanford University captivated the entire skating community with her creativity, determination, and athleticism. More often than not, photographs showed her with an anatomy book under one arm and her skates under the other. Though she did not retain her titles in 1987, she was a medalist in the Winter Olympics in 1988.

In swimming, Alabama A&M University continued to be in the news. Its womens team won the National Black College title for the sixth time running in 1987, under coach Fred Wyckoff, who is an Alabama native and graduate of Alabama State University. The Lady Bulldogs' stars are Lori Reid and Tania Carlton.

Black fencers quietly wrote their names in the record books. On March 24, 1987, Columbia University won its ninth NCAA title and Bob Cottingham finished second in the Individual Saber competition. Michael Lofton of New York University, became the first collegian to win four straight NCAA Individual Saber crowns, with his 18–0 victory at Notre Dame University on March 17.

In motor racing, Willie T. Ribbs won the Columbus 500 in November 1986. He continues as the top black driver and still dreams of winning the Indianapolis 500 one day.

Among the nation's black keglers, George Branham III of Arleta, California, became the first to win a Professional Bowlers Association (PBA) event, the $200,000 Brunswick Memorial World Open at Glendale Heights, Illinois. He defeated Mark Roth 195–191, to capture the first prize of $33,260, in January 1987. Branham also won the AC-Delco Classic at Union City, California, over Steve Wunderlich 225–182.

The saddest note concerns Flo Hyman, star of our United States silver medal–winning Volleyball Team at the 1984 Los Angeles Olympics. Hyman died on January 24, 1986, in Matsue, Japan, of complications from marfan's syndrome, a cardiac disorder that particularly affects tall thin people. Hyman, who was 6-foot 5-inches tall and thirty-one years old, had planned to participate in the 1988 Olympics.

Off the fields and courts there were other developments that had a material affect on the future of black athletes. In 1987, the NCAA reported a surplus of $5.8 million, attesting to the drawing power of the large percentage of blacks on varsity teams. The NCAA also reduced the number of football scholarships from thirty to twenty-five, and the number of basketball scholarships from fifteen to thirteen. It did, however, keep the total number of scholarships at ninety-five, and allowed for additional financial aid for needy student-athletes. Part of this new interpretation may have come from the concerns expressed by the University of Maryland president John B. Slaughter. Slaughter, who is black, is also president of the NCAA's President's Commission and is a public advocate of abolishing varsity eligibility for first year student-athletes.

Black colleges have been the most vocal about these new developments. Strapped by smaller stadiums, local cable television—if any—and smaller budgets, they want to be able to compete in NCAA tournaments, but most find it extremely difficult. The negative affect of NCAA Rule 5 (1) (j) alone caused SWAC schools to lose fifty players and the MEAC to lose forty for football. However, the consensus for tighter and stronger minimum academic entrance and eligibility standards remains firm.

Of more interest than any other subject, though, has been the issue of illegal substance abuse, trafficking, and addiction—cocaine in particular—by amateur and professional athletes. Black athletes have been mentioned in nearly every instance that has made the headlines. Among amateur performers the most startling case was that of the late Len Bias of the University of Maryland.

Bias, a 6-foot 8-inch basketball prodigy in the mold of Michael Jordan, died on June 19, 1986, after taking a substantial amount of cocaine. He had been signed to play as a first-round draft choice with the Boston Celtics, and the nation was stunned by his passing. Maryland's president John B. Slaughter accepted the resignation of Charles "Lefty" Driesell as coach and Dick Dull as athletic director. Bias had been dismissed from the University at the time of his death because he had failed or withdrawn from all five of his courses. More than 10,000 students and friends attended a memorial service in his honor at Cole Field House.

In football, Barry Word of the of the University of Virginia and the Atlantic Coast Conference's Player of the Year for 1985, was charged with cocaine trafficking in July 1986. At the University of Tennessee, quarterback Tony Robinson and Kenneth "B.B." Cooper were convicted of cocaine trafficking on November 6, 1986. Both are spending time on a penal farm.

In the professional ranks, black athletes continue to fall prey to dope dealers who induce them to try drugs or sell it, by first offering illegal narcotics for free. In baseball, the most startling revelation was that involving Dwight Gooden, the Cy Young Award winner for the New York Mets. On December 14, 1986, Gooden was jailed for resisting arrest in Tampa, Florida, while driving with friends. His blood alcohol level was found to be .11, just barely over the minimum for citation for driving under

the influence, in Florida. Claiming police harrassment, the Tampa branch of the NAACP asked Attorney General Edwin Meese to investigate. On January 23, 1987, Gooden was sentenced to three years probation by Judge John P. Griffin.

However, on April 1, 1987, the results of a voluntary drug test were released, and they proved positive for Gooden. The shock was similar to that of the death of Len Bias. His agent, James Meadows, arranged for him to enter the Smithers Clinic at New York City's Roosevelt Hospital. Another Cy Young winner, Vida Blue, was also troubled by cocaine problems. On January 21, 1987, Blue signed a one-year $300,000 contract with the Oakland Athletics, only to see that rescinded because his drug test also proved positive. Blue resigned.

In basketball, Lewis Lloyd and Mitchell Wiggins of the Houston Rockets were banned from the NBA on January 17, 1987, for two years, on cocaine charges, joining John Drew and Michael Ray Richardson as the only banned NBA stars. John Lucas of the Milwaukee Bucks has made good on his comeback after drug rehabilitation. He now heads an organization called STAND (Students Taking Action Not Drugs) that assists hospitals and individuals.

Professional boxers have also had their problems with drugs. During 1984 and part of 1985 Tyrell Biggs, the 1984 Olympic heavyweight gold medalist, became a cocaine addict, but luckily overcame the problem. Michael Dokes, the former WBA Heavyweight champion, pleaded guilty on January 16, 1987, to possession of cocaine in Las Vegas, Nevada. Unfortunately, he was rearrested in April 1987, for driving under the influence plus violation of his probation.

In football, Don Rogers age twenty-three, of the Cleveland Browns, died of a cocaine induced heart attack on June 27, 1986, just eight days following the death of Len Bias. Rogers was to have been married the next day. Lawrence Taylor, the game's premier linebacker and member of the Giants roster, admitted his addiction to cocaine for a time in the 1985 season, but rehabilitated himself and had an outstanding season in 1986. This 6-foot 4-inch All-Pro, who attended Lafayette High School in Williamsburg, Virginia, and the University of North Carolina, is considered by some to be football's best player—bar none. Warren McVea, a former running back for the Cincinnati Bengals and the Kansas City Chiefs, was jailed on cocaine charges, in December 1986.

No issue in sports—not even racism—has quite caught the attention of the public like the use of illegal drugs by athletes. The NCAA, the NAIA, and the commissioners of the major team sports have publicly pledged to rid their organizations of the drug menace. As such, more black athletes can be expected to fall victim to false promises and the mistaken idea that a few quick dollars can be innocently made by dealing in drugs, or that cocaine can be used socially and intermittently without penalty or harm.

There were also reports of physical assault by black athletes. Quentin Dailey, who at thirteen lost both of his parents and later left the University of San Francisco because he allegedly attacked a nurse, had a difficult adjustment into the NBA after drug rehabilitation.

On November 26, 1986, Al Wilson, twenty-three, a former wide receiver for UCLA, committed suicide by jumping into the path of oncoming cars on a Los Angeles Freeway, just moments after intentionally crashing his pick-up truck. Friends said he was despondent over not making it into the NFL. Johnny Rodgers, the 1972 Heisman Trophy winner, was jailed on a felony gun charge, in February 1987. Elvin Bethea, the former Dallas Cowboy, received a four-year suspended sentence and two years probation in February 1987, for stealing his mother's life savings of $64,000.

Albert Reese (among others), a tight end at Southern Methodist University (SMU), allegedly and illegally received a free apartment and cash for enrolling. In a situation reminiscent of that at the University of Maryland, SMU president L. Donald Shields resigned on November 21, 1986, and the school later dropped its football program until further notice. Reese's transgressions, however, seem to pale in comparison to those of Texas Governor Bill Clements, who admitted discussing SMU's illegal payments in a Board of Regents meeting. To the amazement of many, Clements reportedly advised SMU athletic authorities to continue making illegal payments in cases of prior agreements, but counseled that no such new agreements be promulgated.

The foregoing are but the latest in a continuing stream of poor judgment and decisions by black athletes. The facts show that the overwhelming majority of them are from what sociologists would term the "underclass." Professor Allen Sack of the University of New Haven found that sixty-seven percent of these athletes think it is acceptable to take under-the-table payments in college, while forty-two percent of upper class whites agreed.[4] Whatever their moral standards, it is clear there will be more of the same among black athletes.

The African-American athletes' rise to prominence has been difficult. The future holds more victories on the playing fields and more misery off it. However, no one can refute the indisputable fact that for 368 years, their trip to fame has been A Hard Road To Glory.

Notes

1. Ted Koppel interview ABC Television "Nightline" with Al Campanis, April 1987.
2. *New York Times,* 15 April 1987.
3. *USA Today,* 16 April 1987.
4. *The Sporting News,* "Headliners," 24 November 1986.

Reference Section

Author's Note

Because of space limitations, the bulk of the reference material relating to athletes' or team performances in college conferences in the period since 1946 will be found in the Reference Section of Volume II.

Baseball

Key to abbreviations
Column heads: G = games, AB = at bats, H = hits, 2B = doubles, 3B = triples, HR = home runs, HR% = home run percentage, R = runs, RBI = runs bated in, BB = bases on balls, SO = strikeouts, SB = stolen bases, BA = batting average, SA = slugging average, G by POS = games by position
Body of table: N = National League, A = American League, C = catcher, 1B = first base, 2B = second base, 3B = third base, SS = shortstop, OF = outfield, DH = designated hitter

Jackie Robinson

JACK ROOSEVELT ROBINSON
B. Jan. 31, 1919, Cairo, Ga.   D. Oct. 24, 1972, Stamford, Conn.
Inducted into the Baseball Hall of Fame 1962.

	G	AB	H	2B	3B	HR	HR %	R	RBI	BB	SO	SB	BA	SA	Pinch Hit AB	Pinch Hit H	G by POS
1946 Montr. (Int.)	124	444	155			3		113	66			29	.349				
1947 BKN N	151	590	175	31	5	12	2.0	125	48	74	36	29	.297	.427	0	0	1B-151
1948	147	574	170	38	8	12	2.1	108	85	57	37	22	.296	.453	2	1	2B-116, 1B-30, 3B-6
1949	156	593	203	38	12	16	2.7	122	124	86	27	37	.342	.528	0	0	2B-156
1950	144	518	170	39	4	14	2.7	99	81	80	24	12	.328	.500	2	1	2B-144
1951	153	548	185	33	7	19	3.5	106	88	79	27	25	.338	.527	3	1	2B-153
1952	149	510	157	17	3	19	3.7	104	75	106	40	24	.308	.465	2	0	2B-146
1953	136	484	159	34	7	12	2.5	109	95	74	30	17	.329	.502	5	1	OF-76, 3B-44, 2B-9, 1B-6, SS-1
1954	124	386	120	22	4	15	3.9	62	59	63	20	7	.311	.505	7	1	OF-64, 3B-50, 2B-4
1955	105	317	81	6	2	8	2.5	51	36	61	18	12	.256	.363	9	1	3B-84, OF-10, 2B-1, 1B-1
1956	117	357	98	15	2	10	2.8	61	43	60	32	12	.275	.412	10	1	3B-72, 2B-22, 1B-9, OF-2
10 yrs.	1382	4877	1518	273	54	137	2.8	947	734	740	291	197	.311	.474	40	7	2B-751, 3B-256, 1B-197, OF-152, SS-1
WORLD SERIES																	
1947 BKN N	7	27	7	2	0	0	0.0	3	3	2	4	2	.259	.333	0	0	1B-7
1949	5	16	3	1	0	0	0.0	2	2	4	2	0	.188	.250	0	0	2B-5
1952	7	23	4	0	0	1	4.3	4	2	7	5	2	.174	.304	0	0	2B-7
1953	6	25	8	2	0	0	0.0	3	2	1	0	1	.320	.400	0	0	OF-6
1955	6	22	4	1	1	0	0.0	5	1	2	1	1	.182	.318	0	0	3B-6
1956	7	24	6	1	0	1	4.2	5	2	5	2	0	.250	.417	0	0	3B-7
6 yrs.	38	137	32	7 8th	1	2	1.5	22 9th	12	21 8th	14	6	.234	.343	0	0	3B-13, 2B-12, 1B-7, OF-6

Roy Campanella

ROY CAMPANELLA
B. Nov. 19, 1921, Philadelphia, Pa.
Inducted into the Baseball Hall of Fame 1969.

	G	AB	H	2B	3B	HR	HR %	R	RBI	BB	SO	SB	BA	SA	Pinch Hit AB	H	G by POS
1946 Nashua (N. Eng.)	113	396	115			13		75	96				.290				
1947 Montr. (Int.)	135	440	120			13		64	75				.273				
1948 St. Paul (Amer. Ass.)	35	123	40			13		31	39				.325				
1948 BKN N	83	279	72	11	3	9	3.2	32	45	36	45	3	.258	.416	4	1	C-78
1949	130	436	125	22	2	22	5.0	65	82	67	36	3	.287	.498	3	1	C-127
1950	126	437	123	19	3	31	7.1	70	89	55	51	1	.281	.551	3	2	C-123
1951	143	505	164	33	1	33	6.5	90	108	53	51	1	.325	.590	5	2	C-140
1952	128	468	126	18	1	22	4.7	73	97	57	59	8	.269	.453	6	1	C-122
1953	144	519	162	26	3	41	7.9	103	142	67	58	4	.312	.611	9	5	C-140
1954	111	397	82	14	3	19	4.8	43	51	42	49	1	.207	.401	1	0	C-111
1955	123	446	142	20	1	32	7.2	81	107	56	41	2	.318	.583	3	2	C-121
1956	124	388	85	6	1	20	5.2	39	73	66	61	1	.219	.394	7	0	C-121
1957	103	330	80	9	0	13	3.9	31	62	34	50	1	.242	.388	4	1	C-100
10 yrs.	1215	4205	1161	178	18	242	5.8	627	856	533	501	25	.276	.500	45	15	C-1183
WORLD SERIES																	
1949 BKN N	5	15	4	1	0	1	6.7	2	2	3	1	0	.267	.533	0	0	C-5
1952	7	28	6	0	0	0	0.0	0	1	1	6	0	.214	.214	0	0	C-7
1953	6	22	6	0	0	1	4.5	6	2	2	3	0	.273	.409	0	0	C-6
1955	7	27	7	3	0	2	7.4	4	4	3	3	0	.259	.593	0	0	C-7
1956	7	22	4	1	0	0	0.0	2	3	3	7	0	.182	.227	0	0	C-7
5 yrs.	32	114	27	5	0	4	3.5	14	12	12	20	0	.237	.386	0	0	C-32

Monte Irvin

MONFORD MERRILL IRVIN
B. Feb. 25, 1919, Columbia, Ala.
Inducted into the Baseball Hall of Fame 1973.

	G	AB	H	2B	3B	HR	HR %	R	RBI	BB	SO	SB	BA	SA	Pinch Hit AB	H	G by POS
1949 Jersey C. (Int.)	63	203	76			9		55	52				.373				
1950	18	51	26			10		28	33				.510				
1949 NY N	36	76	17	3	2	0	0.0	7	7	17	11	0	.224	.316	13	0	OF-10, 3B-5, 1B-5
1950	110	374	112	19	5	15	4.0	61	66	52	41	3	.299	.497	4	1	1B-59, OF-49, 3B-1
1951	151	558	174	19	11	24	4.3	94	121	89	44	12	.312	.514	1	1	OF-112, 1B-39
1952	46	126	39	2	1	4	3.2	10	21	10	11	0	.310	.437	14	2	OF-32
1953	124	444	146	21	5	21	4.7	72	97	55	34	2	.329	.541	8	2	OF-113
1954	135	432	113	13	3	19	4.4	62	64	70	23	7	.262	.438	9	3	OF-128, 3B-1, 1B-1
1955	51	150	38	7	1	1	0.7	16	17	17	15	3	.253	.333	6	1	OF-45
1956 CHI N	111	339	92	13	3	15	4.4	44	50	41	41	1	.271	.460	18	7	OF-96
8 yrs	764	2499	731	97	31	99	4.0	366	443	351	220	28	.293	.475	73	17	OF-585, 1B-104, 3B-7
WORLD SERIES																	
1951 NY N	6	24	11	0	1	0	0.0	4	2	2	1	2	.458	.542	0	0	OF-6
1954	4	9	2	1	0	0	0.0	1	2	0	3	0	.222	.333	0	0	OF-4
2 yrs.	10	33	13	1	1	0	0.0	5	4	2	4	2	.394	.485	0	0	OF-10

Willie Mays

WILLIE HOWARD MAYS, JR. (Say Hey)
B. May 6, 1931, Westfield, Ala.
Inducted into the Baseball Hall of Fame 1979.

	G	AB	H	2B	3B	HR	HR %	R	RBI	BB	SO	SB	BA	SA	Pinch Hit AB	Pinch Hit H	G by POS
1950 Trenton (Int.)	81	305	108			4		50	55				.353				
1951 Mnpolis (Amer. Ass.)	35	149	71			8		38	30				.477				
1951 NY N	121	464	127	22	5	20	4.3	59	68	56	60	7	.274	.472	0	0	OF-121
1952	34	127	30	2	4	4	3.1	17	23	16	17	4	.236	.409	0	0	OF-34
1954	151	565	195	33	13	41	7.3	119	110	66	57	8	.345	.667	0	0	OF-151
1955	152	580	185	18	13	51	8.8	123	127	79	60	24	.319	.659	0	0	OF-152
1956	152	578	171	27	8	36	6.2	101	84	68	65	40	.296	.557	0	0	OF-152
1957	152	585	195	26	20	35	6.0	112	97	76	62	38	.333	.626	1	0	OF-150
1958 SF N	152	600	208	33	11	29	4.8	121	96	78	56	31	.347	.583	2	0	OF-151
1959	151	575	180	43	5	34	5.9	125	104	65	58	27	.313	.583	4	2	OF-147
1960	153	595	190	29	12	29	4.9	107	103	61	70	25	.319	.555	1	0	OF-152
1961	154	572	176	32	3	40	7.0	129	123	81	77	18	.308	.584	1	1	OF-153
1962	162	621	189	36	5	49	7.9	130	141	78	85	18	.304	.615	1	0	OF-161
1963	157	596	187	32	7	38	6.4	115	103	66	83	8	.314	.582	2	0	OF-157, SS-1
1964	157	578	171	21	9	47	8.1	121	111	82	72	19	.296	.607	3	1	OF-155, SS-1, 3B-1
1965	157	558	177	21	3	52	9.3	118	112	76	71	9	.317	.645	6	0	OF-151
1966	152	552	159	29	4	37	6.7	99	103	70	81	5	.288	.556	4	1	OF-150
1967	141	486	128	22	2	22	4.5	83	70	51	92	6	.263	.453	11	1	OF-134
1968	148	498	144	20	5	23	4.6	84	79	67	81	12	.289	.488	3	2	OF-142, 1B-1
1969	117	403	114	17	3	13	3.2	64	58	49	71	6	.283	.437	12	3	OF-109, 1B-1
1970	139	478	139	15	2	28	5.9	94	83	79	90	5	.291	.506	10	2	OF-129, 1B-5
1971	136	417	113	24	5	18	4.3	82	61	112	123	23	.271	.482	15	4	OF-84, 1B-48
1972 2 teams SF N (19G — .184) NY N (69G — 2.67)																	
" total	88	244	61	11	1	8	3.3	35	22	60	48	4	.250	.402	11	4	OF-63, 1B-11
1973 NY N	66	209	44	10	0	6	2.9	24	25	27	47	1	.211	.344	7	2	OF-45, 1B-17
22 yrs.	2992	10881	3283	523	140	660	6.1	2062	1903	1463	1526	338	.302	.557	94	23	OF-2843, 1B-84, S: 3B-1
	6th	6th	9th		3rd			5th	7th					10th			

LEAGUE CHAMPIONSHIP SERIES

	G	AB	H	2B	3B	HR	HR %	R	RBI	BB	SO	SB	BA	SA	Pinch Hit AB	Pinch Hit H	G by POS
1971 SF N	4	15	4	2	0	1	6.7	2	3	3	3	1	.267	.600	0	0	OF-4
1973 NY N	1	3	1	0	0	0	0.0	1	1	0	0	0	.333	.333	1	1	OF-1
2 yrs.	5	18	5	2	0	1	5.6	3	4	3	3	1	.278	.556	1	1	OF-5

WORLD SERIES

	G	AB	H	2B	3B	HR	HR %	R	RBI	BB	SO	SB	BA	SA	Pinch Hit AB	Pinch Hit H	G by POS
1951 NY N	6	22	4	0	0	0	0.0	1	1	2	2	0	.182	.182	0	0	OF-6
1954	4	14	4	1	0	0	0.0	4	3	4	1	1	.286	.357	0	0	OF-4
1962 SF N	7	28	7	2	0	0	0.0	3	1	1	5	1	.250	.321	0	0	OF-7
1973 NY N	3	7	2	0	0	0	0.0	1	1	0	1	0	.286	.286	1	0	OF-2
4 yrs.	20	71	17	3	0	0	0.0	9	6	7	9	2	.239	.282	1	0	OF-19

Hank Aaron

HENRY LOUIS AARON
Brother of Tommie Aaron.
B. Feb. 5, 1934, Mobile, Ala.
Inducted into the Baseball Hall of Fame 1982.

	G	AB	H	2B	3B	HR	HR %	R	RBI	BB	SO	SB	BA	SA	Pinch Hit AB	Pinch Hit H	G by POS
1952 E. Claire (North)	87	345	116			9		79	61				.336				
1953 J'ville (Sally)	137	574	208			22		115	125				.362				
1954 MIL N	122	468	131	27	6	13	2.8	58	69	28	39	2	.280	.447	6	1	OF–116
1955	153	602	189	37	9	27	4.5	105	106	49	61	3	.314	.540	2	1	OF–126, 2B–27
1956	153	609	200	34	14	26	4.3	106	92	37	54	2	.328	.558	1	0	OF–152
1957	151	615	198	27	6	44	7.2	118	132	57	58	1	.322	.600	0	0	OF–150
1958	153	601	196	34	4	30	5.0	109	95	59	49	4	.326	.546	0	0	OF–153
1959	154	629	223	46	7	39	6.2	116	123	51	54	8	.355	.636	0	0	OF–152, 3B–5
1960	153	590	172	20	11	40	6.8	102	126	60	63	16	.292	.566	0	0	OF–153, 2B–2
1961	155	603	197	39	10	34	5.6	115	120	56	64	21	.327	.594	1	0	OF–154, 3B–2
1962	156	592	191	28	6	45	7.6	127	128	66	73	15	.323	.618	2	1	OF–153, 1B–1
1963	161	631	201	29	4	44	7.0	121	130	78	94	31	.319	.586	0	0	OF–161
1964	145	570	187	30	2	24	4.2	103	95	62	46	22	.328	.514	1	0	OF–139, 2B–11
1965	150	570	181	40	1	32	5.6	109	89	60	81	24	.318	.560	2	1	OF–148
1966 ATL N	158	603	168	23	1	44	7.3	117	127	76	96	21	.279	.539	1	1	OF–158, 2B-2
1967	155	600	184	37	3	39	6.5	113	109	63	97	17	.307	.573	3	0	OF–152, 2B–1
1968	160	606	174	33	4	29	4.8	84	86	64	62	28	.287	.498	2	0	OF–151, 1B–14
1969	147	547	164	30	3	44	8.0	100	97	87	47	9	.300	607	0	0	OF–144, 1B–4
1970	150	516	154	26	1	38	7.4	103	118	74	63	9	.298	574	9	1	OF–125, 1B–11
1971	139	495	162	22	3	47	9.5	95	118	71	58	1	.327	.669	8	2	1B–71, OF–60
1972	129	449	119	10	0	34	7.6	75	77	92	55	4	.265	.514	5	2	1B–109, OF–15
1973	120	392	118	12	1	40	10.2	84	96	68	51	1	.301	.643	11	3	OF–105
1974	112	340	91	16	0	20	5.9	47	69	39	29	1	.268	.491	17	1	OF–89
1975 MIL A	137	465	109	16	2	12	2.6	45	60	70	51	0	.234	.355	5	1	DH–128, OF–3
1976	85	271	62	8	0	10	3.7	22	35	35	38	0	.229	.369	10	2	DH–74, OF–1
23 yrs.	3298 3rd	12364 2nd	3771 3rd	624 8th	98	755 1st	6.1	2174 2nd	2297 1st	1402	1383	240	.305	.555	86	17	OF–2760, 1B–210, DH–202, 2B–43, 3B–7

LEAGUE CHAMPIONSHIP SERIES

	G	AB	H	2B	3B	HR	HR %	R	RBI	BB	SO	SB	BA	SA	Pinch Hit AB	Pinch Hit H	G by POS
1969 ATL N	3	14	5	2	0	3	21.4	3	7	0	1	0	.357	1.143	0	0	OF–3

WORLD SERIES

	G	AB	H	2B	3B	HR	HR %	R	RBI	BB	SO	SB	BA	SA	Pinch Hit AB	Pinch Hit H	G by POS
1957 MIL N	7	28	11	0	1	3	10.7	5	7	1	6	0	.393	.786	0	0	OF–7
1958	7	27	9	2	0	0	0.0	3	2	4	6	0	.333	.407	0	0	OF–7
2 yrs.	14	55	20	2	1	3	5.5	8	9	5	12	0	.364	.600 10th		0 4th	0	OF–14

Lou Brock

LOUIS CLARK BROCK
B. June 18, 1939, El Dorado, Ark.
Inducted into the Baseball Hall of Fame 1985.

	G	AB	H	2B	3B	HR	HR %	R	RBI	BB	SO	SB	BA	SA	Pinch Hit AB	H	G by POS
1961 CHI N	4	11	1	0	0	0	0.0	1	0	1	3	0	.091	.091	0	0	OF-3
1962	123	434	114	24	7	9	2.1	73	35	35	96	16	.263	.412	15	2	OF-106
1963	148	547	141	19	11	9	1.6	79	37	31	122	24	.258	.382	10	2	OF-140
1964 2 teams	CHI N (52G — .251)		STL N (103G — .348)														
" total	155	634	200	30	11	14	2.2	111	58	40	127	43	.315	.464	1	0	OF-154
1965 STL N	155	631	182	35	8	16	2.5	107	69	45	116	63	.288	.445	1	0	OF-153
1966	156	643	183	24	12	15	2.3	94	46	31	134	74	.285	.429	1	0	OF-154
1967	159	689	206	32	12	21	3.0	113	76	24	109	52	.299	.472	4	0	OF-157
1968	159	660	184	46	14	6	0.9	92	51	46	124	62	.279	.418	3	1	OF-156
1969	157	655	195	33	10	12	1.8	97	47	50	115	53	.298	.434	2	1	OF-157
1970	155	664	202	29	5	13	2.0	114	57	60	99	51	.304	.422	3	2	OF-152
1971	157	640	200	37	7	7	1.1	126	61	76	107	64	.313	.425	2	1	OF-157
1972	153	621	193	26	8	3	0.5	81	42	47	93	63	.311	.393	4	1	OF-149
1973	160	650	193	29	8	7	1.1	110	63	71	112	70	.297	.398	1	0	OF-159
1974	153	635	194	25	7	3	0.5	105	48	61	88	118	.306	.381	3	1	OF-152
1975	136	528	163	27	6	3	0.6	78	47	38	64	56	.309	.400	8	3	OF-128
1976	133	498	150	24	5	4	0.8	73	67	35	75	56	.301	.394	12	3	OF-123
1977	141	489	133	22	6	2	0.4	69	46	30	74	35	.272	.354	18	7	OF-130
1978	92	298	66	9	0	0	0.0	31	12	17	29	17	.221	.252	15	4	OF-79
1979	120	405	123	15	4	5	1.2	56	38	23	43	21	.304	.398	22	5	OF-98
19 yrs.	2616	10332 9th	3023	486	141	149	1.4	1610	900	761	1730 5th	938 1st	.293	.410	125	33	OF-2507
WORLD SERIES																	
1964 STL N	7	30	9	2	0	1	3.3	2	5	0	3	0	.300	.467	0	0	OF-7
1967	7	29	12	2	1	1	3.4	8	3	2	3	7	.414	.655	0	0	OF-7
1968	7	28	13	3	1	2	7.1	6	5	3	4	7	.464	.857	0	0	OF-7
3 yrs.	21	87	34 8th	7	2	4	4.6	16	13	5	10	14 1st	.391 2nd	.655 5th	0	0	OF-21

Reference Section

Frank Robinson

FRANK ROBINSON
B. Aug. 31, 1935, Beaumont, Tex.
Manager 1975-77, 1981-84
Inducted into the Baseball Hall of Fame 1982.

	G	AB	H	2B	3B	HR	HR %	R	RBI	BB	SO	SB	BA	SA	Pinch Hit AB	Pinch Hit H	G by POS
1953 Ogden (Pion.)	72	270	94			17		70	83				.348				
1954 Tulsa (Tex.)	8	30	8			0		4	1				.267				
1954 Columbia (Sally)	132	491	165			25		112	110				.336				
1955 Columbia (Sally)	80	243	64			12		50	52				.263				
1956 CIN N	152	572	166	27	6	38	6.6	122	83	64	95	8	.290	.558	0	0	OF-152
1957	150	611	197	29	5	29	4.7	97	75	44	92	10	.322	.529	0	0	OF-136, 1B-24
1958	148	554	149	25	6	31	5.6	90	83	62	80	10	.269	.504	5	0	OF-138, 3B-11
1959	146	540	168	31	4	36	6.7	106	125	69	93	18	.311	.583	0	0	1B-125, OF-40
1960	139	464	138	33	6	31	6.7	86	83	82	67	13	.297	.595	10	5	1B-78, OF-51, 3B-3
1961	153	545	176	32	7	37	6.8	117	124	71	64	22	.323	.611	4	2	OF-150, 3B-1
1962	162	609	208	51	2	39	6.4	134	136	76	62	18	.342	.624	0	0	OF-161
1963	140	482	125	19	3	21	4.4	79	91	81	69	26	.259	.442	2	2	OF-139, 1B-1
1964	156	568	174	38	6	29	5.1	103	96	79	67	23	.306	.548	0	0	OF-156
1965	156	582	172	33	5	33	5.7	109	113	70	100	13	.296	.540	1	1	OF-155
1966 BAL A	155	576	182	34	2	49	8.5	122	122	87	90	8	.316	.637	1	1	OF-151, 1B-3
1967	129	479	149	23	7	30	6.3	83	94	71	84	2	.311	.576	0	0	OF-126, 1B-2
1968	130	421	113	27	1	15	3.6	69	52	73	84	11	.268	.444	12	4	OF-117, 1B-3
1969	148	539	166	19	5	32	5.9	111	100	88	62	9	.308	.540	3	2	OF-134, 1B-19
1970	132	471	144	24	1	25	5.3	88	78	69	70	2	.306	.520	6	3	OF-120, 1B-7
1971	133	455	128	16	2	28	6.2	82	99	72	62	3	.281	.510	8	0	OF-92, 1B-37
1972 LA N	103	342	86	6	1	19	5.6	41	59	55	76	2	.251	.442	5	0	OF-95
1973 CAL A	147	534	142	29	0	30	5.6	85	97	82	93	1	.266	.489	2	1	DH-127, OF-17
1974 2 teams CAL A (129G — .251) CLE A (15G — .200)																	
" total	144	477	117	27	3	22	4.6	81	68	85	95	5	.245	.453	6	0	DH-134, 1B-4, OF-1
1975 CLE A	49	118	28	5	0	9	7.6	19	24	29	15	0	.237	.508	6	2	DH-42
1976	36	67	15	0	0	3	4.5	5	10	11	12	0	.224	.358	16	5	DH-18, 1B-2, OF-1
21 yrs.	2808	10006	2943	528	72	586 4th	5.9	1829 10th	1812	1420	1532	204	.294	.537	87	28	OF-2132, DH-321, 1B-305, 3B-13

LEAGUE CHAMPIONSHIP SERIES

	G	AB	H	2B	3B	HR	HR %	R	RBI	BB	SO	SB	BA	SA	Pinch Hit AB	Pinch Hit H	G by POS
1969 BAL A	3	12	4	2	0	1	8.3	1	2	3	3	0	.333	.750	0	0	OF-3
1970	3	10	2	0	0	1	10.0	3	2	5	2	0	.200	.500	0	0	OF-3
1971	3	12	1	1	0	0	0.0	2	1	1	4	0	.083	.167	0	0	OF-3
3 yrs.	9	34	7	3	0	2	5.9	6	5	9	9	0	.206	.471	0	0	OF-9

WORLD SERIES

	G	AB	H	2B	3B	HR	HR %	R	RBI	BB	SO	SB	BA	SA	Pinch Hit AB	Pinch Hit H	G by POS
1961 CIN N	5	15	3	2	0	1	6.7	3	4	3	4	0	.200	.533	0	0	OF-5
1966 BAL A	4	14	4	0	1	2	14.3	4	3	2	3	0	.286	.857	0	0	OF-4
1969	5	16	3	0	0	1	6.3	2	1	4	3	0	.188	.375	0	0	OF-5
1970	5	22	6	0	0	2	9.1	5	4	0	5	0	.273	.545	0	0	OF-5
1971	7	25	7	0	0	2	8.0	5	2	2	8	0	.280	.520	0	0	OF-7
5 yrs.	26	92	23	2	1	8 7th	8.7 3rd	19	14	.11	23 10th	0	.250	.554	0	0	OF-26

Frank Robinson as Manager

	G	W	L	Pct	Standing	
1975 CLE A	159	79	80	.497	4	
1976	159	81	78	.509	4	
1977	57	26	31	.456	6	5
1981 SF N	59	27	32	.458	5	(1st)
1981	52	29	23	.558	3	(2nd)
1982	162	87	75	.537	3	
1983	162	79	83	.488	5	
1984	106	42	64	.396	6	6
7 yrs.	916	450	466	.491		

Ernie Banks

ERNEST BANKS
B. Jan. 31, 1931, Dallas, Tex.
Inducted into the Baseball Hall of Fame 1977.

	G	AB	H	2B	3B	HR	HR %	R	RBI	BB	SO	SB	BA	SA	Pinch Hit AB	Pinch Hit H	G by POS
1953 CHI N	10	35	11	1	1	2	5.7	3	6	4	5	0	.314	.571	0	0	SS-10
1954	154	593	163	19	7	19	3.2	70	79	40	50	6	.275	.427	0	0	SS-154
1955	154	596	176	29	9	44	7.4	98	117	45	72	9	.295	.596	0	0	SS-154
1956	139	538	160	25	8	28	5.2	82	85	52	62	6	.297	.530	0	0	SS-139
1957	156	594	169	34	6	43	7.2	113	102	70	85	8	.285	.579	0	0	SS-100, 3B-58
1958	154	617	193	23	11	47	7.6	119	129	52	87	4	.313	.614	0	0	SS-154
1959	155	589	179	25	6	45	7.6	97	143	64	72	2	.304	.596	1	0	SS-154
1960	156	597	162	32	7	41	6.9	94	117	71	69	1	.271	.554	0	0	SS-156
1961	138	511	142	22	4	29	5.7	75	80	54	75	1	.278	.507	4	1	SS-104, OF-23, 1B-7
1962	154	610	164	20	6	37	6.1	87	104	30	71	5	.269	.503	4	2	1B-149, 3B-3
1963	130	432	98	20	1	18	4.2	41	64	39	73	0	.227	.403	5	1	1B-125
1964	157	591	156	29	6	23	3.9	67	95	36	84	1	.264	.450	0	0	1B-157
1965	163	612	162	25	3	28	4.6	79	106	55	64	3	.265	.453	2	1	1B-162
1966	141	511	139	23	7	15	2.9	52	75	29	59	0	.272	.432	8	1	1B-130, 3B-8
1967	151	573	158	26	4	23	4.0	68	95	27	93	2	.276	.455	5	1	1B-147
1968	150	552	136	27	0	32	5.8	71	83	27	67	2	.246	.469	4	1	1B-147
1969	155	565	143	19	2	23	4.1	60	106	42	101	0	.253	.416	2	2	1B-153
1970	72	222	56	6	2	12	5.4	25	44	20	33	0	.252	.459	9	2	1B-62
1971	39	83	16	2	0	3	3.6	4	6	6	14	0	.193	.325	18	2	1B-20
19 yrs.	2528	9421	2583	407	90	512	5.4 10th	1305	1636	763	1236	50	.274	.500	62	14	1B-1259, SS-1125, 3B-69, OF-23

Reggie Jackson

REGINALD MARTINEZ JACKSON (Mr. October)
B. May 18, 1946, Wyncote, Pa.

	G	AB	H	2B	3B	HR	HR %	R	RBI	BB	SO	SB	BA	SA	Pinch Hit AB	H	G by POS
1967 KC A	35	118	21	4	4	1	0.8	13	6	10	46	1	.178	.305	2	0	OF-34
1968 OAK A	154	553	138	13	6	29	5.2	82	74	50	171	14	.250	.452	1	0	OF-151
1969	152	549	151	36	3	47	8.6	123	118	114	142	13	.275	.608	2	1	OF-150
1970	149	426	101	21	2	23	5.4	57	66	75	135	26	.237	.458	7	2	OF-142
1971	150	567	157	29	3	32	5.6	87	80	63	161	16	.277	.508	5	1	OF-145
1972	135	499	132	25	2	25	5.0	72	75	59	125	9	.265	.473	0	0	OF-135
1973	151	539	158	28	2	32	5.9	99	117	76	111	22	.293	.531	4	0	OF-145, DH-3
1974	148	506	146	25	1	29	5.7	90	93	86	105	25	.289	.514	3	0	OF-127, DH-19
1975	157	593	150	39	3	36	6.1	91	104	67	133	17	.253	.511	1	0	OF-147, DH-9
1976 BAL A	134	498	138	27	2	27	5.4	84	91	54	108	28	.277	.502	2	1	OF-121, DH-11
1977 NY A	146	525	150	39	2	32	6.1	93	110	74	129	17	.286	.550	3	0	OF-127, DH-18
1978	139	511	140	13	5	27	5.3	82	97	58	133	14	.274	.477	1	1	OF-104, DH-35
1979	131	465	138	24	2	29	6.2	78	89	65	107	9	.297	.544	3	1	OF-125, DH-11
1980	143	514	154	22	4	41	8.0	94	111	83	122	1	.300	.597	3	1	OF-94, DH-46
1981	94	334	79	17	1	15	4.5	33	54	46	82	0	.237	.428	1	1	OF-61, DH-33
1982 CAL A	153	530	146	17	1	39	7.4	92	101	85	156	4	.275	.532	11	6	OF-139, DH-5
1983	116	397	77	14	1	14	3.5	43	49	52	140	0	.194	.340	10	2	DH-62, OF-47
1984	143	525	117	17	2	25	4.8	67	81	55	141	8	.223	.406	7	1	DH-134, OF-3
18 yrs.	2430	8649	2293	410	46	503	5.8	1380	1516	1172 1st	2247	224	.265	.498	66	18	OF-1997, DH-386

DIVISIONAL PLAYOFF SERIES

	G	AB	H	2B	3B	HR	HR %	R	RBI	BB	SO	SB	BA	SA	Pinch Hit AB	H	G by POS
1981 NY A	5	20	6	0	0	2	10.0	4	4	1	5	0	.300	.600	0	0	OF-5

LEAGUE CHAMPIONSHIP SERIES

	G	AB	H	2B	3B	HR	HR %	R	RBI	BB	SO	SB	BA	SA	Pinch Hit AB	H	G by POS
1971 OAK A	3	12	4	1	0	2	16.7	2	2	0	1	0	.333	.917	0	0	OF-3
1972	5	18	5	1	0	0	0.0	1	2	1	6	2	.278	.333	0	0	OF-5
1973	5	21	3	0	0	0	0.0	0	0	0	6	0	.143	.143	0	0	OF-5
1974	4	12	2	1	0	0	0.0	0	1	5	2	0	.167	.250	0	0	OF-1
1975	3	12	5	0	0	1	8.3	1	3	0	2	0	.417	.667	0	0	OF-3
1977 NY A	5	16	2	0	0	0	0.0	1	1	2	2	1	.125	.125	1	1	OF-4
1978	4	13	6	1	0	2	15.4	5	6	3	4	0	.462	1.000	0	0	OF-1
1980	3	11	3	1	0	0	0.0	1	0	1	4	0	.273	.364	0	0	OF-3
1981	2	4	0	0	0	0	0.0	1	1	1	0	1	.000	.000	0	0	OF-2
1982 CAL A	5	18	2	0	0	1	5.6	2	2	2	7	0	.111	.278	0	0	OF-5
10 yrs.	39	137	32	5	0	6	4.4	14	18	15	34	4	.234	.401	1	1	OF-32

WORLD SERIES

	G	AB	H	2B	3B	HR	HR %	R	RBI	BB	SO	SB	BA	SA	Pinch Hit AB	H	G by POS
1973 OAK A	7	29	9	3	1	1	3.4	3	6	2	7	0	.310	.586	0	0	OF-7
1974	5	14	4	1	0	1	7.1	3	1	5	3	1	.286	.571	0	0	OF-5
1977 NY A	6	20	9	1	0	5	25.0	10	8	3	4	0	.450	1.250	0	0	OF-6
1978	6	23	9	1	0	2	8.7	2	8	3	7	0	.391	.696	0	0	DH-6
1981	3	12	4	1	0	1	8.3	3	1	2	3	0	.333	.667	0	0	OF-3
5 yrs.	27	98	35	7 8th	1	10 5th	10.2 2nd	21 10th	24 8th	15	24 8th	1	.357	.755 8th	0 1st	0	OF-21, DH-6

Key to abbreviations (pitchers)
Column heads: W = wins, L = losses, PCT = percentage, ERA = earned run average, G = games pitched in, GS = games started, CG = complete games, IP = innings pitched, H = hits allowed, BB = bases on balls allowed, SO = strikeouts, ShO = shutouts, SV = saves, AB = at bats, H (under Batting) = hits, HR = home runs, BA = batting average
Body of table: N = National League, A = American League

Satchel Paige

LEROY ROBERT PAIGE
B. July 7, 1906, Mobile, Ala.   D. June 8, 1982, Kansas City, Mo.
Inducted into the Baseball Hall of Fame 1971.

	W	L	PCT	ERA	G	GS	CG	IP	H	BB	SO	ShO	Relief Pitching W	L	SV	Batting AB	H	HR	BA
1948 CLE E	6	1	.857	2.48	21	7	3	72.2	61	25	45	2	2	1	1	23	2	0	.087
1949	4	7	.364	3.04	31	5	1	83	70	33	54	0	3	4	5	16	1	0	.063
1951 STL A	3	4	.429	4.79	23	3	0	62	67	29	48	0	3	2	5	16	2	0	.125
1952	12	10	.545	3.07	46	6	3	138	116	57	91	2	8	8	10	39	5	0	.128
1953	3	9	.250	3.53	57	4	0	117.1	114	39	51	0	2	8	11	29	2	0	.069
1965 KC A	0	0	—	0.00	1	1	0	3	1	0	1	0	0	0	0	1	0	0	.000
6 yrs.	28	31	.475	3.29	179	26	7	476	429	183	290	4	18	23	32	124	12	0	.097
WORLD SERIES 1943 CLE A	0	0	—	0.00	1	0	0	.2	0	0	0	0	0	0	0	0	0	0	—

Reference Section

Vida Blue

VIDA ROCHELLE BLUE
B. July 28, 1949, Mansfield, La.

	W	L	PCT	ERA	G	GS	CG	IP	H	BB	SO	ShO	Relief Pitching			Batting			BA
													W	L	SV	AB	H	HR	
1969 OAK A	1	1	.500	6.21	12	4	0	42	49	18	24	0	0	0	1				
1970	2	0	1.000	2.08	6	6	2	39	20	12	35	2	0	0	0				
1971	24	8	.750	1.82	39	39	24	312	209	88	301	8	0	0	0				
1972	6	10	.375	2.80	25	23	5	151.1	117	43	111	4	0	1	0				
1973	20	9	.690	3.28	37	37	13	263.2	214	105	158	4	0	0	0				
1974	17	15	.531	3.26	40	40	12	282	246	98	174	1	0	0	0				
1975	22	11	.667	3.01	39	38	13	278	243	99	189	2	0	0	1	0	0	0	—
1976	18	13	.581	2.36	37	37	20	298	268	63	166	6	0	0	0	0	0	0	—
1977	14	19	.???	3.83	38	38	16	230	284	86	157	1	0	0	0	1	0	0	.000
1978 SF N	18	10	.643	2.79	35	35	9	258	233	70	171	4	0	0	0	79	6	1	.076
1979	14	14	.500	5.01	34	34	10	237	246	111	138	0	0	0	0	83	10	1	.120
1980	14	10	.583	2.97	31	31	10	224	202	61	129	3	0	0	0	68	5	0	.074
1981	8	6	.571	2.45	18	18	1	125	97	54	63	0	0	0	0	35	7	0	.200
1982 KC A	13	12	.520	3.78	31	31	6	181	163	80	103	2	0	0	0	0	0	0	—
1983	0	5	.000	6.01	19	14	1	85.1	96	35	53	0	0	0	0	0	0	0	—
15 yrs.	191	143	.572	3.21	441	425	142	3056.1	2687	1028	1972	37	0	1	2	439	45	3	.103
LEAGUE CHAMPIONSHIP SERIES																			
1971 OAK A	0	1	.000	6.43	1	1	0	7	7	2	8	0	0	0	0	3	0	0	.000
1972	0	0	—	0.00	4	0	0	5.1	4	1	5	0	0	0	1	1	0	0	.000
1973	0	1	.000	10.29	2	2	0	7	8	5	3	0	0	0	0	0	0	0	—
1974	1	0	1.000	0.00	1	1	1	9	2	0	7	1	0	0	0	0	0	0	—
1975	0	0	—	9.00	1	1	0	3	6	0	2	0	0	0	0	0	0	0	—
5 yrs.	1	2	.333	4.60	9	5	1	31.1	27	8	25	1	0	0	1	4	0	0	.000
WORLD SERIES																			
1972 OAK A	0	1	.000	4.15	4	1	0	8.2	8	5	5	0	0	0	1	1	0	0	.000
1973	0	1	.000	4.91	2	2	0	11	10	3	8	0	0	0	0	4	0	0	.000
1974	0	1	.000	3.29	2	2	0	13.2	10	7	9	0	0	0	0	4	0	0	.000
3 yrs.	0	3	.000	4.05	8	5	0	33.1	28	15	22	0	0	0	1	9	0	0	.000

Bob Gibson

ROBERT GIBSON (Hoot)
B. Nov. 9, 1935, Omaha, Neb.
Inducted into the Baseball Hall of Fame 1981.

	W	L	PCT	ERA	G	GS	CG	IP	H	BB	SO	ShO	Relief Pitching			Batting			BA
													W	L	SV	AB	H	HR	
1959 STL N	3	5	.375	3.33	13	9	2	75.2	77	39	48	1	1	0	0	26	3	0	.115
1960	3	6	.333	5.61	27	12	2	86.2	97	48	69	0	1	0	0	28	5	0	.179
1961	13	12	.520	3.24	35	27	10	211.1	186	119	166	2	0	1	1	66	13	1	.197
1962	15	13	.536	2.85	32	30	15	233.2	174	95	208	5	1	0	1	76	20	2	.263
1963	18	9	.667	3.39	36	33	14	254.2	224	96	204	2	1	0	0	87	18	3	.207
1964	19	12	.613	3.01	40	36	17	287.1	250	86	245	2	1	1	1	96	15	0	.156
1965	20	12	.625	3.07	38	36	20	299	243	103	270	6	0	0	1	104	25	5	.240
1966	21	12	.636	2.44	35	35	20	280.1	210	78	225	5	0	0	0	100	20	1	.200
1967	13	7	.650	2.98	24	24	10	175.1	151	40	147	2	0	0	0	60	8	0	.133
1968	22	9	.710	1.12	34	34	28	304.2	198	62	268	13	0	0	0	94	16	0	.170
1969	20	13	.606	2.18	35	35	28	314	251	95	269	4	0	0	0	118	29	1	.246
1970	23	7	.767	3.12	34	34	23	294	262	88	274	3	0	0	0	109	33	2	.303
1971	16	13	.552	3.04	31	31	20	246	215	76	185	5	0	0	0	87	15	2	.172
1972	19	11	.633	2.46	34	34	23	278	226	88	208	4	0	0	0	103	20	5	.194
1973	12	10	.545	2.77	25	25	13	195	159	57	142	1	0	0	0	65	12	2	.185
1974	11	13	.458	3.83	33	33	9	240	236	104	129	1	0	0	0	81	17	0	.210
1975	3	10	.231	5.04	22	14	1	109	120	62	60	0	1	2	2	28	5	0	.179
17 yrs.	251	174	.591	2.91	528	482	255	3884.2	3279	1336	3117 8th	56	6	4	6	1328	274	24	.206
WORLD SERIES																		
1964 STL N	2	1	.667	3.00	3	3	2	27	23	8	31	0	0	0	0	9	2	0	.222
1967	3	0	1.000	1.00	3	3	3	27	14	5	26	1	0	0	0	11	1	1	.091
1968	2	1	.667	1.67	3	3	3	27	18	4	35	1	0	0	0	8	1	1	.125
3 yrs.	7 2nd	2	.778	1.89	9	9 6th	8 3rd	81 6th	55 9th	17	92 2nd	2 4th	0	0	0	28	4	2	.143

PERCENTAGE OF AFRICAN-AMERICAN PLAYERS ON MAJOR LEAGUE BASEBALL TEAMS
1960–1971

Team	Average, 1960–71	1971	1970	1969	1968	1967	1966	1965	1964	1963	1962	1961	1960
NATIONAL LEAGUE													
Atlanta	27	40	40	32	28	28	24	32	16	24	20	16	24
Chicago	19	12	20	20	24	24	28	16	20	16	20	16	16
Cincinnati	25	32	28	36	28	32	24	24	16	20	20	20	20
Houston	24	36	36	32	28	28	32	16	12	12	12	—	—
Los Angeles	22	24	24	16	20	12	32	24	20	24	20	24	20
New York	18	16	16	20	16	12	16	24	16	20	20	—	—
Philadelphia	26	20	24	28	24	28	20	32	20	20	24	32	28
Pittsburgh	35	48	44	36	44	56	44	32	28	32	28	16	16
San Francisco	28	24	20	28	32	32	32	32	32	28	28	20	28
St. Louis	28	32	44	36	36	40	24	24	16	24	20	16	24
Montreal	20	8	20	32	—	—	—	—	—	—	—	—	—
San Diego	24	16	24	32	—	—	—	—	—	—	—	—	—
Average	25	26	28	29	28	29	28	26	20	22	21	20	22
AMERICAN LEAGUE													
Baltimore	17	36	36	36	24	12	12	8	12	8	8	4	12
Boston	14	12	12	12	24	24	24	12	12	12	8	8	4
California	17	24	20	20	16	16	20	24	16	16	8	8	—
Chicago	18	28	20	24	16	20	20	20	20	12	12	20	8
Cleveland	21	20	16	24	40	32	20	16	16	28	12	20	12
Detroit	18	16	20	28	16	20	24	20	20	16	20	16	4
Minnesota	22	24	32	24	24	32	24	24	20	16	16	12	16
New York	17	20	20	28	20	20	20	16	16	12	12	12	8
Oakland	21	24	28	24	12	24	24	16	24	24	20	8	—
Washington	17	28	24	16	24	16	16	12	16	16	8	16	—
Kansas City	24	16	28	28	—	—	—	—	—	—	—	—	—
Milwaukee	19	20	12	24	—	—	—	—	—	—	—	—	—
Average	18	22	22	24	22	22	20	17	17	16	12	12	9

TOP AFRICAN-AMERICAN BATTERS
1969–1984

Batters	Years	Games	.300 + Yrs.	20 + HRs	75 + RBIs
Dusty Baker	14	1,845	3	6	6
Don Baylor	14	1,770	1	7	7
Bobby Bonds	15	1,849	1	10	9
Cecil Cooper	14	1,545	9	5	6
Andre Dawson	9	1,174	3	5	5
George Foster	16	1,761	5	9	9
George Hendrick	14	1,727	4	6	8
Reggie Jackson	18	2,430	1	15	13
Lee May	18	2,071	0	11	11
John Mayberry	15	1,620	0	8	6
Hal McRae	16	1,842	6	2	5
Joe Morgan	22	2,649	2	4	5
Eddie Murray	8	1,206	4	8	8
Al Oliver	17	2,272	11	2	11
Amos Otis	17	1,998	2	2	7
Dave Parker	12	1,457	5	4	7
Jim Rice	11	1,493	6	9	9
George Scott	14	2,034	2	6	9
Ken Singleton	15	2,082	4	5	7
Reggie Smith	17	1,987	7	8	6
Willie Stargell	21	2,360	3	15	12
Andre Thornton	11	1,285	0	5	5
Bob Watson	19	1,832	6	1	6
Dave Winfield	12	1,655	3	7	9
Jim Wynn	15	1,849	1	10	9

To qualify, batters must fall into two or more of the following categories:
1. 15 or more seasons
2. 5 seasons or more of .300 or more in batting average
3. 5 seasons or more of 20 or more home runs
4. 5 seasons or more of 75 or more runs batted in

TOP AFRICAN-AMERICAN PITCHERS
1969–1984

Pitchers	Yrs.	W	L	Pct.	ERA	CG	SHO	SO	Walks
Jim Bibby	12	111	101	.524	3.76	56	19	1,079	723
Vida Blue	15	191	143	.572	3.21	142	37	1,972	1,028
Ray Burris	13	93	114	.449	4.04	41	10	942	667
Dock Ellis	12	138	119	.536	3.45	71	14	1,136	674
Jim Grant	14	145	119	.549	3.63	89	18	1,267	849
Grant Jackson	18	86	75	.534	3.46	16	5	889	511
Rudy May	16	152	156	.494	3.46	87	24	1,760	958
Lynn McGlothen	11	86	93	.480	3.98	41	13	939	572
Mike Norris	9	57	59	.491	3.91	52	7	620	490
John Odom	13	84	85	.497	3.70	40	15	857	788
J.R. Richard	10	107	71	.601	3.15	76	19	1,493	770
Don Wilson	9	104	92	.532	3.15	78	20	1,283	640

To qualify, pitchers must fall into two or more of the following categories:
1. 10 or more seasons
2. 40 or more complete games
3. an earned run average of 3.99 or lower
4. a .500 or more winning percentage

TOP AFRICAN-AMERICAN BASE STEALERS
1969–1984

Player	Years	Stolen Bases	Average/Season
Bobby Bonds	14	461	32.9
Rickey Henderson	6	493	82.2
Rudy Law	3	185	61.6
Ron LeFlore	9	455	50.6
Dave Lopes	13	483	37.2
Willie McGee	3	106	35.3
Joe Morgan	22	489	22.0
Bill North	11	395	35.9
Tim Raines	6	321	53.5
Gary Redus	3	98	32.6
Gene Richards	8	247	30.9
Lonnie Smith	7	221	31.6
Ozzie Smith	7	241	34.4
Alan Wiggins	4	171	42.8
Bump Wills	6	196	32.6
Mookie Wilson	5	189	37.8
Willie Wilson	9	393	43.6

To qualify, a base stealer must fall into one of the two categories below:
1. an average of 30 or more steals per season, or
2. 400 or more career steals

CATEGORICAL COMPARISONS FOR STOLEN-BASE RECORD-HOLDERS

Name	AB	H	TSB	CS	2B	3B	HO	SR
Ty Cobb (1915)	563	208	96	38	74	18	4	71.6%
Maury Wills (1962)	695	208	104	13	86	16	2	88.9%
Lou Brock (1974)	635	194	118	33	112	6	0	78.1%
Rickey Henderson (1982)	536	143	130	42	95	33	2	75.6%

AB = at-bats; H = hits; TSB = total stolen bases; CS = caught stealing; 2B = stole 2nd base; 3B = stole 3rd base; HO = stole home; SR = stolen base success rate.

AFRICAN-AMERICAN BASEBALL NOTABLES

Cy Young Award Winners

National League

1956	Don Newcombe	Brooklyn Dodgers
1968	Bob Gibson	St. Louis Cardinals
1970	Bob Gibson	St. Louis Cardinals

American League

1971	Vida Blue	Oakland A's

Triple Crown Winner

American League

1966	Frank Robinson	Baltimore Orioles

Record-holders for Consecutive Games Played

Rank	Player	Games
4th	Billy Williams	1,117
12th	Ernie Banks	717
26th	Vada Pinson	508

Most Valuable Players

National League

1949	Jackie Robinson	Brooklyn Dodgers	Second Base
1951	Roy Campanella	Brooklyn Dodgers	Catcher
1953	Roy Campanella	Brooklyn Dodgers	Catcher
1954	Willie Mays	New York Giants	Centerfielder
1955	Roy Campanella	Brooklyn Dodgers	Catcher
1956	Don Newcombe	Brooklyn Dodgers	Pitcher
1957	Henry Aaron	Milwaukee Braves	Outfielder
1958	Ernie Banks	Chicago Cubs	Shortstop
1959	Ernie Banks	Chicago Cubs	Shortstop
1961	Frank Robinson	Cincinnati Reds	Outfielder
1962	Maury Wills	Los Angeles Dodgers	Shortstop
1965	Willie Mays	San Francisco Giants	Centerfielder
1968	Bob Gibson	St.Louis Cardinals	Pitcher
1969	Willie McCovey	San Francisco Giants	First Base
1975	Joe Morgan	Cincinnati Reds	Second Base
1976	Joe Morgan	Cincinnati Reds	Second Base
1977	George Foster	Cincinnati Reds	Outfielder
1978	Dave Parker	Pittsburgh Pirates	Outfielder
1979	Willie Stargell	Pittsburgh Pirates	First Base

American League

1963	Elston Howard	New York Yankees	Catcher
1966	Frank Robinson	Baltimore Orioles	Outfielder
1971	Vida Blue	Oakland A's	Pitcher
1972	Richie Allen	Chicago White Sox	First Base
1973	Reggie Jackson	Oakland A's	Outfielder
1978	Jim Rice	Boston Red Sox	Outfielder

Rookie of the Year

National League

1947	Jackie Robinson	Brooklyn Dodgers	Second Base
1949	Don Newcombe	Brooklyn Dodgers	Pitcher
1950	Sam Jethroe	Boston Braves	Outfielder
1951	Willie Mays	New York Giants	Outfielder
1952	Joe Black	Brooklyn Dodgers	Pitcher
1953	Junior Gilliam	Brooklyn Dodgers	Second Base
1956	Frank Robinson	Cincinnati Reds	Outfielder
1959	Willie McCovey	San Francisco Giants	First Base
1961	Billy Williams	Chicago Cubs	Outfielder
1964	Richie Allen	Philadelphia Phillies	Third Base
1971	Earl Williams	Atlanta Braves	Catcher
1973	Gary Matthews	San Francisco Giants	Outfielder
1974	Bake McBride	St. Louis Cardinals	Outfielder
1977	Andre Dawson	Montreal Expos	Outfielder
1983	Darryl Strawberry	New York Mets	Outfielder
1984	Dwight Gooden	New York Mets	Pitcher

American League

1966	Tommie Agee	Chicago White Sox	Outfielder
1971	Chris Chambliss	Cleveland Indians	First Base
1973	Al Bumbry	Baltimore Orioles	Outfielder
1977	Eddie Murray	Baltimore Orioles	First Base
1978	Lou Whitaker	Detroit Tigers	Second Base
1984	Alvin Davis	Seattle Mariners	First Base

Basketball

Key to abbreviations:

NCAA = National Collegiate Athletic Association, NBA = National Basketball Association, G. = games, Min. = minutes, FGA = field goal attempts, FGM = field goals made, Pct. = percentage, Reb. = rebounds, Ast. = assists, PF = personal fouls, Disq. = disqualifications, Pts. = points, Avg. = average, W. = wins, L. = losses, Pos. = position of finish

AFRICAN-AMERICAN COLLEGE BASKETBALL
PLAYER OF THE YEAR

1959-1965 U.S. Basketball Writer's Association
1966-1984 Associated Press

Year	Name	Position	College	Year	Name	Position	College
1959	Oscar Robertson	Guard	University of Cincinnati	1975	David Thompson	Forward	N.C. State
1960	Oscar Robertson	Guard	University of Cincinnati	1976	Scott May	Forward	Indiana
1964	Walt Hazzard	Guard	UCLA	1977	Marques Johnson	Forward	UCLA
1966	Cazzie Russell	Forward	Michigan	1978	Alfred "Butch" Lee	Guard	Marquette
1967	Lew Alcindor	Center	UCLA	1980	Mark Aguirre	Forward	DePaul
1968	Elvin Hayes	Forward	Houston	1981	Ralph Sampson	Center	Virginia
1969	Lew Alcindor	Center	UCLA	1982	Ralph Sampson	Center	Virginia
1971	Austin Carr	Guard	Notre Dame	1983	Ralph Sampson	Center	Virginia
1974	David Thompson	Forward	N.C. State	1984	Michael Jordan	Guard	North Carolina

BLACK CONSENSUS
ALL-AMERICA BASKETBALL SELECTIONS

1953-1984

1953 Walt Dukes, Seton Hall
1955 Bill Russell, San Francisco
      Si Green, Duquesne
1956 Bill Russell, USF
      Si Green, Duquesne
1957 Wilt Chamberlain, Kansas

1958 Bob Boozer, Kansas State
      Elgin Baylor, Seattle
      Wilt Chamberlain, Kansas
      Guy Rodgers, Temple
1959 Bob Boozer, Kansas State
      Oscar Robertson, Cinn.

1960 Oscar Robertson, Cinn.
1961 Chet Walker, Bradley
1962 Billy McGill, Utah
      Chet Walker, Bradley
1963 Jerry Harkness, Loyola (Ill)
      Tom Thacker, Cinn.
1964 Dave Stallworth, Kansas
      Walt Hazzard, UCLA
1965 Cazzie Russell, Michigan
1966 Dave Bing, Syracuse
      Cazzie Russell, Michigan
      Jim Walker, Providence
1967 Lew Alcindor, UCLA
      Elvin Hayes, Houston
      Jim Walker, Providence
      Clem Haskins, W. Kentucky
1968 Wes Unseld, Louisville
      Elvin Hayes, Houston
      Lew Alcindor, UCLA
1969 Lew Alcindor, UCLA
      Spencer Haywood, Detroit
      Calvin Murphy, Niagara
1970 Bob Lanier, St. Bonaventure
      Calvin Murphy, Niagara
1971 Austin Carr, Notre Dame
      Sidney Wicks, UCLA
      Artis Gilmore, Jacksonville
      Dean Meminger, Marquette
      Jim McDaniels, W. Kentucky
1972 Dwight Lamar, SW Louisiana
      Ed Ratleff, Long Beach State
      Bob McAdoo, UNC
      Jim Chones, Marquette
      Henry Bibby, UCLA
1973 Ed Ratleff, Long Beach State
      Dwight Lamar, SW Louisiana
      David Thompson, NC State
      Keith Wilkes, UCLA
1974 Keith Wilkes, UCLA
      John Shumate, Notre Dame
      David Thompson, NC State
      Marvin Barnes, Providence
1975 David Thompson, NC State

      Adrian Dantley, Notre Dame
      Scott May, Indiana
      John Lucas, Maryland
1976 Scott May, Indiana
      Richard Washington, UCLA
      John Lucas, Maryland
      Adrian Dantley, Notre Dame
1977 Otis Birdsong, Houston
      Marques Johnson, UCLA
      Rickey Green, Michigan
      Phil Ford, UNC
      Bernard King, Tennessee
1978 Phil Ford, UNC
      Butch Lee, Marquette
      David Greenwood, UCLA
      Mychal Thompson, Minnesota
1979 David Greenwood, UCLA
      Earvin "Magic" Johnson, Michigan State
      Sidney Moncreif, Arkansas
1980 Mark Aguirre, DePaul
      Michael Brooks, LaSalle
      Joe Barry Carroll, Purdue
      Darrell Griffith, Louisville
1981 Mark Aguirre, DePaul
      Steve Johnson, Oregon State
      Ralph Sampson, Virginia
      Isiah Thomas, Indiana
1982 Terry Cummings, DePaul
      Quintin Dailey, San Francisco
      Eric Floyd, Georgetown
      Ralph Sampson, Virginia
      James Worthy, UNC
1983 Dale Ellis, Tennessee
      Pat Ewing, Georgetown
      Michael Jordan, UNC
      Sam Perkins, UNC
      Ralph Sampson, Virginia
      Waymon Tisdale, Oklahoma
      Keith Lee, Memphis State
1984 Waymon Tisdale, Oklahoma
      Sam Perkins, UNC
      Pat Ewing, Georgetown
      Akeem Olajuwon, Houston
      Michael Jordan, UNC

MEN'S BASKETBALL AFRICAN-AMERICAN JOHN WOODEN AWARD WINNERS

1977	Marques Johnson	UCLA	1982	Ralph Sampson	University of Virginia
1978	Phil Ford	North Carolina	1983	Ralph Sampson	University of Virginia
1980	Darrell Griffith	Louisville			

WOMEN'S COLLEGE BASKETBALL AFRICAN-AMERICAN ALL-AMERICAS, KODAC-WBCA, 1975–1985

1975
Lusia Harris, Delta State

1976
Lusia Harris, Delta State
Pearl Worrell, Wayland Baptist

1977
Lusia Harris, Delta State
Charlotte Lewis, Illinois State
Patricia Roberts, Tennessee

1978
Althea Gwynn, Queens
Lynette Woodard, Kansas

1979
Susan Taylor, Valdosta State
Franci Washington, Ohio State
Rosie Walker, Stephen F. Austin

1980
Pam Kelly, Louisiana Tech
Rosie Walker, Stephen F. Austin
Lynette Woodard, Kansas

1981
Pam Kelly, Louisiana Tech
Valerie Walker, Cheyney State
Lynette Woodard, Kansas

1982
Janet Harris, Georgia
Pam Kelly, Louisiana Tech

Barbara Kennedy, Clemson
Valerie Still, Kentucky
Angela Turner, Louisiana Tech
Valerie Walker, Cheyney State

1983
Priscilla Gary, Kansas State
Janice Lawrence, Louisiana Tech
Paula McGee, Southern California
Cheryl Miller, Southern California
LaTaunya Pollard, Long Beach State
Valerie Still, Kentucky
Joyce Walker, Louisiana State

1984
Tresa Brown, North Carolina
Janet Harris, Georgia
Becky Jackson, Auburn
Yolanda Laney, Cheyney State
Janice Lawrence, Louisiana Tech
Pam McGee, Southern California
Cheryl Miller, Southern California
Annette Smith, Texas
Marilyn Stephens, Temple
Joyce Walker, Louisiana State

1985
Medina Dixon, Old Dominion
Anucha Browne, Northwestern
Pam Gant, Louisiana Tech
Sheila Collins, Tennessee
Teresa Edwards, Georgia

BLACK COLLEGE WOMEN'S NCAA
DIVISION II ALL-AMERICAS
(BASKETBALL)

1982–Jackie White, Tuskegee

1983–Paris McWhirter, Virginia Union

       Barvenia Wooten, Virginia Union

1984–Veta Williams, Virginia Union

BLACK COLLEGE NATIONAL BASKETBALL
CHAMPIONSHIPS

	School		Coach
1957	Tennessee State (men)	NAIA	John McLendon
1958	Tennessee State (men)	NAIA	John McLendon
1959	Tennessee State (men)	NAIA	John McLendon
1961	Grambling (men)	NAIA	Fred Hobdy
1962	Prairie View (men)	NAIA	Leroy Moore
1965	Central State (men)	NAIA	William Lucas
1967	Winston-Salem (men)	NCAA II	Big House Gaines
1968	Central State (men)	NAIA	William Lucas
1974	Morgan State (men)	NCAA II	Nat Frazier
1975	LeMoyne-Owen (men)	NCAA III	Jerry Johnson
1976	Coppin State (men)	NAIA	John Bates
1977	Texas Southern (men)	NAIA	Robert Moreland
1978	Cheyney State (men)	NCAA II	John Chaney
1979	S.C. State (women)	AIAW II	Willie Simon
1980	Virginia Union (men)	NCAA II	Dave Robbins
1982	University of The District of Columbia (men)	NCAA II	Will Jones
1983	Virginia Union (women)	NCAA II	Louis Hearn

Final-Four Tournament Appearances

NAIA Men		Finish
1956	Texas Southern	2nd
1958	Texas Southern	3rd
1960	Tennessee State	3rd
1963	Grambling	3rd
1966	Grambling	3rd
	Norfolk State	4th
1969	Elizabeth City	4th
	Maryland State	2nd*
1973	Maryland Eastern Shore	2nd*
1974	Alcorn State	2nd
1975	Alcorn State	3rd
1980	Alabama State	2nd
1982	Hampton Institute	3rd

*Same school

NAIA Women		
1981	Texas Southern	2nd
1984	Dillard	3rd

NCAA Men Div. II		
1984	St. Augustine's	2nd

NCAA Women Div. II		
1982	Tuskegee Institute	2nd
1984	Virginia Union	2nd

JOHN McLENDON'S CAREER COACHING RECORD

College	W	L	Pct.	Titles, Years
North Carolina College (now North Carolina Central University), 1941–1952	246	60	.815	CIAA, 1941, 1942, 1944, 1947, 1949, 1951; Black Champions 1950
Hampton Institute, 1953–1954	31	20	.608	
Tennessee State A&I University, 1955–1959	144	23	.862	NAIA Champions 1957, 1958, 1959; 1958 NAIA Coach of the Year
Kentucky State College, 1963–1966	51	30		
Cleveland State University, 1967–1969	27	41		
Professional				
Cleveland Pipers (semi-pro) National Industrial League, 1959–1961	72	32	.692	1961 AAU Champions; 1961 Tournament Playoff Champions
Cleveland Pipers American Basketball League	27	20	.574	1961 Eastern Division Professional Champions
Denver Nuggets, 1969	9	19	.321	

WINNINGEST ACTIVE DIVISION II MEN'S BASKETBALL COACHES (By Victories)

(Minimum 5 years as a head coach; includes record at 4-year colleges only.)

Name	School	Won	Name	School	Won
1. Clarence Gaines	Winston-Salem	769	4. Oliver Jones	Albany State (Ga.)	231
2. Charles Christian	Norfolk State	244	5. Dave Robbins	Virginia Union	208
3. Robert Moore	Johnson C. Smith	236			

WINNINGEST DIVISION I MEN'S BASKETBALL COACH ALL-TIME (By Percentage)

(Minimum 10 head coaching seasons in Division I)

Coach	College coached, tenure	Yrs.	Won	Lost	Pct.
John Thompson	Georgetown, 1973–	15	350	120	.745

AFRICAN-AMERICAN BASKETBALL COACHES WHO WON AT LEAST 500 GAMES THROUGH 1987, REGARDLESS OF CLASSIFICATION OR ASSOCIATION, AT 4-YEAR COLLEGES

Coach (alma mater)—Colleges coached, tenure	Yrs.	Won–Lost	Pct.
1. Clarence "Bighouse" Gaines (Morgan State, 1945)—Winston-Salem 1947–	41	769–354	.685
2. Ed Adams (Tuskegee, 1933)—NC Central, 1935–1936; Tuskegee, 1937–1949; Texas Southern, 1950–1958	24	645–153	.808
3. Fred Hobdy (Grambling, 1949)—Grambling, 1957–1986	30	571–287	.666
4. Jerry Johnson (Fayetteville State, 1951)—LeMoyne-Owen, 1959–	29	544–235	.698
5. John McLendon, Jr. (Kansas, 1936)—NC Central 1941–1952; Hampton Inst., 1953–1954; Tennessee State, 1955–1959; Kentucky, 1964–1966; Cleveland State, 1967–1969	25	523–165	.760
6. Ed Martin (North Carolina A&T, 1951)—South Carolina, 1956–1958; Tennessee State, 1969–1985	30	501–253	.664
7. Robert Vaughn (Virginia State, 1948)—Elizabeth City State, 1952–1986	34	501–363	.580

AFRICAN-AMERICANS ON U.S. OLYMPIC BASKETBALL TEAMS

Men's Team

1956	K.C. Jones
	Bill Russell
	Carl Cain

1960	Walt Bellamy
	Bob Boozer
	Oscar Robertson

1964	Jim Barnes
	Joe Caldwell
	Walt Hazzard
	Luke Jackson
	George Wilson

1968	Jo Jo White
	Spencer Haywood
	Charlie Scott
	James King
	Calvin Fowles

1972	Tom Henderson
	Mike Bantom
	Dwight Jones
	Jim Brewer
	Ed Ratleff
	James Forbes

1976	Phil Ford
	Steve Sheppard
	Walter Davis
	Quinn Buckner
	Adrian Dantley
	Kenny Carr
	Scott May
	Phil Hubbard

1984	Patrick Ewing
	Michael Jordan
	Waymon Tisdale
	Alvin Robertson
	Sam Perkins
	Leon Wood
	Vern Fleming

Women's Team

1976	Lusia Harris
	Gail Marquis
	Charlotte Lewis
	Patricia Roberts

1984	Cheryl Miller
	Lynette Woodard
	Janice Lawrence
	Pam McGee
	Teresa Edwards
	Cathy Boswell

TOP AFRICAN-AMERICANS IN THE NATIONAL BASKETBALL ASSOCIATION
(Through 1984)

Scoring

Player	Pts.	OR	Player	Pts.	OR
1. Kareem Abdul-Jabbar	33,262	1	16. Earl Monroe	17,454	23
2. Wilt Chamberlain	31,419	2	17. Moses Malone	16,577	25
3. Elvin Hayes	27,313	3	18. Nate Archibald	16,481	26
4. Oscar Robertson	26,710	4	19. Randy Smith	16,262	28
5. Elgin Baylor	23,149	7	20. Julius Erving	16,019	29
6. Hal Greer	21,586	8	21. World B. Free	15,711	32
7. Walt Bellamy	20,941	9	22. Adrian Dantley	15,669	33
8. George Gervin	19,383	11	23. Walt Frazier	15,581	34
9. Bob Lanier	19,248	13	24. Bob Dandridge	15,530	35
10. Chet Walker	18,831	15	25. Sam Jones	15,411	36
11. Bob McAdoo	18,493	16	26. Dick Barnett	15,358	37
12. Dave Bing	18,327	18	27. John Drew	15,291	38
13. Calvin Murphy	17,949	19	28. Spencer Haywood	14,592	42
14. Lou Hudson	17,940	20	29. Jamaal Wilkes	14,569	43
15. Len Wilkens	17,772	21	30. Bill Russell	14,522	44

Pts. = points   OR = overall ranking

Rebounds

Player	Rbds.	OR	Player	Rbds.	OR
1. Wilt Chamberlain	23,924	1	5. Nate Thurmond	14,464	5
2. Bill Russell	21,620	2	6. Walt Bellamy	14,241	6
3. Elvin Hayes	16,279	3	7. Wes Unseld	13,769	7
4. Kareem Abdul-Jabbar	15,627	4	8. Paul Silas	12,357	10

Rbds. = rebounds

Most Games Played

Player	GP	OR	Player	GP	OR
1. Elvin Hayes	1,303	1	5. Len Wilkens	1,077	6
2. Paul Silas	1,254	3	6. Johnny Green	1,057	8
3. Kareem Abdul-Jabbar	1,249	4	7. Leroy Ellis	1,048	10
4. Hal Greer	1,122	5			

GP = games played

Most Field Goals

Player	FG	OR	Player	FG	OR
1. Kareem Abdul-Jabbar	13,729	1	5. Elgin Baylor	8,693	7
2. Wilt Chamberlain	12,681	2	6. Hal Greer	8,504	8
3. Elvin Hayes	10,976	3	7. Walt Bellamy	7,914	9
4. Oscar Robertson	9,508	5	8. Bob Lanier	7,761	10

FG = field goals

Most Minutes Played

Player	Min.	OR		Player	Min.	OR
1. Elvin Hayes	50,000	1		5. Bill Russell	40,726	6
2. Kareem Abdul-Jabbar	48,373	2		6. Hal Greer	39,788	7
3. Wilt Chamberlain	47,859	3		7. Walt Bellamy	38,940	8
4. Oscar Robertson	43,886	5		8. Len Wilkens	38,064	9

Min. = total minutes played

Career Scoring Average

Player	Avr.	OR		Player	Avr.	OR
1. Wilt Chamberlain	30.1	1		5. Adrian Dantley	26.1	7
2. Elgin Baylor	27.4	2		6. Oscar Robertson	25.7	8
3. George Gervin	27.3	3		7. Moses Malone	23.9	10
4. Kareem Abdul-Jabbar	26.6	4				

Avr. = average points scored per game

Highest Field Goal Percentage

Player	Pct.	OR		Player	Pct.	OR
1. Artis Gilmore	.599	1		5. Buck Williams	.557	5
2. Darryl Dawkins	.567	2		6. Bill Cartwright	.557	6
3. Kareem Abdul-Jabbar	.562	3		7. Adrian Dantley	.548	9
4. Cedric Maxwell	.559	4		8. Earvin Johnson	.545	10

Pct. = percentage

Highest Free Throw Percentage

Player	Pct.	OR		Player	Pct.	OR
1. Calvin Murphy	.892	2		3. James Silas	.852	9
2. Fred Brown	.858	7		4. Flynn Robinson	.849	10

Most Free Throws Made

Player	FT	OR		Player	FT	OR
1. Oscar Robertson	7,694	1		4. Elgin Baylor	5,763	7
2. Wilt Chamberlain	6,957	5		5. Len Wilkens	5,394	8
3. Kareem Abdul-Jabbar	5,804	6		6. Elvin Hayes	5,356	10

FT = free throws

Most Assists

Player	Assists	OR		Player	Assists	OR
1. Oscar Robertson	9,887	1		5. Norm Nixon	5,471	8
2. Len Wilkens	7,211	2		6. Dave Bing	5,397	9
3. Guy Rodgers	6,917	4		7. Kevin Porter	5,314	10
4. Nate Archibald	6,476	5				

Most Steals

Player	Stls.	OR		Player	Stls.	OR
1. Gus Williams	1,525	1		5. Quinn Buckner	1,297	5
2. Randy Smith	1,403	2		6. Maurice Cheeks	1,283	6
3. M. Ray Richardson	1,338	3		7. Calvin Murphy	1,165	7
4. Julius Erving	1,319	4		8. Fred Brown	1,149	10

Stls. = steals

Most Blocked Shots

Player	Blk.	OR		Player	Blk.	OR
1. Kareem Abdul-Jabbar	2,785	1		6. Robert Parish	1,320	6
2. George Johnson	2,045	2		7. Harvey Catching	1,227	7
3. Tree Rollins	1,844	3		8. Elmore Smith	1,183	8
4. Elvin Hayes	1,771	4		9. Caldwell Jones	1,168	9
5. Artis Gilmore	1,514	5		10. Sam Lacey	1,160	10

Blk. = blocked shots

Most Personal Fouls

Player	F	OR		Player	F	OR
1. Elvin Hayes	4,193	1		5. Sam Lacey	3,473	7
2. Hal Greer	3,855	2		6. Bill Bridges	3,375	8
3. Kareem Abdul-Jabbar	3,752	3		7. Len Wilkens	3,285	9
4. Walt Bellamy	3,536	5				

F = fouls

TOP AFRICAN-AMERICANS IN THE NATIONAL BASKETBALL ASSOCIATION AND AMERICAN BASKETBALL ASSOCIATION COMBINED

Scoring Average

Player	Avr.	OR		Player	Avr.	OR
1. Wilt Chamberlain	30.1	1		5. George Gervin	25.8	7
2. Elgin Baylor	27.4	2		6. Oscar Robertson	25.7	8
3. Kareem Abdul-Jabbar	26.6	4		7. Julius Erving	25.0	9
4. Adrian Dantley	26.1	6				

All-Time Scoring

Player	Pts.	OR		Player	Pts.	OR
1. Kareem Abdul-Jabbar	33,262	1		6. George Gervin	25,270	9
2. Wilt Chamberlain	31,419	2		7. Elgin Baylor	23,149	11
3. Julius Erving	27,681	3		8. Artis Gilmore	22,588	12
4. Elvin Hayes	27,313	5		9. Hal Greer	21,586	13
5. Oscar Robertson	26,710	6		10. Walt Bellamy	20,941	14

Most Field Goals

Player	FG	OR	Player	FG	OR
1. Kareem Abdul-Jabbar	13,729	1	4. Julius Erving	10,897	4
2. Wilt Chamberlain	12,681	2	5. George Gervin	9,849	7
3. Elvin Hayes	10,976	3	6. Oscar Robertson	9,508	9

Highest Free Throw Percentage

Player	Pct.	OR	Player	Pct.	OR
1. Calvin Murphy	.892	2	3. Fred Brown	.858	8
2. Mack Calvin	.863	6	4. James Silas	.855	9

Most Minutes Played

Player	Min.	OR	Player	Min.	OR
1. Elvin Hayes	50,000	1	5. Artis Gilmore	41,441	7
2. Kareem Abdul-Jabbar	48,373	2	6. Julius Erving	40,835	8
3. Wilt Chamberlain	47,859	3	7. Bill Russell	40,726	9
4. Oscar Robertson	43,886	5	8. Hal Greer	39,788	10

PROFESSIONAL BASKETBALL
HALL OF FAMERS

PERFORMER   YEAR INDUCTED

Players

Elgin Baylor	1976
Wilt Chamberlain	1978
Charles Cooper	1976
Hal Greer	1981
Sam Jones	1983
Willis Reed	1981
Oscar Robertson	1979
Bill Russell	1974
Nate Thurmond	1984
Walter Frazier	1986
Earl Monroe	1986

Coaches

Clarence "Bighouse" Gaines	1981

Teams

New York Renaissance	1963

Contributors

John McLendon	1978

ELGIN GAY BAYLOR

Born September 16, 1934 at Washington, D.C.
High Schools–Washington, D.C., Phelps Vocational (Fr.-Jr.) and Spingarn (Sr.).
Colleges–The College of Idaho, Caldwell, Idaho, and Seattle University, Seattle, Wash.
Inducted into the Basketball Hall of Fame, 1976
Chosen to the NBA 35th Anniversary All-Time Team, 1980
Chosen the Most Outstanding Player in the 1958 NCAA Tournament

Collegiate Record

College of Idaho

Year	G	Min.	FGA	FGM	Pct.	FTA	FTM	Pct.	Reb.	Pts.	Avg.
54-55	26	—	651	332	.510	232	150	.647	492	814	31.3

Seattle

Year	G.	Min.	FGA	FGM	Pct.	FTA	FTM	Pct.	Reb.	Pts.	Avg.
55-56				Did Not Play–Transfer Student							
56-57	25	—	555	271	.488	251	201	.801	508	743	29.7
57-58	29	—	697	353	.506	308	237	.769	559	943	32.5
Totals	54	—	1252	624	.498	559	438	.784	1067	1686	31.2
College Totals	80	—	1903	956	.502	791	588	.743	1559	2500	31.3

NOTE: 1954-55 rebound figures are for 24 games. Baylor played for Westside Ford, an AAU team in Seattle, during 1955-56 season (averaged 34 points per game).

NBA Regular Season Record

Sea.–Team	G	Min.	FGA	FGM	Pct.	FTA	FTM	Pct.	Reb.	Ast.	PF	Disq.	Pts.	Avg.
58-59–Minneapolis	70	2855	1482	605	.408	685	532	.777	1050	287	270	4	1742	24.9
59-60–Minneapolis	70	2873	1781	755	.424	770	564	.732	1150	243	234	2	2074	29.6
60-61–Los Angeles	73	3133	2166	931	.430	863	676	.783	1447	371	279	3	2538	34.8
61-62–Los Angeles	48	2129	1588	680	.428	631	476	.754	892	222	155	1	1836	38.3
62-63–Los Angeles	80	3370	2273	1029	.453	790	661	.837	1146	386	226	1	2719	34.0
63-64–Los Angeles	78	3164	1778	756	.425	586	471	.804	936	347	235	1	1983	25.4
64-65–Los Angeles	74	3056	1903	763	.401	610	483	.792	950	280	235	0	2009	27.1
65-66–Los Angeles	65	1975	1034	415	.401	337	249	.739	621	224	157	0	1079	16.6
66-67–Los Angeles	70	2706	1658	711	.429	541	440	.813	898	215	211	1	1862	26.6
67-68–Los Angeles	77	3029	1709	757	.443	621	488	.786	941	355	232	0	2002	26.0
68-69–Los Angeles	76	3064	1632	730	.447	567	421	.743	805	408	204	0	1881	24.8
69-70–Los Angeles	54	2213	1051	511	.486	357	276	.773	559	292	132	1	1298	24.0
70-71–Los Angeles	2	57	19	8	.421	6	4	.667	11	2	6	0	20	10.0
71-72–Los Angeles	9	239	97	42	.433	27	22	.815	57	18	20	0	106	11.8
Totals	846	33863	20171	8693	.431	7391	5763	.780	11463	3650	2596	14	23149	27.4

NBA Playoff Record

Sea.–Team	G.	Min.	FGA	FGM	Pct.	FTA	FTM	Pct.	Reb.	Ast.	PF	Disq.	Pts.	Avg.
58-59–Minneapolis	13	556	303	122	.403	113	87	.770	156	43	52	0	331	25.5
59-60–Minneapolis	9	408	234	111	.474	94	79	.840	128	31	38	0	301	33.4
60-61–Los Angeles	12	540	362	170	.470	142	117	.824	183	55	44	1	457	38.1
61-62–Los Angeles	13	571	425	186	.428	168	130	.774	230	47	45	1	502	38.6
62-63–Los Angeles	13	562	362	160	.442	126	104	.825	177	58	58	0	424	32.6
63-64–Los Angeles	5	221	119	45	.378	40	31	.775	58	28	17	0	121	24.2
64-65–Los Angeles	1	5	2	0	.000	0	0	.000	0	1	0	0	0	0.0
65-66–Los Angeles	14	586	328	145	.442	105	85	.810	197	52	38	0	375	26.8
66-67–Los Angeles	3	121	76	28	.368	20	15	.750	39	9	6	0	71	23.7
67-68–Los Angeles	15	633	376	176	.468	112	76	.679	218	60	41	0	428	28.5
68-69–Los Angeles	18	640	278	107	.385	100	63	.630	166	74	56	0	277	15.4
69-70–Los Angeles	18	667	296	138	.466	81	60	.741	173	83	50	1	336	18.7
Totals	134	5510	3161	1388	.439	1101	847	.769	1725	541	445	3	3623	27.0

NBA All-Star Game Record

Sea.–Team	Min.	FGA	FGM	Pct.	FTA	FTM	Pct.	Reb.	Ast.	PF	Disq.	Pts.
1959–Minneapolis	32	20	10	.500	5	4	.800	11	1	3	0	24
1960–Minneapolis	28	18	10	.556	7	5	.714	13	3	4	0	25
1961–Los Angeles	27	11	3	.273	10	9	.900	10	4	5	0	15
1962–Los Angeles	37	23	10	.435	14	12	.857	9	4	2	0	32
1963–Los Angeles	36	15	4	.267	13	9	.692	14	7	0	0	17
1964–Los Angeles	29	15	5	.333	11	5	.455	8	5	1	0	15
1965–Los Angeles	27	13	5	.385	8	8	1.000	7	0	4	0	18
1967–Los Angeles	20	14	8	.571	4	4	1.000	5	5	2	0	20
1968–Los Angeles	27	13	8	.615	7	6	.857	6	1	5	0	22
1969–Los Angeles	32	13	5	.385	12	11	.917	9	5	2	0	21
1970–Los Angeles	26	9	2	.222	7	5	.714	7	3	3	0	9
Totals	321	164	70	.427	98	78	.796	99	38	31	0	218

NBA Coaching Record

Sea.–Club	Regular Season				Playoffs	
	W.	L.	Pct.	Pos.	W.	L.
1974-75–New Orleans	0	1	.000	–†	—	—
1976-77–New Orleans	21	35	.375	5†	—	—
1977-78–New Orleans	39	43	.476	5†	—	—
1978-79–New Orleans	26	56	.317	6†	—	—
Totals (4 seasons)	86	135	.389		—	—

†Central Division.

WILLIS REED, JR.

Born June 25, 1942 at Hico, La.
High School–Lillie, La., West Side.
College–Grambling College, Grambling, La.
Inducted into the Basketball Hall of Fame, 1981
NBA Most Valuable Player, 1970
NBA All-Star Game Most Valuable Player, 1970
NBA Rookie of the Year, 1965

Collegiate Playing Record

Year	G	Min.	FGA	FGM	Pct.	FTA	FTM	Pct.	Reb.	Pts.	Avg.
60-61	35	—	239	146	.611	122	86	.705	312	378	10.8
61-62	26	—	323	189	.585	102	80	.784	380	458	17.6
62-63	33	—	489	282	.565	177	135	.763	563	699	21.2
63-64	28	—	486	301	.619	199	143	.719	596	745	26.6
Totals	122	—	1537	918	.597	600	444	.740	1851	2280	18.7

NBA Regular Season Record

Sea.–Team	G	Min.	FGA	FGM	Pct.	FTA	FTM	Pct.	Reb.	Ast.	PF	Disq.	Pts.	Avg.
64-65–New York	80	3042	1457	629	.432	407	302	742	1175	133	339	14	1560	19.5
65-66–New York	76	2537	1009	438	.434	399	302	.757	883	91	323	13	1178	15.5
66-67–New York	78	2824	1298	635	.489	487	358	.735	1136	126	293	9	1628	20.9
67-68–New York	81	2879	1346	659	.490	509	367	.721	1073	159	343	12	1685	20.8
68-69–New York	82	3108	1351	704	.521	435	325	.747	1191	190	314	7	1733	21.1
69-70–New York	81	3089	1385	702	.507	464	351	.756	1126	161	287	2	1755	21.7
70-71–New York	73	2855	1330	614	.462	381	299	.785	1003	148	228	1	1527	20.9
71-72–New York	11	363	137	60	.438	39	27	.692	96	22	30	0	147	13.4
72-73–New York	69	1876	705	334	.474	124	92	.742	590	126	205	0	760	11.0

Sea.–Team	G	Min.	FGA	FGM	Pct.	FTA	FTM	Pct.	–Rebounds– Off.	–Rebounds– Def.	–Rebounds– Tot.	Ast.	PF	Dq.	Stl.	Blk.	Pts.	Avg.
73-74–New York	19	500	184	84	.457	53	42	.792	47	94	141	30	49	0	12	21	210	11.1
Totals	650	23073	10202	4859	.476	3298	2465	.747			8414	1186	2411	58			12183	18.7

NBA Playoff Record

Sea.–Team	G	Min.	FGA	FGM	Pct.	FTA	FTM	Pct.	Reb.	Ast.	PF	Disq.	Pts.	Avg.
66-67–New York	4	148	80	43	.538	25	24	.960	55	7	19	1	110	27.5
67-68–New York	6	210	98	53	.541	30	22	.733	62	11	24	1	128	21.3
68-69–New York	10	429	198	101	.510	70	55	.786	141	19	40	1	257	25.7
69-70–New York	18	732	378	178	.471	95	70	.737	248	51	60	0	426	23.7
70-71–New York	12	504	196	81	.413	39	26	.667	144	27	41	0	188	15.7
72-73–New York	17	486	208	97	.466	21	18	.857	129	30	65	1	212	12.5

Sea.–Team	G	Min.	FGA	FGM	Pct.	FTA	FTM	Pct.	Off.	Def.	Tot.	Ast.	PF	Dq.	Stl.	Blk.	Pts.	Avg.
									–Rebounds–									
73-74–New York	11	132	45	17	.378	5	3	.600	4	18	22	4	26	0	2	0	37	3.4
Totals	78	2641	1203	370	.474	285	218	.765			801	149	275	4			1358	17.4

NBA All-Star Game Record

Sea.–Team	Min.	FGA	FGM	Pct.	FTA	FTM	Pct.	Reb.	Ast.	PF	Disq.	Pts.
1965–New York	25	11	3	.273	2	1	.500	5	1	2	0	7
1966–New York	23	11	7	.636	2	2	1.000	8	1	3	0	16
1967–New York	17	6	2	.333	0	0	.000	9	1	0	0	4
1968–New York	25	14	7	.500	3	2	.667	8	1	4	0	16
1969–New York	14	8	5	.625	0	0	.000	4	2	2	0	10
1970–New York	30	18	9	.500	3	3	1.000	11	0	6	1	21
1971–New York	27	16	5	.313	6	4	.667	13	1	3	0	14
Totals	161	84	38	.452	16	12	.750	58	7	20	1	88

NBA Coaching Record

Sea.–Club	Regular Season				Playoffs	
	W.	L.	Pct.	Pos.	W.	L.
1977-78–New York	43	39	.524	2†	2	4
1978-79–New York	6	8	.429	–†	—	—
Totals (2 seasons)	49	47	.510		2	4

Collegiate Coaching Record

Sea.–Club	Regular Season				Playoffs	
	W.	L.	Pct.	Pos.	W.	L.
1981-82–Creighton	7	20	.259	‡8		
1982-83–Creighton	8	19	.296	‡10		
1983-84–Creighton	17	14	.548	‡4		
Totals (3 seasons)	32	53	.376			

†Atlantic Division.
‡Missouri Valley Conference.

OSCAR PALMER ROBERTSON
(Big O)

Born November 24, 1938 at Charlotte, Tenn. Height 6:05 Weight 220
High School–Indianapolis, Ind., Crispus Attucks
College–University of Cincinnati, Cincinnati, O.
Inducted into the Basketbell Hall of Fame, 1979
Chosen to the NBA 35th Anniversary All-Time Team, 1980
NBA Most Valuable Player, 1964
NBA All-Star Game Most Valuable Player, 1961, 1964, 1969
United Press International College Player of the Year, 1958, 1959, 1960
Member of the 1960 United States Olympic Basketball Team
NBA Rookie of the Year, 1961

Collegiate Record

Year	G	Min.	FGA	FGM	Pct.	FTA	FTM	Pct.	Reb.	Pts.	Avg.
56-57†	13	—	—	151	—	178	127	.713	—	429	33.0
57-58	28	1085	617	352	.571	355	280	.789	425	984	35.1
58-59	30	1172	650	331	.509	398	316	.794	489	978	32.6
59-60	30	1155	701	369	.526	361	273	.756	424	1011	33.7
Varsity Totals	88	3412	1968	1052	.535	1114	869	.780	1338	2973	13.8

NBA Regular Season Record

Sea.–Team	G	Min.	FGA	FGM	Pct.	FTA	FTM	Pct.	Reb.	Ast.	PF	Disq.	Pts.	Avg.
60-61–Cincinnati	71	3012	1600	756	.473	794	653	.822	716	690	219	3	2165	30.5
61-62–Cincinnati	79	3503	1810	866	.478	872	700	.803	985	899	258	1	2432	30.8
62-63–Cincinnati	80	3521	1593	825	.518	758	614	.810	835	758	293	1	2264	28.3
63-64–Cincinnati	79	3559	1740	840	.483	938	800	.853	783	868	280	3	2480	31.4
64-65–Cincinnati	75	3421	1681	807	.480	793	665	.839	674	861	205	2	2279	30.4
65-66–Cincinnati	76	3493	1723	818	.475	881	742	.842	586	847	227	1	2378	31.3
66-67–Cincinnati	79	3468	1699	838	.493	843	736	.873	486	845	226	2	2412	30.5
67-68–Cincinnati	65	2765	1321	660	.500	660	576	.873	391	633	199	2	1896	29.2
68-69–Cincinnati	79	3461	1351	656	.486	767	643	.838	502	772	231	2	1955	24.7
69-70–Cincinnati	69	2865	1267	647	.511	561	454	.809	422	558	175	1	1748	25.3
70-71–Milwaukee	81	3194	1193	592	.496	453	385	.850	462	668	203	0	1569	19.4
71-72–Milwaukee	64	2390	887	419	.472	330	276	.836	323	491	116	0	1114	17.4
72-73–Milwaukee	73	2737	983	446	.454	281	238	.847	360	551	167	0	1130	15.5

Sea.–Team	G	Min.	FGA	FGM	Pct.	FTA	FTM	Pct.	–Rebounds– Off.	–Rebounds– Def.	–Rebounds– Tot.	Ast.	PF	Dq.	Stl.	Blk.	Pts.	Avg.
73-74–Milwaukee	70	2477	772	338	.438	254	212	.835	71	208	279	446	132	0	77	4	888	12.7
Totals	1040	43866	19620	9508	.485	9185	7694	.838			7804	9887	2931	18			26710	25.7

NBA Playoff Record

Sea.–Team	G	Min.	FGA	FGM	Pct.	FTA	FTM	Pct.	Reb.	Ast.	PF	Disq.	Pts.	Avg.
61-62–Cincinnati	4	185	81	42	.519	39	31	.795	44	44	18	1	115	28.8
62-63–Cincinnati	12	570	264	124	.470	154	133	.864	156	108	41	0	381	31.8
63-64–Cincinnati	10	471	202	92	.455	127	109	.858	89	84	30	0	293	29.3
64-65–Cincinnati	4	195	89	38	.427	39	36	.923	19	48	14	0	112	28.0
65-66–Cincinnati	5	224	120	49	.408	68	61	.897	38	39	20	1	159	31.8
66-67–Cincinnati	4	183	64	33	.516	37	33	.892	16	45	9	0	99	24.8
70-71–Milwaukee	14	520	210	102	.486	69	52	.754	70	124	39	0	256	18.3
71-72–Milwaukee	11	380	140	57	.407	36	30	.833	64	83	29	0	144	13.1
72-73–Milwaukee	6	256	96	48	.500	34	31	.912	28	45	21	1	127	21.2

Sea.–Team	G	Min.	FGA	FGM	Pct.	FTA	FTM	Pct.	–Rebounds– Off.	Def.	Tot.	Ast.	PF	Dq.	Stl.	Blk.	Pts.	Avg.
73-74–Milwaukee	16	689	200	90	.450	52	44	.846	15	39	54	149	46	0	15	4	224	14.0
Totals	86	3673	1466	675	.460	655	560	.855			578	769	267	3			1910	22.2

NBA All-Star Game Record

Sea.–Team	Min.	FGA	FGM	Pct.	FTA	FTM	Pct.	Reb.	Ast.	PF	Disq.	Pts.
1961–Cincinnati	34	13	8	.615	9	7	.778	9	14	5	0	23
1962–Cincinnati	37	20	9	.450	14	8	.571	7	13	3	0	26
1963–Cincinnati	37	15	9	.600	4	3	.750	3	6	5	0	21
1964–Cincinnati	42	23	10	.435	10	6	.600	14	8	4	0	26
1965–Cincinnati	40	18	8	.444	13	12	.923	6	8	5	0	28
1966–Cincinnati	25	12	6	.500	6	5	.833	10	8	0	0	17
1967–Cincinnati	34	20	9	.450	10	8	.800	2	5	4	0	26
1968–Cincinnati	22	9	7	.778	7	4	.571	1	5	2	0	18
1969–Cincinnati	32	16	8	.500	8	8	1.000	6	5	3	0	24
1970–Cincinnati	29	11	9	.818	4	3	.750	6	4	3	0	21
1971–Milwaukee	24	6	2	.333	3	1	.333	2	2	3	0	5
1972–Milwaukee	24	9	3	.333	10	5	.500	3	3	4	0	11
Totals	380	172	88	.512	98	70	.714	69	81	41	0	246

HAL GREER

Born June 26, 1936 at Huntington, W. Va.
High School–Huntington, W. Va.; Douglass College–Marshall University, Huntington, W. Va.
Inducted into the Basketball Hall of Fame, 1981
NBA All Star Game Most Valuable Player, 1968

Collegiate Record

Year	G	Min.	FGA	FGM	Pct.	FTA	FTM	Pct.	Reb.	Pts.	Avg.
54-55†	—	—	—	—	—	—	—	—	—	—	18.0
55-56	23	—	213	128	.601	145	101	.697	153	357	15.5
56-57	24	—	329	167	.508	156	119	.763	332	453	18.9
57-58	24	—	432	236	.546	114	95	.833	280	567	23.6
Varsity Totals	71	—	974	531	.545	415	315	.759	765	1377	19.4

NBA Regular Season Record

Sea.–Team	G	Min.	FGA	FGM	Pct.	FTA	FTM	Pct.	Reb.	Ast.	PF	Disq.	Pts.	Avg.
58-59–Syracuse	68	1625	679	308	.454	176	137	.778	196	101	189	1	756	11.1
59-60–Syracuse	70	1979	815	388	.476	189	148	.783	303	188	208	4	924	13.2
60-61–Syracuse	79	2763	1381	623	.451	394	305	.774	455	302	242	0	1551	19.6
61-62–Syracuse	71	2705	1442	644	.446	404	331	.819	524	313	252	2	1619	22.8
62-63–Syracuse	80	2631	1293	600	.464	434	362	.834	457	275	286	4	1562	19.5
63-64–Philadelphia	80	3157	1611	715	.444	525	435	.829	484	374	291	6	1865	23.3
64-65–Philadelphia	70	2600	1245	539	.433	413	335	.811	355	313	254	7	1413	20.2
65-66–Philadelphia	80	3326	1580	703	.445	514	413	.804	473	384	315	6	1819	22.7
66-67–Philadelphia	80	3086	1524	699	.459	466	367	.788	422	303	302	5	1765	22.1
67-68–Philadelphia	82	3263	1626	777	.478	549	422	.769	444	372	289	6	1976	24.1
68-69–Philadelphia	82	3311	1595	732	.459	543	432	.796	435	414	294	8	1896	23.1
69-70–Philadelphia	80	3024	1551	705	.455	432	352	.815	376	405	300	8	1762	22.0
70-71–Philadelphia	81	3060	1371	591	..431	405	326	.805	364	369	289	4	1508	18.6
71-72–Philadelphia	81	2410	866	389	.449	234	181	.774	271	316	268	10	959	11.8
72-73–Philadelphia	38	848	232	91	.392	39	32	.821	106	111	76	1	214	5.6
Totals	1122	39788	18811	8504	.452	5717	4578	.801	5665	4540	3855	72	21586	19.2

NBA Playoff Record

Sea.–Team	G.	Min.	FGA	FGM	Pct.	FTA	FTM	Pct.	Reb.	Ast.	PF	Disq.	Pts.	Avg.
58-59–Syracuse	9	277	93	39	.419	32	26	.813	47	20	35	2	104	11.6
59-60–Syracuse	3	84	43	22	.512	4	3	.750	14	10	5	0	47	15.7
60-61–Syracuse	8	232	106	41	.387	40	33	.825	33	19	32	1	115	14.4
61-62–Syracuse	1	5	0	0	.000	0	0	.000	0	0	1	0	0	0.0
62-63–Syracuse	5	214	87	44	.506	35	29	.829	27	21	21	1	117	23.4
63-64–Philadelphia	5	211	95	37	.389	39	33	.846	28	30	19	1	107	21.4
64-65–Philadelphia	11	505	222	101	.455	87	69	.793	81	55	45	2	271	24.6
65-66–Philadelphia	5	226	91	32	.352	23	18	.783	36	21	21	0	82	16.4
66-67–Philadelphia	15	688	375	161	.429	118	94	.797	88	79	55	1	416	27.7
67-68–Philadelphia	13	553	278	120	.432	111	95	.858	79	55	49	1	335	25.8
68-69–Philadelphia	5	204	81	26	.321	36	28	.778	30	23	23	0	80	16.0
69-70–Philadelphia	5	178	74	33	.446	13	11	.846	17	27	16	0	77	15.4
70-71–Philadelphia	7	265	112	49	.438	36	27	.750	25	33	35	4	125	17.9
Totals	92	3642	1657	705	.425	574	466	.812	505	393	357	13	1876	20.4

NBA All-Star Game Record

Sea.-Team	Min.	FGA	FGM	Pct.	FTA	FTM	pct.	Reb.	Ast.	PF	Disq.	Pts.
1961–Syracuse	18	11	7	.636	0	0	.000	6	2	2	0	14
1962–Syracuse	24	14	3	.214	7	2	.286	10	9	3	0	8
1963–Syracuse	15	7	3	.429	0	0	.000	3	2	4	0	6
1964–Philadelphia	20	10	5	.500	4	3	.750	3	4	1	0	13
1965–Philadelphia	21	11	5	.455	4	3	.750	4	1	2	0	13
1966–Philadelphia	23	13	4	.308	1	1	1.000	5	1	4	0	9
1967–Philadelphia	31	16	5	.313	8	7	.875	4	1	5	0	17
1968–Philadelphia	17	8	8	1.000	7	5	.714	3	3	2	0	21
1969–Philadelphia	17	1	0	.000	5	4	.800	3	2	2	0	4
1970–Philadelphia	21	11	7	.636	1	1	1.000	4	3	4	0	15
Totals	207	102	47	.461	37	26	.703	45	28	29	0	120

CBA Coaching Record

Sea.-Club	Regular Season				Playoffs	
	W.	L.	Pct.	Pos.	W.	L.
1980-81–Phila. Kings	17	23	.425	3†	6	6

†Eastern Division.

WILTON NORMAN CHAMBERLAIN
(Wilt)

Born August 21, 1936 at Philadelphia, Pa.
High School–Philadelphia, Pa., Overbrook.
College–University of Kansas, Lawrence, Kan.
Inducted into the Basketball Hall of Fame, 1978
Chosen to the NBA 35th Anniversary All-Time Team, 1980
NBA Most Valuable Player, 1960, 1966, 1967, 1968
NBA All-Star Game Most Valuable Player, 1960
NBA Rookie of the Year, 1960
Played with Harlem Globetrotters during 1958-59 season.

Collegiate Record

Year	G	Min.	FGA	FGM	Pct.	FTA	FTM	Pct.	Reb.	Pts.	Avg.
55-56†			(Freshmen team did not play an intercollegiate schedule)								
56-57	27	—	588	275	.468	399	250	.627	510	800	26.6
57-58	21	—	482	228	.473	291	177	.608	367	633	30.1
Varsity Totals	48	—	1070	503	.470	690	427	.619	877	1433	29.9

NBA Regular Season Record

Sea.–Team	G	Min.	FGA	FGM	Pct.	FTA	FTM	Pct.	Reb.	Ast.	PF	Disq.	Pts.	Avg.
59-60–Philadelphia	72	3338	2311	1065	.461	991	577	.582	1941	168	150	0	2707	37.6
60-61–Philadelphia	79	3773	2457	1251	.509	1054	531	.504	2149	148	130	0	3033	38.4
61-62–Philadelphia	80	3882	3159	1597	.505	1363	835	.613	2052	192	123	0	4029	50.4
62-63–San Francisco	80	3806	2770	1463	.528	1113	660	.593	1946	275	136	0	3586	44.8
63-64–San Francisco	80	3689	2298	1204	.524	1016	540	.531	1787	403	182	0	2948	36.9
64-65–S.F.-Phila.	73	3301	2083	1063	.510	880	408	.464	1673	250	146	0	2534	34.7
65-66–Philadelphia	79	3737	1990	1074	.540	976	501	.513	1943	414	171	0	2649	33.5
66-67–Philadelphia	81	3682	1150	785	.683	875	386	.441	1957	630	143	0	1956	24.1
67-68–Philadelphia	82	3836	1377	819	.595	932	354	.380	1952	702	160	0	1992	24.3
68-69–Los Angeles	81	3669	1099	641	.583	857	382	.446	1712	366	142	0	1664	20.5
69-70–Los Angeles	12	505	227	129	.568	157	70	.446	221	49	31	0	328	27.3
70-71–Los Angeles	82	3630	1226	668	.545	669	360	.538	1493	352	174	0	1696	20.7
71-72–Los Angeles	82	3469	764	496	.649	524	221	.422	1572	329	196	0	1213	14.8
72-73–Los Angeles	82	3542	586	426	.727	455	232	.510	1526	365	191	0	1084	13.2
Totals	1045	47859	23497	12681	.540	11862	6057	.511	23924	4643	2075	0	31419	30.1

NBA Playoff Record

Sea.–Team	G.	Min.	FGA	FGM	Pct.	FTA	FTM	Pct.	Reb.	Ast.	PF	Disq.	Pts.	Avg.
59-60–Philadelphia	9	415	252	125	.496	110	49	.445	232	19	17	0	299	33.2
60-61–Philadelphia	3	144	96	45	.469	38	21	.553	69	6	10	0	111	37.0
61-62–Philadelphia	12	576	347	162	.467	151	96	.636	319	37	27	0	420	35.0
63-64–San Francisco	12	558	322	175	.543	139	66	.475	302	39	27	0	416	34.7
64-65–Philadelphia	11	536	232	123	.530	136	76	.559	299	48	29	0	322	29.3
65-66–Philadelphia	5	240	110	56	.509	68	28	.412	151	15	10	0	140	28.0
66-67–Philadelphia	15	718	228	132	.579	160	62	.388	437	135	37	0	326	21.7
67-68–Philadelphia	13	631	232	124	.534	158	60	.380	321	85	29	0	308	23.7
68-69–Los Angeles	18	832	176	96	.545	148	58	.392	444	46	56	0	250	13.9
69-70–Los Angeles	18	851	288	158	.549	202	82	.406	399	81	42	0	398	22.1
70-71–Los Angeles	12	554	187	85	.455	97	50	.515	242	53	33	0	220	18.3
71-72–Los Angeles	15	703	142	80	.563	122	60	.492	315	49	47	0	220	14.7
72-73–Los Angeles	17	801	116	64	.552	98	49	.500	383	60	48	0	177	10.4
Totals	160	7559	2728	1425	.522	1627	757	.465	3913	673	412	0	3607	22.5

NBA All-Star Game Record

Sea.–Team	Min.	FGA	FGM	Pct.	FTA	FTM	Pct.	Reb.	Ast.	PF	Disq.	Pts.
1960–Philadelphia	30	20	9	.450	7	5	.714	25	2	1	0	23
1961–Philadelphia	38	8	2	.250	15	8	.533	18	5	1	0	12
1962–Philadelphia	37	23	17	.739	16	8	.500	24	1	4	0	42
1963–San Francisco	35	11	7	.636	7	3	.429	19	0	2	0	17
1964–San Francisco	37	14	4	.286	14	11	.786	20	1	2	0	19
1965–San Francisco	31	15	9	.600	8	2	.250	16	1	4	0	20
1966–Philadelphia	25	11	8	.727	9	5	.556	9	3	2	0	21
1967–Philadelphia	39	7	6	.857	5	2	.400	22	4	1	0	14
1968–Philadelphia	25	4	3	.750	4	1	.250	7	6	2	0	7
1969–Los Angeles	27	3	2	.667	1	0	.000	12	2	2	0	4
1971–Los Angeles	18	1	1	1.000	0	0	.000	8	5	0	0	2
1972–Los Angeles	24	3	3	1.000	8	2	.250	10	3	2	0	8
1973–Los Angeles	22	2	1	.500	0	0	.000	7	3	0	0	2
Totals	388	122	72	.590	94	47	.500	197	36	23	0	191

ABA Coaching Record

Sea.–Club	Regular Season				Playoffs	
	W.	L.	Pct.	Pos.	W.	L.
1973-74–San Diego	37	47	.440	T4	2	4

WILLIAM FENTON RUSSELL
(Bill)

Born February 12, 1934 at Monroe, La.
High School–Oakland, Calif., McClymonds
College–University of San Francisco, San Francisco, Calif.
Inducted into the Basketball Hall of Fame, 1974
Chosen to the NBA 25th Anniversary All-Time Team, 1970
Chosen to the NBA 35th Anniversary All-Time Team, 1980
NBA Most Valuable Player, 1958, 1961, 1963, 1965
NBA All-Star Game Most Valuable Player, 1963
Member of the 1956 United States Olympic Basketball Team
Chosen the Most Outstanding Player in the 1955 NCAA Tournament

Collegiate Record

Year	G	Min.	FGA	FGM	Pct.	FTA	FTM	Pct.	Reb.	Pts.	Avg.
52-53†	23	—	—	—	—	—	—	—	—	461	20.0
53-54	21	—	309	150	.485	212	117	.552	403	417	19.9
54-55	29	—	423	229	.541	278	164	.590	594	622	21.4
55-56	29	—	480	246	.513	212	105	.495	609	597	20.6
Totals	79	—	1212	625	.516	702	386	.550	1606	1636	20.7

NBA Regular Season Record

Sea.–Team	G	Min.	FGA	FGM	Pct.	FTA	FTM	Pct.	Reb.	Ast.	PF	Disq.	Pts.	Avg.
56-57–Boston	48	1695	649	277	.427	309	152	.492	943	88	143	2	706	14.7
57-58–Boston	69	2640	1032	456	.442	443	230	.519	1564	202	181	2	1142	16.6
58-59–Boston	70	2979	997	456	.457	428	256	.598	1612	222	161	3	1168	16.7
59-60–Boston	74	3146	1189	555	.467	392	240	.612	1778	277	210	0	1350	18.2
60-61–Boston	78	3458	1250	532	.426	469	258	.550	1868	268	155	0	1322	16.9
61-62–Boston	76	3433	1258	575	.457	481	286	.594	1790	341	207	3	1436	18.9
62-63–Boston	78	3500	1182	511	.432	517	287	.555	1843	348	189	1	1309	16.8
63-64–Boston	78	3482	1077	466	.433	429	236	.550	1930	370	190	0	1168	15.0
64-65–Boston	78	3466	980	429	.438	426	244	.573	1878	410	204	1	1102	14.1
65-66–Boston	78	3386	943	391	.415	405	223	.551	1779	371	221	4	1005	12.9
66-67–Boston	81	3297	870	395	.454	467	285	.610	1700	472	258	4	1075	13.4
67-68–Boston	78	2953	858	365	.425	460	247	.537	1451	357	242	2	977	12.5
68-69–Boston	77	3291	645	279	.433	388	204	.526	1484	374	231	2	762	9.9
Totals	963	40726	12930	5687	.440	5614	3148	.561	21620	4100	2592	24	14522	15.1

Reference Section

NBA Playoff Record

Sea.–Team	G.	Min.	FGA	FGM	Pct.	FTA	FTM	Pct.	Reb.	Ast.	PF	Disq.	Pts.	Avg.
56-57–Boston	10	409	148	54	.365	61	31	.508	244	32	41	1	139	13.9
57-58–Boston	9	355	133	48	.361	66	40	.606	221	24	24	0	136	15.1
58-59–Boston	11	496	159	65	.409	67	41	.612	305	40	28	1	171	15.5
59-60–Boston	13	572	206	94	.456	75	53	.707	336	38	38	1	241	18.5
60-61–Boston	10	462	171	73	.427	86	45	.523	299	48	24	0	191	19.1
61-62–Boston	14	672	253	116	.458	113	82	.726	370	70	49	0	314	22.4
62-63–Boston	13	617	212	96	.453	109	72	.661	326	66	36	0	264	20.3
63-64–Boston	10	451	132	47	.356	67	37	.552	272	44	33	0	131	13.1
64-65–Boston	12	561	150	79	.527	76	40	.526	302	76	43	2	198	16.5
65-66–Boston	17	814	261	124	.475	123	76	.618	428	85	60	0	324	19.1
66-67–Boston	9	390	86	31	.360	52	33	.635	198	50	32	1	95	10.6
67-68–Boston	19	869	242	99	.409	130	76	.585	434	99	73	1	274	14.4
68-69–Boston	18	829	182	77	.423	81	41	.506	369	98	65	1	195	10.8
Totals	165	7497	2335	1003	.430	1106	667	.603	4104	770	546	8	2673	16.2

NBA All-Star Game Record

Sea.–Team	Min.	FGA	FGM	Pct.	FTA	FTM	Pct.	Reb.	Ast.	PF	Disq.	Pts.
1958–Boston	26	12	5	.417	3	1	.333	11	2	5	0	11
1959–Boston	27	10	3	.300	1	1	1.000	9	1	4	0	7
1960–Boston	27	7	3	.429	2	0	.000	8	3	1	0	6
1961–Boston	28	15	9	.600	8	6	.750	11	1	2	0	24
1962–Boston	27	12	5	.417	3	2	.667	12	2	2	0	12
1963–Boston	37	14	8	.571	4	3	.750	24	5	3	0	19
1964–Boston	42	13	6	.462	2	1	.500	21	2	4	0	13
1965–Boston	33	12	7	.583	9	3	.333	13	5	6	1	17
1966–Boston	23	6	1	.167	0	0	.000	10	2	2	0	2
1967–Boston	22	2	1	.500	0	0	.000	5	5	2	0	2
1968–Boston	23	4	2	.500	0	0	.000	9	8	5	0	4
1969–Boston	28	4	1	.250	2	1	.500	6	3	1	0	3
Totals	343	111	51	.459	34	18	.529	139	39	37	1	120

NBA Coaching Record

Sea.–Club	Regular Season				Playoffs	
	W.	L.	Pct.	Pos.	W.	L.
1966-67–Boston	60	21	.741	2†	4	5
1967-68–Boston*	54	28	.659	2†	12	7
1968-69–Boston*	48	34	.585	4†	12	6
1973-74–Seattle	36	46	.439	3‡	—	—
1974-75–Seattle	43	39	.524	2‡	4	5
1975-76–Seattle	43	39	.524	2‡	2	4
1976-77–Seattle	40	42	.488	4‡	—	—
Totals (7 seasons)	324	249	.565		34	27

*Won NBA championship.   †Eastern Division.   ‡Pacific Division.

WILT CHAMBERLAIN vs BILL RUSSELL
Per Game

	CHAMBERLAIN	RUSSELL		CHAMBERLAIN	RUSSELL
Regular Season			*Playoffs*		
YEARS	14	13	YEARS	13	13
MINUTES	45.8	42.3	MINUTES	47.2	45.4
FIELD GOALS	12.1	5.9	FIELD GOALS	8.9	6.1
F.G. ATTEMPTS	22.5	13.4	F.G. ATTEMPTS	17	14.1
F.G. PERCENTAGE	.540	.440	F.G. PERCENTAGE	.522	.430
FREE THROWS MADE	5.8	3.3	FREE THROWS MADE	4.7	4
F.T. ATTEMPTS	11.4	5.8	F.T. ATTEMPTS	10.2	6.7
F.T. PERCENTAGE	.511	.561	F.T. PERCENTAGE	.465	.603
REBOUNDS	22.8	22.5	REBOUNDS	24.4	24.9
ASSISTS	4.4	4.3	ASSISTS	4.2	4.7
POINTS	30.1	15.1	POINTS	22.5	16.2
FOULS	2	2.7	FOULS	2.6	3.3

KAREEM ABDUL-JABBAR
1967, 1968, 1969 NCAA All-America
1967, 1969 United Press International College "Player of the Year"
1967, 1968, 1969 Most Outstanding Player in the NCAA Tournament
1970 NBA Rookie of the Year
NBA All-Star 1970–1974, 1976–1988
1971, 1972, 1974, 1976, 1977, 1980 NBA Most Valuable Player
1980, Chosen for the NBA 35th Anniversary Team
All-time leading scorer in the history of the NBA

Kareem's Top Career Performances

SCORING

1. 55 vs Boston (12-10-71)
2. 53 @ Cleveland (2-9-72)
3. 53 vs Philadelphia (2-18-72)
4. 53 @ Cleveland (11-4-70)
5. 53 @ Boston (1-27-71)
6. 52 vs Atlanta (1-2-75)
7. 51 @ Boston (2-13-72)
8. 51 vs Seattle (2-21-70)
9. 50 @ Los Angeles (3-17-72)
10. 50 vs Portland (1-19-75)

REBOUNDING

1. 34 vs Detroit (12-14-75)
2. 30 vs New Jersey (2-3-78)
3. 30 @ Boston (2-28-71)
4. 29 @ Philadelphia (10-23-71)
5. 29 @ Seattle (2-19-71)
6. 28 vs Detroit (12-28-71)
7. 27 @ Chicago (3-16-73)
8. 27 @ Seattle (3-1-72)
9. 27 @ Baltimore (12-11-71)
10. 27 @ New York (11-1-69)

Reference Section

NBA Regular Season

Season	TEAM	G	MIN	FGM-FGA	PCT	3-PT	FTM-FTA	PCT	OFF	DEF	TOT	AST	PF-OQ	ST	TO	BS	PTS	AVG
1969-70	Mil	82	3534	938-1810	.518	—	485-743	.653	—	—	1190	337	283-8	—	—	—	2361	28.8
1970-71	Mil	82	3288	1063-1843	.577	—	470-681	.690	—	—	1311	272	254-4	—	—	—	2596	31.7
1971-72	Mil	81	3583	1159-2019	.574	—	504-732	.598	—	—	1346	370	235-1	—	—	—	2822	34.8
1972-73	Mil	76	3254	982-1772	.554	—	328-460	.713	—	—	1224	379	207-0	—	—	—	2292	30.2
1973-74	Mil	81	3548	948-1759	.539	—	295-120	.702	287	891	1178	386	238-2	112	—	282	2191	27.0
1974-75	Mil	65	2747	812-1584	.513	—	325-426	.763	194	718	912	264	205-2	65	—	212	1949	30.0
1975-76	LA	82	3379	914-1728	.529	—	447-636	.703	272	1111	1383	413	292-6	119	—	338	2275	27.7
1976-77	LA	82	3016	888-1533	.579	—	376-536	.701	266	824	1090	319	252-4	101	—	261	2152	26.2
1977-78	LA	62	2265	662-1205	.550	—	274-350	.738	185	615	801	269	182.1	103	208	185	1600	25.8
1978-79	LA	80	3157	777-1347	.577	—	349-474	.736	207	818	1025	431	230-3	76	282	315	1903	23.9
1979-80	LA	82	3143	835-1383	.504	0-1	364-476	.765	190	696	886	371	216.2	81	297	280	2034	24.8
1980-81	LA	80	2976	836-1457	.573	0-1	423-553	.756	197	524	821	272	244-4	59	249	228	2095	26.2
1981-82	LA	76	2677	753-1301	.579	0-3	312-442	.706	172	487	659	225	224-0	53	230	207	1818	23.0
1982-83	LA	79	2554	722-1228	.588	0-2	278-371	.749	167	425	592	200	220-1	61	200	170	1722	21.8
1983-84	LA	80	2622	716-1238	.578	0-1	235-394	.723	169	418	587	211	211-1	55	221	143	1717	21.5
1984-85	LA	79	2630	723-1207	.599	0-1	289-396	.732	162	460	622	249	238-3	53	197	162	1735	22.0
Totals		1249	48373	13729-24414	.582	0-9	5804-3088	.718	2469	8087	13827	4968	3752-42	958	1884	2785	33252	26.6

Playoff

Season	TEAM	G	MIN	FGM-FGA	PCT	3-PT	FTM-FTA	PCT	OFF	DEF	TOT	AST	PF-OQ	ST	TO	BS	PTS	AVG
1969-70	Mil	10	435	139-245	.567	—	74-101	.783	—	—	168	41	25-1	—	—	—	352	35.2
1970-71	Mil	14	577	152-295	.515	—	68-101	.673	—	—	238	35	45-0	—	—	—	372	26.6
1971-72	Mil	11	510	139-318	.437	—	38-54	.704	—	—	200	56	35-0	—	—	—	316	28.7
1972-73	Mil	6	276	59-138	.428	—	19-35	.543	—	—	97	17	26-0	—	—	—	137	22.8
1973-74	Mil	16	758	224-402	.557	—	67-91	.736	67	186	253	78	41-0	20	—	39	515	32.2
1976-77	LA	11	467	147-242	.507	—	87-120	.725	51	144	195	45	42-0	19	—	38	381	34.6
1977-78	LA	3	134	38-73	.521	—	5-9	.556	14	27	41	11	14-1	2	14	12	81	27.0
1978-79	LA	8	367	88-152	.579	—	52-62	.839	18	83	101	38	25-0	8	29	33	228	28.5
1979-80	LA	15	618	198-346	.572	0-0	83-105	.790	51	130	181	46	51-0	17	55	58	479	31.9
1980-81	LA	3	134	30-65	.462	0-0	20-28	.714	13	37	50	12	14-0	3	11	8	80	25.7
1981-82	LA	14	493	115-221	.520	0-0	55-87	.632	33	86	119	51	45-0	14	41	45	285	20.4
1982-83	LA	15	588	163-287	.568	0-1	80-106	.755	25	90	115	42	51-1	17	50	55	406	27.1
1983-84	LA	21	767	206-371	.555	0-0	90-120	.750	56	117	173	79	71-2	23	45	45	502	23.9
1984-85	LA	19	810	168-300	.550	0-0	80-103	.777	50	104	154	76	67-1	23	52	36	416	21.9
Totals		188	5734	1853-3455	540	0-1	818-1122	.728	378	1004	2085	827	383-8	146	297	369	4550	27.4

AFRICAN-AMERICANS
IN PROFESSIONAL BASKETBALL

Atlanta Hawks
Atlanta, Georgia

Coaches
Reed, Willis (Assistant) 1985–87

All-Stars
Wilkens, Lenny 1963–68
Beatty, Zelmo 1966, 1968
Bridges, Bill 1967–68, 1970
Hudson, Lou 1969–71, 1973–74
Drew, John 1976, 1980
Johnson, Eddie 1980–81
Roundfield, Dan 1980–82
Wilkens, Dominique 1986–87

All-Time Roster of the Atlanta Hawks
Barker, Tom, University of Hawaii, 1976–77
Battle, John, Rutgers University, 1985–86
Beard, Alfred "Butch," University of Louisville, 1969–70
Behagan, Ron, University of Minnesota, 1977–78
Bellamy, Walter, Indiana University, 1969–74
Bracey, Steven, University of Tulsa, 1972–74
Bradshaw, Clyde, DePaul University, 1981–82
Bridges, William, University of Kansas, 1968–72
Brown, Rickey, Mississippi State University, 1982–85
Caldwell, Joe, Arizona State University, 1968–70
Carr, Antoine, Wichita State University, 1984–86
Chambers, Jerry, University of Utah, 1970–71
Charles, Ken, Fordham University, 1976–78
Charles, Lorenzo, North Carolina State University, 1985–86
Christian, Robert, Grambling State University, 1970–73
Collins, Don, Washington State University, 1980–81
Criss, Charles, New Mexico State University, 1977–85
Davis, John, University of Dayton, 1982–84
Drew, John, Gardner-Webb College, 1974–82
DuVal, Dennis, Syracuse University, 1975–76
Eaves, Jerry, University of Louisville, 1984–85
Edmonson, Keith, Purdue University, 1982–83
Furlow, Terry, Michigan State University, 1978–80
Gilliam, Herm, Michigan State University, 1978–80
Givens, Jack, University of Kentucky, 1978–80
Glenn, Michael, Southern Illinois University, 1981–86

Granger, Stewart, Villanova University, 1984–85
Haliburton, Jeff, Drake University, 1971–73
Halimon, Shaler, University of Utah, 1971–72
Hawkins, Connie, Iowa University, 1975–76
Hazzard, Walter (Mahdi Abdul-Rahman), University of California, LA, 1968–71
Henderson, Tom, University of Hawaii, 1974–77
Herron, Keith, Villanova University, 1978–79
Hill, Armond, Princeton University, 1976–84
Holland, Wilbur, University of New Orleans, 1975–76
Hudson, Lou, University of Minnesota, 1968–77
Jackson, Tracey, University of Notre Dame, 1985–86
Johnson, Eddie, Auburn University, 1977–85
Johnson, George, Dillard University, 1982–83
Johnson, Ollie, Temple University, 1977–78
Jones, Dwight, University of Houston, 1973–76
Lee, Alfred "Butch," Marquette University, 1978–79
Lee, Ron, University of Oregon, 1979–80
Levingston, Cliff, Wichita State University, 1984–87
Lowe, Sidney, North Carolina State University, 1984–85
Macklin, Durand "Rudy," Louisiana State University, 1981–83
Matthews, Wes, University of Wisconsin, 1980–84
McElroy, James, Central Michigan University, 1979–82
Meminger, Dean, Marquette University, 1974–75
Meriweather, Joe C., Southern Illinois University, 1976–77
Payne, Tom, University of Kentucky, 1971–72
Pellom, Sam, University of Buffalo, 1979–83
Rivers, Glenn "Doc," Marquette University, 1983–87
Robertson, Tony, West Virginia University, 1977–78
Robinson, Leonard, Tennessee State University, 1976–77
Rollins, Wayne "Tree," Clemson University, 1977–87
Roundfield, Dan, Central Michigan University, 1976–77
Russell, Walker D., Western Michigan University, 1984–85
Shelton, Craig, Georgetown University, 1980–82
Silas, Paul, Creighton University, 1968–69
Smith, Randy, Buffalo State University, 1982–83
Sojourner, Michael, University of Utah, 1974–77
Sparrow, Rory, Villanova University, 1981–83
Toney, Sedric, University of Dayton, 1985
Trapp, George, Long Beach State University, 1971–73

Waller, Dwight, Tennessee State University, 1968–69
Washington, Jim, Villanova University, 1971–75
Wilkins, Dominique, University of Georgia, 1982–87
Williams, Freeman, Portland State University, 1981–82
Williams, Milt, Lincoln University, 1971–72
Williams, Sylvester, University of Rhode Island, 1983–85

Willis, Kevin, Michigan State University, 1984–87
Willoughby, William, Dwight Morrow High School, N.J., 1975–77
Wilson, Rick, University of Louisville, 1978–80
Wood, Al, University of North Carolina, 1981–82

Boston Celtics
Boston, Massachusetts

Coaches
Russell, William (Head) 1966–69
Sanders, Thomas "Satch" (Head) 1978–79
Jones, K.C. (Head) 1983–87
Sanders, Thomas "Satch" (Assistant) 1977–78
Jones, K.C. (Assistant) 1977–83

All-Stars
Russell, William 1959–69
Jones, Sam 1962, 1964-66, 1968
White, JoJo 1971–77
Archibald, Nate 1980–82
Parrish, Robert 1981–87
Johnson, Dennis 1985–87

All-Time Roster of The Boston Celtics
Abdul-Aziz, Zaid, Iowa State University, 1977–78
Anderson, Jerome, West Virginia University, 1975–76
Archibald, Nate, University of Texas, El Paso, 1978–83
Ard, Jim, University of Cincinnati, 1974–78
Barker, Tom, University of Hawaii, 1978–79
Barksdale, Don, University of California, LA, 1953–55
Barnes, Jim "Bad News," Texas Western University, 1968–70
Barnes, Marvin, Providence College, 1978–79
Bing, David, Syracuse University, 1977–78
Boswell, Thomas, University of South Carolina, 1975–78
Bradley, Charles, University of Wyoming, 1981–83
Bryant, Emmette, DePaul University, 1968–70
Buckner, Quinn, Indiana University, 1982–85
Carr, M.L., Guilford College, 1979–85
Chaney, Don, University of Houston, 1968–80
Clark, Carlos, University of Kansas, 1976–77
Cook, Norm, University of Houston, 1968–80
Cooper, Charles, Duquesne University, 1950–54

Downing, Steven, Indiana University, 1973–75
Duerod, Terry, University of Detroit, 1980–82
Embry, Wayne, University of Miami (Ohio), 1966–68
Glover, Clarence, Western Kentucky University, 1971–72
Green, Si Hugo, Duquesne University, 1965–66
Hankinsojn, Phil, University of Pennsylvania, 1973–75
Henderson, Gerald, Virginia Commonwealth University, 1979–85
Jackson, Tracy, University of Notre Dame, 1981–82
Johnson, Dennis, Pepperdine University, 1983–87
Johnson, Rich, Grambling College, 1968–71
Jones, John, Los Angeles State University, 1967–68
Jones, K.C., University of San Francisco, 1958–67
Jones, Sam, North Carolina Central University, 1957–69
King, Maurice, University of Kansas, 1959–60
Knight, Billy, University of Pittsburgh, 1978–79
Maxwell, Cedric, University of North Carolina, Charlotte, 1977–85
McAdoo, Robert, University of North Carolina, 1978–79
McDonald, Glenn, Long Beach State University, 1974–76
Naulls, Willie, University of California, LA, 1963–66
Parrish, Robert, Cenatary College, 1980–87
Rowe, Curtis, University of California, LA, 1976–79
Russell, William, University of San Francisco, 1956–69
Sanders, Frank, Southern University, 1978–79
Sanders, Tom, New York University, 1960–73
Sauldsberry, Woodrow, Texas Southern University, 1965–66
Scott, Charles, University of North Carolina, 1975–78
Searcy, Ed, St. John's University, 1975–76
Silas, Paul, Creighton University, 1972–76
Smith, Garfield, University of Kentucky, 1970–72
Swain, Ben, Texas Southern University, 1958–59
Tatum, Earl, Marquette University, 1978–79
Thacker, Tom, University of Cincinnati, 1967–68

Thompson, John, Providence College, 1964–66
Tillis, Darren, Cleveland State University, 1981–83
Vincent, Sam, Michigan State University, 1985–87
Washington, Kermit, American University, 1977–78
White, Joseph, University of Kansas, 1969–79
Wicks, Sidney, University of California, LA, 1976–78

Williams, Art, California Poly, 1971–74
Williams, Earl, Winston-Salem State University, 1978–79
Williams, Sylvester, University of Rhode Island, 1985
Williams, Willie, Florida State University, 1970–71
Wilson, Robert, Wichita State University, 1976–77

Chicago Bulls
Chicago, Illinois

Board of Directors
Gardner, Edward

All-Stars
Rodgers, Guy 1967
Walker, Chet 1970–74
Love, Robert 1971–73
Gilmore, Artis 1978–80
Theus, Reginald 1980–83
Jordan, Michael 1985–87

All-Time Roster of The Chicago Bulls
Ard, Jim, University of Cincinnati, 1977–78
Barnes, Jim, Texas Western University, 1967–69
Baum, John, Temple University, 1969–71
Benbow, Leon, Jacksonville University, 1974–76
Blume, Ray, University of Oregon, 1981–82
Boozer, Robert, Kansas State University, 1966–69
Bowman, Nate, Wichita State University, 1966–67
Bradley, Dudley, University of North Carolina, 1982–83
Brown, Roger, University of Kansas, 1979–80
Bryant, Wallace, University of San Francisco, 1983–84
Collins, Jimmy, New Mexico State University, 1970–72
Colter, Steve, New Mexico State University, 1986–87
Dailey, Quintin, University of San Francisco, 1982–86
Dickey, Derrick, University of Cincinnati, 1977–78
Dudley, Charles, University of Washington, 1978–79
Garrett, Rowland, New Mexico State University, 1972–75
Gilmore, Artis, Jacksonville University, 1976–82
Green, Sidney, University of Nevada, Las Vegas, 1983–86
Greenwood, David, University of California, 1979–85
Halimon, Shaler, Utah State University, 1969–71
Harding, Reginald, 1967–68
Haskins, Clem, Western Kentucky University, 1967–70

Heard, Garfield, University of Oklahoma, 1972–73
Higgins, Rod, Fresno State University, 1982–85
Holland, Wilbur, University of New Orleans, 1976–79
Jackson, Tracy, University of Notre Dame, 1981–82
Johnson, Mickey, Aurora College, 1974–79
Johnson, Ollie, 1978–79
Johnson, Steven, Oregon State University, 1983–85
Jones, Caldwell, Albany State College, 1984–87
Jones, Charles, University of Louisville, 1984–85
Jones, Dwight, University of Houston, 1979–83
Jordan, Michael, University of North Carolina, 1984
Kenon, Larry, Memphis State University, 1980–82
Lester, Ron, University of Iowa, 1980–84
Love, Robert, Southern University, 1968–76
Mack, Oliver, East Carolina University, 1979–81
Manning, Ed, Jackson State University, 1969–70
Matthews, Wes, University of Wisconsin, 1984–85
May, Scott, Indiana University, 1976–81
McIntosh, Ken, Michigan State University, 1971–73
Oakley, Charles, Virginia Union University, 1985–87
Paulk, Charles, 1971–72
Pondexter, Cliff, University of Nevada, Las Vegas, 1975–78
Porter, Howard, Villanova University, 1971–74
Ray, Clifford, University of Oklahoma, 1971–74
Robinson, Flynn, University of Wyoming, 1967–69
Robinson, Jackie, University of Nevada, Las Vegas, 1981–82
Rodgers, Guy, Temple University, 1966–67
Russell, Cazzie, University of Michigan, 1977–78
Sheppard, Steve, University of Maryland, 1977–78
Smith, Sam, 1979–80
Smith, Willie, University of Missouri, 1976–77
Sobers, Ricky, University of Nevada, Las Vegas, 1979–80
Spriggs, Larry, Howard University, 1982–83
Starr, Keith, University of Pittsburgh, 1976–77

Theus, Reginald, University of Nevada, Las Vegas, 1978–84
Thurmond, Nate, Bowling Green State University, 1974–76
Van Lier, Norm, St. Francis College, 1971–78
Wakefield, Andre, Loyola University, Chicago, 1978–79
Walker, Chet, Bradley University, 1969–75
Washington, Jim, Villanova University, 1966–69
Weatherspoon, Nick, University of Illinois, 1977–78
Wesley, Walter, University of Cincinnati, 1969–70

Whatley, Ennis, University of Alabama, 1983–85
Wiggins, Mitchell, Florida State University, 1983–84
Wiburn, Mitchell, Central State University (Ohio), 1967–69
Wilkerson, Bob, Indiana University, 1980–81
Wilkes, James, University of California, LA, 1980–82
Wilson, George, University of Cincinnati, 1966–67
Woolridge, Orlando, University of Notre Dame, 1981–86
Worthen, Sam, Marquette University, 1980–81

Cleveland Cavaliers
Richfield, Ohio

Coaches
Littles, Eugene (Assistant) 1982–86
Littles, Eugene (Interim Head Coach) 1986

All-Stars
Johnson, John 1971–72
Beard, Alfred "Butch" 1972
Wilkens, Len 1973
Carr, Austin 1974
Russell, Campy 1979
Mitchell, Michael 1981

All-Time Roster of The Cleveland Cavaliers
Anderson, Cliff, St. Joseph's University, 1970–71
Anderson, Ron, Fresno State University, 1984–86
Bagley, John, Boston College, 1982–87
Beard, Alfred "Butch," University of Louisville,
    1971–72,1974–75
Bennett, Melvin, University of Pittsburgh, 1981–82
Brewer, Jim, University of Minnesota, 1973–79
Brewer, Ron, University of Arkansas, 1981–83
Brokaw, Gary, University of Notre Dame, 1976–77
Calvin, Mack, University of Southern California, 1980–81
Carr, Austin, University of Notre Dame, 1971–80
Chones, Jim "Sweets," Marquette University, 1974–79
Cleamons, Jim, Ohio State University, 1972–77
Crompton, Geff, University of North Carolina, 1983–84
Davis, Charles, Wake Forest University, 1971–73
Davis, Dwight, University of Houston, 1972–75
Davis, John, University of Dayton, 1984–86
Edwards, James, University of Washington, 1981–83
Evans, Michael, Kansas State University, 1981–82
Frazier, Walter, Southern Illinois University, 1977–80
Free, World B., Guilford College, 1983–86

Furlow, Terry, Michigan State University, 1977–79
Garrett, Rowland, Florida State University, 1975–77
Garris, John, Boston College, 1983–84
Granger, Stewart, Villanova University, 1983–84
Graves, Earl "Butch," Yale University, 1985–86
Herron, Keith, Villanova University, 1981–82
Higgs, Ken, Louisiana State University, 1978–79
Hinson, Roy, Rutgers University, 1983–86
Howard, Greg, University of New Mexico, 1971–72
Howard, Maurice "Mo," University of Maryland, 1976–77
Hubbard, Phil, University of Michigan, 1982–86
Huston, Geoff, Texas Tech University, 1980–85
Johnson, John, University of Iowa, 1970–73
Johnson, Reginald, University of Tennessee, 1981–82
Jones, Edgar, University of Nevada, Reno, 1984–86
Jordan, Ed, Rutgers University, 1977–78
Kenon, Larry, Memphis State University, 1982–83
Kinch, Chad, University of North Carolina, Charlotte, 1980–81
Lacy, Sam, New Mexico State University, 1982–83
Lee, Alfred "Butch," Marquette University, 1978–80
Lee, Keith, Memphis State University, 1985–87
McLemore, McCojy, Drake University, 1970–71
Minniefield, Dirk, University of Kentucky, 1985–86
Mitchell, Michael, Auburn University, 1978–82
Moore, Lowes, West Virginia University, 1981–82
Nicks, Carl, Indiana State University, 1982–83
Packley, Luther, Xavier Ohio University, 1970–72
Roberson, Rick, University of Cincinnati, 1971–73
Robinson, Cliff, University of Southern California, 1981–84
Robinzine, Bill, DePaul University, 1980–81
Rule, Robert, Colorado State University, 1972–74
Russell, Michael "Campy," University of Michigan, 1974–80,
    1984–85
Shelton, Lonnie, Oregon State University, 1983–86

Silas, James, Steven F. Austin State University, 1981–82
Smith, Bobby, University of Tulsa, 1970–80
Smith, Elmore, Kentucky State University, 1976–79
Smith, Randy, Buffalo State, 1979–81
Smith, Robert, University of Nevada, Las Vegas, 1980–81, 1984–85
Smith, William C., University of Missouri, 1979–80
Tatum, Earl, Marquette University, 1979–80
Thompson, Paul, Tulane University, 1983–85
Thurmond, Nate, Bowling Green State University, 1975–77
Tillis, Darren, Cleveland State University, 1975–77
Turpin, Melvin, University of Kentucky, 1984–87
Walker, Clarence "Foots," West Georgia State College, 1974–80

Warner, Cornell, Jackson State University, 1972–74
Warren, John, St. John's University, 1970–74
Washington, Richard, University of California, LA, 1981–83
Wesley, Walter, University of Kansas, 1970–77
West, Mark, Old Dominion University, 1985–86
Whatley, Ennis, University of Alabama, 1985–86
Whitehead, Jerome, Marquette University, 1980–81
Wilkens, Lenny, Providence College, 1972–74
Wilkerson, Bobby, Indiana University, 1981–83
Williams, Chuckie, Kansas State University, 1976–77
Williams, Kevin, St. John's University, 1984–85
Willoughby, William "Wesley," Dwight Morrow H.S. (Englewood, N.J.), 1979–80
Wilson, Michael, Marquette University, 1984–85

Dallas Mavericks
Dallas, Texas

All-Stars
Aguirre, Mark 1984–87
Blackmon, Rolando 1985–87

All-Time Roster of The Dallas Mavericks
Aguirre, Mark, DePaul University, 1981–87
Allums, Darrell, University of California, LA, 1980–81
Blackmon, Rolando, Kansas State University, 1981–87
Boynes, Winford, University of San Francisco, 1980–81
Bryant, Wallace, University of San Francisco, 1984–86
Carr, Austin, University of Notre Dame, 1980–81
Carter, Howard, Louisiana State University, 1984–85
Cooper, Wayne, University of New Orleans, 1981–82
Davis, Monti, Tennessee State University, 1980–81
Duerod, Terry, University of Detroit, 1980–81
Ellis, Dale, University of Tennessee, 1983–86
Harper, Derek, University of Illinois, 1983–87

Huston, Geoff, Texas Tech University, 1980–81
Jeelani, Abdul (Gary Cole), University of Wisconsin-Parkside, 1980–81
Kea, Clarence, Lamar University, 1980–82
Kinch, Chad, University of North Carolina, Charlotte, 1980–81
Mack, Oliver, East Carolina University, 1980–82
Perkins, Sam, University of North Carolina, 1984–87
Ransey, Kelvin, Ohio State University, 1982–83
Robinzine, Bill, DePaul University, 1980–81
Sluby, Tom, University of Notre Dame, 1984–85
Tarply, Roy, University of Michigan, 1986–87
Thompson, Corny, University of Connecticut, 1982–83
Turner, Elston, University of Mississippi, 1981–84
Vincent, Jay, Michigan State University, 1981–86
Washington, Richard, University of California, LA, 1980–81
West, Mark, Old Dominion University, 1983–84
Whitehead, Jerome, Marquette University, 1980–81

Denver Nuggets
Denver, Colorado

All-Stars (American Basketball Association Until 1975)
Haywood, Spencer 1970
Simpson, Ralph 1972–76
Jabali, Warren 1973

Calvin, Mack 1975
Thompson, David 1976–79
McGinnis, George 1979
English, Alex 1982–87
Natt, Calvin 1985

All-Time Roster of The Denver Nuggets

Anderson, Cliff, St. Joseph's College, 1969–70
Anderson, Dwight, University of Southern California, 1982–83
Barnhill, John, Tennessee State University, 1970–71
Boswell, Thomas, University of South Carolina, 1978–80
Bowens, Thomas, Grambling College, 1967–68
Bradley, Jim, Northern Illinois University, 1975–76
Brown, Roger, University of Kansas, 1975–76
Burns, David, St. Louis University, 1981–82
Calvin, Mack, University of Southern California, 1974–78
Card, Frank, South Carolina State University, 1971–73
Carter, Howard, Louisiana State University, 1983–84
Cook, Norman, University of Kansas, 1977–78
Cooper, Wayne, University of New Orleans, 1984–87
Crompton, Geoff, University of North Carolina, 1978–79
Cross, Russell, Purdue University, 1984–85
Dorsey, Jackie, University of Georgia, 1977–78
Dunn, T.R., University of Alabama, 1980–87
Edmondson, Keith, Purdue University, 1983–84
Ellis, Maurice "Bo," Marquette University, 1977–80
English, Alex, University of South Carolina, 1979–87
Evans, Michael, Kansas State University, 1982–87
Garland, Gary, DePaul University, 1979–80
Green, Michael, Louisiana Tech University, 1973–75
Haywood, Spencer, University of Detroit, 1969–70
Higgs, Ken, Louisiana State University, 1980–82
Hightower, Wayne, University of Kansas, 1967–69
Hillman, Darnell, San Jose State University, 1977–78
Hordges, Cedric, University of Kansas, 1980–82
Jabali, Warren, Wichita State University, 1972–74
Johnson, George, St. John's University, 1979–80
Jones, Steven, University of Oregon, 1973–74
Keye, Julius, Alcorn A&M University, 1969–74
Lever, Lafayette, Arizona State University, 1984–87

Long, Willie, University of New Mexico, 1972–74
McClain, Ted, Tennessee State University, 1976–77
McGill, Bill, University of Utah, 1968–69
McGinnis, George, Indiana University, 1978–80
McKinney, Bill, Northwestern University, 1980–83
Murrell, Willie, Kansas State University, 1967–68
Natt, Calvin, Northeast Louisiana University, 1984–86
Nicks, Carl, Indiana State University, 1980–81
Price, Jim, University of Louisville, 1976–78
Ray, James, Jacksonville University, 1980–83
Roberts, Anthony, Oral Roberts University, 1977–80, 1983–84
Scott, Charles, University of North Carolina, 1978–80
Silas, Paul, Creighton University, 1976–77
Simpson, Ralph, Michigan State University, 1970–76, 1977–78
Smith, Robert, University of Nevada, Las Vegas, 1977–79
Tart, Levern, Bradley University, 1968–69
Taylor, Brian, Princeton University, 1977–78
Taylor, Roland "Fatty," La Salle College, 1974–77
Theard, Floyd, Kentucky State University, 1969–70
Thompson, David, North Carolina State University, 1975–81
Trapp, John Q., University of Nevada, Las Vegas, 1972–73
Turner, Elston, University of Mississippi, 1984–87
Valentine, Ron, Old Dominion University, 1980–81
Waller, Dwight, Tennessee State University, 1969–72
Warley, Ben, Tennessee State University, 1969–70
Washington, Donald, University of North Carolina, 1974–75
Webster, Marvin, Morgan State University, 1975–77
White, Willie, University of Tennessee-Chattanooga, 1984–86
Wilburn, Ken, Central State University (Ohio), 1968–69
Wilkerson, Bobby, Indiana University, 1977–80
Williams, Rob, University of Houston, 1982–84
Wise, Willie, Drake University, 1976–77
Wright, Lonnie, Colorado State University, 1967–71

Detroit Pistons
Pontiac, Michigan

Front Office Personnel

Robinson, Will (Administrative Assistant to the General
    Manager/Director of Community Relations), 1982–present

Coaches

Lloyd, Earl (Assistant) 1971–73
Scott, Ray 1973–76

All-Stars

Dukes, Walter 1960, 1962
Miles, Eddie 1966
Bing, David 1968–69, 1971–73
Walker, Jimmy, 1970–72
Lanier, Robert 1972–75, 1977–79
Rowe, Curtis 1976
Thomas, Isiah 1982–87

All-Time Roster of The Detroit Pistons

Barnes, Marvin, Providence College, 1976–78
Barnhill, John, Tennessee State University, 1965–66
Behagan, Ron, University of Minnesota, 1978–79
Bellamy, Walter, Indiana University, 1968–70
Bing, David, Syracuse University, 1966–76
Black, Norman, St. Joseph's College, 1980–81
Brewer, Jim, University of Minnesota, 1978–79
Britt, Wayman, University of Michigan, 1977–78
Brown, Roger, University of Kansas, 1975–77
Buntin, Bill, University of Michigan, 1965–66
Caldwell, Joe, Arizona State University, 1964–66
Campbell, Tony, Ohio State University, 1984–87
Carr, Kenneth, North Carolina State University, 1981–82
Carr, M.L., Guilford College, 1976–79
Cash, Cornelius, Bowling Green State University, 1976–77
Clark, Archie, University of Minnesota, 1975–76
Clifton, Nat, Xavier University (Louisiana), 1957–58
Cureton, Earl, University of Detroit, 1983–85
Douglas, Leon, University of Alabama, 1976–80
Dove, Sonny, St. John's University, 1967–69
Drew, Larry, University of Missouri, 1980–81
Duerod, Terry, University of Detroit, 1979–80
Dukes, Walter, Seton Hall University, 1957–63
Dumars, Joe, McNeese State University, 1985–87
Evans, Earl, University of Nevada, Las Vegas, 1979–80
Green, Ricky, University of Michigan, 1978–79
Hagan, Glen, St. Bonaventure University, 1981–82
Harding, Reginald, No College, 1963–65
Hardy, Alan, University of Michigan, 1981–82
Hairston, Happy, New York University, 1967–70
Hairston, Lindsay, Michigan State University, 1975–76
Hamilton, Roy, University of California, LA, 1979–80
Hawkins, Bubbles, Illinois State University, 1978–79
Herron, Keith, Villanova University, 1980–81
Hightower, Wayne, University of Kansas, 1966–67
Hollins, Lionel, Arizona State University, 1983–84
Hollis, Essie, St. Bonaventure University, 1978–79
Howard, Otis, Austin Peay State University, 1978–79
Hubbard, Phil, University of Michigan, 1979–82
Johnson, Lee, East Tennessee State University, 1980–81
Johnson, Vinnie, Baylor University, 1981–87
Jones, Edgar, University of Nevada, Reno, 1981–83
Jones, Major, Albany State College, Georgia, 1984–85
Jones, Wali, Villanova University, 1975–76
Jones, Willie, Northwestern University, 1960–65
Kelser, Gregory, Michigan State University, 1979–82
Lanier, Robert, St. Bonaventure University, 1970–80

Lee, Ron, University of Oregon, 1979–82
Levingston, Cliff, Wichita State University, 1982–84
Lloyd, Earl, West Virginia State University, 1958–60
Long, John, University of Detroit, 1978–85
Lowe, Sidney, North Carolina State University, 1984–85
Mahorn, Rick, Hampton University, 1985–87
May, Scott, Indiana University, 1982–83
McAdoo, Robert, University of North Carolina, 1979–81
McElroy, James, Central Michigan University, 1979–80
McLemore, McCoy, Drake University, 1968–70
McNeill, Larry, Marquette University, 1978–79
Mengelt, John, Auburn University, 1972–76
Miles, Eddie, Seattle University, 1963–70
Money, Eric, University of Arizona, 1974–78, 1979–80
Moore, Otto, Pan American University, 1968–71, 1974–75
Murrey, Dorie, University of Detroit, 1966–67
Norwood, Willie, Alcorn A&M University, 1971–75, 1977–78
Pierce, Rick, Rice University, 1982–83
Porter, Howard, Villanova University, 1974–78
Porter, Kevin, St. Francis College, Pennsylvania, 1975–79
Price, Jim, University of Louisville, 1977–78
Robinson, Jackie, University of Nevada, Las Vegas, 1979–80
Robinson, Wayne, Virginia Tech University, 1980–81
Rodman, Dennis, Central Oklahoma State University, 1986–87
Romar, Lorenzo, University of Washington, 1984–85
Roundfield, Dan, Central Michigan University, 1984–85
Rowe, Curtis, University of California, LA, 1971–76
Russell, Walker, Western Michigan University, 1982–84
Salley, John, Georgia Tech University, 1986–87
Scott, Ray, University of Portland, 1961–67
Sellers, Phil, Rutgers University, 1976–77
Sheppard, Steven, University of Maryland, 1978–79
Shumate, John, University of Notre Dame, 1977–80
Simpson, Ralph, Michigan State University, 1976–78
Skinner, Al, University of Massachusetts, 1977–78
Smith, Jim, Ohio State University, 1982–83
Tatum, Earl, Marquette University, 1978–79
Teagle, Terry, Baylor University, 1984–86
Tolbert, Ray, Indiana University, 1982–84
Trapp, George, Long Beach State University, 1973–77
Tresvant, John, Seattle University, 1965–68
Tyler, Terry, University of Detroit, 1978–85
Wakefield, Andre, Loyola University of Chicago, 1978–79
Walker, Jimmy, Providence College, 1967–72
Wilkes, James, University of California, LA, 1982–83
Williams, Earl, Winston-Salem State University, 1975–76
Wright, Larry, Grambling State University, 1980–82

Golden State Warriors
Oakland Coliseum Arena
Oakland, California

Front Office Personnel

Attles, Alvin (General Manager) 1983–present
Thurmond, Nate (Director of Community Relations) 1981–87

Coaches

Attles, Alvin (Head) 1970–83

All-Stars

Sauldsberry, Woody 1959
Rodgers, Guy 1963–64, 1966
Chamberlain, Wilt 1965
Thurmond, Nate 1965–67, 1970, 1973–74
Russell, Cazzie 1972
Wilkes, Jamall 1976
Smith, Phil 1976–77
King, Bernard 1982
Short, Purvis 1986
Floyd, Eric 1987

All-Time Roster of The Golden State Warriors

Abdul-Rahman, Mahdi (Walt Hazzard), University of
    California, LA, 1972–73
Allen, Odis, University of Nevada, Las Vegas, 1971–72
Attles, Alvin, North Carolina A&T University, 1960–72
Beard, Alfred "Butch," University of Louisville, 1973–76
Bracey, Steven, University of Tulsa, 1974–75
Brewer, Ron, University of Arkansas, 1982–83
Bridges, William, University of Kansas, 1974–75
Brown, Rick, Mississippi State University, 1980–83
Burtt, Steven, Iona College, 1984–85
Carroll, Joe Barry, Purdue University, 1980–84, 1985–87
Chamberlain, Wilt, University of Kansas, 1959–65
Chenier, Phil, University of California, Berkeley, 1980–81
Coleman, E.C., Houston Baptist University, 1977–78
Collins, Don, Washington State University, 1983–84
Conner, Lester, Oregon State University, 1982–85
Cooper, Wayne, University of New Orleans, 1978–80
Cox, Westley, University of Louisville, 1977–79
Cross, Russell, Purdue University, 1983–84
Davis, Dwight, University of Houston, 1975–77
Dickey, Derrick, University of Cincinnati, 1973–78
Dudley, Charles, University of Washington, 1974–78
Duerod, Terry, University of Detroit, 1982–83

Ellis, Joe, University of San Francisco, 1966–74
Epps, Ray, Norfolk State University, 1978–79
Floyd, Eric, Georgetown University, 1982–87
Fontaine, Levi, Maryland State College, 1970–71
Frazier, Wilbert, Grambling State University, 1965–66
Free, World B., Guilford College, 1980–83
Gale, Michael, Elizabeth City State University, 1981–83
Green, Ricky, University of Michigan, 1977–78
Hawkins, Robert "Bubbles," Illinois State University, 1975–76
Hightower, Wayne, University of Kansas, 1962–65
Hillman, Darnell, San Jose State University, 1979–80
Johnson, Charles, University of California, Berkeley, 1972–78
Johnson, George, Dillard University, 1972–77
Johnson, Lynbert, Wichita State University, 1979–80
Johnson, Mickey, Aurora College, 1982–85
Kenon, Larry, Memphis State University, 1982–83
King, Bernard, University of Tennessee, 1980–82
Lattin, David, Texas Western University, 1967–68
Lear, Hal, Temple University, 1956–57
Lloyd, Lewis, Drake University, 1981–83
Lucas, John, University of Maryland, 1978–81
Marsh, Ricky, Manhattan College, 1977–78
Mayfield, William, University of Iowa, 1980–81
McLemore, McCoy, Drake University, 1964–66
McNeill, Larry, Marquette University, 1976–78
Moore, Jackie, LaSalle College, 1954–57
Naulls, Willie, University of California, LA, 1962–63
Parker, Sonny, Texas A&M University, 1976–82
Parrish, Robert, Centenary College, 1976–80
Plummer, Gary, Boston University, 1984–86
Ray, Clifford, University of Oklahoma, 1974–81
Richardson, Michael Ray, University of Montana, 1982–83
Robertson, Tony, University of West Virginia, 1978–79
Rodgers, Guy, Temple University, 1958–66
Rogers, Marshall, Pan American University, 1976–77
Romar, Lorenzo, University of Michigan, 1971–74
Russell, Cazzie, University of Michigan, 1971–74
Sauldesberry, Woody, Texas Southern University, 1957–60
Short, Purvis, Jackson State University, 1978–87
Smith, Derek, University of Louisville, 1982–83
Smith, Larry, Alcorn State University, 1980–86
Smith, Phil, University of San Francisco, 1974–80
Teagle, Terry, Baylor University, 1984–86

Thibeaux, Peter, St. Mary's College, 1984–86
Thurmond, Nate, Bowling Green State University, 1963–74
Tillis, Darren, Cleveland State University, 1983–84
White, Hubie, Villanova University, 1962–63
White, JoJo, University of Kansas, 1978–80
White, Rudy, Arizona State University, 1980–81

Whitehead, Jerome, Marquette University, 1984–85
Wilkes, Jamaal, University of California, LA, 1974–77
Williams, Gus, University of Southern California, 1975–77
Williams, Nate, Utah State University, 1977–79
Williams, Ron, West Virginia University, 1968–73
Williams, Sam, Arizona State University, 1981–84

Houston Rockets
Houston, Texas

All-Stars
Hayes, Elvin 1969–72
Malone, Moses 1978–82
Murphy, Calvin 1979
Sampson, Ralph 1984–87

All-Time Roster of The Houston Rockets
Abdul-Aziz, Zaid, Iowa State University, 1972–75, 1977–78
Adams, Don, Northwestern University, 1970–71
Bailey, Gus, University of Texas, El Paso, 1974–76
Bailey, James, Rutgers University, 1982–85
Barker, Tom, University of Hawaii, 1978
Barnes, Harry, Northeastern University, 1968–69
Behagan, Ron, University of Minnesota, 1977
Bond, Phil, University of Louisville, 1977
Bradley, Alonzo, Texas Southern University, 1977–80
Britt, Tyrone, Johnson C. Smith University, 1967–68
Bryant, Joe, LaSalle University, 1982–83
Coleman, E.C., Houston Baptist University, 1973–74, 1978
Davis, Jim, University of Colorado, 1971
Dorsey, Jackie, University of Georgia, 1978–79
Ford, Phil, University of North Carolina, 1983–84
Garrett, Calvin, Oral Roberts University, 1980–82
Green, John, Michigan State University, 1967–68
Harris, Steve, University of Tulsa, 1985–87
Hayes, Elvin, University of Houston, 1968–72
Henderson, Tom, University of Hawaii, 1972–76
Johnson, George, Stephen F. Austin State University, 1973–74
Johnson, John, University of Iowa, 1975–77
Johnson, Lee, East Texas State University, 1980
Jones, Caldwell, Albany State College, 1982–85
Jones, Dwight, University of Houston, 1976–79
Jones, Major, Albany State College, 1979–85
Jones, Nick, University of Oregon, 1967–68

Jones, Robin, St. Louis University, 1971
Kennedy, Eugene, Texas Christian University, 1976–77
Lantz, Stu, University of Nebraska, 1968–72
Lloyd, Lewis, Drake University, 1983–86
Lucas, John, University of Maryland, 1976–78, 1984–85
Malone, Moses, Petersburg H.S. (Virginia), 1976–82
McCray, Rodney, University of Louisville, 1983–87
McKenzie, Stan, New York University, 1972–73
McWilliams, Eric, Long Beach State University, 1972–73
Meely, Cliff, University of Colorado, 1971–76
Meriweather, Joe C., University of Southern Illinois, 1975–76
Moffett, Larry, Long Beach State University, 1977–78
Moore, Otto, Pan American University, 1972–74
Murphy, Calvin, Niagara University, 1970–83
Perry, Curtis, S.W. Missouri State University, 1970–71
Ratleff, Ed, Long Beach State University, 1973–78
Reid, Robert, St. Mary's (Texas), 1977–87
Riley, Ron, University of Southern California, 1973–76
Sampson, Ralph, University of Virginia, 1983–87
Shumate, John, University of Notre Dame, 1979–80
Smith, Bobby, University of Tulsa, 1969–70
Spriggs, Larry, Howard University, 1982
Taylor, Jeff, Texas Tech University, 1982–83
Teagle, Terry, Baylor University, 1982–85
Trapp, John, Nevada Southern, 1968–71
Watts, Slick, Xavier University, 1978–79
Wells, Owen, University of Detroit, 1974–75
White, Rudy, Arizona State University, 1'⁻⁻–79
Wiggins, Mitchell, Florida State University, 1985–86
Williams, Art, California Poly, 1967–70
Williams, Bernie, LaSalle University, 1969–71
Willoughby, Bill, Dwight Morrow H.S. (Englewood, N.J.), 1980–82

Indiana Pacers
Indianapolis, Indiana

Front Office Personnel
Embry, Wayne (Vice President/Basketball Consultant) 1985–87

Coaches
Daniels, Mel (Assistant) 1984–86

All-Stars (American Basketball Association Until 1975)
Brown, Roger 1968, 1970–71
Daniels, Mel 1969–71, 1973
McGinnis, George 1973–75
Knight, Billy 1977

All-Time Roster of The Detroit Pistons
Anderson, Jerome, West Virginia University, 1976–77
Armstrong, Warren, Wichita State University, 1970–71
Bantom, Michael, St. Joseph's University, 1977–82
Barnhill, John, Tennessee State University, 1969–72
Baum, John, Temple University, 1973–74
Behagan, Ron, University of Minnesota, 1977–78
Bennett, Mel, University of Pittsburgh, 1976–78
Bradley, Dudley, University of North Carolina, 1979–81
Brown, Roger, University of Dayton, 1967–75
Brown, Tony, University of Arkansas, 1984–86
Buckner, Quinn, Indiana University, 1985
Calhoun, Corky, University of Pennsylvania, 1978–80
Carrington, Robert, Boston College, 1977–78
Carter, Butch, Indiana University, 1981–84
Carter, Ron, Virginia Military Institute, 1979–80
Chenier, Phil, University of California, Berkeley, 1979–80
Combs, Leroy, Oklahoma State University, 1983–84
Daniels, Mel, University of New Mexico, 1968–74
Dantley, Adrian, University of Notre Dame, 1977–78
Darden, Oliver, University of Michigan, 1967–70
Davis, John, University of Dayton, 1978–82
Duren, John, Georgetown University, 1982–83
Edelin, Kenton, University of Virginia, 1984–85
Edmonds, Bobby Joe, University of Virginia, 1984–85
Edwards, James, University of Washington, 1977–81
Elmore, Len, University of Maryland, 1974–79
English, Alexander, University of South Carolina, 1978–80
Fleming, Vern, University of Georgia, 1984–86

Freeman, Don, University of Illinois, 1972–74
Grant, Travis, Kentucky State University, 1975–76
Hackett, Rudy, Syracuse University, 1976–77
Harding, Reginald, No College, 1967–68
Harkness, Gerald, Loyola University of Chicago, 1967–69
Hillman, Darnell, San Jose State University, 1971–77
Jackson, Ralph, University of California, LA, 1984–85
Jackson, Tracey, University of Notre Dame, 1983–84
Johnson, Clemon, Florida A&M University, 1979–83
Johnson, Gus, University of Idaho, 1972–73
Johnson, Mickey, Aurora College, 1979–80
Jones, Wilbert, Albany State College (Georgia), 1976–77
Kellogg, Clark, Ohio State University, 1982–86
Kelly, Arvesta, Lincoln University (Missouri), 1971–72
Kelser, Gregory, Michigan State University, 1984–85
Knight, Billy, University of Pittsburgh, 1974–83
Lamar, Dwight, University of Southwestern Louisiana, 1975–76
Lewis, Freddie, Arizona State University, 1967–77
Lowe, Sidney, North Carolina State University, 1983–84
Manning, Ed, Jackson State University, 1975–76
Mayes, Clyde, Furman University, 1976–77
McGinnis, George, Indiana University, 1971–82
Morgan, Guy, Wake Forest University, 1982–83
Natt, Ken, N.E. Louisiana University, 1980–81
Orr, Louis, Syracuse University, 1980–82
Pearson, Chuck, Auburn University, 1986–87
Radford, Wayne, Indiana University, 1978–79
Roundfield, Dan, Central Michigan University, 1975–78
Slaughter, Jose, University of Portland, 1982–83
Smith, Willie, University of Missouri, 1977–78
Sobers, Ricky, University of Nevada, Las Vegas, 1977–79
Stansbury, Terrence, Temple University, 1984–87
Tatum, Earl, Marquette University, 1977–78
Thacker, Tom, University of Cincinnati, 1968–71
Thomas, Jim, Indiana University, 1983–85
Waiters, Granville, Ohio State University, 1983–85
Williams, Herb, Ohio State University, 1981–87
Williamson, John, New Mexico State University, 1976–78
Wilson, Robert, Wichita State University, 1977–78
Winkler, Marvin, University of Southwestern Louisiana, 1971–72

Los Angeles Clippers
Los Angeles, California
San Diego Clippers 1978–84

Front Office Personnel
Baylor, Elgin (General Manager) 1986–present

Coaches
Chaney, Don (Head) 1985–87

All-Stars
McAdoo, Robert 1974–76
Smith, Randy 1976, 1978
Free, Lloyd 1980
Cummings, Terry 1984
Nixon, Norm 1985

All-Time Roster of The Los Angeles Clippers
Abdul-Aziz, Zaid (Don Smith), Iowa State University, 1976–77
Abdul Rahman, Mahdi (Walt Hazzard), University of California, LA, 1971–73
Archibald, Nate, University of Texas, El Paso, 1977–78 (Injured All Season)
Averitt, William "Bird," Pepperdine University, 1976–78
Barnes, Marvin, Providence College, 1977–80
Benjamin, Benoit, Creighton University, 1985–87
Bibby, Henry, University of California, LA, 1980–81
Bowman, Nate, Wichita State University, 1970–71
Bridgeman, Junior, University of Louisville, 1984–86
Brokaw, Gary, University of Notre Dame, 1977–78
Brooks, Michael, LaSalle College, 1979–82
Bryant, Emmette, DePaul University, 1970–72
Bryant, Joe, LaSalle College, 1979–82
Cage, Michael, San Diego State University, 1984–85
Carrington, Robert, Boston College, 1979–80
Catchings, Harvey, Hardin-Simmons University, 1984–85
Chambers, Jerry, University of Utah, 1971–72
Charles, Ken, Fordham University, 1973–76
Cooper, Joe, University of Colorado, 1982–83
Crawford, Fred, St. Bonaventure University, 1970–71
Criss, Charlie, New Mexico State University, 1981–82
Cummings, Terry, DePaul University, 1982–84
Dantley, Adrian, University of Notre Dame, 1976–77
Davis, Michael, Virginia Union University, 1970–72
Donaldson, James, Washington State University, 1983–85
Douglas, John, University of Kansas, 1983–85

Edwards, Franklin, Cleveland State University, 1984–85
Fox, Harold, Jacksonville University, 1972–73
Free, Lloyd, Guilford College, 1978–80
Garrett, Dick, Southern Illinois University, 1970–73
Gilliam, Herm, Purdue University, 1970–71
Glenn, Michael, Southern Illinois University, 1977–78
Gordon, Lancaster, University of Louisville, 1984–86
Harris, Bernard, Virginia Commonwealth University, 1974–75
Heard, Garfield, University of Oklahoma, 1973–76, 1980–81
Hill, Armond, Princeton University, 1981–82
Hilton, Fred, Grambling State University, 1971–73
Hodges, Craig, Long Beach State University, 1982–84
Hollins, Lionel, Arizona State University, 1982–83
Johnson, George, Dillard University, 1976–77
Johnson, Marques, University of California, LA, 1984–86
Jones, Wil, Albany State College, Georgia, 1977–78
Kelser, Gregory, Michigan State University, 1983–84
Knight, William, University of Pittsburgh, 1977–78
Loder, Kevin, Alabama State University, 1983–84
Malone, Moses, Petersburgh, Virginia H.S., 1976–77
Maxwell, Cedric, University of North Carolina, Charlotte, 1985–86
Mayes, Clyde, Furman University, 1976–77
McAdoo, Robert, University of North Carolina, 1972–77
McClain, Ted, Tennessee State University, 1977–78
McDaniels, Jim, Western Kentucky University, 1977–78
McKinney, Bill, Northwestern University, 1983–84
McMillian, Jim, Columbia University, 1973–76
McNeil, Larry, Marquette University, 1977–78
Moore, Lowes, West Virginia University, 1982–83
Nixon, Norm, Duquesne University, 1983–86
Norman, Coniel, University of Arizona, 1978–79
Owens, Eddie, University of Nevada, Las Vegas, 1977–78
Price, Jim, University of Louisville, 1976–77
Price, Tony, University of Pennsylvania, 1980–81
Shumate, John, University of Notre Dame, 1975–78
Smith, Derek, University of Louisville, 1983–86
Smith, Elmore, Kentucky State University, 1971–73
Smith, Phil, University of San Francisco, 1980–82
Smith, Randy, Buffalo State University, 1971–83
Smith, Robert, University of Nevada, Las Vegas, 1982–83
Smith, Robert "Bingo," University of Tulsa, 1979–80

Taylor, Brian, Princeton University, 1978–82
Towns, Linton, James Madison University, 1983–84
Warner, Cornell, Jackson State University, 1970–73
Warrick, Bryan, St. Joseph's University, 1984–85
Washington, Jim, Villanova University, 1974–76
Washington, Kermit, American University, 1978–79
Weatherspoon, Nick, University of Illinois, 1978–80
White, Rory, University of South Alabama, 1983–86

Whitehead, Jerome, Marquette University, 1978–84
Wicks, Sidney, University of California, LA, 1978–81
Wiley, Michael, Long Beach State University, 1981–82
Williams, Chuck, University of Colorado, 1976–78
Williams, Freeman, Portland State University, 1978–82
Willoughby, Bill, Dwight Morgan H.S. (Englewood, N.J.),
   1977–78
Wood, Al, University of North Carolina, 1981–83

Los Angeles Lakers
Inglewood, California

Front Office Personnel
Jackson, John (Assistant to the Owner) 1982
Harris, Pat (Vice-President, Finance) 1982

Coaches
Jones, K.C. (Assistant) 1971–72
Barnhill, John (Assistant) 1972–75

All-Stars
Baylor, Elgin 1959, 1961–65, 1967–70
Clark, Archie 1968
Chamberlain, Wilt 1969, 1971–73
Abdul-Jabbar, Kareem 1976–77, 1979–87
Johnson, Earvin 1980, 1982–87
Wilkes, Jamaal 1981, 1983
Nixon, Norm 1982
Worthy, James 1986–87

All-Time Roster of The Los Angeles Lakers
Abdul-Jabbar, Kareem, University of California, LA, 1975–87
Allen, Lucius, University of California, LA, 1974–77
Anderson, Cliff, St. Joseph's University, 1967–69
Barnes, Jim, Texas Western University, 1966–68
Barnett, Richard, Tennessee State University, 1962–65
Baylor, Elgin, Seattle University, 1958–72
Boone, Ron, Idaho State University, 1978–79
Branch, Adrian, University of Maryland, 1986–87
Brewer, Jim, University of Minnesota, 1980–82
Bridges, William, University of Kansas, 1972–75
Calhoun, David, University of Pennsylvania, 1974–75
Carr, Kenneth, North Carolina State University, 1977–79
Carter, Butch, Indiana University, 1980–81
Carter, Ron, Virginia Military Institute, 1978–79

Chamberlain, Wilt, University of North Carolina, 1968–73
Chambers, Jerry, University of Utah, 1966–67
Chones, Jim, Marquette University, 1979–81
Clark, Archie, University of Minnesota, 1966–68
Cooper, Michael, New Mexico University, 1978–87
Crawford, Fred, St. Bonaventure University, 1967–69
Dantley, Adrian, University of Notre Dame, 1977–79
Edwards, James, University of Washington, 1977–78
Ellis, Leroy, St. John's University, 1962–66
Felix, Ray, Long Island University, 1960–62
Freeman, Don, University of Illinois, 1975–76
Garrett, Calvin, Oral Roberts University, 1983–84
Garrett, Dick, Southern Illinois University, 1969–70
Grant, Travis, Kentucky State University, 1972–74
Hairston, Happy, New York University, 1969–75
Hardy, Alan, University of Michigan, 1980–81
Hawkins, Connie, University of Iowa, 1973–74
Hawkins, Tom, University of Notre Dame, 1966–69
Haywood, Spencer, University of Detroit, 1979–80
Hazzard, Walt, University of California, LA, 1964–67
Hudson, Lou, University of Minnesota, 1977–79
Johnson, Clay, University of Missouri, 1982–83
Johnson, Earvin, Michigan State University, 1979–87
Jones, Dwight, University of Houston
Jones, Earl, University of the District of Columbia, 1984–85
Jordan, Ed, Rutgers University, 1980–84
Lamar, Dwight, University of Southwestern Louisiana,
   1976–77
Mack, Oliver, East Carolina University, 1979–80
McAdoo, Robert, University of North Carolina, 1981–85
McCarter, Willie, Drake University, 1969–71
McGee, Michael, University of Michigan, 1981–86
McMillian, Jim, Columbia University, 1970–73

Nixon, Norm, Duquesne University, 1977–83
Patrick, Myle
Price, Jim, University of Louisville, 1972–74
Robinson, Flynn, University of Wyoming, 1971–73
Russell, Cazzie, University of Michigan, 1974–77
Scott, Byron, Arizona State University, 1983–87
Smith, Elmore, Kentucky State University, 1973–75
Spriggs, Larry, Howard University, 1983–86

Tatum, Earl, Marquette University, 1976–78
Thompson, Bill, University of Louisville, 1986–87
Trapp, John Q., Long Beach State University, 1972–73
Washington, Kermit, American University, 1973–78
Wiley, Gene, Long Beach State University, 1962–66
Wilkes, Jamaal, University of California, LA, 1977–85
Worthy, James, University of North Carolina, 1982–86

New Jersey Nets
East Rutherford, New Jersey

Front Office Personnel
Doby, Larry (Director of Community Affairs) 1979–present
Bassett, Tim (Regional Sales Manager) 1984–85

Coaches
Silas, Paul (Assistant) 1985

All-Stars (American Basketball Association Before 1975)
Erving, Julius 1974–75
Taylor, Brian 1975
Williams, Charles "Buck" 1982–83, 1986
Richardson, Michael Ray 1985

All-Time Roster of The New Jersey Nets (American Basketball Association Before 1975)
Archibald, Nat, University of Texas, El Paso, 1976–77
Ard, Jim, University of Cincinnati, 1970–73
Austin, John, Boston College, 1967–68
Averitt, William, Pepperdine University, 1977–78
Bailey, James, Rutgers University, 1981–83
Bantom, Michael, St. Joseph's College, 1976–77
Bassett, Tim, University of Georgia, 1976–80
Beard, Al, Norfolk State University, 1967–68
Birdsong, Otis, University of Houston, 1981–87
Bowens, Tom, Grambling State University, 1968–69
Boynes, Winford, University of San Francisco, 1978–80
Brewer, Ron, University of Arkansas, 1985
Carrington, Robert, Boston College, 1977–78
Catchings, Harvey, Hardin-Simmons University, 1978–79
Chones, Jim, Marquette University, 1972–73
Christian, Robert, Grambling College, 1969–70
Cook, Darwin, University of Portland, 1980–86

Cooper, Joe, University of Colorado, 1981–82
Daniels, Mel, University of New Mexico, 1976–77
Darden, Oliver, University of Michigan, 1968–69
Davis, Mel, St. John's University, 1976–77
Dawkins, Darryl, Maynard Evans H.S. (Florida), 1982–87
DePre, Joe, St. John's University, 1969–72
Dove, Lloyd "Sonny," St. John's University, 1969–72
Elliot, Robert, University of Arizona, 1978–81
Elmore, Len, University of Maryland, 1981–83
Erving, Julius, University of Massachusetts, 1973–76
Floyd, Eric "Sleepy," Georgetown University, 1982–83
Ford, Phil, University of North Carolina, 1982–83
Frazier, Wilbert, Grambling College, 1968–69
Gale, Michael, Elizabeth City State University, 1973–75
Green, Luther, Long Island University, 1969–71
Hackett, Rudy, Syracuse University, 1976–77
Hawkins, Robert "Bubbles," Illinois State University, 1976–78
Hillman, Darnell, San Jose State University, 1977–78
Hunter, Les, Loyola University of Chicago, 1969–71
Jackson, Tony, St. John's University, 1967–69
Johnson, Ed, Tennessee State University, 1969–71
Johnson, George, Dillard University, 1977–80
Johnson, Reginald, University of Tennessee, 1982–84
Johnson, Wallace "Micky," Aurora College, 1983, 1985–86
Jones, Edgar, University of Nevada, Reno, 1980–81
Jones, Rich, Memphis State University, 1976–77
Jordan, Ed, Rutgers University, 1977–81
Kenon, Larry, Memphis State University, 1973–75
King, Albert, University of Maryland, 1981–87
King, Bernard, University of Tennessee, 1977–79
Lacey, Sam, New Mexico State University, 1981–82
Lackey, Robert, Marquette University, 1972–74
Leaks, Manny, Niagara University, 1968–72

Love, Robert, Southern University, 1976–77
Lucas, Maurice, Marquette University, 1979–81
Manning, Ed, Jackson State University, 1974–75
Mathis, John, Savannah State University, 1967–68
McAdoo, Robert, University of North Carolina, 1980–81
McClain, Ted, Tennessee State University, 1975–76
McHartley, Maurice, North Carolina A&T University, 1968–69
McNeil, Larry, Marquette University, 1976–77
Money, Eric, University of Arizona, 1978–79
Moore, Lowes, West Virginia University, 1980–81
Natt, Calvin, Northeast Louisiana University, 1979–80
Porter, Kevin, St. Francis College (Pennsylvania), 1977–78
Ransey, Kelvin, Ohio State University, 1983–86
Richardson, Michael Ray, University of Montana, 1983–86
Robinson, Cliff, University of Southern California, 1979–81
Sappleton, Wayne, Loyola University of Chicago, 1984–85
Sherod, Edmund, Virginia Commonwealth University, 1982
Simpson, Ralph, Michigan State University, 1978–80
Skinner, Al, University of Massachusetts, 1976–79

Smith, Robert, University of Nevada, Las Vegas, 1979–80
Sojourner, Willie, Weber State College, 1973–75
Somerset, Willie, Duquesne University, 1968–69
Sparrow, Rory, Villanova University, 1980–81
Spraggins, Bruce, Virginia Union University, 1967–68
Taylor, Brian, Princeton University, 1972–76
Taylor, Ollie, University of Houston, 1970–74
Tolbert, Ray, Indiana University, 1981–82
Walker, Clarence "Foots," West Georgia College, 1980–84
Washington, Tom, Cheyney State University, 1971–73
Washington, Wilson, Old Dominion University, 1977–79
Webster, Elnardo, St. Peters College, 1971–72
Westbrook, Dexter, Providence College, 1967–68
Williams, Charles "Buck," University of Maryland, 1981–87
Williams, Earl, Winston-Salem State University, 1976–77
Williams, Ray, University of Minnesota, 1981–82
Williamson, John, New Mexico State University, 1976–80
Wilson, Michael, Marquette University, 1984–85
Woodson, Michael, Indiana University, 1981–82

New York Knickerbockers
New York, NY

Coaches
Reed, Willie (Head) 1977–79
Jackson, Stu (Assistant) 1987

All-Stars
Barnett, Dick 1968
Clifton, Nat (Sweetwater) 1957
Frazier, Walter 1970–76
Green, John 1962–63, 1965
King, Bernard 1984–85
Monroe, Earl 1975, 1977
Naulis, Willie 1958, 1960–62
Reed, Willis 1965–71
Richardson, Michael Ray 1980–82
Ewing, Pat 1986

All-Time Roster of The New York Knickerbockers
Bailey, James, Rutgers University, 1984–86
Bannister, Ken, St. Augustine's College, 1984–86
Barnes, Jim, Texas Western University, 1964–65
Barnett, Dick, Tennessee State University, 1965–74
Beard, Alfred "Butch," University of Louisville, 1975–79
Behagan, Ron, University of Minnesota, 1978–79

Bellamy, Walter, University of Indiana, 1965–69
Bibby, Henry, University of California, LA, 1972–75
Boozer, Robert, Kansas State University, 1963–65
Bowman, Nate, Wichita State University, 1967–70
Bradley, Alex, Villanova University, 1981–82
Bryant, Emmette, DePaul University, 1964–68
Buckner, Cleveland, Jackson State University, 1961–62
Bunch, Greg, California State University, Fullerton, 1978–79
Burden, Luther "Ticky," University of Utah, 1976–78
Carter, Butch, Indiana University, 1984–85
Carter, Reggie, St. John's University, 1980–82
Cartwright, William, University of San Francisco, 1979–87
Cavenall, Ron, Texas Southern University, 1984–85
Clemons, Jim, Ohio State University, 1977–80
Clifton, Nat, Xavier Louisiana, 1950–57
Copeland, Hollis, Rutgers University, 1979–82
Crawford, Fred, St. Bonaventure University, 1966–68
Dark, Jesse, Virginia Commonwealth University, 1974–75
Davis, Mel, St. John's University, 1973–77
Davis, Mike, University of Maryland, 1982–83
Demic, Larry, University of Arizona, 1979–82
Dukes, Walter, Seton Hall University, 1955–56
Elmore, Len, University of Maryland, 1983–84

Felix, Ray, Long Island University, 1954–60
Fillmore, Greg, Cheyney State University, 1970–72
Fogle, Larry, Canisius College, 1975–76
Frazier, Walter, Southern Illinois University, 1967–77
Garrett, Dick, Southern Illinois University, 1973–74
Glenn, Michael, Southern Illinois University, 1978–81
Green, John, Michigan State University, 1959–65
Harkness, Gerald, Loyola of Chicago, 1963–64
Haywood, Spencer, University of Detroit, 1975–79
Hogue, Paul, University of Cincinnati, 1962–64
Huston, Geoff, Texas Tech University, 1979–80
Jackson, Greg, Guilford College, 1974–75
King, Bernard, University of Tennessee, 1982–87
Knight, Toby, University of Notre Dame, 1977–82
Layton, Dennis, University of Southern California, 1976–77
Lucas, Maurice, Marquette University, 1981–82
Macklin, Durand "Rudy," Louisiana State University, 1983–84
Mayfield, Kendall, Tuskegee Institute, 1975–76
McAdoo, Robert, University of North Carolina, 1976–79
McGill, Bill, University of Utah, 1963–64
McMillian, Jim, Columbia University, 1976–78
Meminger, Dean, Marquette University, 1971–74, 1976–77
Meriweather, Joe C., Southern Illinois University, 1978–80
Miles, Eddie, Seattle University, 1971–72
Monroe, Earl, Winston-Salem State University, 1971–80
Naulls, Willie, University of California, LA, 1956–63
Orr, Louis, Syracuse University, 1982–85

Paulk, Charles, N.E. Oklahoma State, 1971–72
Porter, Howard, Villanova University, 1974–75
Rackley, Luther, Xavier University, Ohio, 1971–73
Ramsey, Cal, New York University, 1959–60
Reed, Willis, Grambling University, 1964–74
Richardson, Michael Ray, University of Montana, 1978–82
Robinson, Leonard, Tennessee State University, 1982–85
Russell, Cazzie, University of Michigan, 1966–71
Russell, Michael "Campy," University of Michigan, 1980–82
Scales, DeWayne, Louisiana State University, 1980–82
Shelton, Lonnie, Oregon State University, 1976–78
Sherod, Edmund, Virginia Commonwealth University, 1982–83
Short, Eugene, Jackson State University, 1975–76
Smith, Randy, Buffalo State University, 1981–82
Sparrow, Rory, Villanova University, 1983–85
Stallworth, David, Wichita State University, 1965–67, 1969–75
Stith, Tom, St. Bonaventure University, 1962–63
Taylor, Vince, Duke University, 1982–83
Tucker, Kelvin (Trent), University of Minnesota, 1982–85
Walker, Darrell, University of Arkansas, 1983–86
Walker, Ken, University of Kentucky, 1986–87
Warren, John, St. John's University, 1969–70
Webster, Marvin, Morgan State University, 1978–84
Wilkins, Gerald, University of Tennessee at Chattanooga, 1985–87
Williams, Milt, Lincoln University, 1970–71
William, Ray, University of Minnesota, 1977–84

Philadelphia 76ers
Philadelphia, Pennsylvania 19147-0240
Syracuse Nationals 1947–63

Front Office Personnel
Shelton, Clayton (Director of Group Sales—Tickets) 1985–86
Barnes, Marlene (Office Manager) 1985

All-Stars
Greer, Hal 1961–70
Jackson, Lucious 1965
Walker, Chet 1965–67
Chamberlain, Wilt 1966–68
McGinnis, George 1976–77
Erving, Julius, 1977–87
Cheeks, Maurice 1983
Malone, Moses 1983–86
Toney, Andrew 1983–84

All-Time Roster of The Philadelphia 76ers
Anderson, Cliff, St. Joseph's University, 1970–71
Anderson, Mitchell, Bradley University, 1982–83
Batom, Michael, St. Joseph's University, 1981–82
Barkley, Charles, Auburn University, 1984–87
Barnett, Richard, Tennessee State University, 1959–61
Bibby, Henry, University of California, LA, 1976–80
Bowman, Nate, Witchita State University, 1966–67
Boyd, Fred, Oregon State University, 1972–76
Bridges, William, University of Kansas, 1971–73
Bryant, Joe, LaSalle College, 1975–80
Carter, Fred, Mount St. Mary's College, 1971–77
Cathings, Harvey, Hardin-Simmons University, 1974–79
Chamberlain, Wilt, University of Kansas, 1964–68

Chambers, Jerry, University of Utah, 1968–69
Cheers, Maurice, West Texas State, 1978–87
Clark, Archie, University of Minnesota, 1968–72
Crawford, Fred, St. Bonaventure University, 1970–71
Cureton, Earl, University of Detroit, 1980–83
Davis, Monti, Tennessee State University, 1980–81
Dawkins, Darryl, Maynard Evans H.S., Orlando, Florida, 1975–82
Durrett, Ken, LaSalle College, 1974–75
Edwards, Franklin, Cleveland State University, 1981–84
Ellis, Leroy, St. John's University,, 1972–76
Erving, Julius, University of Massachusetts, 1976–87
Free, Lloyd, Guilford College, 1975–78
Furlow, Terry, Michigan State University, 1976–77
Green, John, Michigan State University, 1967–69
Green, Luther, Long Island University, 1972–73
Greer, Hal, Marshall University, 1968–69
Halimon, Shaler, Utah State University, 1968–69
Halliburton, Jeff, Drake University, 1972–73
Hinson, Roy, Rutgers University, 1986–87
Hollins, Lionel, Arizona State University, 1979–82
Hopkins, Robert, Grambling State University, 1956–60
Jackson, Lucious, Pan American University, 1964–72
Johnson, Clemon, Florida A&M University, 1982–86
Johnson, George, St. John's University, 1984–86
Johnson, Ollie, Temple University, 1980–82
Johnson, Reggie, University of Tennessee, 1982–83
Jones, Caldwell, Albany State College (Georgia), 1976–82
Jones, Charles, Albany State College (Georgia), 1983–84
Jones, Wally, Villanova University, 1965–72
Leaks, Manny, Niagara University, 1972–73
Lloyd, Earl, West Virginia State College, 1952–58

Malone, Moses, Petersburg H.S. (Virginia), 1982–86
Matthews, Wes, University of Wisconsin, 1983–84
McClain, Ted, Tennessee State University, 1977–78
McGinnis, George, Indiana University, 1975–78
Meriweather, Porter, Tennessee State University, 1962–63
Money, Eric, University of Arizona, 1978–80
Mosley, Glenn, Seton Hall University, 1977–78
Norman, Coniel, University of Arizona, 1974–76
Rackley, Luther, Xavier University (Ohio), 1973–74
Ramsey, Cal, New York University, 1960–61
Redmond, Marlon, University of San Francisco, 1978–79
Richardson, Clint, Seattle University, 1979–85
Robinson, Cliff, University of Southern California, 1986–87
Rule, Robert, Colorado State University, 1971–73
Simpson, Ralph, Michigan State University, 1978–79
Skinner, Al, University of Massachusetts, 1978–80
Threatt, Sedale, West Virginia Tech, 1983–86
Toney, Andrew, University of Southwestern Louisiana, 1980–85
Toone, Bernard, Marquette University, 1979–80
Trapp, John Q., Nevada Southern, 1972–73
Walker, Chet, Bradley University, 1962–69
Warley, Ben, Tennessee State University, 1962–66
Washington, Jim, Villanova University, 1969–72
Washington, Wilson, Old Dominion University, 1977–78
Wesley, Walter, University of Kansas, 1974–75
White, Hubie, Villanova University, 1963–64
Williams, Sam, Arizona State University, 1983–85
Wilson, George, University of Cincinnati, 1968–70
Wingate, David, Georgetown University, 1986–87
Wood, Leon, California State University, Fullerton, 1984–86

Phoenix Suns
Phoenix, Arizona

All-Stars

Hawkins, Connie 1970–73
Silas, Paul 1972
Scott, Charlie 1973–75
Davis, Walter 1978–81
Robinson, Leonard 1981
Johnson, Dennis 1981–82
Lucas, Maurice 1983
Nance, Larry 1985

All-Time Roster of The Phoenix Suns

Bantom, Michael, St. Joseph's University, 1973–76
Bradley, Dudley, University of North Carolina, 1981–82
Calhoun, David "Corky," University of Pennsylvania, 1972–75
Chamberlain, William, University of North Carolina, 1973–74
Chambers, Jerry, University of Utah, 1969–70
Christian, Robert, Grambling State University, 1973–74
Davis, Walter, University of North Carolina, 1977–87
Edwards, James, University of Washington, 1983–86

Foster, Rod, University of California, LA, 1983–86
Green, Lamar, Morehead State University, 1969–74
Haskins, Clem, Western Kentucky University, 1970–74
Hawkins, Connie, University of Iowa, 1969–73
Hawthorne, Nate, Southern Illinois University, 1974–76
Heard, Garfield, University of Oklahoma, 1975–80
High, Johnny, University of Nevada, Reno, 1979–83
Holton, Michael, University of California, LA, 1984–85
Humphries, Jay, University of Colorado, 1984–86
Jackson, Greg, Guilford College, 1974–75
Johnson, Dennis, Pepperdine University, 1980–83
Jones, Charles, University of Louisville, 1984–87
Lattin, David, University of Texas, El Paso, 1968–69
Layton, Dennis, University of Southern California, 1971–73
Lee, Ron, University of Oregon, 1976–79
McClain, Ted, Tennessee State University, 1978–79
McLemore, McCoy, Drake University, 1968–69
Moore, Otto, Pan American University, 1971–72

Nance, Larry, Clemson University, 1984–87
Niles, Michael, California State University, Fullerton, 1980–81
Perry, Curtis, S.W. Missouri State University, 1974–78
Pittman, Charles, University of Maryland, 1982–86
Robinson, Leonard, Tennessee State University, 1978–82
Sanders, Michael, University of California, LA, 1982–86
Scott, Alvin, Oral Roberts University, 1977–86
Scott, Charlie, University of North Carolina, 1971–75
Shumate, John, University of Notre Dame, 1975–76
Silas, Paul, Creighton University, 1969–72
Sobers, Rickey, University of Nevada, Las Vegas, 1975–77
Terrell, Ira, Southern Methodist University, 1976–77
Thompson, Bernard, Fresno State University, 1985–86
Weiley, Walter, University of Kansas, 1972–73
White, Rory, University of South Arizona, 1982–84
Williams, Earl, Winston-Salem State University, 1974–75
Wilson, George, University of Cincinnati, 1968–69

Portland Trailblazers
Portland, Oregon

Front Office Personnel

Scales, Wallace (Director of Community Relations/Special Events Director) 1971–87

Coaches

Wilkens, Leonard (Head) 1974–76

All-Stars

Wicks, Sidney 1972–75
Lucas, Maurice 1977–79
Hollins, Lionel 1978
Washington, Kermit 1980
Drexler, Clyde 1986

All-Time Roster of The Portland Trailblazers

Bailey, Carl, Tuskegee Institute, 1981–82
Bates, Billy Ray, Kentucky State University, 1979–82
Bowie, Sam, University of Kentucky, 1984–86
Brewer, Jim, University of Minnesota, 1979–80
Brewer, Ron, University of Arkansas, 1978–81
Calhoun, Corky, University of Pennsylvania, 1976–78
Carr, Kenneth, North Carolina State University, 1984–86
Colter, Steven, New Mexico State University, 1984–86
Cooper, Wayne, University of New Orleans, 1982–84

Crompton, Geoff, University of North Carolina, 1980–81
Davis, Charles, Wake Forest University, 1972–74
Davis, John, Dayton University, 1976–78
Davis, Robert, Weber State College, 1972–73
Dorsey, Jackie, University of Georgia, 1977–78
Drexler, Clyde, University of Houston, 1984–86
Dunn, T.R., University of Alabama, 1977–80
Ellis, LeRoy, St. John's University, 1970–71
English, Claude, University of Rhode Island, 1970–71
Gale, Michael, Elizabeth City State University, 1980–81
Gilliam, Herman, Purdue University, 1976–77
Gilmore, Walter, Fort Valley State College, 1970–71
Halimon, Shaler, Utah State University, 1970–71
Hamilton, Roy, University of California, LA, 1980–81
Harper, Michael, North Pack College, 1980–81
Hollins, Lionel, Arizona State University, 1975–80
Jeelani, Abdul, University of Wisconsin, Parkside, 1979–80
Johnson, Clemon, Florida A&M University, 1978–79
Johnson, John, University of Iowa, 1973–76
Johnson, Ken, Michigan State University, 1985–86
Johnson, Ollie, Temple University, 1973–74
Jones, Robin, St. Louis University, 1976–77
Jones, Steven, University of Oregon, 1975–77
Jordan, Ed, Rutgers University, 1983–84

Kersey, Jerome, Longwood College, 1984–86
Knight, Ron, Los Angeles State University, 1970–72
Layton, Dennis, University of Southern California, 1973–74
Lever, Lafayette, Arizona State University, 1982–84
Lucas, Maurice, Marquette University, 1976–80
Lumpkin, Paul, University of Miami (Ohio), 1974–75
Manning, Ed, Jackson State University, 1970–71
Martin, LaRue, Loyola University of Chicago, 1972–76
Mayes, Clyde, Furman University, 1976–77
McCarter, Willie, Drake University, 1971–72
McKenzie, Stan, New York University, 1970–73
McMillian, Jim, Columbia University, 1978–79
Murrey, Doris, University of Detroit, 1970–71
Natt, Calvin, Northeast Louisiana University, 1979–85
Neal, Lloyd, Tennessee State University, 1972–79

Norris, Audie, Jackson State University, 1982–85
Norwood, Willie, Alcorn A&M University, 1977–78
Ransey, Kelvin, Ohio State University, 1980–82
Roberson, Rick, University of Cincinnati, 1973–74
Smith, Greg, Western Kentucky University, 1972–76
Smith, Willie, University of Missouri, 1978–79
Terrell, Ira, Southern Methodist University, 1978–79
Thompson, Bernard, Fresno State University, 1984–85
Thompson, Mychal, University of Minnesota, 1978–86
Townes, Linton, James Madison University, 1982–83
Washington, Kermit, American University, 1979–82
Wicks, Sidney, University of California, LA, 1971–76
Wilkens, Lenny, Providence College, 1974–75
Valentine, Darnell, University of Kansas, 1981–86
Yelverton, Charles, Fordham University, 1971–72

Sacramento Kings
Sacramento, California

Rochester Royals, 1949-57
Cincinnati Royals, 1958-72
Kansas City Kings, 1972-85

Coaches
Russell, William (Head) 1987

All-Stars
Stokes, Maurice 1956–58
Robertson, Oscar 1961–70
Archibald, Nate 1972–76
Ford, Phil 1979–80
Birdsong, Otis 1981

All-Time Roster of The Sacramento Kings
Adams, Michael, Boston College, 1985–86
Allen, Lucius, University of California, LA, 1977–79
Archibald, Nate, University of Texas, El Paso, 1970–76
Behagan, Ron, University of Minnesota, 1973–75
Birdsong, Otis, University of Houston, 1977–81
Boone, Ron, Idaho State University, 1976–78
Boozer, Robert, Kansas State University, 1960–64
Buckhalter, Joe, Tennessee State University, 1961–63
Catlett, Sid, University of Notre Dame, 1971–72
Doblas, Leon, University of Alabama, 1980–83
Drew, Larry, University of Missouri, 1981–85
Elmore, Len, University of Maryland, 1979–80

Embry, Wayne, University of Miami (Ohio), 1957–66
Evans, Michael, Kansas State University, 1978–79
Ford, Phil, University of North Carolina, 1978–82
Gilliam, Herman, Purdue University, 1969–70
Green, John, Michigan State University, 1969–73
Green, Michael, Louisiana Tech University, 1979–80
Green, Sihugo, Duquesne University, 1956–59
Hairston, Harold "Happy," New York University, 1964–68
Hawkins, Tom, University of Notre Dame, 1962–66
Hillman, Darnell, San Jose State University, 1978–79
Jackson, Al, Wilberforce University, 1965–66
Johnson, Eddie, University of Illinois, 1981–86
Johnson, Ollie, Temple University, 1974–77
Johnson, Reggie, University of Tennessee, 1981–83
Johnson, Steve, Oregon State University, 1979–83
King, Reggie, University of Alabama, 1979–83
Knight, Billy, University of Pittsburgh, 1981–85
Lacey, Sam, New Mexico State University, 1970–82
Lewis, Freddie, Arizona State University, 1966–67
Loder, Kevin, Alabama State University, 1981–83
Love, Robert, Southern University, 1966–68
McCarter, Andre, University of California, LA, 1976–78
McKinney, Bill, Northwestern University, 1978–80

McNeill, Larry, Marquette University, 1973–76
Meriweather, Joe C., Southern Illinois University, 1980–85
Moore, Otto, Pan American University, 1973–74
Natt, Ken, N.E. Louisiana University, 1984–85
Paulk, Charles, N.E. Oklahoma State University, 1970–71
Pope, David, Norfolk State University, 1984–85
Rackley, Luther, Xavier University (Ohio), 1969–70
Ratiff, Michael, Eau Claire State University, 1972–73
Redmond, Marlon, University of San Francisco, 1978–80
Roberson, Rick, University of Cincinnati, 1975–76
Robertson, Oscar, University of Cincinnati, 1960–70
Robinson, Cliff, University of Southern California, 1981–82
Robinson, Flynn, University of Wyoming, 1966–68, 1970–77
Robinzine, Bill, DePaul University, 1975–80
Rodgers, Guy, Temple University, 1967–68
Sanders, Frankie, Southern University, 1980–81
Sibert, Sam, Kentucky State University, 1972–73
Smith, Don (Zaid Abdul-Aziz), Iowa State University, 1968–69
Suttle, Dane, Pepperdine University, 1983–85

Taylor, Brian, Princeton University, 1976–77
Thacker, Tom, University of Cincinnati, 1963–66
Theus, Reginald, University of Nevada, Las Vegas, 1983–86
Thompson, LaSalle, University of Texas, 1982–86
Thorpe, Otis, Providence College, 1984–86
Tucker, Al, Oklahoma Baptist University, 1968–69
Van Lier, Norm, St. Francis College (Pennsylvania), 1969–72
Walker, James, Providence College, 1973–76
Walton, Lloyd, Marquette University, 1980–81
Washington, Richard, University of California, LA, 1976–79
Wesley, Walter, University of Kansas, 1966–69
White, Joseph (Jo Jo), University of Kansas, 1980–81
Whitney, Charles, North Carolina State University, 1980–82
Williams, Nate, Utah State University, 1971–75
Williams, Ray, University of Minnesota, 1982–83
Williams, Willie, Florida State University, 1970–71
Wilson, George, University of Cincinnati, 1964–67
Woodson, Michael, Indiana University, 1981–87

San Antonio Spurs
San Antonio, Texas

All-Stars
Powell, Cincy 1968
Freeman, Don 1971–72
Silas, James 1975–76
Gervin, George 1975–85
Kenon, Larry 1978–79
Gilmore, Artis 1983
Robertson, Alvin 1986

All-Time Roster of The San Antonio Spurs
Averitt, William, Pepperdine University, 1973–74
Banks, Eugene, Duke University, 1981–85
Bassett, Tim, 1979–80
Bennett, Willis, 1968–69
Boone, Ron, 1968–71
Brewer, Ron, University of Arkansas, 1983–85
Brown, Roger, University of Dayton, 1973–74
Calvin, Mack, University of Southern California, 1976–77
Chambers, Jerry, University of Utah, 1973–74
Christian, Robert, Grambling College, 1969–70
Crompton, Jeff, University of North Carolina, 1982–83
Davis, Willie, 1970–71
Edmonson, Keith, Purdue University, 1983–84

Evans, Michael, Kansas State University, 1979–80
Freeman, Don, University of Illinois, 1970–72, 1974–75
Gale, Michael, Elizabeth City State University, 1975–81
Gervin, George, Eastern Michigan University, 1974–85
Gilmore, Artis, Jacksonville University, 1982–87
Green, Michael, Louisiana Tech University, 1977–79
Hallmon, Shaler, Utah State University, 1971–73
Hightower, Wayne, University of Kansas, 1970–71
Hill, Simmie, 1971–72
Johnson, George, St. John's University, 1980–82
Johnson, Reginald, University of Tennessee, 1980–82
Jones, Collis, University of Notre Dame, 1971–73
Jones, Edgar, University of Nevada, Reno, 1982–85
Jones, Ozell, California State University, Ful., 1984–86
Jones, Rich, 1969–75
Jones, Steve, University of Oregon, 1971–72
Kenjon, Larry, Memphis State University, 1975–80
Kennedy, Eugene, 1971–74
Knight, Billy, University of Pittsburgh, 1984–85
Layton, Dennis, University of Southern California, 1971–78
Leaks, Manny, 1968–70
Lockhart, Darrell, Auburn University, 1983–84
Lucas, John, University of Maryland, 1983–84

Maloy, Michael, Davidson College, 1972–73
McGill, William, Auburn University, 1983–84
McHartley, Maurice, 1967–70
Miller, Robert, University of Cincinnati, 1983–84
Mitchell, Michael, Auburn University, 1982–86
Moore, Gene, 1970–72
Moore, John, University of Texas, 1980–86
Mosley, Glenn, St. Bonaventure University, 1978–79
Nelson, Lou, University of Washington, 1976–77
Peck, Wiley, Mississippi State University, 1979–80
Powell, Cincy, 1967–70
Robertson, Alvin, University of Arkansas, 1984–86
Robinson, Oliver, University of Alabama, Birmingham, 1982–83
Sanders, Frank, Southern University, 1978–79
Sanders, Michael, University of California, LA, 1982–83

Scott, Willie, 1969–70
Shumate, John, University of Notre Dame, 1979–81
Silas, James, Elizabeth City State, 1972–81
Smith, Robert, University of Nevada, Las Vegas, 1982–83
Tart, Lavern, Bradley University, 1970–71
Temple, Collis, Louisiana State University, 1974–75
Thirdkill, David, Bradley University, 1984–85
Townes, Linton, James Madison University, 1984–85
Truitt, Ansley, University of California, Berkeley, 1972–73
Wiley, Gene, 1967–68
Wiley, Michael, Long Beach State University, 1980–81
Williams, Kevin, St. John's University, 1983–84
Willoughby, William, Dwight Morrow H.S. (Englewood, N.J.), 1982–83
Wise, Alan, Clemson University, 1975–76

Seattle Supersonics
Seattle, Washington

Front Office Personnel
Wilkens, Lenny (Vice-President/General Manager) 1985–86

Coaches
Wilkens, Lenny (Head) 1978–85
Bickerstaff, Bernie (Head) 1985–87

All-Stars
Hazzard, Walt 1968
Wilkens, Lenny 1969–71
Rule, Robert 1970
Haywood, Spencer 1972–75
Brown, Fred 1976
Johnson, Dennis 1979–80
Shelton, Lonnie 1982
Williams, Gus 1982–83

All-Time Roster of The Seattle Supersonics
Abdul-Aziz, Zaid (Don Smith), Iowa State University, 1970–72, 1975–76
Abdul-Rahman, Mahdi (Walt Hazzard), University of California, LA, 1967–68, 1973–74
Allen, Lucius, University of California, LA, 1969–70
Bailey, James, Rutgers University, 1979–82
Bamton, Michael, St. Joseph's University, 1975–77
Beard, Alfred "Butch," University of Louisville, 1972–73

Blackwell, Cory, University of Wisconsin, 1984–85
Boozer, Robert, Kansas State University, 1969–70
Bradley, Charles, University of Wyoming, 1983–84
Brisker, John, University of Toledo, 1972–75
Brown, Fred, University of Iowa, 1971–84
Clark, Archie, University of Minnesota, 1974–75
Cooper, Joe, University of Colorado, 1984–85
Donaldson, James, Washington State University, 1980–87
Dorsey, Jackie, University of Georgia, 1980–81
Dudley, Charles, University of Washington, 1972–73
Ellis, Dale, University of Tennessee, 1986–87
Fleming, Al, University of Arizona, 1977–78
Ford, Jake, Maryland State College, 1970–72
Gilliam, Herm, Purdue University, 1975–76
Gray, Leonard, Long Beach State University, 1974–77
Green, Michael, Louisiana Tech University, 1976–78
Haywood, Spencer, University of Detroit, 1970–75
Heard, Garfield, University of Oklahoma, 1970–72
Henderson, Gerald, Virginia Commonwealth University, 1984–85
Hill, Armond, Princeton University, 1980–82
Johnson, Clay, University of Missouri, 1983–84
Johnson, Dennis, Pepperdine University, 1976–80
Johnson, John, University of Iowa, 1977–82
Johnson, Vinnie, Baylor University, 1979–82
Kelser, Gregory, Michigan State University, 1981–83

King, Reggie, University of Alabama, 1983–85
Love, Robert, Southern University, 1976–77
McCray, Scooter, University of Louisville, 1983–85
McDaniel, Xavier, Wichita State University, 1985–87
McDaniels, Jim, Western Kentucky University, 1971–74
McIntosh, Kennedy, Eastern Michigan University, 1972–75
Norwood, Willie, Alcorn State University, 1975–77
Robinson, Jackie, University of Nevada, Las Vegas, 1978–79
Rule, Robert, Colorado State University, 1967–72
Shelton, Lonnie, Oregon State University, 1978–83
Short, Eugene, Jackson State University, 1975–76
Shumate, John, University of Notre Dame, 1980–81
Silas, Paul, Creighton University, 1977–80
Skinner, Talvin, University of Maryland, Eastern Shore, 1974–75
Smith, Phil, University of San Francisco, 1981–83
Sobers, Ricky, University of Nevada, Las Vegas, 1984–85
Stallworth, Bud, University of Kansas, 1972–74

Thompson, David, North Carolina State University, 1982–84
Tolbert, Ray, Indiana University, 1981–83
Tresvant, John, Seattle University, 1968–70
Tucker, Al, California Batiste University, 1967–69
Watts, Don, Xavier University, 1973–78
Weatherspoon, Nick, University of Illinois, 1976–77
White, Rudy, Arizona State University, 1980–81
Wilkens, Lenny, Providence College, 1968–72
Wilkerson, Bobby, Indiana University, 1976–77
Williams, Gus, University of Southern California, 1977–83
Williams, Kevin, St. John's University, 1986–87
Williams, Milt, Lincoln University, 1973–74
Wilson, George, University of Cincinnati, 1967–68
Winfield, Lee, North Texas State University, 1969–73
Wise, Willie, Drake University, 1977–78
Wood, Al, University of North Carolina, 1983–87
Wright, Toby, Indiana University, 1972–73
Young, Danny, Wake Forest University, 1984–87

Utah Jazz
Salt Lake City, Utah
New Orleans Jazz 1974-80
Utah Jazz 1980

All-Stars
Robinson, Leonard 1978
Dantley, Adrian 1980–86
Green, Rick 1984

All-Time Roster of The Utah Jazz
Anderson, Mitchell "J.J.," Bradley University, 1982–86
Bailey, Gus, 1977–78
Bailey, Thurl, North Carolina State University, 1983–86
Behagan, Ron, University of Minnesota, 1975–77
Bellamy, Walter, Indiana University, 1974
Bennett, Melvin, University of Pittsburgh, 1980–81
Bibby, Henry, University of California, LA, 1975–76
Boone, Ron, 1979–81
Boswell, Thomas, South Carolina State University, 1979–80, 1983–84
Boyd, Fred, 1975–78
Calvin, Mack, University of Southern California, 1979–80
Cattage, Robert, 1981–82
Coleman, E.C., Central Michigan University, 1974–77
Cooper, Wayne, University of New Orleans, 1980–81

Dantley, Adrian, University of Notre Dame, 1979–86
Dawkins, Paul, Northern Illinois University, 1979–80
Drew, John, Gardner-Webb College, 1982–85
Duren, John, Georgetown University, 1980–82
Eaves, Jerry, University of Louisville, 1982–84
Furlow, Terry, Michigan State University, 1979–80
Green, Lamar, 1974
Green, Ricky, University of Michigan, 1980–86
Green, Tom, 1978–79
Griffith, Darrell, University of Louisville, 1980–86
Hardy, James, University of San Francisco, 1978–82
Haywood, Spencer, University of Detroit, 1979
Howard, Maurice, University of Maryland, 1977
James, Aaron, Grambling College, 1974–79
Johnson, Ollie, Temple University, 1974–75
King, Bernard, University of Tennessee, 1979–80
Lee, Ron, University of Oregon, 1979
Lee, Russell, Marshall University, 1974
Malone, Karl, Louisiana Tech University, 1985–87
McElroy, James, Central Michigan University, 1975–79
McKinney, Bill, Northwestern University, 1980

Meriweather, Joe, Southern Illinois University, 1979
Moore, Otto, Pan American University, 1974–77
Natt, Ken, Northeast Louisiana University, 1982–85
Nelson, Louis, University of Washington, 1974–76
Nicks, Carl, University of Cincinnati, 1974–75
Robinson, Leonard, Tennessee State University, 1977–79
Robinzine, William, DePaul University, 1981–82
Smith, Robert, University of Nevada, Las Vegas, 1979
Stallworth, Bud, University of Kansas, 1974–77
Terrell, Ira, 1978–79

Wakefield, Andre, 1979
Watts, Don, Xavier University, 1978
Whitehead, Jerome, Marquette University, 1980
Wilkins, Jeff, Illinois State University, 1980–86
Williams, Don, University of Notre Dame, 1979–80
Williams, Nate, Portland State University, 1982
Williams, Ricky, 1982–83
Wood, Howard, University of Tennessee, 1981–82
Worthen, Sam, Marquette University, 1981

Washington Bullets
Landover, Maryland

Chicago Packers 1961–62
Chicago Zephyrs 1962–63
Baltimore Bullets 1963–73
Capital Bullets 1973–74
Washington Bullets 1974

Front Office Personnel
Unseld, Westley (Vice President/Assistant to the Chief/Administrative Officer) 1983–Present
Rascoe, Vivian (Administrative Officer) 1981–Present

Coaches
Jones, K.C. (Head) 1974–76
Carter, Fred (Assistant) 1985–87

All-Stars
Bellamy, Walter 1962–65
Johnson, Gus 1965–71
Unseld, Westley 1969–75
Monroe, Earl 1969, 1971
Clark, Archie 1972
Hayes, Elvin 1973–80
Chenier, Phil 1974–75, 1977
Bing, David 1976
Dandridge, Robert 1979
Malone, Jeff 1986
Malone, Moses 1987

All-Time Roster of The Washington Bullets
Adams, Michael, Boston College, 1986–87
Austin, John, Boston College, 1966–67
Bates, Billy Ray, Kentucky State University, 1982–83

Bailey, Gus, 1979–80
Ballard, Greg, University of Oregon, 1977–85
Barksdale, Don, University of California, LA, 1951–53
Barnes, Jim "Bad News," Texas Western University, 1965–66, 1970–71
Barnhill, John, Tennessee State University, 1979–80
Behagen, Ron, University of Minnesota, 1979–80
Bellamy, Walter, Indiana University, 1961–66
Bing, David, Syracuse University, 1975–77
Boston, Lawrence, University of Maryland, 1979–80
Brown, Lewis, University of Nevada, Las Vegas, 1980–81
Carr, Austin, University of Notre Dame, 1980–81
Carter, Fred, Mount St. Mary's College, 1969–72
Chenier, Phil, University of California, Berkeley, 1971–80
Chones, Jim, Marquette University, 1981–82
Clark, Archie, University of Minnesota, 1971–74
Barksdale, Don, University of California, LA, 1951–53
Barnes, Jim "Bad News," Texas Western University, 1965–66, 1970–71
Barnhill, John, Tennessee State University, 1979–80
Behagen, Ron, University of Minnesota, 1979–80
Bellamy, Walter, Indiana University, 1961–66
Bing, David, Syracuse University, 1975–77
Boston, Lawrence, University of Maryland, 1979–80
Brown, Lewis, University of Nevada, Las Vegas, 1980–81
Carr, Austin, University of Notre Dame, 1980–81

Carter, Fred, Mount St. Mary's College, 1969–72
Chenier, Phil, University of California, Berkeley, 1971–80
Chones, Jim, Marquette University, 1981–82
Clark, Archie, University of Minnesota, 1971–74
Cox, Chubby, Villanova University, 1982–83
Dandridge, Robert, Norfolk State University, 1977–81
Davis, Charles, Vanderbilt University, 1981–85
Daye, Darren, University of California, LA, 1983–85
DuVal, Dennis, Syracuse University, 1974–75
Ellis, Leroy, St. John's University, 1966–70
Felix, Ray, Long Island University, 1953–54
Gibson, Michael, University of South Carolina, Spartanburg, 1983–84
Gray, Leonard, Long Beach State University, 1976–77
Green, John, Michigan State University, 1965–67
Green, SiHugo, Duquesne University, 1961–65
Hardnett, Charles, Grambling College, 1962–65
Haskins, Clem, Western Kentucky University, 1974–76
Hayes, Elvin, University of Houston, 1972–81
Haywood, Spencer, University of Detroit, 1981–83
Henderson, Tom, University of Hawaii, 1976–79
Hightower, Wayne, University of Kansas, 1964–66
Hogue, Paul, University of Cincinnati, 1963–64
Hunter, Leslie, Loyola (Chicago), 1964–65
Johnson, Charles, University of California, Berkeley, 1977–79
Johnson, George, Stephen F. Austin State University, 1970–71
Johnson, Gus (Honeycomb), 1963–72
Johnson, Frank, Wake Forest University, 1981–85
Jones, Charles, Albany State College, 1984–86
Jones, Jimmy, Grambling College, 1974–77
King, Maurice, University of Kansas, 1962–63
Leaks, Manny, 1973–74
Lucas, John, University of Maryland, 1981–83
Mahorn, Rick, Hampton University, 1980–85
Malone, Jeff, Mississippi State University, 1983–87

Malone, Moses, Petersburg H.S. (Virginia), 1986–87
Manning, Ed, Jackson State University, 1967–70
Matthews, Wes, University of Wisconsin, 1980–81
McCarter, Andre, University of California, LA, 1980–81
McGill, Bill, University of Utah, 1962–64
Miles, Eddie, 1969–71
Monroe, Earl, Winston-Salem State University, 1967–72
Murrey, Dorie, University of Detroit, 1970–72
Nelson, Louis, University of Washington, 1973–74
Pace, Joe, Coppin State University, 1976–78
Porter, Kevin, St. Francis College (Pennsylvania), 1972–75, 1979–83
Roberts, Anthony, Oral Roberts University, 1980–81
Robinson, Cliff, University of Southern California, 1984–86
Robinson, Flynn, University of Wyoming, 1972–73
Sauldsberry, Woody, Texas Southern University, 1961–62
Scale, DeWayne, Louisiana State University, 1983–84
Scott, Ray, 1966–70
Sewell, Tom, Lamar University, 1984–86
Sobers, Ricky, University of Nevada, Las Vegas, 1982–84
Somerset, Willie, 1965–66
Stallworth, David, Witchita State University, 1971–74
Terry, Carlos, Winston-Salem State University, 1980–83
Tresvant, John, 1970–73
Unseld, Westly, University of Louisville, 1968–81
Walker, Phil, Millersville State University, 1977–78
Warley, Ben, 1965–67
Warrick, Bryan, St. Joseph's College, 1982–84
Weatherspoon, Nick, University of Illinois, 1973–77
Wesley, Walter, University of Kansas, 1973–74
Williams, Gus, University of Southern California, 1984–86
Williams, Guy, Washington State University, 1983–85
Williamson, John, New Mexico State University, 1979–80
Wilson, Michael, Marquette University, 1983–84
Wright, Larry, Grambling College, 1976–80

Boxing

Key to abbreviations:

TB = total bouts, KO = knockouts, W = win, WD = wins by decision, WF = wins on fouls, D = draws, L = loss, LD = losses by decision, LF = losses by fouls, KOBO = knockouts by opponents, TKO = technical knockout, ND = no decision, NC = no contest, Exh. = exhibition match, WBA = World Boxing Association, NABF = North American Boxing Federation, AAU = Amateur Athletic Union, WBC = World Boxing Council, UBSA = United States Boxing Association, NBA = National Boxing Association, IBF = International Boxing Federation

BEAU JACK

(Sidney Walker)
Born, April 1, 1921, Augusta, Georgia. Weight, 132-145 lbs.
Height, 5 ft. 6 in. Managed by Joe Caron (1940-1941). Bowman
Milligan (1941-1942). Chick Wergeles (1942-1951).

1940

May	20–Frankie Allen, Holyoke	D 4
May	27–Billy Bannick, Holyoke	KO 3
June	17–Jackie Parker, Holyoke	L 4
July	14–Joe Polowitzer, New Haven	L 6
July	21–Joe Polowitzer, New Haven	W 6
Aug.	19–Jackie Parker, Holyoke	L 4
Aug.	26–Carlo Daponde, Holyoke	W 4
Sept.	2–Jackie Small, Holyoke	KO 4
Sept.	16–Ollie Barbour, Holyoke	KO 3
Sept.	30–Tony Dupre, Holyoke	KO 2
Oct.	14–Abe Cohen, Holyoke	KO 3
Oct.	21–Ritchie Jones, Holyoke	KO 3
Nov.	14–Joey Stack, Holyoke	W 6
Dec.	2–Jimmy Fox, Holyoke	W 6
Dec.	16–Young Johnny Buff, Holyoke	KO 1
Dec.	30–Mel Neary, Holyoke	KO 5

1941

Jan.	27–Joey Silva, Holyoke	L 6
Feb.	10–Mexican Joe Rivers, Holyoke	KO 4
Feb.	24–Lenny Isrow, Holyoke	KO 3
Mar.	10–Nickey Jerome, Holyoke	KO 3
Mar.	24–Joey Silva, Holyoke	W 6
Apr.	7–Tony Iacovacci, Holyoke	KO 6
Apr.	21–Bob Reilly, Holyoke	KO 7

Apr.	28–Harry Gentile, Holyoke	KO 1
May	5–Chester Rico, Holyoke	D 8
May	19–George Salamone, Holyoke	KO 8
June	2–Tommy Spiegel, Holyoke	W 8
June	16–George Zengaras, Holyoke	W 8
Aug.	5–Minnie DeMore, Brooklyn	KO 3
Aug.	14–Al Roth, Brooklyn	KO 6
Aug.	26–Guillermo Puente, New York	W 6
Sept.	19–Al Reid, New York	KO 7
Oct.	14–Tommy Spiegel, Brooklyn	W 8
Oct.	31–Guillermo Puente, New York	W 8
Dec.	1–Mexican Joe Rivers, Brooklyn	KO 3
Dec.	8–Freddie Archer, New York	L 8
Dec.	29–Freddie Archer, New York	L 8

1942

Jan.	5–Carmelo Fenoy, Holyoke	W 10
May	22–Bobby (Poison) Ivy, New York	W 8
June	23–Guillermo Puente, New York	KO 1
July	3–Bobby McIntire, Fort Hamilton	KO 6
July	7–Cosby Linson, Long Island City	KO 8
Aug.	1–Ruby Garcia, Elizabeth, N.J.	KO 6
Aug.	18–Carmine Fatta, New York	KO 1
Aug.	28–Billy Murray, New York	W 10
Sept.	22–Joe Torres, Washington, D.C.	KO 4
Oct.	2–Chester Rico, New York	W 8

Oct. 12–Terry Young, New York . . . . W 10
Nov. 13–Allie Stolz, New York . . . . KO 7
Dec. 18–Tippy Larkin, New York . . . . KO 3
    (Won Vacant New York World Lightweight Title)

1943

Feb. 5–Fritzie Zivic . . . . W 10
Mar. 5–Fritzie Zivic, New York . . . . W 12
Apr. 2–Henry Armstrong, New York . . . . W 10
May 21–Bob Montgomery, New York. . . . . L 15
    (Lost New York World Lightweight Title)
June 21–Maxie Starr, Washington, D.C. . . . . KO 6
July 19–Johnny Hutchinson, Philadelphia . . . . KO 6
Oct. 4–Bobby Ruffin, New York. . . . . L 10
Nov. 19–Bob Montgomery, New York . . . . W 15
    (Regained New York World Lightweight Title)

1944

Jan. 7–Lulu Costantino, New York . . . . W 10
Jan. 28–Sammy Angott, New York . . . . D 10
Feb. 15–Maxie Berger, Cleveland. . . . . W 10
Mar. 3–Bob Montgomery, New York . . . . L 15
    (Lost New York World Lightweight)
Mar. 17–Al Davis, New York. . . . . W 10
Mar. 31–Juan Zurita, New York . . . . W 10
Aug. 4–Bob Montgomery, New York . . . . W 10

1945

Dec. 14–Willie Joyce, New York . . . . W 10

1946

Jan. 4–Morris Reif, New York . . . . KO 4
Feb. 8–Johnny Greco, New York. . . . . D 10
May 31–Johnny Greco, New York. . . . . W 10
July 8–Sammy Angott, Washington . . . . KO 7
Aug. 19–Danny Kapilow, Washington. . . . . W 10
Oct. 22–Bustler Tyler, Elizabeth . . . . L 10

1947

Feb. 21–Tony Janiro, New York . . . . KO by 4
Nov. 3–Humberto Zavala, St. Louis. . . . . KO 4
Dec. 16–Frankie, Vigeant, Hartford . . . . W 10
Dec. 29–Billy Kearns, Providence. . . . . W 10

1948

Jan. 5–Jimmy Collins, New Haven . . . . KO 2
Jan. 28–Johnny Bratton, Chicago . . . . KO 8
Feb. 20–Terry Young, New York . . . . L 10
Apr. 9–Johnny Greco, Montreal . . . . W 10

May 24–Tony Janiro, Washington . . . . W 10
July 12–Ike Williams, Philadelphia. . . . . KO by 6
    (For World Lightweight Title)
Oct. 28–Eric Boon, Washington, D.C. . . . . KO 3
Nov. 23–Chuck Taylor, Philadelphia. . . . . KO 3
Dec. 17–Leroy Willis, Detroit. . . . . W 10

1949

Jan. 17–Jackie Weber, Boston. . . . . W 10
Mar. 28–Johnny Greco, Montreal . . . . L 10
July 19–Eddie Giosa, Washington . . . . W 10
Aug. 31–Johnny Gonsalves, Oakland. . . . . W 10
Sept. 6–Tote Martinez, Los Angeles . . . . W 10
Sept. 30–Livie Minelli, Chicago. . . . . W 10
Oct. 14–Kid Gavilan, Chicago . . . . L 10
Dec. 16–Tuzo Portugez, New York . . . . L 10

1950

Apr. 3–Joey Carkido, Hartford . . . . L 10
Apr. 14–Lew Jenkins, Washington . . . . KO 5
May 8–Jackie Weber, Providence . . . . KO 7
May 22–Johnny Potenti, Boston. . . . . W 10
JUne 28–Ronnie Harper, Indianapolis . . . . KO 5
July 17–Bobby Timpson, Atlanta . . . . KO 6
Oct. 4–Philip Kim, Honolulu . . . . W 10
Nov. 14–Frankie Fernandez, Honolulu . . . . L 10

1951

Jan. 1–Fitzie Pruden, Milwaukee . . . . L 10
Jan. 18–Del Flanagan, Minneapolis. . . . . L 10
Jan. 31–Emil Barao, Oakland, Calif. . . . . W 10
Mar. 5–Ike Williams, Providence. . . . . L 10
Mar. 30–Leroy Williams, New Orleans . . . . W 10
Apr. 16–Gil Turner, Philadelphia. . . . . L 10
May 21–Gil Turner, Philadelphia . . . . KO by 8

1952-1954

(Inactive)

1955

Jan. 20–Eddie Green, Columbia, S.C. . . . . W 10
Apr. 9–Ike Williams, Augusta, Ga. . . . . D 10
July 4–Willie Johnson, Dayton Beach . . . . W 10
Aug. 12–Ike Williams, Augusta, Ga. . . . . KO by 9

TB	KO	WD	WF	D	LD	LF	KOBO	ND	NC
112	40	43	0	5	20	0	4	0	0

Elected to Boxing Hall of Fame, 1972

BOB MONTGOMERY

Born, February 10, 1919, Sumter, South Carolina. Weight,
133-134 lbs. Height, 5 ft. 8 in. Managed by Frankie Thomas
(1938-1944), Joe Gramby (1944-1947).

1938

Oct.	23–Young Johnny Buff, Atlantic City .... KO	2
Oct.	27–Pat Patucci, Atlantic City .... KO	2
Nov.	4–Eddie Stewart, Philadelphia .... KO	2
Nov.	10–Joe Beltrante, Atlantic City .... KO	3
Nov.	17–Red Rossi, Atlantic City .... KO	2
Dec.8	–Jackie Sheppard, Atlantic City .... W	8

1939

Jan.	19–Harvey Jacobs, Atlantic City .... KO	1
Feb.	2–Charley Burns, Atlantic City .... W	8
Feb.	23–Jay Macedon, Atlantic City .... W	8
Mar.	9–Billy Miller, Atlantic City .... KO	2
Mar.	16–Frankie Saia, Philadelphia .... KO	4
Mar.	30–Benny Berman, Atlantic City .... W	8
Apr.	13–Young Raspi, Atlantic City .... KO	6
Apr.	20–Eddie Guerra, Atlantic City .... W	8
May	1–George Zengaras, Philadelphia .... D	10
May	23–Norment Quarles, Philadelphia .... KO	4
June	15–Charley Burns, Atlantic City .... KO	2
June	21–Tommy Rawson, Philadelphia .... KO	1
July	3–Frankie Wallace, Philadelphia .... W	10
Aug.	14–Jimmy Murray, Philadelphia .... KO	3
Aug.	24–Ray Ingram, Atlantic City .... W	10
Oct.	5–Charles Gilley, Atlantic City .... KO	6
Oct.	23–Mike Evans, Philadelphia .... W	10
Nov.	10–Tommy Spiegel, Philadelphia L	10
Nov.	17–Mike Evans, Philadelphia .... KO	1

1940

Jan.	29–Al Nettlow, Philadelphia .... D	10
Mar.	11–Al Nettlow, Philadelphia .... W	10
June	3–Al Nettlow, Philadelphia .... W	12
July	5–Jimmy Vaughn, Atlantic City .... KO	2
Sept.	16–Lew Jenkins, Philadelphia L	10
Nov.	7–Norment Quarles, Atlantic City .... D	10
Nov.	25–Sammy Angott, Philadelphia L	10

1941

Jan.	29–Julie Kogon, Brooklyn .... W	8
Feb.	7–Al Nettlow, New York .... W	8
Mar.	3–George Zengaras, Philadelphia .... KO	3
Apr.	28–Nick Peters, Philadelphia .... KO	3

May	16–Lew Jenkins, New York .... W	10
June	16–Manuel Villa, Baltimore .... KO	1
June	30–Wishy Jones, Washington, D.C. .... KO	6
July	3–Frankie Wallace, Atlantic City .... KO	3
July	14–Luther (Slugger) White, Baltimore ...... W	10
Sept.	8–Mike Kaplan, Philadelphia .... W	10
Oct.	10–Davey Day, Chicago, Ill .... KO	1
Oct.	24–Julie Kogon, Chicago, Ill .... W	10
Oct.	30–Frankie Wallace, Williamsport .... KO	5
Dec.	8–Jimmy Garrison, Philadelphia .... KO	4

1942

Jan.	5–Mayon Padlo, Philadelphia .... KO	8
Mar.	6–Sammy Angott, New York L	12
Apr.	20–Joey Peralta, Philadelphia .... W	10
May	8–Carmen Notch, Toledo, Ohio .... W	10
July	7–Sammy Angott, Philadelphia L	12
Aug.	13–Bobby Ruffin, New York .... W	10
Oct.	6–Maxie Shapiro, Philadelphia L	10
Dec.	1–Maxie Shapiro, Philadelphia .... W	10

1943

Jan.	8–Chester Rico, New York .... KO	8
Feb.	22–Lulu Costantino, Philadelphia .... W	10
Apr.	5–Roman Alvarez, Philadelphia .... KO	4
Apr.	30–Gene Johnson, Scranton, Pa. .... W	10
May	3–Henry Vasquez, Holyoke, Mass .... W	8
May	21–Beau Jack, New York .... W	15
	(Won New York World Lightweight Title)	
July	4–Al Reasoner, New Orleans .... KO	6
July	30–Frankie Wills, Washington .... W	10
Aug.	23–Fritzie Zivic, Philadelphia .... W	10
Oct.	25–Petey Scalzo, Philadelphia .... KO	6
Nov.	19–Beau Jack, New York L	15
	(Lost New York World Lightweight Title)	

1944

Jan.	7–Joey Peralta, Detroit .... W	10
Jan.	25–Ike Williams, Philadelphia .... KO	12
Feb.	18–Al Davis, New York .... KO by	1
Mar.	3–Beau Jack, New York .... W	15
	(Regained New York World Lightweight Title)	
Apr.	28–Joey Peralta, Chicago .... W	10
Aug.	4–Beau Jack, New York L	10

1945

Feb. 13–Cecil Hudson, Los Angeles .... W 10
Mar. 20–Genaro Rojo, Los Angeles.............. KO 8
May 8–Nick Moran, Los Angeles................ L 10
July 9–Nick Moran, Philadelphia .... W 10

1946

Feb. 3–Bill Parsons, New Orleans .... W 10
Feb. 15–Leo Rodak, Chicago, Ill................. W 10
Mar 8–Tony Pellone, New York .... W 10
Mar. 21–Ernie Petrone, New Haven .... KO 4
June 28–Allie Stolz, New York .... KO 13
(Retained New York World Lightweight Title)
July 29–George LaRover, Springfield, Mass........ W 10
Aug. 19–Wesley Mouzon, Philadelphia .... KO by 2
Nov. 26–Wesley Mouzon, Philadelphia........... KO 8
(Retained New York World Lightweight Title)

1947

Jan. 20–Eddie Giosa, Philadelphia .... KO 5
Feb. 7–Tony Pellone, Detroit .... L 10

Feb. 25–Joey Barnum, Los Angeles .... KO 7
Mar. 31–Jesse Flores, San Francisco .... KO 3
May 12–George LaRover, Philadelphia .... W 10
June 2–Julie Kogon, New Haven, Conn. .... W 10
June 9–Frankie Cordino, Springfield .... W 10
Aug. 4–Ike Williams, Philadelphia............ KO by 6
(For Vacant World Lightweight Title)
Nov. 24–Livio Minelli, Philadelphia .... L 10
Dec. 22–Joey Angelo, Boston, Mass.............. L 10

1948-1949

(Inactive)

1950

Feb. 3–Aldo Minelli, Washington................. L 10
Feb. 27–Johnny Greco, Montreal .... L 10
Mar. 9–Don Williams, Worcester................. L 10
Mar. 27–Eddie Giosa, Philadelphia .... L 10

TB	KO	WD	WF	D	LD	LF	KOBO	ND	NC
97	37	38	0	3	16	0	3	0	0

ISIAH (IKE) WILLIAMS

Born, August 2, 1923, Brunswick, Georgia. Weight, 125-150
lbs. Height, 5 ft. 9 ½ in. Managed by Connie McCarthy
(1940-1946), Frank (Blinky) Palermo (1946-1955).

1940

Mar. 15–Carmine Fiotti, New Brunswick.......... W 4
Mar. 29–Billy George New Brunswick............. W 4
Apr. 1–Patsy Gall, Hazleton, Pa .... D 6
may 10–Billy Hildebrand, Morristown............. L 6
June 17–Billy Hildebrand, Mt. Freedom .... KO 6
July 19–Joe Romero, Mt. Freedom, N.J. .... KO 2
Sept. 9–Pete Kelly, Trenton, N.J................ KO 2
Nov. 11–Tony Maglione, Trenton................. L 8

1941

Jan. 6–Tommy Fontana, Trenton .... W 8
Feb. 19–Carl Zullo, Perth Amboy .... KO 2
Mar. 5–Joey Zodda, Perth Amboy .... L 6
Mar. 19–Joe Genovese, Perth Amboy .... W 5
Apr. 9–Johnny Rudolph, Perth Amboy........... W 6
Apr. 14–Hugh Civatte, Trenton.................. KO 3
Oct. 1–Freddie Archer, Perth Amboy............ L 8
Oct. 27–Benny Williams, Newark .... D 6

Nov. 3–Vince DiLeo, Newark, N.J. .... W 6
Dec. 16–Eddie Dowl, Perth Amboy............... W 6

1942

–Ruby Garcia, Atlantic City............... W 6
Mar. 26–Pedro Firpo, Atlantic City .... W 8
Apr. 10–Angelo Panatellas, Atlantic City .... KO 5
Apr. 24–Willie Roache, Perth Amboy .... W 8
May 7–Abie Kaufman, Atlantic City .... W 8
June 29–Ivan Christie, Newark .... KO 5
July 29–Angelo Maglione, Trenton .... KO 3
Sept. 10–Charley Davis, Elizabeth................ W 8
Oct. 20–Gene Burton, White Plains .... KO 4
Dec. 7–Bob Gunther, Trenton.................. W 8
Dec. 21–Sammy Daniels, Baltimore .... W 6

1943

Jan. 29–Jerry Moore, New York .... W 6
Feb. 22–Sammy Daniels, Philadelphia............ KO 2

Feb.   23–Bobby McQuillar, Cleveland............ KO   3
Mar.   8–Bill Speary, Philadelphia............... KO   2
Apr.   2–Rudy Giscombe, New York .... KO   3
Apr.   5–Ruby Garcia, Philadelphia.............. W   8
Apr.   21–Joe Genovese, Cleveland .... KO   4
May   7–Maurice LaChance, Boston............. W   8
May   17–Ray Brown, Philadelphia............... W   10
July   19–Jimmy Hatcher, Philadelphia .... KO   6
Aug.   24–Tommy Jessup, Hartford............... KO   5
Aug.   31–Johnny Bellus, Hartford .... W   10
Sept. 13–Jerry Moore, W. Springfield .... W   10
Oct.   1–Maurice LaChance, Boston .... KO   4
Oct.   22–Ed Perry, New Orleans................ KO   2
Oct.   29–Gene Johnson, New Orleans .... W   10
Nov.   8–Johnny Hutchinson, Philadelphia .... KO   3
Dec.   13–Mayon Padlo, Philadelphia .... W   10

1944

Jan.   25–Bob Montgomery, Philadelphia .... KO by 12
Feb.   28–Ellis Phillips, Philadelphia............. KO   1
Mar.   13–Leo Francis, Trenton, N.J. .... W   8
Mar.   27–Joey Peralta, Philadelphia .... KO   9
Apr.   10–Leroy Saunders, Holyoke .... KO   5
Apr.   17–Mike Delis, Philadelphia............... KO   1
May   16–Slugger White, Philadelphia .... W   10
June   7–Sammy Angott, Philadelphia .... W   10
June   23–Cleo Shans, New York .... KO   10
July   10–Joey Pirrone, Philadelphia............. KO   1
July   20–Julie Kogon, New York .... W   10
Aug.   29–Jimmy Hatcher, Washington .... W   10
Sept. 6–Sammy Angott, Philadelphia .... W   10
Sept. 19–Freddie Dawson, Philadelphia .... KO   4
Oct.   18–Johnny Green, Buffalo, N.Y. .... KO   2
Nov.   2–Ruby Garcia, Baltimore, Md............ KO   7
Nov.   13–Willie Joyce, Philadelphia L   10
Dec.   5–Lulu Costantino, Cleveland............. W   10
Dec.   12–Dave Castilloux, Buffalo .... KO   5

1945

Jan.   8–Willie Joyce, Philadelphia............. W   12
Jan.   22–Mike Berger, Philadelphia............. KO   4
Mar.   2–Willie Joyce, New York L   12
Mar.   26–Dorsey Lay, Philadelphia .... KO   3
Apr.   18–Juan Zurita, Mexico City.............. KO   2
        (Won NBA Lightweight Title)
June   8–Willie Joyce, New York L   10
Aug.   14–Charley Smith, Union City .... W   10

Aug.   28–Gene Burton, Philadelphia .... W   10
Sept. 7–Nick Moran, New York .... W   10
Sept. 19–Sammy Angott, Pittsburgh .... KO by   6
Nov.   26–Wesley Mouzon, Philadelphia........... D   10

1946

Jan.   8–Charley Smith, Trenton................ W   10
Jan.   20–Johnny Bratton, New Orleans .... W   10
Jan.   28–Freddie Dawson, Philadelphia .... D   10
Feb.   14–Cleo Shans, Orange, N.J. .... W   10
Feb.   22–Ace Miller, Detroit, Mich............... W   10
Mar.   11–Eddie Giosa, Philadelphia .... KO   1
Apr.   8–Eddie Giosa, Philadelphia .... KO   4
Apr.   30–Enrique Bolanos, Los Angeles.......... KO   8
        (Retained NBA Lightweight Title)
June   12–Bobby Ruffin, Brooklyn, N.Y............ KO   5
Aug.   6–Ivan Christie, Norwalk, Conn........... KO   2
Sept. 4–Ronnie James, Cardiff, Wales .... KO   9
        (Retained NBA Lightweight Title)

1947

Jan.   27–Gene Burton, Chicago, Ill L   10
Apr.   14–Frankie Conti, Allentown, Pa. .... KO   7
Apr.   25–Willie Russell, Columbus, Ohio........... W   10
May   9–Ralph Zannelli, Boston, Mass. .... W   10
May   26–Juste Fontaine, Philadelphia .... KO   4
June   20–Tippy Larkin, New York................ KO   4
Aug.   4–Bob Montgomery, Philadelphia .... KO   6
        (Won Vacant World Lightweight Title)
Sept. 29–Doll Rafferty, Philadelphia.............. KO   4
Oct.   10–Talmadge Bussey, Detroit .... KO   9
Dec.   12–Tony Pellone, New York .... W   10

1948

Jan.   13–Doug Carter, Camden, N.J............... W   10
Jan.   26–Freddie Dawson, Philadelphia........... W   10
Feb.   9–Livio Minelli, Philadelphia............. W   10
Feb.   27–Kid Gavilan, New York .... W   10
May   5–Rudy Cruz, Oakland, Calif. .... W   10
May   25–Enrique Bolanos, Los Angeles .... W   15
        (Retained World Lightweight Title)
July   12–Beau Jack, Philadelphia .... KO   6
        (Retained World Lightweight Title)
Sept. 23–Jesse Flores, New York .... KO   10
        (Retained World Lightweight Title)
Nov.   8–Buddy Garcia, Philadelphia .... KO   1
Nov.   18–Billy Nixon, Philadelphia .... KO   4

1949

Jan.	17-Johnny Bratton, Philadelphia	W 10
Jan.	28-Kid Gavilan, New York	L 10
Apr.	1-Kid Gavilan, New York	L 10
Apr.	23-Vince Turpin, Cleveland	KO 6
June	21-Irvin Steen, Los Angeles	W 10
July	21-Enrique Bolanos, Los Angeles	KO 4
	(Retained World Lightweight Title)	
Aug.	3-Benny Walker, Oakland	W 10
Sept.	30-Doug Ratford, Philadelphia	W 10
Oct.	24-Al Mobley, Trenton, N.J.	W 10
Nov.	14-Jean Walzack, Philadelphia	W 10
Dec.	5-Freddie Dawson, Philadelphia	W 15
	(Retained World Lightweight Title)	

1950

Jan.	20-Johnny Bratton, Chicago	KO 8
Feb.	17-Sonny Boy West, New York	KO 8
Feb.	27-John L. Davis, Seattle	W 10
June	2-Lester Felton, Detroit	W 10
July	12-George Costner, Philadelphia	L 10
Aug.	7-Charley Salas, Washington	L 10
Sept.	26-Charley Salas, Washington	W 10
Oct.	2-Joe Miceli, Milwaukee	L 10
Nov.	23-Joe Miceli, Milwaukee	W 10
Dec.	12-Dave Marsh, Akron, Ohio	KO 9
Dec.	18-Rudy Cruz, Philadelphia	W 10

1951

Jan.	5-Jose Marcia Gatica, New York	KO 1
Jan.	22-Ralph Zannelli, Providence	KO 5
Jan.	31-Vic Cardell, Detroit, Mich.	KO 9

Feb.	19-Joe Miceli, Philadelphia	L 10
Mar.	5-Beau Jack, Providence	W 10
Apr.	11-Fitzie Pruden, Chicago	W 10
May	25-James Carter, New York	KO by 14
	(Lost World Lightweight Title)	
Aug.	2-Don Williams, Worcester	L 10
Sept.	10-Gil Turner, Philadelphia	KO by 10

1952

Mar.	17-Johnny Cunningham, Baltimore	KO 5
Mar.	26-Chuck Davey, Chicago	KO by 5
Nov.	24-Pat Manzi, Syracuse	KO 7

1953

Jan.	12-Carmen Basilio, Syracuse	L 10
Mar.	9-Claude Hammond, Trenton	W 10
Mar.	28-Vic Cardell, Philadelphia	W 10
Apr.	20-Billy Andy, Trenton	W 10
May	18-Billy Andy, Erie, Pa	W 10
June	8-George Johnson, Trenton	KO by 8
Sept.	17-Dom Zimbardo, Newark	KO 2
Nov.	9-Jed Black, Fort Wayne	L 10

1954

July	2-Rafael Lastre, Havana	L 10

1955

Apr.	9-Beau Jack, Augusta	D 10
Aug.	12-Beau Jack, Augusta	KO 9

TB	KO	WD	WF	D	LD	LF	KOBO	ND	NC
153	60	64	0	5	18	0	6	0	0

Elected to Boxing Hall of Fame, 1978.

HAROLD DADE

Born Oct. 9, 1924, Chicago, Ill. Height 5 ft. 5 in. Bantam weight. Managed by Gus Wilson. Fought as amateur, 1940-1941

1940 National Golden Gloves Bantamweight Champion

1942

Dec.	18-Caferino Robleto, Hollywood	W 4

1943

Jan.	4-Joe Robleto, Ocean Pk., Cal.	D 6
Jan.	8-Orville Young, Hollywood	KO 4
Jan.	18-Ceferino Robleto, Ocean Pk., Cal.	D 8

Feb.	19-Chester Ellis, San Diego	W 10
Mar.	22-Victor Flores, Ocean Pk., Cal.	W 8
Apr.	22-Victor Flores, San Diego	W 10
May	11-Dave Hernandez, Los Angeles	W 10
May	14-Joey Dolan, Portland, Ore.	W 10
	-Ceferino Robleto, Los Angeles	W 4
	-Pedro Ramirez, Hollywood	L 6
	-Joe Robleto, Hollywood	W 10

1944

U.S. Marines

–Al Gregorio, Overseas .... KO	2
–Mc. Don, Overseas .... KO	1

1946

Apr.	9–Ruperto Garcia, San Jose .... KO	3
Apr.	16–Billy Clark, Fresno .... KO	2
Apr.	26–Jess Salazar, Hollywood .... KO	3
Apr.	30–Joe Borjon, Fresno .... W	8
May	7–Billy Gibson, Fresno.................... W	8
Sept.	9–Juan Leanos, Ocean Park .... W	10
Dec.	13–Joey Dolan, Portland .... W	10
	–Chivo Carvajal, San Diego .... KO	7

1947

Jan.	6–Manuel Ortiz, San Francisco............. W	15
	(Won Bantamweight Title)	
Feb.	12–Speedy Cabanella, Oakland............. W	10
Mar.	11–Manuel Ortiz, Los Angeles L	15
	(Lost Bantamweight Title)	
Apr.	2–Tony Olivera, Oakland .... W	10
May	6–Carlos, Chavez, Los Angeles .... D	12
May	27–Jackie McCoy, San Jose .... W	10
July	22–Carlos Chavez, Los Angeles L	12
Aug.	26–Simon, Los Angeles L	10
Oct.	18–Spedy Cabanella, Manila............... W	10
Nov.	19–Star Navan, Manila.................... W	10
Dec.	23–Manny Ortega, Los Angeles .... W	10

1948

Jan.	6–Bobby Jackson, Los Angeles .... KO	7
Mar.	3–Lauro Salas, Sacramento .... W	10
Mar.	16–Jackie McCoy, San Jose .... W	10
Apr.	3–Luis Galvani, Havana .... L Dis.	8
Apr.	14–Carlos Chavez, Los Angeles............. L	10
June	3–Jackie Graves, Minneapolis L	10
June	21–Charley Riley, Chicago .... W	10
Juky	12–Charley Riley, St. Louis................. D	10
Aug.	28–Luis Galvani, Havana.................. L	10
Sept.	28–Henry Davis, Honolulu L	10
Oct.	29–Charley Riley, Chicago .... W	8
Dec.	–Lauro Salas, Los Angeles .... W	12

1949

Jan.	18–Joey Clemo, Seattle .... W	10

Feb.	16–Joe Valdez, Spokane 3	10
Mar.	1–Aaron Joshua, Portland............... KO	5
Apr.	14–Joey Ortega, Tacoma .... W	10
May	31–Jesus Fonseca, Los Angeles .... W	10
July	21–Corky Gonzales, Denver L	10
Sept.	2–Sandy Saddler, Chicago L	10
Sept.	30–Frank Flannery, Melbourne.............. W	12
Oct.	17–Elley Bennett, Sydney .... W	12
Nov.	22–Cork Gonzalez, St. Paul............... L	10
Dec.	12–Willie Pep, St. Louis.................. L	10

1950

Jan.	2–Keith Nuttall, Salt Lake City L	10
Jan.	18–Baby Leroy, Sacramento .... D	10
Jan.	31–Keith Nuttall, Salt Lake City L	10
Feb.	14–Chico Rosa, San Jose .... D	10
Mar.	7–Manuel Ortiz, Los Angeles L	10
Apr.	4–Eddie Chavez, San Jose .... KO by	5
Apr.	24–Eddie Chavez, San Francisco L	10
July	14–Rudy Garcia, Hollywood .... KO by	11
Sept.	–Kid Chocolate, Panama................. W	10
Oct.	4–Rocky McKay, Panama L	10
Dec.	3–Rocky McKay, Balboa.................. L	10

1951

Jan.	30–Percy Bassett, Phila................. KO by	8
Mar.	6–Felix Ramirez, San Jose L	10
Apr.	22–Memo Valero, Mex. City............. L Dis.	5
June	1–Fabala Chavez, Hollywood L	10
June	28–Diego Sosa, Havana L	10

1952

Feb.	28–Bobby Woods, Spokane .... W	10
June	22–Lauro Salas, Monterey .... KO by	3
Nov.	27–Bobby Woods, Vancouver............... L	10

1953

Apr.	9–Ernie Kemick, Calgary.................. L	10

1955

Mar.	29–Paul Jorgensen, Houston .... KO by	4

TB	KO	WD	WF	D	LD	LF	KOBO	ND	NC
77	9	32	0	6	23	2	5	0	0

Died, July 17, 1962, Los Angeles, Calif.

SUGAR RAY ROBINSON

(Walker Smith, Jr.)

Born, May 3, 1921, Detroit, Mich. Weight, 145-157 lbs.
Height, 5 ft. 11½ in. Managed by George Gainford.

1939 New York Golden Gloves Featherweight
Champion.
1940 New York Golden Gloves Lightweight Champion
1939, 1940 New York vs. Chicago Inter-City Golden
Gloves Lightweight Champion

1940

Oct.	4–Joe Escheverria, New York	KO	2
Oct.	8–Silent Stefford, Savannah	KO	2
Oct.	22–Mistos Grispos, New York	W	6
Nov.	11–Bobby Woods, Philadelphia	KO	1
Dec.	9–Norment Quarles, Philadelphia	KO	4
Dec.	12–Oliver White, New York	KO	3

1941

Jan.	4–Henry LaBarba, Brooklyn	KO	1
Jan.	13–Frankie Wallace, Philadelphia	KO	1
Jan.	31–George Zengaras, New York	W	6
Feb.	8–Benny Cartegena, Brooklyn	KO	1
Feb.	21–Bobby McIntire, New York	W	6
Feb.	27–Gene Spencer, Detroit	KO	5
Mar.	3–Jimmy Tygh, Philadelphia	KO	8
Apr.	14–Jimmy Tygh, Philadelphia	KO	1
Apr.	24–Charley Burns, Atlantic City	KO	1
Apr.	30–Joe Ghnouly, Washington, D.C.	KO	3
May	10–Vic Troise, Brooklyn	KO	1
May	19–Nick Castiglione, Philadelphia	KO	1
June	16–Mike Evans, Philadelphia	KO	2
July	2–Pete Lello, New York	KO	4
July	21–Sammy Angott, Philadelphia	W	10
Aug.	27–Carl (Red) Guggino, Long Island City	KO	3
Aug.	29–Maurice Arnault, Atlantic City	KO	1
Sept.	19–Maxie Shapiro, New York	KO	3
Sept.	25–Marty Servo, Philadelphia	W	10
Oct.	31–Fritzie Zivic, New York	W	10

1942

Jan.	16–Fritzie Zivic, New York	KO	10
Feb.	20–Maxie Berger, New York	KO	2
Mar.	20–Norman Rubio, New York	KO	7
Apr.	17–Harvey Dubs, Detroit	KO	6
Apr.	30–Dick Banner, Minneapolis	KO	2
May	28–Marty Servo, New York	W	10
July	31–Sammy Angott, New York	W	10

Aug.	21–Ruben Shank, New York	KO	2
Aug.	27–Tony Motisi, Chicago	KO	1
Oct.	2–Jake LaMotta, New York	W	10
Oct.	19–Izzy Jannazzo, Philadelphia	W	10
Nov.	6–Vic Dellicurti, New York	W	10
Dec.	1–Izzy Jannazzo, Cleveland	KO	8
Dec.	14–Al Nettlow, Philadelphia	KO	3

1943

Feb.	5–Jake LaMotta, Detroit	L	10
Feb.	19–Jackie Wilson, New York	W	10
Feb.	26–Jake LaMotta, Detroit	W	10
Apr.	30–Freddie Cabral, Boston	KO	1
July	1–Ralph Zannelli, Boston	W	10
Aug.	27–Henry Armstrong, New York	W	10

1944

Oct.	13–Izzy Jannazzo, Boston	KO	2
Oct.	27–Sgt. Lou Woods, Chicago	KO	9
Nov.	17–Vic Dellicurti, Detroit	W	10
Dec.	12–Sheik Rangel, Philadelphia	KO	2
Dec.	22–Georgia Martin, Boston	KO	7

1945

Jan.	10–Billy Furrone, Washington, D.C.	KO	2
Jan.	16–Tommy Bell, Cleveland	W	10
Feb.	14–George Costner, Chicago	KO	1
Feb.	24–Jake LaMotta, New York	W	10
May	14–Jose Basora, Philadelphia	D	10
June	15–Jimmy McDaniels, New York	KO	2
Sept.	18–Jimmy Mandell, Buffalo	KO	5
Sept.	26–Jake LaMotta, Chicago	W	12
Dec.	4–Vic Dellicurti, Boston	W	10

1946

Jan.	14–Dave Clark, Pittsburgh	KO	2
Feb.	5–Tony Riccio, Elizabeth	KO	4
Feb.	15–O'Neill Bell, Detroit	KO	2
Feb.	26–Cliff Beckett, St. Louis	KO	4
Mar.	4–Sammy Angott, Pittsburgh	W	10
Mar.	14–Izzy Jannazzo, Baltimore	W	10
Mar.	21–Freddy Flores, New York	KO	5
June	12–Freddy Wilson, Worcester	KO	2
June	25–Norman Rubio, Union City	W	10

July   12–Joe Curcio, New York . . . . KO   2
Aug.   15–Vinnie Vines, Albany . . . . KO   6
Sept.   25–Sidney Miller, Elizabeth . . . . KO   3
Oct.   7–Ossie Harris, Pittsburgh . . . . W 10
Nov.   1–Cecil Hudson, Detroit . . . . KO   6
Nov.   6–Artie Levine, Cleveland . . . . KO 10
Dec.   20–Tommy Bell, New York . . . . W 15
        (Won Vacant World Welterweight Title)

1947

Mar.   27–Bernie Miller, Miami . . . . KO   3
Apr.   3–Fred Wilson, Akron . . . . KO   3
Apr.   8–Eddie Finazzo, Kansas City . . . . KO   4
May   16–Georgia Abrams, New York . . . . W 10
June   24–Jimmy Doyle, Cleveland . . . . KO   8
        (Retained World Welterweight Title)
Aug.   21–Sammy Secreet, Akron . . . . KO   1
Aug.   29–Flashy Sebastian, New York . . . . KO   1
Oct.   28–Jackie Wilson, Los Angeles . . . . KO   7
Dec.   10–Billy Nixon, Elizabeth . . . . KO   6
Dec.   19–Chuck Taylor, Detroit . . . . KO   6
        (Retained World Welterweight Title)

1948

Mar.   4–Ossie Harris, Toledo . . . . W 10
Mar.   16–Henry Brimm, Buffalo . . . . W 10
June   28–Bernard Docusen, Chicago . . . . W 15
        (Retained World Welterweight Title)
Sept.   23–Kid Gavilan, New York . . . . W 10
Nov.   15–Bobby Lee, Philadelphia . . . . W 10

1949

Feb.   10–Gene Buffalo, Wilkes-Barre . . . . KO   1
Feb.   15–Henry Brimm, Buffalo . . . . D 10
Mar.   25–Bobby Lee, Chicago . . . . W 10
Apr.   11–Don Lee, Omaha . . . . W 10
Apr.   20–Earl Turner, Oakland . . . . KO   8
May   16–Al Tribuani, Wilmington . . . . Exh.   4
June   7–Freddie Flores, New Bedford . . . . KO   3
June   20–Cecil Hudson, Providence . . . . KO   5
July   11–Kid Gavilan, Philadelphia . . . . W 15
        (Retained World Welterweight Title)
Aug.   24–Steve Belloise, New York . . . . KO   7
Sept.   2–Al Mobley, Chicago . . . . Exh.   4
Sept.   9–Benny Evans, Omaha . . . . KO   5
Sept.   12–Charley Dotson, Houston . . . . KO   3
Nov.   9–Don Lee, Denver . . . . W 10
Nov.   13–Vern Lester, New Orleans . . . . KO   5

Nov.   15–Gene Burton, Shreveport . . . . Exh.   6
Nov.   16–Gee Burton, Dallas . . . . Exh.   6

1950

Jan.   30–George LaRover, New Haven . . . . KO   4
Feb.   13–Al Mobley, Miami . . . . KO   6
Feb.   22–Aaron Wade, Savannah . . . . KO   3
Feb.   27–Jean Walzack, St Louis . . . . W 10
Mar.   22–George Costner, Philadelphia . . . . KO   1
Apr.   21–Cliff Beckett, Columbus . . . . KO   3
Apr.   28–Ray Barnes, Detroit . . . . W 10
June   5–Robert Villemain, Philadelphia . . . . W 15
        (Won Vacant Pennsylvania World Middleweight Title)
Aug.   9–Charley Fusari, Jersey City . . . . W 15
        (Retained World Welterweight Title)
Aug.   25–Jose Basora, Scranton . . . . KO   1
        (Retained Pennsylvania World Middleweight Title)
Sept.   4–Billy Brown, New York . . . . W 10
Oct.   16–Joe Rindone, Boston . . . . KO   6
Oct.   28–Carl (Bobo) Olson, Philadelphia . . . . KO 12
        (Retained Pennsylvania World Middleweight Title)
Nov.   8–Bobby Dykes, Chicago . . . . W 10
Nov.   27–Jean Stock, Paris . . . . KO   2
Dec.   9–Luc Van Dam, Brussels . . . . KO   4
Dec.   16–Jean Walzack, Geneva . . . . W 10
Dec.   22–Robert Villemain, Paris . . . . KO   9
Dec.   25–Hans Stretz, Frankfort . . . . KO   5

1951

Feb.   14–Jake LaMotta, Chicago . . . . KO 13
        (Won World Middleweight Title)
Apr.   5–Holley Mims, Miami . . . . W 10
Apr.   9–Don Ellis, Oklahoma City . . . . KO   1
May   21–Kid Marcel, Paris . . . . KO   5
May   26–Jean Wanes, Zurich . . . . W 10
June   10–Jan de Bruin, Antwerp . . . . KO   8
June   16–Jean Walzack, Liege . . . . KO   6
June   24–Gerhard Hecht, Berlin . . . . NC   2
July   1–Cyrille Delannoit, Turin . . . . KO   3
July   10–Randy Turpin, London . . . . L 15
        Lost World Middleweight Title)
Sept.   12–Randy Turpin, New York . . . . KO 10
        (Regained World Middleweight Title)

1952

Mar.   13–Carl (Bobo) Olson, San Francisco . . . . W 15
        (Retained World Middleweight Title)

Apr. 16–Rocky Graziano, Chicago . . . . KO 3
      (Retained World Middleweight Title)
June 25–Joey Maxim, New York . . . . KO by 14
      (For World Light Heavyweight Title)
Dec. 18–Announced retirement

1953

(Inactive)

1954

Oct. 20–Announced return to ring
Nov. 29–Gene Burton, Hamilton . . . . Exh. 6

1955

Jan.   5–Joe Rindone, Detroit . . . . KO 6
Jan. 19–Ralph (Tiger) Jones, Chicago . . . . L 10
Mar. 29–Johnny Lombardo, Cincinnati . . . . W 10
April 14–Ted Olla, Milwaukee . . . . TKO 3
May   4–Garth Panter, Detroit . . . . W 10
July 22–Rocky Castellani, San Francisco . . . . W 10
Dec.   9–Carl (BoBo) Olson, Los Angeles . . . . KO 4
      (Regained World Middleweight Title)

1956

May   18–Carl (Bobo) Olson, Los Angeles . . . . KO 4
      (Retained World Middleweight Title)
Nov. 10–Bob Provizzi, New Haven . . . . W 10

1957

Jan.   2–Gene Fullmer, New York . . . . L 15
      (Lost World Middleweight Title)
May   1–Gene Fullmer, Chicago . . . . KO 5
      (Regained World Middleweight Title)
Sept. 10–Otis Woodard, Philadelphia. . . . . Exh. 2
Sept. 10–Lee Williams, Philadelphia . . . . Exh. 2
Sept. 23–Carmen Basilio, New York . . . . L 15
      (Lost World Middleweight Title)

1958

Mar. 25–Carmen Basilio, Chicago. . . . . W 15
      (Regained World Middleweight Title)

1959

Dec. 14–Bob Young, Boston . . . . TKO 2

1960

Jan. 22–Paul Pender, Boston . . . . L 15
      (Lost World Middleweight Title)
Apr.   2–Tony Baldoni, Baltimore . . . . KO 1

June 10–Paul Pender, Boston . . . . L 15
      (For World Middleweight Title)
Dec.   3–Gene Fullmer, Los Angeles . . . . D 15
      (For the National Boxing Association Middleweight Title)

1961

Mar.   4–Gene Fullmer, Las Vegas . . . . L 15
      (For the National Boxing Association Middleweight Title)
Sept. 25–Wilf Greaves, Detroit . . . . W 10
Oct. 21–Denny Moyer, New York . . . . W 10
Nov. 20–Al Hauser, Providence. . . . . TKO 6
Dec.   8–Wilf Greaves, Pittsburgh . . . . KO 8

1962

Feb. 17–Denny Moyer, New York . . . . L 10
Apr. 27–Bobby Lee, Port of Spain . . . . KO 2
July   9–Phil Moyer, Los Angeles . . . . L 10
Sept. 25–Terry Downes, London . . . . L 10
Oct. 17–Diego Infantes, Vienna . . . . KO 2
Nov. 10–George Estatoff, Lyons . . . . TKO 6

1963

Jan. 30–Ralph Dupas, Miami Beach . . . . W 10
Feb. 25–Bernie Reynolds, Santo Domingo. . . . . KO 4
Mar. 11–Billy Thornton, Lewiston. . . . . KO 3
May   5–Maurice Robinet, Sherbrooke . . . . KO 3
June 24–Joey Giadello, Philadelphia . . . . L 10
Oct. 14–Armand Vanucci, Paris . . . . W 10
Nov.   9–Fabio Bettini, Lyons . . . . D 10
Nov. 16–Emile Saerens, Brussels. . . . . KO 8
Nov. 29–Armand Davier, Grenoble . . . . W 10
Dec.   9–Armand Vanucci, Paris . . . . W 10

1964

May   19–Gaylord Barnes, Portland . . . . W 10
July   8–Clarence Riley, Pittsfield . . . . KO 6
July 27–Art Hernandez, Omaha . . . . D 10
Sept. 3–Mick Leahy, Paisley, Scot. . . . . L 10
Sept. 28–Yolande Leveque, Paris . . . . W 10
Oct. 12–Johnny Angel, London. . . . . TKO 6
Oct. 24–Jackie Cailleau, Nice . . . . W 10
Nov.   7–Jean Baptiste Roland, Caen . . . . W 10
Nov. 14–Jean Beltritti, Marseilles . . . . W 10
Nov. 27–Fabio Bettini, Rome . . . . D 10

1965

Mar.   6–Jimmy Beecham, Kingston . . . . KO 2
Apr.   4–East Basting, Savannah . . . . KO 1

Apr.	28–Rocky Randall, Norfolk	KO 3
May	5–Rocky Randall, Jacksonville	W 8
May	24–Memo Ayon, Tijuana	L 10
June	1–Stan Harrington, Honolulu	L 10
June	24–Harvey McCullough, Richmond	W 10
July	12–Ferd Hernandez, Las Vegas	L 10
Aug.	10–Stan Harrington, Honolulu	L 10
Sept.	15–Bill Henderson, Norfolk	NC 2
Sept.	23–Harvey McCullough, Philadelphia	W 10

Oct.	1–Peter Schmidt, Johnstown	W 10
Oct.	5–Neil Morrison, Richmond	TKO 2
Oct.	20–Rudolph Bent, Steubenville	KO 3
Nov.	10–Joey Archer, Pittsburgh	L 10
Dec.	10–Announced retirement	

TB	KO	WD	WF	D	LD	LF	KOBO	ND	NC
202	110	65	0	6	18	0	1	0	2

Elected to Boxing Hall of Fame, 1967

ARCHIE MOORE
(Archibald Lee Wright)
(The Old Mongoose)

Born, December 13, 1913, Benoit, Mississippi. Weight, 157-192 lbs, Height, 5 ft. 11 in. Managed by Kid Bandy, George Wilsman, Cal Thompson, Felix Thurman, Jack Richardson Jimmy Johnson, Charley Johnston, Jack Kearns.

1935

	–Piano Man Jones, Hot Springs	KO 2

1936

Jan.	31–Pocohontas Kid, Hot Springs	KO 2
Feb.	7–Dale Richards, Poplar Bluffs	KO 1
Feb.	18–Ray Halford, St. Louis	KO 3
Feb.	20–Willie Harper, St. Louis	KO 3
Feb.	21–Courtland Sheppard, St. Louis	L 6
	–Kneibert Davidson	KO 2
	–Ray Brewster	KO 3
	–Billy Simms	KO 2
	–Johnny Leggs	KO 1
Apr.	15–Peter Urban, Cleveland	KO 6
Apr.	16–Frankie Nelson, Cleveland	L 6
May	4–Tiger Brown, St. Louis	L 6
May	18–Thurman Martin, St. Louis	W 5
	–Ferman Burton	KO 1
	–Billy Simms	KO 1
July	14–Murray Allen, Quincy, Ill.	KO 6
	–Julius Kemp	KO 3
	–Four H. Posey	KO 6
Oct.	9–Sammy Jackson, St. Louis	W 6
	–Dick Putnam	KO 3
Dec.	8–Sammy Jackson, St. Louis	D 6
Dec.	–Sammy Christian, St. Louis	KO 6

1937

Jan.	5–Dynamite Payne, St. Louis	KO 1
Jan.	18–Johnny Davis, Quincy, Ill	KO 3
Feb.	2–Joe Huff, St. Louis	KO 2
	–Murray Allen, Keokuk, Iowa	KO 2
Apr.	9–Charley Dawson, Indianapolis	KO 5
Apr.	23–Karl Martin, Indianapolis	KO 1
	–Frank Hatfield	KO 1
	–Al Dublinsky	KO 1
Aug.	19–Deacon Logan, St. Louis	KO 3
Sept.	9–Sammy Slaughter, Indianapolis	W 10
	–Sammy Slaughter, Jenkins	W 10
	–Billy Adams, Cincinnati	L 10
Nov.	16–Sammy Christian, St. Louis	W 5
	–Sammy Jackson	KO 8

1938

Jan.	7–Carl Lautenschlager, St. Louis	KO 2
May	20–Jimmy Brent, San Diego	KO 1
May	27–Ray Vargas, San Diego	KO 3
June	24–Johnny Romero, San Diego	L 10
July	22–Johnny Sykes, San Diego	KO 1
Aug.	5–Lorenzo Pedro, San Diego	W 10
Sept.	2–Johnny Romero, San Diego	KO 8
Sept.	16–Frank Rowsey, San Diego	KO 3
Sept.	27–Tom Henry, Los Angeles	KO 4
	–Bobby Yannes	KO 2

Nov. 22–Ray Lyle, St. Louis . . . . KO 2
Dec. 8–"Irish" Bob Turner, St. Louis . . . . KO 2

1939

Jan. 20–Jack Moran, St. Louis . . . . KO 1
Mar. 2–Domenic Ceccarelli, St. Louis . . . . KO 1
Mar. 16–Marty Simmons, St. Louis . . . . W 10
Apr. 20–Teddy Yarosz, St. Louis . . . . L 10
July 21–Jack Coggins, San Diego . . . . NC 8
Sept. 1–Jack Coggins, San Diego . . . . W 10
Sept. 22–Bobby Seaman, San Diego . . . . KO 7
Dec. 7–Honeyboy Jones, St. Louis . . . . W 10
Dec. 29–Shorty Hogue, San Diego . . . . L 6

1940

Mar. 30–Jack McNamee, Melbourne . . . . KO 4
Apr. 18–Ron Richards, Sydney . . . . Ko 10
May 9–Atiloio, Sabatino, Sydney . . . . KO 5
May 12–Joe Delaney, Adelaide . . . . KO 7
June 2–FrankLindsay, Tasmania . . . . KO 4
June 27–Fred Henneberry, Sydney . . . . KO 7
July 11–Ron Richards, Sydney . . . . W 12
Oct. 18–Pancho Ramirez, San Diego . . . . KO 5

1941

Jan. 17–Clay Rowan, San Diego . . . . KO 1
Jan. 31–Shorty Hogue, San Diego . . . . L 10
Feb. 21–Eddie Booker, San Diego . . . . D 10
–Freddie Dixon, Phoenix . . . . KO 5

1942

Jan. 28–Bobby Britton, Phoenix . . . . KO 3
Feb. 27–Guero Martinez, San Diego . . . . KO 2
Mar. 17–Jimmy Casino, Oakland . . . . KO 5
Oct. 30–Shorty Hogue, San Diego . . . . KO 2
Nov. 6–Tabby Romero, San Diego . . . . KO 2
Nov. 27–Jack Chase, San Diego . . . . W 10
Dec. 11–Eddie Booker, San Diego . . . . D 12

1943

May 8–Jack Chase, San Diego . . . . W 15
(Won California Middleweight Title)
July 22–Big Boy Hogue, San Diego . . . . KO 5
July 28–Eddie Cerda, San Diego . . . . KO 3
Aug. 2–Jack Chase, San Francisco . . . . L 15
(Lost California Middleweight Title)
Aug. 16–Aaron (Tiger) Wade, San Francisco . . . . L 10
Nov. 5–Kid Hermosillo, San Diego . . . . KO 5
Nov. 26–Jack Chase, Hollywood . . . . W 10

1944

Jan. 7–Amado Rodriguez, San Diego . . . . KO 1
Jan. 21–Eddie Booker, Hollywood . . . . KO by 8
Mar. 24–Roman Starr, Hollywood . . . . KO 2
Apr. 21–Charley, Burley, Hollywood . . . . L 10
May 19–Kenny LaSalle, San Diego . . . . W 10
Aug. 11–Louie Mays, San Diego . . . . KO 3
Aug. 18–Jimmy Hayden, San Diego . . . . KO 5
Sept. 1–Battling Monroe, San Diego . . . . KO 6
Dec. 18–Nate Bolden, New York . . . . W 10

1945

Jan. 11–Joey Jones, Boston . . . . KO 1
Jan. 29–Bob Jacobs, New York . . . . KO 9
Feb. 12–Nap Mitchell, Boston . . . . KO 6
Apr. 2–Nate, Bolden, Baltimore . . . . W 10
Apr. 23–Teddy Randolph, Baltimore . . . . KO 9
May 21–Lloyd Marshall, Baltimore . . . . W 10
June 18–George Kochan, Baltimore . . . . KO 6
June 26–Lloyd Marshall, Cleveland . . . . KO 10
Aug. 22–Jimmy Bivins, Cleveland . . . . KO by 6
Sept. 17–Cocoa Kid, Baltimore . . . . KO 8
Oct. 22–Holman Williams, Baltimore . . . . L 10
Nov. 12–Odell Riley, Detroit . . . . KO 6
Nov. 26–Holman Williams, Baltimore . . . . KO 11
Dec. 13–Colion Chaney, St. Louis . . . . KO 5

1946

Jan. 28–Curtis Sheppard, Baltimore . . . . W 12
Feb. 5–Georgie Parks, Washington, D.C. . . . . KO 1
May 2–Verne Escoe, Orange, N.J. . . . . KO 7
May 20–Ezzard Charles, Pittsburgh . . . . L 10
Aug. 19–Buddy Walker, Baltimore . . . . KO 4
Sept. 9–Shamus O'Brien, Baltimore . . . . KO 2
Oct. 23–Billy Smith, Oakland . . . . D 12
Nov. 6–Jack Chase, Oakland . . . . D 10

Mar. 18–Jack Chase, Los Angeles . . . . KO 9
Apr. 11–Rusty Payne, San Diego . . . . W 10
May 5–Ezzard Charles, Cincinnati . . . . L 10
June 16–Curtis Sheppard, Washington, D.C. . . . . W 10
July 14–Bert Lytell, Baltimore . . . . W 10
July 30–Bobby Zander, Oakland . . . . W 12
Sept. 8–Jimmy Bivins, Baltimore . . . . KO 9
Nov. 10–George Fitch, Baltimore . . . . KO 6

1947

Jan. 13–Ezzard Charles, Cleveland . . . . KO by 8
Apr. 12–Dusty Wilkerson, Baltimore . . . . KO 7

Apr.	19–Doc Williams, Newark	KO	7
May	5–Billy Smith, Cincinnati	W	10
June	2–Leonard Morrow, Oakland	KO by	1
June	28–Jimmy Bivins, Baltimore	W	10
Aug.	2–Ted Lowry, Baltimore	W	10
Sept.	20–Billy Smith, Baltimore	KO	4
Oct.	15–Henry Hall, New Orleans	L	10
Nov.	1–Lloyd Gibson, Washington, D.C.	LF	4
Nov.	15–Henry Hall, Baltimore	W	10
Dec.	6–Bob Amos, Washington, D.C.	W	10
Dec.	27–Charley Williams, Baltimore	KO	7

1949

Jan.	10–Alabama Kid, Toledo	KO	4
Jan.	31–Bob Satterfield, Toledo	KO	3
Mar.	4–Alabama Kid, Columbus	KO	3
Mar.	23–Dusty Wilkerson, Philadelphia	KO	6
Apr.	11–Jimmy Bivins, Toledo	KO	8
Apr.	26–Harold Johnson, Philadelphia	W	10
June	13–Clinton Bacon, Indianapolis	LF	6
June	27–Bob Sikes, Indianapolis	KO	3
July	29–Esco Greenwood, North Adams	KO	2
Oct.	4–Bob Amos, Toledo	W	10
Oct.	24–Phil Muscato, Toledo	KO	6
Dec.	6–Doc Williams, Hartford	KO	8
Dec.	13–Leonard Morrow, Toledo	KO	10

1950

Jan.	31–Bert Lytell, Toledo	W	10
July	31–Vernon Williams, Chicago	KO	2

1951

Jan.	2–Billy Smith, Portland, Ore.	TKO	8
Jan.	28–John Thomas, Panama City	KO	1
Feb.	21–Jimmy Bivins, New York	TKO	9
Mar.	13–Abel Cestac, Toledo	W	10
Apr.	26–Herman Harris, Flint	TKO	4
May	14–Art Henri, Baltimore	TKO	4
June	9–Abel Cestac, Buenos Aires	TKO	10
June	23–Karel Sys, Buenos Aires	D	10
July	8–Alberto Lovell, Buenos Aires	KO	1
July	15–Vincente Quiroz, Montevideo	KO	6
July	26–Victor Carabajal, Cordoba	TKO	3
July	28–Americo Capitanelli, Tucuman	TKO	3
Aug.	5–Rafael Miranda, Argentina	TKO	4
Aug.	17–Alfredo Lagay, Bahia Blanca	KO	3
Sept.	3–Embrell Davison, Detroit	KO	1
Sept.	24–Harold Johnson, Philadelphia	W	10
Oct.	29–Chubby Wright, St. Louis	TKO	7

Dec.	10–Harold Johnson, Milwaukee	L	10

1952

Jan.	29–Harold Johnson, Toledo	W	10
Feb.	27–Jimmy Slade, St. Louis	W	10
May	19–Bob Dunlap, San Francisco	KO	6
June	26–Clarence Henry, Baltimore	W	10
July	25–Clint Bacon, Denver	TKO	4
Dec.	17–Joey Maxim, St. Louis	W	15
	(Won World Light Heavyweight Title)		

1953

Jan.	27–Toxie Hall, Toledo	KO	4
Feb.	16–Leonard Dugan, San Francisco	TKO	8
Mar.	3–Sonny Andrews, Sacramento	TKO	5
Mar.	11–Nino Valdes, St. Louis	W	10
Mar.	17–Al Spaulding, Spokane	KO	3
Mar.	30–Frank Buford, San Diego	TKO	9
June	24–Joey Maxim, Ogden, Utah	W	15
	(Retained World Light Heavyweight Title)		
Aug.	22–Reinaldo Ansaloni, Buenos Aires	TKO	4
Sept.	12–Dogomar Martinez, Buenos Aires	W	10

1954

Jan.	27–Joey Maxim, Miami	W	15
	(Retained World Light Heavyweight Title)		
Mar.	9–Bob Baker, Miami Beach	TKO	9
June	7–Bert Whitehurst, New York	KO	6
Aug.	11–Harold Johnson, New York	TKO	14
	(Retained World Light Heavyweight Title)		

1955

May	2–Nino Valdes, Las Vegas	W	15
June	22–Carl (Bobo) Olson, New York	KO	3
	(Retained World Light Heavyweight Title)		
Sept.	21–Rocky Marciano, New York	KO by	9
	(For World Heavyweight Title)		
Oct.	22–Dale Hall, Philadelphia	Exh.	4

1956

Feb.	2–Dale Hall, Fresno	Exh.	4
Feb.	20–Howard King, San Francisco	W	10
Feb.	27–Bob Dunlap, San Diego	KO	1
Mar.	17–Frankie Daniels, Hollywood	W	10
Mar.	27–Howard King, Sacramento	W	10
Apr.	10–Willie Bean, Richmond, Cal.	TKO	5
Apr.	16–George Parmenter, Seattle	TKO	3
Apr.	26–Sonny Andrews, Edmonton	KO	4
Apr.	30–Gene Thompson, Tucson	TKO	3

June   5–Yolande Pompey, London . . . . TKO 10
     (Retained World Light Heavyweight Title)
July   25–James J. Parker, Toronto . . . . TKO   9
Sept.   8–Roy Shire, Ogden, Utah . . . . TKO   3
Nov.   30–Floyd Patterson, Chicago . . . . KO by   5
     (For Vacant World Heavyweight Title)

1957

May   1–Hans Kalbfell, Essen . . . . W 10
June   2–Alain Cherville, Stuttgart . . . . TKO   6
Sept. 20–Tony Anthony, Los Angeles . . . . TKO   7
     (Retained World Light Heavyweight Title)
Oct.   31–Bob Mitchell, Vancouver . . . . TKO   5
Nov.   5–Eddie Cotton, Seattle . . . . W 10
Nov.   29–Roger Rischer, Portland . . . . KO   4

1958

Jan.   18–Luis Ignacio, Sao Paulo . . . . W 10
Feb.   1–Julio Neves, Rio de Janeiro . . . . KO   3
Mar.   4–Bert Whitehurst, San Bernardino . . . . TKO 10
Mar.   10–Bob Albright, Vancouver . . . . TKO   7
May   2–Willi Besmanoff, Louisville . . . . W 10
May   17–Howard King, San Diego . . . . W 10
May   26–Charlie Norkus, San Francisco . . . . W 10
June   9–Howard King, Sacramento . . . . W 10
Aug.   4–Howard King, Reno . . . . D 10
Dec.   10–Yvon Durelle, Montreal . . . . KO 11
     (Retained World Light Heavyweight Title)

1959

Feb.   5–Eddie Cotton, Victoria . . . . Exh.   5
Mar.   9–Sterling Davis, Odessa, Texas . . . . TKO   3
Aug.   12–Yvon Durelle, Montreal . . . . KO   3
     (Retained World Light Heavyweight Title)

1960

May   25–Willi Besmanoff, Indianapolis . . . . TKO 10
Sept. 13–George Abinet, Dallas . . . . TKO   3
Oct.   25–National Boxing Association vacated Light Heavy-
     weight Title . . . .
Oct.   29–Giulio Rinaldo, Rome . . . . L 10
Nov.   28–Buddy Turman, Dallas . . . . W 10

1961

Mar.   25–Buddy Turman, Manila . . . . W 10
May   8–Dave Furch, Tucson . . . . Exh.   4
May   12–Clifford Gray, Nogales . . . . KO   4
June   10–Giulio Rinaldi, New York . . . . W 15
     (Retained World Light Heavyweight Title)
Oct.   23–Pete Rademacher, Baltimore . . . . TKO   6

1962

Feb.   10–New York State Athletic Commission vacates
     Light Heavyweight Title . . . .
Mar.   30–Alejandro Lavorante, Los Angeles . . . . TKO 10
May   7–Howard King, Tijuana . . . . KO   1
May   28–Willie Pastrano, Los Angeles . . . . D 10
Nov.   15–Cassius Clay, Los Angeles . . . . KO by   4

1963

Mar.   15–Mike DiBiase, Phoenix . . . . KO   3

1964

(Inactive)

1965

Aug.   27–Nap Mitchell, Michigan City . . . . Exh. KO 3

TB	KO	WD	WF	D	LD	LF	KOBO	ND	NC
215	129	54	0	9	13	2	7	0	1

Elected to Boxing Hall of Fame, 1966

FLOYD PATTERSON

Born, January 4, 1935, Waco, North Carolina. Weight, 164-196
lbs. Height, 5 ft. 11 in. Managed by Cus D'Amato

*1952 United States National Amateur Athletic Union
Middleweight Champion*
*1952 United States Olympic Middleweight
Gold Medalist*

1952

Sept.	12–Eddie Godbold, New York	KO	4
Oct.	6–Sammy Walker, Brooklyn	KO	2
Oct.	21–Lester, Jackson, New York	KO	3
Dec.	29–Lalu Sabotin, Brooklyn	KO	5

1953

Jan.	28–Chester Mieszala, Chicago	KO	5
Apr.	3–Dick Wagner, Brooklyn	W	8
June	1–Gordon Wallace, Brooklyn	KO	3
Oct.	19–Wes Bascom, Brooklyn	W	8
Dec.	14–Dick Wagner, Brooklyn	KO	5

1954

Feb.	15–Yvon Durelle, Brooklyn	W	8
Mar.	30–Sam Brown, Washington, D.C.	KO	2
Apr.	19–Alvin Williams, Brooklyn	W	8
May	10–Jesse Turner, Brooklyn	W	8
June	7–Joey Maxim, Brooklyn	L	8
July	12–Jacques Royer-Crecy, New York	KO	7
Aug.	2–Tommy Harrison, Brooklyn	KO	1
Oct.	11–Esau Ferdinand, New York	W	8
Oct.	22–Joe Gannon, New York	W	8
Nov.	19–Jimmy Slade, New York	W	8

1955

Jan.	7–Willie Troy, New York	KO	5
Jan.	17–Don Grant, Brooklyn	KO	5
Mar.	17–Esau Ferdinand, Oakland	KO	10
June	23–Yvon Durelle, Newcastle	KO	5
July	6–Archie McBride, New York	KO	7
Sept.	8–Alvin Williams, Moncton	KO	8
Sept.	29–Dave Whitlock, San Francisco	KO	3
Oct.	13–Calvin Brad, Las Angeles	KO	1
Dec.	8–Jimmy Slade, Los Angeles	KO	7

1956

Mar.	12–Jimmy Walls, New Britain	KO	2
Apr.	10–Alvin Williams, Kansas City	KO	3
June	8–Tommy Jackson, New York	W	12

Nov.	30–Archie Moore, Chicago	KO	5
	(Won Vacant World Heavyweight Title)		

1957

July	29–Tommy Jackson, New York	KO	10
	(Retained World Heavyweight Title)		
Aug.	22–Pete Rademacher, Seattle	KO	6
	(Retained World Heavyweight Title)		

1958

Aug.	18–Roy Harris, Los Angeles	KO	12
	(Retained World Heavyweight Title)		

1959

May	1–Brian London, Indianapolis	KO	11
	(Retained World Heavyweight Title)		
June	26–Ingemar Johansson, New York	KO by	3
	(Lost World Heavyweight Title)		

1960

June	20–Ingemar Johansson, New York	KO	4
	(Regained World Heavyweight Title)		

1961

Mar.	13–Ingemar Johansson, Miami Beach	KO	6
	(Retained World Heavyweight Title)		
Dec.	4–Tom McNeeley, Toronto	KO	4
	(Retained World Heavyweight Title)		

1962

Sept.	25–Sonny Liston, Chicago	KO by	1
	(Lost World Heavyweight Title)		

1963

July	22–Sonny Liston, Las Vegas	KO by	1
	(For World Heavyweight Title)		

1964

Jan.	6–Sante Amonti, Stockholm	KO	8
July	5–Eddie Machen, Stockholm	W	12
Dec.	12–Charley Powell, San Juan	KO	6

1965

Feb.	1–George Chuvalo, New York	W	12
May	14–Tod Herring, Stockholm	KO	3

Nov. 22–Muhammad Ali, Las Vegas .... KO by 12
(For World Heavyweight Title)

1966

Sept. 20–Henry Cooper, London .... KO 4

1967

Feb. 13–Willie Johnson, Miami Beach .... KO 3
Mar. 30–Bill McMurray, Pittsburgh .... KO 1
June 9–Jerry Quarry, Los Angeles .... D 10
Oct. 28–Jerry Quarry, Los Angeles............. L 12
(WBA Heavyweight Elimination Tournament)

1968

Sept. 14–Jimmy Ellis, Stockholm .... L 15
(For WBA Heavyweight Title)

1969

(Inactive)

1970

Sept. 15–Charlie Green, New York .... KO 10

1971

Jan. 16–Levi Forte, Miami Beach............... KO 2
Mar. 29–Roger Russell, Philadelphia............. KO 9
May 26–Terry Daniels, Cleveland................ W 10
July 17–Charlie Polito, Erie .... W 10
Aug. 21–Vic Brown, Buffalo.................... W 10
Nov. 23–Charlie Harris, Portland .... KO 6

1972

Feb. 11–Oscar Bonavena, New York............. W 10
May 16–Charlie Harris, Washington, D.C. .... Exh. 5
July 14–Pedro Agosto, New York .... KO 6
Sept. 20–Muhammad Ali, New York........... KO by 7
(For NABF Heavyweight Title)

TB	KO	WD	WF	D	LD	LF	KOBO	ND	NC
64	40	15	0	1	3	0	5	0	0

Elected to Boxing Hall of Fame, 1976.

BOB FOSTER

Born, December 15, 1938, Albuquerque, New Mexico.
Weight, 170-188 lbs. Height, 6 ft. 3 in.

1959 Pan American Games Middleweight Silver Medalist

1961

Mar. 27–Duke Williams, Washington, D.C. .... KO 2
Apr. 3–Clarence Ryan, New York .... W 4
May 8–Billy Johnson, New York................. W 4
June 22–Ray Bryan, Montreal................... KO 2
Aug. 8–Floyd McCoy, Montreal................. W 6
Nov. 22–Ernie Knox, Norfolk .... KO 4
Dec. 4–Clarence Floyd, Toronto .... KO 4

1962

May 19–Billy Tisdale, New York................. KO 2
June 27–Bertt Whitehurst, New York .... W 8
Oct. 20–Doug Jones, New York .... KO by 8

1963

Feb. 18–Richard Benjamin, Washington .... KO 1
Apr. 29–Curtis Bruce, Washington, D.C........... KO 4

Nov. 6–Mauro Mina, Lima, Peru .... L 10
Dec. 11–Willi Besmanoff, Norfolk............... KO 3

1964

Feb. 25–Dave Bailey, Miami Beach............... KO 1
May 8–Allen Thomas, Chicago .... KO 1
July 10–Ernest Terrell, New York .... KO by 7
Nov. 12–Don Quinn, Norfolk .... KO 1
Nov. 23–Norm Letcher, San Francisco .... KO 1
Dec. 11–Henry Hank, Norfolk.................. KO 10

1965

Feb. 15–Roberto Rascon, Albuquerque........... KO 2
Mar. 21–Dave Russell, Norfolk................. KO 6
May 24–Chuck Leslie, New Orleans............. KO 3
July 26–Henry Hank, New Orleans .... W 12
Dec. 6–Zora Folley, New Orleans .... L 10

1966

Dec. 6–Leroy Green, Norfolk .... KO 2

1967

Jan.	16–Jim Robinson, Washington, D.C. .... KO	1
Feb.	27–Andres Selpa, Washington, D.C. .... KO	2
May	8–Eddie Cotton, Washington, D.C. .... KO	3
June	9–Henry Mathews, Roanoke, Va. .... KO	2
Oct.	25–Levan Roundtree, Washington .... KO	8
Nov.	20–Eddie Vick, Providence. .... W	10
Dec.	5–Sonny Moore, Washington, D.C. .... KO	2

1968

May 24–Dick Tiger, New York .... KO 4
    (Won World Light Heavyweight Title)
July 29–Charley Polite, West Springfield. .... KO 3
Aug. 26–Eddie Vick, Albuquerque .... KO 9
Sept. 9–Roger Rouse, Washington, D.C. .... KO 5

1969

Jan. 22–Frank DePaula, New York .... KO 1
    (Retained World Light Heavyweight Title)
May 24–Andy Kendall, West Springfield .... KO 4
    (Retained World Light Heavyweight Title)
June 19–Levan Roundtree, Atlanta .... KO 4
Nov. 2–Chuck Leslie, New Orleans .... KO 5

1970

Feb 24–Bill Hardney, Orlando .... KO 4
Mar. 9–Cookie Wallace, Tampa .... KO 6
Apr. 4–Roger Rouse, Missoula .... KO 4
    (Retained World Light Heavyweight Title)
June 27–Mark Tessman, Baltimore .... KO 10
    (Retained World Light Heavyweight Title)
Nov. 18–Joe Frazier, Detroit .... KO by 2
    (For World Heavyweight Title)

1971

Mar. 2–Hal Carroll, Scranton .... KO 4
    (Retained World Light Heavyweight Title)
Apr. 24–Ray Anderson, Tampa. .... W 15
    (Retained World Light Heavyweight Title)
Aug. 17–Vernon McIntosh, Miami Beach .... KO 3
Oct. 29–Tommy Hicks, Scranton .... KO 8
    (Retained World Light Heavyweight Title)

Dec. 16–Brian Kelly, Oklahoma City .... KO 3
    (Retained World Light Heavyweight Title)

1972

Apr. 7–Vicente Rondon, Miami Beach. .... KO 2
    (Retained World Light Heavyweight Title)
June 27–Mike Quarry, Las Vegas .... KO 4
    (Retained World Light Heavyweight Title)
Sept. 26–Chris Finnegan, London .... KO 14
    (Retained World Light Heavyweight Title)
Nov. 21–Muhammad Ali, Stateline .... KO by 8
    (For NABF Heavyweight Title)

1973

Aug. 21–Pierre Fourie, Albuquerque .... W 15
    (Retained World Light Heavyweight Title)
Dec. 1–Pierre Fourier, Johannesburg .... W 15
    (Retained World Light Heavyweight Title)

1974

June 17–Jorge Ahumada, Albuquerque .... D 15
    (Retained World Light Heavyweight Title)
Sept. 16–Announced retirement. ....

1975

June 28–Bill Hardney, Santa Fe .... KO 3

1976

May 8–Al Bolden, Missoula .... KO 3
Aug. 28–Harold Carter, Missoula .... W 10
Sept. 25–Al Bolden, Spokane .... KO 6

1977

Sept. 2–Bob Hazelton, Curacao .... KO 10

1978

Feb. 9–Mustapha Wassaja, Copenhagen .... KO by 5
June 3–Bob Hazelton, Wichita .... KO by 2

TB	KO	WD	WF	D	LD	LF	KOBO	ND	NC
65	46	10	0	1	2	0	6	0	0

Elected to Boxing Hall of Fame, 1983.

MUHAMMAD ALI

(Cassius Marcellus Clay, Jr.)
(The Louisville Lip)
Born, January 17, 1942, Louisville, Ky. Weight, 186-230 lbs.
Height, 6 ft. 3 in.

1959 National Golden Gloves Light Heavyweight
   Champion
1959, 1960 United States National Amateur Athletic
   Union Light Heavyweight Champion
1960 United States Olympic Light Heavyweight
   Gold Medalist

1960

Oct. 29–Tunney Hunsaker, Louisville . . . . W   6
Dec. 27–Herb Siler, Miami Beach . . . . KO   4

1961

Jan. 17–Tony Esperti, Miami Beach . . . . KO   3
Feb. 7–Jim Robinson, Miami Beach . . . . KO   1
Feb. 21–Donnie Fleeman, Miami Beach . . . . KO   7
Apr. 19–Lamar Clark, Louisville . . . . KO   2
June 26–Duke Sabedong, Las Vegas . . . . W   10
July 22–Alonzo Johnson, Louisville . . . . W   10
Oct. 7–Alex Miteff, Louisville . . . . KO   6
Nov. 29–Willi Besmanoff, Louisville . . . . KO   7

1962

Feb. 10–Sonny Banks, New York . . . . KO   4
Feb. 28–Don Warner, Miami Beach . . . . KO   4
Apr. 23–George Logan, Los Angeles . . . . KO   4
May 19–Billy Daniels, New York . . . . KO   7
July 20–Alejandro Lavorante, Los Angeles . . . . KO   5
Nov. 15–Archie Moore, Los Angeles . . . . KO   4

1963

Jan. 24–Charlie Powell, Pittsburgh . . . . KO   3
Mar. 13–Doug Jones, New York . . . . W   10
June 18–Henry Cooper, London . . . . KO   5

1964

Feb. 25–Sonny Liston, Miami Beach . . . . KO   7
(Won World Heavyweight Title)

1965

May 25–Sonny Liston, Lewiston, Me . . . . KO   1
(World Heavyweight Title)
July 31–Jimmy Ellis, San Juan P.R. . . . . Exh.   3
July 31–Cody Jones, San Juan, P.R. . . . . Exh.   3

Aug. 16–Cody Jones, Gothenburg . . . . Exh.   2
Aug. 16–Jimmy Ellis, Gothenburg . . . . Exh.   2
Aug. 20–Jimmy Ellis, London, England . . . . Exh.   4
Aug. 20–Cody Jones, Paisley, Scotland . . . . Exh.   4
Nov. 22–Floyd Patterson, Las Vegas . . . . KO   12
(Retained World Heavyweight Title)

1966

Mar. 29–George Chuvalo, Toronto . . . . W   15
(Retained World Heavyweight Title)
May 21–Henry Cooper, London, England . . . . KO   6
(Retained World Heavyweight Title)
Aug. 6–Brian London, London, England . . . . KO   3
(Retained World Heavyweight Title)
Sept. 10–Karl Mildenberger, Frankfurt . . . . KO   12
(Retained World Heavyweight Title)
Nov. 14–Cleveland Williams, Houston . . . . KO   3
(Retained World Heavyweight Title)

1967

Feb. 6–Ernest Terrell, Houston . . . . W   15
(Retained World Heavyweight Title)
Mar. 22–Zora Folley, New York . . . . KO   7
(Retained World Heavyweight Title)
June 15–Alvin (Blue) Lewis, Detroit . . . . Exh.   3
June 15–Orvill Qualls, Detroit . . . . Exh.   3

1968-1969

(Inactive)

1970

Feb. 3–Announced retirement . . . .
Oct. 26–Jerry Quarry, Atlanta . . . . KO   3
Dec. 7–Oscar Bonavena, New York . . . . KO   15

1971

Mar. 8–Joe Frazier, New York L   15
(For World Heavyweight Title)
June 25–J.D.McCauley, Dayton . . . . Exh.   2
June 25–Eddie Brooks, Dayton . . . . Exh.   3
June 25–Rufus Brassell, Dayton . . . . Exh.   3
June 30–Alex Mack, Charleston . . . . Exh.   3
June 30–Eddie Brooks, Charleston . . . . Exh.   4

July 26–Jimmy Ellis, Houston . . . . KO 12
        (Won Vacant NABF Heavyweight Title)
Aug. 21–Lancer Johnson, Caracas . . . . Exh. 4
Aug. 21–Eddie Brooks, Caracas . . . . Exh. 4
Aug. 23–Lancer Johnson, Port of Spain . . . . Exh. 4
Aug. 23–Eddie Brooks, Port of Spain . . . . Exh. 2
Nov. 6–James Summerville, Buenos Aires . . . . . . Exh. 5
Nov. 6–Miguel Angel Paez, Buenos Aires . . . . Exh. 5
Nov. 17–Buster Mathis, Houston . . . . W 12
        (Retained NABF Heavyweight Title)
Dec. 26–Jurgen Blin, Zurich, Switzerland . . . . KO 7

1972

Apr. 1–Mac Foster, Tokyo, Japan . . . . W 15
May 1–George Chuvalo,Vancouver, B.C. . . . . W 12
        (Retained NABF Heavyweight Title)
June 27–Jerry Quarry, Las Vegas . . . . KO 7
        (Retained NABF Heavyweight Title)
July 1–Lonnie Bennett, Los Angeles . . . . Exh. 2
July 1–Eddie Jones, Los Angeles . . . . Exh. 2
July 1–Billy Ryan, Los Angles . . . . Exh. 2
July 1–Charley James, Los Angeles . . . . Exh. 2
July 1–Rahaman Ali, Los Angeles . . . . Exh. 2
July 19–Alvin (Blue) Lweis, Dublin . . . . KO 11
Aug. 24–Obie English, Baltimore . . . . Exh. 4
Aug. 24–Ray Anderson, Baltimore . . . . Exh. 2
Aug. 24–Alonzo Johnson, Baltimore . . . . Exh. 2
Aug. 24–George Hill, Baltimore . . . . Exh. 2
Aug. 28–Alonzo Johnson, Cleveland . . . . Exh. 2
Aug. 28–Amos Johnson, Cleveland . . . . Exh. 2
Sept. 20–Floyd Patterson, New York . . . . KO 7
        (Retained NABF Heavyweight Title)
Oct. 11–John (Dino) Denis, Boston . . . . Exh. 2
Oct. 11–Cliff McDonald, Boston . . . . Exh. 2
Oct. 11–Doug Kirk, Boston . . . . Exh. 2
Oct. 11–Ray Anderson, Boston . . . . Exh. 2
Oct. 11–Paul Raymond, Boston . . . . Exh. 2
Nov. 21–Bob Foster, Stateline, Nev. . . . . KO 8
        (Retained NABF Heavyweight Title)

1973

Feb. 14–Joe Bugner, Las Vegas . . . . W 12
Mar. 31–Ken Norton, San Diego . . . . L 12
        (Lost NABF Heavyweight Title)
Sept. 10–Ken Norton, Los Angeles . . . . W 12
        (Regained NABF Heavyweight Title)
Oct. 20–Rudi Lubbers, Jakarta . . . . W 12

1974

Jan. 28–Joe Frazier, New York . . . . W 12
        (Retained NABF Heavyweight Title)
Oct. 30–George Foreman, Kinshasa, Zaire . . . . KO 8
        (Regained World Heavyweight Title)

1975

Mar. 24–Chuck Wepner, Cleveland . . . . KO 15
        (Retained World Heavyweight Title)
May 16–Ron Lyle, Las Vegas . . . . KO 11
        (Retained World Heavyweight Title)
July 1–Joe Bugner, Kuala Lumpur . . . . W 15
        (Retained World Heavyweight Title)
Oct. 1–Joe Frazier, Manila . . . . KO 14
        (Retained World Heavyweight Title)

1976

Feb. 20–Jean Pierre Coopman, San Juan . . . . KO 5
        (Retained World Heavyweight Title)
Apr. 30–Jimmy Young, Landover . . . . W 15
        (Retained World Heavyweight Title)
May 24–Richard Dunn, Munich . . . . KO 5
        (Retained World Heavyweight Title)
June 25–Antonio Inoki, Tokyo . . . . Exh. D 15
        (Above match was a boxer against a wrestler.)
Sept. 28–Ken Norton, New York . . . . W 15
        (Retained World Heavyweight Title)

1977

Jan. 29–Peter Fuller, Boston . . . . Exh. 4
Jan. 29–Walter Haines, Boston . . . . Exh. 1
Jan. 29–Jeyy Houston, Boston . . . . Exh. 2
Jan. 29–Ron Drinkwater, Boston . . . . Exh. 2
Jan. 29–Matt Ross, Boston . . . . Exh. 2
Jan. 29–Frank Smith, Boston . . . . Exh. 1
May 16–Alfredo Evangelista, Landover . . . . W 15
        (Retained World Heavyweight Title)
Sept. 29–Earnie Shavers, New York . . . . W 15
        (Retained World Heavyweight Title)
Dec. 2–Scott LeDoux, Chicago . . . . Exh. 5

1978

Feb. 15–Leon Spinks, Las Vegas . . . . L 15
        (Lost World Heavyweight Title)
Sept. 15–Leon Spinks, New Orleans . . . . W 15
        (Regained World Heavyweight Title)

1979

–Announced retirement..................

1980

Oct. 2–Larry Holmes, Las Vegas .... KO by 11
(For World Heavyweight Title)

1981

Dec. 11–Trevor Berbick, Nassau.................. L 10

TB	KO	WD	WF	D	LD	LF	KOBO	ND	NC
61	37	19	0	0	4	0	1	0	0

Elected to the Boxing Hall of Fame, 1987

JOSEPH FRAZIER

(Smokin' Joe)

Born, January 12, 1944, Beaufort, S.C. Weight, 205 lbs.
Height, 5 ft. 11½ in.

1964 United States Olympic Heavyweight Gold Medalist

1965

Aug. 16–Woody Goss, Philadelphia .... KO 1
Sept. 20–Mike Bruce, Philadelphia .... KO 3
Sept. 28–Ray Staples,Philadelphia .... KO 2
Nov. 11–Abe Davis, Philadelphia................. KO 1

1966

Jan. 17–Mel Turnbow, Philadelphia .... KO 1
Mar. 4–Dick Wipperman, New York............. KO 5
Apr. 4–Charley Polite, Philadelphia............. KO 2
Apr. 28–Don (Toro) Smith, Pittsburgh .... KO 3
May 19–Chuck Leslie, Los Angeles .... KO 3
May 26–Memphis Al Jones, Los Angeles .... KO 1
July 25–Billy Daniels, Philadelphia.............. KO 6
Sept. 21–Oscar Bonavena, New York.............. W 10
Nov. 21–Eddie Machen, Los Angeles .... KO 10

1967

Feb. 21–Doug Jones, Philadelphia .... KO 6
Apr. 11–Jeff Davis, Miami Beach .... KO 5
May 4–George Johnson, Los Angeles........... W 10
July 19–George Chuvalo, New York .... KO 4
Oct. 17–Tony Doyle, Philadelphia............... KO 2
Dec. 18–Marion Connors, Boston............... KO 3

1968

Mar. 4–Buster Mathis, New York .... KO 11
(Won Vacant New York World Heavyweight Title)
June 24–Manuel Ramos, New York .... KO 2
(Retained New York World Heavyweight Title)
Dec. 10–Oscar Bonavena, Philadelphia........... W 15
(Retained New York World Heavyweight Title)

1969

Apr. 22–Dave Zyglewicz, Houston............... KO 1
(Retained New York World Heavyweight Title)
June 23–Jerry Quarry, New York .... KO 7
(Retained New York World Heavyweight Title)

1970

Feb. 16–Jimmy Ellis, New York .... KO 5
(Won Vacant World Heavyweight Title)
Nov. 18–Bob Foster, Detroit .... KO 2
(Retained World Heavyweight Title)

1971

Mar. 8–Muhammad Ali, New York............... W 15
(Retained World Heavyweight Title)
July 15–Cleveland Williams, Houston........... Exh. 3
July 15–James Helwig, Houston .... Exh. 3

1972

Jan. 15–Tery Daniels, New Orleans .... KO 4
(Retained World Heavyweight Title)
May 25–Ron Stander, Omaha.................. KO 5
(Retained World Heavyweight Title)

1973

Jan. 22–George Foreman, Kingston .... KO by 2
(Lost World Heavyweight Title)
July 2–Joe Bugner, London................... W 12

1974

Jan. 28–Muhammad Ali, New York .... L 12
(For NABF Heavyweight Title)
June 17–Jerry Quarry, New York .... KO 5

1975

Mar. 1–Jimmy Ellis, Melbourne .... KO 9
Oct. 1–Muhammad Ali, Manila .... KO by 14
(For World Heavyweight Title)

1976

June 15–George Foreman, Uniondale .... KO by 5

1977-1980

(Inactive)

1981

Dec. 3–Jumbo Cummings, Chicago .... D 10

TB	KO	WD	WF	D	LD	LF	KOBO	ND	NC
37	27	5	0	1	1	0	3	0	0

Elected to Boxing Hall of Fame, 1980.

LARRY HOLMES

(The Easton Assassin)
Born, November 3, 1949, Cuthbert, Georgia. Weight, 196-224
lbs. Height, 6 ft. 3 in.

1973

Mar. 21–Rodell Dupree, Scranton .... W 4
May 2–Art Savage, Scranton .... KO 3
June 20–Curtis Whitner, Scranton .... KO 1
Aug. 22–Don Branch, Scranton .... W 6
Sept. 10–Bob Bozic, New York .... W 6
Nov. 14–Jerry Judge, Scranton .... W 6
Nov. 28–Kevin Isaac, Cleveland .... KO 3

1974

Apr. 24–Howard Darlington, Scranton .... KO 4
May 29–Bob Mashburn, Scranton .... KO 7
Dec. 11–Joe Hathaway, Scranton .... KO 1

1975

Mar. 24–Charley Green, Cleveland .... KO 2
Apr. 10–Oliver Wright, Honolulu .... KO 3
Apr. 26–Robert Yarborough, Toronto .... KO 3
May 16–Ernie Smith, Las Vegas................. KO 3
Aug. 16–Obie English, Scranton................. KO 7
Aug. 26–Charlie James, Honolulu................ W 10
Oct. 1–Rodney Bobick, Manila .... KO 6
Dec. 9–Leon Shaw, Washington D.C............. KO 1
Dec. 20–Billy Joiner, San Juan .... KO 3

1976

Jan. 29–Joe Gholston, Easton .... KO 8
Apr. 5–Fred Ashew, Landover .... KO 2
Apr. 30–Roy Williams, Landover .... W 10

1977

Jan. 16–Tom Prater, Pensacola .... W 8
(U.S. Championship Tournament)
Mar. 17–Horacio Robinson, San Juan .... KO 5
Sept. 14–Young Sanford Houpe, Las Vegas......... KO 7
Nov. 5–Ibar Arrington, Las Vegas .... KO 10

1978

Mar. 25–Earnie Shavers, Las Vegas .... W 12
June 9–Ken Norton, Las Vegas................. W 15
(Won WBC Heavyweight Title)
Nov. 10–Alfredo Evangelista, Las Vegas .... KO 7
(Retained WBC Heavyweight Title)

1979

Mar. 23–Osvaldo Ocasio, Las Vegas .... KO 7
(Retained WBC Heavyweight Title)
June 22–Mike Weaver, New York .... KO 12
(Retained WBC Heavyweight Title)
Sept. 28–Earnie Shavers, Las Vegas .... KO 11
(Retained WBC Heavyweight Title)

1980

Feb. 3–Lorenzo Zanon, Las Vegas.............. KO 6
(Retained WBC Heavyweight Title)
Mar. 31–Leroy Jones, Las Vegas................ KO 8
(Retained WBC Heavyweight Title)
July 7–Scott LeDoux, Bloomington .... KO 7
(Retained WBC Heavyweight Title)

Oct.   2–Muhammad Ali, Las Vegas . . . . KO 11
     (Won Vacant World Heavyweight Title)

1981

Apr.   11–Trevor Berbick, Las Vegas . . . . W 15
     (Retained World Heavyweight Title)
June 12–Leon Spinks, Detroit . . . . TKO 3
     (Retained World Heavyweight Title)
Nov.   6–Renaldo Snipes, Pittsburgh . . . . TKO 11
     (Retained World Heavyweight Title)

1982

June 11–Gerry Cooney, Las Vegas . . . . TKO 13
     (Retained World Heavyweight Title)
Nov. 26–Randall (Tex) Cobb, Houston . . . . W 15
     (Retained World Heavyweight Title)

1983

Mar. 27–Lucien Rodriguez, Scranton . . . . W 12
     (Retained World Heavyweight Title)
May   20–Tim Witherspoon, Las Vegas . . . . W 12
     (Retained World Heavyweight Title)

Sept. 10–Scott Frank, Atlantic City . . . . TKO 5
     (Retained World Heavyweight Title)
Nov. 25–Marvis Frazier, Las Vegas . . . . TKO 1
     (Retained World Heavyweight Title)

1984

Nov.   9–James Smith, Las Vegas . . . . TKO 12
     (Retained World Heavyweight Title)

1985

Mar. 15–David Bey, Las Vegas . . . . TKO 10
     (Retained World Heavyweight Title)
May   20–Carl Williams, Reno 15
     (Retained World Heavyweight Title)
Sept. 22–Michael Spinks, Las Vegas . . . . L 15
     (Lost World Heavyweight Title)

1986

Apr. 19–Michael Spinks, Las Vegas . . . . L 15
     (For World Heavyweight Title)

TB	KO	WD	WF	D	LD	LF	KOBO	ND	NC
50	34	14	0	0	2	0	0	0	0

THOMAS HEARNS

(The Motor City Cobra)
(Hit Man)
Born, October 18, 1958, Memphis, Tenn. Weight, 145-175 lbs.
Height, 6 ft. 1 in. Managed by Emanuel Steward.

***1977 U.S. National Amateur Athletic Union Light
   Welterweight Champion***
1977 National Golden Gloves Welterweight Champion

1977

Nov. 25–Jerone Hill, Detroit . . . . KO 2
Dec.   7–Jerry Strickland, Mt. Clemens . . . . KO 3
Dec. 16–Willie Wren, Detroit . . . . KO 3

1978

Jan. 29–Anthony House, Detroit . . . . KO 2
Feb. 10–Robert Adams, Detroit . . . . KO 3
Feb. 17–Billy Goodman, Detroit . . . . KO 2
Mar. 17–Ray Fields, Detroit . . . . KO 2
Mar. 31–Tyrone Phelps, Saginaw . . . . KO 3
June   8–Jimmy Rothwell, Detroit . . . . KO 1
July 20–Raul Aguirre, Detroit . . . . KO 3
Aug.   3–Eddie Marcelle, Detroit . . . . KO 2

Sept. 7–Bruce Finch, Detroit . . . . KO 3
Oct. 26–Pedro Rojas, Detroit . . . . KO 1
Dec.   9–Rudy Barro, Detroit . . . . KO 4

1979

Jan. 13–Clyde Gray, Detroit . . . . KO 10
Jan. 31–Sammy Ruckard, Detroit . . . . KO 8
Mar.   3–Segundo Murillo, Detroit . . . . KO 8
Apr.   3–Alfonso Hayman, Philadelphia . . . . W 10
May   20–Harold Weston Jr., Las Vegas . . . . KO 6
June 28–Bruce Curry, Detroit . . . . KO 3
Aug. 23–Mao DeLa Rosa, Detroit . . . . KO 2
Sept. 22–Jose Figueroa, Los Angeles . . . . KO 3
Oct. 18–Saensak Muangsurin, Detroit . . . . KO 3
Nov. 30–Mike Colbert, New Orleans . . . . W 10

1980

Feb.   3–Fighting Jim Richards, Las Vegas . . . . KO 3

Mar.   2–Angel Espada, Detroit .... KO 4
        (Won Vacant USBA Welterweight Title)
Mar.   31–Santiago Valdez, Las Vegas .... KO 1
May   3–Eddie Gazo, Detroit .... KO 1
Aug.   2–Pipino, Cuevas, Detroit................ KO 2
        (Won WBA Welterweight Title)
Nov.   29–William (Cavemen) Lee, L.A. .... Exh.
Dec.   6–Luis Primera, Detroit .... KO 6
        (Retained WBA Welterweight Title)

1981

Apr.   25–Randy Shields, Phoenix................ KO 13
        (Retained WBA Welterweight Title)
June   25–Pablo Baez, Houston .... KO 4
        (Retained WBA Welterweight Title)
Sept. 16–Ray Leonard, Las Vegas .... KO by 14
        (For World Welterweight Title)
Dec.   11–Ernie Singletary, Nassau .... W 10

1982

Feb.   27–Marcos Geraldo, Las Vegas............ KO 1
July   25–Jeff McCracken, Detroit .... KO 8
Dec.   3–Wilfred Benitez, New Orleans........... W 15
        (Won WBC Junior Middleweight Title)

1983

July   10–Murray Sutherland, Atlantic City.......... W 10

1984

Feb.   11–Luigi Minchillo, Detroit .... W 12
        (Retained WBC Junior Middleweight Title)
June   15–Roberto Duran, Las Vegas............... KO 2
        (Won Vacant World Junior Middleweight Title)
Sept. 15–Fred Hutchings, Saginaw............... KO 3
        (Retained World Junior Middleweight Title)

1985

Apr.   15–Marvin Hagler, Las Vegas .... TKO by 3
        (For World Middleweight Title)

1986

Mar.   10–James Shuler, Las Vegas.............. KO 1
        (Won NABF Middleweight Title)
June   23–Mark Medal, Las Vegas............... TKO 8
        (Retained World Junior Middleweight Title)
Sept.   –Relinquished World Junior Middleweight Title
Oct.   17–Doug DeWitt, Detroit.................. W 12
        (Retained NABF Middleweight Title)

1987

Feb.   –Dennis Andries, Detroit .... TKO 10
        (Won WBC Light Heavyweight Title)

TB	KO	WD	WF	D	LD	LF	KOBO	ND	NC
46	37	7	0	0	0	0	2	0	0

SUGAR RAY LEONARD

(Ray Charles Leonard)
Born, May 17, 1956, Wilmington, S.C. Weight 141-153 lbs.
Height, 5 ft. 10 in.

1973 National Golden Gloves Lightweight Champion
1974 National Golden Gloves Light Welterweight
   Champion
1974, 1975 United States National Amateur Athletic
   Union Light Welterweight Champion
1975 Pan American Games Light Welterweight
   Gold Medalist
1976 United States Olympic Light Welterweight
   Gold Medalist

1977

Feb.   5–Luis Vega, Baltimore................ W 6
May   14–Willie Rodriguez, Baltimore.......... W 6
June   10–Vinnie DeBarros, Hartford........... KO 3

Sept. 24–Frank Santore, Baltimore .... KO 5
Nov.   5–Augustin Estrada, Las Vegas .... KO 5
Dec.   17–Hector Diaz, Washington D.C. .... KO 2

1978

Feb.   4–Rocky Ramon, Baltimore .... W 8
Mar.   1–Art McKnight, Dayton .... KO 7
Mar.   19–Javier Muniz, New Haven............. KO 1
Apr.   13–Bobby Haymon, Landover .... KO 3
May   13–Randy Milton, Utica................. KO 8
June   3–Rafael Rodriguez, Baltimore .... W 10
July   18–Dick Eckland, Boston .... W 10
Sept.   9–Floyd Mayweather, Providence .... KO 9
Oct.   6–Randy Shields, Baltimore .... W 10

Nov. 3–Bernardo Prada, Portland, Me . . . . W 10
Dec. 9–Armando Muniz, Springfield . . . . KO 6

1979

Jan. 11–Johnny Gant, Landover . . . . KO 8
Feb. 11–Fernand Marcotte, Miami Beach . . . . . . KO 8
Mar. 24–Daniel Gonzales, Tuscan . . . . KO 1
Apr. 21–Adolfo Viruet, Las Vegas . . . . W 10
May 20–Marcos Geraldo, New Orleans . . . . W 10
June 24–Tony Chiaverini, Las Vegas . . . . KO 4
Aug. 12–Pete Ranzany, Las Vegas . . . . KO 4
    (Won NABF Welterweight Title)
Sept. 28–Andy Price, Las Vegas . . . . KO 1
    (Retained NABF Welterweight Title)
Nov. 30–Wilfred Benitez, Las Vegas . . . . KO 15
    (Won World Welterweight Title)

1980

Mar. 31–Dave (Boy) Green, Landover . . . . KO 4
    (Retained World Welterweight Title)
June 20–Roberto Duran, Montreal . . . . L 15
    (Lost World Welterweight Title)
Nov. 25–Roberto Duran, New Orleans . . . . KO 8
    (Regained World Welterweight Title)

1981

Mar. 28–Larry Bonds, Syracuse . . . . KO 10
    (Retained World Welterweight Title)
June 25–Ayub Kalule, Houston . . . . KO 9
    (Won World Junior Middleweight Title)
Sept. 16–Thomas Hearns, Las Vegas . . . . KO 14
    (Retained World Welterweight Title)

1982

Feb. 15–Bruce Finch, Reno, Nev. . . . . KO 3
    (Retained World Welterweight Title)
Nov. 9–Announced retirement. . . . .

1983

(Inactive)

1984

May 11–Kevin Howard, Worcester . . . . KO 9

1987

Apr. 6–Marvin Hagler, Las Vegas . . . . W 12
    (Won WBC Middleweight Title)

TB	KO	WD	WF	D	LD	LF	KOBO	ND	NC
35	24	10	0	0	1	0	0	0	0

MARVIN HAGLER

(Marvelous Marvin)

Born, May 23, 1954, Newark, N.J. Weight, 155-162 lbs.
Height, 5 ft. 9½ in. Southpaw. Managed by Goody and Pat
Petronelli.

1973 U.S. National AAU Middleweight Champion

1973

May 18–Terry Ryan, Brockton . . . . KO 2
July 25–Sonny Williams, Boston . . . . W 6
Aug. 8–Muhammad Smith, Boston . . . . KO 2
Oct. 6–Don Wigfall, Brockton . . . . W 8
Oct. 26–Cove Green, Brockton . . . . KO 4
Nov. 18–Cocoa Kid, Brockton . . . . KO 2
Dec. 7–Manny Freitas, Portland, Me . . . . KO 1
Dec. 18–James Redford, Boston . . . . KO 4

1974

Feb. 5–Bob Harrington, Boston . . . . KO 5
Apr. 5–Tracy Morrison, Boston . . . . KO 8

May 4–Jim Redford, Brockton . . . . KO 2
May 30–Curtis Phillips, Portland . . . . KO 5
July 16–Robert Williams, Boston . . . . KO 3
Aug. 13–Peachy Davis, New Bedford . . . . KO 1
Aug. 30–Ray Seales, Boston . . . . W 10
Oct. 29–Morris Jordan, New Bedford . . . . KO 4
Nov. 16–George Green, Brockton . . . . KO 1
Nov. 26–Ray Seales, Seattle . . . . D 10
Dec. 20–D.C. Walker, Boston . . . . KO 2

1975

Feb. 15–Don Wigfall, Brockton . . . . KO 5
Mar. 31–Joey Blair, Boston . . . . KO 2
Apr. 14–Jimmy Owens, Boston . . . . W 10
May 24–Jimmy Owens, Boston . . . . W disq 6

Aug. 7–Jesse Bender, Portland . . . . KO 1
Sept. 30–Lamont Lovelady, Boston . . . . KO 7
Dec. 20–Johnny Baldwin, Boston . . . . W 10

1976

Jan. 13–Bobby Watts, Philadelphia . . . . L 10
Feb. 7–Matt Donovan, Boston . . . . KO 2
Mar. 9–Willie Monroe, Philadelphia . . . . L 10
June 2–Bob Smith, Taunton . . . . KO 5
Aug. 3–D.C. Walker, Providence . . . . KO 6
Sept. 14–Eugene Hart, Philadelphia . . . . KO 8
Dec. 21–George Davis, Boston . . . . KO 6

1977

Feb. 15–Willie Monroe, Boston . . . . KO 12
Mar. 16–Reginald Ford, Boston . . . . KO 3
June 10–Roy Jones, Hartford . . . . KO 3
Aug. 23–Willie Monroe, Philadelphia . . . . KO 2
Sept. 24–Ray Phillips, Boston . . . . KO 7
Oct. 15–Jim Henry, Providence . . . . W 10
Nov. 26–Mike Colbert, Boston . . . . KO 12

1978

Mar. 4–Kevin Finnegan, Boston . . . . KO 9
Apr. 7–Doug Demmings, Los Angeles . . . . KO 8
May 13–Kevin Finnegan, Boston . . . . KO 7
Aug. 24–Bennie Briscoe, Philadelphia . . . . W 10
Nov. 11–Willie Warren, Boston . . . . KO 7

1979

Feb. 3–Ray Seales, Boston . . . . KO 1
Mar. 12–Bob Patterson, Providence . . . . KO 3
May 26–Jaime Thomas, Portland, Me . . . . KO 3
June 30–Norberto Cabrera, Monte Carlo . . . . KO 8
Nov. 30–Vito Antuofermo, Las Vegas . . . . D 15
      (For World Middleweight Title)

1980

Feb. 16–Loucif Hammani, Portland . . . . KO 2
Apr. 19–Bobby Watts, Portland . . . . KO 2
May 17–Marcos Geraldo, Las Vegas . . . . W 10
Sept. 27–Alan Minter, London . . . . KO 3
      (Won World Middleweight Title)

1981

Jan. 17–Fulgencio Obelmejias, Boston . . . . KO 8
      (Retained World Middleweight Title)
June 13–Vito Antuoferno, Boston . . . . KO 5
      (Retained World Middleweight Title)
Oct. 3–Mustafa Hamsho, Rosemont . . . . KO 11
      (Retained World Middleweight Title)

1982

Mar. 7–Wm. (Caveman) Lee, Atlantic City . . . . KO 1
      (Retained World Middleweight Title)
Oct. 30–Fulgencio Obelmejias, San Remo . . . . KO 5
      (Retained World Middleweight Title)

1983

Feb. 11–Tony Sibson, Worcester, Mass . . . . KO 6
      (Retained World Middleweight Title)
May 27–Wilford Scypion, Providence . . . . KO 4
      (Retained World Middleweight Title)
Nov. 10–Roberto Duran, Las Vegas . . . . W 15
      (Retained World Middleweight Title)

1984

Mar. 30–Juan Domingo Roldan, Las Vegas . . . . KO 10
      (Retained World Middleweight Title)
Oct. 19–Mustafa Hamsho, New York . . . . KO 3
      (Retained World Middleweight Title)

1985

Apr. 15–Thomas Hearns, Las Vegas . . . . TKO 3
      (Retained World Middleweight Title)

1986

Mar. 10–John Mugabi, Las Vegas . . . . KO 11
      (Retained World Middleweight Title)

1987

Apr. 6–Sugar Ray Leonard, Las Vegas . . . . L 12
      (Lost WBC Middleweight Title)

TB	KO	WD	WF	D	LD	LF	KOBO	ND	NC
67	52	9	1	2	3	0	0	0	0

MICHAEL SPINKS

Born, July 13, 1956, St. Louis, Mo. Weight, 165-200 lbs.
Height, 6 ft. 2½ in.

1976 National Golden Gloves Middleweight Champion
1976 United States Olympic Middleweight Gold
Medalist

1977

Apr.	17–Eddie Benson, Las Vegas	KO	1
May	9–Luis Rodriguez, St. Louis	W	6
June	1–Joe Borden, Montreal, Qbc.	KO	2
Aug.	23–Jasper Brisbane, Philadelphia	KO	1
Sept.	13–Ray J. Elson, Los Angeles	KO	1
Oct.	21–Gary Summerhays, Las Vegas	W	8

1978

| Feb. | 15–Tom Bethea, Las Vegas, Nev. | W | 8 |
| Dec. | 15–Eddie Phillips, White Plains | KO | 4 |

1979

| Nov. | 24–Marc Hans, Bloomington | KO | 1 |

1980

Feb.	1–Johnny Wilburn, Louisville, Ky	W	8
Feb.	24–Ramon Ronquillo, Atlantic City	TKO	6
May	4–Murray Sutherland, Kiamesha Lake	W	10
Aug.	2–David Conteh, Baton Rouge, La.	KO	9
Oct.	18–Yaqui Lopez, Atlantic City	KO	7

1981

Jan.	24–Willie Taylor, Philadelphia	KO	8
Mar.	28–Marvin Johnson, Atlantic City	KO	4
July	18–Mustafa Muhammad, Las Vegas	W	15

(Won WBA Light Heavyweight Title)

| Nov. | 7–Vonzell Johnson, Atlantic City | TKO | 7 |

(Retained WB Light Heavyweight Title)

1982

| Feb. | 13–Mustapha Wasajja, Atlantic City | TKO | 6 |

(Retained WBA Light Heavyweight Title)

| Apr. | 11–Murray Sutherland, Atlantic City | TKO | 8 |

(Retained WBA Light Heavyweight Title)

| June | 12–Jerry Celestine, Atlantic City | TKO | 8 |

(Retained WBA Light Heavyweight Title)

| Sept. | 18–Johnny Davis, Atlantic City | TKO | 9 |

(Retained WBA Light Heavyweight Title)

1983

| Mar. | 18–Dwight Braxton, Atlantic City | W | 15 |

(Won Vacant World Light Heavyweight Title)

| Nov. | 25–Oscar Rivadeneyra, Vancouver | TKO | 10 |

(Retained World Light Heavyweight Title)

1984

| Feb. | 25–Eddie Davis, Atlantic City | W | 12 |

(Retained World Light Heavyweight Title)

1985

| Feb. | 23–David Sears, Atlantic City | TKO | 3 |

(Retained World Light Heavyweight Title)

| June | 6–Jim MacDonald, Las Vegas | TKO | 8 |

(Retained World Light Heavyweight Title)

| Sept. | 22–Larry Holmes, Las Vegas | W | 15 |

(Won World Heavyweight Title)

1986

| Apr. | 19–Larry Holmes, Las Vegas | W | 15 |

(Retained World Heavyweight Title)

| Sept. | 6–Steffen Tangstad, Las Vegas | TKO | 4 |

(Retained World Heavyweight Title)

1987

| June | 15–Gerry Cooney, Atlantic City | TKO | 5 |

(Retained World Heavyweight Title)

TB	KO	WD	WF	D	LD	LF	KOBO	ND	NC
31	21	10	0	0	0	0	0	0	0

MICHAEL GERALD TYSON

Born, June 30, 1966, Brooklyn, N.Y. Weight, 212-221 lbs.
Height, 5 ft. 11 in. Managed by Jim Jacobs and Bill Cayton.

1984 National Golden Gloves Heavyweight Champion

1985

Mar.	6 – Hector Mercedes, Albany	TKO	1
Apr.	10 – Trent Singleton, Albany	TKO	1
May	23 – Don Halpin, Albany	KO	4
June	20 – Rick Spain, Atlantic City	KO	1
July	11 – John Alderson, Altantic City	TKO	2
July	19 – Larry Sims, Poughkeepsie, N.Y.	KO	3
Aug.	15 – Lorenzo Canady, Atlantic City	TKO	1
Sept.	5 – Mike Johnson, Atlantic City	KO	1
Oct.	9 – Donnie Long, Atlantic City	KO	1
Oct.	25 – Robert Colay, Atlantic City	KO	1
Nov.	1 – Sterling Benjamin, Latham, N.Y.	TKO	1
Nov.	13 – Eddie Richardson, Houston	KO	1
Nov.	22 – Conroy Nelson, Latham, N.Y.	TKO	2
Dec.	6 – Sammy Scaff, New York	TKO	1
Dec.	27 – Mark Young, Latham, N.Y.	TKO	1

1986

Jan.	11 – David Jaco, Albany	TKO	1
Jan.	24 – Mike Jameson, Atlantic City	TKO	5
Feb.	16 – Jesse Ferguson, Troy, N.Y.	TKO	6
Mar.	10 – Steve Zouski, E. Rutherford	KO	3
May	3 – James Tillis, Glens Falls	W	10
May	20 – Mitchell Green, New York	W	10
June	13 – Reggie Gross, New York	TKO	1
June	28 – William Hosea, Troy, N.Y.	KO	1
July	11 – Lorenzo Boyd, Swan Lake	KO	2
July	26 – Marvis Frazier, Glens Falls	KO	1
Aug.	17 – Jose Ribalta, Atlantic City	TKO	10
Sept.	6 – Alfonzo Ratliff, Las Vegas	TKO	2
Nov.	22 – Trevor Berbick, Las Vegas	TKO	2

(Won WBC Heavyweight Title)

1987

Mar.	3 – James Smith, Las Vegas	W	12

(Unified WBC & WBA Heavyweight Titles)

May	30 – Pinklon Thomas, Las Vegas	KO	6

(Retained the WBC & WBA Heavyweight Titles)

Aug.	1 – Tony Tucker, Las Vegas	W	15

(Won the IBF Heavyweight Title)

TB	KO	WD	WF	D	LD	LF	KOBO	ND	NC
31	27	4	0	0	0	0	0	0	0

Football

BOBBY MITCHELL'S CAREER RECORD

Born in Hot Springs, Arkansas, June 6, 1935
College—University of Illinois
Position—Halfback, Wide Receiver
Inducted into the Pro Football Hall of Fame, 1983

RUSHING

Year	Team	Att.	Yards	Avg.	Long	TD
1958	Cleveland	80	500	6.3	63t	1
1959	Cleveland	131	743	5.7	90t	5
1960	Cleveland	111	506	4.6	50	5
1961	Cleveland	101	548	5.4	65t	5
1962	Washington	1	5	5.0	5	0
1963	Washington	3	24	8.0	21	0
1964	Washington	2	33	16.5	19	0
1965	Washington	0	0	0.0	0	0
1966	Washington	13	141	10.8	48	1
1967	Washington	61	189	3.1	16	1
1968	Washington	10	46	4.6	13	0
Totals		513	2,735	5.3	90t	18

RECEIVING

Year	Team	No.	Yards	Avg.	Long	TD
1958	Cleveland	16	131	8.2	25	3
1959	Cleveland	35	351	10.0	76t	4
1960	Cleveland	45	612	13.6	69t	6
1961	Cleveland	32	368	11.5	55	3
1962	Washington	72	1,384	19.2	81t	11
1963	Washington	69	1,436	20.8	99t	7
1964	Washington	60	904	15.1	60	10
1965	Washington	60	867	14.5	80t	6
1966	Washington	58	905	15.6	70t	9
1967	Washington	60	866	14.4	65t	6
1968	Washington	14	130	9.3	18	0
Totals		521	7,954	15.3	99t	65

PUNT RETURNS
69, 699 Yards, 10.1 Avg., 78 Long, 3 TD

KICKOFF RETURNS
102, 2,690 Yards, 26.4 Avg., 98 Long, 5 TD

SCORING
91 TD, 546 Points

EMLEN TUNNELL'S CAREER RECORD

Born in Bryn Mawr, Pennsylvania, March 29, 1925
College—Iowa University
Position—Safety
Inducted into the Pro Football Hall of Fame, 1967
Died July 23, 1975

INTERCEPTIONS

Year	Team	No.	Yards	Avg.	Long	TD
1948	NY Giants	7	116	16.6	43t	1
1949	NY Giants	10	251	25.1	55t	2
1950	NY Giants	7	167	23.9	35	0
1951	NY Giants	9	74	8.2	30	0
1952	NY Giants	7	149	21.3	40	0
1953	NY Giants	6	117	19.5	44	0
1954	NY Giants	8	108	13.5	43	0

t = return interception for touchdown

Year	Team	No.	Yards	Avg.	Long	TD
1955	NY Giants	7	76	10.9	26	0
1956	NY Giants	6	87	14.5	23	0
1957	NY Giants	6	87	14.5	52t	1
1958	NY Giants	1	8	8.0	8	0
1959	Green Bay	2	20	10.0	18	0
1960	Green Bay	3	22	7.3	22	0
1961	Green Bay	0	0	0.0	0	0
Totals	....	79	1,282	16.2	55t	4

Year	Team	No.	Yards	Avg.	Long	TD
1952	NY Giants	30	411	13.7	60	0
1953	NY Giants	38	223	5.9	37	0
1954	NY Giants	21	70	3.3	12	0
1955	NY Giants	25	98	3.9	66t	1
1956	NY Giants	22	120	5.5	14	0
1957	NY Giants	12	60	5.0	23	0
1958	NY Giants	6	0	0.0	0	0
1959	Green Bay	1	3	3.0	3	0
1960	Green Bay	0	0	0.0	0	0
1961	Green Bay	0	0	0.0	0	0
Totals	....	258	2,209	8.6	81t	5

PUNT RETURNS

1948	NY Giants	12	115	9.6	25	0
1949	NY Giants	26	315	12.1	67t	1
1950	NY Giants	31	305	9.8	43	0
1951	NY Giants	34	489	14.4	81t	3

KICKOFF RETURNS

46, 1,215 Yards, 26.4 Avg., 100 Long, 1 TD

CHARLEY TAYLOR'S CAREER RECORD

Born in Grand Prairie, Texas, September 28, 1941
College—Arizona State University
Position—Wide Receiver, Halfback
Inducted into the Pro Football Hall of Fame, 1984
Chosen to the All-Pro Squad of the 1960s in the National Football
    League

RECEIVING

Year	Team	No.	Yards	Avg.	Long	TD
1964	Washington	53	814	15.4	80t	5
1965	Washington	40	577	14.4	69	3
1966	Washington	72	1,119	15.5	86t	12
1967	Washington	70	990	14.1	86t	9
1968	Washington	48	650	13.5	47	5
1969	Washington	71	883	12.4	88t	8
1970	Washington	42	593	14.1	41	8
1971	Washington	24	370	15.4	71t	4
1972	Washington	49	673	13.7	70t	7
1973	Washington	59	801	13.6	53	7
1974	Washington	54	738	13.7	51	5
1975	Washington	53	774	14.6	64	6
1976	Did not play football					
1977	Washington	14	158	11.3	19	0
Totals	....	649	9,140	14.1	88t	79

RUSHING

442 Att., 1,488 yards, 3.4 Avg., 11 TD

SCORING

90 TD, 540 Points

t = return interception for touchdown

DICK LANE'S CAREER RECORD

Born in Austin, Texas, April 16, 1928
College—Scottsbluff Junior College
Position—Cornerback
Inducted into the Pro Football Hall of Fame, 1974
Chosen as an All-Time All-Pro in the National Football League in 1969

INTERCEPTIONS

Year	Team	No.	Yards	Avg.	Long	TD
1952	LA Rams	14	298	21.3	80	2
1953	LA Rams	3	9	3.0	8	0
1954	Chi. Cardinals	10	181	18.1	64	0
1955	Chi. Cardinals	6	69	11.5	26	0
1956	Chi. Cardinals	7	206	29.4	66t	1
1957	Chi. Cardinals	2	47	23.5	33	0
1958	Chi. Cardinals	2	0	0.0	0	0
1959	Chi. Cardinals	3	125	41.7	69	1
1960	Detroit	5	102	20.4	80t	1
1961	Detroit	6	73	12.2	32	0
1962	Detroit	4	16	4.0	13	0
1963	Detroit	5	70	14.0	33	0
1964	Detroit	1	11	11.0	11	0
1965	Detroit	0	0	0.0	0	0
Totals		68	1,207	17.8	80t	5

JIM BROWN'S CAREER RECORD

Born in St. Simons, Georgia, February 17, 1936
College—Syracuse University
Position—Fullback
Inducted into the Pro Football Hall of Fame, 1971
Chosen as an All-Time All-Pro in the National Football League, 1969
1963 Bert Bell Trophy recipient as the Most Valuable Player in the
National Football League (the first African-American to win this
award)

RUSHING

Year	Team	Att.	Yards	Avg.	Long	TD
1957	Cleveland	202	942	4.7	69t	9
1958	Cleveland	257	1,527	5.9	65t	17
1959	Cleveland	290	1,329	4.6	70t	14
1960	Cleveland	215	1,257	5.8	71t	9
1961	Cleveland	305	1,408	4.6	38	8
1962	Cleveland	230	996	4.3	31	13
1963	Cleveland	291	1,863	6.4	80t	12
1964	Cleveland	280	1,446	5.2	71	7
1965	Cleveland	289	1,544	5.3	67	17
Totals		2,359	12,312	5.2	80t	106

KICKOFF RETURNS
29,648 Yards, 22.3 Avg., 35 Long, 0 TD

RECEIVING

Year	Team	No.	Yards	Avg.	Long	TD
1957	Cleveland	16	55	3.4	12	1
1958	Cleveland	16	138	8.6	46	1
1959	Cleveland	24	190	7.9	25	0
1960	Cleveland	19	204	10.7	37t	2
1961	Cleveland	46	459	10.0	77t	2
1962	Cleveland	47	517	11.0	53t	5
1963	Cleveland	24	268	11.2	83t	3
1964	Cleveland	36	340	9.4	40t	2
1965	Cleveland	34	328	9.6	32t	4
Totals		262	2,499	9.5	83t	20

SCORING
126 TD, 756 Points

t = return interception for touchdown

WILLIE BROWN'S CAREER RECORD

Born in Yazoo City, Mississippi, December 2, 1940
College—Grambling College
Position—Cornerback
Inducted into the Pro Football Hall of Fame, 1984
Member of the All-Time American Football League Team

INTERCEPTIONS

Year	Team	No.	Yards	Avg.	Long	TD	Year	Team	No.	Yards	Avg.	Long	TD
1963	Denver	1	0	1.0	0	0	1971	Oakland	2	2	1.0	2	0
1964	Denver	9	140	15.6	45	0	1972	Oakland	4	26	6.5	13	0
1965	Denver	2	18	9.0	18	0	1973	Oakland	3	–1	–0.3	0	0
1966	Denver	3	37	12.3	31	0	1974	Oakland	1	31	31.0	31	0
1967	Oakland	7	33	4.7	25t	1	1975	Oakland	4	–1	–0.3	0	0
1968	Oakland	2	27	13.5	27t	1	1976	Oakland	3	25	8.3	22	0
1969	Oakland	5	111	22.2	30	0	1977	Oakland	4	24	6.0	18	0
1970	Oakland	3	0	0.0	0	0	1978	Oakland	1	0	0.0	0	0
							Totals		54	472	8.7	45	2

HERB ADDERLEY'S CAREER RECORD

Born in Philadelphia, Pennsylvania, June 8, 1939
College—Michigan State University
Position—Cornerback
Inducted into the Pro Football Hall of Fame, 1980
Chosen to the National Football League All-Pro Squad of the 1960s

INTERCEPTIONS

Year	Team	No.	Yards	Avg.	Long	TD	Year	Team	No.	Yards	Avg.	Long	TD
1961	Green Bay	1	9	9.0	9	0	1969	Green Bay	5	169	33.8	80t	1
1962	Green Bay	7	132	18.9	50t	1	1970	Dallas	3	69	23.0	30	0
1963	Green Bay	5	86	17.2	39	0	1971	Dallas	6	182	30.3	46	0
1964	Green Bay	4	56	14.0	35	0	1972	Dallas	0	0	0.0	0	0
1965	Green Bay	6	175	29.2	44	3	Totals		48	1,046	21.8	80t	7
1966	Green Bay	4	125	31.3	68t	1							
1967	Green Bay	4	16	4.0	12t	1							
1968	Green Bay	3	27	9.0	17	0							

KICKOFF RETURNS
120, 3,080 Yards, 25.7 Avg., 103 Long, 2 TD

t = return interception for touchdown

KEN HOUSTON'S CAREER RECORD

Born in Lufkin, Texas, November 12, 1944
College—Prairie View A&M University
Position—Safety
Inducted into the Pro Football Hall of Fame, 1986

INTERCEPTIONS

Year	Team	No.	Yards	Avg.	Long	TD
1967	Houston	4	151	37.8	78	2
1968	Houston	5	160	32.0	66t	2
1969	Houston	4	87	21.8	51t	1
1970	Houston	3	32	10.7	11	0
1971	Houston	9	220	24.4	48t	4
1972	Houston	0	0	0.0	0	0
1973	Washington	6	32	5.3	22	0
1974	Washington	2	40	20.0	37	0
1975	Washington	4	33	8.3	19	0
1976	Washington	4	25	6.3	12	0
1977	Washington	5	69	13.8	31	0
1978	Washington	2	29	14.5	29	0
1979	Washington	1	20	20.0	20	0
1980	Washington	0	0	0.0	0	0
Totals		49	898	18.3	78	9

PAUL WARFIELD'S CAREER RECORD

Born in Warren, Ohio, November 28, 1942
College—Ohio State University
Position—Wide Receiver
Inducted into the Pro Football Hall of Fame, 1983

RECEIVING

Year	Team	No.	Yards	Avg.	Long	TD
1964	Cleveland	52	920	17.7	62t	9
1965	Cleveland	3	30	10.0	13	0
1966	Cleveland	36	741	20.6	51	5
1967	Cleveland	32	702	21.3	49t	8
1968	Cleveland	50	1,067	21.3	65t	12
1969	Cleveland	42	886	21.1	82t	10
1970	Miami	28	703	25.1	54	6
1971	Miami	43	996	23.2	86t	11
1972	Miami	29	606	20.9	47	3
1973	Miami	29	514	17.7	45t	11
1974	Miami	27	536	19.9	54	2
1975	Memphis (WFL)	25	422	16.9	47t	3
1976	Cleveland	38	613	16.1	37t	6
1977	Cleveland	18	251	13.9	52t	2
NFL Totals		427	8,565	20.1	86t	85
Pro Totals		452	8,987	19.9	86t	88

t = return interception for touchdown

JOE PERRY'S CAREER RECORD

Born in Stevens, Arkansas, January 27, 1927
College—Compton Junior College
Position—Fullback
Inducted into the Pro Football Hall of Fame, 1969

RUSHING

Year	Team	Att.	Yards	Avg.	Long	TD
1948	San Francisco (AAFC).	77	562	7.3		10
1949	San Francisco (AAFC).	115	783	6.8		8
1950	San Francisco.......	124	647	5.2	78t	5
1951	San Francisco.......	136	677	5.0	58t	3
1952	San Francisco.......	158	725	4.6	78t	8
1953	San Francisco.......	192	1,018	5.3	51t	10
1954	San Francisco.......	173	1,049	6.1	58	8
1955	San Francisco.......	156	701	4.5	42	2
1956	San Francisco.......	115	520	4.5	39	3
1957	San Francisco.......	97	454	4.7	34	3
1958	San Francisco.......	125	758	6.1	73t	4
1959	San Francisco.......	139	602	4.4	40	3
1960	San Francisco.......	36	95	2.6	21	1
1961	Baltimore..........	168	675	4.0	27	3
1962	Baltimore..........	94	359	3.8	21	0
1963	San Francisco.......	24	98	4.1	16	0
NFL Totals...............		1,737	8,378	4.8	78t	53
Pro Totals		1,929	9,723	5.0	78t	71

SCORING
NFL–61 TD, 1 FG, 6 PAT, 375 Points
Pro–84 TD, 1 FG, 6 PAT, 513 Points

RECEIVING

Year	Team	No.	Yards	Avg.	Long	TD
1948	San Francisco (AAFC) .	8	79	9.9		1
1949	San Francisco (AAFC) .	11	146	13.3		3
1950	San Francisco	13	69	5.3	16	1
1951	San Francisco	18	167	9.3	35	1
1952	San Francisco	15	81	5.4	17	0
1953	San Francisco	19	191	10.1	60t	3
1954	San Francisco	26	203	7.8	70	0
1955	San Francisco	19	55	2.9	19	1
1956	San Francisco	18	104	5.8	20	0
1957	San Francisco	15	130	8.7	17	0
1958	San Francisco	23	218	9.5	64t	1
1959	San Francisco	12	53	4.4	15	0
1960	San Francisco	3	–3	–1.0	3	0
1961	Baltimore...........	34	322	9.5	27	1
1962	Baltimore...........	22	194	8.8	32	0
1963	San Francisco	4	12	3.0	8	0
NFL Totals		241	1,796	7.4	70	8
Pro Totals................		260	2,021	7.8	70	12

KICKOFF RETURNS
NFL–15,276 Yards, 18.4 Avg., 0 TD
Pro–33,758 Yards, 23.0 Avg., 1 TD

---

t = return interception for touchdown

O.J. SIMPSON'S CAREER RECORD

Born in San Francisco, California, July 9, 1947
College—University of Southern California
Position—Halfback
Inducted into the Pro Football Hall of Fame, 1985
1973 Bert Bell Trophy recipient as Most Valuable Player in the
    National Football League
1972, 1973, and 1974 United Press International American Football
    Conference Player of the Year

RUSHING

Year	Team	Att.	Yards	Avg.	Long	TD
1969	Buffalo............	181	697	3.9	32t	2
1970	Buffalo............	120	488	4.1	56t	5
1971	Buffalo............	183	742	4.1	46t	5
1972	Buffalo............	292	1,251	4.3	94t	6
1973	Buffalo............	332	2,003	6.0	80t	12
1974	Buffalo............	270	1,125	4.2	41t	3
1975	Buffalo............	329	1,817	5.5	88t	16
1976	Buffalo............	290	1,503	5.2	75t	8
1977	Buffalo............	126	557	4.4	39	0
1978	San Francisco.......	161	593	3.7	34	1
1979	San Francisco.......	120	460	3.8	22	3
	Totals	2,404	11,236	4.7	94t	61

RECEIVING
203, 2,142 Yards, 10.6 Avg., 64 Long, 14 TD

KICKOFF RETURNS
33,990 Yards, 30.0 Avg., 95 Long, 1 TD

SCORING
76 TD, 456 Points

OLLIE MATSON'S CAREER RECORD

Born in Trinity, Texas, May 1, 1930
College—University of San Francisco
Position—Halfback
Inducted into the Pro Football Hall of Fame, 1972
Chosen to the National Football League All-Pro Squad of the 1950s

RUSHING

Year	Team	Att.	Yards	Avg.	Long	TD
1952	Chi. Cardinals	96	344	3.6	25	3
1953	Military service					
1954	Chi. Cardinals	101	506	5.0	79t	4
1955	Chi. Cardinals	109	475	4.4	54	1
1956	Chi. Cardinals	192	924	4.8	79t	5
1957	Chi. Cardinals	134	577	4.3	56t	6
1958	Chi. Cardinals	129	505	3.9	55t	5
1959	LA Rams	161	863	5.4	50	6
1960	LA Rams	61	170	2.9	27	1
1961	LA Rams	24	181	7.5	69t	2
1962	LA Rams	3	0	0.0	2	0
1963	Detroit............	13	20	1.5	9	0
1964	Philadelphia	96	404	4.2	63	4
1965	Philadelphia	22	103	4.7	22	2
1966	Philadelphia	29	101	3.5	28	1
	Totals	1,170	5,173	4.4	79t	40

RECEIVING

Year	Team	No.	Yards	Avg.	Long	TD
1952	Chi. Cardinals	11	187	17.0	47t	3
1953	Military service					
1954	Chi. Cardinals	34	611	18.0	70	3
1955	Chi. Cardinals	17	237	13.9	70t	2
1956	Chi. Cardinals	15	199	13.3	45t	2
1957	Chi. Cardinals	20	451	22.6	75t	3
1958	Chi. Cardinals	33	465	14.1	59	3
1959	LA Rams	18	130	7.2	49	0

t = return interception for touchdown.

Year	Team	No.	Yards	Avg.	Long	TD
1960	LA Rams	15	98	6.5	24	0
1961	LA Rams	29	537	18.5	96t	3
1962	LA Rams	3	49	16.3	20t	1
1963	Detroit	2	20	10.0	17	0
1964	Philadelphia	17	242	14.2	32	1
1965	Philadelphia	2	29	14.5	20	1
1966	Philadelphia	6	30	5.0	11	1
Totals		222	3,285	14.8	96t	23

1956	Chi. Cardinals	13	362	27.8	105t	1
1957	Chi. Cardinals	7	154	22.0	32	0
1958	Chi. Cardinals	14	497	35.5	101t	2
1959	LA Rams	16	367	22.9	48	0
1960	LA Rams	9	216	24.0	42	0
1961	LA Rams	0	0	0.0	0	0
1962	LA Rams	0	0	0.0	0	0
1963	Detroit	3	61	20.3	30	0
1964	Philadelphia	3	104	34.7	43	0
1965	Philadelphia	0	0	0.0	0	0
1966	Philadelphia	26	544	20.9	31	0
Totals		143	3,746	26.2	105t	6

KICKOFF RETURNS

Year	Team	No.	Yards	Avg.	Long	TD
1952	Chi. Cardinals	20	624	31.2	100t	2
1953	Military service					
1954	Chi. Cardinals	17	449	26.4	91t	1
1955	Chi. Cardinals	15	368	24.5	37	0

PUNT RETURNS

65,595 Yards, 9.2 Avg., 78 Long, 3 TD

GALE SAYERS' CAREER RECORD

Born in Wichita, Kansas, May 30, 1943
College—University of Kansas
Position—Halfback
Inducted into the Pro Football Hall of Fame, 1977

RUSHING

Year	Team	Att.	Yards	Avg.	Long	TD
1965	Chi. Bears	166	867	5.2	61t	14
1966	Chi. Bears	229	1,231	5.4	58t	8
1967	Chi. Bears	186	880	4.7	70t	7
1968	Chi. Bears	138	856	6.2	63	2
1969	Chi. Bears	236	1,032	4.4	28	8
1970	Chi. Bears	23	52	2.3	15	0
1971	Chi. Bears	13	38	2.9	9	0
Totals		991	4,956	5.0	70t	39

PUNT RETURNS

Year	Team	No.	Yards	Avg.	Long	TD
1965	Chi. Bears..........	16	238	14.9	85t	1
1966	Chi. Bears..........	6	44	7.3	27	0
1967	Chi. Bears..........	3	80	26.7	58	1
1968	Chi. Bears..........	2	29	14.5	18	0
1969	Chi. Bears..........	0	0	0.0	0	0
1970	Chi. Bears..........	0	0	0.0	0	0
1971	Chi. Bears..........	0	0	0.0	0	0
Totals		27	391	14.5	85t	2

RECEIVING

Year	Team	No.	Yards	Avg.	Long	TD
1965	Chi. Bears..........	29	507	17.5	80t	6
1966	Chi. Bears..........	34	447	13.1	80t	2
1967	Chi. Bears..........	16	126	7.9	32	1
1968	Chi. Bears..........	15	117	7.8	21	0
1969	Chi. Bears..........	17	116	6.8	25	0
1970	Chi. Bears..........	1	−6	−6.0	−6	0
1971	Chi. Bears..........	0	0	0.0	0	0
Totals		112	1,307	11.6	80t	9

KICKOFF RETURNS

Year	Team	No.	Yards	Avg.	Long	TD
1965	Chi. Bears..........	21	660	31.4	96t	1
1966	Chi. Bears..........	23	718	31.2	93t	2
1967	Chi. Bears..........	16	603	37.7	103t	3
1968	Chi. Bears..........	17	461	27.1	46	0
1969	Chi. Bears..........	14	339	24.2	52	0
1970	Chi. Bears..........	0	0	0.0	0	0
1971	Chi. Bears..........	0	0	0.0	0	0
Totals		91	2,781	30.6	103t	6

SCORING

56 TD, 336 Points

LENNY MOORE'S CAREER RECORD

Born in Reading, Pennsylvania, November 25, 1933
College—Pennsylvania State University
Position—Halfback
Inducted into the Pro Football Hall of Fame, 1975
Chosen to the National Football League All-Pro Squad of the 1950s

RUSHING

Year	Team	Att.	Yards	Avg.	Long	TD
1956	Baltimore	86	649	7.5	79t	8
1957	Baltimore	98	488	5.0	55t	3
1958	Baltimore	82	598	7.3	73t	7
1959	Baltimore	92	422	4.6	31t	2
1960	Baltimore	91	374	4.1	57t	4
1961	Baltimore	92	648	7.0	54t	7
1962	Baltimore	106	470	4.4	25	2
1963	Baltimore	27	136	5.0	25t	2
1964	Baltimore	157	584	3.7	32t	16
1965	Baltimore	133	464	3.5	28t	5
1966	Baltimore	63	209	3.3	18	3
1967	Baltimore	42	132	3.1	21	4
Totals		1,069	5,174	4.8	79t	63

RECEIVING

Year	Team	No.	Yards	Avg.	Long	TD
1956	Baltimore	11	102	9.3	27	1
1957	Baltimore	40	687	17.2	82t	7
1958	Baltimore	50	938	18.5	77t	7
1959	Baltimore	47	846	18.0	71	6
1960	Baltimore	45	936	20.8	80t	9
1961	Baltimore	49	728	14.9	72t	8
1962	Baltimore	18	215	11.9	80t	2
1963	Baltimore	21	288	13.7	34	2
1964	Baltimore	21	472	22.5	74t	3
1965	Baltimore	27	414	15.3	52t	3
1966	Baltimore	21	260	12.4	36	0
1967	Baltimore	13	153	11.8	37	0
Totals		363	6,039	16.6	82t	48

SCORING

113 TD, 678 Points

KICKOFF RETURNS

49, 1,180 Yards, 24.1 Avg., 92 Long, 1 TD

---

t = return interception for touchdown.

BLACK COLLEGE FOOTBALL PLAYERS IN THE NATIONAL FOOTBALL LEAGUE

School	Player	Teams	Position	Years
Alabama A&M	Bill Kindricks	Cincinnati	DE	1968
	Ernest French	Pittsburgh	S	1982
	Franky Smith	Kansas City	T	1980
	John Stallworth	Pittsburgh	WR	1974-
	Mike Williams	Washington	TE	1982-1984
	Oliver Ross	Denver	RB	1973-1975
		Seattle		1976
	Ronnie Coleman	Houston	RB	1974-1981
	Thomas Hopkins	Cleveland	T	1983
	Wayne Mosley	Buffalo	RB	1974
Alabama State	Art Davis	Chicago	T	1953
	Curtis Green	Detroit	DT	1981-1986
	Karl Powe	Dallas	WR	1985-1986
	Ralph Miller	Houston	G	1972-1973
	Ricky Smith	New England	DB	1982-1984
		Washington		1984-1986
	Rodell Thomas	Miami	LB	1981, 1983-1984
		Seattle		1981-1982
Albany State	Arthur Green	New Orleans	RB	1972
	Mike White	Cincinnati	DT	1979-1980
		Seattle		1981-1982
Alcorn State	Billy Howard	Detroit	DT	1974-1976
	Bob Brown	St. Louis	TE	1969
		Minnesota		1971
		New Orleans		1972-1973
	Boyd Brown	Denver	TE	1974-1976
		N.Y. Giants		1977
	Dave Washington	Denver	LB	1970-1971
		Buffalo		1972-1974
		San Francisco		1975-1977
		Detroit		1978-1979
		New Orleans		1980
	David Hadley	Kansas City	CB	1970-1972
	Elbert Foules	Philadelphia	CB	1983-1985
	Elex Price	New Orleans	DT	1973-1980
	Floyd Rice	Houston	LB/TE	1971-1973
		San Diego		1973-1975
		Oakland		1976-1977
		New Orleans		1978
	Frank Purnell	Green Bay	FB	1957
	Henry Bradley	Cleveland	DT	1979-1982

School	Player	Teams	Position	Years
	Issac Holt	Minnesota	CB	1985
	Jack Spinks	Pittsburgh	G	1952
		Chicago Cardinals		1953
		Green Bay		1955-1956
		N.Y. Giants		1956-1957
	Jim Williams	Cincinnati	DB	1968
	Jimmie Giles	Houston	TE	1977
		Tampa Bay		1978-1986
	Joe Owens	San Diego	DE	1970
		New Orleans		1971-1975
		Houston		1976
	Larry Watkins	Detroit	RB	1969
		Philadelphia		1970-1972
		Buffalo		1973-1974
		N.Y. Giants		1975-1977
	Lawrence Estes	New Orleans	DE	1970-1971
		Philadelphia		1972
		Kansas City		1975-1977
	Lawrence Pillers	N.Y. Jets	DE	1976-1980
		San Francisco		1980-1984
		Atlanta		1985
	Leon Garror	Buffalo	S	1972-1973
	Leonard Fairley	Houston	S	1974
		Buffalo		1974
	Leslie Frazier	Chicago	CB	1981-1986
	Otis Wonsley	Washington	RB	1981-1985
	Rich Sowells	N.Y. Jets	CB	1971-1976
		Houston		1977
	Robert Penchion	Buffalo	G/T	1972-1973
		San Francisco		1974-1975
		Seattle		1976
	Roynell Young	Philadelphia	CB	1980-
	Willie Alexander	Houston	CB	1971-1979
	Willie Banks	Washington	G	1968-1969
		N.Y. Giants		1970
		New England		1973
	Willie McGee	San Diego	WR	1973
		L.A. Rams		1974-1975
		San Francisco		1976-1977
		Detroit		1978
	Willie Young	Buffalo	T	1971
		Miami		1973

School	Player	Teams	Position	Years
Allen University	Charlie Bryant	St. Louis Atlanta	RB	1966-1967 1968-1969
	George Harold	Baltimore Washington	DB	1966-1967 1968
	John Cash	Denver	DE	1961-1962
	Sam Davis	Pittsburgh	G	1967-1979
Arkansas, Pine Bluff	Bob Brown	Green Bay San Diego Cincinnati	DE	1966-1973 1974 1975-1976
	Caeser Belser	Kansas City San Francisco	DB	1968-1971 1974
	Clarence Washington	Pittsburgh	DT	1969-1970
	Cleo Miller	Kansas City Cleveland	RB	1974-1975 1975-1982
	Gene Jeter	Denver	LB	1965-1967
	L. C. Greenwood	Pittsburgh	DE	1969-1981
	Manny Sistrunk	Washington Philadelphia	DT	1970-1975 1976-1979
	Mike Lewis	Atlanta Green Bay	DE/DT	1971-1979 1980
	Monk Williams	Cincinnati	DB/KR	1968
	Terry Nelson	L.A. Rams	TE	1973-1980
	Wallace Francis	Buffalo Atlanta	WR	1973-1974 1975-1981
	Willie Frazier	Houston San Diego Kansas City	TE	1964-1965, 1971, 1975 1966-1970 1971-1972
	Willie Parker	Houston	DT	1967-1970
Bethune Cookman	Al Haywood	Denver	RB	1975
	Albert Burton	Houston N.Y. Jets	DE	1976-1977 1977
	Alvin Wyatt	Oakland Buffalo Houston	CB	1970 1971-1972 1973
	Boobie Clark	Cincinnati Houston	RB	1973-1978 1979-1980
	Booker Reese	Tampa Bay L.A. Rams	DE	1982-1984 1984-1986
	Charles Cornelius	Miami San Francisco	CB	1977-1978 1979-1980

School	Player	Teams	Position	Years
	Charlie White	N.Y. Jets	RB	1977
		Tampa Bay		1978
	Dick Washington	Miami	DB	1968
	Earl Inmon	Tampa Bay	LB	1978
	Jack McClairen	Pittsburgh	SE	1955-1960
	Jerry Simmons	Pittsburgh	WR	1965-1966
		New Orleans		1967
		Atlanta		1967-1969
		Chicago		1969
		Denver		1971-1974
	Jonathan Bostic	Detroit	CB	1985
	Larry Little	San Diego	G	1967-1968
		Miami		1969-1980
	Lee Williams	San Diego	DE	1984-1985
	Leon Gonzalez	Dallas	WR	1985
	Maulty Moore	Miami	DT	1972-1974
		Cincinnati		1975
		Tampa Bay		1976
	Rickey Claitt	Washington	RB	1980-1981
	Roger Jackson	Denver	S	1982-1985
	Rudy Barber	Miami	LB	1968
	Terry Anderson	Miami	WR	1977-1978
		Washington		1978
	Tony Samuels	Kansas City	TE	1977-1980
		Tampa Bay		1980
	Willie Lee	Kansas City	DT	1976-1977
Bishop	Bobby Brooks	N.Y. Giants	DB	1974-1976
	Bobby Moten	Denver	WR	1968
	Dennis DeVaughn	Philadelphia	DB	1982-1983
	Emmitt Thomas	Kansas City	CB	1966-1978
	Henry Hooligan	Houston	RB	1965
	Ike Thomas	Dallas	WR/DB	1971
		Green Bay		1972-1973
		Buffalo		1975
	Leroy Howard	Houston	DB	1971
	Tony McGee	Chicago	DE/NT	1971-1973
		New England		1974-1981
		Washington		1982-1985
Bowie State	Marco Tongue	Baltimore	DB	1983
Central State (Ohio)	Curtis Anderson	Kansas City	DE	1979
	David West	N.Y. Jets	DE	1963

School	Player	Teams	Position	Years
Central State (Ohio) (continued)	Donnie Walker	Buffalo N.Y. Jets	S	1973-1974 1975
	Mel Lunsford	New England	DE	1973-1980
	Vince Heflin	Miami	WR	1982-1985
Cheyney State	Andre Waters	Philadelphia	KR/CB	1984-1985
Delaware State	Alphonso Lawson	N.Y. Jets	FL	1964
	Clarence Weathers	New England Cleveland	WR	1983-1984 1985-1986
	Gordon Wright	Philadelphia N.Y. Jets	G	1967 1969
	Steve Coleman	Denver	DE	1974
	Steve Davis	Pittsburgh N.Y. Jets	RB	1972-1974 1975-1976
	Vic Heflin	St. Louis	CB	1982-1984
	Walter Tullis	Green Bay	WR	1978-1979
Edward Waters	Jim Butler	Pittsburgh Atlanta St. Louis	RB	1965-1967 1968-1971 1972
Elizabeth City State	Jethroe Pugh	Dallas	DT	1965-1978
	Jim Greer	Denver	SE	1960
	Johnnie Walton	Philadelphia	QB	1976-1979
	Reginald Langhorne	Cleveland	WR	1985-1986
Fayetteville State	Blenda Gay	San Diego Philadelphia	DE	1974 1975-1976
Fisk	Andy Bolton	Seattle Detroit	RB	1976 1976-1978
	J.J. Jones	N.Y. Jets	QB	1975
	Neal Craig	Cincinnati Buffalo Cleveland	CB	1971-1973 1974 1975-1976
	Robert James	Buffalo	CB	1969-1974
Florida A&M	Al Denson	Denver Minnesota	WR	1964-1970 1971
	Al Frazier	Denver	FL	1961-1963
	Alfred Sykes	New England	WR	1971
	Andre White	Denver Cincinnati San Diego	TE	1967 1968 1968
	Bob Hayes	Dallas San Francisco	WR	1965-1974 1975

School	Player	Teams	Position	Years
	Bobby Felts	Baltimore Detroit	RB	1965 1965-1967
	Carleton Oats	Oakland Green Bay	DE/DT	1965 1972 1973
	Charles Goodrum	Minnesota	G/T	1972-1978
	Clarence Childs	N.Y. Giants Chicago	DB	1964-1967 1968
	Clarence Hawkins	Oakland	RB	1979
	Dave Daniels	Oakland	DT	1966
	Don Smith	Denver	G	1967
	Frank Marion	N.Y. Giants	LB	1977-1983
	Frank Middleton	Indianapolis	RB	1984-1986
	Freddie Woodson	Miami	DE	1967-1969
	Gene Milton	Miami	WR	1968-1969
	Gene Thomas	Kansas City	RB	1966-1967
	Gene White	Oakland	RB	1962
	Glen Edwards	Pittsburgh San Diego	S	1971-1977 1978-1981
	Greg Coleman	Cleveland Minnesota	P	1977 1978
	Henry Lawrence	Oakland L.A. Raiders	T	1974-1981 1982-1985
	Herman Lee	Pittsburgh Chicago	T	1957 1958-1966
	Hewritt Dixon	Denver Oakland	FB	1963-1965 1966-1970
	Hubert Ginni	Miami Baltimore Oakland	RB	1970-1975 1973 1976-1977
	John Eason	Oakland	WR	1968
	John Holmes	Miami	DE	1966
	John Kelly	Washington	T	1966-1967
	Ken Riley	Cincinnati	CB	1969-1983
	Major Hazelton	Chicago New Orleans	DB	1968-1969 1970
	Mel Rogers	San Diego L.A. Rams Chicago	LB	1971, 1973-1974 1976 1977
	Nathaniel James	Cleveland	CB	1968
	Preston Johnson	Boston	RB	1968
	Ralph Hill	N.Y. Giants	C	1976-1977
	Ray Alexander	Denver	WR	1984-1986

School	Player	Teams	Position	Years
Florida A&M (continued)	Riley Morris	Oakland	LB	1960-1962
	Robert Paremore	St. Louis	RB	1963-1964
	Roger Finnie	N.Y. Jets	G/T	1969-1972
		St. Louis		1973-1978
		New Orleans		1979
	Ronnie Blye	N.Y. Giants	RB	1968
		Philadelphia		1969
	Tyrone McGriff	Pittsburgh	G	1980-1982
	Walt Highsmith	Denver	G/T	1968-1969
		Houston		1972
	Willie Erwin	Philadelphia	E	1953
	Willie Galimore	Chicago	HB	1957-1963
	Willie McClung	Pittsburgh	T	1955-1957
		Cleveland		1958-1959
		Detroit		1960-1961
Fort Valley State	Allen Smith	Buffalo	RB	1966-1967
	Dean Brown	Cleveland	DB	1969
		Miami		1970
	Leroy Moore	Buffalo	DE	1960, 1962-1963
		Boston		1961-1962
		Denver		1964-1965
	Rayfield Wright	Dallas	T/TE	1967-1979
Grambling	Al Dennis	San Diego	G	1973
		Cleveland		1976-1977
	Albert Lewis	Kansas City	CB	1983-1986
	Alphonse Dotson	Kansas City	DT	1965
		Miami		1966
		Oakland		1968-1970
	Alvin Richardson	Boston	DE	1960
	Bill Bryant	N.Y. Giants	DB	1976-1978
	Billie Newsome	Baltimore	DE	1970-1972
		New Orleans		1973-1974
		N.Y. Jets		1975-1976
		Chicago		1977
	Bob Atkins	St. Louis	CB	1968-1969
		Houston		1970-1976
	Bob Barber	Green Bay	DE	1976-1979
	Bobby Simon	Houston	T	1976
	Bruce Radford	Denver	DE	1979
		Tampa Bay		1980
		St. Louis		1981

School	Player	Teams	Position	Years
	Buck Buchanan	Kansas City	DT	1963-1975
	Carlos Pennywell	New England	WR	1978-1981
	Charles Johnson	San Francisco	CB	1979-1980
		St. Louis		1981
	Charley Smith	Philadelphia	WR	1974-1981
	Charlie Joiner	Houston	WR	1969-1972
		Cincinnati		1972-1975
		San Diego		1976-1985
	Clifton McNeil	Cleveland	WR	1964-1967
		San Francisco		1968-1969
		N.Y. Giants		1970-1971
		Washington		1971-1972
		Houston		1973
	Coleman Zeno	N.Y. Giants	WR	1971
	Delles Howell	New Orleans	CB	1970-1972
		N.Y. Jets		1973-1975
	Doug Williams	Tampa Bay	QB	1978-1982
	Dwight Scales	L.A. Rams	WR	1976-1978
		N.Y. Giants		1979
		San Diego		1981-1983
	Ed Watson	Houston	LB	1969
	Ernest Sterling	Dallas	DE	1969
	Ernie Ladd	San Diego	DT	1961-1965
		Houston		1966-1967
		Kansas City		1967-1968
	Essex Johnson	Cincinnati	RB	1968-1975
		Tampa Bay		1976
	Everson Walls	Dallas	CB	1981-
	Frank Cornish	Chicago	DT	1966
		Miami		1970-1971
		Buffalo		1972
	Frank Lewis	Pittsburgh	WR	1971-1977
		Buffalo		1978-1983
	Garland Boyette	St Louis	LB	1962-1963
		Houston		1966-1972
	Gary Johnson	San Diego	DT	1975-1984
		San Francisco		1984-1985
	Glenn Alexander	Buffalo	WR	1970
	Goldie Sellers	Denver	DB	1966-1967
		Kansas City		1968-1969
	Greg Fields	Baltimore	DE	1979-1980

School	Player	Teams	Position	Years
Grambling (continued)	Guy Prather	Green Bay	LB	1981-1986
	Henry Davis	N.Y. Giants Pittsburgh	LB	1968-1969 1970-1973
	Henry Dyer	L.A. Rams Washington	RB	1966, 1968 1969
	Henry Jones	Denver	RB	1969
	Hilton Crawford	Buffalo	DB	1969
	J.D. Garrett	Boston	HB	1964-1967
	James Harris	Buffalo L.A. Rams San Diego	QB	1969-1971 1973-1976 1977-1981
	James Hunter	Detroit	DB	1976-1982
	Jamie Caleb	Cleveland Minnesota	RB	1960, 1965 1961
	Jerry Robinson	San Diego N.Y. Jets	SE	1962-1964 1965
	Jim Griffin	San Diego Cincinnati	DE	1966-1967 1968
	John Mendenhall	N.Y. Giants Detroit	DT	1972-1979 1980
	Kerry Parker	Kansas City	CB	1984
	Lane Howell	N.Y. Giants Philadelphia	T	1963-1964 1965-1969
	Leon Simmons	Denver	LB	1983
	Mike Howell	Cleveland Miami	CB	1965-1972 1972
	Mike Smith	Atlanta	WR	1980
	Mike St. Clair	Cleveland Cincinnati	DE	1976-1979 1980-1982
	Nemiah Wilson	Denver Oakland Chicago	CB	1965-1967 1968-1974 1975
	Norman Davis	Baltimore New Orleans Philadelphia	G	1967 1969 1970
	Paul "Tank" Younger	L.A. Rams Pittsburgh	FB/LB	1949-1957 1958
	Preston Powell	Cleveland	FB	1961
	Richard Harris	Philadelphia Chicago Seattle	DE	1971-1973 1974-1975 1976-1977

School	Player	Teams	Position	Years
	Robert Pennywell	Atlanta	LB	1977-1980
	Robert Smith	Minnesota	DE	1985
	Robert Woods	Houston	WR	1978
		Detroit		1979
	Roger Williams	L.A. Rams	DB	1971-1972
	Ron Singleton	San Diego	T	1976
		San Francisco		1977-1980
	Roosevelt Taylor	Chicago	DB	1961-1969
		San Diego		1969
		San Francisco		1970-1971
		Washington		1972
	Sam Holden	New Orleans	T	1971
	Sammy Taylor	San Diego	FL	1965
	Sammy White	Minnesota	WR	1976-1986
	Scott Lewis	Houston	DE	1971
	Solomon Freelon	Houston	G	1972-1974
	Trumaine Johnson	San Diego	WR	1985-1986
	Vern Roberson	Miami	S	1977
		San Francisco		1978
	Virgil Robinson	New Orleans	RB	1971-1972
	Willie Brown	Denver	CB	1963-1966
		Oakland		1967-1978
	Willie Davis	Cleveland	T/DE	1958-1959
		Green Bay		1960-1969
	Willie Williams	N.Y. Giants	CB	1965, 1967-1973
		Oakland		1966
	Willie Young	N.Y. Giants	T/G	1966-1975
	Woody Peoples	San Francisco	G	1968-1977
		Philadelphia		1978-1980
Hampton University	Donovan Rose	Kansas City	CB	1980
	Lucien Reeberg	Detroit	T	1963
	Reggie Doss	L.A. Rams	DE	1978-
	Tom Casey	N.Y. Yankees (AAFC)	HB	1948
Howard University	Robert Sowell	Miami	CB	1983-1985
	Ron Mabry	Atlanta	DB	1975-1976
		N.Y. Jets		1977
	Steve Wilson	Dallas	CB/WR	1979-1981
		Denver		1982-
Jackson State	Al Greer	Detroit	SE	1963
	Ben McGee	Pittsburgh	DE	1964-1972
	Bill Houston	Dallas	WR	1974
	Bob Hughes	Atlanta	DE	1967-1969

School	Player	Teams	Position	Years
Jackson State (continued)	Buster Barnett	Buffalo	TE	1981-1985
	Charlie Williams	Philadelphia	CB	1978
	Chris Burkett	Buffalo	WR	1985
	Claudis James	Green Bay	WR	1967-1968
	Cleo Simmons	Dallas	TE	1983
	Coy Bacon	L.A. Rams	DE	1968-1972
		San Diego		1973-1975
		Cincinnati		1976-1977
		Washington		1978-1981
	Dan Pride	Chicago	LB	1968-1969
	Don Reese	Miami	DE	1974-1976
		New Orleans		1978-1980
		San Diego		1981
	Eddie Payton	Cleveland	RB	1977
		Detroit		1977
		Kansas City		1978
		Minnesota		1980-1982
	Edgar Hardy	San Francisco	G	1973
	Emanuel Zanders	New Orleans	G	1974-1980
		Chicago		1981
	Ernie Jackson	Detroit	CB	1979
	Frank Molden	L.A. Rams	DT	1965
		Philadelphia		1968
		N.Y. Giants		1969
	Gloster Richardson	Kansas City	WR	1967-1970
		Dallas		1971
		Cleveland		1972-1974
	Harold Jackson	L.A. Rams	WR	1968, 1973-1977
		Philadelphia		1969-1972
		New England		1978-1981
		Minnesota		1982
		Seattle		1983
	Jackie Slater	L.A. Rams	T	1976-
	James Marshall	New Orleans	CB	1980
	Jeff Moore	Seattle	RB	1979-1981
		San Francisco		1982-1983
		Washington		1984
	Jerome Barkum	N.Y. Jets	WR/TE	1972-1983
	Jim Hayes	Houston	DT	1965-1966
	Jimmy Holifeld	N.Y. Giants	DB	1968-1969
	John Tate	N.Y. Giants	LB	1976

School	Player	Teams	Position	Years
	Johnny Outlaw	Boston	CB	1969-1970
		New England		1971-1972
		Philadelphia		1973-1978
	Larry Cowan	Miami	RB	1982
		New England		1982
	Larry Franklin	Tampa Bay	WR	1978
	Larry Hardy	New Orleans	TE	1978-1985
	Lee Thomas	San Diego	DE	1971-1972
		Cincinnati		1973
	Lem Barney	Detroit	CB	1967-1977
	Leon Gray	New England	T	1973-1978
		Houston		1979-1981
		New Orleans		1982-1983
	Leslie Duncan	San Diego	S	1964-1970
		Washington		1971-1974
	Louis Bullard	Seattle	T	1978-1980
	Mike Jones	Seattle	LB	1977
	Oakley Dalton	New Orleans	DT	1977
	Perry Harrington	Philadelphia	RB	1980-1983
		St. Louis		1984-1985
	Richard Caster	N.Y. Jets	WR/TE	1970-1977
		Houston		1978-1980
		New Orleans		1981
		Washington		1981-1982
	Richard Harvey	Philadelphia	DB	1970
		New Orleans		1971
	Rickey Young	San Diego	RB	1975-1977
		Minnesota		1978-1983
	Rick Patton	Atlanta	RB	1978-1979
		Green Bay		1979
		San Francisco		1980-1982
	Robert Brazile	Houston	LB	1975-1985
	Robert Hardy	Seattle	DT	1979-1982
	Rod Phillips	L.A. Rams	RB	1975-1978
		St. Louis		1979-1980
	Roscoe Word	N.Y. Jets	DB	1974-1976
		Buffalo		1976
		N.Y. Giants		1976
		Tampa Bay		1976
	Roy Curry	Pittsburgh	FL	1963

School	Player	Teams	Position	Years
Jackson State (continued)	Roy Hilton	Baltimore N.Y. Giants Atlanta	DE	1965-1973 1974 1975
	Sylvester Stamps	Atlanta	WR	1984-
	Taft Reed	Philadelphia	RB	1967
	Tom Funchess	Boston Houston Miami	T	1968-1970 1971-1973 1974
	Tom Richardson	Boston	WR	1969-1970
	Tom Strauthers	Philadelphia	DE	1983-1985
	Verlon Biggs	N.Y. Jets Washington	DE	1965-1970 1971-1974
	Vernon Perry	Houston New Orleans	S	1979-1982 1983
	Walter Payton	Chicago	RB	1975-
	Willie Richardson	Baltimore Miami	WR	1963-1969, 1971 1970
Johnson C. Smith	Benny Johnson	Houston New Orleans	CB	1970-1973 1976
	Bill Dusenberry	New Orleans	RB	1970
	Harris Jones	San Diego Houston	G	1971 1973-1974
	Pettis Norman	Dallas San Diego	TE	1962-1970 1971-1973
	Robert Wells	San Diego	T	1968-1970
	Tim Beamer	Buffalo	S	1971
Kentucky State	Council Rudolph	Houston St. Louis Tampa Bay	DE	1972 1973-1975 1976-1977
	D'Artagnan Martin	New Orleans	DB	1971
	Ezzret Anderson	L.A. Dons (AAFC)	E	1947
	Frank Oliver	Buffalo Tampa Bay	DB	1975 1976
	John Kenerson	L.A. Rams Pittsburgh N.Y. Titans (AFL)	G	1960 1962 1962
	Rod Hill	Dallas Buffalo	CB	1982-1983 1984-1986
	Royce McKinney	Buffalo	DB	1975
Knoxville College	Ken Johnson	Buffalo	DE	1979-1984

School	Player	Teams	Position	Years
Langston University	Ed Williams	Cincinnati Tampa Bay	RB	1974-1975 1976-1977
	Gene Howard	New Orleans L.A. Rams	DB	1968-1970 1971-1972
	Gerard Williams	Washington San Francisco St. Louis	CB	1976-1978 1979-1980 1980
	Ken Payne	Green Bay Philadelphia	WR	1974-1977 1978
	Maurice Bassett	Cleveland	BF	1954-1956
	Odell Lawson	Boston New England New Orleans	RB	1970 1971 1973-1974
	Ricky Williams	L.A. Raiders	CB	1985
	Thomas Henderson	Dallas San Francisco Houston	LB	1975-1979 1980 1980
Lincoln (Missouri)	Bill Robinson	Green Bay	HB	1952
	Bob Waters	N.Y. Titans (AFL) N.Y. Jets	DE	1962 1963-1964
	Jim Sullivan	Atlanta	DT	1970
	Jim Tolbert	San Diego Houston St. Louis	DB	1966-1971, 1976 1972 1973-1975
	John McDaniel	Cincinnati Washington	WR	1974-1977 1978-1980
	Larry Shears	Atlanta	CB	1971-1972
	Lemar Parris	Cincinnati Washington Buffalo	CB	1970-1977 1978-1981 1982
	Zeke Moore	Houston	CB	1967-1977
Livingstone	Johnny Miller	San Francisco	G	1977-1978
Maryland Eastern Shore	Art Laster	Buffalo New England	T	1970 1971
	Art Shell	Oakland L.A. Raiders	T	1968-1981 1982
	Bill Belk	San Francisco	DE	1968-1974
	Billy Thompson	Denver	CB	1969-1981
	Bob Taylor	N.Y. Jets	DT	1963-1964
	Carl Hairston	Philadelphia Cleveland	DE	1976-1983 1984-1985

School	Player	Teams	Position	Years
Maryland Eastern Shore (continued)	Charlie Stukes	Baltimore L.A. Rams	S	1967-1972 1973-1974
	Curtis Gentry	Chicago	DB	1966-1968
	Doug Goodwin	Buffalo Atlanta	RB	1966 1968
	Earl Christy	N.Y. Jets	DB	1966-1968
	Emerson Boozer	N.Y. Jets	RB	1966-1975
	Erwin Williams	Pittsburgh	WR	1969
	Gerald Irons	Oakland Cleveland	LB	1970-1975 1976-1979
	Jimmy Duncan	Baltimore	DB	1969-1971
	Johnny Sample	Baltimore Pittsburgh Washington N.Y. Jets	CB	1958-1960 1961-1962 1963-1965 1966-1968
	Mack Alston	Washington Houston Baltimore	TE	1970-1972 1973-1976 1977-1980
	Marshall Cropper	Pittsburgh	WR	1967-1969
	Moses Denson	Washington	RB	1974-1975
	Roger Brown	Detroit L.A. Rams	DT	1960-1966 1967-1969
	Roy Kirksey	N.Y. Jets Philadelphia	G	1971-1972 1973-1974
	Sherman Plunkett	Baltimore N.Y. Titans (AFL) N.Y. Jets	T	1958-1960 1961-1962 1963-1967
	Willie Belton	Atlanta St. Louis	RB	1971-1972 1973-1974
Miles College	Ed McCall	Cincinnati	DB	1968
Mississippi Valley State	Bob Gaddis	Buffalo	WR	1976
	Dave McDaniels	Dallas	WR	1968
	Deacon Jones	L.A. Rams San Diego Washington	DE	1961-1971 1972-1973 1974
	Fred Bohannon	Pittsburgh	CB	1982
	James Haynes	New Orleans		1984-1985
	Jeff Stanciel	Atlanta	RB	1969
	Jerry Rice	San Francisco	WR	1985-
	Lou Rash	Philadelphia	CB	1984
	Melvin Morgan	Cincinnati San Francisco	DB	1976-1978 1979-1980
	Nate Korsey	New England	DE	1973

School	Player	Teams	Position	Years
	Parnell Dickinson	Tampa Bay	QB	1976
	Phil Darns	Tampa Bay	DE	1984
	Ricky Feacher	New England	WR	1976
		Cleveland		1976-1984
	Sam Washington	Pittsburgh	CB	1982-1985
		Cincinnati		1985
	Ted Washington	Houston	LB	1973-1982
Morehouse	David Graham	Seattle	DE	1982
Morgan State	Alvin Mitchell	Cleveland	DB	1968-1969
		Denver		1970
	Bob Wade	Pittsburgh	DB	1968
		Washington		1969
		Denver		1970
	Bobby Hammond	N.Y. Giants	RB	1976-1979
		Washington		1979-1980
	Carlton Dabney	Atlanta	DT	1968
	Charley Robinson	Baltimore	G/LB	1954
	Clarence Scott	Boston	DB	1969-1970
		New England		1971-1972
	Darryl Johnson	Boston	DB	1968-1970
	Ed Hayes	Philadelphia	DB	1970
	Elmore Harris	Brooklyn (AAFC)	HB	1947
	Elvis Franks	Cleveland	DE	1980-1984
		L.A. Raiders		1985-1986
	George Nock	N.Y. Jets	RB	1969-1971
		Washington		1972
	Greg Latta	Chicago	TE	1975-1980
	Jeff Queen	San Diego	RB	1969-1971
		Oakland		1972-1973
		Houston		1974
	John Andrews	Miami	DE	1975-1976
	John Fuqua	N.Y. Giants	RB	1969
		Pittsburgh		1970-1976
	John Sykes	San Diego	RB	1972
	Leroy Kelly	Cleveland	RB	1964-1973
	Mark Washington	Dallas	CB	1970-1978
		New England		1979
	Maurice Tyler	Buffalo	DB	1972
		Denver		1973-1974
		San Diego		1975
		Detroit		1976
		N.Y. Jets/N.Y. Giants		1977/1978

School	Player	Teams	Position	Years
Maryland State (continued)	Michael Holston	Houston Kansas City	WR	1981-1985 1985
	Mike Collier	Pittsburgh Buffalo	RB	1975 1977-1979
	Ollie Dobbins	Buffalo	DB	1964
	Raymond Chester	Oakland Baltimore	TE	1970-1972, 1978-1981 1973-1977
	Ron Mayo	Houston Baltimore	TE	1973 1974
	Roosevelt Brown	N.Y. Giants	T	1953-1965
	Sonny Person	St. Louis	TE	1972
	Stan Cherry	Baltimore	LB	1973
	Tim Baylor	Baltimore Minnesota	S	1976-1978 1979
	Tom Carr	New Orleans	DT	1968
	Willie Germany	Atlanta Detroit Houston New England	S	1972 1973 1975 1976
	Willie Lanier	Kansas City	LB	1967-1977
Morris Brown	Alfred Jenkins	Atlanta	WR	1975-1983
	Charlie Bivins	Chicago Pittsburgh Buffalo	HB	1960-1966 1967 1967
	Ezra Johnson	Green Bay	DE	1977-1986
	Fernanza Burgess	Miami N.Y. Jets	DB	1984 1984
	George Atkinson	Oakland	DB	1966-1977
	Henry Mosley	Chicago	HB	1955
	Herb Christopher	Kansas City	S	1979-1982
	Jerry Davis	N.Y. Jets	DB	1975
	Solomon Brannon	Kansas City	DB	1965-1966
	Tommy Hart	San Francisco Chicago	DE	1968-1977 1978-1979
Norfolk State	Alex Moore	Denver	DB	1968
	Earl Jones	Atlanta	CB	1980-1983
	Gene Ferguson	San Diego Houston	T	1969-1970 1971-1972
	Joe Bell	Oakland	DE	1979
	John Baker	N.Y. Giants	DE	1970

School	Player	Teams	Position	Years
	Ken Reaves	Atlanta New Orleans St. Louis	CB	1966-1973 1974 1974-1977
	LaRue Harrington	San Diego	RB	1980
	Leroy Jones	San Diego	DE	1976-1983
	Ray Jarvis	Atlanta Buffalo Detroit	WR	1971-1972 1973 1974-1978
	Ricky Ray	New Orleans Miami	CB	1979-1981 1981-1982
	Ron Bolton	New England Cleveland	CB	1972-1975 1976-1982
North Carolina A&T	Bob Jackson	N.Y. Giants	FB	1950-1951
	Cornell Gordon	N.Y. Jets Denver	DB	1965-1969 1970-1972
	Dick Westmoreland	San Diego Miami	DB	1963-1965 1966-1969
	Dwaine Board	San Francisco	DE	1979-1986
	Elvin Bethea	Houston	DE	1968-1983
	George Ragsdale	Tampa Bay	RB	1977-1979
	George Small	N.Y. Giants	DT	1980
	J.D. Smith	Chicago San Francisco Dallas	FB	1956 1956-1964 1965-1966
	Joe Taylor	Chicago	DB	1967-1974
	Mel Holmes	Pittsburgh	G/T	1971-1973
	Mel Phillips	San Francisco	S	1966-1977
	Ralph Coleman	Dallas	LB	1972
	Tom Day	St. Louis Buffalo San Diego	DE	1960 1961-1966, 1968 1967
	Willie Pearson	Miami	DB	1969
North Carolina Central	Aaron Martin	L.A. Rams Philadelphia Washington	DB	1964-1965 1966-1967 1968
	Arnold Brown	Detroit	CB	1985
	Bob McAdams	N.Y. Jets	DT	1963-1964
	Charles Romes	Buffalo	CB	1977-
	Chuck Hinton	Pittsburgh N.Y. Jets Baltimore	DE	1964-1971 1971 1972

School	Player	Teams	Position	Years
North Carolina Central (continued)	Darius Helton	Kansas City	G	1977
	Doug Wilkerson	Houston	G	1970
		San Diego		1971-1986
	Ernie Barnes	N.Y. Titans (AFL)	G	1960
		San Diego		1961-1962
		Denver		1963-1964
	Ernie Warlick	Buffalo	TE	1962-1965
	Frank Tate	San Diego	LB	1975
	Jerry Gantt	Buffalo	T	1970
	Jim Brewington	Oakland	T	1961
	John Baker	L.A. Rams	DE	1958-1961
		Philadelphia		1962
		Pittsburgh		1963-1967
		Detroit		1968
	John Brown	L.A. Dons (AAFC)	C	1947-1949
	Louis Breeden	Cincinnati	CB	1978-1986
	Luther Jeralds	Dallas Texans (AFL)	DE	1961
	Maurice Spencer	St. Louis	CB	1974
		L.A. Rams		1974
		New Orleans		1974-1976, 1978
	Myron Dupree	Denver	CB	1983
	Paul Winslow	Green Bay	HB	1960
	Reggie Smith	Atlanta	KR	1980-1981
	Richard Sligh	Oakland	DT	1967
	William Frizzell	Detroit	CB	1984-1985
Paul Quinn College	Walter Napier	Dallas Texans (AFL)	DT	1960-1961
Philander Smith College	Elijah Pitts	Green Bay	RB	1961-1969, 1971
		L.A. Rams		1970
		New Orleans		1970
Prairie View A&M	Allen Aldridge	Houston	DE	1971-1972
		Cleveland		1974
	Alvin Reed	Houston	TE	1967-1972
		Washington		1973-1975
	Bivian Lee	New Orleans	DB	1971-1975
	Bo Farrington	Chicago	SE	1960-1963
	C.L. Whittington	Houston	S	1974-1976, 1978
	Charley Warner	Kansas City	DB	1963-1964
		Buffalo		1964-1966
	Charlie Brackins	Green Bay	QB	1955
	Charlie Williams	L.A. Rams	WR	1970
	Clarence Williams	Green Bay	DE	1970-1977
	Claude Harvey	Houston	LB	1970

School	Player	Teams	Position	Years
	Clem Daniels	Dallas Texans (AFL)	FB	1960
		Oakland		1961-1967
		San Francisco		1968
	Dave Webster	Dallas Texans (AFL)	DB	1960
	Fred Anderson	Pittsburgh	DE	1978
		Seattle		1980-1982
	Glenn Woods	Houston	DT	1969
	Hise Austin	Green Bay	CB	1973
		Kansas City		1975
	Jim Hunt	Boston	DE	1960-1970
	Jim Kearney	Detroit	CB	1965-1966
		Kansas City		1967-1975
		New Orleans		1976
	Jim Mitchell	Atlanta	TE	1969-1979
	Jim Wolf	Pittsburgh	DE	1974
		Kansas City		1976
	Kenny Houston	Houston	S	1967-1972
		Washington		1973-1980
	Leroy Clark	Houston	K	1976
	Louie Neal	Atlanta	WR	1973-1974
	Matthew Teague	Atlanta	DE	1980-1981
	Otis Taylor	Kansas City	WR	1965-1975
	Otto Brown	Dallas	DB	1969
		N.Y. Giants		1970-1973
	Rufus Granderson	Dallas Texans (AFL)	DT	1960
	Sam Adams	New England	G	1972-1980
		New Orleans		1981
Savannah State	Tim Walker	Seattle	LB	1980
South Carolina State	Al Young	Pittsburgh	WR	1971-1972
	Angelo King	Dallas	LB	1981-1983
		Detroit		1984-1985
	Barney Chavous	Denver	DE	1973-1986
	Charlie Brown	Washington	WR	1982-1984
		Atlanta		1985-1986
	Clifford McClain	N.Y. Jets	RB	1970-1973
	Dextor Clinkscale	Dallas	S	1980-1986
	Donnie Shell	Pittsburgh	S	1974-1986
	Edwin Bailey	Seattle	G	1981-1986
	Ervin Parker	Buffalo	LB	1980-1983
	Harry Carson	N.Y. Giants	LB	1976-
	Henry Odom	Pittsburgh	RB	1983

School	Player	Teams	Position	Years
South Carolina State (continued)	John Gilliam	New Orleans St. Louis Minnesota Atlanta Chicago	WR	1967-1968, 1977 1969-1971 1972-1975 1976 1977
	Louis Ross	Buffalo Kansas City	DE	1971-1972 1975
	Mickey Sims	Cleveland	DT	1977-1979
	Nate Rivers	N.Y. Giants	RB	1980
	Phil Murphy	L.A. Rams	DT	1980-1981
	R.C. Gamble	Boston	RB	1968-1969
	Ricky Anderson	San Diego	RB	1978
	Rufus Bess	Oakland Buffalo Minnesota	CB	1979 1980-1981 1982-1986
	Tom Tutson	Atlanta	CB	1983
	Wendel Tucker	L.A. Rams	WR	1967-1970
	William Judson	Miami	CB	1982-1986
	Willie Grate	Buffalo	TE	1969-1970
	Willie Holman	Chicago Washington	DE	1968-1973 1973
	Zack Thomas	Denver Tampa Bay	WR	1983-1984 1984-1985
Southern University	Al Beauchamp	Cincinnati St. Louis	LB	1968-1975 1976
	Alden Roche	Denver Green Bay Seattle	DE	1970 1971-1976 1977-1978
	Alvin Haymond	Baltimore Philadelphia L.A. Rams Washington Houston	DB/KR	1964-1967 1968 1969-1971 1972 1973
	Brian Williams	New England	TE	1982
	Calvin Magee	Tampa Bay	TE	1985
	Charlie Granger	Dallas St. Louis	T	1961 1961
	Cleveland Green	Miami	T	1979-1986
	Clyde Williams	St. Louis	T	1967-1971
	Conrad Rucker	Houston Tampa Bay L.A. Rams	TE	1978-1979 1980 1980

School	Player	Teams	Position	Years
	Donnie Davis	Dallas	WR/TE	1962
		Houston		1970
	Ed Mitchell	San Diego	G	1965-1967
	Frank Pitts	Kansas City	WR	1965-1970
		Cleveland		1971-1973
		Oakland		1974
	George Farmer	L.A. Rams	WR	1982-1984
	George McGee	Boston	T	1960
	Godwin Turk	N.Y. Jets	LB	1975
		Denver		1976-1978
	Harold Carmichael	Philadelphia	WR	1971-1983
		Dallas		1984
	Harold McClinton	Washington	LB	1969-1978
	Harvey Nairn	N.Y. Jets	WR	1968
	Herb Williams	San Francisco	DB	1980
		St. Louis		1981-1982
	Isaac Hagins	Tampa Bay	WR	1976-1980
	James Davis	L.A. Raiders	CB	1982-1985
	Jerry Broadnax	Houston	TE	1974
	Jim Battle	Cleveland	T	1966
	Jim Osborne	Chicago	DT	1972-1984
	Johnny Jackson	Philadelphia	DE	1977
	Jubilee Dunbar	New Orleans	WR	1973
		Cleveland		1974
	Ken Ellis	Green Bay	CB	1970-1975
		Houston/Miami		1976
		Cleveland		1977
		Detroit/L.A. Rams		1979
	Ken Times	San Francisco	DT	1980
		St. Louis		1981
	Lewis Porter	Kansas City	DB	1970
	Mack Lee Hill	Kansas City	FB	1964-1965
	Marvin Davis	Houston	LB	1974
	Mel Blount	Pittsburgh	CB	1970-1983
	Perry Brooks	Washington	DT	1978-1985
	Pete Barnes	Houston	LB	1967-1968
		San Diego		1969-1972
		St. Louis		1973-1975
		New England		1976-1977
	Ralph Williams	Houston	G/T	1982-1983
		New Orleans		1985
	Ray Jones	Philadelphia	DB	1970
		Miami		1971

School	Player	Teams	Position	Years
Southern University (continued)		San Diego New Orleans		1972 1973
	Rich Jackson	Oakland Denver Cleveland	LB/DE	1966 1967-1972 1972
	Richard Neal	New Orleans N.Y. Jets	DE/DT	1969-1972, 1978 1973-1977
	Robert Holmes	Kansas City Houston San Diego	RB	1968-1971 1971-1972 1973
	Sid Williams	Cleveland Washington Baltimore Pittsburgh	LB	1964-1966 1967 1968 1969
	Willie Brister	N.Y. Jets	TE	1974-1975
St. Augustine College	Ike Lassiter	Denver Oakland Boston	DE/DT	1962-1964 1965-1969 1970
Tennessee State University	Larry Barnes	San Diego St. Louis Philadelphia	RB	1977-1978 1978 1978-1979
	Al Coleman	Minnesota Cincinnati Philadelphia	DB	1967 1969-1971 1972-1973
	Al Davis	Philadelphia	RB	1971-1972
	Bill Tucker	San Francisco Chicago	RB	1967-1970 1971
	Bill West	Denver	DB	1972
	Brian Ramson	Houston	QB	1983-1985
	Bryan Howard	Minnesota	S	1982
	Carl Wafer	Green Bay N.Y. Giants	DE/DT	1974 1974
	Charley Ferguson	Cleveland Minnesota Buffalo	SE	1961 1962 1963, 1965-1966, 1969
	Charlie Thomas	Kansas City	RB	1975
	Charlie Wade	Chicago Green Bay Kansas City	WR	1974 1975 1977
	Chuck Gavin	Denver	DE	1960-1963

School	Player	Teams	Position	Years
	Cid Edwards	St. Louis San Diego Chicago	RB	1968-1971 1972-1974 1975
	Claude Humphrey	Atlanta Philadelphia	DE	1968-1974, 1976-1978 1979-1981
	Cleveland Elam	San Francisco Detroit	DE	1975-1978 1979
	Clifford Brooks	Cleveland	CB	1972-1974
	Danny Johnson	Green Bay	LB	1978
	Darryl Caldwell	Buffalo	T	1983
	Dave Davis	Green Bay Pittsburgh New Orleans	WR	1971-1972 1973 1974
	Dave Little	Kansas City Philadelphia	TE	1984 1985
	Donald Laster	Washington Detroit	T	1982 1984
	Dwight Wheeler	New England L.A. Raiders	T/C	1978-1983 1984
	Ed "Too Tall" Jones	Dallas	DE	1974-1986
	Elbert Drungo	Houston Buffalo	T	1969-1971, 1973-1977 1978
	Elridge Dickey	Oakland	QB/WR	1968, 1971
	Fletcher Smith	Kansas City Cincinnati	DB	1966-1967 1968-1971
	Franklin McRae	Chicago	DT	1967
	George Gilchrist	Chicago Cardinals	T	1953
	Greg Kindle	St. Louis Atlanta	T/G	1974-1975 1976-1977
	Hal Turner	Detroit	DE	1954
	Harold Rice	Oakland	DE	1971
	Herman Hunter	Philadelphia	WR	1985
	Homer Elias	Detroit	G	1978-1984
	Izzy Lang	Philadelphia L.A. Rams	FB	1964-1968 1969
	James Thaxton	San Diego Cleveland New Orleans St. Louis	TE	1973-1974 1974 1976-1977 1978
	Jerrold McRae	Kansas City Philadelphia	WR	1978 1979

School	Player	Teams	Position	Years
Tennessee State University (continued)	Jim Kelly	Chicago	TE	1974
	Jim Marsalis	Kansas City New Orleans	CB	1969-1975 1977
	Joe Gilliam	Pittsburgh	QB	1972-1975
	Joe Jones	Cleveland Philadelphia Washington	DE	1970-1971, 1973, 1975-1978 1974-1975 1979-1980
	Joe Sweet	L.A. Rams New England San Diego	WR	1972-1973 1974 1975
	John Holland	Minnesota Buffalo	WR	1974 1975-1977
	John Smith	Cleveland	WR	1979
	Johnnie Robinson	Detroit	DB	1966-1967
	Larry Dorsey	San Diego Kansas City	WR	1976-1977 1978
	Larry Kinnebrew	Cincinnati	FB	1983-1985
	Larry Mallory	N.Y. Giants	S	1976-1978
	Larry Woods	Detroit Miami N.Y. Jets Seattle	T	1971-1972 1973 1974-1975 1976
	Leo Johnson	San Francisco	WR	1969-1970
	Loaird McCreary	Miami N.Y. Giants	TE	1976-1978 1979
	Mack Lamb	Miami	CB	1967-1968
	Malcolm Taylor	Houston	DE	1982-1983
	McDonald Oden	Cleveland	TE	1980-1982
	Melvin Mitchell	Miami Detroit Minnesota	G/C	1976-1978 1977 1980
	Mike Hegman	Dallas	LB	1976-1985
	Mike Jones	Minnesota	WR	1983-1985
	Nate Simpson	Green Bay	RB	1977-1979
	Nolan Smith	Kansas City San Francisco	KR	1967-1969 1969
	Oliver Davis	Cleveland Cincinnati	DB	1977-1980 1981-1982
	Ollie Smith	Baltimore Green Bay	WR	1973-1974 1976-1977
	Richard Dent	Chicago	DE	1983

School	Player	Teams	Position	Years
	Robert Reed	N.Y. Giants	RB	1965-1966
	Robert Woods	N.Y. Jets	T	1973-1977
		New Orleans		1977-1980
		Washington		1981
	Rodney Parker	Philadelphia	WR	1980-1981
	Roosevelt Davis	N.Y. Giants	DE	1965-1967
	Stan Johnson	Kansas City	DT	1978
	Steve Moore	New England	G/T	1983-1985
	Sylvester Hicks	Kansas City	DT	1978-1981
	Vernon Holland	Cincinnati	T	1971-1979
		Detroit		1980
		N.Y. Giants		1980
	Waymond Bryant	Chicago	LB	1974-1977
	William Winn	Philadelphia	DE	1973-1976
		Washington		1977
	Willie Carter	Chicago Cardinals	HB	1953
	Willie Mitchell	Kansas City	D	1964-1970
	Willie Walker	Detroit	FL	1966
Texas Southern University	Andy Rice	Kansas City	DT	1966-1967
		Houston		1967
		Cincinnati		1968-1969
		San Diego		1970-1971
		Chicago		1972-1973
	Art Strahan	Atlanta	DT	1968
	Arthur Cox	Atlanta	TE	1983-1985
	B.W. Cheeks	Houston	RB	1965
	Boyd Jones	Green Bay	T	1984
	Brett Maxie	New Orleans	CB	1985
	Burt Askson	Pittsburgh	DE	1971
		New Orleans		1973
		Green Bay		1975-1977
	Calvin Muhammad	L.A. Raiders	WR	1982-1983
		Washington		1984-1985
	Charles Philyaw	Oakland	DE	1976-1979
	Charley Frazier	Houston	SE	1962-1968
		Boston		1969-1970
	Dave Mays	Cleveland	QB	1976-1977
		Buffalo		1978
	David Rackley	New Orleans	CB	1985
	Ernie Calloway	Philadelphia	DT	1969-1972
	Ernie Holmes	Pittsburgh	DT	1972-1977
		New England		1978

School	Player	Teams	Position	Years
Texas Southern University (continued)	Ernie Pough	Pittsburgh N.Y. Giants	WR	1976-1977 1978
	Fred Dean	Chicago Washington	G	1977 1978-1982
	Gene Branton	Tampa Bay	WR	1983
	Harold Hart	Oakland N.Y. Giants	DB/RB	1974-1975, 1978 1977
	Homer Jones	N.Y. Giants Cleveland	SE	1964-1969 1970
	Jack Holmes	New Orleans	RB	1978-1982
	James Young	Houston	DE	1977-1979
	Jim Ford	New Orleans	RB	1971-1972
	Jim Sorey	Buffalo	G	1960-1962
	Jimmy Hines	Miami	WR	1969
	John Douglas	New Orleans Houston	CB	1967-1968 1969
	John White	Houston Oakland	TE	1960-1961 1962
	Julius Adams	New England	DE	1971-1985
	Keith Baker	Philadelphia	WR	1985
	Ken Burrough	New Orleans Houston	WR	1970 1971-1981
	Larry Crowe	Philadelphia Atlanta	RB	1972 1975
	Leroy Mitchell	Boston Houston Denver	DB	1967-1969 1970 1971-1973
	Lloyd Mumphord	Miami Baltimore	CB	1969-1974 1975-1978
	Lonnie Hepburn	Baltimore Denver	CB	1971-1972 1974
	Mel Baker	Miami New Orleans New England San Diego Houston	WR	1974 1975 1975 1975 1976
	Mike Holmes	San Francisco Buffalo Miami	DB	1974-1975 1976 1976
	Nate Allen	Kansas City San Francisco Minnesota	CB	1971-1974 1975 1976-1978

School	Player	Teams	Position	Years
	Ray Strahan	Houston	DE	1965
	Raymond Baylor	San Diego	DE	1974
	Roy Hopkins	Houston	RB	1967-1970
	W.K. Hicks	Houston	DB	1964-1969
		N.Y. Jets		1970-1972
	Warren Wells	Detroit	SE	1964
		Oakland		1967-1970
	Willie Ellison	L.A. Rams	RB	1967-1972
		Kansas City		1973-1974
	Willie Porter	Boston	DB	1968
	Willis Perkins	Boston	G	1961
		Houston		1961-1963
	Winston Hill	N.Y. Jets	T	1963-1976
		L.A. Rams		1977
Tuskegee University	Art May	New England	DE	1971
	Cecil Leonard	N.Y. Jets	DB	1969-1970
	Ken Woodard	Denver	LB	1982-1985
	Leon Crenshaw	Green Bay	DT	1968
	Ricky Jones	Cleveland	DB	1977-1979
		Baltimore		1980-1983
	Walter Johnson	San Francisco	DE	1967
Virginia State	Ben Whaley	L.A. Dons (AAFC)	G	1949
	Jim Mitchell	Detroit	DE	1970-1977
	Larry Brooks	L.A. Rams	DT	1972-1982
	Leo Miles	N.Y. Giants	DB	1953
	Ron Davis	St. Louis	DE	1973
	Rufus Crawford	Seattle	RB	1978
Virginia Union	Bob Jones	Cincinnati	S	1973-1974
		Atlanta		1975-1976
	Carl Bland	Detroit	WR	1984-1985
	Cornelius Johnson	Baltimore	G	1968-1973
	Herman Lewis	Denver	DE	1968
	Hezekiah Braxton	San Diego	RB	1962-1963
		Buffalo		1963
	Herbert Scott	Dallas	G	1975-1984
	Irvin Mallory	New England	DB	1971
	Malcolm Barnwell	Oakland	WR	1981
		L.A. Raiders		1982-1984
		Washington		1985
		New Orleans		1985
	Roger Anderson	N.Y. Giants	DT	1964-1965
				1967-1968
	Tony Leonard	San Francisco	DB	1976-1977

School	Player	Teams	Position	Years
West Virginia State	Warren Anderson	Houston	WR	1977
		St. Louis		1978
Wiley College	Floyd Inglehart	L.A. Rams	DB	1958
	George Kinney	Houston	DE	1965
	Kelton Winston	L.A. Rams	DB	1967-1968
Winston-Salem State	Arrington Jones	San Francisco	RB	1981
	Bill Murrell	St. Louis	TE	1979
	Bob Shaw	New Orleans	WR	1970
	Jack Cameron	Chicago	WR	1984
	Timmy Newsome	Dallas	RB	1980-

COLLEGE FOOTBALL
AWARD WINNERS

African-American Recipients of the Vince Lombardi/Rotary Award

Year	Name	College	Position
1972	Rich Glover	University of Nebraska	Middle Guard—1st black American to win Vince Lombardi/Rotary Award
1973	John Hicks	Ohio State University	Offensive Tackle
1975	Lee Roy Selmon	University of Oklahoma	Defensive Tackle
1976	Wilson Whitley	University of Houston	Defensive Tackle
1977	Ross Browner	University of Notre Dame	Defensive End
1978	Bruce Clark	Pennsylvania State University	Defensive Tackle
1980	Hugh Green	University of Pittsburgh	Defensive End
1981	Kenneth Sims	University of Texas	Defensive Tackle
1986	Cornelius Bennett	University of Alabama	Linebacker

African-American Recipients of the Outland Trophy

Year	Name	College	Position
1955	Calvin Jones	University of Iowa	Guard—1st black American to win Outland Trophy
1956	Jim Parker	Ohio State University	Guard
1962	Bobby Bell	University of Minnesota	Tackle
1972	Rich Glover	University of Nebraska	Middle Guard
1973	John Hicks	Ohio State University	Offensive Tackle
1975	Lee Roy Selmon	University of Oklahoma	Defensive Tackle
1976	Ross Browner	University of Notre Dame	Defensive End
1978	Greg Roberts	University of Oklahoma	Guard
1980	Mark May	University of Pittsburgh	Offensive Tackle
1984	Bruce Smith	Virginia Polytechnic Institute	Defensive Tackle

African-American Recipients of the Heisman Memorial Trophy

Year	Name	College	Position
1961	Ernest Davis	Syracuse University	Halfback—1st black American to win Heisman Memorial Trophy
1965	Michael Garrett	University of Southern California	Halfback
1968	O.J. Simpson	University of Southern California	Halfback
1972	Johnny Rodgers	University of Nebraska	Flanker
1974	Archie Griffin	Ohio State University	Halfback
1975	Archie Griffin	Ohio State University	Halfback
1976	Tony Dorsett	University of Pittsburgh	Halfback
1977	Earl Campbell	University of Texas	Halfback
1978	Billy Sims	University of Oklahoma	Halfback
1979	Charles White	University of Southern California	Halfback
1980	George Rodgers	University of South Carolina	Halfback
1981	Marcus Allen	University of Southern California	Halfback
1982	Herschel Walker	University of Georgia	Halfback
1983	Michael Rozier	University of Nebraska	Halfback
1985	Bo Jackson	Auburn University	Halfback

CIAA FOOTBALL CHAMPIONS

Year	School	Coach	Year	School	Coach
1950	North Carolina A&T	William Bell	1968	Morgan State	Earl Banks
1951	W. Va. State	Mark Caldwell	1969	Johnson C. Smith	Ed McGirt
1952	Virginia State	Sal Hall	1970	Virginia State	Walter Lovett
1953	North Carolina College	Herman Riddick	1971	Elizabeth City	Tom Caldwell
1954	North Carolina College	Herman Riddick	1972	Virginia State	Walter Lovett
1955	Maryland State	Vernon McCain	1973	Virginia Union	Willard Bailey
1956	North Carolina College	Herman Riddick	1974	Norfolk State	Dick Price
1957	Maryland State	Vernon McCain	1975	Norfolk State	Dick Price
1958	North Carolina A&T	Bert Piggott	1976	Norfolk State	Dick Price
1959	Norht Carolina A&T	Bert Piggott	1977	Winston-Salem	William Hayes
1960	Maryland State	Vernon McCain	1978	Winston-Salem	William Hayes
1961	North Carolina College	Herman Riddick	1979	Virginia Union	Willard Bailey
1962	Morgan State	Earl Banks	1980	North Carolina Central	Henry Lattimore
1963	North Carolina College	Herman Riddick	1981	Virginia Union	Willard Bailey
1964	North Carolina A&T	Bert Piggott	1982	Virginia Union	Willard Bailey
1965	Morgan State	Earl Banks	1983	Virginia Union	Willard Bailey
1966	Morgan State	Earl Banks	1984	Norfolk State	Willard Bailey
1967	Morgan State	Earl Banks			

SIAC FOOTBALL CHAMPIONS

Year	School	Coach	Year	School	Coach
	NCAA Division II		1970	Tuskegee Institute	Haywood Cissum
1950	Florida A&M University	Jake Gaither	1971	Alabama A&M University	Louis Crews
1951	Morris Brown University	Artis Graves	1972	Alabama A&M University	Louis Crews
1952	Bethune-Cookman	Rev. Bunky Matthews	1973	Bethune-Cookman	Wesley Moore
1953	Florida A&M University	Jake Gaither	1974	Tuskegee Institute	Haywood Cissum
1954	Florida A&M University	Jake Gaither	1975	Bethune-Cookman	Wesley Moore
1955	Florida A&M University	Jake Gaither	1976	Bethune-Cookman	Andy Henson
1956	Florida A&M University	Jake Gaither	1977	Florida A&M University	Rudy Hubbard
1957	Florida A&M University	Jake Gaither	1978	Florida A&M University	Rudy Hubbard
1958	Florida A&M University	Jake Gaither	1979	Alabama A&M University	Ray Green
1959	Florida A&M University	Jake Gaither	1980	Alabama A&M University	Ray Green
1960	Florida A&M University	Jake Gaither	1981	Alabama A&M University	Ray Green
1961	Florida A&M University	Jake Gaither	1982	Fort Valley State	Douglas Porter
1962	Florida A&M University	Jake Gaither	1983	Fort Valley State	Douglas Porter
1963	Florida A&M University	Jake Gaither	1984	Albany State	Hampton Smith
1964	Florida A&M University	Jake Gaither		*NCAA Division III*	
1965	Florida A&M University	Jake Gaither	1966	Alabama State	Whitney Van Cleve
1966	Alabama A&M University	Louis Crews	1967	Tuskegee Institute	Haywood Cissum
1967	Florida A&M University	Jake Gaither	1968	Tuskegee Institute	Haywood Cissum
1968	Florida A&M University	Jake Gaither	1969	Tuskegee Institute	Haywood Cissum
1969	Florida A&M University	Jake Gaither	1970	Fort Valley State	Leon Lomax

Year	School	Coach	Year	School	Coach
1971	Fort Valley State	Leon Lomax	1978	Clark College	Jesse McClardy
1972	Fort Valley State	Leon Lomax	1979	Morehouse College	Maurice Hunt
1973	Fisk University	Sam Whitman	1980	Fort Valley State	Douglas Porter
1974	Clark College	Jesse McClardy	1981	Knoxville College	Joe Cornelius
1975	Fisk University	Sam Whitman	1982	Lane College	Neal McCall
1976	Fort Valley State	Leon Lomax	1983	Knoxville College	Marion Quinn
1977	Clark/Miles College	McClardy/Ocie Moore	1984	Miles College	Don Harris

SWAC FOOTBALL CHAMPIONS

Year	School	Coach	Year	School	Coach
1950	Southern University	A.W. Mumphord	1967	Grambling/Alcorn/ Texas Southern	Robinson/Casem/Durley
1951	Prairie View A&M	Billy Nicks	1968	Texas Southern/Alcorn/ Grambling	Durley/Casem/Robinson
1952	Prairie View A&M	Billy Nicks			
1953	Prairie View A&M	Billy Nicks	1969	Alcorn State University	Marino Casem
1954	Prairie View A&M	Billy Nicks	1970	Alcorn State University	Marino Casem
1955	Southern University	A.W. Mumphord	1971	Grambling University	Eddie Robinson
1956	Texas Southern/Wiley College	Alexander Durley/ Fred Long	1972	Grambling/Jackson State	Robinson/Bob Hill
1957	Wiley College	Fred Long	1973	Grambling/Jackson State	Robinson/Bob Hill
1958	Prairie View A&M	Billy Nicks	1974	Grambling/Alcorn State	Robinson/Casem
1959	Southern University	A.W. Mumphord	1975	Southern/Jackson State	Bates/Bob Hill
1960	Southern/Grambling/ Prairie View	Mumphord/ Eddie Robinson/Nicks	1976	Alcorn State University	Marino Casem
			1977	Grambling University	Eddie Robinson
1961	Jackson State	John Merritt	1978	Grambling University	Eddie Robinson
1962	Jackson State	John Merritt	1979	Grambling/Alcorn	Robinson/Casem
1963	Prairie View A&M	Billy Nicks	1980	Grambling/Jackson State	Robinson/W.C. Gorden
1964	Prairie View A&M	Billy Nicks	1981	Jackson State University	W.C. Gorden
1965	Grambling University	Eddie Robinson	1982	Jackson State University	W.C. Gorden
1966	Grambling/Southern/ Prairie View	Robinson/Smith/Nicks	1983	Grambling University	Eddie Robinson
			1984	Alcorn State University	Marino Casem

MEAC FOOTBALL CHAMPIONS

Year	School	Coach	Year	School	Coach
1971	Morgan State University	Earl Banks	1977	South Carolina State	Willie Jeffries
1972	North Carolina Central	George Quiett	1978	South Carolina State	Willie Jeffries
1973	North Carolina Central	Willie Smith	1979	Morgan State University	Clarence Thomas
1974	South Carolina State	Willie Jeffries	1980	South Carolina State	Bill Davis
1975	N. Car. A&T/S. Car. State	Hornsby Howell/ Willie Jeffries	1981	South Carolina State	Bill Davis
			1982	South Carolina State	Bill Davis
1976	S. Car. St./Morgan State	Willie Jeffries/ Coach Henry	1983	South Carolina State	Bill Davis
			1984	Bethune-Cookman	Larry Little

ORANGE BLOSSOM CLASSIC

Year	Winner		Opponent		Site
1946	Lincoln (Pa.)	20	Florida A&M	12	Tampa, Fla.
1947	Florida A&M	7	Hampton Inst.	0	Miami, Fla.
1948	Virginia Union	10	Florida A&M	6	Miami, Fla.
1949	N.C. A&T	20	Florida A&M	14	Miami, Fla.
1950	Central State	13	Florida A&M	6	Miami, Fla.
1951	Florida A&M	67	N.C. College	6	Miami, Fla.
1952	Florida A&M	29	Virginia State	7	Miami, Fla.
1953	Prairie View	33	Florida A&M	27	Miami, Fla.
1954	Florida A&M	67	Maryland State	19	Miami, Fla.
1955	Grambling	28	Florida A&M	21	Miami, Fla.
1956	Tennessee State	41	Florida A&M	29	Miami, Fla.
1957	Florida A&M	27	Maryland State	21	Miami, Fla.
1958	Prairie View	26	Florida A&M	8	Miami, Fla.
1959	Florida A&M	28	Prairie View	7	Miami, Fla.
1960	Florida A&M	40	Langston	26	Miami, Fla.
1961	Florida A&M	14	Jackson State	8	Miami, Fla.
1962	Jackson State	22	Florida A&M	6	Miami, Fla.
1963	Florida A&M	30	Morgan State	7	Miami, Fla.
1964	Florida A&M	42	Grambling	15	Miami, Fla.
1965	Morgan State	36	Florida A&M	7	Miami, Fla.
1966	Florida A&M	43	Alabama A&M	26	Miami, Fla.
1967	Grambling	28	Florida A&M	25	Miami, Fla.
1968	Alcorn State	36	Florida A&M	9	Miami, Fla.
1969	Florida A&M	23	Grambling	19	Miami, Fla.
1970	Jacksonville St	21	Florida A&M	7	Miami, Fla.
1971	Florida A&M	27	Kentucky State	9	Miami, Fla.
1972	Florida A&M	41	Maryland E-S	21	Miami, Fla.
1973	Florida A&M	23	S.C. State	12	Miami, Fla.
1974	Florida A&M	17	Howard U.	13	Miami, Fla.
1975	Florida A&M	40	Kentucky State	3	Miami, Fla.
1976	Florida A&M	26	Central State	21	Miami, Fla.
1977	Florida A&M	37	Delaware State	15	Miami, Fla.
1978	Florida A&M	31	Grambling	7	Miami, Fla.
1979	Florida A&M	18	Southern U.	6	Miami, Fla.
1980	Florida A&M	57	Delaware State	9	Tallahassee, Fla.
1981	S.C. State	16	Florida A&M	15	Miami, Fla.
1982	Florida A&M	35	N.C. A&T	7	Miami, Fla.
1983	Florida A&M	31	Southern U.	14	Tampa, Fla.
1984	Alcorn State	51	Florida A&M	14	Tampa, Fla.

BLACK COLLEGE COACHES TITLES TOTALS (through 1984)

Name	School	Conf.	Total
Jake Gaither	Florida A&M	SIAC	23
Eddie Robinson	Grambling University	SWAC	13
Billy Nicks	Prairie View A&M	SWAC	8
Marino Casem	Alcorn State	SWAC	8
Willard Bailey	Va. Union/Norfolk State	CIAA	6
Earl Banks	Morgan State	CIAA	6
Willie Jeffries	South Carolina State	MEAC	5
Haywood Cissum	Tuskegee Institute	SIAC	5
Herman Riddick	North Carolina Cent.	CIAA	5
Bill Davis	South Carolina State	MEAC	4
W.C. Gorden	Jackson State	SWAC	3

BLACK COLLEGE CAREER LEADERS (through 1984)

Rushing

Conf.	Player	School	Years	Yards
CIAA	Joseph White	Livingstone	1981-84	4,075
CIAA	Timmy Newsome	Winston-Salem	1976-79	3,843
CIAA	Judge Thomas	Virginia Union	1975-78	3,795
CIAA	Larue Harrington	Norfolk State	1976-79	3,612
CIAA	George Leonard	Virginia State	1976-79	3,575
CIAA	Dennis Mahan	Hampton Institute	1979-82	3,064
CIAA	Arrington Jones	Winston-Salem	1977-80	2,668
CIAA	James Godwin	Fayetteville State	1973-75	2,633
CIAA	Larry Roberts	Virginia Union	1971-74	2,626
CIAA	Oliver Reynolds	Elizabeth City	1968-71	2,618
SWAC	Walter Payton	Jackson State	1971-74	3,563
SWAC	Robert Parham	Grambling	1977-80	3,449
SWAC	Augusta Lee	Alcorn State	1971-74	2,653
MEAC	Gene Lake	Delaware State	1982-84	3,123
MEAC	Robert Hammond	Morgan State	1971-74	2,548
MEAC	Anthony Reed	S. Carolina State	1979-82	2,435
MEAC	Chris Raglund	S. Carolina State	1977-80	2,334
MEAC	Lloyd McCleave	Morgan State	1975-78	2,210
MEAC	Charlie Sutton	N. Carolina A&T	1978-81	2,159
MEAC	Ricky Anderson	S. Carolina State	1975-77	2,017
MEAC	James Breakfield	Howard	1974-77	2,012

Passing

Conf.	Player	School	Years	TD's	Yards
CIAA	Gerald Fraylon	N.C. Central	1981-84	45	5,794
CIAA	Elroy Duncan	J.C. Smith	1967-70	53	5,414
CIAA	John Williams	Elizabeth City	1975-78	43	5,122
CIAA	John Thomas	J.C. Smith	1979-82	29	4,900
CIAA	Samuel Cosby	St. Paul's	1974-77	40	4,818
CIAA	Russell Seaton	Va. St./Hampton	1973-77	57	4,786
SWAC	Willie Totten	Miss. Valley State	1982-84	102	9,475
SWAC	Doug Williams	Grambling	1974-77	93	8,411
SWAC	Parnell Dickinson	Miss. Valley State	1972-75	34	6,326
MEAC	Bernard Hawk	Bethune-Cookman	1982-84	41	5,299
MEAC	Elsworth Turner	N. Carolina A&T	1974-77	41	5,268
MEAC	Michael Banks	Howard	1973-76	42	4,484
MEAC	Nathaniel Koonce	Florida A&M	1980-82	18	3,707
MEAC	Ron Wilson	Howard	1977-80	18	3,298
MEAC	Sandy Nichols	Howard	1980-83	19	3,188
MEAC	Pat Spencer	Delaware State	1981-84	30	3,040

FIRST AFRICAN-AMERICANS ON NATIONAL FOOTBALL LEAGUE TEAMS AFTER 1945

Year	Team	Player	Position
1946	Los Angeles Rams	Kenny Washington	RB
		Woody Strode	E
1948	New York Giants	Emlen Tunnel	DB
	Detroit Lions	Melvin Grooms	RB
		Bob Mann	E
1949	New York Yankees	Sherman Howard	RB
1951	Green Bay Packers	Bob Mann	E
1952	Chicago Bears	Eddie Macon	RB
1952	Chicago Cardinals	Clifton Anderson	E
		Ollie Matson	RB
		Wally Triplett	RB
1952	Philadelphia Eagles	Ralph Goldston	RB
		Donald Stevens	RB

Year	Team	Player	Position
1952	Pittsburgh Steelers	Jack Spinks	G
1953	Baltimore Colts	Melvin Embree	E
		George Taliaferro	RB
		Claude "Buddy" Young	RB
1962	Washington Redskins	Bobby Mitchell	RB
		Ron Hatcher	RB

RB = running back
E = end
G = guard
T = tackle
DB = defensive back

FIRST AFRICAN-AMERICANS ON ALL AMERICAN FOOTBALL CONFERENCE TEAMS

Year	Player	Position	Team	College
1946	Marion Motley	Fullback/ Linebacker	Cleveland Browns	Univ. Nevada– Reno
1946	Bill Willis	Guard	Cleveland Browns	Ohio State Univ.
1947	Claude Young	Halfback	N.Y. Yankees	Univ. Illinois
1947	Elmore Harris	Halfback	Brooklyn Dodgers	Morgan State Univ.
1947	Ezzret Anderson	End	Los Angeles Dons	Kentucky State Univ.
1947	Bert Piggott	Halfback	Los Angeles Dons	Univ. Illinois
1947	John Brown	Center	Los Angeles Dons	N.C. Central Univ.
1947	Bill Bass	Halfback	Chicago Rockets	Univ. Nevada– Reno
1947	Horace Gillom	End-Punter	Cleveland Browns	Univ. Nevada– Reno
1948	Tom Casey	Halfback	N.Y. Yankees	Hampton Institute
1948	Len Ford	End/Defensive End	Los Angeles Dons	Univ. Michigan
1948	Lin Sexton	Halfback	Los Angeles Dons	Wichita State Univ.
1948	Robert Mike	Tackle	San Francisco 49ers	Univ. Cal., Los Angeles
1949	Joe Perry	Fullback	San Francisco 49ers	Compton Jr. College
1949	Ben Whaley	Guard	Los Angeles Dons	Virginia State Univ.

AMERICAN FOOTBALL
CONFERENCE LEADERS 1960-1984
TOP TEN

Rushing					*Receiving*				
Year	Player	Yards	Attempts	Touchdowns	Year	Player	Catches	Yards	Touchdowns
1973	O.J. Simpson	2,003	332	12	1980	Kellen Winslow	89	1,290	9
1980	Earl Campbell	1,934	373	13	1981	Kellen Winslow	88	1,075	10
1975	O.J. Simpson	1,817	329	16	1965	Lionel Taylor	85	1,131	6
1979	Earl Campbell	1,697	368	19	1963	Lionel Taylor	78	1,101	10
1976	O.J. Simpson	1,503	290	8	1970	Marlin Briscoe	57	1,036	8
1966	Jim Nance	1,458	299	11	1984	Ozzie Newsome	89	1,001	5
1983	Curt Warner	1,449	335	13	1962	Lionel Taylor	77	908	4
1981	Earl Campbell	1,376	361	10	1975	Reggie Rucker	60	770	3
1972	O.J. Simpson	1,251	292	6	1979	Joe Washington	82	750	3
1967	Jim Nance	1,216	269	7	1982	Kellen Winslow	54	721	6

Pass Interceptions

Year	Player	Number	Yards
1962	Lee Riley	11	122
1975	Mel Blount	11	121
1967	Miller Farr	10	264
1967	Dick Westmoreland	10	127
1968	Dave Grayson	10	195
1978	Thomas Darden	10	200
1981	John Harris	10	155
1984	Kenny Easley	10	126
1965	W.K. Hicks	9	156
1969	Emmit Thomas	9	146
1971	Kenny Houston	9	220

Punt Returns

Year	Player	Number	Avg. Yardage
1969	Bill Thompson	19	31.3
1974	Lamar Parrish	18	18.8
1975	Billy Johnson	40	18.8
1967	Floyd Little	16	16.9
1982	Rick Upchurch	15	16.1
1984	Mike Martin	24	15.7
1977	Billy Johnson	30	15.4
1973	Ron Smith	27	15.0
1968	Noland Smith	18	15.0
1980	J.T. Smith	40	14.5

PLAYERS WITH 1,000 YARDS (OR MORE) RUSHING SEASONS

African-Americans in Capitals

Player	Team	Number of Seasons	Career Seasons
WALTER PAYTON	Chicago	8	10
FRANCO HARRIS	Pittsburgh	8	13
JIM BROWN	Cleveland	7	9
TONY DORSETT	Dallas	7	8
OTTIS ANDERSON	St. Louis	5	6
EARL CAMPBELL	Houston	5	7
O.J. SIMPSON	Buffalo	5	11
Jim Taylor	Green Bay	5	10

Player	Team	Number of Seasons	Career Seasons
John Riggins	N.Y. Jets, Washington	5	14
MIKE PRUITT	Cleveland	4	9
WILLIAM ANDREWS	Atlanta	4	6
LAWRENCE MCCUTCHEON	L.A. Rams	4	10

PLAYERS WITH 1,000 YARDS RECEIVING SEASONS

African-Americans in Capitals

Player	Teams	Number of Seasons	Career Seasons	Player	Team	Number of Seasons	Career Seasons
Lance Alworth	San Diego	7	11	JOHN STALLWORTH	Pittsburgh	3	12
Steve Largent	Seattle	6	9				
ART POWELL	N.Y. Titans, Oakland	5	10	Tommy McDonald	Phila., L.A. Rams	3	12
Don Maynard	N.Y. Jets	5	16	WES CHANDLER	N. Orleans, S. Diego	3	7
CHARLIE JOINER	San Diego	4	16				
JAMES LOFTON	Green Bay	4	7	Charlie Hennigan	Houston	3	7
Del Shofner	N.Y. Giants	4	11	KELLEN WINSLOW	San Diego	3	6
LIONEL TAYLOR	Denver	3	10				
HOMER JONES	N.Y. Giants	3	7				
HAROLD JACKSON	Phila., N. England	3	16	Steve Watson	Denver	3	6
HAROLD CARMICHAEL	Philadelphia	3	14				

Note: In 1978, rules were changed so that defensive players were not allowed to make contact with the receiver five yards beyond their side of the line of scrimmage.

TOP TEN PUNT CAREER RUTURNERS

African-Americans in Capitals

Player	Rank	Years	No.	Yards	Return Average	TD's
HENRY ELLARD	1	3	83	1,121	13.5	4
George McAfee	2	8	112	1,431	12.8	2
Jack Christiansen	3	8	85	1,084	12.8	8
Claude Gibson	4	5	110	1,381	12.6	3
LOUIS LIPPS	5	2	89	1,093	12.3	3
Bill Dudley	6	9	124	1,515	12.2	3
BILLY JOHNSON	7	11	250	3,036	12.1	6
RICK UPCHURCH	8	9	248	3,008	12.1	8
MACK HERRON	9	3	84	982	11.7	0
BILLY THOMPSON	10	13	157	1,814	11.6	0

TOP TEN PLAYERS IN CAREER INTERCEPTIONS
African-Americans in Capitals

Player	Rank	Years	No.	Yards	Return Average	TD's
Paul Krause	1	16	81	1,185	14.6	3
EMLEN TUNNELL	2	14	79	1,282	16.2	4
DICK LANE	3	14	68	1,207	17.8	5
KEN RILEY	4	15	65	596	9.2	5
Dick LeBeau	5	13	62	762	12.3	3
EMMITT THOMAS	6	13	58	937	16.2	5
Bobby Boyd	7	9	57	994	17.4	4
Johnny Robinson	8	12	57	741	13.0	1
MEL BLOUNT	9	14	57	736	12.9	2
LEM BARNEY	10	11	56	1,077	19.2	7

TOP TEN CAREER KICKOFF RETURNERS
African-Americans in Capitals

Player	Rank	Years	No.	Yards	Average	TD's
GALE SAYERS	1	7	91	2,781	30.6	6
Lynn Chandnois	2	7	92	2,720	29.6	3
ABE WOODSON	3	9	193	5,538	28.7	5
CLAUDE YOUNG	4	6	90	2,514	27.9	2
TRAVIS WILLIAMS	5	5	102	2,801	27.5	6
Joe Arenas	6	7	139	3,798	27.3	1
CLARENCE DAVIS	7	8	79	2,140	27.1	0
Steve Van Buren	8	8	76	2,030	26.7	3
LENNY LYLES	9	12	81	2,161	26.7	3
EUGENE MORRIS	10	8	111	2,947	26.5	3

INDIVIDUAL PROFESSIONAL RECORDS

Rushing

Player	Years	Attempts	Yards	Average	Touchdowns
Joe Perry	15	1,929	9,732	5.0	71
Lenny Moore	12	1,069	5,174	4.8	63
Jim Brown	9	2,359	12,312	5.2	106
Gale Sayers	7	991	4,956	5.0	39
O.J. Simpson	11	2,404	11,236	4.7	61
Franco Harris	13	2,949	12,120	4.1	84
Walter Payton	10	3,047	13,309	4.4	89
Tony Dorsett	8	2,136	9,525	4.5	59
Earl Campbell	7	2,029	8,764	4.3	73

Receiving

Player	Years	Catches	Yards	Average	Touchdowns
Lenny Moore	12	363	6,039	16.6	48
Charley Taylor	13	649	9,110	14.0	79
Paul Warfield	13	427	8,565	20.6	85
Charlie Joiner*	17	716	11,706	16.3	63

* as of 1985

NFL AFRICAN-AMERICAN ALL-PRO'S, 1950-84

1950

Offense

G– Bill Willis, Cleveland
FB– Marion Motley, Cleveland

1951

FB– Deacon Dan Towler, LA Rams
DE– Lenny Ford, Cleveland
MG– Bill Willis, Cleveland
LB– Paul Younger, LA Rams

1952

FB– Deacon Dan Towler, LA Rams
DE– Lenny Ford, Cleveland
MG– Bill Willis, Cleveland
DB– Ollie Matson, Chi. Cards
DB– Emlen Tunnell, NY Giants

1953

FB– Deacon Dan Towler, LA Rams
FB– Joe Perry, San Francisco

Defense

DE– Lenny Ford, Cleveland
MG– Bill Willis, Cleveland

1954

Offense

HB– Ollie Matson, Chi. Cards
FB– Joe Perry, San Francisco

Defense

DE– Lenny Ford, Cleveland

1955

Offense

HB– Ollie Matson, Chi. Cards

Defense

DE– Lenny Ford, Cleveland
DB– Emlen Tunnell, NY Giants

1956

Offense

OT– Roosevelt Brown, NY Giants
HB– Ollie Matson, Chi. Cards

Defense

DT– Rosey Grier, NY Giants
DB– Dick Lane, Chi. Cards
DB– Emlen Tunnell, NY Giants

1957

Offense

OT– Roosevelt Brown, NY Giants
HB– Ollie Matson, Chi. Cards
FB– Jim Brown, Cleveland

Defense

DB– Milt Davis, Baltimore

1958

Offense

OT– Roosevelt Brown, NY Giants
OT– Jim Parker, Baltimore
HB– Lenny Moore, Baltimore
FB– Jim Brown, Cleveland

Defense

DT–   Gene "Big Daddy" Lipscomb, Baltimore

1959

Offense

OT–   Roosevelt Brown, NY Giants
OT–   Jim Parker, Baltimore
HB–   Lenny Moore, Baltimore
FB–   Jim Brown, Cleveland

Defense

DT–   Gene Lipscomb, Baltimore
DB–   Abe Woodson, San Francisco

1960

Offense

OT–   Jim Parker, Baltimore
OT–   Roosevelt Brown, NY Giants
HB–   Lenny Moore, Baltimore
FB–   Jim Brown, Cleveland

Defense

DB–   Abe Woodson, San Francisco
DB–   Dick Lane, Detroit

1960 AFL

Offense

E–   Lionel Taylor, Denver
HB–   Abner Haynes, Dallas Texans
HB–   Paul Lowe, LA Chargers

1961

Offense

OT–   Roosevelt Brown, NY Giants
OT–   Jim Parker, Baltimore
HB–   Lenny Moore, Baltimore
FB–   Jim Brown, Cleveland

Defense

DT–   Gene Lipscomb, Pittsburgh
DB–   Dick Lane, Detroit
DB–   Johnny Sample, Pittsburgh
DB–   Erich Barnes, NY Giants

1961 AFL

E–   Lionel Taylor, Denver
HB–   Abner Haynes, Dallas Texans

Defense

DB–   Tony Webster, Dallas Texans

1962

FL–   Bobby Mitchell, Washington
OT–   Roosevelt Brown, NY Giants
OT–   Jim Parker, Baltimore
RB–   Don Perkins, Dallas
RB–   Dick Bass, LA Rams

Defense

DE–   Willie Davis, Green Bay
DT–   Roger Brown, Detroit
CB–   Dick Lane, Detroit
CB–   Herb Adderley, Green Bay
CB–   Abe Woodson, San Francisco

1962 AFL

Offense

HB–   Abner Haynes, Dallas Texans
FB–   Cookie Gilchrist, Buffalo

Defense

CB–   Fred Williamson, Oakland

1963

Offense

FL–   Bobby Mitchell, Washington
OT–   Roosevelt Brown, NY Giants
OG–   Jim Parker, Baltimore
FB–   Jim Brown, Cleveland

Defense

DT–   Roger Brown, Detroit
CB–   Herb Adderley, Green Bay
CB–   Abe Woodson, San Francisco
CB–   Dick Lane, Detroit
S–   Roosevelt Taylor, Chicago
S–   Willie Wood, Green Bay

1963 AFL

Offense

SE–   Art Powell, Oakland
HB–   Clem Daniels, Oakland

Defense

DT–   Houston Antwine, Boston
CB–   Dave Grayson, Kansas City
CB–   Fred Williamson, Oakland
DT–   Earl Faison, San Diego

1964

SE– Paul Warfield, Cleveland
SE– Frank Clarke, Dallas
SE– Bobby Mitchell, Washington
OG– Jim Parker, Baltimore
HB– Lenny Moore, Baltimore
FB– Jim Brown, Cleveland

Defense

DE– Willie Davis, Green Bay
CB– Erich Barnes, NY Giants
S– Willie Wood, Green Bay

1964 AFL

Offense

SE– Art Powell, Oakland
FB– Cookie Gilchrist, Buffalo

Defense

DT– Earl Faison, San Diego
DE– Bobby Bell, Kansas City
DT– Ernie Ladd, San Diego
CB– Willie Brown, Denver
CB– Dave Grayson, Kansas City
CB– Fred Williamson, Kansas City

1965

Offense

OT– Bob Brown, Philadelphia
OG– Jim Parker, Baltimore
HB– Gale Sayers, Chicago
FB– Jim Brown, Cleveland

Defense

DE– Willie Davis, Green Bay
DE– Deacon Jones, LA Rams
CB– Herb Adderley, Green Bay
S– Willie Wood, Green Bay
S– Mel Renfro, Dallas

1965 AFL

Offense

SE– Lionell Taylor, Denver
SE– Art Powell, Oakland
TE– Willie Frazier, Houston
HB– Paul Lowe, San Diego
FB– Cookie Gilchrist, Denver

Defense

DT– Earl Faison, San Diego
DT– Ernie Ladd, San Diego
LB– Bobby Bell, Kansas City
CB– Dave Grayson, Oakland
CB– Fred Williamson, Kansas City

1966

Offense

SE– Bob Hayes, Dallas
TE– John Mackey, Baltimore
OT– Bob Brown, Philadelphia
RB– Leroy Kelly, Cleveland
RB– Gale Sayers, Chicago

Defense

DE– Willie Davis, Green Bay
DE– Deacon Jones, LA Rams
CB– Herb Adderley, Green Bay
CB– Cornell Green, Dallas
S– Willie Wood, Green Bay

1966 AFL

Offense

SE– Otis Taylor, Kansas City
SE– Art Powell, Oakland
OT– Sherman Plunkett, NY Jets
HB– Clem Daniels, Oakland
FB– Jim Nance, Boston

Defense

DT– Houston Antwine, Boston
DE– Verlon Biggs, NY Jets
DT– Buck Buchanon, Kansas City
LB– Bobby Bell, Kansas City
CB– Dave Grayson, Oakland

1967

Offense

WR– Charlie Taylor, Washington
WR– Homer Jones, NY Giants
WR– Willie Richardson, Baltimore
TE– John Mackey, Baltimore
RB– Leroy Kelly, Cleveland
RB– Gale Sayers, Chicago

Defense

DE– Willie Davis, Green Bay
DE– Deacon Jones, LA Rams

LB– Dave Robinson, Green Bay
CB– Bob Jeter, Green Bay
CB– Cornell Green, Dallas
S– Willie Wood, Green Bay

1967 AFL

Offense
RB– Mike Garrett, Kansas City
FB– Jim Nance, Boston

Defense
DT– Buck Buchanon, Kansas City
LB– George Webster, Houston
LB– Bobby Bell, Kansas City
CB– Miller Farr, Houston

1968

Offense
WR– Clifton McNeil, San Francisco
WR– Paul Warfield, Cleveland
WR– Bob Hayes, Dallas
TE– John Mackey, Baltimore
OT– Bob Brown, Philadelphia
RB– Leroy Kelly, Cleveland
RB– Gale Sayers, Chicago

Defense
DE– Deacon Jones, LA Rams
DE– Carl Eller, Minnesota
LB– Dave Robinson, Green Bay
CB– Lem Barney, Detroit
CB– Cornell Green, Dallas
S– Willie Wood, Green Bay

1968 AFL
OG– Gene Upshaw, Oakland
RB– Paul Robinson, Cincinnati
RB– Hewritt Dixon, Oakland

Defense
DE– Rich Jackson, Denver
DT– Buck Buchanon, Kansas City
LB– Willie Lanier, Kansas City
LB– George Webster, Houston
LB– Bobby Bell, Kansas City
CB– Miller Farr, Houston
CB– Willie Brown, Oakland
S– Dave Grayson, Oakland

1969
WR– Roy Jefferson, Pittsburgh
WR– Paul Warfield, Cleveland
OT– Bob Brown, LA Rams
RB– Gale Sayers, Chicago
RB– Calvin Hill, Dallas
RB– Leroy Kelly, Cleveland

Defense
DE– Carl Eller, Minnesota
DE– Deacon Jones, LA Rams
DT– Alan Page, Minnesota
LB– Dave Robinson, Green Bay
CB– Lem Barney, Detroit
CB– Herb Adderley, Green Bay
CB– Cornell Green, Dallas
CB– Jimmy Johnson, San Francisco
S– Mel Renfro, Dallas

1969 AFL

Offense
WR– Warren Wells, Oakland
OT– Winston Hill, NY Jets
OG– Gene Upshaw, Oakland
RB– Floyd Little, Denver
RB– Matt Snell, NY Jets

Defense
DE– Rich Jackson, Denver
DT– Buck Buchanon, Kansas City
LB– Bobby Bell, Kansas City
LB– George Webster, Houston
CB– Willie Brown, Oakland
S– Dave Grayson, Oakland

1970

Offense
WR– Gene Washington, San Fran.
WR– Dick Gordon, Chicago
TE– Charlie Sanders, Detroit
OT– Bob Brown, LA Rams
OG– Gene Upshaw, Oakland
RB– Larry Brown, Washington
RB– Ron Johnson, NY Giants

Defense
DE– Carl Eller, Minnesota
DE– Rich Jackson, Denver

DT– Alan Page, Minnesota
LB– Bobby Bell, Kansas City
CB– Willie Brown, Oakland
CB– Jimmy Johnson, San Fran.

1971

Offense

WR– Otis Taylor, Kansas City
WR– Paul Warfield, Miami
TE– Charlie Sanders, Detroit
OT– Rayfield Wright, Dallas
OG– Larry Little, Miami
FB– John Brockington, Green Bay

Defense

DE– Carl Eller, Minnesota
DE– Bubba Smith, Baltimore
DT– Alan Page, Minnesota
LB– Willie Lanier, Kansas City
CB– Jimmy Johnson, San Fran.
CB– Willie Brown, Oakland

1972

Offense

WR– Gene Washington, San Fran.
WR– Otis Taylor, Kansas City
WR– Paul Warfield, Miami
OT– Rayfield Wright, Dallas
OT– Bob Brown, Oakland
OG– Larry Little, Miami
OG– Gene Upshaw, Oakland
RB– Larry Brown, Washington
RB– O.J. Simpson, Buffalo

Defense

DE– Claude Humphrey, Atlanta
DT– Joe Greene, Pittsburgh
CB– Willie Brown, Oakland
CB– Jimmy Johnson, San Fran.

1973

Offense

WR– Harold Jackson, LA Rams
WR– Harold Carmichael, Philadelphia
WR– John Gilliam, Minnesota
TE– Charlie Young, Philadelphia
TE– Riley Odoms, Denver
OT– Rayfield Wright, Dallas

OT– Art Shell, Oakland
OG– Larry Little, Miami
OG– Reggie McKenzie, Buffalo
RB– O.J. Simpson, Buffalo
RB– Calvin Hill, Dallas
RB– John Brockington, Green Bay

Defense

De– Claude Humphrey, Atlanta
DE– Alan Page, Minnesota
DT– Joe Greene, Pittsburgh
LB– Isiah Robertson, LA Rams
CB– Willie Brown, Oakland
CB– Mel Renfro, Dallas

1974

Offense

WR– Cliff Branch, Oakland
WR– Drew Pearson, Dallas
WR– Mel Gray, St. Louis
TE– Riley Odoms, Denver
OT– Art Shell, Oakland
OG– Larry Little, Miami
RB– O.J. Simpson, Buffalo
RB– Otis Armstrong, Denver
RB– Lawrence McCutcheon, LA Rams

Defense

DE– L.C. Greenwood, Pittsburgh
DE– Claude Humphrey, Atlanta
DT– Joe Greene, Pittsburgh
DT– Alan Page, Minnesota
LB– Willie Lanier, Kansas City
CB– Robert James, Buffalo
CB– Emmitt Thomas, Kansas City
S– Ken Houston, Washington

1975

Offense

WR– Lynn Swann, Pittsburgh
WR– Mel Gray, St. Louis
WR– Cliff Branch, Oakland
WR– Isaac Curtis, Cincinnati
TE– Charlie Young, Philadelphia
OT– Rayfield Wright, Dallas
OG– Larry Little, Miami
RB– O.J. Simpson, Buffalo
RB– Chuck Foreman, Minnesota

Defense

DE– L.C. Greenwood, Pittsburgh
DE– Curley Culp, Kansas City
DT– Alan Page, Minnesota
DT– Wally Chambers, Chicago
LB– Willie Lanier, Kansas City
LB– Isiah Robertson, LA Rams
CB– Mel Blount, Pittsburgh
CB– Emmitt Thomas, Kansas City
S– Ken Houston, Washington

1976

Offense

WR– Cliff Branch, Oakland
WR– Drew Pearson, Dallas
WR– Isaac Curtis, Cincinnati
RB– O.J. Simpson, Buffalo
RB– Walter Payton, Chicago
RB– Chuck Foreman, Minnesota

Defense

DE– Tommy Hart, San Francisco
DT– Wally Chambers, Chicago
LB– Robert Brazile, Houston
LB– Isiah Robertson, LA Rams
CB– Monte Jackson, LA Rams
CB– Lamar Parrish, Cincinnati
S– Ken Houston, Washington

1977

Offense

WR– Drew Pearson, Dallas
WR– Nat Moore, Miami
WR– Cliff Branch, Oakland
OT– Art Shell, Oakland
OG– Gene Upshaw, Oakland
OG– Larry Little, Miami
RB– Franco Harris, Pittsburgh
RB– Walter Payton, Chicago

Defense

DE– Harvey Martin, Dallas
DE– Claude Humphrey, Atlanta
DT– Cleveland Elam, San Francisco
DT– Larry Brooks, LA Rams
LB– Tom Jackson, Denver
LB– Robert Brazile, Houston
CB– Rolland Lawrence, Atlanta

CB– Monte Jackson, LA Rams
CB– Mel Blount, Pittsburgh
S– Ken Houston, Washington
S– Bill Thompson, Denver

1978

Offense

WR– Lynn Swann, Pittsburgh
WR– Wesley Walker, NY Jets
OT– Leon Gray, New England
OT– Russ Washington, San Diego
RB– Earl Campbell, Houston
RB– Walter Payton, Chicago
RB– Delvin Williams, Miami

Defense

DE– Bubba Baker, Detroit
LB– Robert Brazile, Houston
CB– Louis Wright, Denver
CB– Willie Buchanon, Green Bay
CB– Mike Haynes, New England
S– Thom Darden, Cleveland
S– Ken Houston, Washington

1979

Offense

WR– John Jefferson, San Diego
WR– John Stallworth, Pittsburgh
TE– Raymond Chester, Oakland
TE– Ozzie Newsome, Cleveland
OT– Leon Gray, Houston
OT– Marvin Powell, NY Jets
RB– Earl Campbell, Houston
RB– Ottis Anderson, St. Louis
RB– Walter Payton, Chicago
KR– Rick Upchurch, Denver
KR– Tony Nathan, Miami
PR– J.T. Smith, Kansas City

Defense

DE– Lee Roy Selmon, Tampa Bay
DT– Larry Brooks, LA Rams
DT– Joe Greene, Pittsburgh
DT– Charlie Johnson, Philadelphia
LB– Robert Brazile, Houston
CB– Lemar Parrish, Cincinnati
CB– Louis Wright, Denver
S– Donnie Shell, Pittsburgh

1980

Offense

WR– John Jefferson, San Diego
WR– James Lofton, Green Bay
WR– Charlie Joiner, San Diego
TE– Kellen Winslow, San Diego
OT– Leon Gray, Houston
OG– Herbert Scott, Dallas
RB– Earl Campbell, Houston
RB– Walter Payton, Chicago
KR– Horace Ivory, New England
PR– J.T. Smith, Kansas City

Defense

DE– Lee Roy Selmon, Tampa Bay
DE– Art Still, Kansas City
DE– Fred Dean, San Diego
DT– Gary Johnson, San Diego
DT– Charlie Johnson, Philadelphia
LB– Robert Brazile, Houston
LB– Matt Blair, Minnesota
CB– Lester Hayes, Oakland
CB– Lemar Parrish, Cincinnati
CB– Pat Homas, LA Rams
S– Donnie Shell, Pittsburgh

1981

offense

WR– James Lofton, Green Bay
WR– Alfred Jenkins, Atlanta
TE– Kellen Winslow, San Diego
T– Marvin Powell, NY Jets
G– Herb Scott, Dallas
RB– Tony Dorsett, Dallas
RB– Billy Sims, Detroit
RB– George Rogers, New Orleans
KR– LeRoy Irvin, LA Rams

Defense

DE– Fred Dean, San Francisco
DE– Ed Jones, Dallas
DT– Gary Johnson, San Diego
NT– Charlie Johnson, Philadelphia
LB– Lawrence Taylor, NY Giants
LB– Jerry Robinson, Philadelphia
CB– Ronnie Lott, San Francisco
CB– Mel Blount, Pittsburgh
CB– Mark Haynes, NY Giants

1982

Offense

WR– Wes Chandler, San Diego
TE– Kellen Winslow, San Diego
OT– Marvin Powell, NY Jets
OG– Doug Wilkerson, San Diego
RB– Marcus Allen, LA Raiders
RB– Freeman McNeil, NY Jets
KR– Mike Nelms, Washington

Defense

DE– Lee Roy Selmon, Tampa Bay
DE– Ed Jones, Dallas
LB– Lawrence Taylor, NY Giants
LB– Hugh Green, Tampa Bay
LB– Rod Martin, LA Raiders
CB– Louis Breeden, Cincinnati
CB– Mark Haynes, NY Giants
CB– Mike Haynes, New England
S– Donnie Shell, Pittsburgh
S– Kenny Easley, Seattle

1983

Offense

WR– Roy Green, St. Louis
WR– Mike Quick, Philadelphia
WR– James Lofton, Green Bay
C– Dwight Stevenson, Miami
RB– Eric Dickerson, LA Rams
RB– William Andrews, Atlanta
KR– Mike Nelms, Washington
KR– Fulton Walker, Miami
PR– Billy Johnson, Atlanta

Defense

LB– Mike Singletary, Chicago
LB– Lawrence Taylor, NY Giants
LB– Chip Banks, Cleveland
LB– Rod Martin, LA Raiders
CB– Gary Green, Kansas City
CB– Ronnie Lott, San Francisco
CB– Ken Riley, Cincinnati
CB– Everson Walls, Dallas
CB– Louis Wright, Denver
S– Kenny Easley, Seattle
S– Johnnie Johnson, LA Rams

<u>1984</u>

Offense

WR–	Roy Green, St. Louis
WR–	Art Monk, Washington
WR–	James Lofton, Green Bay
TE–	Ozzie Newsome, Cleveland
C–	Dwight Stevenson, Miami
RB–	Eric Dickerson, LA Rams
RB–	Walter Payton, Chicago
KR–	Henry Ellard, LA Rams
KR–	Bobby Humphrey, NY Jets
PR–	Louis Lipps, Pittsburgh

Defense

LB–	E.J. Junior, St. Louis
LB–	Mike Singletary, Chicago
LB–	Lawrence Taylor, NY Giants
LB–	Rod Martin, LA Raiders
CB–	Mike Haynes, LA Raiders
CB–	Mark Haynes, NY Giants
CB–	Lester Hayes, LA Raiders
S–	Kenny Easley, Seattle
S–	Deron Cherry, Kansas City
S–	Michael Downs, Dallas
S–	Wes Hopkins, Philadelphia
P–	Reggie Roby, Miami

AFRICAN-AMERICANS ENSHRINED IN THE
PRO FOOTBALL HALL OF FAME

Year Inducted	Name	Position	College	Team(s)	Year(s)
1967	Emlen Tunnell	Defensive Back	Univ. of Iowa	New York Giants	1948-1958
				Green Bay Packers	1959-1961
1968	Marion Motley	Fullback & Linebacker	Univ. of Nevada–Reno	Cleveland Browns	1946-1953
				Pittsburgh Steelers	1954-1955
1969	Joe Perry	Fullback	Compton Jr. College	San Francisco 49ers	1948-1960
				Baltimore Colts	1961-1963
1971	Jim Brown	Fullback	Syracuse Univ.	Cleveland Browns	1957-1965
1972	Ollie Matson	Halfback	Univ. of San Fran.	Chicago Cardinals	1952, 1954-1958
				Los Angeles Rams	1959-1962
				Detroit Lions	1963
				Philadelphia Eagles	1964-1966
1973	Jim Parker	Guard	Ohio State Univ.	Baltimore Colts	1957-1967
1974	Dick "Night Train" Lane	Defensive Back	Scottsbluff Jr. College	Los Angeles Rams	1952-1953
				Chicago Cardinals	1954-1959
				Detroit Lions	1960-1965
1975	Roosevelt Brown	Tackle	Morgan State Univ.	New York Giants	1953-1966
1975	Lenny Moore	Halfback	Penn State Univ.	Baltimore Colts	1956-1967
1976	Len Ford	Offensive End	Univ. of Michigan	Los Angeles Dons	1948-1949
				Cleveland Browns	1950-1958
1977	Gale Sayers	Halfback	Univ. of Kansas	Chicago Bears	1965-1971
1977	Bill Willis	Guard	Ohio State Univ.	Cleveland Browns	1946-1953
1980	Herb Adderley	Cornerback	Mich. State Univ.	Green Bay Packers	1961-1969
				Dallas Cowboys	1970-1972
1980	David "Deacon" Jones	Defensive End	S. Carolina State College	Los Angeles Rams	1961-1971
				San Diego Chargers	1972-1973
				Washington Redskins	1974

Year Inducted	Name	Position	College	Team(s)	Year(s)
1981	Willis Davis	Defensive End	Grambling State Univ.	Cleveland Browns	1958-1959
				Green Bay Packers	1960-1969
1983	Bobby Bell	Linebacker	Univ. of Minnesota	Kansas City Chiefs	1963-1974
1983	Bobby Mitchell	Running Back	Univ. of Illinois	Cleveland Browns	1958-1961
				Washington Redskins	1962-1968
1983	Paul Warfield	Wide Receiver	Ohio State Univ.	Cleveland Browns	1964-1969, 1976-1977
				Miami Dolphins	1970-1974
1984	Willie Brown	Defensive Back	Grambling State Univ.	Denver Broncos	1963-1966
				Oakland Raiders	1967-1978
1984	Charley Taylor	Wide Receiver	Arizona State Univ.	Washington Redskins	1964-1975, 1977
1985	O.J. Simpson	Halfback	University of Southern California	Buffalo Bills	1969-1977
				San Francisco 49ers	1978-1979
1986	Ken Houston	Safety	Prairie View A&M	Houston Oilers	1967-1972
				Washington Redskins	1973-1980
1986	Willie Lanier	Linebacker	Morgan State College	Kansas City Chiefs	1967-1977
1987	Joe Greene	Defensive Tackle	North Texas State University	Pittsburgh Steelers	1969-1981
1987	John Henry Johnson	Fullback	Arizona State Univ.	San Francisco 49ers	1954-1956
				Detroit Lions	1957-1959
				Pittsburgh Steelers	1960-1965
				Houston Oilers	1966

AFRICAN-AMERICANS IN PROFESSIONAL FOOTBALL

Atlanta Falcons

Sowanee, Georgia 30174

Coaches		Years
Harrison, Robert	(Assistant Coach)	1984-1986
Daniel, Horace	(Assistant Equipment Manager)	1967-1986

All-Pro or Pro Bowl Selections

	Years
Humphrey, Claude	1970-1974, 1977
Mitchell, Jim	1972
Lawrence, Rolland	1974, 1977
Jenkins, Alfred	1980, 1981
Andrews, William	1980-1984
Miller, Junior	1981
Johnson, Billy	1983

All-Time Team Roster

Player	College	Years
Allen, Anthony	University of Washington	1985-1986
Anderson, Anthony	Temple University	1980
Andrews, William	Auburn University	1979-1986

Player	College	Years
Austin, Cliff	Clemson University	1984-1986
Bailey, Stacy	Stanford University	1982-1986
Bean, Bubba	Texas A&M University	1976-1980
Belton, Willie	Maryland State College	1971-1972
Benson, Cliff	Purdue University	1984-1986
Benson, Thomas	University of Oklahoma	1984-1986
Brook, Jonathan	Clemson University	1980
Brown, Charles	South Carolina State University	1985-1986
Brown, Ray	West Texas State University	1971-1978
Brown, Reginald	University of Oregon	1982
Bryant, Charles	Allen University	1969
Bryant, Warren	University of Kentucky	1978-1983
Burley, Gary	University of Pittsburgh	1984-1986
Butler, Bobby	Florida State University	1981-1986
Butler, Jim	Edward Waters College	1968-1971
Cain, Lynn	University of Southern California	1979-1986
Cason, Wendell	University of Oregon	1985-1986
Childs, Henry	Kansas State University	1974
Coffey, Junior	University of Washington	1966-1967, 1969
Collins, Sonny	University of Kentucky	1976
Cox, Arthur	Texas Southern University	1983-1986
Croudip, David	San Diego State University	1985-1986
Crowe, Larry	Texas Southern University	1975
Dabney, Carlton	Morgan State University	1968
Ellis, Clarence	University of Notre Dame	1972-1974
Francis, Wallace	Arkansas AM&N	1975-1981
Frye, David	Purdue University	1983-1986
Germany, Willie	Morgan State University	1972
Gilliam, John	South Carolina State College	1976
Goodwin, Doug	Maryland State College	1968
Harris, Roy	University of Florida	1984-1986
Hilton, Roy	Jackson State University	1975
Hodge, Floyd	University of Utah	1982-1986
Homer, Rudy	Drake University	1974
Humphrey, Claude	Tennessee State University	1968-1974, 1976-1978
Jackson, Alfred	University of Texas	1978
Jackson, Ernest	Duke University	1978
Jackson, Jeff	Auburn University	1984-1986
Jenkins, Alfred	Morris Brown College	1975-1983
Jarvis, Ray	Norfolk State University	1971-1972
Johnson, Billy	Widener College	1982-1986
Johnson, Ken	Mississippi State University	1980-1986
Jones, Robert	Virginia Union University	1975-1976
Jones, Earl	Norfolk State University	1980-1983
Kindle, Gregg	Tennessee State University	1976
Lavan, Al	Colorado State University	1969-1970
Lawrence, Rolland	Tabor	1973-1980

Player	College	Years
Lewis, Michael	Arkansas AM&N	1971-1979
Mabra, Ron	Howard University	1975-1976
Malancon, Rydell	Louisiana State University	1984-1985
Malone, Art	Arizona State University	1970-1974
Matthews, Al	Vanderbilt University	1983-1986
McCrary, Greg	Clark College	1975-1977
Meyers, Eddie	U.S. Naval Academy	1982-1986
Miller, Junior	University of Nebraska	1980-1983
Mitchell, Jim	Prairie View A&M University	1969-1979
Neal, Louis	Prairie View A&M University	1974
Patton, Ricky	Jackson State University	1978
Pennywell, Robert	Grambling State University	1977-1980
Pitts, Michael	University of Alabama	1983-1986
Profit, Joseph	North East Louisiana	1971-1973
Reaves, Ken	Norfolk State University	1966-1973
Reed, Oscar	Colorado State University	1975
Richardson, Al	Georgia Tech University	1980-1986
Riggs, Gerald	Arizona State University	1982-1986
Robinson, Bo	West Texas State University	1981-1983
Scott, David	University of Kansas	1976-1982
Seay, Virgil	Troy State University	1984-1986
Simmons, Jerry	Bethune-Cookman College	1967-1969
Small, Gerald	San Jose State University	1984-1986
Smith, Reginald	North Carolina Central University	1980-1981
Stamps, Sylvester	Jackson State University	1984-1986
Stanciel, Jeff	Mississippi Valley State University	1969
Straham, Art	Texas Southern University	1968
Sullivan, James	Lincoln University (Missouri)	1970
Tate, Rodney	University of Texas	1984-1986
Taylor, John	University of Hawaii	1984-1986
Teague, Matthew	Prairie View A&M University	1981
Thompson, Woody	University of Miami (Florida)	1975-1977
Tinker, Gerald	Kent State University	1974-1975
Tuttle, Perry	Clemson University	1984-1985
Washington, Ron	North East Louisiana	1985-1986
Wheelwright, Ernest	Southern Illinois University	1966-1967
Wright, Nate	San Diego State University	1969

Buffalo Bills

Orchard Park, N.Y. 14127

Coaches		Years
Pitts, Elijah	(Assistant)	1978-1980, 1985
Debenion, Elbert	(Assistant)	1985-1986

All-Pro or Pro Bowl Selections
(American Football League before 1970)

Joe, Billy	1966
Gilchrist, Cookie	1962, 1963, 1964
Dubenion, Elbert	1964
Simpson, O.J.	1969, 1972, 1973, 1974, 1975, 1976
Briscoe, Marlin	1970
James, Robert	1972, 1973, 1974
McKenzie, Reginald	1973, 1974, 1975
Green, Tony	1974
Cribbs, Joe	1980, 1981, 1983
Butler, Jerry	1980
Lewis, Frank	1981
Williams, Ben	1982

All-Time Team Roster

Player	*College*	*Years*
Alexander, Glenn	Grambling State University	1970
Baker, Mel	Texas Southern University	1977
Barnett, Buster	Jackson State University	1981-1986
Bayless, Martin	Bowling Green State University	1984-1986
Beamer, Tim	Johnson C. Smith University	1971
Bell, Greg	University of Notre Dame	1984-1986
Bellinger, Rodney	University of Miami (Florida)	1984-1986
Bess, Rufus	South Carolina State University	1980-1981
Bivins, Charles	Morris Brown College	1967
Braxton, Hezekiah	Virginia Union University	1963
Braxton, Jim	West Virginia University	1971-1978
Briscoe, Marlin	Omaha University	1969-1971
Brookins, Mitchell	University of Illinois	1984-1986
Brooks, Clifford	Tennessee State University	1976
Butler, Jerry	Clemson University	1979-1983, 1985-1986
Byrd, George	Boston University	1964-1970
Caldwell, Darryl	Tennessee State University	1983
Carpenter, Brian	University of Michigan	1984
Clark, Mario	University of Oregon	1976-1983
Collier, Michael	Morgan State University	1977-1979
Cornish, Frank	Alcorn A&M	1972
Cowling, Al	University of Southern California	1970-1972
Crawford, Hilton	Grambling State University	1969
Cribbs, Joe	Auburn University	1980-1983, 1985
Dawkins, Julius	University of Pittsburgh	1983-1985
Day, Thomas	North Carolina A&T University	1961-1966, 1968
Dennard, Preston	University of New Mexico	1984-1986
Dubbins, Oliver	Morgan State University	1964
Drungo, Elbert	Tennessee State University	1978

Player	College	Years
Dubenion, Elbert	Bluffton	1960-1968
Edwards, Earl	Wichita State University	1973-1975
Ferguson, Charles	Tennessee State University	1963-1969
Francis, Wallace	Arkansas AM&N	1973-1974
Franklin, Byron	Auburn University	1981, 1983-1985
Gaddis, Robert	Mississippi Valley State University	1976
Gant, Reuben	Oklahoma State University	1974-1980
Gilchrist, Cookie	(no college)	1962-1964
Goodwin, Doug	Maryland State College	1966
Grate, Willie	South Carolina State University	1969-1970
Green, Tony	University of Maryland	1971-1979
Harrison, Dee	University of North Carolina	1978-1980
Harris, Jim	Grambling State University	1969-1971
Harrison, Dwight	Texas A&M University	1972-1977
Hill, J.D.	Arizona State University	1971-1975
Holland, John	Tennessee State University	1975-1977
Holmes, Michael	Texas Southern University	1976
Hooks, Roland	North Carolina State University	1976-1982
Hunter, Tony	University of Notre Dame	1983-1984
James, Robert	Fisk University	1969-1974
Jarvis, Ray	Norfolk State University	1973
Jessie, Ron	University of Kansas	1980-1981
Joe, Billy	Villanova University	1965
Johnson, Ken	Knoxville College	1979-1984
Johnson, Lawrence	University of Wisconsin	1984
Laster, Art	Maryland State College	1970
Leaks, Roosevelt	University of Texas	1980-1983
Lewis, Frank	Grambling State University	1978-1983
Marve, Eustive	Saginaw Valley State	1982-1985
Mays, David	Texas Southern University	1978
McCutheon, Lawrence	Colorado State University	1981
McKenzie, Reginald	University of Michigan	1972-1982
McKinney, Royce	Kentucky State University	1975
Miller, Terry	Oklahoma State University	1978-1980
Moore, Boozer	Pennsylvania State University	1982-1985
Moore, Leroy	Fort Valley State College	1960, 1962-1963
Moses, Haven	San Diego State University	1968-1972
Mosley, Wayne	Alabama A&M University	1974
Neal, Speedy	University of Miami (Florida)	1984-1985
Norris, Ulysses	University of Georgia	1984-1985
Oliver, Frank	Kentucky State University	1975
Parker, Ervin	South Carolina State University	1980-1983
Parker, Willie	North Texas State University	1973-1979
Parrish, Lamar	Lincoln University	1982
Penchion, Robert	Alcorn A&M University	1972-1973
Rashad, Ahmad	University of Oregon	1974-1975
Riddick, Robb	Millersville State University	1981, 1983-1985

Player	College	Years
Robertson, Bo	Cornell University	1965
Robertson, Isiah	Southern University	1979-1980
Romes, Charles	North Carolina Central University	1977-1986
Ross, Louis	South Carolina State University	1971-1972
Sanford, Lucius	Georgia Tech University	1978-1985
Simpson, O.J.	University of Southern California	1979-1977
Smith, Tody	University of Southern California	1976
Sorey, Jim	Texas Southern University	1960-1962
Talley, Darryl	West Virginia University	1983-1986
Thomas, Ike	Bishop College	1975
Tuttle, Perry	Clemson University	1982-1983
Tyler, Maurice	Morgan State University	1972-1973
Walker, Donnie	Central State University (Ohio)	1973-1974
Walton, Larry	Arizona State University	1978
Warlick, Ernest	North Carolina Central University	1962-1965
Warner, Charles	Prairie View A&M University	1964-1966
Washington, David	Alcorn State University	1972-1974
Watkins, Larry	Alcorn State University	1973-1974
White, Sherman	University of California (Berkeley)	1976-1983
Williams, Ben	University of Mississippi	1976-1985
Williams, Van	Carson-Newman	1983-1984
Willis, Len	Ohio State University	1977-1979
Wilson, Don	North Carolina State University	1984
Word, Roscoe	Jackson State University	1976
Wyatt, Alvin	Bethune-Cookman College	1970-1973
Young, David	Purdue University	1983
Young, Willie	Alcorn State University	1981

Chicago Bears

55 East Jackson Boulevard Suite 1200
Chicago, Illinois 60604

	Coaches	Years
Roland, John	(Assistant)	1983-1986
Graves, Rod	(Regional Scout)	1983-1986

All-Pro or Pro Bowl Selections

Hill, Harlon	1954, 1955, 1956
Taylor, Roosevelt	1963
Sayers, Gale	1965, 1966, 1967, 1969
Gordon, Dick	1970
Chambers, Wally	1975, 1976
Payton, Walter (All-Time National Football League Leading Rusher)	1976, 1977, 1978, 1979, 1980, 1981, 1984, 1985, 1986

Singletary, Michael   1984, 1985, 1986
Dent, Richard   1985, 1986
Bell, Todd   1985
Wilson, Otis   1986

All-Time Team Roster

Player	*College*	*Years*
Anderson, Marcus	Tulane University	1981
Anderson, Neal	University of Florida	1986
Antoine, Lionel	Southern Illinois University	1972-1976, 1978
Atkins, Kelvin	University of Illinois	1983
Bell, Todd	Ohio State University	1981-1985
Berry, Royce	University of Houston	1976
Best, Art	Kent State University	1977-1978
Bivins, Charles	Morris Brown College	1960-1966
Bryant, Waymond	Tennessee State University	1974-1977
Calland, Lee	University of Louisville	1969
Caroline, J.C.	University of Illinois	1956-1965
Castete, Jesse	McNeese State University	1956
Chambers, Wally	Eastern Kentucky University	1973-1977
Chesley, Al	University of Pittsburgh	1982
Childs, Clarence	Florida A&M University	1968
Clemons, Craig	University of Iowa	1972-1977
Cobb, Michael	Michigan State University	1978-1981
Cornish, Frank	Grambling State University	1966-1969
Cotton, Craig	Youngstown State University	1973
Dean, Fred	Texas Southern University	1977
Dent, Richard	Tennessee State University	1983-1986
Douthitt, Earl	University of Iowa	1975
Duerson, David	University of Notre Dame	1983-1986
Edwards, Cid	Tennessee State University	1975
Ellis, Allan	University of California Los Angeles	1973-1979
Evans, Vince	University of Southern California	1977-1982
Farrington, John	Prairie View A&M University	1960-1963
Ford, Charles	University of Houston	1971-1973
Forrest, Tom	University of Cincinnati	1974
Frazier, Leslie	Alcorn State University	1981-1986
Gaines, Wentford	University of Cincinnati	1978-1980
Galimore, Willie	Florida A&M University	1957-1963
Garrett, Carl	New Mexico Highland University	1973-1974
Gault, Willie	University of Tennessee	1983-1986
Gayle, Shaun	Ohio State University	1984-1986
Gentry, Dennis	Baylor University	1982-1986
Gordon, Dick	Michigan State University	1965-1971
Graham, Conrad	University of Tennessee	1973
Grandberry, Ken	Washington State University	1974
Gunn, Jim	University of Southern California	1970-1975

Player	College	Years
Harper, Roland	Louisiana Tech University	1975-1982
Harris, Al	Arizona State University	1979-1983
Harris, Richard	Grambling State University	1974-1975
Hart, Tommy	Morris Brown College	1978
Hartnett, Perry	Southern Methodist University	1982-1983
Hazelton, Major	Florida A&M University	1968-1969
Henderson, Reuben	San Diego State University	1981-1982
Herron, Bruce	New Mexico University	1978-1982
Hill, Harlon	Florence State Teachers College	1954-1961
Hill, Ike	Catawba	1973-1974
Hodgins, Norm	Louisiana State University	1974
Holman, Willie	South Carolina State University	1968-1973
Humphries, Stefan	University of Michigan	1984-1986
Hutchinson, Anthony	Texas Tech University	1983
Jackson, Bobby	University of Alabama	1961
Jackson, Noah	University of Tampa	1975-1982
Jeter, Bob	University of Iowa	1971-1973
Jiggetts, Dan	Harvard University	1976-1982
Kelly, Jim	Tennessee State University	1974
Keys, Tyrone	Mississippi State University	1983-1986
Kinney, Steve	Utah State University	1973-1974
Knox, Bill	Purdue University	1974-1976
Latta, Greg	Morgan State University	1975-1980
Lee, Herman	Florida A&M University	1958-1966
Livers, Virgil	Western Kentucky University	1975-1979
Lyle, Garry	George Washington University	1968-1974
Marshall, Wilbur	University of Florida	1984-1986
Mayes, Rufus	Ohio State University	1969
McClendon, Willis	University of Georgia	1969
McGee, Tony	Bishop College	1979-1982
McKinney, Bill	West Texas State	1971-1973
McKinnon, Dennis	Florida State University	1982-1986
McCrae, Bennie	University of Michigan	1962-1970
McCrae, Franklin	Tennessee State University	1967
Montgomery, Randy	Weber State College	1974
Moore, McNeil	Sam Houston State University	1954-1956
Moorehead, Emery	University of Colorado	1981-1986
Mosley, Henry	Morris Brown College	1955
Newsome, Billy	Grambling State University	1977
Osborne, Jim	Southern University	1972-1983
Page, Alan	University of Notre Dame	1978-1981
Payton, Walter	Jackson State University	1975-1986
Perrin, Lonnie	University of Illinois	1979
Perry, William	Clemson University	1985-1986
Phillips, Reggie	Southern Methodist University	1985-1986

Player	College	Years
Pickins, Bob	University of Nebraska	1967-1968
Potter, Kevin	University of Missouri	1983
Pride, Dan	Jackson State University	1968-1969
Rather, Bo	University of Michigan	1974-1978
Rice, Andy	Texas Southern University	1972-1973
Richardson, Michael	Arizona State University	1983-1986
Roberts, Willie	University of Houston	1973
Roger, Mel	Florida A&M University	1977
Sanders, Thomas	Texas A&M University	1985-1986
Sayers, Gale	University of Kansas	1965-1971
Scott, James	Henderson Junior College	1976-1982
Seals, George	University of Missouri	1965-1971
Shanklin, Ron	North Texas State University	1975-1976
Shy, Don	San Diego State University	1970-1972
Simmons, J.	Bethune-Cookman College	1969
Simmons, David	University of North Carolina	1983
Singletary, Michael	Baylor University	1981-1983
Smith, J.D.	North Carolina A&T University	1956
Sorey, Revie	University of Illinois	1975-1982
Spivey, Michael	University of Colorado	1977-1979
Taylor, Clifton	Memphis State University	1974
Taylor, Joe	North Carolina A&T University	1967-1974
Taylor, Ken	Oregon State University	1985-1986
Taylor, Lionel	Highland University	1959
Taylor, Roosevelt	Grambling State University	1961-1968
Thomas, Calvin	University of Illinois	1982-1986
Thomas, Earl	University of Houston	1971-1973
Thrower, Willie	Michigan State University	1953
Tucker, Bill	Tennessee State University	1971
Turner, Cecil	California Poly	1968-1973
Wade, Charles	Tennessee State University	1974
Wallace, Bob	University of Texas-El Paso	1968-1972
Watts, Rickey	University of Tulsa	1979-1983
Wheeler, Ted	West Texas State University	1980
White, Wilford	Arizona State University	1951-1952
Williams, Perry	Purdue University	1974
Williams, Walter	New Mexico State University	1982-1983
Williams, Oliver	University of Illinois	1983
Wilson, Nehemiah	Grambling State University	1975
Wilson, Otis	University of Louisville	1980-1986
Zanders, Emanuel	Jackson State University	1981

Cincinnati Bengals
Cincinnati, Ohio

All-Pro or Pro Bowl Selections

Player	*Years*
Parrish, Lamar	1971, 1972, 1973, 1974, 1975, 1976, 1977
Curtis, Isaac	1974, 1975, 1976, 1977
Johnson, Peter	1982

All-Time Team Roster

Player	*College*	*Years*
Alexander, Charles	Louisiana State University	1979-1986
Bacon, Coy	Jackson State University	1976-1977
Barker, Leo	New Mexico State University	1984-1985
Bass, Don	University of Houston	1978-1981
Beauchamp, Al	Southern University	1968-1975
Breeden, Louis	North Carolina Central University	1978-1986
Brooks, Billy	University of Oklahoma	1976-1979
Brooks, James	Auburn University	1984-1986
Brown, Eddie	University of Miami	1986
Brown, Robert	Arkansas AM&N	1975-1976
Browner, Jim	University of Notre Dame	1979-1980
Browner, Ross	University of Notre Dame	1979-1986
Buncom, Frank	University of Southern California	1968
Chandler, Al	Eastern Michigan University	1973-1974
Chapman, Clarence	Eastern Michigan University	1980-1982
Clark, Boobie	Bethune-Cookman College	1973-1978
Cobb, Marvin	University of Southern California	1975-1979
Coleman, Al	Tennessee State University	1969-1971
Collins, Glen	Mississippi State University	1982-1985
Cornish, Frank	Grambling College	1970
Craig, Neal	Fisk University	1971-1973
Curtis, Isaac	San Diego State University	1973-1984
Davis, Charles	University of Colorado	1974-1975
Davis, Oliver	Tennessee State University	1981-1982
Davis, Tony	University of Nebraska	1976-1978
Edwards, Eddie	University of Miami (Florida)	1977-1986
Elliot, Lenvil	N.E. Missouri State University	1973-1978
Farley, John	California State University (Sacramento)	1984
Frazier, Guy	University of Wyoming	1981-1985
Griffin, Archie	Ohio State University	1976-1983
Griffin, Ray	Ohio State University	1978-1984
Griffin, Jim	Grambling College	1968-1969
Harris, Bo	Louisiana State University	1975-1982
Harris, M.L.	Kansas State University	1980-1985
Holden, Steven	Arizona State University	1977
Holman, Rodney	Tulane University	1982-1985

Player	College	Years
Holland, Vernon	Tennessee State University	1971-1979
Horton, Ray	University of Washington	1983-1985
Jackson, Bernard	Washington State University	1972-1976
Jackson, Robert	Central Michigan University	1981-1986
Jennings, Stanford	Furman University	1984-1986
Johnson, Essex	Grambling College	1968-1975
Johnson, Jim	South Carolina State University	1968-1975
Johnson, Peter	Ohio State University	1977-1983
Johnson, Walter	Los Angeles State University	1977
Joiner, Charles	Grambling College	1972-1975
Jones, Robert	Virginia Union University	1973
Jones, Willie Lee	University of Kansas	1968-1971
Kemp, Robert	California State University, Fullerton	1981-1985
Kern, Don	Arizona State University	1984-1985
Kindricks, William	Alabama A&M University	1968
King, Arthur	Grambling State University	1982
Kinnebrew, Larry	Tennessee State University	1983-1986
Martin, Michael	University of Illinois	1983-1985
Mayes, Rufus	Ohio State University	1970-1978
McDaniel, John	Lincoln University	1974-1977
McVea, Warren	University of Houston	1968
Moore, Maury	Bethune-Cookman College	1975
Morgan, Melvin	Mississippi Valley State University	1976-1978
Parrish, Lemar	Lincoln University	1970-1978
Peacock, Elvis	University of Oklahoma	1981
Pureforty, David	Eastern Michigan University	1978
Rice, Andy	Texas Southern University	1968-1969
Riley, Ken	Florida A&M University	1969-1983
Robinson, Paul	University of Arizona	1968-1972
Shelby, Willie	University of Alabama	1976-1985
Simmons, John	Southern Methodist University	1981-1985
Simpkins, Ron	University of Michigan	1980-1985
Smith, Fletcher	Tennessee State University	1968-1971
Smith, Gary	Virginia Tech University	1984-1986
Smith, Tommie	San Jose State University	1969
St. Clair, Michael	Grambling State University	1980-1982
Suggs, Shafer	Ball State University	1980
Tate, Rodney	University of Texas	1982-1983
Thomas, Lee	Jackson State University	1973
Turner, James	University of California, Los Angeles	1983-1985
Verser, David	University of Kansas	1981-1985
Walker, Rick	University of California, Los Angeles	1977-1979
Weaver, Emanuel	University of South Carolina	1982-1983
White, Andre	Florida A&M University	1968
White, Sherman	University of California, Berkeley	1972-1975
Whitley, Wilson	University of Houston	1977-1982
Williams, Ed	Langston University	1974

Player	College	Years
Williams, Gary	Wilmington College	1983-1985
Williams, James	Alcorn A&M University	1968
Williams, Monk	Arkansas AM&N	1968
Williams, Reginald	Dartmouth College	1976-1986
Wilson, Stanley	University of Oklahoma	1983-1986
Wright, Ernest	Ohio State University	1968-1971

Cleveland Browns
Cleveland Stadium
Cleveland, Ohio 44114

Front Office Personnel

		Years
Warfield, Paul	(Assistant Director of Pro Personnel)	1979-1980
	(Assistant to the President)	1981-1982
	(Director of Player Relations)	1982-1986
Feacher, Ricky	(Player Relations)	1986
Tabor, Alva	(Scout)	1978-1979
Garcia, Charles	(Scout)	1980-1982
Chappelle, Ted	(Director of Security)	

Coaches

Tabor, Alva	(Assistant)	1972-1977
Buchanan, Junius	(Assistant)	1978
Mann, Richard	(Assistant)	1985-1986

All-Pro or Pro Bowl Selections

	Years
Motley, Marion	1951
Willis, Bill	1951-1953
Ford, Len	1953-1955
Gillon, Horace	1953
Brown, Jim	1957-1961
Mitchell, Robert	1961
Warfield, Paul	1965, 1970
Wooton, John	1966, 1967
Green, Ernest	1967, 1968
Kelley, Leroy	1967-1972
Barnes, Erich	1969
Pruitt, Gregg	1974-1975, 1977-1978
Scott, Clarence	1974
Darden, Thomas	1979
Pruitt, Michael	1980, 1981
Newsome, Ozzie	1982, 1985
Banks, Chip	1983, 1984

All-Time Team Roster

Player	College	Years
Adams, Willis	University of Houston	1979-1985
Anderson, Stuart	University of Virginia	1984
Aldridge, Allen	Prairie View A&M University	1974
Baldwin, Keith	Texas A&M University	1982-1985
Banks, Chip	University of Southern California	1982-1986
Barnes, Erich	Purdue University	1965-1971
Barney, Eppie	Iowa State University	1967-1968
Bassett, Maurice	Langston University	1954-1956
Battle, Jim	Southern University	1966
Beach, Walter	Central Michigan University	1963-1966
Beamon, Autry	East Texas State University	1980-1981
Belk, Rocky	University of Miami	1983
Bolden, Leroy	Michigan State University	1958-1959
Bolden, Ricky	Southern Methodist University	1984-1985
Bolton, Ron	Norfolk State University	1976-1982
Bradley, Harold	University of Iowa	1954-1956
Braziel, Larry	University of Southern California	1982-1985
Brooks, Clifford	Tennessee State University	1972-1974
Brown, Dean	Fort Valley State College	1969
Brown, Jim	Syracuse University	1957-1965
Brown, John	Syracuse University	1962-1966
Brown, Ken	(no college)	1970-1975
Brown, Stan	Purdue University	1971
Brown, Thomas	Baylor University	1981, 1983
Burell, Clinton	Louisiana State University	1979-1984
Caleb, Jamie	Grambling College	1960, 1965
Camp, Reginald	University of California	1983-1986
Campbell, Milton	Indiana University	1957
Carver, Dale	University of Georgia	1983
Clarke, Frank	University of Colorado	1957-1959
Cole, Emerson	University of Toledo	1950-1952
Coleman, Gregory	Florida A&M University	1977
Collins, Larry	Texas A&I University	1978
Craig, Neal	Fisk University	1975-1976
Crews, Ron	University of Nevada, Las Vegas	1980
Crosby, Cleveland	University of Arizona	1980
Darden, Thomas	University of Michigan	1972-1974, 1976-1981
Davis, Ben	Defiance	1967-1968, 1970-1973
Davis, Bruce	Baylor University	1984
Davis, John	University of Alabama	1982-1985
Davis, Oliver	Tennessee State University	1977-1980
Davis, Willie	Grambling College	1958-1959
Dennis, Al	Grambling College	1976-1977
Dixon, Hanford	University of Southern Mississippi	1981-1986

Player	*College*	*Years*
Dunbar, Jubilee	Southern University	1974
Edwards, Earl	Wichita State University	1976-1978
Ellis, Ken	Southern University	1977
Feacher, Ricky	Mississippi Valley State University	1976-1984
Ferguson, Charles	Tennessee A&I University	1961
Ferguson, Vagas	University of Notre Dame	1983
Flint, Judson	Memphis State University	1980-1982
Ford, Len	University of Michigan	1950-1957
Franks, Elvis	Morgan State University	1980-1984
Fulton, Dan	University of Nebraska, Omaha	1981-1982
Gautt, Prentice	University of Oklahoma	1960
Gillom, Horace	University of Nevada	1947-1956
Goode, Don	University of Kansas	1980-1981
Goosby, Tom	Baldwin-Wallace	1963
Grant, Wes	University of California, Los Angeles	1972
Green, Boyce	Carson-Newman	1983-1985
Green, David	Edinboro State	1982
Green, Ernest	University of Louisville	1962-1968
Green, Van	Shaw University	1973-1976
Gross, Al	University of Arizona	1983-1985
Hairston, Carl	University of Maryland, Eastern Shore	1984-1986
Hall, Charles	University of Houston	1971-1980
Harraway, Charles	San Jose State University	1966-1968
Hawkins, Ben	Arizona State University	1974
Hill, Calvin	Yale University	1978-1981
Hill, Jim	Texas A&I University	1975
Holden, Steven	Arizona State University	1973-1976
Holt, Harry	University of Arizona	1983-1986
Hooker, Fair	Arizona State University	1969-1974
Hopkins, Thomas	Alabama A&M University	1983
Howell, Michael	Grambling College	1965-1972
Irons, Gerald	University of Maryland, Eastern Shore	1976-1979
Jackson, Rich	Southern University	1972
Jackson, Robert L.	Texas A&M University	1978-1981
James, Nathaniel	Florida A&M University	1968
Johnson, Ed	University of Louisville	1981-1985
Johnson, Lawrence	University of Wisconsin	1979-1983
Johnson, Ron	University of Michigan	1969
Johnson, Walter	California State University, Los Angeles	1965-1976
Jones, Homer	Texas Southern University	1970
Jones, Joe	Tennessee State University	1970-1971, 1973, 1975-1978
Jones, Ricky	Tuskegee Institute	1977-1979
Kelly, Leroy	Morgan State University	1964-1973
LeFear, William	Henderson State College	1972-1975
Leigh, Charles	(no college)	1968-1969
Lewis, Darryl	University of Texas, Arlington	1984
London, Tom	North Carolina State University	1978

Player	College	Years
Long, Mel	University of Toledo	1972-1974
Marshall, David	Eastern Michigan University	1984
Marshall, Jim	Ohio State University	1960
Mays, David	Texas Southern University	1976-1977
McClung, Willie	Florida A&M University	1958-1959
McKinnis, Hugh	Arizona State University	1973-1975
McNeil, Clifton	Grambling College	1964-1967
Miller, Cleo	Arkansas AM&N	1975-1982
Miller, Willie	Colorado State University	1975-1976
Mitchell, Alvin	Morgan State University	1968-1969
Mitchell, Robert	University of Illinois	1958-1961
Mitchell, Mack	University of Houston	1975-1978
Motley, Marion	University of Nevada	1946-1953
Newsome, Ozzie	University of Alabama	1978-1986
Oden, McDonald	Tennessee State University	1980-1982
Odom, Clifton	University of Texas, Arlington	1980
Payton, Eddie	Jackson State University	1977
Pena, Robert	University of Massachusetts	1972
Perry, Rod	University of Colorado	1983-1984
Peters, Tony	University of Oklahoma	1975-1978
Pitts, Frank	Southern University	1971-1973
Pitts, John	Arizona State University	1975
Poole, Larry	Kent State University	1975-1977
Powell, Preston	Grambling College	1961
Pritchett, William	West Texas State University	1975
Pruitt, Greg	University of Oklahoma	1973-1981
Pruitt, Michael	Purdue University	1976-1984
Raimey, David	University of Michigan	1964
Roan, Oscar	Southern Methodist University	1975-1978
Roberts, Walter	San Jose State University	1964-1966
Rockins, Chris	Oklahoma State University	1984-1985
Rogers, Don	University of California, Los Angeles	1984-1985
Rucker, Reginald	Boston University	1975-1981
St. Clair, Michael	Grambling State University	1976-1979
Scales, Charles	Indiana University	1962-1965
Scott, Bo	Ohio State University	1969-1974
Scott, Clarence	Kanas State University	1971-1983
Shorter, Jim	University of Detroit	1962-1963
Smith, John	Tennessee State University	1979
Summers, Fred	Wake Forest University	1969-1971
Tidmore, Sam	Ohio State University	1962-1963
Walker, Dwight	Nicholls State University	1982-1984
Ward, Carl	University of Michigan	1967-1968
Warfield, Paul	Ohio State University	1964-1969, 1976-1977
Weathers, Clarence	Delaware State University	1985
Weathers, Curtis	University of Mississippi	1979-1986
White, Charles	University of Southern California	1980-1982, 1984

Player	College	Years
Williams, A.D.	College of Pacific	1960
Williams, Sidney	Southern University	1964-1966
Willis, Bill	Ohio State University	1946-1953
Wilson, Tom	(no college)	1962
Wooten, John	University of Colorado	1959-1967
Young, Glen	Mississippi State University	1984-1985
Youngblood, George	California State University, Los Angeles	1967

Dallas Cowboys
Dallas, Texas 75206

Coaches

		Years
Lavan, Al	(Assistant)	1983-1986

All-Pro or Pro Bowl Selections

	Years
Perkins, Don	1962
Renfro, Mel	1965, 1967
Hayes, Robert	1965-1969, 1971, 1973
Green, Cornell	1966-1969
Hill, Calvin	1969, 1970, 1973-1975
Wright, Rayfield	1971-1973, 1975
Pearson, Drew	1974, 1976-1977
Martin, Harvey	1977
Scott, Herbert	1980, 1981
Dorsett, Tony	1979, 1981-1984
Jones, Ed	1981, 1982-1984
Walls, Everson	1982, 1983-1986
Downs, Michael	1984

All-Time Team Roster

Player	College	Years
Adderly, Herb	Michigan State University	1970-1972
Albritton, Vince	University of Washington	1984-1986
Allen, Gary	University of Hawaii	1983-1984
Banks, Gordon	Stanford University	1985-1986
Barnes, Rodrigo	Rice University	1973-1974
Blackwell, Alois	University of Houston	1978-1979
Brooks, Kevin	University of Michigan	1985-1986
Brown, Guy	University of Houston	1977-1982
Brown, Otto	Prairie View A&M University	1969
Carmichael, Harold	Southern University	1984
Clack, Darryl	Arizona State University	1986
Clinkscale, Dexter	South Carolina State University	1980, 1982-1984

Player	College	Years
Cole, Larry	University of Hawaii	1968-1980
Coleman, Ralph	North Carolina A&T University	1972
Collier, Reggie	University of Southern Mississippi	1986
Davis, Don	Southern University	1962
Dickerson, Anthony	Southern Methodist University	1980-1986
Dorsett, Anthony	University of Pittsburgh	1977-1986
Downs, Michael	Rice University	1981-1985
DuPree, Bill Joe	Michigan State University	1972-1983
Fellows, Ron	University of Missouri	1981-1986
Fuggett, Jean	Amherst College	1972-1975
Granger, Norman	University of Iowa	1984
Green, Cornell	Utah State University	1962-1974
Harris, Duriel	New Mexico State University	1984-1985
Hayes, Robert	Florida A&M University	1965-1974
Hayes, Wendell	Humboldt State University	1963
Henderson, Thomas	Langston University	1975-1979
Heyman, Michael	Tennessee State University	1976-1986
Hill, Calvin	Yale University	1969-1974
Hill, Rod	Kentucky State University	1982-1983
Hill, Tony	Stanford University	1977-1986
Houston, William	Jackson State University	1974
Howard, Carl	Rutgers University	1984
Howard, Percy	Austin Peay State University	1975
Hunter, Monty	Salem College	1982
Jeffcoat, Jim	Arizona State University	1983-1986
Johnson, Butch	University of California, Riverside	1976-1983
Jones, Ed	Tennessee State University	1974-1978, 1980-1986
Jones, James	Mississippi State University	1980-1982, 1984-1985
King, Angelo	South Carolina State University	1981-1983
Lavette, Robert	Georgia Tech University	1985-1986
Lockhart, Eugene	University of Houston	1984-1986
Martin, Harvey	East Texas State University	1973-1983
McDaniels, David	Mississippi Valley State University	1968
McSwain, Charles	Clemson University	1983-1985
Mitchell, Aaron	University of Nevada, Las Vegas	1979-1980
Newhouse, Robert	University of Houston	1972-1983
Newsome, Tim	Winston-Salem State University	1980-1986
Norman, Pettis	Johnson C. Smith University	1962-1970
Pearson, Drew	University of Tulsa	1973-1983
Pearson, Preston	University of Illinois	1975-1980
Penn, Jesse	Virginia Tech University	1985-1986
Perkins, Don	University of New Mexico	1961-1968
Phillips, Kirk	University of Tulsa	1984-1985
Pinder, Cyril	University of Illinois	1973
Powe, Karl	Alabama State University	1985-1986
Pugh, Jethro	Elizabeth City State University	1965-1978

Player	*College*	*Years*
Reece, Beasley	North Texas State University	1976
Renfro, Mel	University of Oregon	1964-1977
Richards, Howard	University of Missouri	1981-1986
Richardson, Gloster	Jackson State University	1971
Rucker, Reggie	Boston University	1970-1971
Scott, Herbert	Virginia Union University	1975-1984
Scott, Victor	University of Colorado	1984-1986
Sherrod, Michael	University of California, Los Angeles	1986
Simmons, Cleo	Jackson State University	1983
Smith, J.D.	North Carolina A&T University	1965-1966
Smith, Tody	University of Southern California	1971-1972
Springs, Ron	Ohio State University	1979-1983
Stowe, Otto	Iowa State University	1973
Thomas, Duane	West Texas State University	1970-1971
Thomas, Ike	Bishop College	1971
Thurman, Dennis	University of Southern California	1978-1985
Turner, James	Presbyterian College	1984
Walker, Herschel	University of Georgia	1986
Walls, Everson	Grambling State University	1981-1986
Washington, Mark	Morgan State University	1970-1978
Wilson, Steven	Howard University	1979-1981
Wright, Rayfield	Fort Valley State University	1967-1979
Young, Charles	North Carolina State University	1974-1976

Denver Broncos

Denver, Colorado 80204

Front Office Personnel

Years

Lee, Charles   (Director of Player and Community Relations)

Coaches

West, Charles   (Assistant)   1986

All-Pro or Pro Bowl Selections
(American Football League until 1970)

		Years
Taylor, Lionel	All-AFL	1960-1962, 1965
Brown, Willie	All-AFL	1964
Gilchrist, Cookie	All-AFL	1965
Denson, Al	All-AFL	1967
Wilson, Nemiah	All-AFL	1967
Jackson, Rich	All-AFL	1968-1971
Little, Floyd	All-AFL	1968-1973
Moses, Haven		1973
Odoms, Riley		1973-1975, 1978

Armstrong, Otis	1974, 1976
Upchurch, Rich	1976, 1978, 1979, 1982
Jackson, Tom	1977-1979, 1984
Thompson, William	1977-1978, 1981
Wright, Louis	1977-1979, 1983
Winder, Sam	1984
Smith, Dennis	1984

All-Time Team Roster

Player	College	Years
Alexander, Ray	Florida A&M University	1984-1985
Armstrong, Otis	Purdue University	1973-1980
Atkinson, George	Morris Brown College	1979
Barnes, Ernest	North Carolina College	1963-1964
Bowyer, Walter	Arizona State University	1983-1985
Brewer, Chris	University of Arizona	1984-1985
Briscoe, Marlin	University of Omaha	1968
Brown, Boyd	Alcorn A&M University	1974-1976
Brown, Willie	Grambling College	1963-1966
Canada, Larry	University of Wisconsin	1978-1979, 1981
Carter, Rubin	University of Miami (Florida)	1975-1985
Charous, Barney	South Carolina State University	1973-1985
Coleman, Steven	Delaware State University	1974
Comeaux, Darren	Arizona State University	1982-1986
Crenshaw, Willis	Kansas State University	1982-1985
Davis, Marvin	Wichita State University	1966
Denson, Al	Florida A&M University	1964-1970
Dixon, Hewritt	Florida A&M University	1963-1965
Dixon, Zachary	Temple University	1979
Dupree, Myron	North Carolina Central University	1983
Farr, Miller	Wichita State University	1965
Fletcher, Simon	University of Houston	1985-1986
Frazier, Al	Florida A&M University	1961-1963
Gavin, Charles E.	Tennessee State University	1960-1963
Gilbert, Fred	(no college)	1986
Gilchrist, Cookie	(no college)	1965-1967
Gordon, Cornell	North Carolina A&T University	1970-1972
Graves, Marsharne	University of Arizona	1984-1985
Greer, James D.	Elizabeth City State University	1960
Harden, Michael	University of Michigan	1980-1986
Harrison, Dwight	Texas A&I University	1971-1972
Hayes, Wendell	Humboldt State University	1965-1967
Hayes, Abner	North Texas State University	1965-1966
Haywood, Alfred	Bethune-Cookman College	1975
Hepburn, Lonnie	Texas Southern University	1974
Highsmith, Walter	Florida A&M University	1968-1969

Player	College	Years
Hood, Winford	University of Georgia	1984-1986
Hunley, Rick	University of Arizona	1984-1986
Hunter, Daniel	Henderson State College	1985-1986
Jackson, Bernard	Washington State University	1977-1980
Jackson, Mark		1986
Jackson, Richard	Southern University	1967-1972
Jackson, Roger	Bethune-Cookman College	1982-1985
Jackson, Tom	University of Louisville	1973-1986
Jeter, Eugene	Arkansas AM&N	1966-1967
Joe, William (Billy)	Villanova University	1963-1964
Johnson, Michael (Butch)	University of California, Riverside	1984-1985
Johnson, Vance	University of Arizona	1985
Jones, Henry	Grambling University	1969
Kay, Clarence	University of Georgia	1984-1986
Kyle, Aaron	University of Wyoming	1980-1982
Lang, Gene	Louisiana State University	1984-1986
Lanier, Ken	Florida State University	1981-1986
Lassiter, Ike T	St. Augustine's College	1926-1964
Lewis, Herman	Virginia Union University	1968
Little, Floyd	Syracuse University	1967-1975
Manning, Wade	Ohio State University	1981-1982
McCutcheon, Lawrence	Colorado State University	1980
Mitchell, Leroy	Texas Southern University	1971-1973
Mobley, Orson		1986
Moore, Alex	Norfolk State University	1968
Moore, Leroy	Fort Valley State College (Georgia)	1964-1965
Moorehead, Emery	University of Colorado	1980
Moses, Haven	San Diego State University	1972-1981
Moten, Robert	Bishop College	1968
Myers, Wilbur	Delta State College	1963
Myles, Jesse	Louisiana State University	1983-1985
Parish, Don	Stanford University	1972
Parros, Rick	Utah State University	1981-1985
Radford, Bruce	Grambling State University	1979
Robbins, Randy	University of Arizona	1984-1986
Roche, Alden	Southern University	1970
Ross, Oliver	Alabama A&M University	1973-1975
Sampson, Clint	San Diego State University	1983-1986
Seller, Goldie	Grambling State University	1966-1967
Sewell, Steve	University of Oklahoma	1985-1986
Simmons, Jerry	Bethune-Cookman College	1971-1974
Simmons, Leon	Grambling College	1973
Smith, Aaron	Utah State University	1984-1985
Smith, Dennis	University of Southern California	1981-1986
Smith, Don	Florida A&M University	1967
Stowe, Otto	Iowa State University	1974
Taylor, Lionel T.	New Mexico Highlands	1960-1966

Player	College	Years
Thomas, Earlie	Colorado State University	1975
Thomas, J.T.	Florida State University	1982
Thomas, Zack		
Thompson, William	Maryland State College	1969-1981
Townsend, Andre	University of Mississippi	1984-1986
Turk, Godwin	Southern University	1976-1978
Tyler, Maurice	Morgan State University	1973-1974
Wade, Robert	Morgan State University	1970
Washington, David	Alcorn A&M University	1971
West, William	Tennessee State University	1972
White, Andre	Florida A&M University	1967
Willhite, Gerald	San Jose State University	1982-1986
Wilson, Nemiah	Grambling State University	1965-1967
Wilson, Steven	Howard University	1982-1986
Winder, Sam	University of Southern Mississippi	1982-1986
Woodward, Ken	Tuskegee Institute	1982-1986
Wright, James	Texas Christian University	1980-1985
Wright, Louis	San Jose State University	1975-1986

Detroit Lions
Pontiac, Michigan 48057

Front Office Personnel		*Years*
Lane, Richard	(Administrative Assistant)	
Canty, Otis	(Office Superintendent)	

Coaches

Shaw, Willie	(Assistant)	1985-1986
Raye, Jimmy	(Assistant)	1978-1979
Phillips, Mel	(Assistant)	1980-1984
Williams, Ivy	(Assistant)	1985-1986

All-Pro or Pro Bowl Selections

	Years
Lane, Dick	1961-1963
Brown, Roger	1963-1967
Barney, Lem	1968-1970, 1973-1974, 1976-1977
Farr, Mel	1968, 1971
Sanders, Charles	1969-1972, 1975, 1977
Hill, David	1978, 1979
Baker, Al	1978-1980
Sims, Billy	1980-1982
Gay, William	1983

All-Time Team Roster

Player	College	Years
Allen, Jimmy	University of California, Los Angeles	1978-1981
Allen, Nate	Texas Southern University	1979
Baker, Al	Colorado State University	1978-1982
Baker, John	North Carolina College	1968
Barnes, Al	New Mexico State University	1971-1973
Barnes, Roosevelt	Purdue University	1982-
Barney, Lem	Jackson State University	1967-1977
Bell, Robert	University of Cincinnati	1971-1973
Bland, Carl	Virginia Union University	1984-1986
Blue, Luther	Iowa State University	1977-1979
Bolton, Andy	Fisk University	1976-1978
Bostic, John	Bethune Cookman College	1985-1986
Bradley, Luther	University of Notre Dame	1978-1981
Briscoe, Marlin	University of Nebraska, Omaha	1975-1976
Brooks, Jon	Clemson University	1979
Brown, Charles	Northern Arizona University	1970
Brown, Lomas	University of Florida	1985-1986
Brown, Marvin	East Texas State University	1957
Brown, Roger	Maryland State College	1960-1966
Burns, Michael	University of Southern California	1978
Bussey, Dexter	University of Texas, Arlington	1974-1984
Caver, James	University of Missouri	1983
Clark, Al	Eastern Michigan University	1971
Clark, Ernest	Michigan State University	1963-1967
Cobb, Gary	University of Southern California	1979-
Cofer, Michael	University of Tennessee	1983-1986
Cole, Eddie	University of Mississippi	1979-1980
Cotton, Craig	Youngston College	1969-1972
Cottrell, William	Delaware Valley College	1967-1970
Cole, Curley	Arizona State University	1980-1981
Davis, Ben	Defiance	1974-1976
Dunlap, Leonard	North Texas State University	1975
Elam, Cleveland	Tennessee State University	1979
Elias, Homer	Tennessee State University	1978-
Ellis, Ken	Southern University	1979-
Evans, Leon	University of Miami	1985-1986
Farr, Mel	University of California, Los Angeles	1967-1973
Farr, Miller	Wichita State University	1973
Fells, Robert	Florida A&M University	1965-1967
Ferguson, Keith	Ohio State University	1985-1986
Franklin, Dennis	University of Michigan	1975-1976
Gaines, Lawrence	University of Wyoming	1976-1979
Galloway, Duane	Arizona State University	1985-1986
Gay, William	University of Southern California	1978-
Germany, Willie	Morgan State University	1973

Player	College	Years
Gibson, Paul	University of Houston	1971
Graham, William	University of Texas	1982-1986
Gray, Hector	Florida State University	1981-1983
Green, Curtis	Alabama State University	1981-1986
Greer, Albert	Jackson State University	1963
Griffin, James	Middle Tennessee State University	1986
Groomes, Melvin	Indiana University	1948-1949
Hall, Alvin	University of Miami (Ohio)	1981-
Harrell, James	University of Florida	1979-1986
Harvey, Maurice	Ball State University	1983
Henderson, John	University of Michigan	1965-1967
Hicks, R.C.	Humboldt State University	1975
Hill, David	Texas A&I University	1962-1982
Hill, J.D.	Arizona State University	1976-1978
Hill, Jimmy	Sam Houston State University	1965
Holland, Vernon	Tennessee State University	1980
Hooks, Jim	Central State University (Oklahoma)	1973-1976
Howard, Billy	Alcorn A&M University	1974-1976
Hunter, James	Grambling State University	1976-1982
Jackson, Ernest	Jackson State University	1979
James, Gary	Louisiana State University	1986
Jarvis, Ray	Norfolk State University	1974-1978
Jenkins, Keiv	Bucknell University	1983
Jenkins, Leon	West Virginia University	1972
Jessie, Ron	University of Kansas	1971-1974
Johnson, Demitrious	University of Missouri	1983-1986
Johnson, James	San Diego State University	1985-1986
Johnson, John Henry	Arizona State University	1957-1959
Johnson, Levi	Texas A&I University	1973-1977
Jones, James	University of Florida	1983-
Jones, Jimmie	University of California, Los Angeles	1974
Kearney, Jim	Prairie View A&M University	1965-1966
King, Angelo	South Carolina State College	1984-1986
King, Horace	University of Georgia	1975-1983
Lane, Dick	Scottsbluff Junior College	1960-1965
Laster, Don	Tennessee State University	1984-
Latimer, Al	Clemson University	1982-
Lee, Edward	South Carolina State University	1983
Lee, Larry	University of California, Los Angeles	1981-
Leonard, Tony	Virginia Union University	1978-1979
Lewis, Dan	University of Wisconsin	1958-1964
Lewis, David	University of California, Berkeley	1984-1986
Lewis, Eddie	University of Kansas	1979-1980
Mandley, Peter	Northern Arizona University	1984-1986
Mann, Robert	University of Michigan	1948-1949
Marsh, Amos	Oregon State University	1965-1967

Player	College	Years
Matson, Ollie	University of San Francisco	1963
Maxwell, Vernon	Arizona State University	1985-1986
McCall, Reese	Auburn University	1983-1985
McClung, Willie	Florida A&M University	1960-1961
McCray, Prentice	Arizona State University	1980
McCullough, Earl	University of Southern California	1968-1973
McNorton, Bruce	Georgetown (Kentucky)	1982-1986
Meade, Michael	Pennsylvania State University	1984-
Mendenhall, John	Grambling State University	1980
Mitchell, Devon	Iowa University	1986
Mitchell, Melvin	Tennessee State University	1977
Mitchell, Jim	Virginia State University	1970-1977
Moore, Alvin	Arizona State University	1985-1986
Moss, Martin	University of California, Los Angeles	1982-
Nichols, Mark	San Jose State University	1981-
Norris, Ulysses	University of Georgia	1979-1983
Parson, Ray	University of Minnesota	1971
Pinckney, Reginald	East Carolina University	1977-1978
Porter, Tracy	Louisiana State University	1981-1982
Potts, Charles	Purdue University	1972
Price, Ernest	Texas A&I University	1973-1978
Pureifory, David	Eastern Michigan University	1978-1982
Randolph, Al	University of Iowa	1972
Redmond, Rudy	University of Pacific	1972-1973
Reeberg, Lucien	Hampton University	1963
Rhodes, Bruce	San Francisco State University	1978
Robinson, Bo	West Texas State University	1979-1980
Robinson, John	Tennessee State University	1966-1967
Robinson, Shelton	University of North Carolina	1986
Rush, Jerry	Michigan State University	1965-1971
Sanders, Charles	University of Minnesota	1968-1977
Scott, Fred	Amherst College	1978-1983
Sims, Billy	University of Oklahoma	1980-
Smith, Wayne	Purdue University	1980-1982
Staggers, Jon	University of Missouri	1975
Taylor, Altie	Utah State University	1969-1976
Teal, Jim	Purdue University	1973
Tearly, Larry	Wake Forest University	1978-1979
Thompson, Robert	University of Arizona	1964-1968
Thompson, Jesse	University of California, Berkeley	1978-1981
Thompson, Leonard	Oklahoma State University	1975-1986
Thrower, Jim	East Texas State University	1973-1975
Todd, Jim	Ball State University	1966
Triplett, William	University of Miami (Ohio)	1968-1972
Triplett, Wallace	Pennsylvania State University	1949-1950
Turner, Harold	Tennessee State University	1954
Tyler, Maurice	Morgan State University	1976

Player	College	Years
Vaughn, Tom	Iowa State University	1965-1971
Walker, Willie	Tennessee State University	1966
Walton, Larry	Arizona State University	1969-1976
Washington, David	Alcorn State University	1978-1979
Washington, Eugene	Stanford University	1979
Watkins, Robert	Southwest Texas State University	1982-1985
Watkins, Larry	Alcorn A&M University	1969
Wells, Warren	Texas Southern University	1964
West, Charles	University of Texas, El Paso	1974-1977
White, Darryl	University of Nebraska	1974
Williams, Robert	Central State University	1969-1971
Williams, Jimmy	University of Nebraska	1982-1986
Williams, Walt	New Mexico State University	1977-1981
Woods, Larry	Tennessee State University	1971-1972
Woods, Robert	Grambling State University	1979

Green Bay Packers

1265 Lombardi Avenue
Green Bay, Wisconsin 54303-1231

Coaches		Years
Roland, John	(Assistant)	1974
Colbert, Jim	(Assistant)	1975
McMillan, Ernest	(Assistant)	1979-1983
Riley, Ken	(Assistant)	1984

All-Pro or Pro Bowl Selections

	Years
Davis, Willie	1962, 1964, 1965, 1966, 1967
Adderley, Herb	1962, 1963, 1965, 1966, 1969
Wood, Willie	1963, 1964, 1965, 1966, 1967, 1968
Robinson, David	1967, 1968, 1969
Jeter, Robert	1967
Brockington, John	1971, 1972, 1973
Ellis, Ken	1972, 1973, 1974
Carr, Fred	1974
Buchanon, Willie	1978
Lofton, James	1980, 1981, 1982, 1983
Douglass, Michael	1982

All-Time Team Roster

Player	College	Years
Adderley, Herb	Michigan State University	1961-1969
Aldridge, Lionel	Utah State University	1963-1971
Anderson, Vickey Ray	University of Oklahoma	1980
Askson, Bert	Texas Southern University	1975
Barber, Robert	Grambling State University	1976-1979
Barnes, Emery	University of Oregon	1956
Boyd, Elmo	Eastern Kentucky University	1978
Boyd, Greg	San Diego State University	1983
Brackins, Charles	Prairie View A&M University	1955
Braggs, Byron	University of Alabama	1981-1983
Brockington, John	Ohio State University	1971-1977
Brown, Aaron	University of Minnesota	1973-1974
Brown, Bob	Arkansas AM&N	1966-1973
Brown, Robert L.	Virginia Tech University	1982-1986
Brown, Tim	Ball State University	1959
Buchanon, Willie	San Diego State University	1972-1978
Butler, Michael	University of Kansas	1977-1982, 1985-1986
Cade, Mossy	University of Texas	1985-1986
Carr, Fred	University of Texas, El Paso	1968-1977
Carreker, Alphonso	Florida State University	1984-1986
Carter, Michael	Sacramento State University	1970-1971
Chesley, Francis	University of Wyoming	1978
Clanton, Chuck	Auburn University	1985-1986
Clark, Jessie	University of Arkansas	1983-1986
Coffey, Junior	University of Washington	1965
Collins, Glen	Mississippi State University	1986
Crenshaw, Leon	Tuskegee Institute	1968
Culbreath, Jim	University of Oklahoma	1977-1979
Cumby, George	University of Oklahoma	1980-1986
Davis, David	Tennessee A&I	1971-1972
Davis, Ken	Texas Christian University	1986
Davis, Willie	Grambling State University	1960-1969
Dennard, Preston	University of New Mexico	1985-1986
Douglass, Michael	San Diego State University	1978
Edwards, Earl	Wichita State University	1979-1985
Ellerson, Gary	University of Wisconsin	1985-1986
Ellis, Gerry	University of Missouri	1980-1986
Epps, Phillip	Texas Christian University	1982-1986
Fields, Angelo	Michigan State University	1982
Fleming, Marv	University of Utah	1963-1969
Ford, Len	University of Michigan	1958
Garrett, Len	New Mexico Highlands	1971-1973
Glass, Leland	University of Oregon	1972-1973
Goodman, Les	Yankton College	1973-1976
Gray, Johnnie	California State University, Fullerton	1975-
Green, Jessie	University of Tulsa	1976

Player	College	Years
Hampton, David	University of Wyoming	1970-1971
Harden, Leon	University of Texas, El Paso	1970
Harrell, Willard	University of Pacific	1975-1977
Harris, Leon	University of Arkansas	1978-
Harrison, Reggie	University of Cincinnati	1978-
Harvey, Maurice	Ball State University	1981-1983
Hayes, Gary	Fresno State University	1984-1986
Highsmith, Don	Michigan State University	1973
Hill, Jim	Texas A&I University	1972-1974
Hood, Estus	Illinois State University	1978-1985
Huckleby, Harlan	University of Michigan	1980
Hudson, Robert	N.E. Oklahoma State	1972
Hunt, Ervin	Fresno State University	1970
Hunt, Sam	Stephen F. Austin State University	1980
Ivery, Eddie Lee	Georgia Tech University	1979-1986
Jackson, Mel	University of Southern California	1976-1980
James, Claudis	Jackson State University	1967-1969
Jefferson, John	San Diego State University	1981-1985
Jeter, Robert	University of Iowa	1963-1970
Johnson, Charles	University of Maryland	1979, 80, 83
Johnson, Danny	Tennessee State University	1978
Johnson, Ezra	Morris Brown College	1977-1986
Jones, Terry	University of Alabama	1978-1985
Landers, Walt	Clark College	1978-1979
Lane, McArthur	Utah State University	1972-1974
Lee, Mark	University of Washington	1980-1986
Lewis, Cliff	Southern Mississippi University	1981-
Lewis, Gary	University of Texas, Arlington	1981-
Lewis, Michael	Arkansas A&M University	1980-
Lewis, Tim	University of Pittsburgh	1983-
Lofton, James	Stanford University	1978-
Luke, Steven	Ohio State University	1975-1980
Mann, Bob	University of Michigan	1950-1954
Martin, Charles	Livingstone College	1984-1986
Matthews, Al	Texas A&I University	1975-1980
McBride, Al	University of Missouri	1973
McCoy, Michael	University of Colorado	1976-1983
McMath, Herb	Morningside College	1977
McMillan, Ernest	University of Illinois	1975
Meade, Michael	Penn State University	1982-1983
Middleton, Terdell	Memphis State University	1977-1981
Monroe, Henry	Mississippi State University	1979
Oats, Carlton	Florida A&M University	1973
Osteen, Dwayne	San Jose State University	1983-1984
Odom, Steven	University of Utah	1974-1979
Patton, Ricky	Jackson State University	1979
Payne, Ken	Langston	1974-1977

Reference Section

Player	College	Years
Peay, Francis	University of Missouri	1968-1972
Pitts, Ellitah	Philander Smith College	1961-1969, 1971
Prather, Guy	Grambling State University	1981-1986
Pureifory, David	Eastern Michigan University	1972-1977
Purnell, Frank	Alcorn A&M University	1957
Randolph, Terry	American International College	1977
Robinson, David	Penn State University	1963-1972
Roche, Alden	Southern University	1971-1976
Rodgers, Del	University of Utah	1982-1986
Rowser, John	University of Michigan	1967-1969
Sampson, Howard	University of Arkansas	1978-1979
Scales, Hurles	North Texas State University	1973
Simmons, David	University of North Carolina	1979-1980
Simpson, Nate	University of Tennessee	1977-1979
Smith, Blane	Purdue University	1977
Smith, Donnell	Southern University	1971
Smith, Ollie	Tennessee State University	1976-1977
Spinks, Jack	Alcorn A&M University	1955-1956
Staggers, John	University of Missouri	1972-1974
Stanley, Walter	Mesa	1985-1986
Stills, Ken	University of Wisconsin	1985-1986
Switzer, Veryl	Kansas State University	1954-1955
Taylor, Cliff	Memphis State University	1976
Thomas, Ike	Bishop College	1972
Thompson, Aundra	East Texas State College	1977-1981
Thompson, John	Utah State University	1979-1982
Tinker, Gerald	Kent State University	1975
Tullis, Walter	University of Delaware	1978-1979
Tunnell, Emlen	University of Iowa	1959-1961
Turner, Wylie	Angelo State University	1979-1980
Vanoy, Vernon	University of Kansas	1972
Walker, Cleo	University of Louisville	1970
Weaver, Gary	Fresno State University	1975-1979
Wells, Terry	Southern Mississippi University	1975
West, Ed	Auburn University	1984-1986
Williams, A.D.	University of Pacific	1959
Williams, Clarence	Prairie View A&M University	1970-1977
Williams, Delvin	University of Kansas	1981
Williams, Howard	Howard University	1962-1963
Williams, Perry	Purdue University	1969-1973
Williams, Travis	Arizona State University	1967-1970
Wilson, Ben	University of Southern California	1967
Winslow, Paul	North Carolina College	1960
Winters, Chet	University of Oklahoma	1983
Wood, Willie	University of Southern California	1960-1971

Houston Oilers
Houston, Texas 77251-1516

Front Office Personnel		Years
Alexander, Willie	(Career Consultant)	1981-1986

Coaches		Years
Gaines, Eugene	(Assistant)	1984-1986
Roberts, Al	(Assistant)	1984-1986
Houston, Ken	(Assistant)	1981-1986

All-Pro or Pro Bowl Selections
(American Football League before 1970)

	Years
Frazier, Willie	1965
Farr, Miller	1967, 1968
Webster, George	1967-1969
Reed, Alvin	1970
Houston, Ken	1971-1972
Bethea, Elvin	1973-1975, 1978-1979
Culp, Curly	1975-1978
Brazille, Robert	1977
Johnson, Billy	1977
Campbell, Earl	1978-1981, 1983
Gray, Leon	1979-1981
Roaches, Carl	1981

All-Time Team Roster

Player	*College*	*Years*
Abraham, Robert	North Carolina State University	1982-1986
Aldridge, Allen	Prairie View A&M University	1971-1972
Alexander, Willie	Alcorn State University	1971-1979
Allen, Patrick	Utah State University	1984-1986
Atkins, Robert	Grambling State University	1970-1975
Baker, Jesse	Jacksonville State University (Alabama)	1979-1986
Baker, Melvin	Texas Southern University	1972
Banks, Chuck	West Virginia Tech	1986
Barnes, Peter	Southern University	1967-1968
Bethea, Elvin	North Carolina A&T University	1968-1983
Blanks, Sid	Texas A&I University	1964-1968
Bostic, Keith	University of Michigan	1983-1986
Brazille, Robert	Jackson State University	1975-1985
Broadwax, Jerry	Southern University	1974
Brooks, Billy	University of Oklahoma	1981
Brown, Steven	University of Oregon	1983-1986
Bryant, Steven	Purdue University	1982-1985
Burrough, Ken	Texas Southern University	1971-1981
Burton, Al	Bethune-Cookman College	1976

Player	*College*	*Years*
Campbell, Earl	University of Texas	1978-1985
Caster, Richard	Jackson State University	1978-1980
Cheeks, B.W.	Texas Southern University	1965
Clark, Boobie	Bethune-Cookman College	1979-1980
Coleman, Ron	Alabama A&M University	1974-1981
Cowlings, Al	University of Southern California	1973-1974
Culp, Curly	Arizona State University	1974-1980
Davis, Donnie	Southern University	1970
Davis, Marvin	Southern University	1974
Dirden, John	Sam Houston University	1978
Douglas, John	Texas Southern University	1969-1970
Drewrey, Willie	West Virginia University	1985-1986
Drungo, Elbert	Tennessee State University	1969-1977
Edwards, Stan	University of Michigan	1982-1985
Fairley, Leonard	Alcorn A&M University	1974
Fairs, Eric	Memphis State University	1986
Farr, Miller	Wichita State University	1967-1969
Ferguson, Eugene	Norfolk State University	1971-1972
Fields, Angelo	Michigan State University	1980-1981
Foster, Jerome	Ohio State University	1983-1985
Frazier, Charles	Texas Southern University	1962-1968
Frazier, Willie	Arkansas AM&N	1964-1965, 1971-1975
Freelon, Solomon	Grambling College	1972-1974
Fuller, William	University of North Carolina	1986
Funchess, Tom	Jackson State University	1971-1973
Germany, Willie	Morgan State University	1975
Giles, Jimmy	Alcorn State University	1977
Givins, Ernest	University of Louisville	1986
Grant, Wes	University of California, Los Angeles	1973
Gray, Leon	Jackson State University	1979-1981
Griffin, Larry	University of North Carolina	1986
Hardeman, Don	Texas A&I University	1975-1977
Harvey, Claude	Prairie View A&M University	1970-1971
Hayes, Jim	Jackson State University	1965-1966
Haymond, Alvin	Southern University	1973
Henderson, Thomas	Langston University	1980
Hicks, W.K.	Texas Southern University	1964-1969
Highsmith, Walter	Florida A&M University	1972
Hill, Drew	Georgia Tech University	1985-1986
Hinton, Eddie	University of Oklahoma	1973
Holigan, Henry	Bishop College	1963
Holmes, Robert	Southern University	1971-1975
Houston, Michael	Morgan State University	1981-1985
Hopkins, Roy	Texas Southern University	1967-1981
Houston, Ken	Prairie View A&M University	1967-1972
Hunt, Darryl	University of Oklahoma	1979-1985

Player	College	Years
Jenkins, Al	Morris Brown College	1973
Johnson, Ben	Johnson C. Smith University	1970-1973
Johnson, Billy	Widener College	1974-1980
Johnson, John H.	Arizona State University	1966
Johnson, Michael	University of Illinois	1984-1985
Joiner, Charles	Grambling College	1969-1972
Jones, Harris	Johnson C. Smith University	1973-1974
Jones, Willie	Kansas State University	1967
Joyner, Willie	University of Maryland	1984-1985
King, Kenny	University of Oklahoma	1979
Ladd, Ernest	Grambling College	1966
Levias, Jerry	Southern Methodist University	1969-1970
Lyday, Allen	University of Nebraska	1984-1985
Lyles, Robert	Texas Christian University	1984-1986
Mayo, Ron	Morgan State University	1973
McMillian, Audrey	University of Houston	1985-1986
McNeil, Clifton	Grambling College	1973
Meadows, Darryl	University of Toledo	1983-1985
Meads, Johnny	Nichols State University	1984-1986
Miller, Ralph	Alabama State University	1972-1973
Mitchell, Leroy	Texas Southern University	1969-1970
Moon, Warren	University of Washington	1984-1986
Moore, Zeke	Lincoln University (Missouri)	1967-1977
Mullins, Eric	Stanford University	1984-1985
Nicholson, Oliver	Texas Southern University	1975
Owens, Joe	Alcorn State University	1976
Parker, Willie	Arkansas AM&N	1967-1970
Perkins, Willie	Texas Southern University	1961-1963
Perry, Vernon	Jackson State University	1979-1982
Queen, Jeff	Morgan State University	1974
Ransom, Brian	Tennessee State University	1983-1985
Reed, Alvin	Prairie View A&M University	1967-1972
Rice, Andy	Texas Southern University	1967
Rice, Floyd	Alcorn A&M University	1971-1973
Riley, Avon	University of California, Los Angeles	1981-1986
Roaches, Carl	Texas A&M University	1981-1984
Robinson, Paul	University of Arizona	1972-1973
Rodgers, Willie	Kentucky State University	1972-1975
Rozier, Michael	University of Nebraska	1984-1986
Rucker, Conrad	Southern University	1978-1979
Rudolph, Council	Kentucky State University	1972
Sledge, Leroy	Baskerfield Junior College	1971
Smith, Charles "Bubba"	Michigan State University	1975-1976
Smith, Doug	Auburn University	1984-1986
Smith, Tody	University of Southern California	1973-1976
Sowells, Rich	Alcorn State University	1977

Player	College	Years
Strahan, Arthur	Texas Southern University	1965
Studaway, Mark	University of Tennessee	1984-1985
Tatum, Jack	Ohio State University	1980
Taylor, Altie	Utah State University	1976
Taylor, Lionel	New Mexico Highlands University	1967-1968
Taylor, Malcolm	Tennessee State University	1982-1983
Thomas, Earl	University of Houston	1976
Thomas, Lee	Jackson State University	1975
Tolbert, Jim	Lincoln University	1972
Towns, Morris	University of Missouri	1977-1983
Tullis, Willie	Troy State University	1981-1985
Walls, Herrie	University of Texas	1981-1985
Washington, Ted	Mississippi Valley State University	1973-1982
Watson, Ed	Grambling College	1969
Webster, George	Michigan State University	1967-1972
White, John	Texas Southern University	1960-1961
Whitely, Wilson	University of Houston	1983
Whittington, C.L.	Prairie View A&M University	1974-1976, 1978
Wilkerson, Doug	North Carolina Central University	1970
Williams, Jamie	University of Nebraska	1984-1986
Williams, Ralph	Southern University	1982-1983
Wilson, J.C.	University of Pittsburgh	1978-1983
Woods, Robert	Grambling State University	1978
Wright, Elmo	University of Houston	1975
Wyatt, Alvin	Bethune-Cookman College	1973
Young, James	Texas Southern University	1977-1979

Indianapolis Colts

Indianapolis, Indiana 46254

Front Office Personnel

		Years
Powers, Clyde	(Pro Personnel Director)	1985-1986

Coaches

		Years
Matthews, Bill	(Assistant)	1985-1986

All-Pro or Pro Bowl Selections

	Years
Lipscomb, Eugene	1958-1960
Moore, Lenny	1958-1960
Parker, Jim	1958-1965
Moore, Len	1959-1961, 1964
Mackey, John	1963-1968
Lyles, Lenny	1966
Richardson, Willie	1967, 1968
Smith, Charles "Bubba"	1970, 1971

Mitchell, Lydell		1975-1977
Washington, Joe		1979
Hinton, Chris		1983

All-Time Team Roster

Player	College	Years
Anderson, Don	Purdue University	1985-1986
Anderson, Larry	Louisiana Tech University	1982-1985
Bailey, Elmer	University of Minnesota	1982
Barnes, Roosevelt	Purdue University	1986
Baylor, Tim	Morgan State University	1976-1978
Benson, Charles	Baylor University	1985-1986
Bentley, Albert	University of Miami	1985-1986
Brown, Tim	Ball State University	1968
Broughton, Willie	University of Miami	1985-1986
Burroughs, James	Michigan State University	1982-1985
Butler, Raymond	University of Southern California	1980-1985
Capers, Wayne	University of Kansas	1985-1986
Cherry, Stan	Morgan State University	1973
Chester, Raymond	Morgan State University	1973-1977
Coleman, Leonard	Vanderbilt University	1985-1986
Cooks, John	Mississippi State University	1982-1986
Danicl, Eugene	Louisiana State University	1984-1986
Davis, Norman	Grambling State University	1967
Davis, Preston	Baylor University	1984-1986
Dickey, Curtis	Texas A&M University	1980-1985
Dixon, Zach	Temple University	1980-1982
Donaldson, Ray	University of Georgia	1984-1986
Doughty, Glen	University of Michigan	1972-1979
Duncan, James	Maryland State College	1969-1971
Felts, Robert	Florida A&M University	1965
Fields, Greg	Grambling State University	1979-1980
Franklin, Cleveland	Baylor University	1981-1982
Gill, Owen	University of Iowa	1985-1986
Ginn, Hubert	Florida A&M University	1973
Glasgow, Nesby	University of Washington	1979-1986
Green, Anthony	North Carolina State University	1981
Harbour, James		1986
Hardeman, Don	Texas A&I University	1978-1979
Harrison, Dwight	Texas A&I University	1978-1979
Hatchett, Derrick	University of Texas	1980-1983
Haymond, Alvin	Southern University	1964-1967
Henry, Bernard	Arizona State University	1982-1985
Hepburn, Lonnie	Texas Southern University	1971-1972
Hilton, Roy	Jackson State University	1965-1973
Hinton, Chris	Northwestern University	1983-1986
Hinton, Ed	University of Oklahoma	1969-1972

Player	College	Years
Jefferson, Roy	University of Utah	1970
Johnson, Cornelius	Virginia Union University	1968-1972
Jones, Rick	Tuskegee Institute	1980-1983
Leaks, Roosevelt	University of Texas	1975-1979
Lee, Keith	Colorado State University	1985-1986
Lipscomb, Eugene	Miller High School	1956-1960
Lorick, Tony	Arizona State University	1964-1967
Lowry, Orlando	Ohio State University	1985-1986
Lyles, Len	University of Louisville	1958, 1961-1969
Mackey, John	Syracuse University	1963-1972
Maxwell, Vernon	Arizona State University	1983-1985
May, Ray	University of Southern California	1970-1972
Mayo, Ron	Morgan State University	1974
McMillan, Randy	University of Pittsburgh	1981-1986
Middleton, Frank	Florida A&M University	1984-1985
Mitchell, Lydell	Pennsylvania State University	1972-1977
Moore, Alvin	Arizona State University	1983-1985
Moore, Lenny	Pennsylvania State University	1956-1967
Mumphord, Lloyd	Texas Southern University	1975-1978
Munsey, Nelson	University of Wyoming	1972-1977
Newsome, William	Grambling State University	1970-1972
Nichols, Rick	East Carolina University	1985-1986
Odom, Cliff	University of Texas, Arlington	1984-1986
Orduna, Joe	University of Nebraska	1974
O'Steen, Dwayne	San Jose State University	1982
Owens, R.C.	College of Idaho	1962
Parker, Jim	Ohio State University	1957-1967
Pearson, Preston	University of Illinois	1967-1968
Perry, Joe	Compton College	1961-1962
Plunkett, Sherman	Maryland State College	1958-1960
Porter, Tracey	Louisiana State University	1983-1985
Richardson, Willie	Jackson State University	1963-1969, 1971
Robinson, Charles	Morgan State University	1954
Salters, Bryant	University of Pittsburgh	1976
Sample, John	Maryland State College	1958-1960
Scott, Chris	Purdue University	1984-1986
Scott, Freddie	Amherst College	1974-1977
Smith, Byron	University of California, Berkeley	1984-1986
Smith, Charles "Bubba"	Michigan State University	1967-1971
Smith, Ollie	Tennessee State University	1973-1974
Stevens, Howard	University of Louisville	1975-1977
Stukes, Charles	Maryland State College	1967-1972
Taliaferro, George	Indiana University	1953-1954
Taylor, Hosea	University of Houston	1981, 1983
Thomas, Jesse	Michigan State University	1955-1957
Thompson, Aundra	East Texas State University	1983
Thompson, Norm	University of Utah	1977-1979

Player	College	Years
Wallace, Jackie	University of Arizona	1975-1976
Washington, Joe	University of Oklahoma	1978-1980
Williams, Kevin	University of Southern California	1981
Williams, Oliver	University of Illinois	1985-1986
Wonsley, George	Mississippi State University	1984-1986
Young, Anthony	Temple University	1985-1986
Young, David	Purdue University	1983-1984

Kansas City Chiefs
Kansas City, Missouri 64129

Front Office Personnel		Years
Taylor, Otis	(Scout)	1977-1986

Coaches		Years
Daniel, Dan	(Assistant)	1983-1984
Peete, Willie	(Assistant)	1983-1986

All-Pro or Pro Bowl Selections
(American Football League before 1970)

	Years
Haynes, Abner	1960-1962
Bell, Robert	1966-1973
Buchanan, Buck	1966-1972
Marsalis, Jim	1970, 1971
Culp, Curly	1971, 1972
Taylor, Otis	1971-1973
Thomas, Emmitt	1971-1973, 1975-1976
Lanier, Willie	1971-1976
Still, Art	1981-1983, 1985
Smith, J.T.	1981
Delaney, Joe	1982
Green, Gary	1983, 1984
Cherry, Deron	1984, 1985
Carson, Carlos	1984

All-Time Team Roster

Player	College	Years
Allen, Nate	Texas Southern University	1971-1974
Anderson, Curtis	Central State University (Ohio)	1979
Austin, Hise	Prairie View A&M University	1975
Bell, Robert	University of Minnesota	1963-1974
Belser, Caesar	Arkansas AM&N	1968-1971
Blanton, Jerry	University of Kentucky	1979-1986
Brannon, Soloman	Morris Brown College	1965-1966

Player	College	Years
Brockington, John	Ohio State University	1977
Brown, Aaron	University of Minnesota	1966-1972
Brown, Theotis	University of California, Los Angeles	1983-1985
Brunson, Larry	University of Colorado	1974-1977
Buchanan, Julius	Grambling College	1963-1975
Burruss, Lloyd	University of Maryland	1981-1986
Carson, Carlos	Louisiana State University	1980-1986
Cherry, Deron	Rutgers University	1981-1986
Christopher, Herb	Morris Brown College	1979-1982
Culp, Curly	Arizona State University	1968-1974
Daniels, Calvin	University of North Carolina	1982-1985
Daniels, Clemon	Prairie View A&M University	1960
Delaney, Joe	N.W. Louisiana University	1981-1982
Dirden, Jon	Sam Houston State University	1979
Dorsey, Larry	Tennessee State University	1978
Ellison, Willie	Texas Southern University	1973-1974
Estes, Lawrence	Alcorn A&M University	1975-1976
Frazier, Willie	Arkansas AM&N	1972
Gaines, Clark	Wake Forest University	1981-1982
Garrett, Michael	University of Southern California	1966-1970
Granderson, Rufus	Prairie View A&M University	1960
Green, Gary	Baylor University	1977-1983
Green, Woody	Arizona State University	1974-1976
Gunter, Michael	University of Tulsa	1984-1985
Hadley, David	Alcorn State University	1970-1972
Hancock, Anthony	University of Tennessee	1982-1985
Harris, Eric	Memphis State University	1980-1982
Hayes, Wendell	Humboldt State University	1968-1974
Haynes, Abner	North Texas State University	1960-1965
Haynes, Louis	North Texas State University	1982-1983
Heard, Herman	University of Southern Colorado	1984-1986
Helton, Darius	North Carolina Central University	1977
Hicks, Sylvester	Tennessee State University	1978-1981
Hill, Jim	Sam Houston University	1966
Hill, Mack Lee	Southern University	1964-1965
Hines, Jim	Texas Southern University	1970
Holmes, Robert	Southern University	1968-1971
Jackson, Billy	University of Alabama	1981-1985
Jeralds, Luther	North Carolina College	1961
Kearney, Jim	Prairie View A&M University	1967-1975
Keyes, Leroy	Purdue University	1973
Lacy, Ken	University of Tulsa	1984-1986
Ladd, Ernest	Grambling College	1967-1968
Lane, MacArthur	Utah State University	1975-1978
Lanier, Willie	Morgan State University	1967-1977

Player	College	Years
Lee, Willie	Bethune-Cookman College	1976-1977
Lewis, Albert	Grambling State University	1983-1986
Lowe, Paul	Oregon State University	1968-1969
Marsalis, Jim	Tennessee State University	1969-1975
Marshall, Henry	University of Missouri	1976-1985
McAlister, Ken	University of San Francisco	1984-1985
McClinton, Curtis	University of Kansas	1962-1969
McKnight, Ted	University of Minnesota, Duluth	1977-1981
McRae, Jerrald	Tennessee State University	1978
McVea, Warren	University of Houston	1969-1973
Miller, Cleophus	Arkansas AM&N	1974-1975
Mitchell, Willie	Tennessee State University	1964-1971
Osley, Willie	University of Illinois	1974
Paige, Stephone	Fresno State University	1983-1985
Parker, Kerry	Grambling State University	1984-1986
Parrish, Don	University of Pittsburgh	1978-1982
Payton, Eddie	Jackson State University	1978
Peay, Francis	University of Missouri	1973-1974
Pitts, Frank	Southern University (Louisiana)	1965-1971
Porter, Lewis	Southern University (Louisiana)	1970
Reed, Tony	University of Colorado	1977-1980
Rice, Andrew	Texas Southern University	1966
Richardson, Gloster	Jackson State University	1967-1970
Rome, Stan	Clemson University	1979-1982
Rose, Donovan	Hampton Institute	1980
Ross, Kevin	Temple University	1984-1986
Ross, Louis	South Carolina State University	1975
Samuels, Tony	Bethune-Cookman College	1981-1984
Scott, Willie	University of South Carolina	1971-1975
Sellers, Goldie	Grambling College	1968-1969
Smith, Fletcher	Tennessee A&I University	1966-1967
Smith, Frankie	Alabama A&M University	1980
Smith, J.T.	North Texas State University	1978-1986
Smith, Lucious	California State University, Fullerton	1983
Smith, Noland	Tennessee State University	1967-1969
Still, Art	University of Kentucky	1978-1986
Stroud, Morris	Clark College	1969-1974
Taylor, Otis	Prairie View A&M University	1965-1975
Thomas, Charles	Tennessee State University	1975
Thomas, Emmitt	Bishop College	1966-1978
Thomas, Eugene	Florida A&M University	1966-1967
Thomas, Jewell	San Jose State University	1983
Thomas, Ken	San Jose State University	1983
Urshaw, Marvin	Trinity College	1970-1975
Wade, Charles	Tennessee State University	1977

Player	College	Years
Warner, Charles	Prairie View A&M University	1963-1964
Webster, David	Prairie View A&M University	1960-1961
White, Walter	University of Maryland	1975-1979
Williamson, Fred	Northwestern University	1965-1967
Wolf, James	Prairie View A&M University	1976
Wright, Almo	University of Houston	1971-1974
Young, Wilbur	William Penn College	1971-1977

Los Angeles Raiders
El Segundo, California 90245

Coaches

		Years
Brown, Willie	(Assistant)	1979-1986
Shell, Art	(Assistant)	1983-1986

All-Pro or Pro Bowl Selections
(American Football League until 1970)

	Years
Williamson, Fred	1962, 1963
Daniels, Clemson	1963
Upshaw, Eugene	1967-1974
Dixon, Hewritt	1968-1973
Brown, Willie	1968-1973
Wells, Warren	1969
Brown, Robert	1971
Shell, Art	1973-1978, 1980
Branch, Cliff	1974, 1975
Tatum, Jack	1973-1975
Chester, Ray	1970-1972, 1979
Hayes, Lester	1980-1984
Allen, Marcus	1982, 1984-1985
Martin, Rod	1984
Haynes, Michael	1984
King, Kenny	1980
Lawrence, Henry	1983, 1984

All-Time Team Roster

Player	College	Years
Adams, Stefon	East Carolina University	
Allen, Marcus	University of Southern California	1982-1986
Atkinson, George	Morris Brown College	1968-1977
Barksdale, Rod	University of Arizona	1985-1986
Barnes, Jeff	University of California, Berkeley	1977-1986
Barnes, Rodrigo	Rice University	1976
Barnwell, Malcolm	Virginia Union University	1981-1984

Player	College	Years
Bell, Joseph	Norfolk State University	1979
Bess, Rufus	Southern Carolina State University	1979
Bradshaw, Morris	Ohio State University	1974-1981
Branch, Cliff	University of Colorado	1972-1985
Brown, Robert	University of Nebraska	1971-1973
Brown, Willie	Grambling College	1967-1968
Brunson, Larry	University of Colorado	1978-1979
Bryant, Warren	University of Kentucky	1984-1985
Caldwell, Tony	University of Washington	1983-1985
Carter, Louis	University of Maryland	1975
Chester, Raymond	Morgan State University	1970-1972, 1978-1981
Colzie, Neal	Ohio State University	1975-1978
Cooper, Earl	Rice University	1986
Daniels, Clemon	Prairie View A&M University	1961-1967
Daniels, David	Florida A&M University	1966
Davis, Bruce	University of California, Los Angeles	1979-1986
Davis, Clarence	University of Southern California	1971-1978
Davis, James	Southern University	1982-1985
Davis, Michael	University of Colorado	1978-1985
Dickey, Eldridge	Tennessee State University	1968-1971
Dixon, Hewritt	Florida A&M University	1966-1970
Dotson, Al	Grambling College	1968-1970
Eason, John	Florida A&M University	1968
Garrett, Carl	New Mexico Highlands University	1976-1977
Ginn, Hubert	Florida A&M University	1976-1978
Hall, Willie	University of Southern California	1975-1978
Hardman, Cedric	North Texas State University	1980-1981
Harrison, Dwight	Texas A&I University	1980
Hart, Harold	Texas Southern University	1974-1975, 1978
Hawkins, Clarence	Florida A&M University	1979
Hawkins, Frank	University of Nevada, Reno	1981-1986
Hayes, Lester	Texas A&M University	1977-1986
Haynes, Michael	Arizona State University	1983-1986
Hester, Jessie	Florida State University	1985-1986
Hipp, I.M.	University of Nebraska	1980
Irons, Gerald	Maryland State College	1970-1975
Jackson, Monte	San Diego State University	1978-1982
Jackson, Richard	Southern University	1966
Jones, Horace	University of Louisville	1971-1975
Jones, Sean	Northeastern University	1984-1986
Jones, Willie	Florida State University	1979-1982
Jordan, Shelby	Washington (Missouri)	1983-1986
King, Kenneth	University of Oklahoma	1980-1985
Kinlaw, Reginald	University of Oklahoma	1979-1985
Lassiter, Isaac	St. Augustine's College	1965-1969
Lawrence, Henry	Florida A&M University	1974-1986
Martin, Rod	University of Southern California	1977-1986

Player	*College*	*Years*
Matthews, Ira	University of Wisconsin	1979-1981
McCall, Jeff	Clemson University	1984-1985
McCall, Joe	University of Pittsburgh	1984-1985
McCallum, Napoleon	U.S. Naval Academy	1986
McKenzie, Reggie	University of Tennessee	1985-1986
McKinney, Odis	University of Colorado	1980-1985
Montgomery, Cle	Abilene Christian University	1981-1985
Moore, Manfred	University of Southern California	1976
Morris, Riley	Florida A&M University	1960-1962
Muhammad, Calvin	Texas Southern University	1982-1983
Oats, Carlton	Florida A&M University	1965-1972
O'Steen, Dwayne	San Jose State University	1980-1981
Owens, Burgess	University of Miami (Florida)	1980-1982
Phillips, Charles	University of Southern California	1975-1980
Phillips, Jess	Michigan State University	1975
Philyaw, Charles	Texas Southern University	1976-1979
Pitts, Frank	Southern University	1974
Pruitt, Gregory	University of Oklahoma	1982-1985
Queen, Jeff	Morgan State University	1973
Ramsey, Derrick	University of Kentucky	1978-1983
Rice, Floyd	Alcorn A&M University	1976-1977
Rice, Harold	Tennessee State University	1971
Roberson, Bo	Cornell University	1962-1965
Robinson, Jerry	University of California, Los Angeles	1985-1986
Russell, Booker	Southwest Texas State University	1978-1979
Seale, Sam	Western State (Colorado)	1984-1986
Sheil, Arthur	Maryland State College	1968-1982
Simpson, Willie	San Francisco State	1962
Sistrunk, Otis	(no college)	1972-1979
Smith, Charles "Bubba"	Michigan State University	1973-1974
Smith, Willie	University of Michigan	1961
Tatum, Jack	Ohio State University	1971-1979
Taylor, Bill	Texas Tech University	1982
Thomas, Skip	University of Southern California	1972-1978
Toran, Stacey	University of Notre Dame	1984-1986
Townsend, Greg	Texas Christian University	1983-1986
Upshaw, Eugene	Texas A&I University	1967-1982
Walker, Fulton	University of West Virginia	1985-1986
Watts, Ted	Texas Tech University	1981-1985
Weathers, Carl	San Diego State University	1970-1971
Wells, Warren	Texas Southern University	1967-1970
Wheeler, Dwight	Tennessee State University	1984-1985
White, Eugene	Florida A&M University	1962
Whittington, Arthur	Southern Methodist University	1978-1981
Williams, Dokie	University of California, Los Angeles	1983-1986
Williams, Howard	Howard University	1964-1969
Williams, Willie	Grambling College	1966

Player	College	Years
Williamson, Fred	Northwestern University	1961-1964
Willis, Chester	Auburn University	1981-1985
Wilson, Nemiah	Grambling College	1968-1974
Wyatt, Alvin	Bethune-Cookman College	1970

Los Angeles Rams
Anaheim, California 92801

Coaches

		Years
Brooks, Larry	(Assistant)	1983-1986
Dixon, Hewritt	(Assistant)	1980-1981
Pitts, Elijah	(Assistant)	1974-1977
Raye, Jimmy	(Assistant)	1983-1984
Taylor, Lionel	(Assistant)	1977-1981

All-Pro or Pro Bowl Selections

	Years
Towler, Dan	1951-1954
Younger, Paul	1951-1953
Wilson, Tom	1956, 1957
Bass, Dick	1962, 1963
Jones, David	1964-1970
Brown, Roger	1967, 1969
Casey, Bernie	1967
Brown, Robert	1969, 1970
Robertson, Isiah	1971, 1973-1977
Ellison, Willie	1971
Jackson, Harold	1973, 1975
McCutcheon, Lawrence	1973-1977
Brooks, Larry	1976, 1978-1980
Jackson, Monte	1976, 1977
Jessie, Ron	1976
Jones, Cody	1978
Perry, Rod	1978, 1980
Thomas, Pat	1978, 1980
Hill, Kent	1980, 1982-1984
Dickerson, Eric	1983-1986
Ellard, Henry	1984
Brown, Ron	1985

All-Time Team Roster

Player	College	Years
Alexander, Kermit	University of California, Los Angeles	1970-1971
Bacon, Coy	Jackson State University	1968-1972
Baker, John	North Carolina College	1958-1961

Player	College	Years
Bass, Dick	University of Pacific	1960-1969
Bishop, Richard	University of Louisville	1983
Brooks, Larry	Virginia State University	1972-1982
Brown, Robert	University of Nebraska	1969-1970
Brown, Roger	Maryland State College	1967-1969
Brown, Ron	Arizona State University	1984-1985
Bryant, Cullen	University of Colorado	1973-1982
Casey, Bernie	Bowling Green State University	1967-1968
Childs, Henry	Kansas State University	1981
Collins, Kirk	Baylor University	1982-1983
Cowan, Charles	New Mexico Highlands University	1961-1975
Cowlings, Al	University of Southern California	1975, 1977
Cross, Irv	Northwestern University	1966-1968
Croodip, David	San Diego State University	1984-1985
Crutchfield, Dwayne	Iowa State University	1984-1985
Davis, Anthony	University of Southern California	1978
DeJurnett, Charles	San Jose State University	1982-1986
Dennard, Preston	University of New Mexico	1978-1983
Dickerson, Eric	Southern Methodist University	1983-1986
Doss, Reginald	Hampton University	1978-1985
Duckworth, Bobby	University of Arkansas	1985-1986
Dyer, Henry	Grambling State University	1966-1968
Ellard, Henry	Fresno State University	1983-1986
Ellis, Ken	Southern University	1979
Ellison, Willie	Texas Southern University	1967-1972
Farmer, George	Southern University	1982-1985
Gordon, Dick	Michigan State University	1972-1973
Grant, Otis	Michigan State University	1983-1984
Gray, Jerry	University of Texas	1985-1986
Green, Gary	Baylor University	1984-1986
Grier, Roosevelt	Pennsylvania State University	1963-1966
Harris, Eric	Memphis State University	1983-1986
Harris, James	Grambling State University	1973-1976
Haymond, Alvin	Southern University	1969-1971
Hill, David	Texas A&I University	1983-1985
Hill, Drew	Georgia Tech University	1979-1985
Hill, Kent	Georgia Tech University	1979-1986
Hill, Winston	Texas Southern University	1977
Howard, Eugene	Langston University	1971-1972
Hunter, Anthony	University of Notre Dame	1985
Inglehart, Floyd	Wiley College	1958
Irvin, LeRoy	University of Kansas	1980-1986
Jackson, Harold	Jackson State University	1968, 1973-1977
Jackson, Monte	San Diego State University	1975-1977
Jessie, Ron	University of Kansas	1975-1979
Jeter, Gary	University of Southern California	1983-1986
Johnson, Johnnie	University of Texas	1980-1986

Player	*College*	*Years*
Jones, A.J.	University of Texas	1982
Jones, Cody	San Jose State University	1974-1978, 1980-1982
Jones, David	South Carolina State College	1961-1971
Jones, Gordon	University of Pittsburgh	1983-1984
Justin, Sid	Long Beach State University	1979
Kenerson, John	Kentucky State University	1960
Lane, Dick	Scottsbluff Junior College	1952-1953
Lang, Israel	Tennessee State University	1969
Lewis, David	University of Southern California	1983
Lipscomb, Eugene	Miller High School (Michigan)	1953-1955
Lundy, Lamar	Purdue University	1957-1969
Martin, Aaron	North Carolina College	1964-1965
Matson, Ollie	University of San Francisco	1959-1962
McCutcheon, Lawrence	Colorado State University	1972-1979
McDonald, James	University of Southern California	1983-1986
McGee, Willie	Alcorn A&M University	1974-1975
McKeever, Marvin	University of Southern California	1961-1966, 1971-1972
Miller, Willie	Colorado State University	1978-1982
Mitchell, Lydell	Pennsylvania State University	1980
Molden, Frank	Jackson State University	1965
Murphy, Phil	South Carolina State University	1980-1981
Nelson, Terry	Arkansas AM&N	1973-1980
Newsome, Vincent	University of Washington	1983-1986
O'Steen, Dwayne	San Jose State University	1978-1979
Pankey, Irv	Pennsylvania State University	1980-1986
Parish, Don	Stanford University	1971
Peacock, Elvis	University of Oklahoma	1979-1980
Perry, Rod	University of Colorado	1975-1982
Phillips, Rod	Jackson State University	1975-1978
Pitts, Elijah	Philander Smith College	1970
Pleasant, Michael	University of Oklahoma	1984-1986
Redden, Barry	University of Richmond	1982-1986
Reed, Doug	San Diego State University	1984-1986
Reese, Booker	Bethune-Cookman College	1984-1986
Richardson, Jerry	West Texas State University	1964-1965
Robertson, Isiah	Southern University	1971-1978
Rogers, Mel	Florida A&M University	1976
Rucker, Conrad	Southern University	1980
Scales, Dwight	Grambling College	1976-1978
Sherman, Rod	University of Southern California	1973
Slater, Jackie	Jackson State University	1976-1986
Smith, Lucious	California State University, Fullerton	1980-1982
Staton, Tony	University of Southern California	1985-1986
Strode, Woody	University of California, Los Angeles	1946
Stukes, Charles	University of Maryland, Eastern Shore	1973-1974
Sully, Ivory	University of Delaware	1979-1984
Sweet, Joe	Tennessee State University	1972-1973

Player	College	Years
Thomas, Jewel	San Jose State University	1980-1982
Thomas, Pat	Texas A&M University	1976-1982
Towler, Dan	Washington & Jefferson University	1950-1955
Tucker, Wendell	South Carolina State College	1967-1970
Tyler, Wendell	University of California, Los Angeles	1977-1982
Vann, Norwood	East Carolina University	1984-1986
Waddy, Billy	University of Colorado	1977-1981
Wallace, Jackie	University of Arizona	1977-1979
Washington, Ken	University of California, Los Angeles	1946-1948
White, Charles	University of Southern California	1985-1986
Wilcher, Michael	University of North Carolina	1983-1986
Williams, Charles	Prairie View A&M University	1970
Williams, Henry	San Diego State University	1983
Williams, Roger	Grambling State University	1971-1972
Williams, Travis	Arizona State University	1971
Wilson, Tom	(no college)	1956-1961
Young, Charles	University of Southern California	1977-1979
Younger, Paul	Grambling College	1949-1957

Miami Dolphins
Miami, Florida

Coaches

		Years
Phillips, Mel	(Assistant)	1985
Wade, Junior	(Assistant)	1983-1985
Davis, Milt	(College Scout)	1977

All-Pro or Pro Bowl Selections

	Years
Warfield, Paul	1970-1974
Little, Larry	1971-1974
Morris, Eugene	1971, 1972
Moore, Nat	1977
Williams, Delvin	1978
Nathan, Tony	1979
Franklin, Andra	1982
Duper, Mark	1983
Stephenson, Dwight	1983, 1984-1986
Clayton, Mark	1984-1986
Duper, Mark	1984-1985
Roby, Reginald	1984-1985
Walker, Fulton	1983

All-Time Team Roster

Player	College	Years
Anderson, Terry	Bethune-Cookman College	1977-1978
Andrews, John	Morgan State College	1975-1976
Baker, Mel	Texas Southern University	1974
Barber, Rudy	Bethune-Cookman College	1968
Barnes, Rodrigo	Rice University	1975
Bennett, Woody	University of Miami (Florida)	1980-1986
Bishop, Richard	University of Louisville	1982
Bowser, Charles	Duke University	1982-1986
Braxton, James	University of West Virginia	1978
Briscoe, Marlin	Omaha University	1972-1974
Brown, Dean	Fort Valley State College	1970
Brown, Mark	Purdue University	1983-1986
Burgess, Fernanza	Morris Brown	1984
Carter, Joe	University of Alabama	1984-1986
Charles, Michael	Syracuse University	1983-1986
Clayton, Mark	Louisville University	1983-1986
Colzie, Neal	Ohio State University	1979
Cornelius, Charles	Bethune-Cookman College	1977-1978
Cornish, Frank	Grambling State University	1979-1981
Cowan, Larry	Jackson State University	1982
Crowder, Randy	Pennsylvania State University	1974-1976
Davenport, Ron	University of Louisville	1985-1986
Dotson, Al	Grambling State University	1966
Duper, Mark	Northwestern State University (Louisiana)	1982-1986
Ellis, Ken	Southern University	1976
Foster, Roy	University of Southern California	1982-1986
Falson, Earl	Indiana University	1966
Fleming, Marv	University of Utah	1970-1974
Foster, Jerome	Ohio State University	1986
Franklin, Andra	University of Nebraska	1981-1985
Funchess, Thomas	Jackson State University	1974
Gilchrist, Cookie	(no college)	1966
Ginn, Hubert	Florida A&M University	1970-1975
Gordon, Larry	Arizona State University	1976-1982
Green, Cleveland	Southern University	1979-1986
Green, Hugh	University of Pittsburgh	1985-1986
Hampton, Lorenzo	University of Florida	1985-1986
Harris, Duriel	New Mexico State University	1976-1983
Harris, Leroy	Arkansas State University	1977-1978
Haynes, Abner	North Texas State University	1967
Heflin, Vincent	Central State University	1982-1985
Hester, Ron	Florida State University	1982-1985
Hill, Eddie	Memphis State University	1981-1985
Hines, Jimmy	Texas Southern University	1969
Holmes, John	Florida A&M University	1966

Player	College	Years
Holmes, Michael	Texas Southern University	1976
Howell, Michael	Grambling State University	1972
Hunt, Darryl	University of Oklahoma	1979
Joe, Billy	Villanova University	1966
Johnson, Curtis	Toledo University	1970-1978
Johnson, Pete	Ohio State University	1984-1985
Judson, William	South Carolina State University	1982-1986
Lamb, Mack	Tennessee State University	1967-1968
Lankford, Paul	Pennsylvania State University	1982-1986
Lee, Ronnie	Baylor University	1979-1982, 1984-1986
Little, George	University of Iowa	1985-1986
Little, Larry	Bethune-Cookman College	1969-1980
Malone, Benny	Arizona State University	1974-1978
Matthews, Bo	University of Colorado	1981
McCreary, Loaird	Tennessee State University	1976-1978
McNeal, Don	University of Alabama	1980-1986
Milton, Gene	Florida A&M University	1968-1969
Mitchell, Melvin	Tennessee State University	1976-1978
Moore, Mack	Texas A&M University	1985-1986
Moore, Maulty	Bethune-Cookman College	1972-1974
Moore, Nat	University of Florida	1974-1986
Morris, Mercury	West Texas State University	1969-1975
Moyer, Alex	Northwestern University	1985-1986
Mumphord, Lloyd	Texas Southern University	1969-1974
Nathan, Tony	University of Alabama	1979-1986
Overstreet, David	University of Oklahoma	1983
Owens, Morris	Arizona State University	1975-1976
Pearson, Willie	North Carolina A&T University	1969
Pruitt, James	California State University, Fullerton	1986
Ray, Ricky	Norfolk State University	1981-1982
Reese, Don	Jackson State University	1974-1976
Rhone, Ernest	Henderson College (Arkansas)	1975-1985
Richardson, Willie	Jackson State University	1970
Roberson, Bo	Cornell University	1966
Robertson, Vernon	Grambling State University	1977
Roby, Reggie	University of Iowa	1983-1986
Rose, Donovan	Hampton University	1985-1986
Salter, Bryant	University of Pittsburgh	1976
Shipp, Jackie	University of Oklahoma	1984-1986
Small, Gerald	San Joe State University	1978-1983
Smith, Michael	University of Texas, El Paso	1985-1986
Soloman, Freddie	University of Tampa	1975-1977
Sowell, Robert	Howard University	1983-1985
Stephenson, Dwight	University of Alabama	1980-1986
Stowe, Otti	Iowa State University	1971-1972
Thomas, Rodell	Alabama State University	1981, 1983-1985
Thompson, Reyna	Baylor University	1986

Player	College	Years
Tillman, Andre	Texas Tech University	1975-1978
Turner, T.J.	University of Houston	1986
Wade, Charles	Tennessee State University	1973
Walker, Fulton	University of West Virginia	1981-1985
Warfield, Paul	Ohio State University	1981-1984
Washington, Dick	Bethune-Cookman College	1968
Westmoreland, Dick	North Carolina A&T University	1966-1969
White, Jeris	University of Hawaii	1974-1976
Williams, Delvin	University of Kansas	1978-1980
Woods, Larry	Tennessee State University	1973
Young, Willie	Alcorn A&M University	1973

Minnesota Vikings

All-Pro or Pro Bowl Selections

	Years
Eller, Carl	1969, 1972, 1974, 1975
Marshall, Jim	1969, 1970
Washington, Gene	1970, 1971
Page, Alan	1969-1977
Gilliam, John	1973-1976
Foreman, Chuck	1974-1978
White, Sammy	1977-1978
Rashad, Ahmad	1979-1982
Blair, Matt	1978-1983
Browner, Joey	1985-1986

All-Time Team Roster

Player	College	Years
Allen, Nate	Texas Southern University	1976-1978
Blair, Matt	Iowa State University	1974-1976
Brown, Robert	Alcorn A&M University	1971
Bess, Rufus	South Carolina State College	1982-1986
Brown, Ted	North Carolina State University	1979-1986
Browner, Joey	University of Southern California	1983-1986
Caleb, Jamie	Grambling State University	1961
Carter, Anthony	University of Michigan	1985-1986
Coleman, Al	Tennessee State University	1967
Coleman, Greg	Florida A&M University	1978-1986
Denson, Al	Florida A&M University	1971
Doleman, Chris	University of Pittsburgh	1985-1986
Eller, Carl	University of Minnesota	1964-1978
Ferguson, Charles	Tennessee State University	1963
Foreman, Chuck	University of Miami	1973-1979
Gilliam, John	South Carolina State College	1972-1975

Player	College	Years
Goodrum, Charles	Florida A&M University	1972-1978
Harris, John	Arizona State University	1986
Hilton, Carl	University of Houston	1986
Holland, John	Tennessee State University	1974
Holt, Issiac	Alcorn State University	1985-1986
Howard, David	Long Beach State University	1985-1986
Jones, Clint	Michigan State University	1967-1972
Jones, Hassan	Florida State University	1986
Jordan, Steve	Brown University	1982-1986
Keys, Brady	Colorado State University	1967
Lee, Carl	Marshall University	1983-1986
Lewis, Leo	University of Missouri	1981-1986
Marshall, Jim	Ohio State University	1961-1979
Martin, Amos	University of Louisville	1972-1976
Martin, Chris	Auburn University	1984-1986
Martin, Doug	University of Washington	1980-1986
McClanahan, Brent	Arizona State University	1973-1979
McCullum, Sam	Montana State University	1974-1975
McNeil, Fred	University of California, Los Angeles	1974-1975
Newton, Tim	University of Florida	1985-1986
Page, Alan	University of Notre Dame	1967-1978
Rhymes, Buster	University of Oklahoma	1985-1986
Rashad, Ahmad	University of Oregon	1976-1982
Reed, Oscar	Colorado State University	1968-1974
Rice, Allen	Baylor University	1984-1986
Robinson, Gerald	Auburn University	1986
Solomon, Jesse	Florida State University	1986
Spencer, Willie	(no college)	1976
Triplett, Mel	University of Toledo	1961-1962
Teal, Willie	Louisiana State University	1980-1986
Warwick, Lonnie	Tennessee State University	1965-1972
White, Sammy	Grambling State University	1976-1986
Willis, Leonard	Ohio State University	1976
Wilson, Wayne	Shepard College	1986
Wright, Nate	San Diego State University	1971-1980

New England Patroits
Foxboro, Massachusetts

Front Office Personnel

		Years
Loudd, Rommie	(Director of Player Personnel)	1971-1972
Kennedy, Katherine	(Administrative Assistant to General Manager)	1984-1986
Greenidge, Jim	(Director of Publicity)	1984-1986
Smith, Claudia	(Director of Public Affairs)	1979-1984
Langhorne, Cheryl	(Coaches Secretary)	1981-1982

Player	College	Years
Grier, Bobby	(Scout)	1982-1984
Garcia, Charles	(Scout)	1984-1986

	Coaches	**Years**
Loudd, Rommie	(Assistant)	1966
Grier, Bobbie	(Assistant)	1981, 1985-1986
Bryant, Cleveland	(Assistant)	1982-1984

All-Pro or Pro Bowl Selections
(American Football League Until 1970)

	Years
Garron, Larry	1961, 1963-1964
Hunt, Jim	1961, 1966-1967, 1969
Antwine, Houston	1963-1968
Nance, Jim	1966-1967
Garrett, Carl	1969
Webb, Don	1969
Gray, Leon	1976, 1978
Haynes, Michael	1976-1980, 1982
Cunningham, Sam	1978
Morgan, Stanley	1979-1981
Adams, Julius	1980
Clayborn, Ray	1983
Collins, Tony	1983
Holloway, Brian	1983-1986
Tippett, Andre	1984-1986

All-Time Team Roster

Player	College	Years
Adams, Julius	Texas Southern University	1971-1985
Adams, Sam	Prairie View	1972-80
Antwine, Houston	Southern Illinois University	1961-1971
Ashton, Josh	University of Tulsa	1972-1974
Atchason, Jack	Western Illinois	1960
Ballou, Mike	University of California, Los Angeles	1970
Banks, Willie	Alcorn A&M University	1973
Barnes, Bruce	University of California, Los Angeles	1973-1974
Barnes, Pete	Southern University	1976-1977
Barnes, Rodrigo	Rice University	1974-1975
Beach, Walter	Central Michigan University	1960-1961
Beverly, Randy	Colorado State University	1970-1971
Bishop, Richard	University of Louisville	1976-1981
Blackmon, Don	University of Tulsa	1981-1986
Blanks, Sid	Texas A&I University	1969-1970
Bolton, Ron	Norfolk State University	1972-1975

Player	College	Years
Boyd, Greg	University of Arizona	1973
Boyd, Greg	San Diego State University	1977-1978
Bradshaw, Morris	Ohio State University	1982
Briscoe, Marlin	University of Nebraska, Omaha	1976
Brown, Preston	Vanderbilt University	1980, 1982
Brown, Sidney	University of Oklahoma	1978
Bryant, Hubie	University of Minnesota	1971-1972
Burton, Ron	Northwestern University	1960-1965
Calhoun, Don	Kansas State University	1975-1981
Carter, Allen	University of Southern California	1975
Carwell, Allen	Iowa State University	1969-1972
Chandler, Al	University of Oklahoma	1976-1979
Charles, John	Purdue University	1967-1969
Clark, Steve	Kansas State University	1981
Clayborn, Raymond	University of Texas	1977-1986
Collins, Tony	East Carolina University	1981-1986
Costict, Ray	Mississippi State University	1977-1979
Cowan, Larry	Jackson State	1982
Crump, George	East Carolina University	1982-1985
Cunningham, Jay	Bowling Green University	1965-1967
Cunningham, Sam	University of Southern California	1973-1979, 1981-1982
Dawson, Lin	North Carolina State University	1981-1986
Dorsey, Nate	Mississippi Valley University	1973
Dressler, Doug	Chico State University	1975
Feacher, Ricky	Mississippi Valley	1976
Ferguson, Vegas	Notre Dame University	1980-1982
Forte, Ike	University of Arkansas	1967-1977
Foster, Will	East Michigan University	1973-1974
Frazier, Charley	Texas Southern University	1969-1970
Fryar, Irving	University of Nebraska	1984-1986
Funchess, Tom	Jackson State University	1968-1970
Fussell, Tom	Louisiana State University	1967
Gamble, R.C.	South Carolina State University	1968-1969
Garrett, Carl	New Mexico Highlands University	1969-1970
Garrett, J.D.	Grambling State University	1964-1967
Garron, Larry	Western Illinois University	1960-1968
Germany, Willie	Morgan State University	1976
Gray, Leon	Jackson State University	1973-1978
Hamilton, Ray	University of Oklahoma	1973-1981
Haynes, Michael	Arizona State University	1976-1982
Herron, Mack	Kansas State University	1973-1975
Hinton, Ed	University of Oklahoma	1974
Huat, Sam	Stephen F. Austin State University	1974-1980
Hawthorne, Greg	Baylor University	1984-1986
Jackson, Harold	Jackson State University	1978-1981
Johnson, Darryl	Morgan State University	1967-1971
Johnson, Preston	Florida A&M University	1968

Player	College	Years
Jordan, Shelby	Washington University (Missouri)	1975
Lassitor, Ike	St. Augustine's College	1970-1971
Lawson, Odell	Langston University	1970-1971
Loudd, Rommie	University of California, Los Angeles	1961-1962
Lunsford, Mel	Central State University (Okla.)	1973-1980
May, Art	Tuskegee University	1971
McAlister, James	University of California, Los Angeles	1978
McCall, Bob	University of Arizona	1973
McCray, Prentice	Arizona State University	1974-1980
McCurry, Dave	Iowa State University	1974
McDougald, Doug	Virginia Polytechnic Institute	1980
McGee, George	Southern University	1960
McGee, Tony	Bishop College (Texas)	1974-1981
McGrew, Larry	University of Southern California	1980-1985
McQuay, Leon	University of Tampa	1975
Mitchell, Leroy	Texas Southern University	1967-1968
Moore, Arthur	University of Tulsa	1973-1977
Moore, Leroy	Fort Valley State University	1961-1962
Moore, Steve	Tennessee State University	1983-1986
Morgan, Stanley	University of Tennessee	1977-1986
Mosier, John	University of Kansas	1973
Moss, Roland	University of Toledo	1971
Nance, Jim	Syracuse University	1965-1971
Osley, Willie	University of Illinois	1974
Outlaw, John	Jackson State University	1969-1972
Owens, Dennis	North Carolina State University	1982-1985
Pennywell, Carlos	Grambling State University	1978-1981
Peoples, George	Auburn	1983
Philips, Jess	Michigan State University	1976-1977
Price, Kenny	University of Iowa	1971
Ramsey, Derrick	University of Kentucky	1983-1986
Rembert, Johnny	Clemson University	1983-1986
Reynolds, Ed	University of Virginia	1983-1985
Reynolds, Tom	San Diego State University	1972
Richardson, Tom	Jackson State University	1969-1970
Rucker, Reggie	Boston University	1971-1974
Scott, Clarence	Morgan State University	1969-1972
Shoate, Rod	University of Oklahoma	1975-1981
Sims, Ken	University of Texas	1982-1986
Singer, Carl	Purdue University	1966-1968
Smith, Ricky	Alabama State University	1982-1984
Spears, Ron	San Diego State University	1982-1983
Starring, Stephen	McNeese State University	1983-1986
Stingley, Darryl	Purdue University	1973-1977
Tarver, John	University of Colorado	1972-1974
Tippett, Andre	University of Iowa	1982-1986
Washington, Clyde	Purdue University	1960-1961

Player	*College*	*Years*
Weathers, Clarence	Delaware State University	1983-1985
Weathers, Robert	Arizona State University	1982-1986
Webb, Don	Iowa State University	1961-1971
Webster, George	Michigan State University	1974-1976
Westbrook, Don	University of Nebraska	1977-1981
Wheeler, Dwight	Tennessee State University	1978-1983
Williams, Brian	Southern University	1982
Williams, Lester	University of Miami	1982-1983
Williams, Toby	University of Nebraska	1983-1986
Wilson, Darryal	University of Tennessee	1983-1986
Witt, Mel	Arlington State University	1967-1970

New Orleans Saints

New Orleans, Louisiana 70112

Coaches

	Years
Buchanann, Buck	1971-1972
Hill, Robert	1978-1979

All-Pro or Pro Bowl Selections

	Years
Childs, Henry	1979
Chandler, Wes	1979
Muncie, Chuck	1979
Rogers, George	1981, 1982
Jackson, Rick	1983, 1984
Clark, Bruce	1984

All-Time Team Roster

Player	*College*	*Years*
Adams, Sam	Prairie View A&M University	1981
Askson, Bert	Texas Southern University	1973
Baker, Melvin	University of Michigan	1975
Banks, Gordon	Stanford University	1980-1981
Bell, Carlos	University of Houston	1971
Brown, Robert	Alcorn A&M University	1972-1973
Brown, Ray	West Texas State University	1978-1980
Burrough, Ken	Texas Southern University	1970
Burton, Larry	Purdue University	1975-1977
Carr, Thomas	Morgan State University	1968
Caster, Richard	Jackson State University	1981
Chandler, Wes	University of Florida	1978-1981
Chapman, Clarence	Eastern Michigan University	1976-1980
Childs, Henry	University of Kansas	1974-1980

Player	College	Years
Clark, Bruce	Pennsylvania State University	1982-1986
Collins, Larry	Texas A&I University	1980
Davis, David	Tennessee State University	1974
Davis, Norman	Grambling College	1969
Douglas, John	Texas Southern University	1967-1968
Dunbar, Jubilee	Southern University	1973
Dusenberry, William	Johnson C. Smith University	1970
Elliot, Tony	North Texas State University	1982-1986
Estes, Lawrence	Alcorn A&M University	1970-1971
Finnie, Roger	Florida A&M University	1978
Ford, James	Texas Southern University	1971-1972
Galbreath, Anthony	University of Missouri	1977-1980
Garrett, Len	New Mexico Highlands University	1973-1975
Gary, Russell	University of Nebraska	1981-1986
Geathers, James	Wichita State University	1984-1986
Gilbert, Daren	California State University, Fullerton	1985-1986
Gilliam, John	South Carolina State University	1967-1968, 1977
Goodlow, Eugene	Kansas State University	1983-1986
Gray, Leon	Jackson State University	1982-1983
Green, Arthur	Albany State University	1972
Green, Sam	University of Florida	1980
Grooms, Elois	Tennessee Tech. University	1975-1981
Hall, Willie	University of Southern California	1972-1973
Harris, Ike	University of Iowa	1978-1981
Hart, Thomas	Morris Brown College	1979-1980
Hazelton, Major	Florida A&M University	1970
Hines, Glen Ray	University of Arkansas	1971-1972
Holden, Sam	Grambling College	1971
Holmes, Jack	Texas Southern University	1978-1982
Howard, Eugene	Langston University	1968-1970
Howell, Delles	Grambling College	1970-1972
Jackson, Ernest	Duke University	1972-1977
Johnson, Bennie	Johnson C. Smith University	1976
Kearney, Jim	Prairie View A&M University	1976
Lawson, Odell	Langston University	1973-1974
Lee, Bivian	Prairie View A&M University	1971-1975
Lorick, Tony	Arizona State University	1968-1969
McCullough, Earl	University of Southern California	1974
McNeill, Rod	University of Southern California	1974-1975
Marsalis, Jim	Tennessee State University	1977
Marshall, James	Jackson State University	1980
Martin, D'Artagnan	Kentucky State University	1971-1972
Mathis, Reginald	University of Oklahoma	1979-1980
Maxson, Alvin	Southern Methodist University	1974-1976
Muncie, Chuck	University of California, Berkeley	1976-1980
Neal, Richard	Southern University	1969-1972, 1978

Player	College	Years
Nevett, Elijah	Clark College	1967-1970
Newsome, William	Grambling College	1973-1974
Owens, Joe	Alcorn A&M University	1971-1975
Perry, Vernon	Jackson State University	1983
Phillips, Jess	Michigan State University	1973-1974
Pitts, Elijah	Philander Smith College	1970
Price, Alex	Alcorn State University	1973-1980
Profit, Joe	Northeast Louisiana	1973
Ray, Ricky	Norfolk State University	1979-1980
Reaves, Ken	Norfolk State University	1974
Reese, Don	Jackson State University	1978-1980
Rice, Floyd	Alcorn State University	1978
Riley, Preston	Memphis State University	1973
Roberts, Walter	San Jose State University	1967
Robinson, Virgil	Grambling College	1971
Rogers, George	University of South Carolina	1981-1984
Shaw, Robert	Winston-Salem State University	1970
Simmons, Jerry	Bethune-Cookman College	1967
Spencer, Maurice	University of North Carolina	1974-1978
Stevens, Howard	University of Louisville	1973-1974
Strachan, Michael	Iowa State University	1975-1980
Thaxton, James	Tennessee State University	1976-1977
Thomas, Charles	Tennessee State University	1975
Thompson, Aundra	East Texas State University	1981-1982
Tyler, Toussaint	University of Washington	1981-1982
Washington, David	Alcorn State University	1980
Welch, Claxton	University of Oregon	1970
Wheelwright, Ernest	Southern Illinois University	1967-1970
Willis, Len	Ohio State University	1977
Zanders, Emanuel	Jackson State University	1974-1980

New York Giants

Giants Stadium
East Rutherford, New Jersey 07073

Coaches		Years
Brown, Roosevelt	(Assistant Coach)	1966-1969, 1971
Crennel, Romeo	(Assistant)	1981-1986
Tunnell, Emlen	(Assistant Coach)	late 1960's

Trainers		Years
Barnes, Ron	(Head Trainer)	1983-1986

All-Pro or Pro Bowl Selections

	Years
Tunnell, Emlen	1951-1952, 1955-1966
Brown, Roosevelt	1956-1963
Grier, Roosevelt	1956
Barnes, Erich	1961, 1964
Jones, Homer	1967
Johnson, Ron	1970
Mendenhall, John	1974
Carson, Harry	1979, 1981, 1982, 1986
Haynes, Mark	1981-1983
Taylor, Lawrence	1981-1986

All-Time Team Roster

Player	*College*	*Years*
Adams, George	University of Kentucky	1985-1986
Anderson, Roger	Virginia Union University	1964-1965, 1967-1968
Banks, Carl	Michigan State University	1984-1986
Banks, Willie	Alcorn A&M University	1970
Barnes, Erich	Purdue University	1961-1964
Belcher, Kevin	University of Texas, El Paso	1983-1984
Bell, Gordon	University of Michigan	1976-1977
Blount, Tony	University of Virginia	1980
Blye, Ron	Florida A&M University	1968
Boston, McKinley	University of Minnesota	1968-1969
Bright, Leon	Florida State University	1981-1983
Brooks, Robert	Bishop College	1974-1976
Brown, Boyd	Alcorn State University	1977
Brown, Otto	Prairie View A&M University	1970-1973
Brown, Roosevelt	Morgan State University	1953-1965
Bryant, William	Grambling State University	1976-1978
Buggs, Dan	West Virginia University	1975-1976
Caldwell, Alan	University of North Carolina	1979
Campbell, Carter	Weber State College	1972-1973
Carpenter, Brian	University of Michigan	1982
Carr, Henry	Arizona State University	1965-1967
Carson, Harry	South Carolina State University	1976-1986
Cephous, Frank	University of California, Los Angeles	1984
Chatman, Cliff	Central State University (Oklahoma)	1982
Childs, Clarence	Florida A&M University	1964-1967
Coffey, Junior	University of Washington	1969-1971
Colbert, Randy	Lamar University	1974-1976
Counts, John	University of Illinois	1962-1963
Daniel, Ken	San Jose State University	1984-1985
Davis, Don	Los Angeles State University	1966-1967
Davis, Henry	Grambling College	1968-1969

Player	College	Years
Davis, Roosevelt	Tennessee A&I	1965-1967
Dawkins, Joe	University of Wisconsin	1974-1975
Dennis, Michael	University of Wyoming	1980-1983
Dixon, Al	Iowa State University	1977-1978
Dixon, Zach	Temple University	1979
Dorsey, Eric	University of Notre Dame	1986
Eddings, Floyd	University of California	1982-1984
Epps, Robert	University of Pittsburgh	1954-1957
Ellison, Mark	University of Dayton	1972-1973
Flowers, Larry	Texas Tech University	1981-1985
Ford, Charles	University of Houston	1975-1976
Forte, Ike	University of Arkansas	1981
Fuqua, John	Morgan State University	1969
Gaithers, Robert	New Mexico State University	1961-1962
Galbreath, Tony	University of Missouri	1984-1986
Garrett, Alvin	Angelo State University	1980
Gatewood, Tom	University of Notre Dame	1972-1973
Glover, Rich	University of Nebraska	1973
Gray, Ernest	Memphis State University	1979-1985
Green, Tony	University of Florida	1979
Grier, Roosevelt	Pennsylvania State University	1955-1956, 1958-1962
Green, Lawrence	University of Tennessee, Chattanooga	1985
Gunn, James	University of Southern California	1975
Hammond, Robert	Morgan State University	1976-1978
Hardison, Dee	University of North Carolina	1981-1985
Harris, Don	Rutgers University	1980
Hart, Harold	Texas Southern University	1977
Haynes, Mark	University of Colorado	1980-1985
Headen, Andy	Clemson University	1983-1986
Heater, Larry	University of Arizona	1980-1983
Hicks, John	Ohio State University	1974-1977
Hill, Ken	Yale University	1984-1986
Hill, Ralph	Florida A&M University	1976-1977
Hilton, Roy	Jackson State University	1974
Hogan, Michael	University of Tennessee, Chattanooga	1980
Holifield, Jimmy	Jackson State University	1968-1969
Houston, Rich	East Texas State University	1969-1973
Howell, Lane	Grambling College	1963-1964
Hunt, Byron	Southern Methodist University	1981-1986
Jackson, Robert	North Carolina A&T University	1950-1951
Jackson, Cleveland	University of Nevada, Las Vegas	1979
Jackson, Louis	Cal. Poly. S.L.O.	1981
Jackson, Terry	San Diego State University	1978-1983
Jacobs, Proverb	University of California	1960
Janarette, Charles	Pennsylvania State University	1961-1962
Jeter, Gary	University of Southern California	1977-1982
Johnson, Bob	University of Kansas	1984-1986

Player	College	Years
Johnson, Dennis	Mississippi State University	1980
Johnson, Ken	University of Miami	1979
Johnson, Ron	University of Michigan	1970-1975
Jones, Ernest	Miami University	1977-1979
Jones, Homer	Texas Southern University	1964-1969
Kelly, Ellison	Michigan State University	1959
Kinard, Terry	Clemson University	1983-1986
King, Jerome	Purdue University	1980
Lakes, Roland	Wichita State University	1971
Lewis, Dan	University of Wisconsin	1966
Lockhart, Carl "Spider"	North Texas State University	1965-1975
Love, Walter	Westminster (Utah)	1973
Lumpkin, Ron	Arizona State University	1973
McCreary, Loaird	Tennessee State University	1979
McDaniel, LeCharles	Cal. Poly. S.L.O.	1983-1984
McGriff, Curtis	University of Alabama	1980-1985
McKinney, Odis	University of Colorado	1978-1979
McNeil, Clifton	Grambling College	1970-1971
McQuay, Leon	University of Tampa	1974
McRae, Bennie	University of Michigan	1971
Mallory, Larry	Tennessee State University	1976-1978
Manuel, Lionel	University of Pacific	1984-1986
Marion, Frank	Florida A&M University	1977-1983
Marshall, Leonard	Louisiana State University	1983-1986
Martin, George	University of Oregon	1975-1986
Matthews, Bo	University of Colorado	1980
Maxson, Alvin	Southern Methodist University	1978
Mendenhall, John	Grambling State University	1972-1979
Magwood, Frank	Clemson University	1984-1985
Miller, Calvin	Oklahoma State University	1979
Miller, Michael	University of Tennessee	1983
Moden, Frank	Jackson State University	1969
Moorehead, Emery	University of Colorado	1977-1979
Morris, Joe	Syracuse University	1982-1985
Mowarr, Joe	Florida State University	1983-1984
Odam, Steven	University of Utah	1979
Orduna, Joe	University of Nebraska	1972-1973
Owens, R.C.	University of Idaho	1964
Parker, Ken	Fordham University	1970
Patterson, Elvis	University of Kansas	1984-1986
Peay, Francis	University of Missouri	1966-1967
Perkins, John	Abilene Christian University	1977-1983
Perry, Leon	University of Mississippi	1980-1982
Puttman, Dan	University of Wyoming	1980-1983
Powers, Clyde	University of Oklahoma	1974-1977
Paugh, Ernest	North Southern University	1978
Reece, Beasley	North Texas State University	1977-1983

Player	*College*	*Years*
Reed, Henry	Weber State College	1971-1974
Reed, Smith	Alcorn A&M University	1965-1966
Rhodes, Ray	University of Tulsa	1974-1979
Rivers, Nate	South Carolina State University	1980
Roberts, William	Ohio State University	1984-1986
Robinson, Stacey	North Dakota State University	1986
Roland, John	University of Missouri	1973
Rucker, Reginald	Boston University	1971
Sally, Jerome	University of Missouri	1982-1986
Scales, Dwight	Grambling State University	1979
Scott, Malcolm	Louisiana State University	1983
Shaw, Peter	Northwestern University	1982-1985
Shy, Les	Long Beach State University	1970
Silas, Sam	Southern Illinois University	1968
Simmons, Roy	Georgia Tech University	1977-1980
Small, Eldridge	Texas A&I University	1972-1974
Small, George	North Carolina A&T University	1980
Smith, Jeff	University of Southern California	1966-1967
Spencer, Willie	(no college)	1977-1978
Spinks, Jack	Alcorn A&M University	1956-1957
Staten, Randy	University of Minnesota	1967
Stucker, Henry	University of Missouri	1975-1976
Tate, John	Jackson State University	1976
Taylor, Lawrence	University of North Carolina	1981-1986
Thompson, Rocky	West Texas State University	1971-1973
Triplett, William	University of Miami (Ohio)	1967
Triplett, Mel	University of Toledo	1955-1960
Tunnel, Emlen	University of Iowa	1948-1958
Turner, J.T.	Duke University	1977-1983
Tyler, Maurice	Morgan State University	1978
Vanoy, Vernon	University of Kansas	1971
Wafer, Carl	Tennessee State University	1974
Watkins, Larry	Alcorn A&M University	1975-1977
Washington, Gene	University of Georgia	1979
Webb, Allen	Arnold	1961-1965
Wheelwright, Ernest	University of Southern Illinois	1964-1965
Williams, Perry	North Carolina State University	1984-1985
Williams, Willie	Grambling College	1965, 1967-1973
Woolfolk, Butch	University of Michigan	1982-1984
Word, Roscoe	Jackson State University	1976
Wyatt, Kervin	University of Maryland	1980
Young, David	Purdue University	1981
Young, Willie	Grambling State University	1966-1975
Zeno, Coleman	Grambling State University	1971

New York Jets Football Club, Inc.

598 Madison Avenue
New York, New York 10022

Front Office Personnel		Years
Washington, Clyde	(Assistant Director of Player Personnel)	1966-1969
Jones, Jimmy	(Assistant Director of Player Personnel)	1971
Rust, Jr., Arthur	(Public Relations Assistant)	1960-1964

Coaches		Years
Ledbetter, Robert	(Assistant)	1977-1982
Hammond, Robert	(Assistant)	1983-1986

All-Pro or Pro Bowl Selections

	Years
Hill, Winston	1964, 1967-1973
Plunkett, Sherman	1964, 1966
Snell, Matt	1964, 1966, 1969
Biggs, Verlon	1966-1967, 1968
Boozer, Emerson	1966, 1968
Caster, Richard	1972, 1974-1975
Barkum, Jerome	1973
Walker, Wesley	1978, 1982
Powell, Marvin	1979-1983
McNeil, Freeman	1982, 1984

All-Time Team Roster

Player	*College*	*Years*
Adkins, Margene	Hutchinson Junior College	1973
Barber, Marion	University of Minnesota	1982-1984
Barkum, Jerome	Jackson State University	1972-1983
Barnes, Ernest	North Carolina College	1960
Bates, Ted	Oregon State University	1963
Batton, Robert	University of Nevada, Las Vegas	1980
Bell, Ed	Pennsylvania State University	1960
Bell, Ed	Idaho State University	1970-1975
Bell, Kevin	Lamar University	1978
Bell, Robert	University of Missouri	1984
Bennett, Woody	University of Miami (Florida)	1979-1980
Beverly, Randy	Colorado State University	1967-1969
Biggs, Verlon	Jackson State University	1965-1970
Bligen, Dennis	St. John's University	1984
Boozer, Emerson	Maryland State College	1966-1975
Brannan, Soloman	Morris Brown College	1967
Brister, Willie	Southern University	1974-1975
Brooks, Robert	Ohio University	1961
Brooks, Clifford	Tennessee State University	1976
Brown, Preston	Vanderbilt University	1983

Player	College	Years
Browning, Charles	University of Washington	1965
Burton, Al	Bethune-Cookman College	1977
Burton, Leon	Arizona State University	1960
Carpenter, Steve	Western Illinois University	1980
Carson, Kern	San Diego State University	1965
Carter, Gerald	Texas A&M University	1980
Carter, Russell	Southern Methodist University	1984-1986
Caster, Richard	Jackson State University	1970-1977
Christy, Earl	Maryland State College	1966-1968
Cruchfield, Dwayne	Iowa State University	1982-1983
Cunningham, Eric	Pennsylvania State University	1979-1980
Darby, Paul	S.W. Texas State University	1979-1980
Davidson, Chy	University of Rhode Island	1984
Davis, Jerry	Morris Brown College	1975
Davis, Steve	Delaware State University	1975-1976
DeLoach, Ralph	University of California, Berkeley	1981
Dennis, Mike	University of Wyoming	1984
Denson, Keith	San Diego State University	1976
Diggs, Shelton	University of Southern California	1977
Dykes, Donald	S.E. Louisiana	1979-1981
Earley, Jim	Michigan State University	1978
Farmer, Roger	Baker (Kansas)	1979
Finnie, Roger	Florida A&M University	1969-1972
Floyd, George	Eastern Kentucky University	1982-1983
Gaffney, Derrick	University of Florida	1978-1984
Gaines, Clark	Wake Forest University	1976-1980
Garrett, Carl	New Mexico Highlands University	1975
Glenn, Howard	Linfield	1960
Gordon, Cornell	North Carolina A&T University	1965-1969
Grant, Reginald	University of Oregon	1978
Gray, Jim	University of Toledo	1966
Gray, Moses	University of Indiana	1961-1962
Gresham, Robert	University of West Virginia	1975-1976
Hardee, Billy	Virginia Tech University	1977
Harmon, Michael	University of Mississippi	1983
Harper, Bruce	Kutztown State University	1977-1985
Harris, Jim	Utah State University	1965-1967
Haslerig, Clint	University of Michigan	1976
Haynes, Abner	North Texas State University	1967
Hector, Johnny	Texas A&M University	1983-1986
Hicks, Wilmer Kenzie (W.K.)	Texas Southern University	1970-1972
Hill, Winston	Texas Southern University	1963-1976
Hinton, Chuck	North Carolina College	1971
Hoey, George	University of Michigan	1975
Holmes, Jerry	University of West Virginia	1980-1984, 1986
Howard, Harry	Ohio State University	1976
Howell, Delles	Grambling State University	1973-1975

Player	College	Years
Humphrey, Bobby	New Mexico State	1984
Jackson, Bobby	Florida State University	1978-1984
Jackson, Clarence	Western Kentucky University	1974-1976
Jackson, Joe	New Mexico State University	1972-1973
Jacobs, Proverb	University of California, Berkeley	1961-1962
Janerette, Charles	Pennsylvania State University	1963
Joe, William	Villanova University	1967-1968
Johnson, Jesse	University of Colorado	1980-1983
Jones, Jimmie	Wichita State University	1969-1970
Jones, John (J.J.)	Fisk University	1975
King, Henry	Utah State University	1967
Kirksey, Roy	Maryland State College	1971-1972
Lawson, Alphonzo	Delaware State College	1964
Lewis, Kenny	Virginia Tech University	1980-1981, 1983
Lewis, Richard	Portland State University	1974-1975
Lewis, Sherman	Michigan State University	1966
Leonard, Cecil	Tuskegee Institute	1969-1970
Little, John	Oklahoma State University	1970-1974
Long, Kevin	University of South Carolina	1977-1981
Lynn, Johnny	University of California, Los Angeles	1979-1986
Mabra, Ron	Howard University	1977
Marshall, Ed	Cameron State University	1976
Marshall, Charles (Tank)	Texas A&M University	1977
Martin, Blanche	Michigan State University	1960
Martin, Saladin	San Diego State University	1980
McAdams, Robert	North Carolina College	1963-1964
McClain, Clifford	South Carolina State College	1970-1973
McElroy, Reginald	West Texas State University	1983-1986
McNeil, Freeman	University of California, Los Angeles	1981-1986
Minter, Cedric	Boise State	1984
Mullen, Davlin	Western Kentucky University	1983
Nance, Jim	Syracuse University	1973
Neil, Ken	Iowa State University	1981-1983
Newsome, Bill	Grambling State University	1975-1976
Newton, Tom	University of California, Berkeley	1977-1982
Nock, George	Morgan State University	1969-1971
Owens, Burgess	University of Miami	1973-1979
Owens, Marv	San Diego State University	1974
Paige, Toney	Virginia Tech	1984
Parket, Artimus	University of Southern California	1977
Perkins, Bill	University of Iowa	1963
Pillers, Lawrence	Alcorn State University	1976-1980
Plunkett, Sherman	Maryland State College	1963-1967
Powell, Art	San Jose State University	1960-1962
Powell, Darnell	University of Tennessee, Chattanooga	1978
Ray, Darrol	University of Southern California	1977-1983
Reese, Steve	University of Oklahoma	1980-1983

Player	College	Years
Richardson, Jeff	Michigan State University	1974-1975
Riley, Larry	Salem (West Virginia)	1967-1968
Rivers, Jamie	Bowling Green State University	1978
Roberts, Wesley	Texas Christian University	1974-1975
Robinson, Jerry	Grambling State University	1980
Rudolph, Ben	Long Beach State University	1965
Russ, Carl	University of Michigan	1981-1984
Salaam, Abdul	Kent State University	1976-1977
Sample, John	Maryland State College	1976-1984
Satterwhite, Howard	Sam Houston State University	1976
Schockley, Bill	West Chester State College	1960-1962
Smith, Allen	Findlay	1966
Snell, Matt	Ohio State University	1964-1972
Sowells, Rich	Alcorn A&M University	1971-1976
Springs, Kirk	University of Miami (Ohio)	1981-1984
Starks, Marshall	University of Illinois	1963-1964
Stephens, Bruce	Columbia University	1978
Stephens, Steve	Oklahoma State University	1981
Suggs, Shafer	Ball State	1976-1980
Taylor, Billy	Texas Tech University	1981
Taylor, Ed	Memphis State University	1975-1979
Taylor, Mike	University of Michigan	1972-1973
Thomas, Earlie	Colorado State	1970-1974
Tiller, Jim	Purdue University	1962
Toon, Al	University of Wisconsin	
Turk, Godwin	Southern University	1974-1975
Tyler, Maurice	Morgan State University	1977
Walker, Donnie	Central State University	1975
Walker, Wesley	University of California, Berkeley	1977-1986
Walton, Sam	East Texas State University	1968-1969
Ward, Chris	Ohio State University	1978-1983
Washington, Al	Ohio State University	1981
Washington, Clyde	Purdue University	1963-1965
Watters, Bob	Lincoln University	1962-1964
West, David	Central State University	1963
West, Mel	University of Missouri	1961-1963
West, Willie	University of Oregon	1964-1965
White, Charlie	Bethune-Cookman	1977
White, Lee	Weber State	1968-1970
Wise, Phil	Nebraska, Omaha	1971-1976
Wood, Richard	University of Southern California	1975
Woods, Larry	Tennessee State University	1974-1975
Woods, Robert	Tennessee State University	1973-1977
Word, Roscoe	Jackson State University	1974-1976
Wright, Gordon	Delaware State University	1969
Yearby, Bill	University of Michigan	1966

Philadelphia Eagles

Philadelphia, Pennsylvania 19148-5201

	Front Office Personnel	*Years*
Graves, Jackie	(Assistant Director of Player Personnel)	1974-1985

	Coaches	*Years*
Cross, Irv	(Assistant)	1969-1970
Hawkins, Ben	(Assistant)	1982
Jackson, Milt	(Assistant)	1985
Roland, John	(Assistant)	1976-1978

All-Pro or Pro Bowl Selections

	Years
Brown, Jim	1963-1964, 1966
Cross, Irv	1965, 1966
Brown, Bob	1967, 1969
Jackson, Harold	1970, 1973
Carmichael, Harold	1974, 1979-1981
Young, Charles	1974-1976
Montgomery, Wilbert	1970, 1980
Henry, Wally	1980
Johnson, Charles	1980, 1982
Logan, Randy	1980, 1981
Robinson, Jerry	1982
Young, Roynell	1982
Harrison, Dennis	1983
Quick, Michael	1984, 1985

All-Time Team Roster

Player	*College*	*Years*
Alexander, Kermit	University of California, Los Angeles	1972-1973
Allison, Henry	San Diego State University	1971-1972
Atwine, Houston	Southern Illinois University	1972
Armstrong, Harvey	Southern Methodist University	1982-1985
Atkins, Steven	University of Maryland	1981
Baker, John	North Carolina College	1962
Baker, Ron	Oklahoma State University	1980-1986
Barnes, Larry	Tennessee State University	1978-1979
Bell, Eddie	University of Pennsylvania	1955-1958
Betterson, James	University of North Carolina	1977-1978
Blue, Luther	Iowa State University	1980
Blye, Ron	University of Notre Dame	1969
Bouggess, Lee	University of Louisville	1970-1973
Bradley, Harold	University of Iowa	1958
Brown, Gregory	Kansas State University	1981-1986
Brooks, Clifford	Tennessee State University	1976-
Brown, Jim	Ball State University	1960-1967

Player	College	Years
Brown, Willie	University of Southern California	1966
Bryant, William	Grambling State University	1978
Budd, Frank	Villanova University	1962
Calloway, Ernest	Texas Southern University	1969-1972
Campfield, William	University of Kansas	1978-1982
Carmichael, Harold	Southern University	1971-1983
Carr, Earl	University of Florida	1979
Chesley, Al	University of Pittsburgh	1979-1982
Clark, Al	Eastern Michigan University	1976
Clarke, Ken	Syracuse University	1978-1985
Cobb, Gary	University of Southern California	1985-1986
Coleman, Al	Tennessee State University	1972
Cooper, Evan	University of Michigan	1984-1986
Cross, Irv	Northwestern University	1961-1965, 1969
Crowe, Larry	Texas Southern University	1972
Cullars, Willie	Kansas State University	1974
Cunningham, Randall	University of Nevada, Las Vegas	1985-1986
Darby, Byron	University of Southern California	1983-1986
Davis, Al	Tennessee State University	1971-1972
Davis, Norman	Grambling State University	1970
Davis, Stan	Memphis State University	1973
DeVaughn, Dennis	Bishop College	1982-1983
Dixon, Zachary	Temple University	1980
Edwards, Herman	San Diego State University	1977-1985
Ellis, Ray	Ohio State University	1981-1985
Estes, Larry	Alcorn State University	1972
Everett, Major	Mississippi College	1983-1985
Foules, Elbert	Alcorn State University	1983-1986
Gay, Brenda	Fayetteville State University	1975-1976
Glover, Richard	University of Nebraska	1975
Gray, James	University of Toledo	1967
Griggs, Anthony	Ohio State University	1982-1985
Haddx, Michael	Mississippi State University	1983-1986
Hairston, Carl	Maryland State College	1976-1983
Hampton, Dave	University of Wyoming	1976
Hardy, Andre	St. Mary's College (California)	1984-1985
Harrington, Perry	Jackson State University	1980-1983
Harris, Leroy	Arkansas State University	1979-1982
Harris, Richard	Grambling State University	1971-1973
Harvey, Richard	Jackson State University	1970
Hawkins, Ben	Arizona State University	1966-1973
Hayes, Ed	Morgan State University	1970
Haymond, Alvin	Southern University	1968
Heath, Jo-Jo	University of Pittsburgh	1981
Henry, Wally	University of California, Los Angeles	1971-1982
Hooks, Alvin	University of California, Los Angeles	1982-1985
Hoover, Mel	Arizona State University	1982-1985

Player	College	Years
Hopkins, Wes	Southern Methodist University	1983-1985
Howard, Robert	San Diego State University	1978-1979
Howell, Lane	Grambling State University	1967-1969
Humphrey, Claude	Tennessee State University	1979-1981
Irvin, Willie	Florida A&M University	1953
Jackson, Harold	Jackson State University	1969-1972
Jackson, Johnny	Southern University	1977
Jackson, Ken	Pennsylvania State University	1984-1986
Jackson, Randy	Wichita State University	1974
James, Po	New Mexico State University	1972-1975
Jiles, Dwayne	Texas Tech University	1985-1986
Johnson, Alonzo	University of Florida	1986
Johnson, Charles	University of Colorado	1977-1981
Johnson, Ron	Long Beach State University	1985-1986
Jones, Joe	Tennessee State University	1974-1975
Jones, Ray	Southern University	1970
Joyner, Seth	University of Texas, El Paso	1986
Keyes, Leroy	Purdue University	1969-1972
Kirksey, Roy	Maryland State College	1973-1974
Long, Israel	Tennessee State University	1964-1968
Lattimer, Al	Clemson University	1979
Lavender, Joseph	San Diego State University	1973-1975
Logan, Randy	University of Michigan	1973-1983
Lusk, Herbert	Long Beach State University	1976-1978
McAlister, James	University of California, Los Angeles	1975-1976
McRae, Jerrold	Tennessee State University	1979
Malone, Art	Arizona State University	1975-1976
Manning, Roosevelt	Northeast Oklahoma	1975
Martin, Aaron	North Carolina College	1966-1967
Matson, Ollie	University of San Francisco	1964-1966
Mitchell, Leonard	University of Houston	1981-1986
Mitchell, Martin	Tulane University	1977
Molden, Frank	Jackson State University	1968
Montgomery, Wilbert	Abilene Christian	1977-1985
Murray, Calvin	Ohio State University	1981-1982
Nelson, Al	University of Cincinnati	1965-1973
Oliver, Hubert	University of Arizona	1981-1985
Outlaw, John	Jackson State University	1973-1978
Parker, Artimus	University of Southern California	1974-1976
Parker, Rodney	Tennessee State University	1980-1981
Payne, Ken	Langston University	1978
Peaks, Clarence	Michigan State University	1957-1963
Peoples, Woody	Grambling State University	1978-1980
Pinder, Cyril	University of Illinois	1960-1970
Powell, Art	San Jose State University	1959
Quick, Michael	North Carolina State University	1982-1986
Ramsey, Nate	Indiana University	1963-1972

Player	*College*	*Years*
Rash, Lou	Mississippi Valley State University	1984
Raye, James	Michigan State University	1969
Reed, Taft	Jackson State University	1967
Reeves, Ken	Texas A&M University	1985-1986
Reeves, Marion	Clemson University	1974
Robinson, Jerry	University of California, Los Angeles	1979-1985
Russell, Booker	Southwest Texas State University	1981
Russell, Rusty	University of South Carolina	1984-1985
Sampleton, Lawrence	University of Texas	1982-1985
Simmons, Clyde	Western Carolina University	1986
Singletary, Reggie	North Carolina State University	1986
Smith, Charles	Grambling State University	1974-1981
Smith, Ron	San Diego State University	1981-1983
Strauthers, Tom	Jackson State University	1983-1986
Thrower, James	East Texas State University	1970-1972
Toney, Anthony	Texas A&M University	1986
Walton, John	Elizabeth City State University	1976-1979
Waters, Andre	Cheyney University of Pennsylvania	1984-1986
Watkins, Larry	Alcorn A&M University	1970-1972
Wells, Harold	Purdue University	1965-1968
White, Reggie	University of Tennessee	1985-1986
Wilkes, Reginald	Georgia Tech University	1978-1985
Williams, Charles	Jackson State University	1978
Williams, Joel	University of Wisconsin, La Crosse	1983-1985
Williams, Michael	Mississippi College	1983-1985
Williams, Roger	Grambling State University	1973
Wilson, Bernard	Vanderbilt University	1979-1986
Woodruff, Tony	Fresno State University	1982-1985
Wright, Gordon	Delaware State University	1967
Wynn, William	Tennessee State University	1973-1976
Young, Charles	University of Southern California	1973-1976
Young, Roynell	Alcorn State University	1980-1986

Pittsburgh Steelers
300 Stadium Circle
Pittsburgh, Pennsylvania 15212

Front Office Personnel		*Years*
Nunn, William	(Assistant Director of Player Personnel)	1968-1986

Coaches		*Years*
Perry, Lowell	(Assistant)	1956
Dungy, Anthony	(Assistant)	1981-1986

All-Pro or Pro Bowl Selections

	Years
McClairen, Jack	1958
Nisby, John	1960, 1962
Johnson, John Henry	1963, 1964, 1965
Lipscomb, Gene	1963
Keys, Brady	1966
McGee, Ben	1967, 1969
Woodson, Marv	1968
Jefferson, Roy	1969, 1970
Greene, Joe	1970-1980
Davis, Henry	1973
Harris, Franco	1973-1981
White, Dwight	1973, 1974
Greenwood, L.C.	1974-1980
Shanklin, Ron	1974
Blount, Mel	1976, 1977, 1979-1980
Edwards, Glen	1976, 1977, 1980
Swann, Lynn	1976, 1977, 1980
Thomas, J.T.	1977
Shell, Donnie	1979-1980
Stallworth, John	1980, 1983
Brown, Larry	1983

All-Time Team Roster

Player	*College*	*Years*
Abercrombie, Walter	Baylor University	1982-1986
Allen, Jim	University of California, Los Angeles	1974-1977
Alley, Don	Adams State	1969
Anderson, Anthony	Temple University	1979
Anderson, Fred	Prairie View A&M University	1978
Anderson, Larry	Louisiana Tech University	1978-1981
Anderson, Ralph	West Texas State University	1971-1972
Asbury, William	Kent State University	1966-1968
Askson, Burt	Texas Southern University	1971
Austin, Ocie	Utah State University	1970-1971
Baker, John	North Carolina College	1963-1967
Barnett, Tom	Purdue University	1959-1960
Barry, Fred	Boston College	1970
Beatty, Charles	North Texas State	1969-1972
Bell, Theo	University of Arizona	1976, 1978-1980
Bingham, Craig	Syracuse University	1982-
Bishop, Don	Los Angeles College	1958-1959
Bivins, Charles	Morris Brown College	1967
Blount, Mel	Southern University	1970-1983
Bohannon, Fred	Mississippi Valley State	1982-

Player	*College*	*Years*
Britt, Jesse	North Carolina A&T University	1986
Brown, David	University of Michigan	1975
Brown, John	Syracuse University	1967-1972
Brown, Larry	University of Kansas	1971-
Brumfield, Jim	Indiana State University	1971
Bryant, Hubie	University of Minnesota	1970
Bullocks, Amos	Southern Illinois University	1966
Butler, Jim	Edward Waters College	1965-1967
Clayton, Harvey	Florida State University	1983-1986
Cobb, Marvin	University of Southern California	1980
Cole, Robin	University of New Mexico	1977-1986
Collier, Michael	Morgan State University	1975
Cunningham, Bennie	Clemson University	1976-
Curry, Roy	Jackson State University	1963
Davis, Charlie	Texas Christian University	1974
Davis, David	Tennessee State University	1973
Davis, Henry	Grambling State University	1970-1973
Davis, Sam	Allen University	1967-1979
Davis, Steve	Delaware State College	1972-1974
Dirden, John	Sam Houston State	1981
Dungy, Tony	University of Minnesota	1977-1978
Edwards, David	University of Illinois	1985-1986
Edwards, Glen	Florida A&M University	1971-1977
Elder, Donnie	Memphis State University	1986
Fisher, Dough	San Diego State University	1969-1970
Ford, Henry	University of Pittsburgh	1956
French, Ernest	Alabama A&M University	1982
Fuqua, John	Morgan State University	1970-1976
Garrett, Reggie	Eastern Michigan University	1974-1975
Gary, Keith	University of Oklahoma	1981-1986
Gilliam, Joe	Tennessee State University	1972-1975
Graves, Tom	Michigan State University	1979
Greene, Joe	North Texas State University	1969-1981
Greenwood, L.C.	Arkansas AM&N	1969-1981
Harris, Franco	Penn State University	1972-1973
Harris, Lou	Kent State University	1968
Harrison, Reggie	University of Cincinnati	1974-1977
Hawthorne, Greg	Baylor University	1979-1981
Henderson, John	Colorado State University	1968-1969
Henton, Anthony	Troy State College	1986
Hinton, Chuck	North Carolina College	1964-1971
Holmes, Ernie	Texas Southern University	1972-1977
Holmes, Mel	North Carolina A&T University	1971-1973
Jefferson, Roy	University of Utah	1965-1969
Jeter, Tony	University of Nebraska	1966, 1968
Johnson, John Henry	St. Mary's (California)/Arizona State	1960-1965
Johnson, Ron	Eastern Michigan University	1978-1983

Player	College	Years
Kemp, Ray	University of Duquesne	1933*
Keys, Brady	Colorado State University	1961-1967
Lewis, Frank	Grambling State University	1971-1977
Lewis, Joe	Compton Junior College	1958-1960
Lipps, Louis	University of Southern Mississippi	1984-1986
Lipscomb, Gene		1961-1962
Little, David	University of Florida	1981-1986
Marion, Jerry	University of Wyoming	1967
Maxson, Alvin	Southern Methodist University	1977-1978
May, Ray	University of Southern California	1967-1969
McCall, Don	University of Southern California	1969
McClairen, Jack	Bethune-Cookman College	1955-1960
McClung, Willie	Florida A&M University	1955-1957
McGriff, Tyrone	Florida A&M University	1980-1982
Merriweather, Michael	University of Pacific	1982-1986
Mingo, Gene		1969-1970
Motley, Marion	University of Nevada, Reno	1955
Nelsun, Edmund	Auburn University	1982-1986
Nisby, John	University of Pacific	1957-1961
Oliver, Clarence	San Diego State University	1969-1970
Peaks, Clarence	Michigan State University	1964-1965
Pearson, Preston	University of Illinois	1970-1973
Perry, Lowell	University of Michigan	1956
Pollard, Frank	Baylor University	1980-1986
Pough, Ernest	Texas Southern University	1976-1977
Rodgers, John	Louisiana Tech University	1982
Rowser, John	University of Michigan	1970-1973
Sanders, Chuck	Slippery Rock	1986
Shanklin, Ron	North Texas State University	1970-1975
Sheffield, Chris	Albany State College	1986
Shell, Donnie	South Carolina State College	1974-1986
Shorter, Jim	University of Detroit	1969
Shy, Don	San Diego State University	1965-1966
Simmons, Jerry	Bethune-Cookman College	1970-1972
Sims, Darryl	University of Wisconsin	1985-1986
Smith, David	Indiana (Pennsylvania)	1970-1972
Smith, Jim	University of Michigan	1977-1982
Smith, Laverne	University of Kansas	1977
Spinks, Jack	Alcorn A&M	1952
Staggers, Jon	University of Missouri	1970-1971
Stallworth, John	Alabama A&M	1974-1986
Swann, Lynn	University of Southern California	1974-1981
Sweeny, Calvin	University of Southern California	1979-1986
Sydnor, Willie	Syracuse University	1982
Taylor, Michael	University of Southern California	1968-1969
Terry, Nat	Florida State University	1978
Thomas, J.T.	Florida State University	1973-1977, 1979-1981

Player	College	Years
Thornton, Sidney	Northwestern (Louisiana)	1977-1984
Valentine, Zack	Eastern Carolina University	1979-1981
Wade, Bob	Morgan State University	1968
Washington, Anthony	Fresno State	1981-1983
Washington, Clarence	Arkansas AM&N	1969-1970
Washington, Sam	Mississippi Valley State University	1982-
Webster, George	Michigan State University	1972-1973
White, Dwight	East Texas State University	1971-1980
Williams, Eric	North Carolina State University	1983-1986
Williams, Erwin	Maryland State College	1969
Williams, Gerald	Auburn University	1986
Willis, Keith	Northeastern	1982
Wilson, Frank	Rice University	1982
Winfrey, Carl	University of Wisconsin	1972
Winston, Dennis	University of Arkansas	1977-1981, 1985-1986
Wolf, Jim	Prairie View A&M	1974
Womack, Joe	California State University, Los Angeles	1962
Woodruff, Dwayne	University of Louisville	1979-1982
Woodson, Marv	Indiana University	1964-1969
Young, Al	South Carolina State College	1971-1972
Younger, Paul	Grambling State University	1958

St. Louis Football Cardinals

St. Louis, Missouri 63102

Coaches

		Years
McMillan, Ernest	(Assistant)	1984-1986
Thomas, Emmit	(Assistant)	1981-1985

All-Pro or Pro Bowl Selections

	Years
McMillan, Ernest	1965, 1967, 1969-1970
Roland, John	1966
Lane, MacArthur	1970
Gray, Mel	1974-1977
Metcalf, Terry	1974-1975, 1977
Anderson, Otis	1979, 1980
Green, Roy	1983, 1984

All-Time Team Roster

Player	College	Years
Anderson, Otis	University of Miami (Florida)	1979
Anderson, Warren	West Virginia State University	1978
Atkins, Robert	Grambling College	1968-1969
Baker, Al	Colorado State University	1983-1986

Player	College	Years
Baker, Charles	University of New Mexico	1980-1986
Barnes, Lawrence	Tennessee State University	1978
Barney, Peter	Southern University	1973-1975
Beauchamp, Al	Southern University	1976
Bell, Gordon	University of Michigan	1978-1979
Belton, Willie	Maryland State College	1973-1974
Boyette, Garland	Grambling College	1962-1963
Brown, Robert	Alcorn A&M University	1969-1970
Brown, Theotis	University of California, Los Angeles	1979-1981
Bryant, Charles	Allen University (South Carolina)	1966-1967
Burns, Leon	California State University, Los Angeles	1972
Butler, James	Edward Waters College	1972
Cain, J.V.	University of Colorado	1974-1977
Clayton, Ralph	University of Michigan	1981
Crenshaw, Willis	Kansas State University	1964-1969
Dardar, Ramsey	Louisiana State University	1984-1985
Davis, Ron	Virginia State University	1973
Day, Thomas	North Carolina A&T University	1960
Duncan, Clyde	University of Tennessee	1984-1985
Edwards, Cid	Tennessee State University	1968-1971
Farr, Miller	Wichita State University	1970-1972
Ferrell, Earl	East Tennessee State University	1982-1985
Finnie, Roger	Florida A&M University	1973-1978
Galloway, David	University of Florida	1982-
Gautt, Prentice	University of Oklahoma	1961-1967
Gilliam, John	South Carolina State University	1969-1971
Goode, John	Youngstown State University	1984-1985
Granger, Charles	Southern University	1961
Gray, Mel	University of Missouri	1971-1982
Green, Roy	Henderson State College	1979-1986
Greer, Curtis	University of Michigan	1980-1986
Griffin, Jeff	University of Utah	1981-1985
Grooms, Elois	Tennessee Tech University	1982-1985
Harrell, Willard	University of Pacific	1978-1986
Harrington, Perry	Jackson State University	1984-1985
Harris, Ike	Iowa State University	1975-1977
Harrison, Reginald	University of Cincinnati	1974
Heflin, Victor	Delaware State College	1983-1985
Holloway, Randy	University of Pittsburgh	1984
Howard, Thomas	Texas Tech University	1984-1986
Hunter, Monte	Salem College	1983
Johnson, Charles	Grambling College	1981
Junior, E.J.	University of Alabama	1981-1986
Kindle, Greg	Tennessee State University	1974-1975
LaFleur, Greg	Louisiana State University	1981-1985
Lane, MacArthur	Utah State University	1968-1971
Lott, Thomas	University of Oklahoma	1979

Player	College	Years
Love, Randy	University of Houston	1979-1985
Mack, Cedric	Baylor University	1983-1986
Marsh, Doug	University of Michigan	1980-1986
Mays, Stafford	University of Washington	1980-1986
McMillan, Ernest	University of Illinois	1961-1974
Metcalf, Terry	California State University, Long Beach	1973-1977
Mitchell, Stump	The Citadel	1981-1986
Morris, Wayne	Southern Methodist University	1976-1983
Murrell, William	Winston-Salem State University	1979
Oliver, Clancy	San Diego State University	1973
Paremore, Robert	Florida A&M University	1963-1964
Person, Ara	Morgan State University	1972
Phillips, Rod	Jackson State University	1979-1980
Pittman, Dan	University of Wyoming	1983-1986
Radford, Bruce	Grambling State University	1981
Ramson, Eason	Washington State University	1978
Rashad, Ahmad	University of Oregon	1972-1973
Reaves, Ken	Norfolk State University	1974-1977
Robbins, Tootie	East Carolina University	1982-1986
Roland, John	University of Missouri	1966-1972
Rudolph, Council	Kentucky State University	1973-1975
Scales, Hurles	North Texas State University	1974
Scott, Carlos	University of Texas, El Paso	1983-1985
Shelby, Willie	University of Alabama	1978
Smith, Leonard	McNeese State University	1983-1986
Smith, Wayne	Purdue University	1982-1986
Spencer, Maurice	North Carolina Central University	1974
Thaxton, James	Tennessee State University	1978
Thomas, Earl	University of Houston	1974-1975
Thompson, Norm	University of Utah	1971-1976
Times, Ken	Southern University	1981
Tolbert, Jim	Lincoln University (Missouri)	1973-1975
Urshaw, Marvin	Trinity College (Texas)	1976
Walker, Quentin	University of Virginia	1984-1985
Washington, Lionel	Tulane University	1983-1986
Williams, Clyde	Southern University	1967-1971
Williams, Gerard	Langston University	1980
Williams, Herb	Southern University	1981-1982
Wright, Nate	San Diego State University	1969-1970

San Diego Chargers
San Diego, California 92120

Front Office Personnel		*Years*
Younger, Paul	(Assistant General Manager)	1975-1986
Brooks, Sid	(Equipment Manager)	1973-1986

Coaches		*Years*
Lundy, Lamar	(Assistant)	1971
Wood, Willie	(Assistant)	1972-1974
Durden, Earnel	(Assistant)	1974-1986

All-Pro or Pro Bowl Selections

	Years
Faison, Earl	1961, 1963-1965
Lowe, Paul	1960, 1965
Ladd, Ernest	1965
Washington, Russ	1978
Jefferson, John	1979, 1980
Dean, Fred	1980
Winslow, Kellen	1980, 1981
Johnson, Gary	1980, 1981
Joiner, Charles	1980
Chandler, Wes	1982, 1984
Wilkerson, Doug	1982, 1983
Jackson, Earnest	1985

All-Time Team Roster

Player	*College*	*Years*
Aldridge, Lionel	Utah State University	1972-1973
Anderson, Gary	University of Arkansas	1985-1986
Anderson, Rickey	Southern Carolina State College	1978
Bacon, Coy	Jackson State University	1973-1975
Baker, Mel	Texas Southern University	1975
Barnes, Earnest	North Carolina College	1960-1962
Barnes, Lawrence	Tennessee State University	1977-1978
Barnes, Peter	Southern University	1970-1972
Bell, Eddie	Idaho State University	1976
Bell, Rickey	University of Southern California	1982
Bendross, Jesse	University of Alabama	1984-1986
Benson, Thomas	University of Oklahoma	1986
Bradley, Carlos	Wake Forest University	1981-1985
Braxton, Hezekiah	Virginia Union University	1962
Briscoe, Marlin	Omaha College	1975
Brooks, Billy	University of Oklahoma	1981
Brooks, James	Auburn University	1981-1983
Brown, Donald	University of Maryland	1986
Brown, Robert	Arkansas AM&N	1974

Player	*College*	*Years*
Brown, Booker	University of Southern California	1975-1977
Buchanon, Willie	San Diego State University	1979-1982
Burns, Leon	Long Beach State University	1971
Burton, Larry	Purdue University	1978-1979
Byrd, Gil	San Jose State University	1983-1986
Chandler, Wes	University of Florida	1981-1986
Dale, Jeffrey	Louisiana State University	1985-1986
Davis, Harrison	University of Virginia	1974
Davis, Thomas	North Carolina A&T University	1967
Davis, Wayne	Indiana State University	1985-1986
Dean, Fred	Louisiana Tech University	1975-1981
DeJurnett, Charles	San Jose State University	1976-1980
Dennis, Al	Grambling State University	1973
Dorsey, Larry	Tennessee State University	1976-1977
Duckworth, Bobby	University of Arkansas	1982-1985
Duncan, Leslie "Speedy"	Jackson State University	1964-1970
Dunlap, Leonard	North Texas State University	1972-1974
Edwards, Cid	Tennessee State University	1972-1974
Edwards, Glen	Florida A&M University	1978-1981
Falson, Earl	University of Indiana	1961-1966
Farr, Miller	Wichita State University	1965-1966
Ferguson, Eugene	Norfolk State University	1969-1970
Ferguson, Keith	Ohio State University	1981-1985
Frazier, Willie	Arkansas AM&N	1966-1970
Garrett, Michael	University of Southern California	1970-1973
Gordon, Dick	Michigan State University	1974
Green, Michael	Oklahoma State University	1983-1985
Griffin, Jim	Grambling State University	1966-1967
Hardison, Dee	University of North Carolina	1986
Harrington, LaRue	Norfolk State University	1980
Harris, James	Grambling State University	1977-1982
Henderson, Reuben	San Diego State University	1983-1985
Hill, Jim	Texas A&I	1969-1971
Holmes, Robert	Southern University	1973
Jackson, Bernard	Washington State University	1980
Jackson, Earnest	Texas A&M University	1983-1985
James, Lionel	Auburn University	1984-1986
Jefferson, John	Arizona State University	1978-1980
Johnson, Gary	Grambling State University	1975-1985
Johnson, Pete	Ohio State University	1984
Johnson, Trumaine	Grambling State University	1985-1986
Joiner, Charles	Grambling State University	1976-1986
Jones, Clint	Michigan State University	1973
Jones, David "Deacon"	South Carolina State College	1972-1973
Jones, Harris	Johnson C. Smith University	1971
Jones, Leroy	Norfolk State University	1976-1983
Jones, Ray	Southern University	1978

Player	College	Years
Ladd, Ernest	Grambling State University	1961-1965
Levias, Jerry	Southern Methodist University	1971-1974
Lewis, David	University of Southern California	1982
Little, Larry	Bethune-Cookman College	1967-1968
Lowe, Paul	Oregon State University	1960-1968
Lowe, Woodrow	University of Alabama	1976-1986
Mackey, John	Syracuse University	1972
McCrary, Gregg	Clark College	1978-1980
McGee, Buford	University of Mississippi	1984-1986
McGee, Willie	Alcorn A&M	1973
McPherson, Miles	New Haven College	1982-1985
Mitchell, Lydell	Pennsylvania State University	1978-1979
Mitchell, Ed	Southern University	1965-1966
Morris, Eugene	West Texas State University	1976
Morris, Wayne	Southern Methodist University	1984
Muncie, Chuck	University of California, Berkeley	1980-1985
Norman, Pettis	Johnson C. Smith University	1971-1973
O'Neal, Leslie	Oklahoma State University	1986
Owens, Joe	Alcorn A&M University	1970
Preston, Ray	Syracuse University	1976-1985
Plunkett, Sherman	Maryland State College	1961-1962
Queen, Jeff	Morgan State University	1969-1971
Reese, Don	Jackson State University	1981
Rice, Andy	Texas Southern University	1970-1971
Rice, Floyd	Alcorn A&M University	1973-1975
Roberson, Bo	Cornell University	1961
Robinson, Fred	University of Miami	1984-1986
Robinson, Jerry	Grambling State University	1962-1964
Rodgers, John	University of Nebraska	1972-1978
Rodgers, Mel	Florida A&M University	1971, 1974
Russell, Booker	Southwest Texas State University	1980
Salter, Bryant	University of Pittsburgh	1971-1973
Selmon, Dewey	University of Oklahoma	1982
Scales, Dwight	Grambling State University	1981-1983
Singleton, Ron	Grambling State University	1976
Smith, John Ray	Lamar University	1984
Smith, Lucious	Fullerton State University	1984
Smith, Sherman	University of Miami, Ohio	1983
Spencer, Tim	Ohio State University	1985-1986
Sykes, John	Morgan State University	1972
Tanner, John	Tennessee State University	1971
Tate, Franklin	North Carolina Central University	1975
Taylor, Ken	Oregon State University	1986
Taylor, Sammie	Grambling State University	1964
Thaxton, James	Tennessee State University	1973-1974
Thomas, Duane	West Texas State University	1972
Thomas, Jewerl	San Jose State University	1984-1985

Player	College	Years
Thomas, Lee	Jackson State University	1971-1972
Thomas, Mitchell	University of Nevada, Las Vegas	1979-1980
Thompson, Audra	East Texas State University	1981
Tolbert, Jim	Lincoln University (Missouri)	1966-1971, 1976
Turner, John	University of Miami (Florida)	1984-1985
Tyler, Maurice	Morgan State University	1975
Walters, Dan	University of Arkansas	1983-1985
Washington, Joe	University of Oklahoma	1976-1977
Washington, Russ	University of Missouri	1968-1982
Wells, Robert	Johnson C. Smith University	1968-1970
Westmoreland, Richard	North Carolina A&T University	1963-1965
White, Andre	Florida A&M University	1968
Wilkerson, Doug	North Carolina Central University	1971-1985
Williams, Clarence	University of South Carolina	1977-1981
Williams, Lee	Bethune-Cookman College	1984-1986
Williams, Lester	University of Miami	1986
Winslow, Kellen	University of Missouri	1979-1986
Woods, Don	University of New Mexico	1974-1980
Wyatt, Kevin	University of Arkansas	1986
Young, Andre	Louisiana Tech University	1982-1985
Young, Ricky	Jackson State University	1975-1977
Young, Wilbur	West Pennsylvania	1978-1980, 1981-1982

San Francisco 49ers

Redwood City, California 94061

Front Office Personnel

		Years
Knox, Rodney	(Publications Coordinator)	
Owens, R.C.	(Executive Assistant)	

Coaches

		Years
Perry, Joe	(Assistant)	1968-1969
Raye, James	(Assistant)	1977
Matthews, Billy	(Assistant)	1979-1982
Rhodes, Ray	(Assistant)	1981-1986
Hart, Tom	(Assistant)	1983-1986
Green, Dennis	(Assistant)	1986
Lewis, Sherman	(Assistant)	1986

All-Pro or Pro Bowl Selections

	Years
Perry, Joe	1953, 1954
McNeil, Clifton	1968
Alexander, Kermit	1968
Johnson, James	1969, 1971-1972, 1974

Washington, Eugene	1969-1972
Taylor, Bruce	1971
Hardeman, Cedric	1971, 1975
Peoples, Woody	1973
Williams, Delvin	1976
Elam, Cleveland	1976, 1977
Hart, Tom	1976
Solomon, Fred	1980
Dean, Fred	1981, 1983
Lott, Ron	1981-1986
Hicks, Dwight	1981-1982, 1984
Turner, Keena	1982, 1984
Board, Dwaine	1983, 1984
Wright, Eric	1983
Tyler, Wendell	1984
Williamson, Carlton	1984
Craig, Roger	1985
Rice, Jerry	1986

All-Time Team Roster

Player	*College*	*Years*
Alexander, Kermit	University of California, Los Angeles	1963-1969
Allen, Nate	Texas Southern University	1975
Anderson, Terry	Bethune-Cookman College	1980
Belser, Ceaser	Arkansas AM&N	1974
Belk, William	Maryland State College	1968-1974
Board, Dwaine	North Carolina A&T University	1979-1986
Carter, Michael	Southern Methodist University	1984-1986
Casey, Bernie	Bowling Green State University	1961-1966
Cherry, Tony	University of Oregon	1986
Clark, Mario	University of Oregon	1984
Coller, Tim	East Texas State University	1982-1983
Cooper, Earl	Rice University	1980-1985
Cornelius, Charles	Bethune-Cookman College	1979-1980
Cowlings, Al	University of Southern California	1979
Craig, Roger	University of Nebraska	1983-1986
Cribbs, Joe	Auburn University	1986
Daniels, Clemon	Prairie View A&M University	1968
Davis, John	University of Alabama	1981
Dean, Fred	Louisiana Tech University	1981-1985
Dungy, Anthony	University of Minnesota	1979
Edwards, Earl	Wichita State University	1969-1972
Elam, Cleveland	Tennessee State University	1976-1978
Elliot, Lenvil	N.E. Missouri State University	1979-1981
Fuller, Jeff	Texas A&M University	1984
Griffin, Don	Middle Tennessee State University	1986

Player	College	Years
Haley, Charles	James Madison University	1986
Hardeman, Cedric	North Texas State University	1970-1979
Hardy, Edgar	Jackson State University	1973
Harmon, Derrick	Cornell University	1984-1986
Harper, Willie	University of Nebraska	1979-1983
Hart, Tom	Morris Brown College	1968-1973
Hayes, Robert	Florida A&M University	1975
Henderson, Thomas	Langston University	1980
Hicks, Dwight	University of Michigan	1979-1985
Holmes, Mitchell	Texas Southern University	1974-1975
Jackson, Wilbur	University of Alabama	1974-1979
Johnson, Charles	Grambling State University	1979-1980
Johnson, Gary	Grambling State University	1984
Johnson, James	University of California, Los Angeles	1961-1976
Johnson, John Henry	St. Mary's College/Arizona State	1954-1956
Johnson, Kermit	University of California, Los Angeles	1975-1976
Johnson, Leo	Tennessee State University	1969-1970
Jones, Arrington	Winston-Salem State University	1981
Lakes, Roland	Wichita State University	1961-1970
Lawrence, Amos	University of North Carolina	1981-1982
Lecount, Terry	University of Florida	1978
Leonard, Anthony	Virginia Union University	1976
Lott, Ron	University of Southern California	1981-1986
Lyles, Leonard	University of Louisville	1959-1960
McGee, Willie	Alcorn State University	1976
McIntrye, Guy	University of Georgia	1984-1986
McKyer, Tin	University of Texas, Arlington	1986
McLemore, Dana	University of Hawaii	1982-1985
McNeil, Clifton	Grambling College	1968-1969
Monroe, Carl	University of Utah	1983-1985
Moore, Manfred	University of Southern California	1974-1975
Moore, Jeff	Jackson State University	1982-1983
Morgan, Melvin	Mississippi Valley State University	1979-1980
Nehemiah, Renaldo	University of Maryland	1982-1985
Norton, Ray	San Jose State University	1960-1961
Paris, William	University of Michigan	1982-1986
Patton, Ricky	Jackson State University	1980-1982
Penchio, Robert	Alcorn A&M University	1974-1975
Peoples, Woody	Grambling State University	1968-1977
Phillips, Mel	North Carolina A&T University	1966-1976
Pillers,	Alcorn A&M University	1980-1984
Ramson, Eason	Washington State University	1979-1983
Reese, Archie	Grambling State University	1978-1981
Rhodes, Ray	University of Tulsa	1980
Rice, Jerry	Mississippi Valley State University	1985-1986
Roberson, Vern	Grambling State University	1978
Simpson, O.J.	University of Southern California	1978-1979

Player	College	Years
Singleton, Ron	Grambling State University	1977-1980
Smith, J.D.	North Carolina A&T University	1956-1964
Smith, Noland	Tennessee State University	1969
Solomon, Fred	University of Tampa	1978-1985
Taylor, Bruce	Boston University	1970-1977
Taylor, Roosevelt	Grambling College	1969-1971
Thomas, Lynn	University of Pittsburgh	1981-1982
Times, Ken	Southern University	1980
Turner, Keena	Purdue University	1980-1986
Tyler, Wendell	University of California, Los Angeles	1983-1985
Walker, Elliott	University of Pittsburgh	1978
Washington, David	Alcorn A&M University	1975-1976
Washington, Eugene	Stanford University	1969-1976
Williams, Delvin	University of Kansas	1974-1977
Williams, Gerard	Langston University	1979-1980
Williams, Herb	Southern University	1963
Williams, Howie	Howard University	1981-1985
Williamson, Carlton	University of Pittsburgh	1981-1986
Wilson, Michael	Washington State University	1981-1986
Woods, Don	University of New Mexico	1980
Wright, Eric	University of Missouri	1981-1986

Seattle Seahawks

Kirkland, Washington

Front Office Personnel

		Years
Perry, Lowell	(Sales and Marketing Coordinator)	1986-1987
McKenzie, Reginald	(Sales and Marketing Assistant)	1987

All-Pro or Pro Bowl Selections

	Years
Brown, Dave	1985
Easley, Ken	1983-1986
Green, Jacob	1986
Warner, Curt	1984-1986
Young, Fred	1985-1986

All-Time Team Roster

Player	College	Years
Anderson, Eddie	Fort Valley State College	1986-1987
Bailey, Edwin	South Carolina State College	1981-1987
Bolton, Andy	Fisk University	1976
Brown, Dave	University of Michigan	1976-1986
Bryant, Jeff	Clemson University	1982-1987

Player	College	Years
Butler, Keith	Memphis State University	1978-1987
Butler, Ray	University of Southern California	1985-1987
Cowlings, Al	University of Southern California	1976
Easley, Ken	University of California, Los Angeles	1981-1987
Franklin, Byron	Auburn University	1985-1987
Green, Jacob	Texas A&M University	1980-1987
Hardy, Robert	Jackson State University	1979-1982
Harris, Richard	Grambling State University	1976-1977
Jackson, Michael	University of Washington	1979-1986
Justin, Kerry	Oregon State University	1979-1983
Kinlaw, Reggie	University of Oklahoma	1986-1987
McKenzie, Reggie	University of Michigan	1983-1984
Moore, Jeff	Jackson State University	1979-1981
Penchion, Robert	Alcorn State University	1976
Robinson, Eugene	Colgate University	1985-1987
Robinson, Shelton	University of North Carolina	1982-1985
Ross, Oliver	Alabama A&M University	1976
Simpson, Keith	Memphis State University	1978-1985
Smith, Sherman	University of Miami, Ohio	1976-1982
Taylor, Terry	Southern Illinois University	1984-1987
Turner, Daryl	Michigan State University	1984-1987
Warner, Curt	Penn State University	1983-1987
Woods, Larry	Tennessee State University	1976
Williams, John L.	University of Florida	1986-1987
Young, Fred	New Mexico State University	1984-1986

Tampa Bay Buccaneers
Tampa, Florida 33607

Coaches

		Years
Raye, James	(Assistant, Offensive Coordinator)	1985

All-Pro or Pro Bowl Selections

	Years
Selmon, Leroy	1979-1984
Giles, Jimmie	1980-1982
Lewis, David	1980
Green, Hugh	1982, 1983
Wilder, James	1984

All-Time Team Roster

Player	College	Years
Acorn, Fred	University of Texas	1984-1985
Armstrong, Adger	Texas A&M University	1983-1984
Bell, Jerry	Arizona State University	1982-1984

Player	College	Years
Bell, Ricky	University of Southern California	1977-1981
Bell, Theo	University of Arizona	1981-1985
Braggs, Byron	University of Alabama	1984
Branton, Eugene	Texas Southern University	1983
Bright, Leon	Florida State University	1984-1985
Brown, Aaron	Ohio State University	1978-1980
Brown, Cedric	Kent State University	1976-1986
Browner, Keith	University of Southern California	1984-1985
Carter, Gerald	Texas A&M University	1981-1986
Carter, Louis	University of Maryland	1976-1978
Carver, Melvin	University of Nevada, Las Vegas	1982-1986
Castille, Jeremiah	University of Alabama	1983-1985
Chambers, Wallace	Eastern Kentucky University	1978-1979
Colzie, Neal	Ohio State University	1980-1983
Crowder, Randy	Pennsylvania State University	1978-1980
Curry, Craig	University of Texas	1984-1985
Darns, Phil	Mississippi Valley State University	1984-1986
Davis, Anthony	University of Southern California	1977
Davis, Charles	University of Colorado	1976
Davis, Jeff	Clemson University	1982-1986
Davis, Johnny	University of Alabama	1978-1980
Dickinson, Parnell	Mississippi Valley State University	1976
Dixon, Dwayne	University of Florida	1984-1985
DuBose, Jimmy	University of Florida	1976-1978
Franklin, Larry	Jackson State University	1978
Giles, Jimmie	Alcorn State University	1978-1985
Grant, Frank	South Colorado State University	1978
Green, Hugh	University of Pittsburgh	1981-1985
Hagins, Isaac	University of Southern California	1976-1980
Holt, John	West Texas State University	1981-1985
Holmes, Ron	University of Washington	1985
House, Kevin	University of Southern Illinois	1980-1985
Inmon, Earl	Bethune-Cookman College	1978
Jackson, Noah	University of Tampa	1984-1986
Johnson, Cecil	University of Pittsburgh	1977-1986
Johnson, Essex	Grambling State University	1976
Jones, Gordon	University of Pittsburgh	1979-1982
Lewis, David	University of Southern California	1977-1981
Lewis, Reggie	North Texas State University	1980-1982
Logan, David	University of Pittsburgh	1979-1985
Maxson, Alvin	Southern Methodist University	1978
McNeil, Rod	University of Southern California	1976
Middleton, Terdell	Memphis State University	1982-1983
Mitchell, Aaron	University of Nevada, Las Vegas	1981
Moore, Maulty	Bethune-Cookman College	1976
Morgan, Karl	University of California, Los Angeles	1984
Morton, Michael	University of Nevada, Las Vegas	1982-1986

Player	*College*	*Years*
Oliver, Frank	Kentucky State University	1976
O'Steen, Dwayne	San Jose State University	1982-1983
Owens, James	University of California, Los Angeles	1982-1985
Owens, Morris	Arizona State University	1976-1979
Peoples, George	Auburn University	1984-1986
Radford, Bruce	Grambling State University	1980
Ragsdale, George	North Carolina A&T University	1977-1979
Reece, Beasley	North Texas State University	1983-1985
Roberts, Greg	University of Oklahoma	1979-1982
Rudolph, Council	Kentucky State University	1976-1977
Samuels, Tony	Bethune-Cookman College	1980
Sanders, Eugene	Texas A&M University	1979, 1985
Selmon, Dewey	University of Oklahoma	1976-1980
Selmon, Lee Roy	University of Oklahoma	1976-1985
Swell, Ray	University of Wisconsin	1980-1983
Thomas, Norris	University of Southern Mississippi	1980-1984
Thomas, Zach	South Carolina State University	1984-1985
Thompson, Robert	University of Michigan	1983-1985
Tuttle, Perry	Clemson University	1976
Washington, Chris	Iowa State University	1984
White, Charles	Bethune-Cookman College	1978
White, Jeris	University of Hawaii	1977-1979
Wilder, James	University of Missouri	1981-1986
Williams, Doug	Grambling State University	1978-1982
Williams, Ed	Langston University	1976-1977
Williams, Punkin	Memphis State University	1985
Wood, Richard	University of Southern California	1976-1986

Washington Redskins
Washington, D.C. 20003

	Front Office Personnel	*Years*
Mitchell, Robert	(Executive Assistant to The President)	1978-1980
	(Assistant General Manager	1981-1986
Daniels, Richard	(Director of Player Personnel)	1983-1986
Morris, Dale	(Director of Stadium Operations)	

	Coaches	*Years*
Taylor, Charles	(Assistant)	1980-1986
Thomas, Emmitt	(Assistant)	1986

All-Pro or Pro Bowl Selections

	Years
Mitchell, Robert	1962-1964
Taylor, Charles	1964-1967, 1972-1975
Brown, Larry	1969-1972
Jefferson, Roy	1971
Duncan, Leslie (Speedy)	1972
Houston, Ken	1973-1978
Mulkey, Herb	1973
Thomas, Michael	1976
Fuggett, Jean	1977, 1978
Green, Tony	1978
Parrish, Lamar	1979
Nelms, Michael	1980-1982
Peters, Tony	1982
Brown, Charles	1982, 1983
Green, Darrell	1984
Monk, Art	1984, 1985
Manley, Dexter	1986

All-Time Team Roster

Player	*College*	*Years*
Adams, Willie	New Mexico State University	1965-1966
Alston, Mack	Maryland State College	1970-1972
Anderson, Terry	Bethune-Cookman College	1978
Bacon, Coy	Jackson State University	1978-1981
Bass, Michael	University of Michigan	1969-1975
Biggs, Verlon	Jackson State University	1971-1975
Brooks, Perry	Southern University	1978-1985
Brown, Charles	South Carolina State College	1982-1985
Brown, Larry	Kansas State University	1969-1976
Buggs, Dan	University of West Virginia	1976-1979
Caster, Richard	Jackson State University	1981
Claitt, Rick	Bethune-Cookman College	1980-1981
Clark, Gary		1986
Cherry, Raphael	University of Hawaii	1985-1986
Coffey, Ken	Southwest Texas State University	1983-1986
Coleman, Monte	Central Arkansas University	1979-1986
Dean, Fred	Texas Southern University	1978-1982
Dean, Vernon	San Diego State University	1982-1986
Denson, Moses	Maryland Eastern Shore	1974-1975
Duncan, Leslie (Speedy)	Jackson State University	1971-1973
Dyer, Henry	Grambling College	1969-1970
Evans, Charles	University of Southern California	1974
Evans, Reginald	University of Richmond	1983
Forte, Ike	University of Arkansas	1978-1980
Fuggett, Jean	Amherst College	1976-1979

Player	College	Years
Garrett, Alvin	Angelo State University	1971-1985
Grant, Darryl	Rice University	1981-1986
Grant, Frank	South Colorado State College	1973-1978
Green, Darryl	Texas A&I	1983-1985
Green, Tony	University of Florida	1978
Griffin, Keith	University of Miami (Florida)	1984-1986
Hammond, Robert	Morgan State University	1979-1980
Hardeman, Buddy	Iowa State University	1979-1980
Harmon, Clarence	Mississippi State University	1977-1982
Harraway, Charles	San Jose State University	1969-1973
Harris, Don	Rutgers University	1978-1979
Haymond, Alvin	Southern University	1972
Haynes, Reginald	University of Nevada, Las Vegas	1978
Hill, Calvin	Yale University	1976-1977
Holman, Willie	South Carolina State University	1971
Houston, Ken	Prairie View A&M University	1973-1980
Jackson, Leroy	Western Illinois University	1962-1963
Jackson, Wilbur	University of Alabama	1980-1982
Jefferson, Roy	University of Utah	1971-1976
Jones, Anthony	Wichita State University	1984
Jones, David	South Carolina State College	1974
Jones, Jimmie	Wichita State University	1971-1973
Jones, Joe	Tennessee State University	1979-1980
Jones, Melvin	University of Houston	1981
Kaufman, Mel	Cal Poly, San Luis Obispo	1981-1985
Laster, Donald	Tennessee State University	1982-1983
Lavender, Joe	San Diego State University	1976-1982
Malone, Ben	Arizona State University	1978-1979
Manley, Dexter	Oklahoma State University	1981-1986
Mann, Charles	University of Nevada, Reno	1983-1986
Martin, Aaron	North Carolina College	1968
May, Mark	University of Pittsburgh	1981-1986
McCrary, Greg	Clark College	1978-1981
McDaniel, John	Lincoln University	1978-1980
McDaniel, LeCharles	Cal Poly, San Luis Obispo	1981-1982
McGee, Tony	Bishop College	1983-1984
McKenzie, Raleigh		1986
McKinney, Zion	University of South Carolina	1980
McLinton, Harold	Southern University	1969-1978
Metcalf, Terry	San Diego State University	1981
Mitchell, Robert	University of Illinois	1962-1968
Monk, Art	Syracuse University	1980-1985
Moore, Jeff	Jackson State University	1984-1985
Muhammad, Calvin	Texas Southern University	1984-1985
Mulkey, Herb	(no college)	1972-1974

Player	*College*	*Years*
Nelms, Michael	Baylor University	1980-1985
Nock, George	Morgan State University	1972
Owens, Brig	University of Cincinnati	1966-1967
Parrish, Lemar	Lincoln University	1978-1981
Perrin, Lonnie	University of Illinois	1979
Peters, Tony	University of Oklahoma	1979-1982, 1984, 1985
Phillips, Joe	University of Kentucky	1985-1986
Reed, Alvin	Prairie View A&M University	1973-1975
Reed, Robert	Tennessee State University	1965
Roberts, Walter	San Jose State University	1969-1970
Robinson, David	Pennsylvania State University	1973-1974
Rogers, George	University of South Carolina	1985-1986
Salters, Bryant	University of Pittsburgh	1974-1975
Sample, John	Maryland State College	1963-1965
Seay, Virgil	Trog State College	1981-1984
Sistruck, Manny	Arkansas AM&N	1970-1975
Smith, Jim (Yazoo)	University of Oregon	1968
Smith, Rick	Alabama State University	1984
Starke, George	Columbia University	1973-1984
Taylor, Charles	Arizona State University	1964-1977
Taylor, Roosevelt	Grambling College	1972
Thomas, Duane	West Texas State University	1973-1974
Thomas, Michael	University of Nevada, Las Vegas	1975-1978
Towns, Morris	University of Missouri	1984-1985
Vactor, Ted	University of Nebraska	1969-1974
Waddy, Ray	Texas A&I University	1979-1980
Wade, Robert	Morgan State University	1969
Walker, Rick	University of California, Los Angeles	1980-1985
Washington, Anthony	Fresno State University	1983-1985
Washington, Joe	University of Oklahoma	1981-1984
White, Jeris	University of Hawaii	1980-1982
Wilburn, Barry	University of Mississippi	1985-1986
Williams, Clarence	University of South Carolina	1982
Williams, Kevin	Iowa State University	1985-1986
Williams, Michael	Alabama A&M University	1982-1984
Williams, Sid	Southern University	1967
Wonsley, Otis	Alcorn State University	1981-1986
Wynn, William	Tennessee State University	1977

Golf

UNITED GOLFERS ASSOCIATION CHAMPIONS

Year	Player	Designation	Site
1926	Harry Jackson	Pro	Stowe, Mass.
1927	Robert "Pat" Ball	Pro	Stowe, Mass.
1928	Frank Gaskins	Amateur	Stowe, Mass.
1929	Frank Gaskins	Amateur	Shady Rest, NJ
1930	George Roddy	Amateur	Casa Loma, Wis.
	Marie Thompson	Amateur	
	Edison Marshall	Pro	
1931	James McKoy	Amateur	Kankakee, Ill.
	Marie Thompson	Amateur	
	Edison Marshal	Pro	
1932	Frank Gaskins	Amateur	Indianapolis, Ind.
	Lucy Williams	Amateur	
	John Dendy	Pro	
1933	Isaac Ellis	Amateur	Kankakee, Ill.
	Julia Siler	Amateur	
	Howard Wheeler	Pro	
1934	Percy Jones	Amateur	Detroit, Mich.
	Ella Able	Amateur	
	Robert "Pat" Ball	Pro	
1935	Frank Radcliffe	Amateur	Yorktown Heights, NY
	Ella Able	Amateur	
	Solomon Hughes	Pro	
1936	Clifford Taylor	Amateur	Philadelphia, Pa.
	Lucy Williams	Amateur	
	John Dendy	Pro	
1937	George Roddy	Amateur	Cleveland, Ohio
	Lucy Williams	Amateur	
	John Dendy	Pro	
1938	Remus Robinson	Amateur	Kankakee, Ill.
	Melanie Moye	Amateur	
	Howard Wheeler	Pro	
1939	Gus Price	Amateur	Los Angeles, Cal.
	Geneva Wilson	Amateur	
	Cliff Strickland	Pro	

Year	Player	Designation	Site
1940	Remus Robinson	Amateur	Chicago, Ill.
	Melanie Moye	Amateur	
	Hugh Smith	Pro	
1941	Cliff Taylor	Amateur	Boston, Mass.
	Cleo Ball	Amateur	
	Robert "Pat" Ball	Pro	

1942-1945 No competition

Year	Player	Designation	Site
1946	Bill Brown	Amateur	Pittsburgh, Pa.
	Lucy Mitchell	Amateur	
	Howard Wheeler	Pro	
1947	Alfred "Tub" Holmes	Amateur	Philadelphia, Pa.
	Thelma Cowan	Amateur	
	Howard Wheeler	Pro	
1948	Gordon Goodson	Amateur	Indianapolis, Ind.
	Mary Brown	Amateur	
	Howard Wheeler	Pro	
1949	Butler Cooper	Amateur	Detroit, Mich.
	Thelma Cowan	Amateur	
	Ted Rhodes	Pro	
1950	Tex Gillory	Amateur	Washington, DC
	Anne Gregory	Amateur	
	Ted Rhodes	Pro	
1951	Joe Louis	Amateur	Cleveland, Ohio
	Eoline Thornton	Amateur	
	Ted Rhodes	Pro	
1952	Gordon Goodson	Amateur	Pittsburgh, Pa.
	Alice Stewart	Amateur	
	Charles Sifford	Pro	
1953	Joe Roach	Amateur	Kansas City, Mo.
	Anne Gregory	Amateur	
	Charles Sifford	Pro	
1954	Joe Roach	Amateur	Dallas, Tex.
	Thelma Cowan	Amateur	
	Charles Sifford	Pro	
1955	Joe Roach	Amateur	Detroit, Mich.
	Thelma Cowan	Amateur	
	Charles Sifford	Pro	
1956	Gordon Goodson	Amateur	Philadelphia, Pa.
	Charles Sifford	Pro	
1957	Howard Brown	Amateur	Washington, DC
	Anne Gregory	Amateur	
	Ted Rhodes	Pro	

Year	Player	Designation	Site
1958	Alfred "Tub" Holmes	Amateur	Pittsburgh, Pa.
	Bernice Turner	Amateur	
	Howard Wheeler	Pro	
1959	Rafe Botts	Amateur	Washington, DC
	Ethel Funches	Amateur	
	Richard Thomas	Pro	
1960	Calvin Turner	Amateur	Chicago, Ill.
	Ethel Funches	Amateur	
	Charles Sifford	Pro	
1961	Willie Greer	Amateur	Boston, Mass.
	Bernice Turner	Amateur	
	Pete Brown	Pro	
1962	Calvin Tanner	Amateur	Memphis, Tenn.
	Carey Jones	Amateur	
	Pete Brown	Pro	
1963	Charles Howard	Amateur	Washington, DC
	Ethel Funches	Amateur	
	Lee Elder	Pro	
1964	Forrest Jones	Amateur	Indianapolis, Ind.
	Renee Power	Amateur	
	Lee Elder	Pro	
1965	Andy Woodard	Amateur	Detroit, Mich.
	Anne Gregory	Amateur	
	Cliff Brown	Pro	
1966	Dave Brown	Amateur	Chicago, Ill.
	Anne Gregory	Amateur	
	Lee Elder	Pro	
1967	James Everitt	Amateur	Miami, Fla.
	Ethel Funches	Amateur	
	Lee Elder	Pro	
1968	Eddie Leonard	Amateur	Washington, DC
	Ethel Funches	Amateur	
	James Black	Pro	
1969	Curtis Walker	Amateur	Turnersville, NJ
	Ethel Funches	Amateur	
	Jim Dent	Pro	
1970	Joe Green	Amateur	New Haven, Conn.
	Exie O'Cher	Amateur	
	James Walker	Pro	
1971	Joe Green	Amateur	Pittsburgh, Pa.
	Exie O'Cher	Amateur	
	Jack Price (white)	Pro	

Year	Player	Designation	Site
1972	James Osborne	Amateur	Chicago, Ill.
	Mary Truett	Amateur	
	James Black	Pro	
1973	Howard Pierson	Amateur	Turnersville, NJ
	Ethel Funches	Amateur	
1974	George O'Rourke	Amateur	Boston, Mass.
	Clara Kliinui	Amateur	
	Charles Owen	Pro	
1975	Dan Bieber	Amateur	Pine Ridge, Md.
	Laura Spokien	Amateur	
	Charles Owen	Pro	
1976	Ashley Smith	Amateur	
	Debra Bennett	Amateur	
	Lou Harve	Pro	
1977	Milton Carswell	Amateur	New Haven, Conn.
	Joy Little	Amateur	
	Floyd Tinsley	Pro	
1978	Billy Osborne	Amateur	San Diego, Cal.
1979	James Sanders	Amateur	San Juan, PR
	Vera Gillespie	Amateur	
	Joe Williams	Pro	
1980	Joe Green	Amateur	Innisbrook, Fla.
1981	Norman Collier	Amateur	Chicago, Ill.
	Wilhemena Stringer	Amateur	
	Leonard Pace	Pro	
1982	Herb Runnels	Amateur	Detroit, Mich.
	Naomi Jenkins	Amateur	
	Leonard Pace	Pro	
1983	Jerry Morgan	Amateur	Rehobeth, Mass.
	Naomi Jenkins	Amateur	
	Curtis Walker	Pro	
1984	Herb Runnels	Amateur	Dayton, Ohio
	Doretha Green	Amateur	
	Curtis Walker	Pro	

Tennis

BLACK NATIONAL AND INTERNATIONAL CHAMPIONS

1948	Oscar Johnson	National Public Parks Juniors
1956-57-59	Reginald Weir	National Senior (45's) Indoors
1956	Althea Gibson	French Singles and Doubles (A. Buxton)
1957	Althea Gibson	Wimbledon Singles
		US Singles
		US Clay Court Singles
		Australian Doubles (Shirley Fry)
		US Mixed Doubles (Kurt Nielsen)
1958	Althea Gibson	Wimbledon Singles and Doubles (M. Bueno)
		US Singles
1960	Arthur Ashe	US Boy's 18 Indoor Singles
1961	Arthur Ashe	US Interscholastic Singles
		US Boy's 18 Indoor Singles
1961-62	Reginald Weir	US Senior (45's) Indoor Doubles (G. Ball)
1961	Doug Sykes	National Public Parks Men's Singles
1963	Arthur Ashe	US Hard Courts
1965	Arthur Ashe	NCAA Singles (UCLA)
		NCAA Doubles (Ian Crookenden)
1967	Arthur Ashe	US Clay Courts
		US Indoor Doubles (Charles Pasarell)
1968	Arthur Ashe	US Amateur
		US Open Singles
1970	Arthur Ashe	Australian Open Singles
		US Indoor Doubles (Stan Smith)
		US Indoor Doubles (Stan Smith), split season
		US Clay Court Doubles (Clark Graebner)
1970	Chip Hooper	US Boy's 12 Doubles (Juan Farrow)
1970	Juan Farrow	US Boy's 12 Singles
		US Boy's 12 Doubles (Chip Hooper)
1971	Arthur Ashe	French Open Doubles (Marty Riessen)
1971	Horace Reid	US Boy's 16 Clay Court Doubles (B. Martin)
1972	Juan Farrow	US Boy's 14 Singles
1972	Diane Morrison	National Public Parks Girl's 16 Singles
		Nat'l Pub. Parks Girl's 16 Doubles (K. Nilsson)
1973	Juan Farrow	US Boy's 16 Indoor Singles

1975	Arthur Ashe	Wimbledon Singles
1977	Chip Hooper	US Boy's 18 Clay Doubles (Mel Purcell)
1977	Andrea Whitmore	Nat'l Pub. Parks Mixed Doubles (K. Simpson)
1977	Arthur Ashe	Australian Doubles (Tony Roche)
1978	Andrea Whitmore	Nat'l Pub. Parks Mixed Doubles (N. Bessent)
1978	Kathy Foxworth	US Girl's 14 Indoor Doubles (Lori Kosten)
1979	Rodney Harmon	US Boy's 18 Doubles (Mike DePalmer)
1979	Rodney Harmon	US Boy's 18 Clay Doubles (Mike DePalmer)
1979	Lori McNeil	US Girl's 16 Hard Court Doubles (Z. Garrison)
1979	Zina Garrison	US Girl's 16 Hard Court Doubles (L. McNeil)
1980	Rodney Harmon	NCAA Doubles, U. of Tennessee (Mel Purcell)
1980	Zina Garrison	US Girl's 16 Singles
		US Girl's 18 Indoor Doubles (Lori McNeil)
		US Girl's 16 Hard Court Doubles (L. McNeil)
		US Girl's 18 Clay Court Doubles (L. McNeil)
1980	Lori McNeil	US Girl's 18 Indoor Doubles (Z. Garrison)
		US Girl's 18 Clay Court Doubles (Z. Garrison)
		US Girl's 16 Hard Court Doubles (Z. Garrison)
1981	Mal Washington	US Boy's 12 Doubles (Al Parker)
1981	Zina Garrison	US Open Junior Girl's Singles
		Wimbledon Junior Girl's Singles
		US Girl's 18 Indoor Singles
		US Girl's 18 Hard Court Doubles (Lori McNeil)
		US Girl's 18 Indoor Doubles (Lori McNeil)
1981	Lori McNeil	US Girl's 18 Indoor Doubles (Z. Garrison)
		US Girl's 18 Hard Court Doubles (Z. Garrison)

AMERICAN TENNIS ASSOCIATION CHAMPIONSHIP ROLL

Women's Singles

Year	Place Played	Names	Year	Place Played	Names
1917	Baltimore	Lucy Slowe	1931	Tuskegee	Ora Washington
1918	New York	M. Rae	1932	Shady Rest, NJ	Ora Washington
1919	New York	M. Rae	1933	Hampton	Ora Washington
1920	New York	M. Rae	1934	Lincoln, PA	Ora Washington
1921	Washington, DC	Lucy Slowe	1935	Institute, WV	Ora Washington
1922	Philadelphia	Isadore Channels	1936	Wilberforce	Lulu Ballard
1923	Chicago	isadore Channels	1937	Tuskegee	Ora Washington
1924	Baltimore	Isadore Channels	1938	Lincoln, PA	Flora Lomax
1925	Bordentown	Lulu Ballard	1939	Hampton	Flora Lomax
1926	St. Louis	Isadore Channels	1940	Wilberforce	Agnes Lawson
1927	Hampton	Lulu Ballard	1941	Tuskegee	Flora Lomax
1928	Bordentown	Lulu Ballard	1942	Lincoln, PA	Flora Lomax
1929	Bordentown	Ora Washington	1944	New York	Roumania Peters
1930	Indianapolis	Ora Washington	1945	New York	Kathryn Irvis

Women's Doubles

Year	Place Played	Names	Year	Place Played	Names
1924	Baltimore	Isadore Channels & Emma Leonard	1935	Institute, WV	Ora Washington & Lulu Ballard
1925	Bordentown	Ora Washington & Lulu Ballard	1936	Wilberforce	Ora Washington & Lulu Ballard
1926	St. Louis	Ora Washington & Lulu Ballard	1937	Tuskegee	Bertha Iassacs & Lilyan Spencer
1927	Hampton	Ora Washington & Lulu Ballard	1938	Lincoln, PA	Margaret Peters & Roumania Peters
1928	Bordentown	Ora Washington & Lulu Ballard	1939	Hampton	Margaret Peters & Roumania Peters
1929	Bordentown	Ora Washington & Lulu Ballard	1940	Wilberforce	Margaret Peters & Roumania Peters
1930	Indianapolis	Ora Washington & Blanche Winston	1941	Tuskegee	Margaret Peters & Roumania Peters
1931	Tuskegee	Ora Washington & Blanche Winston	1942	Lincoln, PA	Lillian Van Buren & Flora Lomax
1932	Shady Rest, NJ	Ora Washington & Lulu Ballard	1944	New York	Margaret Peters & Roumania Peters
1933	Hampton	Ora Washington & Anita Grant	1945	New York	Margaret Peters & Roumania Peters
1934	Lincoln, PA	Ora Washington & Lulu Ballard			

Mixed Doubles

Year	Place Played	Names	Year	Place Played	Names
1924	Baltimore	Nellie Nicholson & B.M. Rhetta	1932	Shady Rest, NJ	Martha Davis & Henry Williams
1925	Bordentown	C.O. Seames & L.C. Downing	1933	Hampton	Emma Leonard & C.O. Hilton
1926	St. Louis	E. Robinson & E. Cole	1934	Lincoln, PA	Emma Leonard & C.O. Hilton
1927	Hampton	Blanche Winston & Louis Jones	1935		
			1936		
1928	Bordentown	Blanche Winston & W.A. Kean	1937	Tuskegee	Flora Lomax & William H. Hall
1929	Bordentown	Anita Grant & O.B. Williams	1938	Lincoln, PA	Lulu Ballard & Gerald Norman, Jr.
1930	Indianapolis	Anita Grant & O.B. Williams	1939	Hampton	Ora Washington & Sylvester Smith
1931	Tuskegee	Anne Roberts & Theodore Thompson	1940	Wilberforce	Flora Lomax & William H. Hall

Year	Place Played	Names	Year	Place Played	Names
1941	Tuskegee	Eoline Thornton & Harold Mitchell	1944	New York	Lillian Van Buren & Delbert Russell
1942	Lincoln, PA	Kathryn Jones & William E. Jones	1945	New York	Lillian Van Buren & Delbert Russell
1943					

Boy's 18 and Under Singles

Year	Place Played	Names	Year	Place Played	Names
1924	Baltimore	Russell Smith	1935	Institute, WV	Earnest McCampbell
1925	Bordentown	Lenoir Cook	1936	Wilberforce	Johnson Wells
1926	St. Louis	Maceo Hill	1937	Tuskegee	Johnson Wells
1927	Hampton	Douglas Turner	1938	Lincoln, PA	Johnson Wells
1928	Bordentown	Reginald Weir	1939	Hampton	Robert Ryland
1929	Bordentown	Nathaniel Jackson	1940	Wilberforce	Joseph King
1930	Indianapolis	Nathaniel Jackson	1941	Tuskegee	Raymond Jackson
1931	Tuskegee	Franklin Jackson	1942	Lincoln, PA	Richard Cunningham
1932	Shady Rest, NJ	Franklin Jackson	1944	New York	Carl Williams
1933	Hampton	Hubert Eaton	1945	New York	Franklin Bailey
1934	Lincoln, PA	Theodore Cousins			

Boy's 16 and Under Singles

Year	Place Played	Names	Year	Place Played	Names
1937	Tuskegee	Marshal Arnold	1941	Tuskegee	John D. Rhodes
1938	Lincoln, PA	Weldon Collins	1942	Lincoln, PA	Matthew Branche
1939	Hampton	Robert Issacs	1944	New York	Clyde Freeman
1940	Wilberforce	Charles Lewis, Jr.	1945	New York	Wilbert Davis

Girl's 18 and Under Singles

Year	Place Played	Names	Year	Place Played	Names
1935	Institute, WV	Mae Hamlin	1940	Wilberforce	Helen Mutchinson
1936	Wilberforce	Angelina Spencer	1941	Tuskegee	Thelma McDaniels
1937	Tuskegee	Mae Hamlin	1942	Lincoln, PA	Nana Davis
1938	Lincoln, PA	Mayme Stanley	1944	New York	Althea Gibson
1939	Hampton	Vivian Murphy	1945	New York	Althea Gibson

Boy's Junior Doubles

Year	Place Played	Names	Year	Place Played	Names
1937	Tuskegee	Eugene Harrington & George Cox	1941	Tuskegee	Jack Points & Richard Cunningham
1938			1942	Lincoln, PA	Jefferson Craig & DeWitt Willis
1939	Hampton	Joseph King & Marshall Arnold	1944	New York	Franklin Bailey & Carl Williams
1940	Wilberforce	Robert Asford & Ronald McDaniel	1945	New York	Fred Wilson & Wilbert Davis

BLACK COLLEGE CONFERENCE CHAMPIONS (TENNIS)

Year	CIAA	Coaches	SIAC	Coaches
1953			S.C. State	Ollie Dawson
1954	na		na	
1955	Hampton	Buck Neilson	na	
1956			na	
1957	Hampton	Buck Neilson	na	
1958	N.C. Central	Jimmy Younge	Tuskegee	Ed Jackson
1959	N.C. Central	Jimmy Younge	na	
1960	J.C. Smith	Winston Coleman	na	
1961	Hampton	Buck Neilson	Florida A & M	Robert Mungeon
1962	N.C. Central	Jimmy Younge	Tuskegee	Ed Jackson
1963	N.C. Central	Jimmy Younge	Fisk	H.B. Thompson
1964	Hampton	Buck Neilson	Clark	na
1965	Hampton	Buck Neilson	Tuskegee	Ed Jackson
1966	Hampton	Buck Neilson	na	
1967	Hampton	Buck Neilson	na	
1968	J.C. Smith	Joe Alston	Florida A & M	Robert Mungeon
1969	Hampton	Buck Neilson	Tuskegee	Henry Holbert
1970	Hampton	Robert Screen	Florida A & M	Robert Mungeon
1971	Hampton	Robert Screen	Florida A & M	Robert Mungeon
1972	Hampton	Robert Screen	Florida A & M	Robert Mungeon
1973	Hampton	Robert Screen	Florida A & M	Robert Mungeon
1974	Hampton	Robert Screen	Fisk	Harry Beamon
1975	Hampton	Robert Screen	Fisk	Harry Beamon
1976	Hampton	Robert Screen	Florida A & M	Robert Mungeon
1977	St. Augustine	Leon Carrington	Morehouse	James Haines
1978	St. Augustine	Leon Carrington	Morehouse	James Haines
1979	St. Augustine	Leon Carrington	Morehouse	James Haines
1980	Hampton	Robert Screen	Morehouse	James Haines
1981	Hampton	Robert Screen	Alabama A & M	Lou Brown
1982	Hampton	Robert Screen	Morehouse	James Haines
1983	Hampton	Robert Screen	Morehouse	James Haines
1984	Hampton	Robert Screen	Morehouse	James Haines

Year	SWAC	Coaches	MEAC	Coaches
1950	Prairie View	Lloyd Scott		
1951	Prairie View	Lloyd Scott		
1952	Prairie View	Lloyd Scott		
1953	Prairie View	Lloyd Scott		
1954	Prairie View	Lloyd Scott		
1955	Prairie View	Lloyd Scott		
1956	na			
1957	Prairie View	Norm Johnson		
1958	Prairie View	Norm Johnson		
1959	Prairie View	Norm Johnson		
1960	Prairie View	Billy Nicks		
1961	Prairie View	Billy Nicks		
1962	Prairie View	Martin Epps		
1963	Prairie View	Martin Epps		
1964	Prairie View	Martin Epps		
1965	Prairie View	Martin Epps		
1966	Prairie View	Martin Epps		
1967	Prairie View	Martin Epps		
1968	Prairie View	Martin Epps		
1969	Prairie View	Martin Epps		
1970	Texas Southern	Herb Provost		
1971	Texas Southern	Herb Provost		
1972	Texas Southern	Herb Provost	N.C. Central	Jimmy Younge
1973	Texas Southern	Herb Provost	N.C. Central	Jimmy Younge
1974	Texas Southern	Herb Provost	N.C. Central	Jimmy Younge
1975	Texas Southern	Herb Provost	N.C. Central	Jimmy Younge
1976	Texas Southern	Herb Provost	na	
1977	Texas Southern	Herb Provost	na	
1978	Texas Southern	Herb Provost	na	
1979	Southern U.	Cliff Johnson	na	
1980	Southern U.	Cliff Johnson	na	
1981	Jackson St.	John Shinall	Howard U.	Larry Strickland
1982	Grambling	Wallace Bly	Howard U.	Larry Strickland
1983	Grambling	Wallace Bly	Howard U.	Larry Strickland
1984	Grambling	Wallace Bly	S.C. State	Tom Saxon

BLACK COLLEGE NATIONAL CHAMPIONS

Year	Player	School	Title
1974	Stan Fracker	Texas Southern	NAIA Singles
1975	Benny Sims & Glenn Moolchan	Texas Southern	NAIA Doubles
1976	Bruce Foxworth & Roger Guedes	Hampton	NCAA II Doubles
1980	Tony Mmoh & Bullus Hussaini	St. Augustine's	NAIA Doubles

DR. ROBERT SCREEN'S RECORD—HAMPTON UNIVERSITY

Year	Title	NCAA Ranking	Record	Percentage
1970	CIAA	6	16-1	.941
1971	CIAA	6	20-3	.870
1972	CIAA	5	20-4	.833
1973	CIAA	6	24-2	.923
1974	CIAA	5	18-4	.818
1975	CIAA	4	19-4	.826
1976	CIAA	1	16-8	.667
1977		3	14-4	.778
1978		2	13-4	.765
1979		3	16-5	.762
1980	CIAA		18-4	.818
1981	CIAA	4	22-7	.759
1982	CIAA	5	26-4	.923
1983	CIAA	4	20-8	.714
1984	CIAA	3	34-7	.829
Totals			296-69	.811

Track and Field

BLACK COLLEGE CONFERENCE CHAMPIONS

CIAA			SWAC	
1950	Morgan St.	Ed Hurt	Prairie View	Jimmy Stephens
1951	Morgan St.	Ed Hurt	Prairie View	Jimmy Stephens
1952	Morgan St.	Ed Hurt	Prairie View	Jimmy Stephens
1953	Morgan St.	Ed Hurt	Prairie View	Hugh McKinnis
1954	Morgan St.	Ed Hurt	Southern U.	Robert Smith
1955	Morgan St.	Ed Hurt	Texas Southern	Stan Wright
1956	Morgan St.	Ed Hurt	Prairie View	Hugh McKinnis
1957	Morgan St.	Ed Hurt	Texas Southern	Stan Wright
1958	Morgan St.	Ed Hurt	Prairie View	Leroy Moore
1959	Winston-Salem	Wilbur Ross	Southern U.	Eugene Thomas
1960	Winston-Salem	Wilbur Ross	Southern U.	Eugene Thomas
1961	Maryland E-S	Wilbur Ross	Texas Southern	Stan Wright
1962	Maryland E-S	Wilbur Ross	Texas Southern	Stan Wright
1963	Maryland E-S	Wilbur Ross	Texas Southern	Stan Wright
1964	N.C Central	Leroy Walker	Southern U.	Robert Smith
1965	N.C. Central	Leroy Walker	Southern U.	Robert Smith
1966	(No Title)		Southern U.	Dick Hill
1967	Maryland E-S	Cap Anderson	Texas Southern	Stan Wright
1968	Maryland E-S	Cap Anderson	Southern U.	Dick Hill
1969	J.C. Smith	Ken Powell	Prairie View	Hoover Wright
1970	J.C. Smith	Ken Powell	Prairie View	Hoover Wright
1971	N.C. Central	Leroy Walker	Southern U.	Dick Hill
1972	Norfolk St.	Dick Price	Texas Southern	Dave Bethany
1973	Norfolk St.	Dick Price	Texas Southern	Dave Bethany
1974	Norfolk St.	Dick Price	Texas Southern	Dave Bethany
1975	Norfolk St.	Dick Price	Jackson St.	Martin Epps
1976	Norfolk St.	Dick Price	Jackson St.	Martin Epps
1977	Virginia St.	George Williams	Jackson St.	Martin Epps
1978	St. Augustine	George Williams	Jackson St.	Martin Epps
1979	St. Augustine	George Williams	Texas Southern	Dave Bethany
1980	St. Augustine	George Williams	Texas Southern	Dave Bethany
1981	Virginia St.	William Bennett	Texas Southern	Dave Bethany
1982	St. Augustine	George Williams	Texas Southern	Dave Bethany
1983	St. Augustine	George Williams	Jackson St.	Martin Epps
1984	St. Augustine	George Williams	Texas Southern	Dave Bethany

SIAC			MEAC	
1951	Xavier (La.)	Al Priestley		
1952	Florida A&M	Robert Griffin		
1953	Xavier (La.)	Al Priestley		
1954	Xavier (La.)	Al Priestley		
1955	Florida A&M	Robert Griffin		
1956	Florida A&M	Robert Griffin		
1957	Xavier (La.)	Al Priestley		
1958	Xavier (La.)	Al Priestley		
1959	Florida A&M	Robert Griffin		
1960	Florida A&M	Robert Griffin		
1961	Florida A&M	Robert Griffin		
1962	Florida A&M	Dick Hill		
1963	Florida A&M	Dick Hill		
1964	Florida A&M	Dick Hill		
1965	Morehouse	Darlington		
1966	Florida A&M	Bobby Lang		
1967	Florida A&M	Bobby Lang		
1968	Florida A&M	Bobby Lang		
1969	Florida A&M	Bobby Lang		
1970	Florida A&M	Bobby Lang		
1971	Florida A&M	Bobby Lang		
1972	Florida A&M	Bobby Lang	N.C. Central	Leroy Walker
1973	Albany State	Robert Cross	N.C. Central	Leroy Walker
1974	Albany State	Robert Cross	N.C. Central	Leroy Walker
1975	Albany State	Robert Cross	(No Title)	
1976	Florida A&M	Bobby Lang	Delaware St.	Joe Burden
1977	Florida A&M	Bobby Lang	S.C. State	Robert Johnson
1978	Albany State	Robert Cross	S.C. State	Robert Johnson
1979	Florida A&M	Bobby Lang	S.C. State	Robert Johnson
1980	Albany State	Robert Cross	Florida A&M	Bobby Lang
1981	Albany State	Robert Cross	S.C. State	Robert Johnson
1982	Albany State	Robert Cross	Florida A&M	Bobby Lang
1983	Albany State	Robert Cross	S.C. State	Robert Johnson
1984	Albany State	Robert Cross	S.C. State	Robert Johnson

BLACK COLLEGE WOMEN'S CONFERENCE CHAMPIONS

SIAC			MEAC	
1980	Alabama A&M	Joe Henderson	Howard	William Moultrie
1981	Alabama A&M	Joe Henderson	Delaware St.	Joe Burden
1982	Alabama A&M	Joe Henderson	S.C. State	Robert Johnson
1983	Alabama A&M	Joe Henderson	S.C. State	Robert Johnson
1984	Alabama A&M	Joe Henderson	S.C. State	Robert Johnson

CIAA			SWAC	
1974			Prairie View	Barbara Jacket
1975			Prairie View	Barbara Jacket
1976			Prairie View	Barbara Jacket
1977	Virginia St.	William Bennett	Prairie View	Barbara Jacket
1978	St. Augustine	George Williams	Prairie View	Barbara Jacket
1979	St. Augustine	George Williams	Prairie View	Barbara Jacket
1980	St. Augustine	George Williams	Prairie View	Barbara Jacket
1981	St. Augustine	George Williams	Texas Southern	Dave Bethany
1982	St. Augustine	George Williams	Prairie View	Barbara Jacket
1983	St. Augustine	George Williams	Jackson St.	Martin Epps
1984	St. Augustine	George Williams	Prairie View	Barbara Jacket

EVOLUTION OF WORLD RECORDS

(African-Americans in Capitals)

100-meter dash

	Runner	Time	Date
1.	HOWARD PORTER DREW	10.4 seconds	JUNE 8, 1912
2.	Charley Paddock	10.4 seconds	APRIL 23, 1921
3.	EDDIE TOLAN	10.4 seconds	AUGUST 8, 1929
4.	Percy Williams (Canada)	10.3 seconds	AUGUST 9, 1930
5.	EDDIE TOLAN	10.3 seconds	AUGUST 1, 1932
6.	RALPH METCALFE	10.3 seconds	AUGUST 12, 1933
7.	EULACE PEACOCK	10.2 seconds	AUGUST 6, 1934
8.	Christian Berger (Neth.)	10.3 seconds	AUGUST 26, 1934
9.	RALPH METCALFE	10.3 seconds	SEPTEMBER 15, 1934
10.	RALPH METCALFE	10.3 seconds	SEPTEMBER 23, 1934
11.	Takayoshi Yoshioka (Jap.)	10.3 seconds	JUNE 15, 1935
12.	JESSE OWENS	10.2 seconds	JUNE 20, 1936
13.	Harold Davis	10.2 seconds	JUNE 6, 1941
14.	Lloyd LaBeach (Panama)	10.2 seconds	MAY 15, 1948
15.	NORWOOD "BARNEY" EWELL	10.2 seconds	JULY 9, 1948
16.	Emm M. Bailey (England)	10.2 seconds	AUGUST 25, 1951
17.	Heinz Futtere (Germany)	10.2 seconds	OCTOBER 31, 1954
18.	Bobby Morrow	10.2 seconds	MAY 19, 1956
19.	Bobby Morrow	10.2 seconds	MAY 26, 1956
20.	IRA MURCHISON	10.2 seconds	JUNE 1, 1956
21.	Bobby Morrow	10.2 seconds	JUNE 22 1956
22.	IRA MURCHISON	10.2 seconds	JUNE 29, 1956

	Runner	Time	Date
23.	Bobby Morrow	10.2 seconds	JUNE 29, 1956
24.	WILLIE WILLIAMS	10.1 seconds	AUGUST 3, 1956
25.	IRA MURCHISON	10.1 seconds	AUGUST 4, 1956
26.	LEAMON KING	10.1 seconds	OCTOBER 27, 1956
27.	RAY NORTON	10.1 seconds	APRIL 18, 1959
28.	Harry Jerome (Canada)	10.0 seconds	JUNE 21, 1960
29.	Armin Hary (Germany)	10.0 seconds	JULY 15, 1960
30.	Horacio Esteves (Ven.)	10.0 seconds	AUGUST 15, 1964
31.	BOB HAYES	10.0 seconds	OCTOBER 15, 1964
32.	JIM HINES	10.0 seconds	MAY 27, 1967
33.	Paul Nash (South Africa)	10.0 seconds	APRIL 2, 1968
34.	OLIVER FORD	10.0 seconds	MAY 31, 1967
35.	CHARLIE GREENE	10.0 seconds	JUNE 10, 1968
36.	Roger Bambuck	10.0 seconds	JUNE 20, 1968
37.	JIM HINES	9.9 seconds	JUNE 10, 1968
38.	RONNIE RAY SMITH	9.9 seconds	JUNE 20, 1968
39.	CHARLIE GREENE	9.9 seconds	JUNE 20, 1968
40.	JIM HINES	9.9 seconds	OCTOBER 14, 1968
41.	EDDIE HART	9.9 seconds	JULY 1, 1972
42.	REY ROBINSON	9.9 seconds	JULY 1, 1972
43.	STEVE WILLIAMS	9.9 seconds	JUNE 21, 1974
44.	Silvio Leonard (Cuba)	9.9 seconds	JUNE 5, 1975
45.	STEVE WILLIAMS	9.9 seconds	JULY 16, 1975
46.	STEVE WILLIAMS	9.9 seconds	AUGUST 22, 1975
47.	STEVE WILLIAMS	9.9 seconds	MARCH 27, 1976
48.	HARVEY GLANCE	9.9 seconds	APRIL 3, 1976
49.	HARVEY GLANCE	9.9 seconds	MAY 1, 1976
50.	Don Quarrie (Jamaica)	9.9 seconds	MAY 22, 1976

200-meter dash

1.	EDDIE TOLAN	21.1 seconds	AUGUST 9, 1929
2.	RALPH METCALFE	21.1 seconds	JULY 28, 1933
3.	JESSE OWENS	21.1 seconds	AUGUST 4, 1936
4.	JESSE OWENS	20.7 seconds	AUGUST 5, 1936
5.	Mel Patton	20.7 seconds	JULY 10, 1948
6.	ANDY STANFIELD	20.6 seconds	MAY 26, 1951
7.	ANDY STANFIELD	20.6 seconds	JUNE 28, 1952
8.	Than Baker	20.6 seconds	JUNE 23, 1956
9.	ANDY STANFIELD	20.6 seconds	JUNE 23, 1956
10.	Bobby Morrow	20.6 seconds	NOVEMBER 27, 1957
11.	Manfred Germar (Ger.)	20.6 seconds	OCTOBER 1, 1958
12.	RAY NORTON	20.6 seconds	MARCH 19, 1960

	Runner	Time	Date
3.	RAY NORTON	20.6 seconds	APRIL 30, 1960
4.	STONE JOHNSON	20.5 seconds	JULY 2, 1960
5.	RAY NORTON	20.5 seconds	JULY 2, 1960
6.	Livio Berruti (Italy)	20.5 seconds	SEPTEMBER 3, 1960
7.	PAUL DRAYTON	20.5 seconds	JUNE 23, 1962
8.	HENRY CARR	20.3 seconds	MARCH 23, 1963
9.	HENRY CARR	20.2 seconds	APRIL 4, 1964
0.	TOMMIE SMITH	20.0 seconds	JUNE 11, 1966
1.	TOMMIE SMITH	19.8 seconds	OCTOBER 16, 1968
2.	Don Quarrie (Jamaica)	19.8 seconds	JUNE 21, 1975
3.	JAMES MALLARD	19.8 seconds	MAY 13, 1979
4.	Pietro Mennea (Italy)	19.8 seconds	SEPTEMBER 3, 1979
5.	JAMES SANFORD	19.7 seconds	APRIL 19, 1980

400-meter dash

	Runner	Time	Date
1.	TED MEREDITH	47.4 seconds	MAY 27, 1916
2.	BINGA DISMOND	47.4 seconds	JUNE 3, 1916
3.	Emerson Spencer	47.0 seconds	MAY 12, 1928
4.	Ben Eastman	46.4 seconds	MARCH 26, 1932
5.	Bill Carr	46.2 seconds	AUGUST 5, 1932
6.	ARCHIE WILLIAMS	46.1 seconds	JUNE 19, 1936
7.	Rudolf Harbig (Germany)	46.0 seconds	AUGUST 12, 1939
8.	Herb McKinley (Jamaica)	45.9 seconds	JULY 2, 1948
9.	George Rhoden (Jamaica)	45.8 seconds	AUGUST 22, 1950
0.	LOU JONES	45.4 seconds	MARCH 18, 1955
1.	LOU JONES	45.2 seconds	JUNE 30, 1956
2.	OTIS DAVIS	44.9 seconds	SEPTEMBER 6, 1960
3.	Mike Larrabee	44.9 seconds	SEPTEMBER 12, 1964
4.	TOMMIE SMITH	44.5 seconds	MAY 20, 1967
5.	LARRY JAMES	44.1 seconds	SEPTEMBER 14, 1968
6.	LEE EVANS	43.8 seconds	OCTOBER 18, 1968

400-meter hurdles

	Runner	Time	Date
.	Gert Potgieter (S. Afr.)	49.3 seconds	APRIL 16, 1960
.	Sal Morale (Italy)	49.2 seconds	SEPTEMBER 14, 1962
.	Warren Cawley	49.1 seconds	SEPTEMBER 13, 1964
.	Geoff Vanderstock	48.1 seconds	SEPTEMBER 11, 1968
.	John Akii-Bua (Uganda)	47.8 seconds	SEPTEMBER 2, 1972
.	EDWIN MOSES	47.64 seconds	JULY 25, 1976

	Runner	Time	Date
7.	EDWIN MOSES	47.45 seconds	JULY 11, 1977
8.	EDWIN MOSES	47.13 seconds	JULY 3, 1980
9.	EDWIN MOSES	47.02 seconds	AUGUST 31, 1983

110-meter hurdles

1.	HARRISON DILLARD	13.6 seconds	APRIL 17, 1948
2.	Dick Attlesley	13.5 seconds	MAY 13, 1950
3.	Jack Davis	13.4 seconds	JUNE 22, 1956
4.	LEE CALHOUN	13.2 seconds	AUGUST 21, 1960
5.	EARL McCULLOCH	13.2 seconds	JULY 16, 1967
6.	WILLIE DAVENPORT	13.2 seconds	JULY 4, 1969
7.	ROD MILBURN	13.0 seconds	JUNE 25, 1971
8.	RENALDO NEHEMIAH	12.93 seconds	AUGUST 19, 1981

long jump

1.	Peter O'Connell	7.61 meters	AUGUST 5, 1901
2.	EDWARD GOURDIN	7.69 meters	JULY 23, 1921
3.	WILLIAM DeHART HUBBARD	7.89 meters	JUNE 13, 1925
4.	Shuhei Nambu (Japan)	7.98 meters	OCTOBER 27, 1931
5.	JESSE OWENS	8.13 meters	MAY 25, 1935
6.	RALPH BOSTON	8.21 meters	AUGUST 12, 1960
7.	RALPH BOSTON	8.24 meters	MAY 27, 1961
8.	RALPH BOSTON	8.28 meters	JULY 16, 1961
9.	Igor T.-Ovanesyan (Rus.)	8.31 meters	JUNE 10, 1962
10.	RALPH BOSTON	8.31 meters	AUGUST 15, 1964
11.	RALPH BOSTON	8.34 meters	SEPTEMBER 12, 19
12.	RALPH BOSTON	8.35 meters	MAY 29, 1965
13.	BOB BEAMON (29' 2½")	8.90 meters	OCTOBER 18, 1968

high jump

1.	George Horine	2.00 meters	MAY 18, 1912
2.	CORNELIUS JOHNSON	2.07 meters	JULY 12, 1936
3.	DAVE ALBRITTON	2.07 meters	JULY 12, 1936
4.	MELVIN WALKER	2.09 meters	AUGUST 12, 1937
5.	Lester Steers	2.11 meters	JUNE 17, 1941
6.	WALTER DAVIS	2.12 meters	JUNE 27, 1953
7.	CHARLES DUMAS	2.15 meters	JUNE 29, 1956
8.	Yuri Styepanov (Russia)	2.16 meters	JULY 13, 1957
9.	JOHN THOMAS	2.17 meters	APRIL 30, 1960

	Runner	Time	Date
10.	JOHN THOMAS	2.18 meters	JUNE 24, 1960
11.	Valeri Brumel (Russia)	2.23 meters	JUNE 18, 1961
12.	Zhu Jianhua (China)	2.38 meters	SEPTEMBER 22, 1983

decathlon

1.	Bob Mathias	7,690 points	JULY 1-2, 1952
2.	RAFER JOHNSON	7,758 points	JUNE 10-11, 1955
3.	Vasiliy Kusnyetsov (Rus.)	7,760 points	MAY 17-18, 1958
4.	RAFER JOHNSON	7,896 points	JULY 27-28, 1958
5.	Vasiliy Kusnyetsov (Rus.)	7,957 points	MAY 16-17, 1959
6.	RAFER JOHNSON	8,063 points	JULY 8-9, 1960

4 X 100-meter relay

1.	I. Moller, C. Luther T. Persson, K. Lindberg	42.5 seconds	JULY 8, 1912
2.	(The record was improved 7 times between 1912 and 1935)		
3.	JESSE OWENS, RALPH METCALFE Frank Wykoff, Fred Draper	39.8 seconds	AUGUST 9, 1936
4.	IRA MURCHISON, LEAMON KING Bobby Morrow, T. Baker	39.5 seconds	DECEMBER 1, 1956
5.	HAYES JONES, Paul Drayton, C. FRAZIER, Frank Budd	39.1 seconds	JULY 15, 1961
6.	Paul Drayton, BOB HAYES G. Ashworth, R. STEBBINS	39.0 seconds	OCTOBER 21, 1964
7.	EARL McCULLOCH, O.J. SIMPSON, F. Kuller, L. Miller	38.6 seconds	JUNE 17, 1967
8.	CHARLIE GREEN, MEL PENDER RONNIE SMITH, JIM HINES	38.2 seconds	OCTOBER 20, 1968
9.	LARRY BLACK, ROBERT TAYLOR, GERALD TINKER, EDDIE HART	38.2 seconds	SEPTEMBER 10, 1972
0.	STEVE RIDDICK, STEVE WILLIAMS, B. COLLINS, CLIFF WILEY	38.03 seconds	SEPTEMBER 3, 1977
1.	EMMITT KING, WILLIE GAULT, CALVIN SMITH, CARL LEWIS	37.86 seconds	AUGUST 10, 1983
2.	RON BROWN, SAM GRADDY, CALVIN SMITH, CARL LEWIS	37.83 seconds	AUGUST, 1984

4 X 400-meter relay

	Runner	Time	Date
1.	Irish-American A.C.	3:18.2 minutes	SEPTEMBER 4, 1911
2.	(The record was lowered 7 times between 1911 and 1959)		
3.	OTIS DAVIS, J. Yerman, E. Young, G. Davis	3:02.2 minutes	SEPTEMBER 8, 1960
4.	HENRY CARR, ULIS WILLIAMS, O. Cassell, M. Larrabee	3:00.7 minutes	OCTOBER 21, 1964
5.	LEE EVANS, TOMMIE SMITH, THERIN LEWIS, R. Frey	2:59.6 minutes	JULY 24, 1966
6.	LEE EVANS, RON FREEMAN, VINCE MATTHEWS, LARRY JAMES	2:56.1 minutes	OCTOBER 20, 1968

Women's 100-meter dash

		Time	Date
1.	Stella Walsh (Poland)	11.7 seconds	AUGUST 26, 1934
2.	(The record was lowered 4 times between 1934 and 1959)		
3.	WILMA RUDOLPH	11.3 seconds	SEPTEMBER 2, 1960
4.	WILMA RUDOLPH	11.2 seconds	JULY 19, 1961
5.	WYOMIA TYUS	11.2 seconds	OCTOBER 15, 1964
6.	Irene Kirszentein (Pol.)	11.1 seconds	JULY 9, 1965
7.	WYOMIA TYUS	11.1 seconds	JULY 31, 1965
8.	BARBARA FERRELL	11.1 seconds	JULY 2, 1967
9.	WYOMIA TYUS	11.0 seconds	OCTOBER 15, 1968
10.	Renate Meissner (GDR)	10.9 seconds	AUGUST 20, 1972
11.	Renate Meissner (GDR)	10.8 seconds	JULY 20, 1973
12.	EVELYN ASHFORD	10.79 seconds	JUNE 3, 1983
13.	EVELYN ASHFORD	10.76 seconds	AUGUST 22, 1984

Women's 200-meter dash

		Time	Date
1.	Stella Walsh (Poland)	23.6 seconds	AUGUST 15, 1935
2.	(The record was lowered 2 times between 1935 and 1959)		
3.	WILMA RUDOLPH	22.9 seconds	JULY 9, 1960

Women's 4 X 100-meter relay

	Runner	Time	Date
1.	Albus, Krauss, Dollinger, Dorffeldt	46.6 seconds	AUGUST 8, 1936
2.	MAE FAGGS, BARBARA JONES, CATHERINE HARDY, Brenda Moreau	45.9 seconds	JULY 27, 1952
3.	(The record was lowered 5 times between 1952 and 1959)		
4.	MARTHA HUDSON, LUCINDA WILLIAMS, BARBARA JONES, WILMA RUDOLPH	44.4 seconds	SEPTEMBER 7, 1960
5.	WILLYE WHITE, WILMA RUDLOPH, ERNESTINE POLLARD, VIVIAN BROWN	44.3 seconds	JULY 15, 1961
6.	WILLYE WHITE, WYOMIA TYUS, MARILYN WHITE, EDITH McGUIRE	43.9 seconds	OCTOBER 21, 1964
7.	BARBARA FERRELL, MILDRETTA NETTER, WYOMIA TYUS, MARGRET BAILES	43.4 seconds	OCTOBER 19, 1968
8.	BARBARA FERRELL, MILDRETTE, WYOMIA TYUS, MARGRET BAILES	42.8 seconds	OCTOBER 20, 1968

AFRICAN-AMERICAN OLYMPIC MEDALISTS IN TRACK AND FIELD, 1948–1984

African-American Medalists: The XIVth Olympiad

	Medal	Event	Time/Distance
HARRISON DILLARD	gold	100–m dash	10.3 seconds, OR*
	gold	400–m relay	40.6 seconds
MAL WHITFIELD	gold	800–m run	1:49.2 minutes, OR
	gold	1600–m relay	3:10.4 minutes
NORWOOD EWELL	gold	400–m relay	40.6 seconds
	silver	100–m dash	10.4 seconds
LORENZO WRIGHT	gold	400–m relay	40.6 seconds
WILLIE STEELE	gold	long jump	25' 8"
ALICE COACHMAN	gold	high jump	5' 6", OR
AUDREY PATTERSON	bronze	200–m dash	25.2 seconds

*OR = Olympic Record

African-American Medalists: The XVth Olympiad

	Medal	Event	Time/Distance/Points
ARRISON DILLARD	gold	110-m hurdles	13.7 seconds, OR*
	gold	400-m relay	40.1 seconds
MAL WHITFIELD	gold	800-m run	1:49.2 minutes, OR
	silver	1600-m relay	3:04 minutes

	Medal	Event	Time/Distance/Points
ANDREW STANFIELD	gold	200-m dash	20.7 seconds, OR
	gold	400-m relay	40.1 seconds
JEROME BIFFLE	gold	long jump	24' 10"
MAE FAGGS	gold	400-m relay	45.9 seconds, OR
CATHERINE HARDY	gold	400-m relay	45.9 seconds, OR
BARBARA JONES	gold	400-m relay	45.9 seconds, OR
MEREDITH GOURDINE	silver	long jump	24' 8¼"
MILTON CAMPBELL	silver	decathlon	7,132 points
OLLIE MATSON	silver	1600-m relay	3:04 minutes
	bronze	400-m run	46.8 seconds

*OR = Olympic Record

African-American Medalists: The XVIth Olympiad

	Medal	Event	Time/Distance/Points
LEE CALHOUN	gold	110-m hurdles	13.5 seconds, OR*
MILDRED McDANIEL	gold	high jump	5' 9-1/4", OR, WR
CHARLES DUMAS	gold	high jump	6' 11-1/4", OR
MILTON CAMPBELL	gold	decathlon	7,708 points
GREG BELL	gold	long jump	25' 8-1/4"
LOU JONES	gold	1600-m relay	3:04.8 minutes
CHARLES JENKINS	gold	1600-m relay	3:04.8 minutes
	gold	400-m run	46.7 seconds
IRA MURCHISON	gold	400-m relay	39.5 seconds, OR, WR
LEAMON KING	gold	400-m relay	39.5 seconds, OR
RAFER JOHNSON	silver	decathlon	7,568 points
ANDREW STANFIELD	silver	200-m dash	20.7 seconds
WILLYE WHITE	silver	long jump	19' 11-3/4"
JOSH CULBREATH	bronze	400-m hurdles	51.6 seconds
MAE FAGGS	bronze	400-m relay	44.9 seconds
MARGRET MATTHEWS	bronze	400-m relay	44.9 seconds
WILMA RUDOLPH	bronze	400-m relay	44.9 seconds
ISABELLE DANIELS	bronze	400-m relay	44.9 seconds

*OR = Olympic Record, WR = World Record

African-American Medalists: The XVIIth Olympiad

	Medal	Event	Time/Distance/Points
RAFER JOHNSON	gold	decathlon	8,001 points, OR*
RALPH BOSTON	gold	long jump	26' 7-1/2", OR

	Medal	Event	Time/Distance/Points
LEE CALHOUN	gold	110-m hurdles	13.8 seconds
OTIS DAVIS	gold	400-m dash	44.9 seconds, OR, WR
	gold	1600-m relay	3:02.2 minutes, OR, WR
WILMA RUDOLPH	gold	100-M dash	11 seconds
	gold	200-m dash	24 seconds
	gold	400-m relay	44.5 seconds
MARTHA HUDSON	gold	400-m relay	44.5 seconds
LUCINDA WILLIAMS	gold	400-m relay	44.5 seconds
BARBARA JONES	gold	400-m relay	44.5 seconds
WILLIE MAY	silver	110-m hurdles	13.8 seconds
LESTER CARNEY	silver	200-m dash	20.6 seconds
IRVIN ROBERSON	silver	long jump	26' 7-1/4"
HAYES JONES	bronze	110-m hurdles	14 seconds
JOHN THOMAS	bronze	high jump	7' 1/4"
EARLENE BROWN	bronze	shot put	53' 10-1/4"

*OR = Olympic Record, WR = World Record

African-American Medalists: The XVIIIth Olypmiad

	Medal	Event	Time/Distance
BOB HAYES	gold	100-m dash	10 seconds, OR, WR*
	gold	400-m relay	39 seconds, OR, WR
HENRY CARR	gold	200-m dash	20.3 seconds, OR
	gold	1600-m relay	3:00.7 minutes, OR, WR
PAUL DRAYTON	gold	400-m relay	39 seconds, OR, WR
	silver	200-m dash	20.5 seconds
HAYES JONES	gold	110-m hurdles	13.6 seconds
ULIS WILLIAMS	gold	1600-m relay	3:00.7 minutes, OR, WR
RICHARD STEBBINS	gold	400-m relay	39 seconds, OR, WR
WYOMIA TYUS	gold	100-m dash	11.4 seconds
	silver	400-m relay	43.9 seconds
EDITH McGUIRE	gold	200-m dash	23 seconds, OR
	silver	100-m dash	11.6 seconds
	silver	400-m relay	43.9 seconds

	Medal	Event	Time/Distance/Point
WILLYE WHITE	silver	400-m relay	43.9 seconds
MARILYN WHITE	silver	400-m relay	43.9 seconds
JOHN THOMAS	silver	high jump	7′ 1-3/4″
RALPH BOSTON	silver	long jump	26′ 4″
JOHN RAMBO	bronze	high jump	7′ 1″

*OR = Olympic Record, WR = World Record

African-American Medalists: The XIXth Olympiad

	Medal	Event	Time/Distance
BOB BEAMON	gold	long jump	29′ 2½″, OR, WR*
JAMES HINES	gold	100-m dash	9.9 seconds, OR, WR
	gold	400-m relay	38.2 seconds, OR, WR
LEE EVANS	gold	400-m dash	43.8 seconds, OR, WR
	gold	1600-m relay	2:56.1 minutes, OR, WR
TOMMIE SMITH	gold	200-m dash	19.8 seconds, OR, WR
WILLIE DAVENPORT	gold	110-m hurdles	13.3 seconds, OR
CHARLES GREENE	gold	400-m relay	38.2 seconds, OR, WR
	bronze	100-m dash	10 seconds
RONNIE SMITH	gold	400-m relay	38.2 seconds, OR, WR
MELVIN PENDER	gold	400-m relay	38.2 seconds, OR, WR
RON FREEMAN	gold	1600-m relay	2:56.1 minutes, OR, WR
	bronze	400-m dash	44.4 seconds
VINCENT MATTHEWS	gold	1600-m relay	2:56.1 minutes, OR, WR
LARRY JAMES	gold	1600-m relay	2:56.1 minutes, OR, WR
	silver	400-m dash	43.9 seconds
WYOMIA TYUS	gold	100-m dash	11 seconds, OR, WR
	gold	400-m relay	42.8 seconds, OR, WR

	Medal	Event	Time/Distance
BARBARA FERRELL	gold	400-m relay	42.8 seconds, OR, WR
	silver	100-m dash	11.1 seconds
MARGARET BAILES	gold	400-m relay	42.8 seconds, OR, WR
MADELINE MANNING	gold	800-m run	2:00.9 minutes, OR
MILDRETTE NETTER	gold	400-m relay	42.8 seconds, OR, WR
ERVIN HALL	silver	110-m hurdles	13.4 seconds
EDWARD CARUTHERS	silver	high hump	7' 3½"
JOHN CARLOS	bronze	200-m dash	20.0 seconds
RALPH BOSTON	bronze	long jump	26' 9¼"

*OR = Olympic Record, WR = World Record

African-American Medalists: The XXth Olympiad

	Medal	Event	Time/Distance
VINCENT MATTHEWS	gold	400-m run	44.66 seconds
ROD MILBURN	gold	110m-hurdles	13.24 seconds, OR, WR*
RANDY WILLIAMS	gold	long jump	27' ¼"
ROBERT TAYLOR	gold	400-m relay	38.19 seconds, OR, WR
	silver	100-m dash	10.24 seconds
LARRY BLACK	gold	400-m relay	38.19 seconds, OR, WR
	silver	200-m dash	20.19 seconds
EDDIE HART	gold	400-m relay	38.19 seconds, OR, WR
GERALD TINKER	gold	400-m relay	38.19 seconds, OR, WR
MADELINE MANNING	silver	1600-m relay	3:25.2 minutes
MABLE FERGUSON	silver	1600-m relay	3:25.2 minutes
CHERYL TOUSSAINT	silver	1600-m relay	3:25.2 minutes
WAYNE COLLETT	silver	400-m dash	44.80 seconds
ARNIE ROBINSON	bronze	long jump	26' 4"

*OR = Olympic Record, WR = World Record

African-American Medalists: The XXIst Olympiad

	Medal	Event	Time/Distance
ARNIE ROBINSON	gold	long jump	27' 4-3/4"
EDWIN MOSES	gold	400-meter hurdles	47.64 seconds, OR, WR*
MILLARD HAMPTON	gold	400-meter relay	38.33 seconds
	silver	200-meter dash	20.29 seconds
STEVE RIDDICK	gold	400-meter relay	38.33 seconds
HARVEY GLANCE	gold	400-meter relay	38.33 seconds
JOHN JONES	gold	400-meter relay	38.33 seconds
HERMAN FRAZIER	gold	1600-meter relay	2:58.7 minutes
	bronze	400-meter dash	44.95 seconds
BENNY BROWN	gold	1600-meter relay	2:58.7 minutes
MAXIE PARKS	gold	1600-meter relay	2:58.7 minutes
FRED NEWHOUSE	gold	1600-meter relay	2:58.7 minutes
	silver	400-meter dash	44.40 seconds
RANDY WILLIAMS	silver	long jump	26' 7-1/4"
JAMES BUTTS	silver	triple jump	56' 8-1/2"
ROSALYN BRYANT	silver	1600-meter relay	3:22.8 minutes
SHEILA INGRAM	silver	1600-meter relay	3:22.8 minutes
PAMELA JILES	silver	1600-meter relay	3:22.8 minutes
DEBRA SAPENTER	silver	1600-meter relay	3:22.8 minutes
DWAYNE EVANS	bronze	200-meter dash	20.43 seconds
WILLIE DAVENPORT	bronze	110-meter hurdles	13.38 seconds

*OR = Olympic Record, WR = World Record

African-American Medalists: The XXIIIrd Olympiad

	Medal	Event	Time/Distance/Points
CARL LEWIS	gold	100-m dash	10.97 seconds
	gold	200-m dash	19.80 seconds, OR*
	gold	long jump	8.54 meters
	gold	400-m relay	37.83 seconds, OR, WR
ALONZO BABERS	gold	400-m run	44.27 seconds
	gold	1600-m relay	2:57.91 minutes
ROGER KINGDOM	gold	110-m hurdles	13.20 seconds
EDWIN MOSES	gold	400-m hurdles	47.75 seconds
AL JOYNER	gold	triple jump	17.26 meters
SAM GRADDY	gold	400-m relay	37.83 seconds, OR, WR
	silver	100-m dash	10.19 seconds

	Medal	Event	Time/Distance/Points
RON BROWN	gold	400-m relay	37.83 seconds, OR, WR
CALVIN SMITH	gold	400-m relay	37.83 seconds, OR, WR
SUNDER NIX	gold	1600-m relay	2:57.91 minutes
RAY ARMSTEAD	gold	1600-m relay	2:57.91 minutes
ANTONIO McKAY	gold	1600-m relay	2:57.91 minutes
	bronze	400-m run	44.71 seconds
EVELYN ASHFORD	gold	100-m dash	10.97 seconds, OR
	gold	400-m relay	41.65 seconds
VALERIE BRISCO-HOOKS	gold	200-m dash	21.81 seconds, OR
	gold	400-m run	48.83 seconds, OR
	gold	1600-m run	3:18.29 minutes, OR
BENITA FITZGERALD-BROWN	gold	100-m hurdles	12.84 seconds
ALICE BROWN	gold	400-m relay	41.65 seconds
	silver	100-m dash	11.13 seconds
JEANETTE BOLDEN	gold	400-m relay	41.65 seconds
CHANDRA CHEESEBOROUGH	gold	400-m relay	41.65 seconds
	gold	1600-m relay	3:18.29 minutes, OR
	silver	400-m run	49.05 seconds
SHERRI HOWARD	gold	1600-m relay	3:18.29 minutes, OR
LILLIE LEATHERWOOD	gold	1600-m relay	3:18.29 minutes, OR
KIRK BAPTISTE	silver	200-m dash	19.96 seconds
GREG FOSTER	silver	110-m hurdles	13.23 seconds
DANNY HARRIS	silver	400-m hurdles	48.13 seconds
MIKE CONLEY	silver	triple jump	17.18 meters
FLORENCE GRIFFITH	silver	200-m dash	22.04 seconds
JUDI BROWN	silver	400-m hurdles	55.20 seconds
JACKIE JOYNER	silver	heptathlon	6,385 points
EARL JONES	bronze	800-run	1:43.83 minutes
KIM TURNER	bronze	100-m hurdles	13.06 seconds

*OR = Olympic Record, WR = World Record

Other Sports

BOWLING

NATIONAL BOWLING ASSOCIATION TOURNAMENT CHAMPIONS

Men's Singles

Year	Bowler	Hometown	Points
1939	Jimmy Jones	Detroit	589
1940	Poindexter Orr	Chicago	593
1941	Issac Thurman	Indianapolis	668
1942	Herbert Cross	Chicago	692
1946	Obra Houston	Chicago	649
1947	Andrew Sharp	Indianapolis	623
1948	John Williams	Chicago	698
1949	Bob Robinson	Chicago	634
1950	Ben Harding	Cleveland	650
1951	Al Levine	New York	608
1952	Luther Hawkshaw	Columbus	637
1953	William Rhodman	Detroit	682
1954	Charles Bedell	Cleveland	610
1955	Floyd Wiggins	Baltimore	621
1956	E.J. Pollack	Detroit	615
1957	Charles Bedell	Cleveland	727
1958	Lovell Walker	Indianapolis	685
1959	Robert Council	Chicago	697
1960	Melwood Davis	Pittsburgh	630
	Lafayette Allen	Detroit	630
1961	Abner Fields	Newark	673
1962	Al Rotunno	Youngstown	716
1963	Robert Sims	Philadelphia	685
1964	Art Greene	Cleveland	676
1965	J. Wilbert Sims	Chicago	678
1966	Lannell Clark	Cleveland	686
1967	Fred McLarty	St. Louis	669

Year	Bowler	Hometown	Points
1968	Ray O'Riley	Buffalo	656
1969	Kenneth Parker	Newark	665
1969	Clyde Wilson	Buffalo	665
1970	Bill Gaume	Akron	638
1971	Joe King	Indianapolis	655
1972	Roger Williams	Akron	649
1973	Henry Goston	Buffalo	673
1974	Joseph Woodlock	Philadelphia	697
1975	John Ervin	Indianapolis	720
1976	Charles E. Chase	Washington, D.C.	725
1977	Jim Kirby	Philadelphia	683
1978	Willie Ridley	Indianapolis	743*
1979	Elton Richardson	Bronx	717
1980	F. Cumberland	Toledo	703
1981	James Clingman	Cincinnati	741
1982	William Tumpkin	Detroit	725
1983	Alphonso T. Harris	Chicago	845
1984	Joe Calloway	Denver	750

No tournaments 1943–45 due to the war

*Tournament record

NATIONAL BOWLING ASSOCIATION TOURNAMENT CHAMPIONS

Men's All-Events

Year	Bowler	Hometown	Points
1939	Merrill Thomas	Chicago	1662
1940	G. Walker	Chicago	1747
1941	G. Walker	Chicago	1696
1942	Merrill Thomas	Chicago	1722
1946	Thomas Washington	Chicago	1910
1947	Ray Strickland	Cleveland	1868
1948	Allen Levins	Newark	1773
1949	Bob Robinson	Chicago	1882
1950	Ben Harding	Cleveland	1843
1951	Pierce Monroe	Cleveland	1696
1952	Charles Bedell	Cleveland	1881
1953	William Rhodman	Detroit	1939
1954	Sterling Scott	Cleveland	1796
1955	Lloyd Thomas	Cleveland	1751

Year	Bowler	Hometown	Points
1956	Robert Ellis	Toledo	1731
1957	Sterling Scott	Cleveland	1937
1958	James Merritt	Jersey City	1824
1959	J. "Lank" Williams	Chicago	1952
1960	Archie DeShields	Detroit	1791
1961	LaRue Abel	Bronx	1910
1962	Al Rotunno	Youngstown	2013*
1963	Gilbert White	Jamesburg	1931
1964	Lorenz Wall	Cleveland	1889
1965	Wilbert Sims	Chicago	1876
1966	Joseph Jordan	New York	1965
1967	T.J. Pollock	Detroit	1804
1968	Edward Newton	Chicago	1931
1969	Clyde Wilson	Buffalo	1826
1970	Lester Smith	Pontiac	1814
1971	James Mosselle	Newark	1845
1972	Charles Gibson	Toledo	1879
1973	Ray Gage	Los Angeles	1920
1974	Joseph Woodlock	Philadelphia	1966
1975	Joe Isaiah	Akron	1985
1976	John Slappy	Detroit	1823
1977	James Burton	Indianapolis	1867
1978	Dave Hughes	Indianapolis	1917
1979	Speller Hall	Washington, D.C.	1970
1980	W. Jackson	San Francisco	1895
1981	Harry Reynolds	Akron	1888
1982	Rick Pollard	Cincinnati	2007
1983	Alphonso T. Harris	Chicago	1968
1984	Rick Pollard	Cinncinati	1997

No tournaments 1943–45 due to the war

*Tournament record

NATIONAL BOWLING ASSOCIATION TOURNAMENT CHAMPIONS

Women's Singles

Year	Bowler	Hometown	Points
1940	Edna Conner	Chicago	483
1941	Hazel Lyman	Detroit	487
1942	Virginia Dolphins	Detroit	550

Year	Bowler	Hometown	Points
1946	Fay Johnson	Detroit	596
1947	Louise Horton	Chicago	561
1948	Connie Ware	Detroit	588
1949	Jean Winbon	Chicago	593
1950	Fay Johnson	Detroit	609
1951	Doris Miller	Cleveland	559
1952	Ruth Coburn	Cleveland	632
1953	Irene Richardson	Columbus	559
1954	Thelma Artis	Toledo	539
1955	Mary Harmon	Cincinnati	604
1956	Beverly Adams	Chicago	557
1957	Lorraine Ramsey	Newark	593
1958	Gladys King	Indianapolis	592
1959	Albera Cable	Washington	651
1960	Jewel Locke	Detroit	591
1961	Dorothy Abbott	Toledo	613
1962	Evelyn Phillips	Cleveland	638
1963	Carol Strickland	St. Albans, N.Y.	625
1964	Marge Adams	Detroit	641
1965	Aileen Carter	Chicago	600
1966	Evelyn Phillips	Cleveland	635
1967	Claudine Roy	Chicago	635
1968	Bettie Garvin	Dayton	639
1969	Ruby Wallace	Detroit	645
1970	Nancy Davison	Buffalo	616
1971	Wanda Bruce	Los Angeles	676
1972	Louise McCluskey	Dayton	645
1973	Mary Schaeffer	Cleveland	629
1974	Dorothy Jackson	Detroit	656
1975	Annatta Ziegler	Cincinnati	614
1976	Vivian Prince	Buffalo	708
1977	Lila Lambert	Indianapolis	626
1978	Mary R. Lloyd	Detroit	718
1979	Mattie Worthy	Buffalo	744*
1980	Laura Jones	Indianapolis	713
1981	Ilona Wyatt	Petersburg	709
1982	Gerrie C. Smith	Rochester	709
1983	Mary Wright	Pasadena	698
1984	Joanna Jackson	Detroit	688

No tournaments 1943–45 due to the war

*Tournament record

NATIONAL BOWLING ASSOCIATION TOURNAMENT CHAMPIONS

Women's All-Events

Year	Bowler	Hometown	Points
1940	Sara Sturdivant	Cleveland	1421
1941	Hazel Lyman	Detroit	1426
1942	Virginia Dolphins	Detroit	1548
1946	Toni Taylor	Chicago	1520
1947	Isabel Baxter	Cincinnati	1782
1948	Ruth Coburn	Cleveland	1555
1949	Doris Largent	Cleveland	1602
1950	Doris Largent	Cleveland	1683
1951	Mae Gordon	Chicago	1593
1952	Ruth Coburn	Cleveland	1725
1953	Sadie Dixon	Wilmington	1594
1954	Dorothy Webb	Cincinnati	1542
1955	Ruth Coburn	Cleveland	1562
1962	Beverly Adams	Chicago	1547
1957	Sadie Dixon	Chester	1601
1958	Mae Gordon	Chicago	1694
1959	Gloria Hurd	Cleveland	1674
1960	Margarette Uncles	Washington	1582
1961	Mary Evans	Detroit	1721
1962	Juanita Warner	Chicago	1734
1963	Joan Oleske	New York	1807
1964	Sadie Dixon	Philadelphia	1772
1965	Rosemary Patch	Chicago	1683
1966	Clara Lane	Cleveland	1741
1967	Hattie Plamer	Cincinnati	1700
1968	Lavolia Brown	Detroit	1755
1969	Loretta Smith	Dayton	1701
1970	Joelia Mitchell	Indianapolis	1662
1971	Wanda Bruce	Los Angeles	1809
1972	Wanda Bruce	Los Angeles	1711
1973	Pat Ingram	Plainfield	1756
1974	Vernas Williams	Bronx	1735
1975	Pearl Valentine	Des Moines	1781
1976	Joelia Mitchell	Indianapolis	1816
1977	Susan Horvath	Detroit	1902*
1978	Julia Grumes	Cincinnati	1744
1979	Martha Howard	Oakland	1870
1980	Laura Jones	Indianapolis	1812
1981	Jewell Butler	Compton	1777

Year	Bowler	Hometown	Points
1982	Daisey Hawkins	Denver	1754
1983	Lula Peoples	Albany	1751
1984	Sarah Woods	Buffalo	1808

No tournaments 1943–45 due to the war

*Tournament record

NATIONAL BOWLING ASSOCIATION MIXED TEAM, DOUBLES AND TOURNAMENT RECORDS

Mixed Teams

Year	Team	Hometown	Points
1970	Meadow Lanes	Pittsburgh	2965
1971	The Real Team	Philadelphia	1985
1972	Mrs. Mort Bowling	Los Angeles	2724
1973	Brown's Garage	Buffalo	3130
1974	The Pin Knockers	Cleveland	3093
1975	Three & Two	Chicago	3072
1976	Black Diamonds	Philadelphia	3076
1977	Levert's Five	Detroit	2938
1978	Zodiac's	Detroit	3050
1979	Fiddlestix No. 2	Plainfield, N.J.	3291
1980	Bowled One	Petersburg, Va.	3149
1981	Fast Breakers	Walnut, Ca.	3092
1982	Manchester/Western Bowl	Los Angeles	3138
1983	Friends	Buffalo	3162

Mixed Doubles

Year	Bowlers	Hometown	Points
1978	Ann Cobb—Herman Terrell	Chicago	1363
1979	D. Penn—M. Clivens	New Orleans	1363
1980	L. Woods—D. Banks	Chicago	1428
1981	Flo Calaway—John Patton	Denver	1340
1982	Barbara Sulter—William Brewer	Buffalo	1343
1983	Shelia Duncan—Gary Jones	Chicago	1412
1984	Judith Seckel—William Cameron	St. Louis	1353

Championship Tournament Records

Men's Team

Year	*Team*	*Hometown*	*Points*
1980	Sandbaggers	Los Angeles, CA	3243

Men's Doubles

1979	W. Jones—Watson	Cleveland, OH	1476

Men's Singles

1983	Alphonso T. Harris	Chicago, ILL	845

All Events

1962	Al Totunno	Youngstown, OH	2013

Women's Team

1979	Strikes And Spares	Detroit, MI	3153

Women's Doubles

1979	L. Matlock—M. Howard	Oakland, CA	1489

Women's Singles

1979	Mattie Worty	Buffalo, NY	744

All Events

	Susan Horvath	Detroit, MI	1902

FENCING

AFRICAN-AMERICAN FENCING CHAMPIONS

National Collegiate Athletic Association

1957	Bruce Davis	Foil	Wayne State University
1958	Bruce Davis	Foil	Wayne State University
1971	Tyrone Simmons	Foil	University of Detroit
1972	Tyrone Simmon	Foil	University of Detroil
	Tyrone Simmons	3-weapon team	University of Detroit
	Ken Blake	3-weapon team	University of Detroit
	Fred Hooker	3-weapon team	University of Detroit
1973	Peter Westbrook	Sabre	New York University
1981	Peter Lewison	Sabre	City University of New York
1984	Michael Lofton	Sabre	New York University

Amateur Fencer's League of America

1969	Ruth White	Foil	New York University
1971	Uriah Jones	Foil	Santelli Club (New York)
1972	Bart Freeman	Foil	U.S. Naval Academy
1973	Edward Ballinger	Foil	New York University
1974	Peter Westbrook	Sabre	
1975	Edward Ballinger	Foil	
	Nikki Franke	Foil	LaSalle Csizar Club
	Peter Westbrook	Sabre	
1979	Peter Westbrook	Sabre	
1980	Nikki Franke	Foil	LaSalle Csizar Club
	Peter Westbrook	Sabre	
1981	Peter Westbrook	Sabre	
	Mark Smith	Foil	
1982	Peter Westbrook	Sabre	
1983	Peter Westbrook	Sabre	
	Mark Smith	Foil	
1984	Peter Westbrook	Sabre	
	Bob Cottingham	Foil (under 20)	Columbia University

National Intercollegiate Women's Fencing Association

1972	Ruth White	Foil	New York University
1984	Sharon Montplasir	Foil	Hunter College

Intercollegiate Fencing Association

1971	Edward Ballinger	Foil	New York University
1977	Mark Smith	Foil	Massachusetts Institute of Technology
1984	Michael Lofton	Sabre	New York University

Olympic Team Members

1968	Uriah Jones	1980	Nikki Franke
1972	Ruth White		Peter Westbrook
	Bart Freeman		Mark Smith
	Tyrone Simmons	1984	Peter Westbrook (bronze medal, sabre)
1976	Edward Ballinger		Michael Lofton
	Edward Wright		Mark Smith
	Peter Westbrook		Peter Lewison
			Sharon Montplasir

RUTH WHITE—FENCING RECORD

*1969 AFLA National Champion, Women's Foil individual
*1971 NIWFA Champion, Women's Foil individual (New York University)
1972 NIWFA Champion, Women's Foil individual (New York University)
*1972 U.S. Olympic Fencing team member

Junior Awards

**1971 World Under-20 Fencing Championships, medalist

*First Black woman
**First American
  AFLA is American Fencers League of America
  NIWFA is National Intercollegiate Women's Fencing Association

PETER WESTBROOK—FENCING RECORD

1974 AFLA Champion, Men's Sabre individual
1975 AFLA Champion, Men's Sabre individual
1976 U.S. Olympic team, member
1979 AFLA Champion, Men's Sabre individual
1980 U.S. Olympic team, member
   AFLA Champion, Men's Sabre individual
1981 AFLA Champion, Men's Sabre individual
1982 AFLA Champion, Men's Sabre individual
1983 AFLA Champion, Men's Sabre individual
1984 U.S. Olympic team, Bronze medalist at Sabre individual
   AFLA Champion, Men's Sabre individual

VOLLEYBALL

AFRICAN-AMERICAN VOLLEYBALL ALL-AMERICAS

NCAA Division I

Years	Athlete	School
1982	Beverly Robinson	U. of Tennessee
1982–83	Deitre Collins	U. of Hawaii
1982–84	Tracy Clark	U. of Southern California
1983–84	Marsha Bond	U. of Kentucky
1983–84	Anita Moss	U. of Arizona
1983–84	Kim Oden	Stanford University

Years	Athlete	School
1984 (2nd Team)	April Chapple	U. of Tennessee

NCAA Division II

Years	Athlete	School
1984 (2nd Team)	Geraldine Mattaur	U. of New Haven

WRESTLING

BLACK COLLEGE CONFERENCE WRESTLING CHAMPIONS

Year	CIAA	Coach	MEAC	Coach
1950	Lincoln	Bob Gardner		
1951	Lincoln	Bob Gardner		
1952	LLincoln	Bob Gardner		
1953	Lincoln	Bob Gardner		
1954	Lincoln	Bob Gardner		
1955	Va. State	Hulon Willis		
1956	Va. State	Hulon Willis		
1957	Va. State	Hulon Willis		
1958	Va. State	Hulon Willis		
1959	Va. State	Hulon Willis		
1960	Lincoln	Bob Gardner		
1961	Va. State	Hulon Willis		
1962	Lincoln	Bob Gardner		
1963	Morgan St.	Ken Jones		
1964	Morgan St.	Ken Jones		
1965	Morgan St.	Ken Jones		
1966	Howard	John Organ		
1967	Howard	John Organ		
1968	Howard	John Organ		
1969	Howard	John Organ		
1970	Howard	John Organ		
1971	Howard	John Organ		
1972	Eliz. City	Thurlis Little	Howard	John Organ
1973	Eliz. City	Thurlis Little	Howard	John Organ
1974	Eliz. City	Thurlis Little	Morgan St.	James Phillips
1975	Eliz. City	Thurlis Little	N.C. A & T	Mel Pinkney
1976	Eliz. City	Thurlis Little	N.C. A & T	Mel Pinkney
1977	Norfolk St.	Earl Powell	Morgan St.	James Phillips
1978	Livingstone	Robert Johnson	Morgan St.	James Phillips
1979	Norfolk St.	Earl Powell	S.C. State	James Raglund
1980	Winston-Salem	Mike Edwards	S.C. State	James Raglund
1981	Winston-Salem	Mike Edwards	S.C. State	James Raglund
1982	Winston-Salem	Mike Edwards	S.C. State	James Raglund
1983	Winston-Salem	Mike Edwards	S.C. State	James Raglund
1984	Winston-Salem	Mike Edwards	Delaware St.	William Collick

ROBERT DOUGLAS, ARIZONA STATE UNIVERSITY WRESTLING COACH

Career Achievements As A Wrestler

1963	World Open Freestyle Champion	138.5 class
1964	U.S. Olympics, 4th place,	138.5 class
	1st Black wrestler.	
1965	Big Eight Champion	147 class
	Oklahoma State U.	
	World Open Freestyle champion	138.5 class
1966	World Open Freestyle, Silver Medal	138.5 class
	World Greco-Roman Champion	138.5 class
1968	Captain U.S. Olympic team, Gold Medal Freestyle	138.5 class
1969	World Open Freestyle, 4th place	149 class
1970	National Open Freestyle Champion	150 class
	United States "Outstanding Wrestler of the Year."	
	World Open Freestyle, 3rd place, 149.5 class.	
Other titles	5 AAU National Championships, 2 Olympic Trials titles.	

Arizona State University Coaching Career (1974-1984)

Record, 141-42-1

Pac-10 titles in 1979 and 1981

Pac-10 Coach of the Year in 1979 and 1981

Coach of Sunkist Kids Wrestling club.

Authored four books on wrestling, will publish an autobiography.

NATIONAL COLLEGIATE ATHLETIC ASSOCIATION CHAMPIONS

Division I

Year	Wrestler	School	Weight Class
1957	Simon Roberts	Iowa	147 pounds
1959	Arthur Baker	Syracuse	191 pounds
1963	Jim Nance	Syracuse	Heavyweight
1964	Joe James	Oklahoma State	Heavyweight
1965	Veryl Long	Iowa State	147 pounds
1965	Jim Nance	Syracuse	Heavyweight
1967	Curley Culp	Arizona State	Heavyweight
1969	Cleo McGlory	Oklahoma	160 pounds
1969	Jason Smith	Iowa State	167 pounds
1970	Jason Smith	Iowa State	167 pounds
1971	Carl Adams	Iowa State	158 pounds
1972	Carl Adams	Iowa State	158 pounds
1973	Jarrett Hubbard	Michigan	150 pounds
1973	Bill Simpson	Clarion State	167 pounds
1974	Jarrett Hubbard	Michigan	150 pounds
1974	Jim Woods	Western Illinois	Heavyweight
1975	Shawn Garel	Oklahoma	118 pounds
1975	Ron Ray	Oklahoma State	167 pounds
1976	Lee Kemp	Wisconsin	158 pounds
1976	Chris Campbell	Iowa	177 pounds
1976	Jimmy Jackson	Oklahoma State	Heavyweight
1977	Lee Kemp	Wisconsin	158 pounds
1977	Chris Campbell	Iowa	177 pounds
1977	Jimmy Jackson	Oklahoma State	Heavyweight
1978	Ken Mallory	Montclair State	134 pounds
1978	Lee Kemp	Wisconsin	158 pounds
1978	Jimmy Jackson	Oklahoma State	Heavyweight
1979	Darryl Burley	Lehigh	134 pounds
1980	Noel Loban	Clemson	190 pounds
1980	Howard Harris	Oregon State	Heavyweight
1981	Nate Carr	Iowa State	150 pounds
1982	Nate Carr	Iowa State	150 pounds
1982	Israel Shephard	Oklahoma	
1983	Darryl Burley	Lehigh	142 pounds
1983	Nate Carr	Iowa State	150 pounds
1984	Kenny Monday	Oklahoma State	150 pounds
1984	Tab Thacker	North Carolina State	Heavyweight

AFRICAN-AMERICAN
NATIONAL ASSOCIATION OF INTERCOLLEGIATE ATHLETICS (NAIA) CHAMPIONS

Year	Wrestler	School	Weight Class
1968	Roy Washington	U. Nebraska-Omaha	145 pounds
1969	Curlee Alexander	U. Nebraska-Omaha	115 pounds
1969	Roy Washington	U. Nebraska-Omaha	145 pounds
1969	Mel Washington	U. Nebraska-Omaha	177 pounds
1970	Roy Washington	U. Nebraska-Omaha	150 pounds
1971	Mel Washington	U. Nebraska-Omaha	177 pounds
1978	Herb Stanley	Adams State (Colorado)	Heavyweight
1979	Herb Stanley	Adams State (Colorado)	Heavyweight
1983	David Marshall	Jamestown (N. Dakota)	190 pounds
1984	Greg Ford	Cen. Washington	118 pounds
1984	Tony Ramsey	Simon Fraser (Canada)	167 pounds

NATIONAL OPEN FREESTYLE CHAMPIONS

Year	Wrestler	Club	Weight Class
1970	Bobby Douglas	Ames, Iowa	150 pounds
1972	Wayne Holmes	Ohio Wrestling Club	105 pounds
1973	Wayne Holmes	Ohio Wrestling Club	105 pounds
1973	Willie Williams	Mayor Daley Y. Fndtn.	198 pounds
1975	Mel Renfro	Louisiana State W. C.	198 pounds
1975	Larry Avery	Michigan Wrestling Club	Heavyweight
1977	Greg Gibson	Oregon Wrestling Club	Heavyweight
1979	Lee Kemp	Wisconsin Wrestling Club	163 pounds
1980	Lee Kemp	Wisconsin Wrestling Club	163 pounds
1981	Lee Kemp	Wisconsin Wrestling Club	163 pounds
1982	Lee Kemp	Wisconsin Wrestling Club	163 pounds
1983	Lee Kemp	Wisconsin Wrestling Club	163 pounds
1983	Chris Campbell	Hawkeye Wrestling Club	180 pounds
1983	Greg Gibson	U. S. Marines	220 pounds
1984	Charlie Heard	Sunkist Kids (Tennessee)	114 pounds
1984	Harold Smith	Wildcat Wrestling Club (Ken.)	220 pounds

NATIONAL OPEN GRECO-ROMAN CHAMPIONS

Year	Wrestler	Club	Weight Class
1969	Johnny Johnson	Mayor Daley Y. Fndtn.	198 pounds
1971	Willie Williams	Mayor Daley Y. Fndtn.	198 pounds
1973	Abdul Raheem Ali	U. S. Army	163 pounds
1973	Willie Williams	Mayor Daley Y. Fndtn.	198 pounds
1974	Abdul Raheem Ali	U. S. Army	163 pounds
1974	Mike Bradley	Rhino Wrestling Club	180 pounds
1974	Willie Williams	Mayor Daley Y. Fndtn.	198 pounds
1974	Ken Levels	Hiram College	220 pounds
1975	Abdul Raheem Ali	U. S. Army	163 pounds
1975	Willie Williams	Mayor Daley Y. Fndtn.	198 pounds
1976	John Matthews	Michigan Wrestling Club	163 pounds
1976	Abdul Raheem Ali	U. S. Army	180 pounds
1976	Willie Williams	Mayor Daley Y. Fndtn.	198 pounds
1976	Jimmy Jackson	Oklahoma State	Heavyweight
1977	John Matthews	Michigan Wrestling Club	163 pounds
1977	Willie Williams	Mayor Daley Y. Fndtn.	198 pounds
1977	Pete Lee	Michigan Wrestling Club	Heavyweight
1978	Willie Williams	Mayor Daley Y. Fndtn.	198 pounds
1981	T.J. Jones	U. S. Navy	105 pounds
1981	Abdul Raheem Ali	Twin Cities Wrestling C.	198 pounds
1982	Greg Gibson	U. S. Marines	220 pounds
1982	Ron Carlisle	U. S. Marines	Heavyweight
1983	T.J. Jones	U. S. Navy	105 pounds
1984	T.J. Jones	U. S. Navy	105 pounds
1984	John Matthews	Michigan Wrestling Club	163 pounds

AFRICAN-AMERICAN OLYMPIC GAMES and PAN AM GAMES WINNERS

Olympians

Year	Wrestler	Event	Medal	Weight Class
1964	Bobby Douglas	Freestyle		138 pounds
1964	Charles Tribble	Freestyle		171 pounds
1968	Bobby Douglas	Freestyle		138 pounds
1972	Jimmy Carr	Freestyle		114 pounds
1972	Wayne Holmes	Greco-Roman		105 pounds
1976	Lloyd Keaser	Freestyle	Silver	149 pounds
1976	Jimmy Jackson	Freestyle		Heavyweight
1976	John Matthews	Greco-Roman		163 pounds
1976	Pete Lee	Greco-Roman		Heavyweight
1980	Lee Kemp	Freestyle		163 pounds
1980	Chris Campbell	Freestyle		180 pounds
1980	John Matthews	Greco-Roman		163 pounds
1984	Greg Gibson	Greco-Roman	Silver	220 pounds

Pan Am Games

1963	Joe James	Freestyle	Gold	Heavyweight
1975	Lloyd Keaser	Freestyle	Gold	149 pounds
1975	Carl Adams	Freestyle	Silver	163 pounds
1975	Willie Williams	Greco-Roman	Gold	198 pounds
1979	Lee Kemp	Freestyle	Gold	163 pounds
1979	Jimmy Jackson	Freestyle	Gold	Heavyweight
1979	Gregg Williams	Greco-Roman	Bronze	105 pounds
1979	John Matthews	Greco-Roman	Gold	163 pounds
1980	Pete Lee	Greco-Roman	Silver	Heavyweight
1983	Charles Heard	Freestyle	Silver	114 pounds
1983	Lee Kemp	Freestyle	Gold	163 pounds
1983	Greg Gibson	Freestyle	Gold	220 pounds
1983	T.J. Jones	Greco-Roman	Silver	105 pounds
1983	Ron Carlisle	Greco-Roman	Bronze	Heavyweight

Sources

BOOKS

Aaron, Henry. *Aaron*. New York: Thomas Y. Crowell Publishers, 1974.

Abdul-Jabbar, Kareem, and Knobler, Peter. *Giant Steps*. New York: Bantam Books, 1983.

Achebe, Chinua. *Things Fall Apart*. New York: McDowell Obolensky, 1959.

Adelman, Bob, and Hall, Susan. *Out of Left Field: Willie Stargell and the Pittsburgh Pirates*. Boston: Little, Brown and Company 1974.

Adelman, Melvin L. *A Sporting Time: New York City and the Rise of Modern Athletics 1820–70*. Urbana, Illinois: University of Illinois Press, 1986.

Adu Boahen, Clark; Desmond, Clarke; John H., Curtin, Philip; Davidson, Basil; Samkange, Stanlake; Schaar, Stuart; Shepperson, George; Shinnie, Margaret; Vansina, Jan; Wallerstein, Immanuel; Willis, John R. *The Horizon History of Africa*. New York: American Heritage Publishing Company, 1971.

Alexander, Charles C. *Ty Cobb*. New York: Oxford University Press, 1984.

Ali, Muhammad. *The Greatest: My Own Story*. New York: Random House, 1975.

Allen, Maury. *Mr. October: The Reggie Jackson Story*. New York: New American Library, 1982.

Anderson, Dave. *Sports of Our Times*. New York: Random House, 1979.

Aptheker, Herbert. *A Documentary History of the Negro People in the United States: 1910–1932*. Secaucus, New Jersey: Citadel Press, 1973.

Ashe, Arthur. *Off the Court*. New York: New American Library, 1981.

——————*Portrait in Motion*. Boston, Massachusetts: Houghton Mifflin Company, 1975.

Astor, Gerald. *And a Credit to His Race: The Hard Life and Times of Joseph Louis Barrow*. New York: Saturday Review Press, 1974.

Baker, William J. *Jesse Owens: An American Life*. New York: The Free Press, 1986.

Barber, Red. *1947: When All Hell Broke Loose in Baseball*. Garden CIty, New York: Doubleday and Company, 1982.

Beart, Charles. *"Jeux et Jouets de L'Ouest Africain"* (a monograph). Tome 1. Number 42.

Behee, John. *Hail to the Victors!* Ann Arbor, Michigan: Ulrich's Books, 1974.

Bell, Marty. *The Legend of Dr. J*. New York: New American Library, 1975.

Bennett, Lerone, Jr. *Wade in the Water: Great Moments in Black History*. Chicago: Johnson Publishing Company, 1979.

Berkow, Ira. *Oscar Robertson: The Golden Year 1964*. Englewood Cliffs, New Jersey: Prentice Hall, 1971.

——————. *The DuSable Panthers*. New York: Atheneum Publishers, 1978.

Blassingame, John W. *Black New Orleans: 1860–1880*. Chicago: University of Chicago Press, 1973.

——————. *Slave Testimony: Two Centuries of Letters, Speeches, Interviews and Autobiographies*. Baton Rouge, Louisiana: Louisiana State University Press, 1977.

Boss, David. *The Pro-Football Experience*. New York: Harry N. Abrams, Inc., 1973.

Broderick, Francis L., and Meier, August. *Negro Protest Thought in the Twentieth Century*. Indianapolis: Bobbs-Merrill Company, 1965.

Brondfield, Jerry. *Kareem Abdul-Jabbar, Magic Johnson and the Los Angeles Lakers*. New York: Scholastic Book Services, 1981.

Brown, Gene. *The Complete Book of Basketball*. New York: Arno Press, 1980.

Brown, Jimmy. *Off My Chest*. New York: Doubleday and Company, 1964.

Brown, Larry. *I'll Always Get Up*. New York: Simon and Schuster, 1973.

Brown, Paul. *PB: The Paul Brown Story*. New York: Atheneum Publishers, 1979.

Butler, Hal. *The Willie Horton Story*. New York: Julian Messner Company, 1970.

Campanella, Roy. *It's Good to Be Alive*. Boston: Little, Brown and Company, 1959.

Carter, Rubin "Hurricane." *The Sixteenth Round*. New York: Viking Press, 1974.

Cashmore, Ernest. *Black Sportsmen*. London: Routledge and Kegan Paul, 1982.

Chalk, Ocania. *Black College Sport*. New York: Dodd, Mead and Company, 1976.

——————. *Pioneers of Black Sport*. New York: Dodd, Mead and Company, 1975.

Chamberlain, Wilt, and Shaw, David. *Wilt: Just Like Any Other 7-Foot Black Millionaire Who Lives Next Door*. New York: Macmillan Publishing Company, 1973.

Chambers, Lucille Arcola. *America's Tenth Men*. New York: Twayne Publishers, 1957.

Chambers, Ted. *The History of Athletics and Physical Education at Howard University*. Washington, D.C.: Vantage Press, 1986.

Chew, Peter. *The Kentucky Derby: The First 100 Years*. Boston: Houghton Mifflin and Company, 1974.

Chisholm, J. Francis. *Brewery Gulch: Frontier Days of Old Arizona, Last Outpost of the Great Southwest*. San Antonio: Naylor Company, 1949.

Cohen, Joel H. *Hammerin' Hank of the Braves*. New York: Scholastic Book Services, 1971.

Considine, Tim. *The Language of Sport*. New York: World Almanac Publications, 1982.

Corbett, J. James. *The Roar of the Crowd: The True Tale of the Rise and Fall of a Champion*. Garden City, New York: Garden City Publishing Company, 1926.

Cottrell, John. *Man of Destiny: The Story of Muhammed Ali*. London: Frederick Muller Press, 1967.

Cummings, John. *Negro Population in the United States, 1790–1915*. New York: Arno Press, 1968.

Cunard, Nancy. *Negro Anthology 1913–1933*. London: Wishart and Company, 1934.

Davies, Marianna W. *Contributions of Black Women to America*. Columbia, South Carolina: Kenday Press, Inc., 1982.

Davis, Edwin Adams, and Hogan, William Ranson. *The Barber of Natchez*. Baton Rouge, Louisiana: Louisiana State University Press, 1973.

Diamond, Wilfred. *How Great Was Joe Louis?* New York: Paebar Company, 1950.

Dolan, Edward F., Jr., and Lyttle, Richard B. *Jimmy Young: Heavyweight Challenge*. Garden City; New York: Doubleday and Company, 1979.

Donaldson, Thomas. *Idaho of Yesterday*. Westport, Connecticut: Greenwood Press, 1970.

Douglass, Frederick. *The Life and Times of Frederick Douglass*. New York: Bonanza Books, 1962.

Drake, St. Clair, and Cayton, Horace R. *Black Metropolis: A Study of Negro Life in a Northern City*. New York: Harcourt, Brace and Company, 1945.

Du Bois, W. E. Burghardt. *The Souls of Black Folk*. New York: Washington Square Press, 1970.

Duncan, Otis Dudley, and Duncan, Beverly. *The Negro Population of Chicago*. Chicago: University of Chicago Press, 1957.

Durant, John, and Bettman, Otto. *Pictorial History of American Sports from Colonial Times to the Present*. Cranberry, New Jersey: A.S. Barnes and Company, 1973.

Durham, Philip, and Jones, Everette L. *The Negro Cowboys*. New York: Dodd, Mead and Company 1965.

Eaton, Hubert A. *Every Man Should Try*. Wilmington North Carolina: Bonaparte Press, 1984.

Edwards, Audrey, and Wohl, Gary. *Muhammad Ali: The People's Champ*. Boston: 1977.

Edwards, Harry. *Sociology of Sport*. Homewood, Illinois: The Dorsey Press, 1973.

——————. *The Revolt of the Black Athlete*. New York: The Free Press, 1970.

——————. *The Struggle That Must Be: An Autobiography*. New York: Macmillan Publishing, 1980.

Egan, Pierce. *Boxiana*. London: G. Smeeton Publishers, 1812.

Ehre, Edward, and *The Sporting News*. *Best Sport Stories 1982*. New York: E. P. Dutton, 1982.

Einstein, Charles. *Willie Mays: Born to Play Ball*. New York: G. P. Putnam's Sons, 1955.

Eisenstadt, Murray. *The Negro in American Life*. New York: Oxford Book Company, 1968.

Farr, Finis. *Black Champion: The Life and Times of Jack Johnson*. London: Macmillan and Company 1964.

——————. *Black Champions: The Life and Times of Jack Johnson*. New York: Charles Scribner Sons, 1964.

Figler, Stephen, and Figler, Howard. *The Athlete's Game Plan for College and Career.* Princeton, New Jersey: Peterson's Guide, 1984.

Fisher, Galen M. *John R. Mott: Architect of Cooperation and Unity.* New York: Associated Press, 1962.

——————. *Public Affairs and the YMCA: 1844–1944.* New York: Association Press, 1948.

Fitzgerald, Ray. *Champions Remembered.* Brattleboro, Vermont: The Stephen Greene Press, 1982.

Fleischer, Nat. *All-Time Ring Record Book.* Norwalk, Connecticut: O'Brian Suburban Press, 1944.

——————. *Black Dynamite: The Story of the Negro in the Prize Ring from 1782 to 1938.* New York: *Ring* magazine, 1947.

——————. *All-Time Ring Record Book.* Norwalk, Connecticut: O'Brian Suburban Press, 1947.

Fletcher, Marvin E. *The Black Soldier Athlete in the United States Army 1890–1916.* Athens, Ohio: 1973.

Flood, Kurt. *The Way It Is.* New York: Trident Press, 1971.

Foner, Philip S. *Paul Robeson Speaks: Writings, Speeches and Interviews.* London: Quartette Books, 1978.

Foreman, Thomas Elton. "Discrimination Against the Negro in American Athletics" (a monograph). Fresno, California: Fresno State College, 1957.

Fox, Larry. *Willis Reed: Take Charge Man of the Knicks.* New York: Grosset and Dunlap, 1970.

Franklin, John Hope. *The Free Negro in North Carolina 1790–1860.* New York: W. W. Norton and Company, 1969.

Frazier, Walt, and Berkow, Ira. *Rockin' Steady.* Englewood Cliffs, New Jersey: Prentice Hall Inc., 1974.

Frazier, Walt, and Jares, Joe. *The Walt Frazier Story: Clyde.* New York: Grosset and Dunlap, 1970.

Frommer, Harvey. *Rickey and Robinson: The Men Who Broke Baseball's Color Barrier.* New York: Macmillan Publishing Company, 1982.

The Fulani of Northern Nigeria. Lagos, Nigeria: Government Printing Office, 1945.

Gallagher, Robert C. *Ernie Davis: The Elmira Express.* Silver Spring, Maryland: Bartleby Press, 1983.

Gary, Lawrence E. *Black Men.* Beverly Hills, California: Sage Publications, 1981.

Gayle, Addison, Jr. *The Black Aesthetic.* Garden City, New York: Anchor Books, 1972.

Genovese, Eugene D. *Roll Jordan Roll: The World the Slaves Made.* New York: Random House, 1974.

Gewecke, Cliff. *Advantage Ashe.* New York: Coward McCann, 1965.

Gibson, Althea. *I Always Wanted to Be Somebody.* New York: Harper and Brothers, 1958.

Gibson, Bob. *From Ghetto to Glory: The Story of Bob Gibson.* Englewood, New Jersey: Prentice Hall Inc., 1968.

Goldstein, Allan. *A Fistful of Sugar.* New York: Coward, McCann and Geoghegan, 1981.

Graffis, Herb. *PGA: Official History of the PGA of America.* New York: Thomas Y. Crowell Publishers, 1975.

Griffin, Archie. *Archie: The Archie Griffin Story.* Garden City, New York: Doubleday and Company, 1977.

Grun, Bernard. *The Timetables of History.* New York: Simon and Schuster, 1979.

Halberstam, David. *The Breaks of the Game.* New York: Alfred A. Knopf, 1981.

Hamilton, Virginia. *Paul Robeson: The Life and Times of a Free Black Man.* New York: Harper and Row, 1974.

Harris, Merv. *On Court with the Superstars of the NBA.* New York: The Viking Press, 1973.

Haskins, James. *Sugar Ray Leonard.* New York: Lothrop, Lee and Shepard, 1982.

Hayes, Elvin, and Gilbert, Bill. *They Call Me "The Big E."* Englewood Cliffs, New Jersey: Prentice Hall, 1978.

Heller, Peter. *In This Corner: Forty World Champions Tell Their Stories.* New York: Simon and Schuster, 1973.

Henderson, Edwin B. *The Negro in Sports.* Washington, D.C.: Associated Publishers Inc., 1949.

Henderson, Edwin B., and *Sport* magazine. *The Black Athlete: Emergence and Arrival.* Cornwell Heights, Pennsylvania: Pennsylvania Publishers Company Inc., 1968.

Henderson, James H. M., and Henderson, Betty F. *Molder of Men: Portrait of a "Grand Old Man"— Edwin Bancroft Henderson.* New York: Vantage Press, 1985.

Hirschberg, Al. *Henry Aaron: Quiet Superstar.* New York: G. P. Putnam's Sons, 1974.

Hollander, Zander. *Great American Athletes of the Twentieth Century.* New York: Random House, 1966.

Holmes, Dwight Oliver Wendell. *The Evolution of the Negro College.* New York: Arno Press, 1969.

Holway, John B. *"Bullet Joe and the Monarchs"* (a monograph). Washington, D.C.: Capitol Press, 1984.

Isaac, Stan. *Jim Brown: The Golden Year 1964.* Englewood Cliffs, New Jersey: Prentice Hall Inc., 1970.

Isaacs, Neil D. *All the Moves: A History of College Basketball.* New York: Harper and Row, 1984.

Jackson, Reggie. *Reggie.* New York: Ballantine Books, 1984.

—————. *Reggie: A Season with a Superstar.* Chicago: Playboy Press Books, 1975.

James, C. L. R. *Beyond a Boundary.* New York: Pantheon Books, 1983.

Jares, Joe. *Basketball: The American Game.* Chicago: Follett Publishing Company, 1971.

"The Jesse Owens Dossier." Obtained from the Federal Bureau of Investigation Under the Freedom of Information Act.

Johnson, Arthur T., and Frey, James H. *Government and Sport: The Public Policy Issues.* Totowa, New Jersey: Rowman and Allanheld, 1985.

Johnson, Charles S. *Patterns of Negro Segregation.* New York: Harper and Brothers, 1943.

Johnson, Earvin "Magic," and Levin, Richard. *Magic.* New York: The Viking Press, 1983.

Johnson, Jack. *Jack Johnson Is a Dandy: An Autobiography.* New York: New American Library, 1969.

—————. *Jack Johnson: In the Ring and Out.* Chicago: National Sports Publishing Company, 1927.

Johnson, James Weldon. *Black Manhattan.* New York: Atheneum Press, 1977.

Jones, Cleon. *Cleon.* New York: Coward-McCann, Inc., 1970.

Jones, Wally, and Washington, Jim. *Black Champions Challenge American Sports.* New York: David McKay Company, Inc., 1972.

Jones, William H. *Recreation and Amusement Among Negros in Washington.* Westport, Connecticut: Negro Universities Press, 1970.

Jordan, Pat. *Black Coach.* New York: Dodd, Mead and Company, 1971.

Kaletsky, Richard. *Ali and Me: Through the Ropes.* Bethany, Connecticut: Andrienne Publications, 1982.

Katz, William Loren. *The Black West.* Garden City, New York: Anchor Books, 1973.

Keeneland Association Library. *Thoroughbred Record.* Lexington, Kentucky: Keeneland Association Library.

Kountze, Mabe "Doc." *Fifty Sport Years Along Memory Lane.* Medford, Massachusetts: Mystic Valley Press, 1979.

Kowet, Don. *Vida Blue: Coming Up Again.* New York: G. P. Putnam's Sons, 1974.

Lapchick, Richard Edward. *The Politics of Race and International Sport: The Case of South Africa.* Westport, Connecticut: Greenwood Press, 1975.

Leach, George B. *Kentucky Derby Diamond Jubilee.* New York: Gibbs Inman Publishers, 1949.

LeFlore, Ron. *Break Out: From Prison to the Big Leagues.* New York: New York. Harper and Row, 1978.

Lewis, David Levering. *When Harlem Was in Vogue.* New York: Alfred A. Knopf, 1981.

Lewis, Dwight, and Thomas, Susan. *A Will to Win.* Mount Juliet, Tennessee: Cumberland Press, 1983.

Lewis, William H. *"How to Play Football"* (a monograph). Boston: 1903.

Libby, Bill, and Haywood, Spencer. *Stand Up for Something: The Spencer Haywood Story.* New York: Grosset and Dunlap, 1972.

Libby, Bill *Goliath: The Wilt Chamberlain Story.* New York: Dodd, Mead and Company, 1977.

Lipman, David, and Wilks, Ed. *Bob Gibson: Pitching Ace.* New York: G. P. Putnam's Sons, 1975.

Lipsyte, Robert. *Free to Be Muhammad Ali.* New York: Harper and Row, 1978.

—————. *Sports World: An American Dreamland.* New York: Quadrangle Books, 1975.

Louis, Joe. *Joe Louis: My Life.* New York: Harcourt Brace Jovanovich, 1978.

Louis, Joe. *My Life Story.* New York: Duell, Sloan and Pearce, 1947.

Lyle, Sparky, and Golenbock, Peter. *The Bronx Zoo.* New York: Crown Publishers Inc., 1979.

Mackler, Bernard. *Black Superstars: Getting Ahead in Today's America.* New York: *Conch* magazine Limited Publishers, 1977.

Mailer, Norman. *The Fight.* Boston: Little, Brown and Company, 1975.

Major, Gerri. *Black Society*. Chicago: Johnson Publishing Company, Inc., 1976.

Matthews, Vincent. *My Race Be Won*. New York: Charter House Publishers, 1974.

Mays, Willie, and Einstein, Charles. *Willie Mays: My Life in and Out of Baseball*. New York: E. P. Dutton and Company, 1966.

McAdoo, Harriett Pipes, and McAdoo, John Lewis. *Black Children: Social, Educational, and Parental Environments*. Beverly Hills, California: Sage Publications, 1985.

McCallum, John D. *The World Heavyweight Boxing Championship: A History*. Radnor, Pennsylvania: Chilton Book Company, 1974.

McPhee, John. *A Sense of Where You Are: A Profile of William Warren Bradley*. New York City: New York. Farrar, Straus and Giroux, 1965.

McPhee, John. *Levels of the Game*. New York: Farrar, Straus and Giroux, 1969.

Michelson, Herb. *Almost a Famous Person*. New York: Harcourt Brace Jovanovich, 1980.

Michener, James A. *Sports in America*. New York: Fawcett Crest, 1976.

Miller, Margery. *Joe Louis: American*. New York: Hill and Wang, 1945.

Moore, Archie, and Pearl, Leonard B. *Any Boy Can: The Archie Moore Story*. Englewood Cliffs, New Jersey: Prentice Hall, Inc., 1971.

Morris, Willie. *The Courting of Marcus Dupree*. Garden City, New York: Doubleday and Company, 1983.

Movius, Geoffrey H. *The Second Book of Harvard Athletics, 1923–1963*. Cambridge, Massachusetts: The Harvard Varsity Club, 1964.

Murray, Florence. *The Negro Handbook, 1944*. New York: Current Reference Publications, 1944.

Nazel, Joseph. *Jackie Robinson: A Biography*. Los Angeles: Holloway House Publishing Company, 1982.

Neft, David S., Cohen, Richard M., and Deutsch, Jordan A. *The Sports Encyclopedia: Pro Football the Modern Era, 1960 to Present*. New York: Simon and Schuster, 1982.

Neft, David S., Cohen, Richard M., and Deutsch, Jordan A. *Pro-Football: The Early Years, 1895–1959*. Ridgefield, Connecticut: Sports Products, Inc., 1978.

Negro Population in the United States, 1790–1915. New York: Arno Press, 1968.

Newcombe, Jack. *Floyd Patterson: Heavyweight King*. New York: Bartholomew House Inc., 1961.

Noll, Roger G. *Government and the Sports Business*. Washington, D.C.: The Brookings Institution, 1974.

Norback, Craig, and Norback, Peter. *The New American Guide to Athletics, Sports, and Recreation*. New York: The New American Library, 1979.

Norman, Gardner L. *Athletics of the Ancient World*. Chicago: Associated Publishers, 1930.

O'Connor, Dick. *Reggie Jackson: Yankee Superstar*. New York: Scholastic Book Services, 1978.

The Official 1985 National Football League Record and Fact Book. New York: National Football League, 1986.

Olsen, Jack. *Black Is Best: The Riddle of Cassius Clay*. New York: G. P. Putnam's Sons, 1967.

Orr, Jack. *The Black Athlete: His Story in American History*. New York: Lion Books Publishing, 1969.

Owens, Jesse. *Blackthink: My Life as Black Man and White Man*. New York: William Morrow and Company, 1970.

——————. *I Have Changed*. New York: William Morrow and Company, 1972.

——————. *Jesse: The Man Who Outran Hitler*. New York: Fawcett Gold Medal Books, 1978.

Pachter, Mark. *Champions of American Sport*. New York: National Portrait Gallery, Smithsonian Institute, 1981.

Parker, Inez Moore, and Callison, Helen Vassy. *The Biddle Johnson C. Smith University Story*. Charlotte, North Carolina: Charlotte Publishing Company, 1975.

Palmer, Charles B. *For Gold and Glory: The Story of Thoroughbred Racing in America*. New York: Karrick and Evans Inc., 1939.

Patterson, Floyd, and Gross, Milton. *Victory Over Myself*. New York: Bernard Geis Associates and Random House, 1962.

Paul Robeson Archives. *Paul Robeson Tribute and Selected Writings*. New York: Paul Robeson Archives, 1976.

Payton, Walter. *Sweetness*. Chicago: Contemporary Books, Inc., 1978.

Pepe, Phil. *Stand Tall: The Lew Alcindor Story*. New York: Grosset and Dunlap, 1970.

Peterson, James A. *Slater of Iowa*. Chicago: Hinkley and Schmitt, 1958.

Peterson, Robert. *Only the Ball Was White.* Englewood Cliffs, New Jersey: Prentice Hall Inc., 1970.

Phillips, Ulrich Bonnell. *American Negro Slavery.* Baton Rouge, Louisiana: Louisiana State University Press, 1966.

Picott, J. Rupert. *"Selected Black Sports Immortals"* (a monograph). Washington, D.C.: Association for the Study of Afro-American Life and History, Inc., 1981.

Plimpton, George. *Sports!* New York: Abbeville Press/Harry N. Abrams, 1978.

Plosky, Harry A., and Brown, Roscoe C., Jr. *The Negro Almanac.* New York: Bellwhether Publishing Company, 1967.

Puckett, Newbell N. *The Magic and Folk Beliefs of the Southern Negro.* New York: Dover Publications, 1969.

Rader, Benjamin G. *American Sports.* Englewood Cliffs, New Jersey: Prentice Hall, 1983.

Randolph, Jack. *"Tom Molineux: America's 'Almost' Champion"* (a monograph).

Randolph, Wilma. *Wilma.* New York: New American Library, 1977.

Reed, Willis. *A View from the Rim: Willis Reed on Basketball.* Philadelphia: J. B. Lippincott, 1971.

Reichler, Joseph L. *The Baseball Encyclopedia.* New York: Macmillan Publishing Company, Inc., 1985.

Reidenbaugh, Lowell. *The Sporting News First Hundred Years, 1886–1986.* St. Louis: Sporting News Publishing Company, 1985.

Reuter, Edward Byron. *The Mulatto in the United States.* New York: Negro Universities Press, 1969.

Ritter, Lawrence, and Honig, Donald. *The 100 Greatest Baseball Players of All Time.* New York: Crown Publishers, 1981.

Roberts, Randy. *Papa Jack: Jack Johnson and the Era of White Hopes.* New York: The Free Press, 1983.

Robertson, Lawson. *College Athletics.* New York: American Sports Publishing Company, 1923.

Robeson, Susan. *The Whole World in His Hands: A Pictorial Biography of Paul Robeson.* Secaucus, New Jersey: Citadel Press, 1981.

Robinson, Frank. *Frank: The First Year.* New York: Holt, Rinehart and Winston, 1976.

Robinson, Frank. *My Life in Baseball.* Garden City, New York: Doubleday and Company, 1968.

Robinson, Jackie. *I Never Had It Made.* Greenwich, Connecticut: Fawcett Publications, 1972.

——————. *Jackie Robinson: My Own Story.* New York: Greenberg Publishers, 1948.

Robinson, Louie, Jr. *Arthur Ashe: Tennis Champion.* Garden City, New York: Doubleday and Company, Inc., 1967.

Rogosin, Don. *Invisible Men: Life in Baseball's Negro Leagues.* New York: Atheneum Publishers, 1983.

Ross, Frank Alexander, and Kennedy, Louise Benable. *A Bibliography of Negro Migration.* New York: Columbia University Press, 1934.

Ruck, Ron. *Sandlot Seasons: Sport in Black Pittsburgh.* Urbana, Illinois: University of Illinois Press, 1987.

Russell, Bill, and Branch, Taylor. *Second Win: The Memoirs of an Opinionated Man.* New York: Random House, 1979.

Russell, Cazzie L., Jr. *Me, Cazzie Russell.* Westwood, New Jersey: Fleming H. Revell, 1967.

Russell, John A. *The Free Negro in Virginia 1619–1865.* New York: Negro Universities Press, 1969.

Rust, Art, Jr. *"Get That Nigger Off the Field!"* New York: Delacorte Press, 1976.

Rust, Art, Jr., and Rust, Edna. *Recollections of a Baseball Junkie.* New York: William Morrow and Company, 1985.

Rust, Edna, and Rust, Art, Jr. *Art Rust's Illustrated History of the Black Athlete.* Garden City, New York. Doubleday and Company Inc., 1985.

Sample, Johnny. *Confessions of a Dirty Ball Player.* New York: The Dial Press, 1970.

Savin, Francine. *Women Who Win.* New York: Dell Publishing Company, 1975.

Saxon, Walt. *Darryl Strawberry.* New York: Dell Books, 1985.

Schapp, Dick. *The Perfect Jump.* New York: New American Library, 1976.

——————. *Sport.* New York: Arbor House, 1975.

Schneider, Russell, Jr. *Frank Robinson: The Making of a Manager.* New York: Coward, McCann and Geoghegan, 1976.

Schoolcraft, M. H. *"Letters on the Condition of the African Race in the United States by a Southern Lady"* (a monograph). Philadelphia: T. K. and P. G. Collins, 1852.

Schoor, Gene. *Dave Winfield: The 23 Million Dollar Man.* Briarcliff Manor, New York: Stein and Day Publishers, 1982.

——————. *Willie Mays: Modest Champion.* New York: G. P. Putnam's Sons, 1960.

Schubert, Frank N. "*The Black Regular Army Regiments in Wyoming, 1885–1912*" (a thesis). Laramie, Wyoming: University of Wyoming, 1970.

Scott, Jack. *The Athletic Revolution.* New York: The Free Press, 1971.

Silvermen, Al. *Best from Sport: An Anthology of Fifteen Years of Sport Magazine.* New York: Bartholomew House, Inc., 1961.

——————. *I Am Third: Gale Sayers.* New York: Viking Press, 1970.

Simpson, O. J. *O.J. : The Education of a Rich Rookie.* New York: The Macmillan Company, 1970.

Sims, Mary S. *The Natural History of a Social Institution—YMCA.* New York: Association Press, 1929.

Smith, Harry Worcester. *Life and Sport in Aiken.* Aiken, South Carolina: Derrydale Press, 1935.

"Softball Hall of Famers" (a monograph). Oklahoma City: Amateur Softball Association.

Sowell, Thomas. *Ethnic America: A History.* New York: Basic Books Inc., 1981.

Spalding's Athletic Library. *Interscholastic Athletic Association Guide Book for 1910, 1911, and 1913.* New York: American Sports Publishing Company.

Spink, J. G. Taylor. *Judge Landis and Twenty-Five Years of Baseball.* New York: Thomas Y. Crowell Publishers, 1947.

Spradling, Mary Mace. *In Black and White.* Detroit: Gale Research Company, 1980.

Stagg, Amos Alonzo, and Williams, H. C. "A Scientific and Practical Treatise on American Football for Schools and Colleges" (a monograph). Chicago: University of Chicago, 1893.

Staples, Robert. *Black Masculinity: The Black Male's Role in American Society.* San Francisco: The Black Scholar Press, 1982.

Stargell, Willie, and Bird, Tom. *Willie Stargell: An Autobiography.* New York: Harper and Row Publishers, 1984.

Stern, Robert. *They Were Number One: A History of the NCAA Basketball Tournament.* New York: Leisure Press, 1983.

Stingley, Darryl. *Darryl Stingley: Happy to be Alive.* New York: Beaufort Books Inc., 1983.

Sugar, Bert Randolph, and *Ring* magazine. *The Great Fights.* New York: Rutledge Press, 1981.

Super, Paul. *Formative Ideas in the YMCA.* New York: Association Press, 1929.

Tatum, Jack. *They Call Me Assassin.* New York: Everest House Publishers, 1979.

Taylor, Marshall W. "Major." *The Fastest Bicycle Rider in the World.* Worcester, Massachusetts: Wormley Publishing Company, 1928.

The Annals of America. Chicago: Encyclopedia Britannica Inc., 1976.

The Horizon History of Africa. New York: American Heritage Publishing Company, 1971.

The International Amateur Athletic Association Federation Statistics Handbook. Los Angeles: International Amateur Athletic Federation, 1984.

The Official Results of the 1984 Olympic Games. Los Angeles: Los Angeles Olympic Committee, 1984.

The Ring Record Book and Boxing Encyclopedia. New York: Atheneum Publishers, 1987.

The *Sporting Life's* Official Baseball Guide: 1890.

The Sporting News Official NBA Guide: 1984–1985. St. Louis: The Sporting News, 1985.

Trengove, Allan. *The Story of the Davis Cup.* London: Stanley Paul Publishers, 1985.

Truehart, William Elton. "The Consequences of Federal and State Resource Allocation and Development Policies for Traditionally Black Land-Grant Institutions: 1862–1954" (a thesis). Cambridge, Massachusetts: Doctoral Thesis for Graduate School of Education, Harvard University, 1979.

Tygiel, Jules. *Baseball's Great Experiment: Jackie Robinson and His Legacy.* New York: Oxford University Press, 1983.

United States Tennis Association. *The Official USTA Year Book and Tennis Guide.* Lynn, Massachusetts: H. O. Zimman Inc., 1986.

Wallechinsky, David. *The Complete Book of the Olympics.* New York: Penguin Books, 1984.

White, Solomon. *Sol White's Official Baseball Guide.* Philadelphia: Camden House, Inc., 1984.

Who's Who Among Black Americans. *Who's Who Among Black Americans, 1975-76.* Northbrook, Illinois: 1976.

Wills, Maury, and Gardner, Steve. *It Pays to Steal.* Englewood Cliffs, New Jersey: Prentice Hall Inc., 1963.

Winters, Manque. *Professional Sports: The Community College Connection.* Inglewood, California: Winnor Press, 1982.

Woodward, Bob, and Armstrong, Scott. *The Brethren: Inside the Supreme Court.* New York: Simon and Schuster, 1979.

Works Projects Administration. *Houston, Texas: A History and Guide.* Houston: Anson Jones Press, 1945.

Yannakis, Andrew; McIntrye, Thomas D.; Melnick, Merrill J.; and Hart, Dale P. *Sport Sociology: Contemporary Themes.* Dubuque, Iowa: Kendall/Hunt Publishing Company, 1976.

Young, A. S. "Doc." *Great Negro Baseball Stars.* New York: Barnes and Company, 1953.

————. *Negro Firsts in Sports.* Chicago: Johnson Publishing Company, 1963.

Zinkoff, Dave. *Go, Man, Go!: Around the World with the Harlem Globetrotters.* New York: Pyramid Books, 1958.

NEWSPAPERS

The Afro-American Newspaper (New York, New York)
The Atlanta Constitution (Atlanta, Georgia)
The Atlanta Independent (Atlanta, Georgia)
The Atlanta Daily World (Atlanta, Georgia)
The Birmingham Reporter (Birmingham, Alabama)
The Boston Chronicle (Boston, Massachusetts)
The Boston Globe (Boston, Massachusetts)
The Boston Guardian (Boston, Massachusetts)
The Brooklyn Daily Union (Brooklyn, New York)
The Brooklyn Times (Brooklyn, New York)
The California Eagle (Los Angeles, California)
The Cape May Star and Wave (Cape May, New Jersey)
The Cedar Rapids Republican (Cedar Rapids, Iowa)
The Chicago Bee (Chicago, Illinois)
The Chicago Defender (Chicago, Illinois)
The Chicago Tribune (Chicago, Illinois)
The City Sun (Brooklyn, New York)
The Cleveland Advocate (Cleveland, Ohio)
The Cleveland Call & Post (Cleveland, Ohio)
The Cleveland Gazette (Cleveland, Ohio)
The Daily Houston Telegraph (Houston, Texas)
The Daily Worker (New York, New York)

The Dallas Times Herald (Dallas, Texas)
The Detroit Free Press (Detroit, Michigan)
The Detroit Plain Dealer (Detroit, Michigan)
The East Tennessee News (Johnson City, Tennessee)
The Galesburg Register (Galesburg, Illinois)
The Harvard Crimson (Harvard University)
The Indianapolis Freeman (Indianapolis, Indiana)
The Interstate Tattler (New York, New York)
The Irish Times (Dublin, Ireland)
The Jamestown Evening Journal (Jamestown, New York)
The London Times (London, England)
The Los Angeles Sentinel (Los Angeles, California)
The Los Angeles Times (Los Angeles, California)
The Louisville Courier Journal (Louisville, Kentucky)
The Macon Telegram (Macon, Georgia)
The Miami Herald (Miami, Florida)
The Minnesota Journal (Mahtomedi, Minnesota)
The Montgomery Advertiser (Montgomery, Alabama)
The Morning Telegraph (New York, New York)
The Morning Transcript (Lexington, Kentucky)
The Nashville Tennessee Banner (Nashville, Tennessee)
The Newark Call (Newark, New Jersey)
The Newark Evening News (Newark, New Jersey)
The New Orleans Daily-Picayune (New Orleans, Louisiana)
The New Orleans Pelican (New Orleans, Louisiana)
The New Orleans Times (New Orleans, Louisiana)
The New Orleans Times-Democrat (New Orleans, Louisiana)
The New Orleans Weekly Louisianian (New Orleans, Louisiana)
The New York Age (New York, New York)
The New York American (New York, New York)
The New York Amsterdam News (New York, New York)
The New York City Illustrated News (New York, New York)
The New York Herald (New York, New York)
The New York Herald-Tribune (New York, New York)
The New York News (New York, New York)
The New York Post (New York, New York)
The New York Sun (New York, New York)
The New York World (New York, New York)
The Norfolk Journal and Guide (Norfolk, Virginia)

The Philadelphia Public Ledger (Philadelphia, Pennsylvania)

The Philadelphia Tribune (Philadelphia, Pennsylvania)

The Pittsburgh American (Pittsburgh, Pennsylvania)

The Pittsburgh Courier (Pittsburgh, Pennsylvania)

The Police Gazette (New York, New York)

The Record and Sun (Pennsylvania)

The Richmond News Leader (Richmond, Virginia)

The Richmond Planet (Richmond, Virginia)

The Richmond Times-Dispatch (Richmond, Virginia)

The Rochester Democrat and Chronicle (Rochester, New York)

The Rocky Mount Telegram (Rocky Mount, North Carolina)

The Rocky Mountain News (Denver, Colorado)

The Rome Tribune-Herald (Rome, Georgia)

The South Side Signal (Long Island, New York)

The Spirit of the Times

The Sporting Life (Philadelphia, Pennsylvania)

The St. Louis Argus (St. Louis, Missouri)

The St. Louis Post-Dispatch (St. Louis, Missouri)

The St. Louis Star (St. Louis, Missouri)

The Syracuse Standard (Syracuse, New York)

The Times Plain Dealer

The Washington Post (Washington, D.C.)

Tombstone Epitaph (Tombstone, Arizona)

MAGAZINES AND MAGAZINE ARTICLES

Abbotts Monthly

Backstretch

Black Enterprise (New York)

Black Sports (New York)

Black Tennis (Houston, Texas)

Boxing Scene (Palisades, New York)

Lowe, Albert S. "Camp Life of The Tenth U.S. Cavalry." The Colored American (Boston, Massachusetts), Volume 7, Number 3, 1904.

Collier's

Commonwealth (Charlottesville, Virginia)

Crisis

Ebony

Edwards, Harry. "Black Athletes and Sports in America." The Western Journal of Black Studies, Volume 6, Number 3, Fall 1982.

Esquire

Garvey, Edward R. "From Chattel to Employee: The Athlete's Quest for Freedom And Dignity." Annals of the American Academy of Political and Social Science. Vol. 445, September 1979.

Harper's Weekly

Hewetson, W. T. "The Social Life of the Southern Negro." Chautauquan Magazine, Volume 26, page 295, October 1897–March 1898.

Inside Sports

Lapchick, Richard E. "South Africa: Sport and Apartheid Politics." Annals of the American Academy of Political and Social Science, September 1979.

Lowe, Albert S. "Camp Life of The Tenth U.S. Cavalry." The Colored American (Boston, Massachusetts), Volume 7, Number 3, 1904.

New Directions: The Howard University Magazine (Washington, D.C.)

New York Times Sunday Magazine

Newsweek

Opportunity

Racquet Quarterly (New York)

Reach's Official Baseball Guide

Roberts, Milton. "50 Years of the Best in Black College Football." Black Sports, June 1976.

——————. "First Black Pro Gridder." Black Sports, November 1975.

Spivey, Donald, "The Black Athlete in Big-Time Intercollegiate Sports, 1941–1968." Phylon, Volume 44, pages 116–25, June 1983.

Sport

Sports Illustrated

Stumpf, Florence, and Cozens, Fred. "Some Aspects of the Role of Games, Sports and Recreational Activites in the Culture of Modern Primitive Peoples." Research Quarterly, 1949.

Tennis (Trumbull; Connecticut)

The Black Scholar (San Francisco)

The Negro History Bulletin

Time

Wiggins, David K. "The Play of Slave Children in the Plantation Communities of the Old South,

1820–1860. *"Journal of Sport History,* Volume 7, Number 2.

——————. "Sport and Popular Pastimes: Shadow of the Slave Quarter." *Canadian Journal of History of Sport and Physical Education,* Vol. 11, May 1980.

ORGANIZATIONS, FOUNDATIONS, AND INSTITUTIONS

The Carter G. Woodson Institute for Afro-American and African Studies, University of Virginia, Charlottesville, Virginia

The Jackie Robinson Foundation

The Jesse Owens Foundation

Moorland Spingarn Research Library, Howard University

Norfolk, Virginia, Public Library

Northern University: Center for the Study of Sport in Society

Schomburg Library for Research in Black Culture

Tuskegee University Archives

Index